THE STORY OF

AMERICA

FREEDOM AND CRISIS FROM
SETTLEMENT TO SUPERPOWER

THE STORY OF
AMERICA

FREEDOM AND CRISIS FROM
SETTLEMENT TO SUPERPOWER

WRITTEN BY

ALLEN WEINSTEIN
DAVID RUBEL

AN AGINCOURT PRESS PRODUCTION

LONDON, NEW YORK, MUNICH, MELBOURNE, and DELHI

Publishers: Sean Moore, Chuck Lang
Creative Director: Tina Vaughan
Art Director: Dirk Kaufman
Editorial Director: Chuck Wills
Production Manager: Chris Avgherinos
DTP Manager: Milos Orlovic
Design Intern: Melissa Chung

AN AGINCOURT PRESS PRODUCTION
President: David Rubel

Senior Image Researcher: Julia Rubel
Image Researchers: Martha Davidson, Margaret Johnson, Joan Mathys, Carol Talbert Peters
Copy Editor and Indexer: Laura Jorstad
Editorial: Donna Gold, Brooke Palmer

Art Direction and Production: Oxygen Design
Design and Map Illustrations: Tilman Reitzle, Sherry Williams
Design Intern: Juliette Vega

For photo credits, see page 688.

First American edition, 2002

00 01 02 03 04 05 10 9 8 7 6 5 4 3 2 1

Published in the United States by DK Publishing, Inc.
375 Hudson Street, New York, New York 10014

DK Publishing offers special discounts for bulk purchases for sales promotions or premiums. Specific, large-quantity needs can be met with special editions, including personalized covers, excerpts of existing guides, and corporate imprints. For more information, contact Special Markets Department, DK Publishing, Inc., 375 Hudson Street, New York, NY 10014 Fax: 212-689-5254.

ISBN 0-7894-8903-1

CATALOGING-IN-PUBLICATION DATA IS AVAILABLE FROM THE LIBRARY OF CONGRESS

Color reproduction by Colourscan, Singapore
Printed and bound by Quebecor World, Taunton, Massachusetts

see our complete product line at
www.dk.com

CONTENTS

INTRODUCTION

Any single volume that covers the length of American history as this one does cannot possibly cover its breadth as well. Too much has happened during the course of five hundred years for all of American history to fit between two covers. Choices have to be made: What to include? What to omit? In order for their books to be as comprehensive as possible, textbook authors often choose a broad strategy, presenting many brief parcels of information linked together with generalizations about periodic trends. This strategy often produces a blur of names and dates that can neither be remembered nor appreciated. But *The Story of America* is not a textbook; rather, as its title states, it is a *story*—or, more precisely, twenty-six stories.

We have structured *The Story of America* around twenty-six significant episodes in American history. Each chapter describes a particular noteworthy period in American history by focusing on a single event—for example, the Boston Massacre in the case of the Revolutionary period, or Charles Lindbergh's transatlantic flight for the 1920s. Concentrating on a single event has allowed us to describe settings, characters, and the routines of daily life during unfamiliar previous ages. We have made space for these details by omitting other people and events in order to deepen the context of each chapter.

If we have done our job properly, as these details accumulate, the larger patterns and themes of American history will become not only clear but vivid. Those themes to which we have paid particular attention include the struggle to expand personal, political, and religious freedoms; the response to urgent national crises, both foreign and domestic; and the redefinition of national goals and values during the five centuries since Christopher Columbus first landed on Guanahani. Because our twenty-six episodes cannot accomplish this task alone, we have integrated into each chapter enough additional information on causes, effects, and contemporary conditions to bring out the significance of each period within the totality of American history.

We have also attempted to strengthen the context of our history through the use of art: contemporary photographs, maps, paintings, cartoons, books, documents, personal effects, and other memorabilia of historical significance. These images have been obtained primarily through the research facilities of two incomparable national storehouses, the Library of Congress and the National Archives, to whose staffs we are indebted. Other items have been collected from the countless smaller institutions that perform the diligent and often thankless task of preserving the physical manifestations of our national heritage. For example, the images of Eugene V. Debs that appear in this book come from the Debs Foundation, a small nonprofit organization that maintains the Debs Home in Terre Haute, Indiana. Similarly, the photograph in Chapter Nine of mid-nineteenth-century Waterloo, New York—the hamlet where Lucretia Mott, Elizabeth Cady Stanton, and three other women planned the 1848 Seneca Falls Convention—is available to scholars today only through the efforts of the Waterloo Library and Historical Society, one of many unheralded local groups formed by neighbors to investigate and protect the history of their towns, villages, and localities.

Why bother? What is the point of preserving and studying the past? Among the obvious reasons, of course, is that the past informs the present. In the words of historian Arthur M. Schlesinger Jr., "History, by putting crisis in perspective, supplies the antidote to every generation's illusion that its own problems are uniquely oppressive." The wisdom and truth of this statement is felt by all who write history because historical research inevitably leads one to identify past preoccupations in the present and present ones in the past. You will no doubt experience this yourself as you read through these pages and recognize in past events issues and situations that presently concern the nation.

Learning from the past, however, is far from simple. "History is not," Henry Kissinger pointed out in his memoir *The White House Years*, "...a cookbook offering pretested recipes. It teaches by analogy, not by maxims. It can illuminate the consequences of actions in comparable situations, yet each generation must discover for itself what situations are in fact comparable." To help encourage this process of discovery, we have written *The Story of America* with a particular attention to storytelling nuance that, we hope, helps reclaim the human quality of past events.

Additionally, because there are so many different historical perspectives, we have invited a number of our colleagues to contribute to this book short biographies of individuals whom they believe merit special attention. Often, these American Profiles reflect aspects of American history that we have otherwise regrettably had to omit.

We are also grateful to Prof. Frank Otto Gatell, coauthor with Allen Weinstein of the textbook *Freedom and Crisis,* once widely used but now out of print—from whose pages many of the insights and tales in this book have been drawn.

The stories that we have told here are not always encouraging. A number deal with episodes of strife, brutality, and confrontation during which the human suffering has been extreme. Nevertheless, such episodes are an integral part of American history and its underlying tale of a basically optimistic people fashioning from their uneven past a hopeful if uncertain future. In this regard, the stunning and frightening events of September 11, 2001—reconstructed in the final chapter of this book—fit a recurring pattern of grave national challenge followed by swiftly mobilized response. Such challenges underscore the importance of remembering that no generation's problems are singularly disheartening. In fact, readers may find surprising solace in our accounts of these episodes, especially as those accounts yield insight that can guide all of us as we move into this country's next historical epoch.

ALLEN WEINSTEIN
DAVID RUBEL

THE STORY OF
AMERICA

1

EXPLORATION AND CONQUEST

Cortés and Moctezuma

THE AZTEC EMPEROR MOCTEZUMA was eating and sleeping badly, awaiting anxiously the return of his envoys to the seacoast. For two months, since March 1519, he had been monitoring closely the approach of the bearded white strangers who had arrived from the east in extraordinary ships. With each new report from his messengers, he had become increasingly persuaded that the strangers, as he had feared, were emissaries of the ancient god Quetzalcóatl. According to an important body of Meso-American myth, Quetzalcóatl had once been a priest-king at Tula, the capital city of the Toltec empire. The Toltecs had ruled the central Mexican valley of Anáhuac for two hundred years before invaders sacked Tula in from the north the mid–twelfth century. But legend didn't ascribe the fall of the Toltecs to a lack of military prowess. Rather, Aztecs believed that the Toltec empire fell because Quetzalcóatl had left Tula for his homeland in the east. It was also said that one day the god would return and reclaim his lost empire.

Although the strangers numbered merely six hundred men, a pittance compared with the hundreds of thousands of warriors available to

***Moctezuma awaits** the arrival of Cortés in this watercolor created for a history of New Spain written in the 1570s by Dominican friar Diego Durán.*

Moctezuma, the fatalistic emperor sat in his palace in the magnificent Aztec capital of Tenochtitlán, brooding over the possibly imminent loss of his wealth and power. A particularly tyrannical king, Moctezuma had taxed his vassals to the limits of their endurance and routinely sacrificed to Huitzilopochtli, the supreme Aztec deity, any who resisted his commands. Recently, though, there had been a number of disturbing omens: A three-headed comet had passed over Anáhuac, a temple in Tenochtitlán had been struck by lightning, the water in Lake Texcoco (in the middle of which sat the island city of Tenochtitlán) had suddenly risen, and other unusual natural events had taken place. These signs, along with dreams and prophecies, had unnerved Moctezuma and persuaded him of his approaching doom.

His attempts to save himself and his people from the return of Quetzalcóatl were at best halfhearted. Hoping to persuade Huitzilopochtli to intervene on the Aztecs' behalf, Moctezuma greatly increased the number of human sacrifices being offered at the temples of Tenochtitlán. A new sacrificial stone, quarried at Coyoacán on the southern shore of Lake Texcoco, was brought to the city, where it was consecrated with the blood of thousands more. Meanwhile,

AT LEFT: ***This anonymous sixteenth-century** oil painting of Hernán Cortés hangs in Mexico City's Hospital de Jesús, where the conquistador's remains are buried.*

Moctezuma sent a party of ambassadors to the strangers. They carried with them greetings and gifts that Moctezuma hoped would placate Quetzalcóatl and persuade him to return home, leaving the Aztecs in peace. These gifts of gold and silver, however, only intrigued the leader of the strangers, Hernán Cortés.

First Contacts

THE SPANISH WERE, OF COURSE, not the first Europeans to reach the New World. Five hundred years before Cortés, Vikings from Scandinavia had also sailed far out into the ocean. Crossing the North Atlantic, they had reached Iceland, where they established a colony in the late ninth century. From there, under the leadership of Erik the Red, the Norsemen had journeyed even farther west, settling Greenland in 986. Sometime after the year 1000, Erik's son Leif finally reached the northeastern shore of North America. He called the place Vinland (it was likely modern Newfoundland) and spent the winter there before returning to Greenland. Later, other Vikings founded a colony of farmers and tradesmen in Vinland, but after spending two or three years fighting off hostile Indians, they abandoned the settlement and never returned.

This woodcut of Erik the Red appeared in Arngrin Jonas's Gronlandia *(1688), the first printed account of the Viking discovery of North America.*

Neither Cortés nor Moctezuma, of course, knew of these early Scandinavian visits. Cortés had gained his awareness of the New World from the exploits of an Italian navigator working for Spain. In 1492, with three small ships, Christopher Columbus had crossed the Atlantic Ocean from Palos, landing at the small Bahamian island of Guanahani. Believing that he had reached "the end of the Orient," Columbus called the inhabitants "Indians." It was an understandable mistake. No one in Europe had ever suspected that there might be an undiscovered continent between Europe and Asia.

FOR CENTURIES, THE FAR EAST, particularly China (then called Cathay) and Japan (Cipangu), had been the source of the Western world's most coveted luxury goods, notably silks, spices, and jewels. Before the sixteenth century, these goods were generally shipped overland along the famous Silk Road to ports in the eastern Mediterranean, from which they were distributed throughout Europe by Italian middlemen. (Some trade goods also reached the Near East via the Indian Ocean, but these, too, were monopolized by the Italians.) Eventually, the exorbitant prices being charged by the Italians and the prospect of great profits prompted the Atlantic nations of Spain and Portugal to seek alternate routes to the East so that they might bypass the Mediterranean (and the Italians) and conduct trade themselves.

A fragment from an Iranian silk scroll of the 1470s. It shows the marriage procession of a Chinese princess sent to wed a barbarian ruler on China's northwestern frontier. The highly prized blue-and-white porcelain in the cart is apparently part of her dowry.

The Portuguese concentrated their efforts on finding a route around Africa to the Indian Ocean. During the early fifteenth century, Prince Henry the

Navigator sponsored a school of navigation devoted to the exploration of Africa's west coast. Year after year, the Portuguese sailed farther and farther south, reaching the Madeiras in 1420, the Cape Verde Islands in 1445, and the Cape of Good Hope at the southern tip of Africa in 1488. Leaving Lisbon in July 1497, Vasco da Gama sailed around the cape, crossed the Indian Ocean, and reached India in May 1498. When he returned to Portugal the following year, his ships carried a rich cargo. Two years later, King Manuel I outfitted another expedition to India, this one commanded by Pedro Cabral. Although Cabral was supposed to follow da Gama's route closely, winds and currents pushed his ships off course, carrying them far to the west. On April 22, Cabral's fleet discovered Brazil, which Cabral claimed for Portugal before resuming his voyage east, passing the Cape of Good Hope in late May and continuing along da Gama's route to India.

The Voyages of Columbus

MEANWHILE, IN SPAIN, Ferdinand and Isabella decided to fund Columbus's pursuit of a different strategy. For years, cartographers in the Mediterranean ports that Columbus frequented had understood that the world was round. They also suspected that the Atlantic Ocean was less wide than most people believed. Having no knowledge of the Western Hemisphere, though, they naturally concluded that a ship sailing westward would sooner or later reach the East. Thus, when Columbus landed in the New World, he was certain he had reached India, or at least some outlying region thereof.

During the next decade, Columbus returned to the New World three more times. On these voyages, he established Spanish colonies on the islands of Hispaniola and Cuba and explored a great deal of the Caribbean. His quest for

This portrait of Christopher Columbus—attributed by some experts to Spanish artist Pedro Berruguete, who lived at the same time as Columbus—agrees remarkably well with written descriptions of the explorer's features.

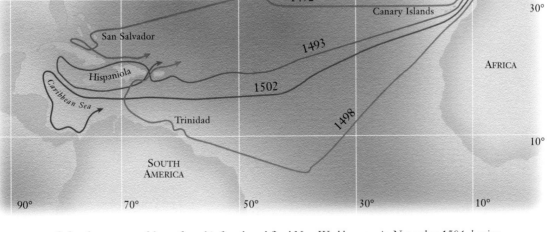

Columbus returned home from his fourth and final New World voyage in November 1504, having failed once again to find China. He died eighteen months later in poverty and neglect.

AMERIGO VESPUCCI
1454–1512

FLORENTINE MERCHANT BANKER Amerigo Vespucci served the Medici family, and as their agent in Seville he helped outfit ships of Columbus's second and third expeditions. Later, between 1497 and 1504, Vespucci made his own voyages to the New World, exploring the Gulf of Mexico and the Atlantic coast from Florida to the Chesapeake Bay as well as some of South America. These experiences led him to conclude that the newly discovered lands were not part of Asia (as Columbus had claimed) but belonged instead to an entirely "new world." This, in turn, prompted mapmaker Martin Waldseemüller to suggest in 1507 that the new territory be named America, after *Americus* (the Latin form of Vespucci's first name) who "invented" it. The name was soon applied to the New World in a planisphere printed by Waldseemüller, and it quickly caught on.

the Asian mainland, however, remained unsuccessful, as did his search for gold and other treasure. All he could offer the rulers of Spain was subjugation of hundreds of native "Indians." But Ferdinand and Isabella, though certainly disappointed with the lack of treasure, were less focused on trade than were the Portuguese or

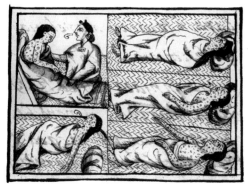

the Dutch or the English. Having only recently chased out the Moors and reunified their country under Catholic rule, the Spanish monarchs contented themselves with the pursuit of Christian expansionism, at least for a time. (The *reconquista* also provided funds that financed Spain's operations in the New World and gave the Spaniards useful experience in suppressing an alien culture and settling conquered lands.)

BETWEEN 1500 AND 1520, as Columbus's colonies on Hispaniola and Cuba stabilized, they attracted a sizable number of adventurers, brigands, penniless noblemen, and others seeking a quick fortune in the New World or perhaps a release from the disciplines of formal Spanish society. When these men arrived to find the storied riches of Cathay and Cipangu as inaccessible as ever, they exploited the local Indians for economic advantage. They divided the land into *encomiendas* (feudalistic plantations) and required Indians who lived on them to work for the benefit of their Spanish overlords. Those Indians who resisted were executed or reduced to chattel slavery. European diseases, particularly smallpox, also decimated the native population, and within a generation, the Indian tribes that had welcomed Columbus were nearly exterminated. (Already, though, the Spaniards had begun importing African slaves to replenish the labor pool.)

This illustration from Franciscan friar Bernardino da Sahagún's Historia Universal de las cosas de Nueva España *shows Aztecs dying from smallpox. Bernardino's bilingual manuscript, written about 1576 in both Castilian and Nahua, is known more commonly as the* Florentine Codex (*because it came to reside in Florence's Biblioteca Medicea Laurenziana*).

It was to find another supply of slaves, in fact, that Cuban governor Diego Velázquez commissioned an expedition in 1517 to explore the Gulf of Mexico. What that expedition found, much to its surprise, was a civilization on the Yucatán Peninsula whose culture and technology far exceeded those of any yet encountered by the Spanish in the New World. The Maya who inhabited the Yucatán wore clothes, lived in stone houses, and adorned themselves with gold jewelry. Encouraged by reports of this Mayan wealth, Velázquez outfitted a second expedition in

1518 under the command of his kinsman Juan de Grijalba. Sailing along the northern shore of the Yucatán, Grijalba bartered with the coastal Indians for gold and listened to stories of a mysterious empire located within the Mexican interior.

In June, Grijalba reached the island of San Juan de Ulúa off the coast of the Mexican mainland, near the southern border of the Aztec empire. From there, he sent a ship back to Cuba carrying the gold he had thus far accumulated. The rest of the fleet continued sailing north along the coastline for several more months before returning to Cuba in November. Meanwhile, in Tenochtitlán, Moctezuma tracked Grijalba's movements as messengers brought him henequen cloths with pictographs of the strangers and the "sea-castles" in which they rode. The Aztec emperor petitioned Huitzilopochtli to remove the strangers; and when Grijalba left, Moctezuma congratulated himself on the effectiveness of his prayers.

The Conquest of Mexico

IN FEBRUARY 1519, though, Velázquez sent Cortés to Mexico with six hundred men; and unlike the tentative Grijalba, Cortés was arrogant and bold. Just nineteen when he arrived on Hispaniola in 1504 (a year after Moctezuma's ascendance to the Aztec throne), Cortés announced when he got there, in response to the offer of an *encomienda*, that he had come to the New World for gold, not to till the soil as a peasant. Yet this conquistador was more than a typical captain of brigands. He was a romantic as well, who labored for glory and God in addition to gold. He had no intention of merely looting and depopulating Mexico, as Cuba and Hispaniola had been. Rather, he wanted to transform Mexico into a Spanish province with a permanent white population that could deliver Spanish civilization to the Indians and, most importantly, convert them to Catholicism. Of course, Cortés's romantic sensibility never prevented him from treating those he considered savages harshly, and he slaughtered as many Indians as he believed necessary.

This drawing of one of Cortés's "sea-castles" appeared in the Codex Azcatitlan.

THE FIRST CIRCUMNAVIGATION

IN SEPTEMBER 1519, working in the service of Spain, Portuguese explorer Fernão de Magalhães sailed for the Spice Islands. Like Columbus, Magalhães (known in English as Ferdinand Magellan) wanted to reach the East by sailing west. First, he navigated his five ships to South America, sighting Brazil in November. Then, after stopping off at Rio de Janeiro and exploring the La Plata estuary (site of modern-day Buenos Aires), he wintered at Puerto San Julián, located at 49°20' south latitude. On Easter Day, Magellan put down a mutiny led by two Spanish captains, one of whom he had executed and the other put ashore. Leaving Puerto San Julián in August, he sailed south until, on October 21, he entered the strait that would later bear his name. A month later, his three remaining ships emerged from the strait into the Pacific Ocean. Magellan is reported to have broken down and cried at this point, having finally found the westward route that had eluded European explorers for a generation. Crossing the Pacific, Magellan arrived on March 6, 1521, at Guam, and ten days later he discovered the Philippines, where he lingered for two months and where, on April 27, he was killed by natives on the island of Mactan. Following Magellan's death, two of his ships reached the Spice Islands, but only one—the *Victoria*, commanded by Juan de Elcano—made it all the way back to Spain, completing in September 1522 the first circumnavigation of the world.

THE ORIGIN OF THE AZTEC EMPIRE

THE BEGINNINGS OF THE Aztec people are uncertain, but they were most likely a tribe of hunters and gatherers who lived quite far north of Anáhuac. During the late twelfth or early thirteenth century, they migrated southward, settling in the area around Lake Texcoco—where, in 1325, they founded Tenochtitlán. Aztec expertise in irrigation and the reclamation of swampland made their city-state rich and populous, and by the fifteenth century, the Aztecs (who were also known as the Mexica) had come to dominate Anáhuac. By 1519, when Cortés arrived, their empire controlled as many as five hundred small states and perhaps six million people.

The migration of the Aztecs probably contributed to the collapse of the Toltec empire centereed at Tula (shown here).

Cortés's fleet touched first at the Yucatán, where the novelty of his purpose became clear. Some of his men went ashore and, finding that the natives had fled, began ransacking the Indians' abandoned homes in the usual manner. When Cortés discovered this, he ordered the Indians' belongings returned to them along with gifts from the Spaniards. According to the account of Bernal Díaz del Castillo, Cortés explained that "we should never pacify the country in that way by robbing the natives of their property." Cortés also learned at this time of a party of Spanish castaways, the survivors of a shipwreck off the coast of Jamaica seven years earlier who had drifted to the Yucatán in an open boat. Most had long since been sacrificed to the Mayan gods, but two were still alive. One had gone native (even to the point of teaching the Maya how to repel a Spanish invasion), but the other, Jeromino de Aguilar, eagerly accepted Cortés's rescue, and the knowledge of the Mayan language that Aguilar had acquired later proved invaluable to Cortés.

The Spanish fleet next sailed west to Tabasco, where the Tabascans—alerted by their Yucatán neighbors to the dangers of white invaders—attacked Cortés's men in great numbers. The Spaniards' arms, especially their cannon and steel swords, gave them a technological advantage sufficient for victory, and Cortés was particularly impressed with the panic that his horses created among the Indians. No Tabascan had ever seen a horse before, and many took them to be supernatural beasts, the horse and rider all part of one animal. Following their defeat, the Tabascans, as was their custom, submitted to Cortés and presented him with gifts, among them twenty young women (whom they immediately baptized because the Spaniards would not sleep with the women otherwise). One of these women, called Marina by the Spaniards, had been living among the Tabascans as a prisoner. By birth, however, she was the daughter of a chief of an interior tribe that spoke Náhuatl, the same language spoken by the Aztecs. Now, through Aguilar and Doña Marina, Cortés would be able to communicate with Moctezuma.

ON APRIL 21, CORTÉS ARRIVED off the island of San Juan de Ulúa, and from this anchorage, he founded on the mainland the town of Villa Rica de la Vera Cruz. More than a symbolic gesture, the founding of Vera Cruz was an important practical step for Cortés. Up to this point, he had been acting under the authority of Diego Velázquez, to whom he was therefore subservient. However, because of

Spanish medieval traditions concerning municipal autonomy, the founding of Vera Cruz gave Cortés a means of escaping the Cuban governor's yoke. After founding the town, Cortés appointed its first officials, who in turn elected him their captain general and authorized him, under the Spanish right of self-government, to conquer and colonize the newly discovered lands. Henceforth, Cortés would be responsible not to Velázquez but directly to King Charles I of Spain, who was more commonly known as the Holy Roman Emperor Charles V. Cortés's disobedience thus had a veneer of legality, but he knew that, should he fail to fill King Charles's coffers, he would likely be returned to Spain in chains.

Some days later, the first of Moctezuma's ambassadors arrived. The gifts they carried for Cortés included a large gold disc in the shape of the sun and an even larger silver disc in the shape of the moon. They pleaded with him to leave, but far from satisfying the captain general, their gifts served only to advertise the Aztecs' wealth. Finally, Cortés told them that he had come a long way to see Moctezuma and that he would not leave without doing so—a message he repeated to the many envoys who followed.

Cortés was particularly confident because he had learned from the Totonacs, who lived nearby, that many local tribes were chafing under the severe rule of the Aztecs and all were potential allies. Meanwhile, Cortés made preparations for a march to Tenochtitlán. These included, significantly, the dispatch of a messenger to King Charles, advising him of Cortés's discoveries and intentions, and the scuttling of the remaining ships so that the fearful among his men would have no choice but to follow him. Only then, accompanied by forty Totonac nobles and two hundred Totonac porters, did Cortés and his men march into the interior. The date was August 16, 1519.

An Indian artist recorded this early 1520s image of Cortés sitting astride El Morzillo, one of the first horses ever seen in the New World.

THE MAYA

ONCE THEY BECAME undisputed overlords of Anáhuac, the Aztecs created a society that incorporated not only the customs of local tribes but also the achievements of neighboring civilizations, most notably the Maya. Mayan civilization prospered from the fourth century until the tenth, when Toltec ascendancy began. Little is known of its history because Mayan hieroglyphics remain poorly understood, but extensive ruins at sites such as Chichén Itzá in the Yucatán yield some insights. Classical Mayan religion, for example, was based on a pantheon of nature gods similar to those worshiped by many Meso-American cultures. Its rituals were elaborate and included bloodletting and self-mutilation as well as human and animal sacrifices. The Maya, who ruled from southern Mexico to northern Belize, were also superior mathematicians and astronomers: They invented positional notation, developed the concept of zero, created an accurate solar calendar, and could predict solar eclipses. Mayan art, too, was the most highly developed among Meso-American cultures.

This Aztec calendar stone made use of Mayan astronomical discoveries.

The Irresistible March

THE FIRST NOTEWORTHY TRIBE Cortés encountered was the Tlaxcala. He had learned from the Totonacs that the Tlaxcalans were traditional enemies of the Aztecs, and he hoped to win their allegiance. But the Tlaxcalans had their own sources of intelligence, and what they had learned troubled them. They knew of the numerous embassies passing between Moctezuma and the strangers, and they suspected an Aztec plot. Therefore, they decided not to take any chances. They allowed the Spaniards to pass through the Tlaxcalan wall, a vast masonry structure nine feet tall that ran from mountain range to mountain range across their valley, but then surrounded and set upon Cortés and his men. The Tlaxcalans had an enormous advantage in numbers, and had they been more interested in killing the whites than in capturing them for use as human sacrifices, they probably would have won. But the Spaniards endured; and after conducting a series of attacks, the Tlaxcalans relented and decided to accept Cortés as a friend. When the captain general eventually left the Tlaxcalans after being feted by their *caciques*, or chiefs, he was escorted by six thousand Tlaxcalan warriors. Later, thousands of additional Indian enemies of the Aztecs joined his march to Anáhuac.

During much of the march, Moctezuma still sent ambassadors to Cortés, hoping to turn him away from Tenochtitlán. These envoys told Cortés that Moctezuma was too poor to entertain him properly, they brought more gifts, and they offered to pay him tribute, but Cortés would not listen. So Moctezuma changed his strategy and sent messengers to the *caciques* of Cholula, Cortés's next stop, urging them to annihilate the strangers. Cortés learned of this conspiracy, however, and massacred the unwary Cholulans in the courtyard of their great temple to Quetzalcóatl. The failure of this conspiracy, which Moctezuma could ascribe only to Cortés's supernatural powers, broke whatever remained of his will. As Cortés drew irresistibly closer to Tenochtitlán, Moctezuma abandoned all efforts to avoid his fate and simply surrendered to it.

From Cholula, the Spaniards passed into the valley of Anáhuac and came to Ixtapalapán, the terminal point of one of three remarkable causeways linking Tenochtitlán to the Lake Texcoco shoreline. Made like the others of concrete with wooden bridges that could be raised or removed, the causeway from Ixtapalapán was five miles long and, according to Bernal Díaz del Castillo, "eight paces in

A glyph from the Codex Mendoza *shows Moctezuma, who ascended to the Aztec throne in 1503, wearing the traditional blue crown of the emperor.*

THE INDIAN WAY

ALTHOUGH INDIAN LIFE differed a great deal from group to group and place to place, certain traits were common to nearly all Indian tribes, setting them apart from other peoples, especially the Europeans. One of these characteristics was the Indian attitude toward land: Although members of a tribe might claim hunting rights to a certain territory, they didn't believe they could own the land any more than they could own the sky above it. Even among the complex farming societies of Central America, land generally belonged to either the community as a whole or perhaps to a god or spirit. (Of course, Cortés and his fellow Spaniards had a much more possessive concept of land ownership.) Indians also had a different attitude about warfare. For many tribes, especially in North America, fighting was as much about ceremony as about conflict. Sioux warriors achieved more glory by touching an enemy in battle than by killing him; and even the Aztecs, to whom the acquisition of territory and tribute was important, considered the basic goal of warfare to be the capture of prisoners for religious sacrifice.

width…but, broad as it is, it was so crowded with people that there was hardly room for them all." On this day, as on most, tens of thousands of tradesmen, priests, nobles, and commoners used the causeway to pass to and from the Aztec capital, and Cortés and his large company had difficulty navigating the crowds. "As we approached the city," another of Cortés's men later wrote, "we could see great towers and churches of the kind they build, and large palaces and dwellings. There were over one hundred thousand houses in this city, each house built over the water on wooden piles, with nothing but a beam connecting one house to another, so that each one was a fortress in itself."

At Xoloc, where the causeway from Ixtapalapán joined that from Coyoacán, Cortés was met by the *caciques* of Texcoco, Tacuba, Coyoacán, and Ixtapalapán, who accompanied him to the city entrance, where more Aztec nobles stood in two parallel files. Between them, in a jeweled litter, sat Moctezuma. Cortés dismounted his horse, the emperor climbed down from his litter, and the two men confronted one another. It was an encounter that, even given Cortés's hubris and Moctezuma's depression, fulfilled the old legends. The captain general had conquered Mexico.

This map accompanied a letter sent by Cortés to King Charles V in 1524. It is the oldest known plan of Tenochtitlán.

ORTÉS WAS WELCOMED as a legitimate ruler returning to his throne, and he entered Tenochtitlán at the head of the first threatening army in more than a century to pass through the city's gates unopposed. The Spaniards and their Tlaxcalan allies were given use of a palace on the western side of the great temple square that dominated life in Tenochtitlán, and they were told by Moctezuma that he would do as Quetzalcóatl commanded. Although the Aztec emperor had probably come to realize by this point that the strangers were not deities but men, he was never able to abandon the idea that the Spaniards represented a fulfillment of ancient prophecy and that their arrival meant the end of his rule and the destruction of his kingdom.

Cortés, however, knew that his hold on the Aztecs was tenuous. At any time, Moctezuma's mood might change, or his own men, greedy and unscrupulous as they were, might provoke the Aztecs into rebellion. To safeguard himself, a few days after his arrival, Cortés went to Moctezuma's palace and kidnapped the emperor, ordering him to return with the Spaniards to their quarters or else be killed on the spot. A weeping Moctezuma complied and became a prisoner in his own capital while Cortés ruled in his name. Thus, without shedding any Aztec blood, a mere four hundred Spaniards gained control over an empire of millions.

Nearly identical in architecture to the Templo Mayor in Tenochtitlán was the great temple at Texcoco, shown here in an illustration from the Codex Ixtlilxóchitl.

This state of affairs continued for six months, until Cortés learned from his garrison on the coast that Velázquez had sent an armada of fifteen ships and nine hundred men—the largest yet assembled in the West Indies—to arrest his impertinent agent. The fleet's commander, Pánfilo de Narváez, had dispatched to Vera Cruz two messengers, who were promptly tied to hammocks and sent via Totonac porters to Cortés in Tenochtitlán. Meanwhile, Narváez told the Totonacs, some Aztec messengers, and anyone else who would listen that Cortés was no god and no loyal subject of Spain.

Another illustration from the Codex Durán, *this watercolor shows Pedro de Alvarado's men massacring Aztec celebrants in the courtyard of the Templo Mayor in June 1520.*

CORTÉS RESPONDED to the crisis with characteristic confidence and cunning. Immediately, he ordered the two emissaries from Narváez released. Next, he showed them Tenochtitlán and, before sending them back to Narváez, told them that they and their companions could share in its riches and pleasures if they joined him. Finally, leaving half his men in Tenochtitlán under the command of Pedro de Alvarado, he returned to the coast to deal with Narváez personally. On a dark and rainy night, he infiltrated Narváez's camp and captured the commander before any real fighting could begin. After that, already having learned from the released messengers what awaited them in Tenochtitlán, Narváez's officers and men swore loyalty to Cortés. Narváez himself was taken to Vera Cruz in chains, and his ships were dismantled so that none might return to inform Velázquez of the recent developments. A few days later, Cortés was preparing to return inland when he received a desperate message from Alvarado carried by two Tlaxcalan messengers.

At first, the Aztecs in Tenochtitlán had seemed willing to wait for news from the coast, hoping that the soldiers of Cortés and Narváez would destroy each other, at which time Alvarado's small force could be easily eliminated. But Alvarado, the man who had led the initial looting on the Yucatán Peninsula a year earlier, again disappointed Cortés. Concerned about his army's reduced numbers, uncertain as to his fate should Narváez imprison Cortés, and fearful that the Aztecs were plotting against him, Alvarado determined to act first. The Aztecs were set to hold a major religious festival at the end of which, Alvarado feared, he and men would be sacrificed to Huitzilopochtli. But Alvarado remembered Cholula; and at the height of the festival, he closed the temple gates and slaughtered thousands of unarmed celebrants before the Aztecs rallied and forced the Spaniards back into their palace. Alvarado's men remained there, besieged, until the return of Cortés from the coast.

La Noche Triste

CORTÉS'S COLUMN, WHICH INCLUDED a thousand Spaniards and many more Indian allies, entered Tenochtitlán without any resistance, the Aztecs apparently hoping to trap all their enemies inside the Spaniards' palace. After chastising Alvarado for his madness, Cortés ordered Moctezuma to arrange food and drink. Moctezuma replied that he could do nothing. A tribal council had replaced him as emperor with his brother Cuitlahuac, who launched a series of vigorous attacks against the Spanish and their allies. The fighting, which went badly for Cortés, lasted a week, during which time Moctezuma died. According to Spanish accounts, he was stoned to death as he pleaded with his former subjects (at Cortés's urging) to allow the Spaniards to leave in peace. According to the Aztecs, the Spaniards strangled him.

Cortés finally decided to abandon Tenochtitlán, fleeing the city on the night of June 30, 1520. The departing Spanish column would have been cumbersome in any case, but this night on the causeway to Tacuba it carried with it not only a good portion of the Aztec treasure but also a portable wooden bridge. (The Aztecs had removed all the permanent bridges from the causeway, and Cortés needed some means of spanning the gaps.) Whatever the merits of Cortés's plan for retreat, its execution was disastrous. The streets of Tenochtitlán were quiet that night, and the captain general apparently hoped to surprise the Aztecs, but sentinels on the causeway sounded the alarm. At the first breach in the causeway, the portable bridge jammed, and at subsequent breaches, the Spaniards and their Indian allies had to swim. This proved impossible for many Spaniards who, weighted down with gold, drowned in the shallow waters of the lake. (Some of their companions scrambled to safety atop their corpses.) Several thousand of the Tlaxcalans and at least six hundred of the Spaniards failed to reach Tacuba. Most of the missing among Cortés's countrymen were soldiers who had accompanied Narváez—either killed in the fighting, drowned, or taken for sacrifice to Huitzilopochtli. Cortés himself remained on the causeway until dawn, gathering the survivors, whom he led back to Tlaxcala. Afterward, the night of June 30 was remembered by the Spaniards as *la noche triste*, "the night of sorrows."

W HEN THE SPANIARDS left Tenochtitlán," wrote one Mexican chronicler, "the Aztecs thought they had departed for good and would never return. Therefore, they repaired and decorated the temple of their god." But Cortés proved a persistent enemy. Several more Spanish ships put in at Vera Cruz, and their crews were persuaded to join a new campaign against the Aztecs. During the next several months, the tribes between Anáhuac and the coast were again subdued (many had abandoned Cortés after his flight from Tenochtitlán), and by the fall the captain general had nine hundred Spanish soldiers, nearly a hundred horses, plenty of guns and ammunition, and the renewed support of his Indian allies. Meanwhile, the Aztecs had been

Cortés was particularly offended by the Aztec ritual of human sacrifice, shown here in an illustration from the Florentine Codex. From the moment he learned of its practice, the Spaniard determined to substitute Christianity for the Indians' paganism.

LEFT: *An Aztec warrior in full battle regalia, as shown in the* Codex Mendoza. *This manuscript was created by native scribes at the request of Spanish viceroy Antonio de Mendoza, who sent it to King Charles by 1542. However, French pirates captured the galleon carrying the codex, which they delivered instead to French king Francis I.*

suffering. One of Narváez's men had been infected with smallpox, and the disease spread throughout Anáhuac, killing thousands. Among the dead was the emperor Cuitlahuac, who was succeeded by Cuauhtémoc, nephew and son-in-law to the late Moctezuma.

In December, Cortés returned to Anáhuac, making his camp at Texcoco. Marching around the lake, he reduced all the towns in the valley, burning Ixtapalapán and isolating Tenochtitlán. In May 1521, he besieged the Aztec capital using thirteen brigantines. These had been built by the Tlaxcalans under Spanish direction and carried in pieces the sixty miles to Texcoco. Once reassembled, they gave Cortés command of the approaches to Tenochtitlán and reduced the ability of the Aztecs to resupply themselves via canoe.

Companies of Spanish soldiers supported by Indian warriors advanced each day along the three causeways to repair the breaches opened by the Aztecs, while Cortés protected them with his brigantines. At night, however, once the Spaniards had retreated to shore, the Aztecs crept out of their city and reopened the breaches. This continued for a few weeks while conditions inside Tenochtitlán, of course, deteriorated. Rotting corpses spread disease, supplies of food and fresh water were running short, and the Aztecs began eating lizards, swallows, corncobs, and the salt grasses of the lake to fill their stomachs. But Cuauhtémoc, a resolute young man in his early twenties, would not countenance any talk of surrender. So, reluctantly, Cortés and his Indian allies set about systematically destroying the island he had called "the most beautiful city in the world." By late June, more than half of Tenochtitlán lay in ruin, for such is the price of resisting the irresistible. The end finally came on August 13, when the Spaniards seized the last autonomous district of the city and drove its Aztec defenders into the lake. Cuauhtémoc was captured in a canoe, and the next day, after the surviving Aztecs were evacuated, Cortés ordered the city cleansed by fire.

This illustration from the Codex Durán *shows Cortés constructing his fleet of brigantines at Texcoco. In the center, the ruler of Texcoco (wearing a diadem) can be seen assisting the Spanish in their efforts.*

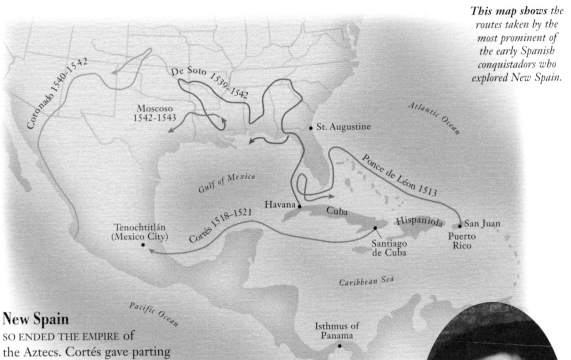

Coronado 1540–1542

De Soto 1539–1542

Moscoso 1542–1543

• St. Augustine

Atlantic Ocean

Gulf of Mexico

Ponce de Léon 1513

Havana • • Cuba

Cortés 1518–1521

Tenochtitlán (Mexico City) •

Hispaniola • San Juan Puerto Rico

Santiago de Cuba

Caribbean Sea

Pacific Ocean

Isthmus of Panama

New Spain

SO ENDED THE EMPIRE of the Aztecs. Cortés gave parting gifts to his Indian allies and sent them home. Then he set about rebuilding Tenochtitlán, henceforth to be called the city of Mexico. Cortés transformed the old temple square into a new central plaza, which became the city's principal marketplace. Using labor forced from the Indians of Anáhuac and hewn stone from the destroyed Aztec buildings, he erected new homes, shops, and a town hall. Farther north, on the site of a pyramid to Huitzilopochtli, he built Mexico City's first cathedral atop a foundation composed of broken Aztec idols. At the same time, he built a new society in Mexico, introducing Spanish government and converting the Indians to Christianity. A party of friars summoned from Spain walked barefoot from Vera Cruz, and when they reached Mexico City, Cortés knelt and kissed the hems of their coarse gray gowns. Later, just as Moctezuma once had, Cortés sent men off in all directions to explore the land and subjugate its inhabitants. The first expeditions went north toward the Gulf of California and southeast into present-day Guatemala and Honduras. What they found, they conquered; and what they conquered they called New Spain. Thus Cortés's westward march—the irresistible march of European civilization—continued.

Yet for every Cortés and Francisco Pizarro who found riches, there were many Spanish explorers who discovered nothing more than some small, impoverished villages. For example, no Spaniard appears to have gotten rich exploring what is now the United States. In 1513, Juan Ponce de León, who had sailed with Columbus on his second voyage to the New World, outfitted an expedition to find Bimini, a fabulous island on which was said to be located the Fountain of Youth. Instead Ponce de León, at the time the governor of Puerto Rico, found Florida. Returning to Florida eight years later, he tried to establish a settlement there but was chased away by the natives. Wounded, he died on the return voyage to Cuba.

Cortés is shown near the end of his life in this anonymous sixteenth-century portrait, now at Madrid's Museo Nacional. He died in 1547.

SIMILARLY, FRANCISCO VÁSQUEZ DE CORONADO left Mexico in 1540 to find the legendary Seven Cities of Cibola, said to be rich beyond measure. Traveling northward, Coronado trekked through Texas and Oklahoma as far north as present-day Kansas without finding any gold. Around the same time, Hernando de Soto, leading a large military expedition from Cuba, landed in Florida and explored west, becoming on May 21, 1540, the first white to look upon the Mississippi River. De Soto had hoped to discover gold and jewels but instead found only suspicious or hostile Indians. When he died in 1542 of a fever near present-day Ferriday, Louisiana, his companions weighted down his body and sank it in the Mississippi to prevent its desecration.

THE INCA

IF THE INTELLECTUALLY GIFTED Maya were the Greeks of the pre-Columbian world, then the imperial, bureaucratic Inca were its Romans. Spreading from their capital, Cuzco, during the fourteenth century, the Inca came to rule an empire that included nearly all of western South America from the Andean Plateau down to the Pacific Ocean. The road system that the Inca built ranged 2,250 miles from Quito in the north to Santiago in the south, and messages carried along it by a sophisticated courier system traveled 150 miles a day. At its height when Francisco Pizarro arrived in 1532, the Inca empire had about twelve million subjects. With so many people and so much territory to control, the Inca had to have an effective military, yet even they had difficulty resisting the ridiculously outnumbered Europeans.

Pizarro first arrived in the New World in 1509, and he was with Vasco Núñez de Balboa when Balboa discovered the Pacific Ocean in 1513. Later, Pizarro served as the mayor of Panama before joining in the late 1520s two expeditions that explored the western coast of South America. During these voyages, Pizarro heard stories of a rich inland empire reminiscent of the tales that Cortés had heard about the Aztecs. In 1531, after obtaining permission from Holy Roman Emperor Charles V to conquer and govern new territory, he led a group of 180 Spaniards to Peru, where he found the Inca in the throes of civil war. Loyalties were divided between two feuding sons of the late emperor Huayna Capac, and the disarray suited Pizarro's aims perfectly. The more successful contender, Atahualpa, was persuaded to meet with the Spaniards; and once Atahualpa was in the Spanish camp, Pizarro had him imprisoned and later executed. The Spanish commander then marched on a leaderless Cuzco, which he captured along with its immense hoard of gold and silver in 1533. By 1535, the Inca empire was little more than a Spanish colonial appendage.

Undiscovered by the Spaniards, *the Inca stronghold of Machu Picchu remained hidden in the Andes until Yale archaeologist Hiram Bingham uncovered it in 1911. Shown here in one of Bingham's original photos, the site has survived nearly intact— a rarity among pre-Columbian settlements.*

In spite of these setbacks, Spaniards continued to arrive in the New World in large numbers, and by 1600, there were a quarter of a million living in the Western Hemisphere. They organized polities and founded municipal governments. They built towns, missions, and military posts. They introduced new crops and livestock but also learned quickly to grow native crops, especially corn, tomatoes, potatoes, beans, cacao, and tobacco. Funding much of this was the gold and silver that was for many decades New Spain's chief export to Europe, coming at first from the Aztec and Inca hoards and later from rich mines discovered in Mexico and Peru during the 1540s.

Meanwhile, those Indians who had survived conquest and epidemic disease were essentially enslaved. Thousands were put to work in the mines, digging and smelting precious metals, while others were forced to farm what was now Spanish land and tend Spanish livestock. Some of the clergy, in the spirit of Cortés, protested this mistreatment, and the Spanish crown issued edicts limiting the abuse of native labor, but these were largely ignored by an arrogant immigrant population intent on the creation of wealth through exploitation. The bloodletting occasioned by Cortés was nothing compared to that which followed him.

During the first century of Spanish rule, the Indian population of Mexico dropped from five million to one million people. As on Cuba and Hispaniola, the lost Indian labor was quickly replaced with that of hundreds of thousands of imported African slaves. Packed tightly into the pestilent holds of cargo ships, many more Africans died of disease during the crossing of the Atlantic than reached the New World, but enough survived the journey to keep the trade profitable. (Africans were preferred to Indians because they had already been exposed to European diseases at home and because they had some agricultural experience, unlike many Indians.)

This gold pendant, carved to resemble a Mexican deity, is the work of Mixtecs who lived in Oaxaca. They were the most accomplished craftsmen of all those who supplied jewelry to the Aztecs.

Mercantilism

THE GOLD AND SILVER THAT FLOWED generously from its American possessions gave Spanish great sway in sixteenth-century Europe, which was then dominated by the economic theory of mercantilism. Mercantilists believed that a nation's strength depended on its stockpile of precious metals—in other words, its capital—and that it should acquire colonies to supply it with raw materials and serve as exclusive markets for its manufactured goods. A positive trade balance—that is, more exports than imports—was considered highly desirable so that foreign exchange would flow into, rather than out of, a country. In general, mercantilists also believed that a nation could grow rich only at the expense of other nations (a belief later challenged by laissez-faire economists, who pointed out that increased trade benefited all parties).

These principles guided Spanish policy, but what the Spaniards (and most Europeans) didn't realize was that too much money could be a bad thing. During the early sixteenth century, Spain and the rest of Europe began experiencing what has been called a "price revolution." In Spain alone, prices rose about 400 percent, an extremely high rate for that time. Such inflation made it difficult for ordinary Spaniards to afford the basic necessities of life and prompted scholars at the University of Salamanca to develop the first quantity theory of money: that money is worth more when it is scarce than when it is abundant. Thus, although the nobility were able to mount great displays of wealth, little of it went toward greater economic production, and Spain remained a relatively poor country.

At the same time, because only Spain had the means to acquire New World gold and silver directly, the other European powers had to rely on trade for the accumulation of specie. Toward this end, the ships of Portugal, Holland, England, and France crossed and recrossed the Atlantic in search of new trade opportunities. (Spain, by contrast, never developed a strong foreign commerce because it expected its New World mines to produce all the gold and silver it needed—a policy that proved unwise when mine yields dropped precipitously after 1600.)

THE PAPAL BULLS OF 1493

ALEXANDER VI, a Spaniard by birth, was one of the most worldly, ambitious, and corrupt Renaissance popes. Among his more notable contributions to world history were his neglect of the church's spiritual life, which contributed significantly to the onset of the Protestant Reformation, and his parentage of Cesare Borgia, who grew up to become Machiavelli's model for *The Prince*. In 1493, a year after his elevation to the papacy, the former Rodrigo Borgia issued a series of bulls designed to please his allies the kings of Spain and Portugal. In these bulls, he drew a line from north to south along the western border of Brazil and extending into the Atlantic. All the new lands to the east of this line, he proclaimed, belonged to Portugal; all the lands to the west, to His Most Catholic Majesty Ferdinand of Spain.

This 1621 woodcut shows Pope Alexander VI blessing the thirteen monks who accompanied Christopher Columbus on his second voyage. Their mission was to Christianize the pagan Indians.

The French and the Dutch in the New World

ALTHOUGH THE POPE HAD DIVIDED the New World between Spain and Portugal in 1493, the excluded European nations—especially the antipapal ones—paid this edict little mind. "Show me the will of Adam dividing the world between Spain and Portugal," Francis I of France demanded. In 1523, challenging Spain's claim to the New World, he sent Florentine navigator Giovanni da Verrazano to explore North America. Verrazano's instructions were to find a water route to China, a "northwest passage," the search for which would fascinate explorers for a century.

Unlike the first Spanish explorers, Verrazano had a fairly good idea of what he would find in the New World. For twenty years, French fishermen had been sailing as far west as Newfoundland to gather codfish, and Verrazano's tour of the east coast from Cape Fear north to Newfoundland established a substantial French claim to North America. Distracted by wars in Europe, France failed to pursue this claim for several generations, but in 1603 King Henry IV sent Samuel de Champlain on a fur-trading mission to the Gulf of St. Lawrence, from which Champlain explored the St. Lawrence River. Five years later, he returned with a group of colonists, founded Quebec, and used that settlement as a base of operation from which to explore northern New York and the lake that bears his name. After 1612, when he was named commandant of New France, Champlain organized a profitable fur trade, consolidated his good relations with the local Indians, and explored the Great Lakes. With the passing of Champlain, French exploration continued at a much more

NORTH AMERICAN CULTURES

COMPARED WITH THE MAYA, the Inca, and the Aztecs, the native peoples of North America generally exhibited much simpler cultures at the time of the European influx. Tribal groupings north of the Rio Grande were relatively small and limited to a particular geographical area. There was one group, however, that approached its Meso-American neighbors in cultural and technological sophistication: the Pueblo people of the Southwest, who lived in adobe houses and built complex irrigation systems as early as the eighth century. Other early North American cultures included the Mound Builders of the Mississippi Valley, who made temples by mounding earth and rubble into pyramids and other structures. Archaeologists have since found remarkable works of art inside these mounds.

With its wide range of climates and topography, North America supported a striking diversity of Indian lifestyles. This photograph shows the ruins of the pueblo settlement at Acoma as they appeared in 1904.

leisurely pace until the late seventeenth century, when René-Robert Cavelier, sieur de La Salle, descended the Mississippi River to the Gulf of Mexico, which he reached on April 9, 1682. La Salle subsequently claimed the entire Mississippi Valley for France and named the region Louisiana in honor of King Louis XIV.

The society of New France differed markedly from that of New Spain. The history of Spain in the New World was one of conquest and exploitation, while the French, who never found gold and had little interest in farming Indian land, focused their efforts on the fur trade, which required amicable relations with the Indians. In New Netherland also, trade was the focus of the colony. In 1609, sailing for the Dutch East India Company aboard the *Half Moon*, Englishman Henry Hudson had discovered the Hudson River and sailed up it as far north as Albany. (He had been attempting at the time, as had Verrazano, to find a northwest passage.) In 1626, the Dutch West India Company, founded largely as a commercial weapon against the Spanish, established a small colony on Manhattan Island, which it purchased from local Indians for sixty guilders, or twenty-four dollars. The Dutch concentrated their efforts on the plunder of Spanish and Portuguese shipping, but the colony prospered as Dutch farmers proved more eager than the French to cross the Atlantic and other immigrants joined them. With this immigration, New Amsterdam grew rapidly, becoming a polyglot colony with residents from many different European nations, all of them competing for an economic foothold in the New World. Of course, their profusion, like Cortés's march, was irresistible.

AMERICAN PROFILE

Francesco-Giuseppe Bressani
1612–1672

by James Axtell

THE MISSIONARIES who followed European explorers to North America found themselves in fierce competition for Indian souls, not only with one another but also with tenacious native holy men. In the colonies of New England, English Protestants were generally content to postpone their proselytizing for years, even decades, until the native peoples were safely subjugated. Not so the members of the Society of Jesus, who launched in New France the earliest assaults on native "paganism" and "superstition." These men literally risked their lives and limbs seeking converts in sovereign native villages, far from the comforts (and troops) in Quebec and Montreal.

The Jesuits enjoyed their greatest successes with large sedentary peoples, such as the five Huron tribes of southern Ontario. To secure military alliances and trade with the French, the Hurons agreed to admit "black robes" to their villages. These missionaries learned the Huron language, insinuated themselves into leading Huron families, and took Huron names. The tribes' traditional religious leadership resisted the change, but the Jesuits used such advantages as their resistance to epidemic disease, their ability to predict eclipses, and their mysterious power of literacy to persuade thousands of Hurons to accept Christianity. Only later did much more significant opposition arise from the tribes of the

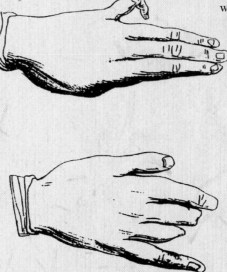

Father Bressani included this drawing of his disfigured hands in a report on his captivity that he wrote in July 1644.

Iroquois Confederation, who were allied with the English and considered the black robes a threat to their domination of northeastern politics.

Among the intrepid missionaries who served Huronia at the height of this Iroquois displeasure was Francesco-Giuseppe Bressani—not a Frenchman at all, but an Italian who had joined the Society of Jesus at age fourteen. During his first three years in the society, Bressani had repeatedly sought missionary work in Canada, only to have his requests denied. But after spending sixteen years in the rigorous Jesuit educational system—first as a student, then as a teacher in Italy and France—he was allowed to sail for New France in 1642.

Bressani spent the next two years ministering to French colonists while learning the Huron tongue from summer visitors. Finally, in late April 1644, he left for Huronia itself, accompanied by six Christian Hurons. Three days later, an Iroquois war party overtook the Hurons' canoes, kidnapping the missionary and his companions. During the next two months, Bressani's captors led him from village to village, subjecting him to some of the most horrendous tortures imaginable. He was eventually condemned to a fiery death but "miraculously" saved by an old woman, who redeemed him for some wampum beads. Bressani sold "cheaply," he said, "because of my want of skill for everything [Indian]" and "because they believed that I would never recover from my wounds."

He described these disfigurements in a letter he wrote from Fort Orange (now Albany, New York) in early July 1644 after he was ransomed by the Dutch. Using a gunpowder solution as ink and "the earth for a table," Bressani apologized to his Jesuit superior for the letter's poor penmanship, explaining that "he who writes it has only one whole finger on his right hand; and it is difficult to avoid staining the paper with the blood which flows from his wounds, not yet healed." Included in Bressani's report was a drawing of his mangled hands—the left one missing a thumb, the right badly truncated.

At each village, Bressani had been forced to run a gauntlet of mocking, jeering Iroquois. Young and old alike would tear out his hair, jab him with sticks, and slice his hands between the fingers. They fed him "filth," pulled out his nails, and suspended him by his feet. Worst of all were the torments by fire—which gave him, he said, "a rough idea of the punishments of Purgatory." The Iroquois "caressed" him (as they called it) with burning coals, pierced his toes with hot irons, and stuck his fingers into lit tobacco pipes, burning them down to successive joints. They also urged him to sing a special song acknowledging his complete powerlessness—though, Bressani wrote, it was "quite impossible to stop screaming."

By November 1644, his wounds had healed sufficiently for the Dutch to put Father Bressani on a ship bound for France. The following autumn, however, he returned to Huronia to resume God's work. Until 1649, when Iroquois

This print of Native Americans in New France appeared in a 1619 edition of Samuel de Champlain's Voyages and Discoveries Made in New France Since the Year 1615.

armies permanently dispersed the Huron tribes, Bressani won numerous converts using his mangled hands to demonstrate the strength and power of his faith. His hands also proved persuasive in Italy, where he preached from 1650 until his death in 1672 with great effect.

MANN

POWHATAN

Held this state & fashion when Capt. Smith
was deliuered to him prisoner
1607

MAN-
GOAGS

CHA
WONS

P O W H A T A N

Powhatan

The Fales

Cattachiptico

Arrohatteck

Orapaks

Passaunkack

Myghtuckpassu

Vtenstank

Accoqueck

Secobeck

Etherston

Bayé

Massawetec

Soackbeck

Cuttatawen

Cheopissoco

Ashwsha

Papisione

Kerahocak

Pissasseck

Nawacaten

Mangoraca

Wecuppom

Matchopick

Pissascack

Cawwentoll

Opiscopanke

Paumkee

Quiyoughcohanock

Mattacoock

Werowacomoco

Cekakawwon

SA-

Cincoteck

PI

Appamatuck

Apocant

Quackcohowaon

Nechanicok

Righkahauk

Weancock

Pamunkee

Attamtuck

Accossiwinck

Mamanahunt

Potauncac

Accomer

Vttamussak

Shakep

Werawahon

Matchut

Menavacant

Kupkipcock

Maltapament flu

Paspahegh

Quiyoughcohanock

Nandtaughtacund

Aurenapeugh

Ozenick

Matchutt

Tanxsnitania

Mattapament

Cinquoteck

Poruptanck

Pasaughtacock

Payankatank flu

Tappahanock flu

Oquanock

Anskenoans

Muttamussinsack

Nandtanghtacund

Warraskoyack

Matho mauk

Mohele

Nandsamund

Mattanock

Teracosick

Sharpes Ile

Mantoughquemec

Chesapeac

Mortons baye

Cape Henry

Cape Charle

Smyths Iles

Ceader Ile

Fleat hope

Keough
tan

Poynt comfort

Osenolds baye

Tindals poynt

Wissins poynt

Poynt Warde

CHE-

Accowmack

Accohanoch

Keals hill

Russels Iles

Wattheus poynt

Kuskar

Kiskiack

Cantaunkack

Capahowasick

Paranka
tank

Pawtecomeoac

Nepawtacum

Kapawnich

Ottachugh

Chesakawon

Cittamawoman

Wighcocomoco

Opament

Rapahanock flu

Vause

Cape harbuor

Washeborne

Reads poynt

Wigheocomoco

Scale of

THE

VIRGINIAN   SEA

2

THE PLANTATION COLONIES

The Founding of Jamestown

JOHN ROLFE LIKED TO SMOKE; but in Jamestown, as in England, tobacco was scarce and expensive. So Rolfe planted a few seeds of a native strain, hoping merely to satisfy his own habit. He had little else to do. The Jamestown settlement was failing, and few of the colonists saw much point in working, other than to escape punishment for violating the strict regulations against laxity. Yet Rolfe discovered something in his horticultural dabblings that would transform the prospects of the English colony in Virginia from dismal to dazzling: Tobacco grew well there.

At the time—the year was 1611 or perhaps 1612—the European trade in tobacco, a crop native to the New World, was a lucrative Spanish monopoly. During his voyages to the West Indies, Columbus had observed Cuban natives smoking small cigars through their nostrils. Eager to please Ferdinand and Isabella with Indian curiosities, he brought some samples of the unusual plant back with him to Spain. A century later, tobacco use in Europe had become widespread, and Spanish colonies in the New World remained the only reliable source for premium leaf. In England, where Walter Raleigh had popularized smoking during the 1580s, there was a substantial back-lash against the habit. King James I considered it "a custom loathsome to the eye, hateful to the

AT LEFT: *A detail of the map of Virginia created by John Smith from surveys he conducted during the summer of 1608. This version of the map accompanied Smith's 1624 memoir,* The Generall Historie of Virginia, New England, and the Summer Isles.

nose, harmful to the brain, dangerous to the lungs, and in the black stinking fume thereof, nearest resembling the horrible Stygian smoke of the pit that is bottomless." As a good mercantilist, King James also worried that his subjects' costly purchases of tobacco from Spanish importers were unnecessarily draining England's gold supplies. Thus, Rolfe's discovery that tobacco flourished in the rich soil and mild climate of the Virginia tidewater had important political and economic implications, not only for Jamestown but for England as well.

The local tobacco that Rolfe grew proved to be "poore and weake, and of a biting taste"; but, after obtaining some seeds from the West Indies, he was able to grow subsequent crops of a much higher quality. By 1613, Rolfe was growing enough tobacco to export, and other settlers quickly began cultivating tobacco themselves—even though there still wasn't enough corn being grown to meet the colonists' dietary needs. During 1616, Virginia exported 2,500 pounds of tobacco; in 1620, those exports jumped to 119,000 pounds; in 1626, the amount was 333,000 pounds; and by 1638, the figure was a whopping 3.1 million pounds per year.

During this time, the tobacco economy came to dominate Virginia, and tobacco itself replaced specie as the most important form of currency. Not only were taxes assessed in pounds of tobacco, but when a ship containing unmarried Englishwomen reached the overwhelmingly male colony in 1619, settlers were offered wives at the price of 120 pounds of tobacco apiece (the approximate cost of each woman's passage). The residents of Jamestown were by this point aware that Rolfe's discovery had saved Virginia from abandonment, but they didn't yet realize that the demands of the tobacco economy, particularly in labor and acreage, had determined a course for them that left little room for correction or deviation.

English Exploration of the New World

ALTHOUGH ENGLAND WAS, like France, late to colonize the New World, its explorations of America began in the immediate aftermath of Columbus's discovery. As early as 1497, King Henry VII sent the Italian navigator Giovanni Caboto (known in England as John Cabot) to the New World in search of a passage to Asia. What Cabot found instead were the rich fishing grounds off Newfoundland (or "New Found Land," as he called it), which the English exploited long before establishing a permanent colony on the North American coast. When Cabot's second voyage, launched in 1498, never returned—it was believed lost at sea—the parsimonious Henry VII refused to finance further expeditions, and his son Henry VIII was too busy with the English Reformation to support colonial ventures. Henry VIII's elder daughter, Mary I, who reigned from 1553 to 1558, reestablished Catholicism in England and promoted trade with Russia but kept English shipping away from the New World because she had no wish to encroach upon the domains of her husband, Philip II of Spain (son of Holy Roman Emperor Charles V). It was, therefore, not until the reign of Mary's sister, Elizabeth I, that English merchant-adventurers were given permission to plunder America.

As committed a Protestant as her sister had been a Catholic, Elizabeth had little respect for Spanish claims to land or property in the New World and no respect at all for the pope's 1493 division of America between Spain and Portugal. Also, the idea of a northwest passage to the Orient appealed to her even more than it had to her grandfather Henry VII. Beginning in 1576, she dispatched Martin Frobisher on three separate voyages to North America, during which he explored Labrador and its environs. Frobisher's results were mixed: As Cabot had, he confirmed the plentiful presence of fish and the disappointing absence of Chinese.

MEANWHILE, although Protestant England and Catholic Spain were not formally at war, the rich Spanish treasure fleets sailing from the New World were targets simply too tempting for the English to resist. Supported and encouraged by their queen, English privateers—chief among them Francis Drake—took to looting Philip II's colonies and shipping, enriching England as they reduced Spanish power. (The privateers operated under royal commissions that entitled them to keep a portion of whatever goods they seized from the Spaniards. They were, in other words, pirates who shared their booty with the Crown.) In 1572, Drake

Elizabeth I appears in her coronation robes in this oil-on-panel work by an unknown artist.

ambushed on the Isthmus of Panama a Spanish mule train carrying a shipment of silver from Peru and became the first English captain to see the Pacific Ocean. In 1577, intending to thwart Spanish interests in the Pacific, he circumnavigated the globe, seizing Spanish treasure as he went. When Drake returned to England in 1580, Spain demanded that he be executed as a pirate, hinting at war should Elizabeth refuse. But the queen knighted Drake and allowed the popular captain to continue his raids on Spanish America.

Elsewhere in America, gentleman-seafarer Humphrey Gilbert, attracted by what he believed to be huge potential profits in the New World, persuaded Elizabeth in 1578 to grant him a six-year charter to discover and settle "heathen lands not possessed by any Christian prince." That November, Gilbert sailed for North America, only to have his poorly outfitted seven-ship fleet broken up by bad weather during the crossing. (Some ships returned to England, while others turned to piracy.) In 1583, Gilbert tried again, this time reaching Newfoundland before perishing when his ship sank in a great storm.

Upon Gilbert's death, his dream of establishing an English colony in America was carried forward by his half brother Walter Raleigh, who obtained in 1584 a new and even more favorable charter from Queen Elizabeth. That same year, Raleigh sent out a reconnaissance mission, which stopped at Puerto Rico before sailing north along the coast of Florida to the Outer Banks off present-day North Carolina. (After Gilbert's misadventures in the North Atlantic, Raleigh had decided to explore farther south.) There, Raleigh's captains found Roanoke Island;

This hand-colored engraving was published in London in 1589. Made by Baptista Boazio from the drawings of a participant (possibly Francis Drake himself), it shows Drake plundering St. Augustine in 1586. Established by Pedro Menéndez de Avilés in 1565, this Florida town is the oldest continuously occupied European settlement on the North American mainland north of Mexico.

and, according to one account, "after thanks given to God for our safe arrival hither, we manned our boats and went to view the land...and to take possession of the same, in the right of the Queen's most excellent Majesty." The explorers noted the abundant game, the "sweet and aromatic smells [that] lay in the air," and the presence of friendly Indians, with whom they traded pots and axes for provisions and animal hides. The Englishmen even transported home two Indians, Manteo and Wanchese, to corroborate their story.

Roanoke

FOLLOWING THEIR RETURN, Raleigh launched a publicity campaign to raise funds for the establishment of a colony on Roanoke. He flattered the unmarried Elizabeth by naming the new land Virginia in her honor, Elizabeth being the Virgin Queen; but already having granted Raleigh a generous charter, Elizabeth had little else to offer him. The monarchs of Spain and France had enough personal wealth to finance colonization themselves, but in England, Parliament controlled the nation's purse strings, and its members had little inclination to bankroll Raleigh's highly speculative adventuring. So Raleigh turned to England's merchant class for money, setting a pattern that would guide future English settlements in North America. Thereafter, English colonization proceeded because of the collaborative efforts of monarchs (who granted the charters), adventurous aristocrats (who established and governed the colonies), and ambitious middle-class entrepreneurs (who risked their own money in colonial joint-stock companies, the forerunners of modern corporations).

The caption that John White inscribed below this watercolor read, "The broyling of their fish over the flame of fier."

In April 1585, Raleigh assembled at Plymouth a fleet of seven ships, which he placed under the command of his cousin Richard Grenville. The fleet carried six hundred men, half of them soldiers. Also among the company were Ralph Lane, an experienced military campaigner who was put in charge of the troops; scientific observer Thomas Hariot, who had learned from Manteo and Wanchese the language of the local tribes; and John White, England's first watercolorist of distinction. Following a few misadventures and some plundering of Spanish ships, the colonists arrived at Roanoke in July and immediately built a fort on the north side of the island. Lane was then left with 107 men to hold the fort while Grenville returned to England for more supplies.

The men who were left behind accomplished little that could be termed colonizing. Most devoted their energies to searching the countryside for gold, while some others explored nearby rivers hoping to find an outlet to the Pacific Ocean. Lane was, of course, ill suited to the work of establishing a permanent colony: He knew nothing of crop raising; he acted belligerently toward the Indians, antagonizing them; and he personally saw no future in a goldless Roanoke. But the lack of communal activity wasn't entirely his fault. As Hariot later noted, the men he commanded were soldiers, not settlers. "Some also," Hariot wrote in *A Briefe and True Report of Virginia* (1588), "were of a nice bringing up, only in cities or towns, and such as never (as I may say) had seen the world before." These men, according to Hariot, missed their "accustomed dainty food," their soft feather beds, and so were miserable. Having come to the New World for treasure, "after gold and silver was not to be found, [they] had little or no care for any other thing but to pamper their bellies." So when Francis Drake happened by after a raid on the Spanish Caribbean, Lane's party decided to abandon Roanoke and returned to England with Drake.

RALEIGH'S THIRD EXPEDITION to North America set out in May 1587, this time with a more stable group of 150 colonists aboard—including some women and children. John White was named governor, and he traveled to Virginia with his pregnant daughter Elenora and her husband, Ananias Dare, who served as White's assistant. (On August 18, Elenora gave birth to Virginia Dare, the first child born to English parents in America.) Finding the original shelters on Roanoke still standing, the 112 colonists who had survived the voyage decided to remain on the island rather than start afresh elsewhere (as Raleigh had planned), and White helped them acclimate. A month later, though, he sailed with the fleet back to England so that he could pressure Raleigh into sending a resupply ship quickly.

Unfortunately, White returned to an England preparing for war. No longer willing to tolerate English raiding of his treasure ships, Philip II of Spain was preparing to send the fabled Spanish Armada against England, and Elizabeth was herself mobilizing her nation's defenses. Overseas voyages were canceled, and

This John White watercolor depicts the Atlantic loggerhead turtle, the only species of sea turtle to breed on the Outer Banks.

THE LOST COLONY

JOHN WHITE'S 1590 RELIEF MISSION arrived at the island of Roanoke at nightfall. "We let fall our Grapnel neere the shore," White wrote in his journal, "& sounded with a trumpet a Call, & afterward many familiar English tunes of Songs, and called to them friendly; but we had no answere." The next morning at daybreak, he rowed ashore and found the island deserted. The only clue to where the colonists had gone was the word CROATOAN carved on a post. Because White had anticipated that the colonists might want to (or have to) leave Roanoke, he had told them to carve a message somewhere indicating their destination. He also told them to add a Maltese cross if they were leaving "in distresse." Because there was no cross beside this message, White hoped that the colony had simply moved on to Croatoan Island, where Manteo was the werowance, or chief. Unfortunately, a storm and some mishaps aboard ship prevented White from searching Croatoan, and Raleigh's attempt to sail past the island in 1595 (after completing an expedition to Guyana) was also unsuccessful. In 1602, a search party sent by Raleigh did look around but discovered nothing. No further trace of the Roanoke colony was ever found.

The failure at Roanoke (shown here in John White's 1590 map) may have indirectly benefited English colonization of North America. Had the Roanoke colony succeeded, the Spanish would surely have attacked it; and in that event, James I would likely have withheld his permission for another expedition to Virginia in 1606.

English ships were ordered to remain in port so that they could join the fleet sailing against the Armada. Not until 1590 was White able to mount a relief expedition to Roanoke, and when he arrived there in August, he found the island deserted and the colonists missing. No trace of them, including White's daughter and granddaughter, was ever found.

Jamestown

ALTHOUGH ENGLAND'S CONFLICT with Spain most likely contributed to the failure at Roanoke—delaying, as it did, White's return for more than two years— the defeat of the Spanish Armada in 1588 played overall a highly positive role in promoting English settlement of North America. The defeat of the Armada proved that England, not Spain, was the Atlantic world's leading naval power—and this, in turn, meant that English colonization could proceed unchallenged. The misfortune at Roanoke dampened enthusiasm for a time, and not much activity took place during the 1590s. But in 1603, James I became king; and as a younger Elizabeth had been, King James was eager to colonize North America. In 1606, he granted a charter to two companies of adventurers, one located in Plymouth and the other in London. In 1607, both of these companies established new colonies on the North American mainland.

This 1621 oil-on-canvas portrait of King James I of England (James VI of Scotland) was painted by Daniel Mytens.

The Plymouth Company settled Sagadahoc on the Kennebec River but lasted only one bitter Maine winter before abandoning its outpost there. The London Company, meanwhile, returned to Raleigh's Virginia. A fleet of three ships commanded by Christopher Newport—the flagship *Susan Constant* and two smaller escort vessels, the *Discovery* and the *Godspeed*—entered the Chesapeake Bay in May 1607, sailed up a river the colonists called the James, and thirty miles along founded a settlement they called Jamestown. The site the colonists chose was a low, marshy peninsula jutting out into the river at a spot where the James narrowed considerably. One advantage of this location was its easy access to deep water (so that large ships could approach it); another was the protection it offered from the Indian attacks that most believed had doomed Roanoke. There was one important disadvantage, however: The peninsula's swampy climate made the colonists prone to malaria, dysentery, and other debilitating diseases.

BESIDES A WARINESS of Indians, other lessons had also been taken from the Roanoke experience. The London Company had made sure, for example, to carry aboard its ships experienced craftsmen—blacksmiths, carpenters, brick-layers, masons—who could accomplish the physical work necessary to build a permanent colony. These men were particularly important because another third of the 144 colonists who sailed to Virginia (104 survived the voyage) were, according to prevailing English standards, "gentlemen"—that is, they enjoyed at least some measure of wealth and status at home and considered their positions in the new settlement to be management rather than labor. They contributed little to the viability of Jamestown as a colony and generally refused to do anything, such as chopping down trees or plowing the soil, that did not directly involve their private gain.

JOHN SMITH
1580?–1631

EVEN BEFORE HIS TRIP to America, John Smith had lived a remarkably adventurous life. At twenty, he had fought in Hungary against the Turks, who captured him. Smith then escaped and spent the next several years wandering across Europe before returning to England in 1604. A relentless self-promoter, he subsequently ingratiated himself with the merchants who were organizing the London Company's expedition to Virginia, and he was hired on as a mercenary. After his return from Jamestown in late 1609, the short, muscular Smith sailed to the New World twice more, these times in the service of the Plymouth Company.

His 1614 voyage mapped the coastline of the region he named New England, and the following year he sailed again, only to be captured by pirates, from whom he escaped three months later penniless. Although Smith never saw North America after that, he wrote and talked about it for the rest of his life. His books, including *Map of Virginia with a Description of the Country* (1612) and *The Generall Historie of Virginia, New England, and the Summer Isles* (1624), are vivid accounts of his experiences; and, although fanciful at times, they have been largely corroborated by modern scholars.

Why did these people—most of whom, incidentally, claimed the title *captain*—come to the New World? Reasons varied, but many shared hopes, nurtured by the London Company, of achieving glory and quick fortunes—the same goals that had motivated the Spanish conquistadores a century earlier. Although some among this ambitious crowd looked for an easy passage to the Pacific, most were obsessed with the search for gold. According to Capt. John Smith, who accompanied the 1607 expedition as a hired soldier, "There was no talk, no hope, no work, but dig gold, wash gold, refine gold, load gold." Of course, it was all talk because there was no gold.

Virtually the only communal activity concerned intrigues over leadership. King James's 1606 charter had given the London Company all the authority it needed to govern Virginia as it wished, and the company council, which remained in England, had set up a local council to exercise that authority on a day-to-day basis. Good leadership was crucial, because the settlers faced grave problems: They had to construct defenses against the Indians, they had to stockpile food for the winter, and they had to find something they could export to England so that the London Company would continue to support them. But the council members merely bickered the time away, neglecting the work that had to be done.

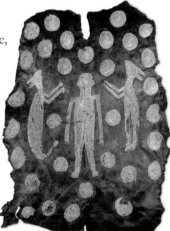

This ceremonial mantle, now in the collection of the Ashmolean Museum at Oxford, once belonged to Powhatan, who died in 1618. It was made of four white-tailed deer hides stitched together; the garment was then decorated with small shells.

The Powhatan Confederacy

IN FACT, TROUBLE WITH THE INDIANS began early, because the Jamestown settlement encroached on some traditional hunting grounds. Just weeks after the colonists arrived, there was an attack, and only cannon fire from the *Godspeed* prevented Indian warriors from overrunning the settlement—more by its terrifying sound than any bloody effect. Thereafter, the settlers reinforced the town's ramshackle fort, but the colony remained at great risk.

Most of the thirty or so tribes in the region that lay between the Potomac River and the Great Dismal Swamp belonged to what Thomas Jefferson later called the Powhatan Confederacy. They gave their allegiance to the great Algonkin werowance (chief) Powhatan, whose capital was at Werowocomoco. It was said that Powhatan controlled more than one hundred villages with about nine thousand inhabitants. His authority was similar to that of a king, and he was an intelligent, capable leader, if also considered somewhat cruel. Powhatan's first personal contact with one of the Jamestown settlers came during the winter of 1607, when John Smith, who had been exploring the Chesapeake, was captured by Indians loyal to Powhatan and brought to the bark-covered house of the chief.

The colonists had had a difficult summer. They had been on their own since late June, when Captain Newport returned to England with the *Susan Constant* and the *Godspeed*. (The pinnace *Discovery* remained with the colonists.) Those ships had been loaded with timber, tar, pitch, and other raw materials available near Jamestown. It was hoped that the cargo would please the colony's sponsors and demonstrate Jamestown's economic potential, but all understood that this was no Spanish treasure hoard, and even the ore samples taken back for testing proved disappointing.

Even worse, once the summer heat set in, so did the epidemic diseases. Many colonists died, and those who didn't were often too fatigued to work. On a given day, only half a dozen or fewer men might be available for watch duty on the fort's palisades. "There were never Englishmen left in a foreign country in such miserie as we were in this new discouvered Virginia," Capt. George Percy later wrote. "[We heard] the pitifull murmurings and outcries of our sick men without reliefe, every night and day for the space of sixe weeks: some departing out of the World, many times three or four in a night; in the morning their bodies being trailed out of their cabines like Dogges, to be buried." So many men were dying that the colonists later began burying them at night, rather than let the Indians know how weakened they had become. The winter that followed, of course, was not much better; and by the end of 1607, only 38 of the original 104 settlers were still alive.

This illustration from John Smith's 1624 Generall Historie glorifies the author's courage in forcing American savages into subjection. Here, Smith "fighteth the King of Pamaunkee" in 1608.

THE SURVIVAL OF JAMESTOWN was now obviously in doubt, and food was the central concern. Apparently only John Smith understood that the colony's fate depended on the procurement of Indian corn. A few friendly tribes had provided some staples in exchange for English metalware, but a much greater supply was needed. So Smith, who had been deprived of his seat on the Jamestown governing council because of his excessive shipboard arrogance, proposed that he lead an expedition to find more trading partners. The leadership at Jamestown, such as it was, concluded that it had nothing to lose: If Smith returned with food, they would eat; if the Indians killed him, his death would be no loss. At first, Smith's forays were highly successful, and the bargeloads of corn and beans he provided increased his influence at Jamestown. During one of these trips, however, he was ambushed by Indians, who killed the other men in the party and took Smith to see Powhatan. A year later, Smith wrote that he had first seen Powhatan *proudly lying upon a bedstead a foot high, upon ten or twelve mats, richly hung with many chains of great pearls about his neck, and with a great covering of [raccoon skins]. At his head sat one woman, at his feet another. On each side, sitting upon a mat upon the ground, were ranged his chief men on each side of the fire, ten in a rank, and behind them as many young women, each with a great chain of white beads over their shoulders, their heads painted in Red.*

Although he could not have reasonably expected to leave Powhatan's camp alive, Smith nevertheless tried to reassure the chief that the people of Jamestown were friendly. He denied that the London Company intended to establish permanent settlements on Powhatan's land and told the chief disingenuously that the colonists had come ashore because their ship had needed repairs and that "wee were inforced to stay to mend her."

It is unlikely that Powhatan believed these or any other Smith fabrications, but he was charmed by the Englishman and decided to welcome him, at least for the time being, as a friend and potential ally against the tribes of the interior who still resisted Powhatan's rule. Guides subsequently returned Smith to Jamestown, where the captain showed them the fort and demonstrated the power of its cannon by firing a load of stones into nearby icicle-laden trees. The display alarmed the Indians, much as Cortés's demonstrations had terrified Moctezuma's envoys.

John Smith Takes Over

ALTHOUGH SMITH may have temporarily solved the colony's Indian problem, Jamestown's circumstances in early 1608 remained desperate. Food was still scarce, and the colony's leadership, which continued to despise Smith, wanted to hang him for causing the slaughter of his companions. Only Newport's serendipitous return from England in January 1608 saved Smith's life. Afterward, Smith became not merely the colony's chief Indian trader but also its chief explorer—welcoming, according to one historian, "any reason to be away from the ill-led colonists." In September 1608, however, Smith was elected president of the Jamestown council because of his previous achievements, the fact that he clearly embodied the colony's best chance to survive the coming winter, and the lack of any suitable alternative candidate.

For the next year, John Smith governed Jamestown firmly. He divided the colonists (who, with new arrivals, now numbered two hundred) into work details of ten to fifteen men each and, despite his frequent absences, imposed a strict discipline upon them. He staged weekly military drills and also frequent musket firings to impress any Indians who might be watching. Meanwhile, he exchanged beads and other European trade goods for food whenever and wherever he could. When the Indians he met proved unwilling to swap food for his baubles, Smith often burned their towns and took the food anyway. Smith suspected that Powhatan was discouraging trade with the whites, and this was probably true; but at the same time, Smith failed to consider another explanation: that the Indians raised corn for food, not for cash, and sometimes there was little surplus.

An illustration from 1622 shows the hand of Fate about to grab an unsuspecting ship. Newport's fleet minimized the risks of early navigation by sailing the middle latitudes and making island stopovers at the Canaries and in the Caribbean. It wasn't until 1609 that Samuel Argall undertook the first direct crossing.

***This goffering iron** was used at Jamestown to spruce up ruffs.*

History has largely credited Smith's stern rule with the rescue of Jamestown. During the winter of 1608–1609, only a handful of the settlers perished—a remarkable feat when one considers the prevalence of death during the early years in Virginia. (Between 1607 and 1623, a total of eighty-five hundred people emigrated to the colony; in 1624, fewer than thirteen hundred of them remained alive.) Using clever bluffs and harsh but effective discipline, Smith proved his mettle as a leader, ruling Jamestown arbitrarily but well. When a relief convoy arrived in July 1609, however, its captain, Samuel Argall, informed Smith that the king had issued a new charter for Virginia and that the London Company (now calling itself the Virginia Company) had formed a new colonial government to replace the Jamestown council over which Smith presided. Two months later, an ailing Smith, suffering from a severe powder burn, sailed for England, never to return.

THE NEW CHARTER REPLACED the elected council president with a governor appointed by the Virginia Company. As the colony's first governor, the Virginia Company chose Thomas West, twelfth baron De La Warre. Because De La Warre was unable to leave immediately, however, Thomas Gates was sent in his place to assume temporary command of Jamestown. Unfortunately, Gates's ship was wrecked off the coast of Bermuda, where he and the other survivors spent the winter of 1609–1610 constructing two new ships to complete their crossing.

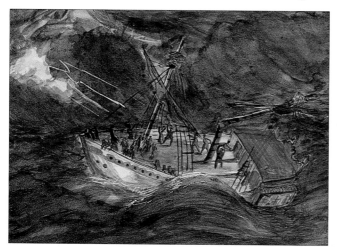

A scene from an early-nineteenth-century promptbook for The Tempest. *It shows the ship-wreck that strands the Italians on Prospero's island. For his source material, Shakespeare used published accounts of Thomas Gates's 1609 shipwreck off the coast of Bermuda.*

Meanwhile, the rest of the fleet reached Jamestown safely, depositing four hundred more colonists, including the first women and children.

The Virginia Company was in the process of changing its mind about the profits it expected to earn from Jamestown. At first, its stockholders had sought quick gains through the acquisition of precious metals, or trade with the Orient, or both. By this point, however, they were beginning to realize that profits would have to come in the long term. So the Virginia Company began restructuring its business to resemble the "plantations" that England had recently placed in Ireland to exploit and control the Irish. These were, in fact, transplantations (hence the word *plantation*) of English society into an alien environment. The Spaniards who came to America adapted in many ways to the Indian cultures they found; the English, however, worked hard to create a microcosm of the Old World in the New that could exist independent of the natives. For example, Jamestown's various governors made it a point to retrieve any colonists who had gone native—humiliating them publicly before executing them, often in a brutal manner, so that others would be discouraged from attempting the same.

With this development of a self-sufficient society in mind, the Virginia Company recruited families for the 1609 crossing, believing that family life would encourage colonists to develop a permanent stake in the colony's welfare. (With families to feed, it was reasoned, the men of Jamestown would have to grow food systematically.) There was still no private ownership of land, but the company made this offer to its colonists (or at least those who could pay their own cost of passage): Contribute seven years of communal labor and receive at the end of that period land of your own. Those who could not afford to pay their own way across the Atlantic were offered a different deal: Receive passage (but no land) in exchange for seven years of labor. In this way, the first white indentured servants came to Virginia.

The Starving Time

WITH SMITH GONE, however, Powhatan sensed an opportunity to rid himself of Jamestown once and for all. Quietly, he ordered the tribes of his confederacy to stop trading with the whites, knowing that without Indian corn the whites could not survive. At the same time, in Jamestown, the bickering resumed; and the vital tasks of food collection and town building, so ably (if harshly) directed by Smith, became largely ignored. The colonists sent out trading missions, but of the eighty-six men who left Jamestown, only fourteen returned. When the colonists demanded that Powhatan explain these disappearances, the Algonkin chief replied that perhaps the missing settlers had met up with the lost Roanoke colony and were reluctant to leave such convivial company.

Without Indian corn, food supplies became so inadequate that the winter of 1609–1610 came to be known as the "starving time." The residents of Jamestown ate cats and dogs, then rats and mice, and finally anything, even horsehide, that might fill their stomachs. There were even accounts of cannibalism. One colonist was reportedly executed for digging up corpses, and another was burned to death for dismembering his pregnant wife and salting those portions of her that he failed to eat immediately. By the time Gates finally arrived in May 1610, the approximately five hundred colonists who had begun the winter in Jamestown had been whittled down to just sixty or so survivors. Observing their condition and the growing hostility of the Indians, Gates decided to abandon the settlement immediately. Just as he was preparing to leave, however, Lord De La Warre arrived with three abundantly provisioned relief ships, and the decision was made to stay.

Although De La Warre himself lasted only a single year in Virginia (his health failed him), the government he established under Gates, though harsh, enabled the colony to survive, if not prosper. The "Laws Divine, Moral and Martiall" promulgated by Gates in 1611 required strict obedience of the Sabbath, forbade immodest dress, and punished laxity. Transgressors were dealt with severely. Some were burned at the stake, others hanged or shot, and still others broken on the wheel. (Under its charter, the Virginia Company was entitled to deny colonists any or all of the rights they had enjoyed in England, including the right to a trial by jury.) Killing an animal without permission was punishable by death; washing filthy items near the village well—the chief source of its fresh water—earned the violator a whipping; and colonists who cursed or fought were "tied head and feete together" every night for a month. This formal body of laws, the first in America, was also known as Dale's Code after Thomas Dale, the marshal who enforced it. (Between 1614 and 1616, Dale also served as the acting governor of Virginia.)

This watercolor painted by John White about 1585 records the clothing and elaborate body painting of an Algonkin man accoutered for a hunt.

SMITH AND POCAHONTAS

WHEN JOHN SMITH LEARNED in 1616 that Pocahontas (now Rebecca Rolfe) would be visiting England, he jumped on the opportunity for self-promotion. Specifically, he wrote a public letter to Queen Anne in which he praised Pocahontas and urged that she be invited to the court of James I. Attempting to dramatize their shared contribution to the pacification of Virginia, Smith related a story that he had never told before, although opportunities had been plentiful. According to Smith's letter, twelve-year-old Pocahontas had saved his life during his 1607 encounter with her father, Powhatan. With great sentimentality, Smith wrote about how Pocahontas had interposed herself between the Englishman and his Indian executioners, cradling his head in her lap as the savages prepared to crush it between two large stones. Thus was Smith's life spared.

This 1616 portrait of Pocahontas in English garb was painted by William Sheppard not long after the Indian princess's arrival in London.

Whatever the truth of this story, Pocahontas was a popular guest in England. She spoke the language well, carried herself with great dignity, and lived in style with her husband and young son thanks to funds provided by the publicity-hungry Virginia Company. Meanwhile, the Indian princess attended masques at court, listened to the poetry of Ben Jonson, and was dazzled by the elegance of London. She would likely have stayed in England indefinitely had the Virginia Company not decided in early 1617 that it was time to send the Rolfes back to Jamestown. On their journey to the port at Gravesend, however, Pocahontas contracted smallpox, and she died in March before her ship could sail.

Relations with the Indians during this period were noticeably more violent. (In general, despite Powhatan's veneer of friendship and the London Company's instructions that the natives be treated fairly, both sides usually behaved as harshly as circumstances allowed.) The colonists resurrected Smith's strong-arm methods of expropriating corn—they were still dependent on the Indians for food—but they exhibited none of Smith's restraint or finesse. Not surprisingly, Powhatan responded in kind, and brutal bloodletting continued for several years. During the winter of 1612–1613, however, Capt. Samuel Argall, while trading for corn with the Potomac Indians, learned that Powhatan's daughter Pocahontas was nearby, visiting friends. Reasoning that she would make a most useful hostage, Argall kidnapped the princess and brought her to Jamestown—where, as ransom negotiations dragged on for more than a year, she became accustomed to life among the English. It turned out that, even as a young girl, Pocahontas had been fascinated by life in the colony; and during her captivity, as this attraction grew, she converted to Christianity and was baptized. In April 1614, she even married John Rolfe. Their union, in turn, initiated a long truce between the whites and the Indians. Powhatan, who reluctantly accepted the marriage but did not attend the wedding, knew that this peace served mainly the interests of the whites (by allowing them to expand their settlement without resistance); but, tired and disheartened, he felt powerless to oppose it.

An assortment of Indian trade beads used by the settlers at Jamestown.

Yet even peace with the Indians wasn't enough to reverse Jamestown's fortunes, and it remained a miserable, deadly place. The fluxes and fevers continued, and so did the food shortages. Because Rolfe had shown the potential profitability of tobacco cultivation, many more colonists were now tilling the soil, but few were sparing even small patches for corn, and yields of food crops stayed low. Dale's Code saw the colony through, but the settlers often referred to the years between 1611 and 1616 as those of "slavery." Conditions began to ease, however, after 1614 when Dale, using the enhanced powers of the governor's office, began transferring some land to private ownership, even before the seven-year communal period had ended. This change in policy, John Rolfe wrote, "giveth all greate content, for now knowing their owne landes, they strive and are prepared to build houses & to cleer their groundes ready to plant, which giveth…them greate incouragement, and the greatest hope to make the Colony florrish."

MARYLAND

AFTER CONVERTING TO CATHOLICISM in 1625, George Calvert, the first baron Baltimore, set about establishing a refuge in America for English Catholics, who were facing repression at home. In 1632, he persuaded King Charles I to grant him land for that purpose in northern Virginia. Calvert died before a formal charter could be issued, but the king followed through despite Calvert's death and issued a charter later that year to Calvert's oldest son, Cecilius, the second lord Baltimore. In gratitude, Cecilius named the new colony Maryland after Charles's wife, Queen Henrietta Maria.

Although the charter named Cecilius Calvert the proprietor of Maryland, it was actually his younger brother Leonard who led the first group of English Catholics to America. Leonard also served as the governor of Maryland from its founding in 1634 until his death in 1647, while Cecilius remained in England to defend the charter and the family against Protestant attack. The Maryland charter granted the Calverts land from the Potomac River north to latitude forty degrees, and Leonard chose as the site of the first settlement a spot near the mouth of the Potomac that he called Saint Marys. Because the Jamestown settlement was nearby and Leonard's relations with the coastal Indians were friendly, the

George Calvert, *a stockholder in the London Company and a favorite of James I, tried unsuccessfully to establish a colony in Newfoundland before petitioning James's son Charles I for land in Virginia.*

Maryland colony managed to avoid Virginia's brutal experiences with starvation and violence.

Despite Maryland's origins as a Catholic refuge, the Calverts always permitted Protestants to settle there and urged that they be treated civilly. During the English Civil War, fought during the 1640s, Maryland took in hundreds of Puritan immigrants who felt unwelcome in Virginia, which remained steadfastly loyal to the Crown. Ironically, the Protestants in Maryland soon came to outnumber the Catholics, prompting the colonial assembly to pass a 1649 law, the Act of Religious Toleration, to safeguard the rights of the Catholic minority. Although the Toleration Act did require Marylanders to accept the divinity of Jesus Christ, it nevertheless endorsed the coexistence of different Christian sects, which was no small thing during a time when England itself was torn by religious violence. Among the English colonies in North America, only Rhode Island practiced comparable tolerance toward religious dissenters.

Following Oliver Cromwell's victory in the English Civil War, Puritans came to power in Maryland as well, and their repeal of the Toleration Act led to a brief civil war. By 1657, however, the second baron Baltimore had recovered his control of the colony, and Maryland returned to its previous policy of religious coexistence.

The Reforms of 1619

FOR VIRGINIA TO FLOURISH, the colony had to grow tobacco; and to grow tobacco, the colonists had to have two things in abundant supply: land (because heavy-feeding tobacco plants quickly depleted the thin tidewater soil) and labor. In 1619, to satisfy these needs, the Virginia Company introduced several important reforms. The most important, the headright system, enticed workers to Jamestown by granting fifty acres of land to anyone who transported himself to the colony and stuck it out for three years. Heads of families could also claim additional fifty-acre parcels for each family member or servant they brought along. Thus, moderately wealthy Englishmen who crossed with their entire households were able to begin life in Virginia with quite sizable estates.

Meanwhile, the Virginia Company continued to offer passage to England's unemployed in exchange for five to seven years of labor. These indentured servants, whose rights were severely restricted (they could not vote or marry), made up the bulk of Virginia's labor force for the next fifty years. The group that eventually replaced them, the African slaves, also began arriving in Virginia at this time. In his diary entry for August 20, 1619, John Rolfe noted, "There came in a Dutch man-of-warre that sold us 20 negars." Actually, these particular Africans, the first in Virginia, may not have been slaves. There is reason to believe that they were treated the same as white indentured servants. But this brief racial equality didn't last long. After 1660, as white servants became increasingly scarce and expensive (and former servants, now freemen, proved socially and politically combustible), large landowners turned more and more to imported African slaves to work their lucrative tobacco crops.

A few of the many early tobacco pipes unearthed during recent excavations at Jamestown.

CAROLINA

FOLLOWING THE RESTORATION of the monarchy in 1660, England began a period of vigorous colonial expansion. In 1663, for example, King Charles II granted eight nobles who had been influential in his restoration vast territory in southern Virginia that they named Carolina after *Carolus*, the Latin form of *Charles*. Some of these men had made large fortunes planting sugar on Barbados, and they were eager to expand their colonial ventures in America. In 1670, they sponsored an expedition that established a settlement at Albemarle Point. (Charles Town, later renamed Charleston, was moved across the Ashley River to its present location in 1680.)

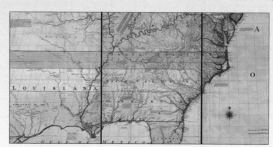

As with many other American colonies, the original Carolina land grant (shown here in a 1755 map) extended all the way to the Pacific.

The plantation society that they created around Charles Town closely resembled the one they had established on Barbados—except that instead of sugar, they now grew rice. Carolina suffered from the same labor shortage as in Virginia, however; and with white indentured servants becoming ever less available, African slaves soon came to dominate the population in the southern half of the colony. Meanwhile, since 1653, malcontents from Virginia, including criminals and runaway slaves, had been settling the land around Albemarle Sound in the colony's northern half. This distinct region, known first as Albemarle and then as North Carolina, became a separate proprietary colony in 1712. (Both North Carolina and South Carolina became royal colonies in 1729.)

GEORGIA

IN 1732, GEORGE II made a grant of land that became the last colony founded on the North American mainland under English royal auspices. He gave the unsettled territory between the Savannah and Altamaha Rivers to a group of English philanthropists who wanted to create a sanctuary for otherwise worthy men who had been sent to debtor's prison. (Many of the colony's early settlers came directly from English jails.) The leader of the colony's trustees, James Oglethorpe, arrived with the first hundred settlers in 1733 and personally founded the city of Savannah near the South Carolina border. South Carolinians were delighted because they saw the new colony of Georgia as a bulwark against the Spanish in Florida.

The trustees of Georgia hoped to attain their humanitarian goals by creating a society of small, industrious farmers not unlike that of New England. Capital to establish this planned society came from Parliament as well as from the trustees themselves. Slavery was outlawed, landholdings were limited to fifty acres, and the settlers were forced to grow silk, which was less profitable than tobacco or rice but did not require slave labor. Not surprisingly, these social and economic controls, especially their prohibition of land speculation, discouraged migration and private investment.

It didn't take long, though, for political opposition to mount, and pressure from both new arrivals and Georgia's colonial neighbors soon forced the abandonment of Oglethorpe's experiment. In 1742, the ban on rum was lifted, and by 1750 slavery was legalized. This led, in turn, to increases in the number of rice plantations and the size of estates. When the trustees surrendered their charter to the Crown in 1752, Georgia was already well on its way to acquiring the social structure common to England's other plantation colonies.

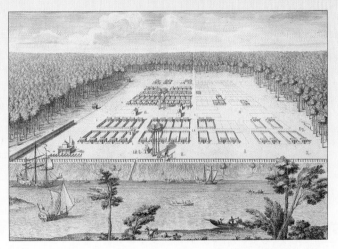

This **View of Savanah** [sic] As It Stood the 20th of March, 1734 *was published in London a year later. Intended to promote investment in and emigration to the colony, it shows the town of Savannah as James Oglethorpe originally laid it out.*

The House of Burgesses

ANOTHER NOTEWORTHY EVENT of 1619 was the introduction by Virginia's new governor, George Yeardley, of greater political rights for the colonists. Until 1619, the residents of Jamestown had lived under martial law; now, Yeardley declared, Virginians would enjoy the same rights as other Englishmen. A representative government was established—the first in the New World—and annual meetings were scheduled. The first of these began on July 30, 1619. Composed of twenty-two men (two from each of Virginia's eleven organized "plantations," or counties), the House of Burgesses met for a full week, acting as a House of Commons to the governor and his council's House of Lords. The chief business that year was reform of Dale's Code, and changes were made in light of eight years' experience and the popular will. When Yeardley approved the changes, they became law.

Nothing like this had ever occurred in a Spanish, French, or Portuguese colony. With it, Virginia's bifurcation began: On the one hand, geographically removed from the influence of the Crown, new social and political institutions—

democratic institutions—were being formed. On the other, the foundation of Virginia's undemocratic slave-labor economy was also being laid.

RELATIONS WITH THE INDIANS turned nasty again in March 1622, when Powhatan's successor, his brother Opechancanough, launched coordinated surprise attacks on the white settlements around Jamestown. It was, Opechancanough believed, the Indians' last chance to save themselves from white domination. He could see the results of the eight-year peace: More Englishmen arriving each year, more land being taken for tobacco, more concessions being demanded from the Indians. So his warriors approached the white villages as though they had goods to trade and then, suddenly, attacked. The raids killed 347 settlers (including women, children, and, it seems, John Rolfe) before the English recovered

BACON'S REBELLION

BY THE MID-1670S, indentured servants who had become freemen in Virginia were finding it increasingly difficult to prosper. The owners of the large tobacco estates had already taken up all the available coastal land, and high transportation costs, as well as high taxes, were making it difficult for yeoman farmers in the interior to get by. This decline in social mobility can be most strikingly seen in the history of the House of Burgesses, where not a single indentured servant arriving in Virginia after 1640 ever became a member. The power of Virginia's oligarchy was such that, beginning in 1661, even elections were ignored, and the burgesses simply retained their seats from year to year without popular consent.

Jamestown never held much interest for Nathaniel Bacon. Even during the 1670s, three generations after its founding, the settlement left much to be desired. Yet it did begin the continuous presence of the English in North America.

Meanwhile, freed servants swelled the ranks of the wandering poor, who traveled from county to county in the Virginia interior, avoiding the tax collector while hunting and stealing to stay alive. Yet the colonial government in Jamestown was not, at least at first, the object of their growing wrath. That was reserved for the Indians, who had likewise been forced out of the tidewater by the spread of the whites. (It was no accident that the Piedmont counties with the most freed servants were also those with the highest Indian populations.) As a result, poor whites often expressed their frustrations with violence against their Indian neighbors.

For the most part, clashes with the Indians proved a sufficient distraction, but attitudes changed in 1675 when Gov. William Berkeley mustered a large force in response to some Indian raiding and then, at the last minute, canceled the campaign. Berkeley's decision to build forts instead (many on land owned by his friends) disgusted Nathaniel Bacon, a twenty-eight-year-old planter and member of the governor's council, who had emigrated from England just two years earlier to farm a thousand-acre estate up the James River. Living near the frontier, Bacon had witnessed both the discontent of the dislocated poor and the self-absorption of Virginia's ruling oligarchy.

As soon as he learned of Berkeley's decision to withdraw, Bacon (a cousin of the governor by and forced an Indian retreat. Even by contemporary Virginian standards, the killings were a special horror because the whites and Indians involved had often known each other for years, having traded peacefully for almost a decade. The merciless English reprisals continued for years; and, as a result, with the exception of a lesser uprising in 1644, the Indians soon ceased to be a threat.

Even so, news of the 1622 massacre disturbed many in London and prompted King James to order an investigation. The exorbitantly high mortality rates discovered by his 1623 commission (fewer than one in six of the settlers who had left England since 1607 was still alive) and the Virginia Company's woeful finances (the colony was still not showing any profit) persuaded him in May 1624 to revoke the company's charter and make Virginia a possession of the Crown, which it remained until 1776.

marriage) applied for a commission to raise a militia himself that he might lead against the Indians. Berkeley refused, but Bacon continued with his preparations regardless. In May 1676, the governor denounced Bacon and, to reinforce his political position, called for new elections, the first in fifteen years. New burgesses, he explained, could air the grievances of the people in a proper legal manner. Meanwhile, Berkeley urged Bacon to repent, and when Bacon refused, Berkeley declared Bacon and his followers to be rebels.

Because of widespread discontent among landless Virginians, however, Berkeley's action proved unwise. Now directly threatened by the authorities in Jamestown, many humble settlers refocused their anger on the colonial government and elected to the House of Burgesses a majority sympathetic to Bacon—including Bacon himself, whom Berkeley had arrested as he tried to take his seat. In order to placate a group of wealthy landowners who thought Indian fighting a perfectly appropriate activity for discontented whites, Bacon was soon pardoned, yet Berkeley still refused him a military commission to subjugate the Indians.

Bacon then raised an army of five hundred men and marched on Jamestown, where he forced Berkeley at gunpoint in June 1676 to grant his request. Meanwhile, the new burgesses enacted reforms granting landless freemen the right to vote and forbidding tax collectors to continue pocketing, as they had been, percentages of the revenues they collected. But Bacon was always more interested in fighting Indians than reforming the colony's politics, and he soon left Jamestown for the frontier. A renewed effort by Berkeley to regain control of the colony brought him back in September, and after forcing the governor to retreat by ship, Bacon burned Jamestown to the ground. The rebellion degenerated a month later, however, when Bacon died of dysentery and his followers, lacking direction, began to switch sides or lay down their arms. In the end, Bacon's Rebellion did little to overthrow the wealthy in Virginia but much to encourage Virginia's planter aristocracy to reduce its reliance on politically unreliable white indentured labor and move instead toward a black labor force that could be kept permanently enslaved.

William Berkeley was not generally a harsh governor, but the revenge he took upon the insurgents following Bacon's death was bloody indeed. As Charles II remarked, "That old fool has taken away more lives in that naked country than I did here for the murder of my father."

AMERICAN PROFILE

Squanto
?–1622

by Elliott West

GENERATIONS OF SCHOOLCHILDREN have heard the story. The spring following the Pilgrims' arrival at Plymouth, a local Indian emerges from the forest, pledges his friendship, and teaches the colonists valuable lessons in survival—how to grow corn, what plants to gather, where to fish, and how to roust eels from the mud using one's feet.

This Indian was Squanto. In many classroom retellings, his life is still used to support the notion that simple, guileless natives greeted America's European colonizers with wide eyes and open hands—that they not merely accepted but positively embraced the good news of the Old World's arrival in the New. One children's biography even has Squanto calling out, "Welcome Englishmen!" Yet there are other meanings and lessons to be found in Squanto's story that are at once much more revealing and far more shadowy.

Also called Tisquantum, Squanto was a member of the Patuxet people, who lived on the shores of Massachusetts Bay. The year of his birth is uncertain, but he was a young man in 1614 when an English sea captain, Thomas Hunt, grabbed him (along with nineteen other Indians) and hauled him off to a slave market in Spain. Squanto's kidnapping reminds us that coastal tribes were well acquainted with European adventurers long before the first settlers arrived. Beginning in the mid–sixteenth century, more than five hundred ships a year fished the teeming waters off Newfoundland and traded with the natives for furs and other exotic valuables. From the start, Europeans also carried away more than a few of the natives—some willingly, some not. The lucky ones were cherished novelties, yet many more became part of a west-to-east slave trade that substantially predated the triangular trade of the seventeenth and eighteenth centuries.

Squanto fared much better than most of those enslaved. He was purchased by Spanish monks, who treated him well. The details of his life over the next three years are mostly lost, but in 1617 he returns to the historical record, living in London. By then he must have learned a great deal about European culture and was probably conversant in several Continental languages. Most of all, he was eager to return home, and he found that his uncommon knowledge was his ticket back. To those Englishmen of means who had transatlantic ambitions, Squanto's store of information was invaluable. One of these men, Sir Ferdinando Gorges, was outfitting an expedition to scout the Massachusetts coastline for possible settlement sites; and when Gorges's ship left England in 1619, Squanto was aboard, presumably to act as a guide and interpreter. Once across the Atlantic, however, Squanto bolted and made his way back to his village, only to find it deserted and in ruins. He later learned that an epidemic disease, perhaps smallpox or bubonic plague, had ravaged the Patuxets, along several other tribes, sometime about 1617. All of Squanto's people had either died or fled. Such scourges were, in fact, powerful tools of conquest. Because native immune systems presented "virgin soil," Indian tribes were appallingly vulnerable to Old World infections, which killed many natives outright and also undermined the economies of those who managed to survive. At the same time, many Europeans considered these epidemics divine endorsements of their moral superiority. One colonist described the process as "the wondrous wisdom and love of God…sweep[ing] away by heaps the savages." The dead were generally left as carrion, and once the flesh was gone, the bones and skulls "made such a pectacle…that… it seemed to me a new found Golgotha."

The author of these words, Thomas Morton, was the Pilgrims' first historian, and the grisly scene he described was the home to which Squanto returned. Morton recalled the tableau so well because it was on the site of the ruined Patuxet village that the Pilgrims established their own town of Plymouth in December 1620. The following spring, they met Squanto, who had been living since 1619 with Massasoit's Wampanoags. Amazed by his fluency in English, the colonists immediately recognized his potential value to their enterprise and asked him to join their community, which he did.

Squanto helped the Pilgrims establish friendly relations with the Wampanoags and other native peoples, taught them how to farm and fish, and introduced them to the fur trade. Indian rivals accused him of subverting tribal interests, and some Pilgrims suspected that he might be exaggerating the danger of Indian violence in order to maximize his own value, but these complaints never rose to the level of endangering either Squanto or his role as a shrewd, respected cultural intermediary. His remarkable life, which ended in November 1622, leaves us no comforting truisms, but it does speak of colonial beginnings and native endings as resistant to easy moralism as everything else that would follow.

A popular engraving from the late nineteenth century of Squanto welcoming the Pilgrims.

3

PURITAN NEW ENGLAND

The Witches of Salem

DRAGGED FROM HER SICKBED by constables on March 23, 1692, seventy-one-year-old Rebecca Nurse found herself the next day sitting before two magistrates in a Salem Village meetinghouse packed with hysterical neighbors. Ailing and nearly deaf, she could barely hear the charge being made against her: "suspicion of having committed…acts of witchcraft." She was not the first Salem woman thus charged—witchmania had been tearing up her community for more than a month—but all of those previously accused had been women of low social standing whose behavior or circumstances had somehow disturbed the town's well-defined social order. Rebecca Nurse, however, was among the first of the "unlikely" witches. A deeply pious woman, she and her husband, Francis, were among Salem Village's most respected residents. With their four sons and four daughters, they worked a prosperous three-hundred-acre farm, and Francis Nurse was often called upon to resolve disputes among his neighbors.

Yet the witch hysteria so gripped Salem Village during the winter of 1692 that, by late March, none of its citizens was beyond suspicion. Emotions ran unchecked, and the atmosphere in the Salem Village meetinghouse was bedlam. The examinations that took place there were often interrupted by the shrieks of the "afflicted" (as the

AT LEFT: *The frontispiece to* Matthew Hopkins's 1647 manual The Discovery of Witches. *The self-appointed Hopkins was England's foremost witch hunter during the rule of Oliver Cromwell. Those who questioned his methods usually came under suspicion themselves.*

accusers were known), and the questioning of the magistrates typically assumed that the accused were guilty. The examination of Rebecca Nurse on March 24 by magistrates John Hathorne and Jonathan Corwin was dutifully recorded by Rev. Samuel Parris, minister of Salem Village:

JOHN HATHORNE: *What do you say (speaking to one afflicted) have you seen this Woman hurt you?*
ABIGAIL WILLIAMS: *Yes, she beat me this morning.*
HATHORNE: *…Have you been hurt by this Woman?*
WILLIAMS: *Yes.*
Ann Putnam in a grievous fit cryed out….
HATHORNE: *Goody Nurse, here are two—Ann Putnam the child and Abigail Williams—complains of your hurting them. What do you say to it?*
REBECCA NURSE: *I can say before my Eternal father I am innocent, & God will clear my innocency…. I am innocent & clear & have not been able to get out of doors these 8 or 9 Dayses.*
HATHORNE: *Mr. Putnam, give in what you have to say.*
Then Mr. Edward Putnam gave in his relate.
HATHORNE: *Is this true Goody Nurse?*
NURSE: *I never afflicted no child never in my life.*
HATHORNE: *You see these accuse you, is it true?*
NURSE: *No.*
HATHORNE: *Are you an innocent person, relating to this Witchcraft?*
Here Tho. Putnam's wife [also named Ann] cryed out, Did you not bring the Black man with you, did you not bid me tempt God & dye? How oft have you eat and drunk y'r own damnation? What do you say to them?… [She] spread out her hands, & the afflicted were greviously vexed.

Stirred by Goodwife Putnam's shouting—*goodwife* was the favored title of respect for married women in Puritan New England—the afflicted girls, most of whom were usually present at the examinations, began howling that Rebecca Nurse's apparition was at that very moment tormenting them. An angry John Hathorne complained to Nurse, "It is very awfull to all to see these agonies,…& yet to see you stand with dry eyes when there are so many whet—"

"You do not know my heart," Nurse snapped back, denying that she had then, or ever, caused the girls any pain. "You would do well if you are guilty to confess & give Glory to God," Hathorne advised. "I am as clear as the child unborn," Nurse replied. Yet with virtually every movement of Rebecca Nurse's body, "the afflicted persons were seized with violent fits of torture," according to Parris's account. Nurse agreed with Hathorne that the afflicted girls seemed bewitched but insisted that she could not explain the cause of their suffering. "I cannot help it," she said, "the Devil may appear in my shape."

Then, exhausted by the questioning, Rebecca Nurse allowed her head to droop to one side. Immediately, seventeen-year-old Elizabeth Hubbard's head drooped in the same manner, causing Abigail Williams to scream, "Set up Goody Nurse's head [or] the maid's [Hubbard's] neck will be broke." Nurse's head was then forcibly raised to an upright position, at which point Elizabeth Hubbard's neck "immediately righted." The examination ended at this point. Afterward, persuaded by what they had heard and seen, Hathorne and Corwin recommended that Rebecca Nurse be indicted for "certaine Detestable Arts of witchcraft & Sorceries."

Origins of the Hysteria

THE TROUBLE IN SALEM VILLAGE began in late January 1692 at the home of Samuel Parris, where first his nine-year-old daughter, Betty, and then his eleven-year-old niece, Abigail Williams, began exhibiting strange behaviors. They dashed oddly about the house, dived under furniture, convulsed with pain, entered trances, screamed blasphemies, and complained of fevers. After several weeks of keeping this matter within the family, Samuel Parris asked a local physician, William Griggs, to examine the girls. Unable to find anything physically wrong with them, Griggs ventured that their afflictions might be the result of witchcraft. While something of a catchall diagnosis, bewitchment was considered a reasonable possibility at the time because seventeenth-century Americans (and Europeans) commonly believed that witches were real and often dangerously close at hand.

During the rest of February, Parris conducted prayer services and community fastings in the hope that these would relieve the evil forces tormenting his niece and daughter. Meanwhile, on February 25, a neighbor of the Parris family, Mary Sibley, persuaded Tituba, a slave acquired by Parris during his merchant days in Barbados, to bake a "witchcake" (a mixture of rye flour and Betty's urine); this was fed to a dog suspected by Sibley of being a familiar. It was believed that feeding a familiar such a urine cake would compel it to reveal the identity of its demoniacal master. Reportedly, when Parris found out about the witchcake episode, he flew into a rage.

Samuel Parris was a marginally successful planter and merchant in Barbados (where he acquired the slave Tituba) before John Putnam invited him to become the minister of Salem Village (now Danvers) in 1688. After a year of salary negotiations, during which Parris won for himself inflationary adjustments and free firewood, he accepted Putnam's offer.

THE GLOVER CASE

THE SCENT OF WITCHCRAFT may have drifted over to Salem from Boston. In 1688, an Irish washerwoman named Mary Glover was executed in Boston for allegedly afflicting four young girls. Cotton Mather, who followed the case closely, wrote extensively on the subject in his *Memorable Providences, Relating to Witchcrafts and Possessions* (1689), which left little doubt that witches were both active in New England and a genuine threat. Perhaps it is no coincidence that Mather's popular book happened to be one of the few volumes in Samuel Parris's meager Salem library. Mather later became involved with the Salem witch trials, objecting to some of the flimsy evidence being admitted yet also expressing great pleasure

Cotton Mather is believed to have been the first author to use the term American *to describe white colonists of European descent.*

at the success the trials were having in apparently reviving piety. On August 19, 1692, Mather became even more directly involved when he attended the execution at Salem of five men and women convicted of witchcraft. One of those sentenced to hang was George Burroughs, a former minister of Salem Village who had long since moved to Maine. As Burroughs stood on the gallows awaiting his noose, he loudly proclaimed his innocence and recited perfectly the Lord's Prayer, which witches and wizards were not supposed to be able to do. Members of the stunned crowd began demanding Burroughs's release, but Mather quickly intervened, reminding the protesters that Burroughs had already been tried and fairly convicted.

AROUND THE SAME TIME, pressured by townspeople to identify the causes of their suffering, the girls named three women as witches. They were Tituba, who had often told the girls stories of magic from her Barbadian childhood; a socially estranged, sharp-tongued young mother named Sarah Good, who had no home and lived wherever she was offered housing; and Sarah Osborne, an older woman with a poor record of church attendance who was widely judged to be a liar. On February 29, arrest warrants were issued; the following day, the three women were examined in the village meetinghouse by Hathorne and Corwin. (The proceedings had been originally set for Ingersoll's tavern, but when hundreds of townspeople showed up, the magistrates were forced to relocate the examinations to the larger hall.)

During these examinations, the afflicted girls described being attacked by the "specters" of the three women, and they contorted often in the presence of the accused. (This came to be a hallmark of their behavior in court.) Good and Osborne adamantly denied being witches, and the matter might have ended there had not Tituba confessed. No one knows why she did. She may have feared that she or her husband, the Parris slave known as John Indian, would be made scapegoats. It has also been suggested that Parris beat the confession out of her. In any case, Tituba's involvement in the witchcake episode certainly raised people's suspicions concerning her, and most were quite ready to believe her tale of an active community of witches in Salem Village. Tituba named Good and Osborne as her accomplices and claimed that they had all flown through the air "upon poalls."

The detailed instructions on how best to discover witches that Cotton Mather included in his Memorable Providences (1689) *gave encouragement to Salem residents who, three years later, thought they had found some.*

SIN IN THE SIXTEENTH CENTURY

NO SINGLE ELEMENT DIFFERENTIATED the Christian theologies of the sixteenth century more than the concept of sin. Although all Catholics and Protestants believed in original sin, symbolized by Adam and Eve's fall from grace, sixteenth-century Catholics accepted humanity's fallen condition with relative tolerance. So long as individuals submitted to the authority of the Roman church, their sins could be absolved with little exertion, often with a modest cash payment. (The trade in indulgences, essentially fees collected by the church in exchange for forgiveness, was one of the chief examples used by Luther to demon-strate Rome's spiritual corruption.) Protestants, however, especially followers of the stern Swiss theologian John Calvin, believed that Christians were obliged to strive relentlessly against every manifestation of sin in their behavior and thoughts. In their view, neither the absolution of priests nor the devotion to ritual could replace the obligation of each person to act in a moral fashion.

At the same time, Calvinists (the English Puritans among them) also believed that God had predestined some for salvation and others for damnation, not specifically because of anything good or bad inherent in their souls but simply of His own volition. The tricky bit was that only God knew for certain which people were which. Therefore, according to the teachings of Calvin, all believers should lead devout lives as they continued to search their hearts for the signs of God's grace that would indicate their membership in the "company of saints."

This 1533 portrait of Martin Luther was painted by Lucas Cranach the Elder (one of Adolf Hitler's favorite artists) when Luther was fifty years old.

With Tituba's confession, more girls came forward with symptoms similar to those of Betty and Abigail. They included Ann Putnam, the twelve-year-old daughter of Thomas and Ann Putnam; seventeen-year-old Mercy Lewis, a servant in the Putnam household; and seventeen-year-old Mary Walcott, one of the child Ann Putnam's closest friends. The presence of young Ann Putnam among the afflicted was important because the Putnam family was one of the most influential in Salem Village. The Putnams had arranged the hiring of Samuel Parris, which later proved divisive; and their support of the girls' accusations added considerably to the impetus behind the prosecutions. It wasn't very long before other townspeople found themselves accused by the "afflicted" of acting in sympathy with the Devil—including Rebecca Nurse.

The Puritans

SALEM VILLAGE WAS IN MOST respects a typical town in Puritan Massachu-setts. In Virginia, where economic advancement had been the draw, most of the settlers belonged to the Church of England, created by King Henry VIII in 1534 after Pope Clement VII, a political rival, refused to grant him a divorce from his first wife, Catherine of Aragon. The Massachusetts Bay Colony, however, was founded in 1630 not by economic adventurers but by a group of extremely pious Protestants who believed that King Henry hadn't gone far enough in reforming the English church. They were called Puritans because they wanted to "purify" the Church of England of all vestiges of popery.

The Protestant Reformation had begun in Europe in October 1517 with the posting of Augustinian monk Martin Luther's ninety-five theses denouncing corruption within the Roman Catholic Church. The religious upheaval these attacks produced, however, spread quickly because it suited the political aims of many secular monarchs. In England, for example, in the guise of spiritual reform, Henry VIII dramatically reduced the political influence of the Roman church, seized many valuable ecclesiastical lands, and enhanced his own personal authority by making the king the spiritual leader of the new Church of England. Meanwhile, the rising English merchant and professional classes welcomed the Reformation because it released them from limits placed upon their advancement by an overbearing Catholic Church hierarchy.

When it came to matters of theology, though, Henry VIII didn't much care, and he found it easiest simply to maintain a great deal of Catholic doctrine and ritual—a policy that his daughter Elizabeth I continued. This irked elements of English society, especially in Parliament and among the intelligentsia, who favored a more Calvinist approach to church governance—that is, one based on representative bodies (presbyteries) rather than hierarchical elites (episcopacies). The Puritans went even farther, agitating for congregational self-governance.

This oil portrait of George Fox was reputedly painted by Peter Lely, who would have sketched Fox from life sometime during the second half of the seventeenth century.

BECAUSE PURITANS BELIEVED that salvation was predestined by God, they had little use for elaborate church rituals or hierarchies. Instead, their ministers emphasized study of the Bible, because Scripture alone expressed the will of God concerning human behavior. George Fox, who founded the Society of Friends (or Quakers) during the late 1640s, pushed this logic to its ultimate conclusion—eliminating entirely the role of the minister, doing away with the sacraments and the liturgy, and instead exalting the believer's unmediated relationship with God.

The Puritans believed that they were members of "the elect," chosen by God for eternal salvation. Yet they also understood that only God knew such things for certain. So, to relieve their anxieties, they did the best they could to observe their conduct and predict their fates, constantly measuring their behavior (and that of others) against mutually accepted standards of righteousness and morality. Every moment of a Puritan's life, therefore, was subject to a spiritual accounting, and the obligation to conduct oneself properly was ongoing. So was the need to look within oneself for signs of the salvation to come. In fact, only those who had undergone transformative experiences—who could declare personally that they had experienced a work of grace—were allowed to join the Puritan church.

To be a Puritan, therefore, was to assess constantly one's moral behavior, because how else could a believer confirm his or her position among the saved? Similarly, the ideal Puritan polity was one organized to serve God's purposes on earth, at least to the extent they could be understood. The Puritans called this a "covenanted community" because it was based upon a covenant between God and the citizenry, as well as among the citizens themselves. Believing that England

LEFT: This 1661 pamphlet, written by Edward Burroughs, describes the persecution of Quakers in Massachusetts. Many Quakers settled in the Bay Colony because of the generous land terms the Puritans offered—only to find out later that the Puritan leadership used jailings, banishments, and even executions to punish those who chose direct communion with God over properly channeled congregational worship.

was an elect nation, chosen by God to complete the work of the Protestant Reformation, the Puritans were dogged in their efforts to establish in their country a model society. But, try as they might, they could persuade neither Elizabeth I nor Parliament of their cause.

When James I, previously king of Calvinist Scotland, became ruler of England in 1603, the Puritans thought that, finally, their opportunity had arrived. Yet King James proved unsympathetic, dismissing Puritan appeals at the 1604 Hampton Court Conference and placing the sect under greater political pressure to conform. Many Puritans got by with minimal conformity; but others, unwilling to compromise their beliefs in any respect, "separated" from England and its church entirely. One congregation of these Separatists, from Scrooby in Nottinghamshire, left their homes for Holland late in 1607. After a frustrating decade in Leyden, however, thirty-five of the Separatists (better known as the Pilgrims) sailed to the New World in 1620 aboard the *Mayflower*.

PENNSYLVANIA

ALTHOUGH FEW QUAKERS tried to settle in Massachusetts Bay during the seventeenth century, the sect proved especially irritating to the Puritans, and their suppression of it was merciless. At first, the Massachusetts General Court passed laws fining and banishing Quakers; then it enacted another condemning any Quakers who returned to death. One imprisoned Quaker was beaten unconscious for his beliefs; another Quaker couple, failing to pay their fines, had their children sold into slavery.

It quickly became obvious to the Quaker leadership in England that a colony of their own was needed. The person who came to provide such a refuge was William Penn— son of Adm. William Penn, a careful man who had managed to land important commissions from both Oliver Cromwell and later Charles II. William the younger converted to the unpopular Quaker faith in the 1660s; yet, like his father, he remained on good terms with the powers at court. During the late 1670s, he became obsessed with the idea of creating a colony in English America that would institutionalize his radical political and religious views. Using his influence among men of rank, Penn applied for and was granted in 1681 a proprietary charter for Pennsylvania. (The favor was also, in part, repayment of a debt that Charles II owed Penn's father.)

Immediately, both in England and on the Continent, Penn began advertising for settlers. Because his land terms were generous, and because

they included promises of religious freedom and representative government, thousands of non-conformists responded, including many who weren't Quakers. In 1682, Penn crossed the Atlantic with some of the first immigrants. Hailing from Ireland, Wales, Holland, and Germany as well as England, these farmers and artisans established Pennsylvania as a truly cosmopolitan haven for dissenters. By 1700, the Quaker capital at Philadelphia had ten thousand residents. Shortly thereafter, it surpassed Boston as the most populous city in North America.

This early-nineteenth-century painting by Quaker folk artist Edward Hicks illustrates the legend that William Penn confirmed his royal land grant by compensating the local Indians as well.

In England, meanwhile, the political position of the Puritans deteriorated. Charles I, who succeeded his father in 1625, appointed a new archbishop of Canterbury, William Laud, who launched a vigorous campaign of suppression against the Puritans. As their political and religious persecution increased, more and more Puritan began looking to the New World for relief. When John Winthrop, a Cambridge-educated lawyer and member of the landed gentry, lost his court-appointed post in 1629 because of his Puritan beliefs, he purchased an interest in the recently formed Massachusetts Bay Company, which had obtained a royal charter earlier that year to plant a colony in New England. (Apparently, Charles didn't know that the company's owners were Puritans.) Winthrop offered to sell his English estate and move his family to Massachusetts if the company would shift its council to America so that the colony could be self-governing. A deal was struck, the stockholders who didn't share Winthrop's vision of a covenanted community sold their shares amicably, and Winthrop himself was elected governor on October 20.

The City upon a Hill

BETTER ORGANIZED, WEALTHIER, and much more aggressive than the Pilgrims, the leadership of the Massachusetts Bay Company had already dispatched during the summer of 1629 six ships bearing more than three hundred well-supplied and well-armed colonists to New England. The following spring, Winthrop arrived with an even greater convoy, carrying nearly a thousand settlers, most in family groups. Under his direction, a colonial capital was established at Boston. Within a decade, more than twenty thousand other Puritans joined the Great Migration from England. By 1640, Massachusetts Bay had nearly twice the population of Virginia.

Their community, Winthrop told the colonists even before they landed in America, would have a special covenant with God. "Wee shall be as a Citty upon a Hill," he declared in a lay sermon delivered during the crossing aboard his ship, the *Arbella*. "The eies of all people are uppon us."

Unlike the founders of Jamestown, who wasted so much time and energy searching for gold and a quick route to Asia, the members of the Massachusetts Bay Company pursued realistic goals from the outset. As their Pilgrim neighbors did, they fished and farmed to sustain themselves, while at the same time developing export trades in fish, fur, and lumber. Labor was not a problem, as it had been in Virginia, because the Puritan work ethic was strong and there were plenty of bodies available. The mix of farmers, artisans, merchants, lawyers, ministers, and others among the immigrants gave each new Massachusetts town (and their number was increasing rapidly) a useful diversity of residents. Nor was capital or administrative talent in short supply; with the colony's success, more and more Puritan resources were being diverted from England.

Between 1631 and 1649 (the year that John Winthrop died), the Massachusetts Bay Colony held nineteen annual elections. In twelve of those, Winthrop was the man chosen to lead. Although some residents questioned his arbitrary rulings (he had no faith in democracy), none doubted his integrity.

IN SHAPING GOVERNMENTS for these towns, the Puritans relied on their religious principles. Accordingly, governance was viewed as the task of restraining humanity's innate sinfulness. The company's royal charter provided for a governor, a deputy governor, and eighteen assistants chosen by the shareholders meeting in general assembly (called the General Court) four times a year. These officials were to manage the colony's affairs, make laws, punish wrongdoers, assign land, and otherwise direct life in Massachusetts.

PILGRIMS

THE PILGRIMS WHO SAILED to America aboard the *Mayflower* were Puritan Separatists who had left England thirteen years earlier rather than submit to the increasing religious pressure there to conform. They had migrated from Scrooby to Leyden because the Dutch practiced religious tolerance. However, life in the Netherlands proved disappointing. The Separatists were allowed to worship freely; but, lacking Dutch citizenship, they could not join local craft guilds and thus were limited to low-paying, unskilled work. When their children began to intermarry and drift away from their church, some decided to leave.

Thirty-five Separatists made arrangements with a London joint-stock company, the

Merchant Adventurers, to finance their passage to America in exchange for repayment of the cost and a share in the settlement's future profits. The Pilgrims (as they later called themselves) would be accompanied by sixty-seven other *Mayflower* passengers, whom William Bradford in his famous *History of Plimouth Plantation* called the "strangers." On September 16, 1620, the *Mayflower* sailed from Plymouth, ostensibly bound for Virginia. The uncomfortable voyage lasted nearly ten weeks. When the ship finally reached the New World, however, it was nowhere near Virginia. Instead, the *Mayflower* dropped anchor November 11 near the tip of Cape Cod. (New England was probably the ship's secret destination all along.) The Strangers were in an

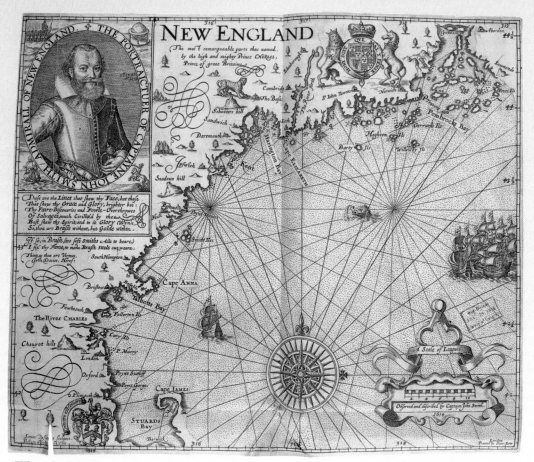

When the Pilgrims sailed for America in 1620, they took with them John Smith's published account of his 1614 voyage to New England (in which this map was printed). Smith himself offered to sail aboard the Mayflower for a price, but he was turned down because, he was told, his book was "better cheap" than he.

uproar because their royal patents named Virginia, not New England. Fearing a mutiny, the Pilgrim leaders of the expedition drafted a document, the Mayflower Compact, to assure all that they would be treated fairly in the new colony. Modeled on the church covenants used by Separatists to form new congregations, this document professed the colonists' continuing allegiance to the Crown while simultaneously establishing the basis for an independent civil government.

Perhaps because few of the Strangers were inclined to remain at sea after more than two months aboard ship, forty-one adult male passengers signed the Mayflower Compact, and the decision to stay was made. (A year later, the reorganized Plymouth Company, now known as the Council of New England, legitimized their presence with promises of one hundred acres of land for each settler at the end of seven years.) Weighing anchor again, the *Mayflower* sailed along the coast of New England, exploring for several weeks before finding on December 21 a site to their liking. John Smith had labeled that particular stretch of coastline "Plimouth" on his 1616 map of New England, and the name was kept.

For many of the same reasons that mortality rates were so high at Jamestown—disease, hunger, exhaustion from the difficult ocean voyage—only half of the original settlers survived the first winter at Plymouth. The harsh New England climate also took its toll; fortunately, Indian attacks were not a problem. In fact, had it not been for the food and kindness provided by the Wampanoag sachem Massasoit, all the colonists might have perished. A year later, those who survived celebrated the colony's first fall harvest with a feast to which they invited ninety-one of their Indian neighbors. It was the first Thanksgiving.

The earliest surviving text of the Mayflower Compact—*written in the hand of William Bradford, one of its original signers.*

The Bible that William Bradford, longtime governor *of the Plymouth Colony, brought with him to the New World aboard the* Mayflower.

CONNECTICUT

DURING THE 1630s, as wave after wave of Puritan immigrants arrived in Massachusetts Bay, many tarried only briefly in the coastal towns of Salem, Boston, Charlestown, and Dorchester before heading inland. Edward Winslow of Plymouth had explored the fertile Connecticut River Valley as early as 1632, and small groups of settlers from Massachusetts soon followed him. In 1635, Rev. Thomas Hooker petitioned the Massachusetts General Court for permission to form a new settlement there.

Political and religious dissatisfaction prompted Hooker's request. He felt that the church and state were too close in Massachusetts and believed that participation in town affairs should not be limited to members of the church.

Fredric Edwin Church *entitled this 1846 painting* Hooker and Company Journeying through the Wilderness from Plymouth to Hartford in 1636. *It was one of a series of landscapes Church created to portray significant events in Connecticut colonial history.*

During the late 1630s, other groups migrated from Massachusetts to join him, founding towns at Hartford, Wethersfield, and Windsor. In 1639, representatives of these towns drafted the Fundamental Orders of Connecticut, a compact that some historians have praised as the first American constitution based on the consent of the governed. The framework it authorized was quite similar to the government of Massachusetts Bay, except that there was no religious test for freemanship. Connecticut finally emerged as a distinct, independent colony in 1662, when Charles II issued a royal charter merging the early Connecticut River Valley towns with the New Haven Colony, founded in 1638.

Inevitably, the Puritans adapted this structure so that citizenship became identified with church membership. In October 1630, during the first meeting of the General Court (when the Massachusetts Bay Company formally became the Massachusetts Bay Colony), a number of colonists applied for status as freemen, or franchised citizens. Not all were granted this estate—generally, one had to be an adult male and a member of the church in good standing—but in May 1631, the first 115 freemen took their prescribed oaths; and within the next few years, the ranks of the freemen expanded with immigration. Meanwhile, each town in the commonwealth was given the right to elect representatives to the General Court, which evolved into a legislative body comparable to Virginia's House of Burgesses.

Although control of the Massachusetts Bay government was kept firmly in the hands of church members, the colony could not properly be called a theocracy because, despite the close relations between church and state, church officials never exercised political power merely by virtue of their church offices. However, Puritan ministers did exercise substantial influence and control within each town because religious worship and the monitoring of moral behavior were such routine and fundamental aspects of Puritan daily life. Every resident had the obligation to attend church services regularly, contribute money or goods for the support of the local minister, and accept graciously whatever scrutiny and criticism other church members had to offer. Rarely have the members of a society watched one another so closely as they did in seventeenth-century New England.

"Puritanism— the haunting fear that someone, somewhere, may be happy."

—

H. L. Mencken

The Late Seventeenth Century

BY THE 1670s, MASSACHUSETTS BAY was in many ways thriving, but "a City upon a Hill" it was not. The English Civil War had ended in 1660, following the demise of first Oliver Cromwell and then his protectorate. Charles II, son of the executed Charles I, had been restored to the throne. The new king's inclination toward entertainments of all sorts had initiated a rather libertine period in English history, during which little attention was paid to the deportment of the oddly pious Puritans in New England. The first generation of Puritan immigrants had also come and gone. Now, most of the residents of Massachusetts were native born and had never known life in England—where, in any case, Puritanism was a rapidly declining faith.

For this and other reasons, the declension in faith among second-generation Puritans became a matter of great concern to church leaders in Massachusetts. Increasingly, second-generation Puritans were finding it difficult to testify to their personal experience of a work of grace. So, in 1662, the church adopted the Half-Way Covenant permitting baptized, moral, and otherwise orthodox Puritans to

ROGER WILLIAMS AND PURITAN DISSENT

TWENTY-EIGHT-YEAR-OLD Roger Williams came to Massachusetts in 1631 as part of the Great Migration, eager to help establish John Winthrop's "City upon a Hill." The trouble was that the Puritans of Massachusetts simply weren't pure enough for Williams, who immediately stirred tempers in Boston when he refused to fill the vacant post of minister because the Boston church, he argued, wasn't separate enough from the Church of England. After a year in Separatist Plymouth, where Williams declared the colony's royal land grant to be invalid because it hadn't come from the Indians (the land's true owners), he moved back to Salem, where he preached for a year, generating even more controversy by opposing the taxes that paid for church expenses and the laws that made church attendance mandatory. Thus, ironically, Williams arrived at a position of religious tolerance through his own personal

No portrait of Roger Williams drawn from life exists. This approximation was used to illustrate David Benedict's A General History of the Baptist Denomination in America *(1813).*

intolerance of the Puritans. Possessing a vision of religious purity far more personal than the communal faith of Massachusetts Bay, he opposed strongly the oligarchical control exercised by Puritan leaders and insisted on a complete separation of church and state.

The Massachusetts Puritans, of course, were far from tolerant themselves. Overly enthusiastic visions, Winthrop and his colleagues feared, might just as easily come from the Devil as from the Lord—and Williams was certainly enthusiastic. In the fall of 1635, the General Court voted to banish him; and in January 1636, Williams set out for Narragansett Bay, where he purchased land from the local Indians and founded the town of Providence. Lacking a colonial charter, Williams devised instead a compact that allowed all residents of Providence to vote without regard to their religious affiliations. Dissenting sects were welcomed, and the right to worship freely was guaranteed to all. In 1643, Williams traveled to England, where he obtained in March 1644 a charter from Parliament for the "Incorporation of Providence Plantations." The towns of Providence, Newport, Warwick, and Aquidneck (later Portsmouth) united under this charter in 1647, and the colony of Rhode Island evolved from their union.

PURITAN ECONOMICS

VIEWING NEARLY everything about their lives in religious terms, the early Massachusetts Bay Puritans considered their prosperity obvious evidence of God's approval of their behavior. In midcentury, the first slaves were brought to the colony, but slavery never became important in Massachusetts (or any other northern colony) because the rocky soil and cold winters made large-scale, labor-intensive farming impractical. Instead, in Puritan New England there were more freemen than servants, more craftsmen than merchants, and more farmers and fishermen than anything else. The class structure in Massachusetts was much more fluid than in England or the plantation colonies, and there were many fewer gradations. The economic life of Puritan New England was at all levels characterized by independence, self-sufficiency, and self-confidence.

The decision of the Massachusetts General Court in May 1652 to establish its own mint in Boston was a profound act of economic defiance. These coins were among those issued by the colony between 1652 and 1682.

share in a lesser form of church membership. The Reverend Cotton Mather (1663–1728), in particular, berated his generation for failing to measure up to their forebears. The problem, though, was really one of cultural transition. Committed to a set of beliefs that seemed to many increasingly archaic, the Puritans of the late seventeenth century were at the same time experiencing an economic success that tempered their faith. Even Cotton Mather could not adequately reconcile his society's past and present.

DURING THE TWO DECADES leading up to the Salem witchcraft trials, the Puritans didn't need a John Winthrop to tell them that God was not pleased with them. The signs of His disfavor were manifest. They included a horribly bloody 1675–1676 war with local Indian tribes and Charles II's decision in 1684 to revoke the Massachusetts Bay charter. Almost from the moment of Charles's 1660 restoration, Massachusetts authorities had alienated the king and his most important advisers. First, they failed to enforce the Navigation Act of 1660 and its later iterations. (These mercantilist laws permitted English ships only to carry American colonial goods and directed that certain enumerated commodities—such as tobacco, sugar, indigo, and cotton—be exported to European markets only through England.) The Massachusetts Puritans also refused to allow other religious groups, including Anglicans, to practice their faiths freely. And there were more insults, such as the coinage of money without permission from the Crown. All this behavior reflected the persistent Massachusetts belief that the colony deserved to be free of English control. In October 1684, however, the Lords of Trade persuaded the Court of Chancery to declare Massachusetts's charter forfeit. By 1687, the charters of Connecticut and Rhode Island had been annulled as well, clearing the way for Charles II to impose direct royal control over all New England.

The frustrations of Puritan leaders in Massachusetts Bay grew daily as they watched their old order crumble. In 1686, the colony's first Anglican congregation began holding services at Boston's historic Old South Church (while that church's Puritan congregation waited outside for the Anglicans to finish). Meanwhile, along with religious humiliation came political subordination. Also in 1686, the king appointed a new royal governor, Edmund Andros, to oversee Charles's entire "Dominion of New England." The hugely unpopular Andros ended representative government in Massachusetts Bay, began enforcing the Navigation Acts, and imposed taxes by fiat. His government also challenged many early New England land titles as part of a campaign to break the economic power of the Puritan oligarchy and their Congregationalist churches.

When Bostonians learned during the spring of 1689 of the Glorious Revolution that had deposed James II (Catholic son of Charles II) and placed William and Mary on the throne in late 1688, they promptly arrested Andros and shipped him back to England. They also sent to England Rev. Increase Mather, Cotton's father and Harvard College's president, to persuade the new Protestant monarchs to restore the old Massachusetts Bay charter. Unfortunately, Mather failed in his mission, returning to Boston in May 1692 in the company of the new royal governor, William Phips. The new 1691 charter under which Phips had been appointed folded the Plymouth Colony into Massachusetts Bay and granted the new merged colony only limited self-rule.

The Court of Oyer and Terminer

With Phips's arrival in Boston, the end of the Puritan era seemed nearly complete. Thanks to Andros, Anglicans were now worshiping freely in the heart of Congregationalist Boston, and many of the colony's new merchant princes were either Anglicans themselves or otherwise alienated from traditional Puritan dogma. This is why many historians interpret the Salem witchcraft trials as the last gasp of the old Puritan order. Even before the trouble began in Salem Village that winter, a general mood of uncertainty and foreboding had overtaken Massachusetts. Made nervous by the collapse of Puritan authority and the imposition of royal control,

Gov. Edmund Andros

KING PHILIP'S WAR

After troops from Connecticut and Massachusetts Bay annihilated the Pequots in 1637, Indian uprisings in New England became rare. In June 1675, however, the Wampanoag sachem Metacom (whom the English called King Philip) began a suicidal war that killed one in sixteen whites and countless Indians before ending in the near-total destruction of Indian culture in New England. In 1620, Philip's father, Massasoit, had welcomed the Pilgrims to his land, giving the whites corn and teaching them how to farm it for themselves. During the next half century, however, Massasoit's kindness was repaid with land grabs and the intrusion of Puritan missionaries into tribal affairs. By 1675, Philip had come to the realization that fighting was better than peace, because peace had only brought his people humiliation and loss. First, Philip attacked the Plymouth town of Swansea; then, acting in concert with other disgruntled New England tribes, he and his warriors wiped out settlements along the western Massachusetts frontier. The English—who were, in a certain sense, relieved that Philip had finally given them an excuse—responded with equal brutality and, of course, much greater force. Within a year, Philip was dead, and most of the original Indian tribes of New England were virtually exterminated. A pattern had also been set—of whites pressuring their Indian neighbors, taking their land and threatening their culture, until finally the Indians responded with war, their violence conveniently providing the rationale for their complete subjugation.

Paul Revere created this 1772 *portrait of King Philip entirely out of his own imagination because he had no accurate likeness from which to work. Revere's concoction has since become the most widely identified image of the Wampanoag leader.*

the warfare with the Indians and the changing economic circumstances, the people of Massachusetts were both ill at ease and ill prepared to contemplate a future without the highly ingrained patterns of Puritan communal behavior.

Phips was immediately confronted with the problem of the witchcraft trials, whose growing number threatened to overwhelm the colony's legal system. On May 27, not knowing what else to do, he established a special Court of Oyer and Terminer to "hear and determine" these cases. Chosen to lead the court was Lt. Gov. William Stoughton, who began the trials at Salem Town on June 2.

FIRST TO BE JUDGED was Bridget Bishop, whose case was taken up first because it was believed to be the strongest for the prosecution. Bishop was notorious about Salem for her extravagance of dress, her licentiousness, and her utter disregard for the accepted norms of Puritan behavior. She had even been accused of witchcraft once before, at the time of her second marriage in 1679, but had escaped without punishment. Now Bishop's presence in the courtroom provoked the usual round of shrieks and complaints from the afflicted—who were joined by a confessed witch, Deliverance Hobbs, in denouncing Bishop's devilish activities. Several reputable men of Salem also testified that she had employed spells and charms against them and that, once they rebuffed her proposals, their loved ones had suffered inexplicable

THE GREAT AWAKENING

THE STEADY DECLENSION IN FAITH among Puritan church members remained a matter of acute concern well into the eighteenth century. As late as the 1740s, in fact, the degree to which expectations in Massachusetts had declined from the time of the founding generation still produced sharp controversy. In 1729, when Jonathan Edwards succeeded his grandfather as pastor of the Congregationalist church in Northampton, Massachusetts, he was appalled at the encroachments theological liberalism was making upon Puritan orthodoxy. For the next two decades,

Edwards devoted himself to defending that orthodoxy and lifting up his church. Aided enormously by the sensational American tours of English evangelist George Whitefield, Edwards and other American theologians initiated a new religious fervor that came to be called the Great Awakening. Following Whitefield's example, the proponents of the Great Awakening, which began in the late 1730s and peaked a decade later, emphasized conversion experiences and emotional release. In addition, the proceedings were remarkably democratic. Itinerant preachers roamed the countryside, offering the prospect of salvation to anyone who cared to attend their open-air meetings. The Great Awakening thus extended the reach of religious experience to groups such as blacks and the poor who understandably felt uncomfortable with the elitist Puritan establishment.

A Faithful
NARRATIVE
OF THE
Surprising Work of GOD.
IN THE
CONVERSION
OF
Many Hundred Souls in Northampton, and the Neighbouring Towns and Villages of the County of Hampshire, in the Province of the Massachusetts-Bay in New-England.

In a LETTER to the Reverend Dr. BENJAMIN COLMAN, of Boston.

Written by the Revd. Mr. EDWARDS, Minister of Northampton, Nov. 6. 1736.

Published with a Large PREFACE by the Rev. Dr. WATTS and Dr. GUYSE of London: To which a Shorter is added by Some of the Reverend Ministers of BOSTON.

Together with an ATTESTATION from Some of the Reverend Ministers of Hampshire.

The THIRD EDITION.

BOSTON: N.E. Printed by S. KNEELAND and T. GREEN, for D. HENCHMAN, in Corn-Hill, 1738.

In 1721, Jonathan Edwards had a transformative religious experience that persuaded him of his own salvation. As chief pastor of the Northampton church, he tightened membership requirements and emphasized the inability of human beings to influence their own fate. He also took to writing books and preaching hell-and-damnation sermons that terrified audiences by pointing out their own helplessness before God.

injury. "There was little occasion to prove the witchcraft, this being evident and notorious to all beholders," Cotton Mather observed of Bishop's trial, which ended the day it began with a verdict of guilty and a sentence of death. On June 10, Bishop became the first of eighteen Salem residents, twelve women and six men, to hang for the crime of witchcraft.

Mather's opinion notwithstanding, Bishop's trial did arouse some controversy. Court member Nathaniel Saltonstall resigned because of his unhappiness with the proceedings; and on June 15, Cotton Mather wrote a letter to John Richards, a judge of the Court of Oyer and Terminer who happened to be a member of Mather's congregation, expressing the growing doubts of a number of local ministers. These largely concerned the admission of what was then called "spectral evidence"—that is, the testimony of the afflicted that apparitions, or "specters," of the accused had been tormenting them. Many around Massachusetts were concerned that spectral evidence was unreliable and too easily used as a vehicle for carrying forward feuds within the Salem community. Without such spectral evidence, Saltonstall had pointed out, it would have been impossible to convict even so mischievous a woman as Bridget Bishop; and Mather, in his letter, urged "a very critical and exquisite caution [in using spectral evidence] lest by too much credulity of things received only upon the devil's authority there be a door opened for a long train of miserable consequences." But Stoughton and his colleagues disregarded these warnings and chose to accept depositions of the afflicted. They also tilted the scales of justice further by continuing the practice of granting leniency to those who confessed, thereby encouraging false testimony against accused witches who steadfastly maintained their innocence.

Some of those who wouldn't confess willingly were forced to do so by means of torture. According to a July 1692 prison letter written by accused wizard John Proctor to a group of concerned Boston ministers, "[Martha] Carrier's Sons…would not confess any thing till they tyed them Neck and Heels till the Blood was ready to come out of their Noses…. My son William Proctor, when he was examin'd, because he would not confess that he was Guilty, when he was Innocent, they tyed him Neck and Heels till the Blood gushed out at his Nose." Another accused wizard, Giles Corey, was "pressed" to death by his jailers, who wanted to punish him for refusing to give testimony at his and his wife's trials. Corey was stripped naked, a board was placed over his chest, and large rocks were piled on top of the board until, after two days, Corey died.

COLONIAL GOVERNMENT

THERE WERE THREE main types of colonies in English America: royal, proprietary, and corporate. In royal colonies, such as Massachusetts after 1691, the Crown appointed a governor, and the governor ruled nearly absolutely in the king's name. In proprietary colonies, such as Maryland until 1691 and Pennsylvania, the Crown gave the land to one or more proprietors, who were permitted to rule as they saw fit. In corporate colonies, such as Virginia before 1624, it was the board of directors of a company that was given land and the leave to rule it.

In practice, however, all the English colonies in North America developed some form of popular government. Colonial governments of the late seventeenth century were typically composed of a governor and a bicameral legislature. (Only Pennsylvania had a single house.) The upper chamber, whose members were usually appointed by the governor, was often called the council; the lower chamber, whose members were generally elected by franchised freemen, was called the assembly.

This is the royal charter, issued in 1691, that Gov. William Phips brought with him to Boston in May 1692.

The Trial of Rebecca Nurse

WHEN THE COURT OF OYER and Terminer reconvened on June 29, it heard five cases in two days, among them the case of Rebecca Nurse. Abigail Williams had been the first of the afflicted girls to name her as a witch. On March 19—at the home of Thomas Putnam, where Abigail had gone to live after Samuel Parris sent his daughter Betty to stay with friends in nearby Salem Town—Abigail suddenly launched into what one observer described as a "grievous fit,"

> *sometimes makeing as if she would fly, stretching up her arms as high as she could and crying "Whish, Whish, Whish" several times; Presently after she said there was Goodw. N [Nurse] and said "Do you not see her? Why, there she stands! And then said Goodw. N offered her The Book, and she was resolved she would not take it, saying Often, "I won't, I won't, I won't take it. I do not know what Book it is; I am sure it is none of God's Book, it is the Devil's Book, for ought I know." After that she run to the Fire, and begun to throw Fire Brands about the house.*

Two days later, young Ann Putnam repeated Abigail's accusation, telling a jammed meetinghouse during the examination of Martha Corey (Giles Corey's wife, whom Ann had also accused of witchcraft) that she thought she had seen Goodwife Nurse praying to the Devil.

At Nurse's June 29–30 trial, several among the afflicted told stories of Nurse's apparition tormenting them, and other witnesses linked her to several unusual deaths in the Salem community. Sarah Holton, for example, told of how her otherwise healthy husband, Benjamin, had taken ill and died three years earlier, shortly after arguing with Nurse about some pigs that had strayed onto her fields.

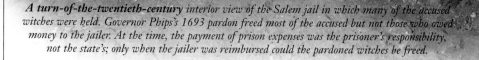

A turn-of-the-twentieth-century interior view of the Salem jail in which many of the accused witches were held. Governor Phips's 1693 pardon freed most of the accused but not those who owed money to the jailer. At the time, the payment of prison expenses was the prisoner's responsibility, not the state's; only when the jailer was reimbursed could the pardoned witches be freed.

THE WITCH'S TEAT

LIKE MOST EUROPEANS of the seventeenth century, the Puritans of New England had no doubt that evil forces of supernatural origin sometimes affected daily life, either directly or through malevolent apparitions. Most of what New Englanders knew about these demons, they learned from a book published two centuries earlier by Dominican friars Heinrich Kraemer and Johann Sprenger. *Malleus maleficarum [The Witches' Hammer]* (1486) folded various folk traditions into a single authoritative text that for nearly three centuries served as the definitive encyclopedia of demonology through-out Christendom.

According to *The Witches' Hammer*, witches' bodies often had extra "teats," or nipples, so that they could suckle their familiars, which craved human blood. In fact, third nipples sometimes occur naturally in men and women, but this bit of anatomical arcanum was not widely known—nor did anyone much care. People wanted tangible proof of witchery; and during witch trials, the discovery of virtually any wart, mole, or swelling on the body of the accused could be entered into evidence.

This early edition of Malleus maleficarum *was published in Paris during the 1510s. It was bound in wood with a leather spine wrap.*

Goodwife Holton said that she now realized that the cause of her husband's death had been Nurse's witchcraft. In fact, grievances of this sort were aired frequently during the witch trials, and long-standing feuds underlay many of the prosecutions. In Rebecca Nurse's case, she may have been targeted because she was a member of the Towne family, whose mutual dislike of the Putnam family was well known. Later, Rebecca's sisters Sarah (Towne) Cloyce and Mary (Towne) Easty were also accused of witchcraft and imprisoned.

THE MOST TANGIBLE and yet the most bizarre evidence presented at Nurse's trial came in an affidavit signed by "J. Barton, Chyrurgen [Surgeon]" and a group of midwives who had examined six of the imprisoned women on June 2. According to their report, they found on Nurse and two other women (Bridget Bishop and Elizabeth Proctor) "a preternaturall Excrescence of flesh between the pudendum and Anus much like to Tetts & not usuall in women." These were the "witches' teats" that professional witch finders of the seventeenth century regularly cited as proof of witchery. Again, Rebecca Nurse proclaimed her innocence, protesting that the marks on her body came not from the Devil but from a simple and natural cause: aging.

Perhaps because of the petition testifying to Nurse's propriety signed by thirty-nine of her neighbors, the jury at first brought back a verdict of not guilty. But the matter did not rest there. According to one account, "Immediately all the accusers in the Court...made a hideous out-cry, to the amazement, not only of the Spectators, but the Court also seemed strangely surprised; one of the Judges expressed himself not satisfied, another of them as he was going off the Bench,

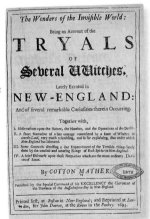

In The Wonders of the Invisible World *(1693), Cotton Mather published his own account of "the grievous molestations by daemons and witchcrafts which have lately annoy'd the countrey."*

said they would have her Indicted anew." Stoughton asked the members of the jury whether they had "considered one Expression of the Prisoner's, when she was upon Tryal, viz. That one [Deliverance] Hobbs, who had confessed her self to be a Witch, was brought into court to testify against her, the Prisoner turning her head to her, said 'What, do you bring her? she is one of us,' or to that effect." Pressed by Stoughton's question and the clamor of the afflicted, the jury withdrew to reconsider its decision. Still unable to reach a guilty verdict, the members returned to the courtroom and asked Nurse to explain her words. Unfortunately, the nearly deaf Nurse, exhausted from the experience, never heard the question put to her, and she failed to reply. The jury retired again, this time returning a finding of guilt. (Later, when the matter was explained to her, Nurse insisted that she had meant only that Deliverance Hobbs was one of her codefendants.) Along with four other women, Nurse was hanged on July 19.

NEW YORK

THAT A NUMBER OF HIGHLY placed residents fled to New York during the witchcraft trials of 1692 was nothing new for Massachusetts. As early as the 1630s, religious dissenters from the Bay Colony had sought refuge in New York (then New Amsterdam), where the Dutch accepted members of all religious faiths, even Jews. The most important governor of New Netherland, Peter Stuyvesant, had taken over the colony in May 1647 and ruled it dictatorially for the next seventeen years. Among his chief accomplishments, in addition to holding the diverse settlement together, was the annexation of New Sweden. A company of fifty Swedes had settled Fort Christina (now Wilmington) on the Delaware River in 1638, and in 1655 Stuyvesant seized New Sweden for the Dutch. He wasn't able to hold it long, however.

In March 1664, displeased with the presence of Dutch settlements among his American colonies, the newly restored Charles II declared that all territory between the Connecticut and Delaware Rivers henceforth belonged to his brother James, the duke of York. When the duke's fleet entered the harbor at New Amsterdam in September 1664, the Dutch, who were in no position to fight, immediately surrendered, and New Netherland became New York. The colony of New Jersey emerged that same year from York's holdings when the duke reassigned to a pair of his cronies, John Berkeley and George Carteret, his land between the Hudson and Delaware Rivers.

New Amsterdam, in a print from the mid–seventeenth century.

Increase Mather's Conscience

AS THE TRIALS CONTINUED, witchcraft ceased to be a problem for merely the community of Salem. By midsummer, it was affecting nearly every town in Essex County and many others around Massachusetts as well. In September 1692, the jails of Boston alone were filled to capacity with more than one hundred accused witches and wizards, all awaiting trial before the Court of Oyer and Terminer. Business was at a standstill, and new suspects were being interrogated daily. The afflicted had by now become grandiose in their charges, accusing some

of the most prominent people in Massachusetts of witchcraft—including the governor's wife. A significant number fled to New York to escape prosecution.

With no other end in sight, and after visiting many of the accused in prison, Increase Mather preached a sermon on October 3 in which he categorically denounced the use of spectral evidence. That sermon, delivered to a conclave of ministers and quickly published as *Cases of Conscience Concerning Evil Spirits Personating Men*, Mather also criticized as inadequate most of the other types of evidence presented at the Salem witch trials. "It were better that ten suspected witches should escape," he wrote, "than that one innocent person should be condemned."

Aware that the matter had gotten out of hand, Governor Phips ordered an end to the use of spectral and other intangible evidence on October 8. Three weeks later, he dissolved the Court of Oyer and Terminer, prohibited further arrests, and ordered the release of all but fifty-two prisoners. This last group was tried before another special court in January 1693, and all but three were acquitted. The last three were pardoned by Phips in May 1693. On December 17, 1696, the General Court adopted a resolution calling for a day of fasting and repentance. On that day—January 14, 1697—Samuel Sewall became the first member of the Court of Oyer and Terminer to admit publicly the injustice of the trials. Others followed, but never William Stoughton.

IN SALEM, MEANWHILE, the afflicted, fearful of the governor's displeasure, ceased complaining of their torments. The supporters and opponents of Samuel Parris continued doing battle for several years, but in April 1695 neighboring ministers began mediating a settlement. Although the visiting clergy urged compassion for all, they were nonetheless quite critical of the "unwarranted and uncomfortable steps" Parris had taken against those accused of witchcraft. Eventually, Parris agreed to resign his post and leave Salem Village in exchange for back pay totaling seventy-nine pounds (several thousand dollars in today's currency). Raising the money proved easy, leading to Parris's departure from Salem in 1697. He became a merchant in Stowe and later other towns on the northern frontier. No record, however, mentions the fate of Betty Parris or whether she ever recovered from her affliction.

This edition of Cases of Conscience *was published by Benjamin Harris in Boston in 1693, not long after the October 1692 sermon on which its text is based.*

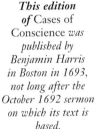

Anne Hutchinson

1591?–1643

by Ann Braude

ANNE MARBURY WAS BORN in Alford, England, probably in 1591. Her father, Anglican clergyman Francis Marbury, was twice imprisoned for challenging the religious authority of the Church of England, which subsequently stripped him of his ministerial living. From her father, Anne received a learned intimacy with Christian doctrine and Scripture, as well as a fearless conscience. In 1612, she married William Hutchinson, a successful cloth merchant who was devoted to his brilliant wife. Over the next twenty-two years, she bore twelve children and followed the Puritan teachings of the Rev. John Cotton.

In 1634, Hutchinson and her family joined the thousands of English Puritans crossing the Atlantic to plant a godly commonwealth in Massachusetts, where John Cotton had already fled to escape Church of England reprisals. In many ways, Hutchinson was a model Puritan, pious and committed. Her neighbors in Boston flocked to her home to hear her explain the more difficult points in Cotton's sermons. Yet these meetings quickly drew the unwelcome attention of local authorities, who became concerned not only with the propriety of a woman speaking on religious matters in public but also with the content of her speech.

Hutchinson embraced the Puritan doctrine of God's absolute sovereignty so vigorously that her theology shocked Boston's ministers and magistrates. In her insistence that sinners could find salvation only through God's grace (and not through specific obedience to the laws of church and state), they saw an emerging threat to their authority. If humans answered to God alone and not to religious or civil leaders, the result they believed, would be anarchy, and their holy commonwealth would fail.

When male clergy expressed such views, their ministerial brethren invited them to discuss their errors in private. Yet when Anne Hutchinson did so, she was imprisoned and tried for heresy and sedition. This discriminatory treatment reflected a difficulty that the Puritan magistrates had separating the fact that Hutchinson was a woman from the essence of what she said. In their minds, the obedience of wives to husbands was a necessary element of the well-ordered society designed by God to promote human welfare—a society in which children obeyed parents, servants obeyed masters, laypeople obeyed ministers, and everyone obeyed the laws of the commonwealth and the will of God. To the leaders of Puritan Boston, a woman speaking in public signified nothing less than religious and civil anarchy.

Anne Hutchinson's trial brought these tensions over religious authority and gender out into the open. It was not a flattering moment for the colony. Hutchinson was specifically charged with disobeying the Fifth Commandment (honor thy father and thy mother) because she had invited her neighbors into her home for religious discourse and thus had failed to respect, or honor, the authority of the ministers and the state. "Put the case, Sir," Hutchinson replied, "that I do fear the Lord and my parents, may I not entertain them that fear the Lord because my parents will not give me leave?" Hutchinson knew the Bible well, and for every verse that the presiding magistrates quoted against her, she quoted another in support of her positions that the Bible sanctioned her behavior. When the court objected that the texts she cited did not fit her case exactly, she responded sarcastically, "Must I shew my name written therein?" Even today, her eloquence sparkles through the brittle pages of

Hutchinson preaches at her home in Boston in this late-nineteenth-century painting by Howard Pyle.

the trial transcript, the only surviving record of her words.

For acting rather as "a Husband than a Wife and a Preacher than a Hearer," Anne Marbury Hutchinson was banished from the Massachusetts Bay Colony in 1638. She moved first to Rhode Island and later to Pelham Bay, New York, a Dutch settlement not far from Manhattan Island. Along with most of her household, she was murdered in 1643 by Native Americans, possibly incited by Puritan authorities. Three centuries later, the same commonwealth that judged her death to be a manifestation of divine judgment erected a monument in her honor on the steps of its statehouse, celebrating her commitment to free speech and religious liberty. Meanwhile, the undercurrents of Hutchinson's case continue to resonate in American society. Even today, the nation's largest religious denominations bar women from ordination, citing some of the same arguments used against Anne Hutchinson. Furthermore, all of us continue to struggle as a society to balance individual rights with communal needs and freedom of conscience with respect for our shared values.

The BLOODY MASSACRE perpetrated in King——t——Street BOSTON on March

Engrav'd Printed & Sold by Pau

pvBoston! fee thy Sons deplore,   If fcalding drops from Rage from Anguish Wrung But

4

THE AMERICAN REVOLUTION

The Boston Massacre

ELEVEN-YEAR-OLD CHRISTOPHER Seider was one of several hundred angry Bostonians gathered outside the home of Ebenezer Richardson on the cold, windy morning of February 22, 1770. He and others were pelting the house with eggs, fruit, sticks, and stones. Trapped inside with his family was Richardson, an informer for the local British customs inspectors. (The inspectors were *British*, rather than *English*, because in 1707 the Act of Union had formally merged England and Scotland into the united kingdom of Great Britain.)

Rocks had already broken most of the windowpanes in the house (and one had even struck Richardson's wife) when Richardson picked up an unloaded musket and pointed it out a front window. The mob responded by breaking down his front door—which, in turn, provoked Richardson into loading his musket and firing birdshot into the crowd. Several people were hurt, most only slightly; but Christopher Seider (or perhaps his name was Christian Snider; sources disagree) fell to the ground with eleven pellets in his chest and abdomen. He died later that day.

After Seider's collapse, the crowd surged into the house and cornered Richardson, who surrendered without further resistance. Surely he would have been lynched right then and there

AT LEFT: **Issued on March 28, 1770,** *Paul Revere's* The Bloody Massacre perpetrated in King Street *became one of the most influential works of propaganda in American history. Of course, its depiction of redcoats slaughtering peaceable colonists bore no relation to the actual event.*

had it not been for the intervention of William Molineux, a leader of the anti-British Sons of Liberty. Using his influence, Molineux saved Richardson for Boston's judicial system. Within the hour, Richardson was taken to Faneuil Hall and arraigned before four justices of the peace and a thousand onlookers. Several witnesses testified, and Richardson was bound over for trial. The initial charge was "giving Christopher Seider a very dangerous wound." After Seider's death, the charge was upgraded to murder.

Before February 22, Seider had been nearly invisible among Boston's sixteen thousand residents. On February 26, however, he received perhaps the best-attended funeral yet held in America. Several thousand Bostonians marched in a lengthy procession through the city's narrow, snow-clogged streets. Samuel Adams, the Sons of Liberty ringleader who had organized the event, staged it carefully: According to his cousin John Adams, a "vast Number of boys" preceded Seider's coffin, with even more numerous adult mourners following behind it.

Four days later—on March 2, 1770— emotions were still running high when a fight broke out between local laborers and off-duty British soldiers at a Boston ropewalk owned by John Gray. Ropewalks were long, low buildings in which unskilled workers walked from one end to the other, playing out fibers, which they braided into rope. Typically, a ropewalk such as Gray's employed a great deal of temporary labor, and the jobs it offered attracted both unemployed townspeople and off-duty redcoats looking to

supplement their unimpressive pay. The job market in Boston was especially tight at this time because patriotic merchants were boycotting British goods. To make matters worse, the off-duty soldiers were willing to work for up to 20 percent less than the going rate. So the locals at Gray's ropewalk had a special reason to be resentful of the redcoat who walked in that day—in addition to all the other reasons Bostonians had for hating the British.

Denis Diderot commissioned this image of a rope-walk to illustrate the article on ropemaking in his famous 1772 Encyclopédie.

Salutary Neglect

AT LEAST AS FAR BACK as the rule of Gov. William Berkeley in Virginia, relations between the American colonists and the royal officials appointed to oversee them had been troubled. Royal governors were generally more concerned with the powerful stresses and strains of the British empire than with local American affairs, and few knew how to respond when American economic interests clashed with imperial trade regulations. What the Crown wanted was simple: obedient colonies that produced valuable raw materials and in exchange bought the mother country's manufactured goods. This relationship was the very basis of mercantilism, and in theory it seemed a reasonable division of labor. However, its presumption that the colonies existed for no other purpose than to benefit the mother country didn't sit well with Americans, who came to oppose parliamentary legislation (such as the Navigation Acts) that limited their commerce.

As a result, during the late seventeenth century, Parliament found it much easier to pass such laws than to enforce them, and smuggling became common. Even after the king's Privy Council created the Board of Trade and Plantations in 1696 to bring some order to the Crown's disorganized system of colonial administration, there were simply too many ships and too many ports for the small number of customs inspectors and coastal patrols to cover. In addition, for much of the early eighteenth century, domestic and international political conflicts distracted London's attention from the less-than-pressing problem of American smuggling. So during the 1720s and 1730s, Britain's first prime minister, Robert Walpole, developed a policy now known as "salutary neglect." In other words, Walpole thought, if the colonial relationship wasn't broken—and British-American trade was still producing high profits for both sides—why fix it?

During the four proxy wars that Britain and France fought in North America between 1689 and 1763, the principal Indian allies of the British were the tribes of the Iroquois Confederation. This 1787 French engraving purports to show an Iroquois warrior in full battle dress, yet its numerous mistakes suggest the artist never saw one.

GREAT BRITAIN'S PRIMARY CONCERN during this period of salutary neglect was its traditional enemy, France. Between 1689 and 1763, the two nations fought four long wars. The first three of these took place largely in Europe, but they affected North America as well. The Puritans in Massachusetts had long been suspicious of their French Catholic neighbors to the north, and the presence of French settlements in the Mississippi and Ohio River Valleys also troubled American colonial authorities. Other causes for concern were the strong alliances the French had made with several powerful Indian tribes— among them the Hurons, with whom they traded furs. Indeed, when the War of the Grand Alliance broke out in Europe in 1689, New France began mobilizing its forces; and a year later, the fighting spread to North America.

On one side were the French Canadians and the Hurons; on the other, the Americans and their principal allies, the tribes of the Iroquois Confederation, who were traditional enemies of the Hurons. King William's War (as the Americans called the conflict) continued off and on for seven years until the 1697 Treaty of Rijswijk ended the inconclusive fighting on both continents. The next round of bloodshed, known as Queen Anne's War in America and the War of the Spanish Succession in Europe, took place between 1701 and 1713, when the Peace of Utrecht transferred to British America a great deal of New France, including Nova Scotia, Newfoundland, and the Hudson Bay region.

The American tradition of echoing European wars with halfhearted conflicts of its own resumed in 1740 with the escalation of fighting along the Georgia–Spanish Florida border. Later, this skirmishing merged into a much wider struggle precipitated by the death of Austrian emperor Charles VI. During the ensuing War of the Austrian Succession, France supported Prussia in its struggle against Austria in the hope of annexing the Netherlands, then under Austrian control; meanwhile, Great Britain supported Austria to block the French from acquiring Holland. The fighting, called King George's War in America, ended in 1748 with the Treaty of Aix-la-Chapelle. The only major action in North America took place in June 1745, when British regulars and American militiamen captured the French fortress of Louisburg on Cape Breton Island. Under the terms of the peace treaty, however, Louisburg and other captured territory was returned to its prewar owners.

This contemporary German woodcut shows the June 1745 British capture of Louisburg during King George's War.

The French and Indian War

THE LAST OF THE FOUR WARS fought during this period was the French and Indian War, also known as the Seven Years' War, which began late in the spring of 1754—not in Europe, but in North America itself. During the previous winter, acting on behalf of Virginia governor Robert Dinwiddie, twenty-one-year-old militia major George Washington had delivered this ultimatum to the French living in the Ohio River Valley: Leave the land, which Great Britain claimed (and colonial speculators coveted), or face the military consequences. When the French refused to leave, Washington (now promoted to lieutenant colonel) returned the following May with 160 armed Virginians. Near Fort Duquesne, a French stronghold on the site of present-day Pittsburgh, he built a crude stockade named Fort Necessity. Shortly thereafter, the French and Indian War began when Washington ordered the capture of a French reconnaissance party, and the French responded with an overwhelming assault on Fort Necessity. After losing a third of his men, Washington surrendered, yielding—at least temporarily—the entire region to the French.

William Pitt rose to power during the 1740s as the leader of Parliament's House of Commons. Known as the Great Commoner, he often opposed the foreign policy machinations of the new Hanoverian kings.

In fact, it was several years before the tide of the war turned. Not until William Pitt became British prime minister in 1756 was a coherent military plan developed. Before Pitt, the American war effort depended on the willingness of reluctant colonial assemblies to contribute troops and funds. Pitt, however, assumed direct control of the fighting; and even though hostilities in Europe also began that year, he kept his focus emphatically on the colonial theaters, beating back the French in India, Africa, and on the high seas, as well as in North America. In military terms, Pitt's global strategy was enormously successful, but it also proved costly, nearly bankrupting the British treasury. For example, Pitt for the first time committed large numbers of British troops to North America. Initially, to offset the cost of provisioning them, he authorized their officers to confiscate needed supplies from the civilian population. British officers in America were also permitted to impress civilians into military service if additional troops were needed. Yet these policies so enraged the colonists that some rioted; and following a 1757 uprising in New York City, Pitt relented, relaxing his policies and agreeing to reimburse colonists for commandeered supplies.

The military turning point of the war came on September 13, 1759, when British general James Wolfe defeated the marquis de Montcalm at Quebec. A year later, at Montreal, the remainder of the French army surrendered to Jeffrey Amherst, and all of Canada passed into British control. The Treaty of Paris, signed in February 1763, confirmed this annexation and also shifted into British hands French Louisiana east of the Mississippi River. (New Orleans and western Louisiana were excluded because France had already ceded these properties to Spain in 1762.)

Benjamin West's The Death of General Wolfe *(1771) depicts the final moments of the British commander's life. James Wolfe was fatally wounded on the Plain of Abraham outside Quebec but lived long enough to learn that the French stronghold had fallen to his army.*

THE ALBANY CONGRESS

BEFORE THE FRENCH AND INDIAN WAR, intercolonial political contacts were rare. From long experience, the Board of Trade knew that, left to themselves, the American colonies would probably remain divided and suspicious of one another. Therefore, in June 1754, it organized a conference at Albany, New York, where representatives from seven colonies met to discuss their common defense.

The British wanted the colonists to talk about military preparedness and how best to coordinate with their Iroquois allies, but Benjamin Franklin of Pennsylvania went well beyond this agenda, proposing a more general scheme of colonial confederation. Under his Plan of Union, each colonial legislature would elect representatives to a Grand Council chaired by a president-general appointed by the Crown. The number of council members

JOIN, or DIE.

Benjamin Franklin published this woodcut, considered the first American political cartoon, in the May 9, 1754, issue of his Pennsylvania Gazette. *It promoted his unsuccessful plan for colonial integration.*

allotted to each colony would depend on its tax payments, and the president-general would have veto power over all council decisions. This new federal union would be empowered to make laws and levy taxes, but only with regard to continental defense, Indian relations, and settlement of the western frontier. In other words, it could raise money to pay for an army and a navy, negotiate treaties with the Indians, and regulate the distribution of land west of the Appalachians.

Although the delegates to the Albany Congress approved Franklin's plan, it was later rejected by the Crown and by the colonial legislatures, which were reluctant to cede any of their authority (especially the power to tax). Instead, each colony looked out for itself, and whatever coordinated military operations did take place were largely the work of the British government, which also paid for them.

IN THE MEANTIME, with so many British ships patrolling the coast of America in support of the troops, it finally became possible for royal customs inspectors to enforce the Navigation Acts—and they did so vigorously, much to the colonists' chagrin. Customs agents on land made particularly effective use of writs of assistance, general warrants that allowed them to enter and search any premises suspected of containing smuggled goods. Because these writs were valid for the entire term of a monarch's reign, Boston merchants hired James Otis in 1760 following the death of George II to challenge the legality of the writs before George III renewed them. Otis lost his case, and the searches continued, but so did the smuggling.

Pitt had hoped that enforcement of the Navigation Acts would produce additional tax revenue that would, in turn, help reduce the government's huge war debt. To the authorities in London, it seemed rather obvious that the American colonies should pay a fair share of the cost of their own defense. That's why, when enforcement of the Navigation Acts failed as a revenue-generating policy, Pitt's successor, George Grenville, proposed another means of achieving the same end: In 1764, confronting a British war debt of £130 million, he persuaded Parliament to pass the Revenue Act.

Also known as the Sugar Act, this law revised import duties (or imposed new ones) on a number of significant colonial commodities, including sugar, molasses, textiles, coffee, and indigo. The revision of the tax on imported molasses was particularly interesting: Under the Molasses Act of 1733, the British government had established an import duty on foreign molasses of sixpence per gallon. The

> "Taxation without representation is tyranny."
> —
> *James Otis, 1763*

Because so many Americans despised having to pay British taxes, royal tax collectors often bore the brunt of colonial rage. This print, entitled The Bostonians Paying the Excise-Man, or Tarring & Feathering, *was first published in London in 1774.*

point was to compel the American colonists to buy their molasses exclusively from the British West Indies, whose sugar planters exercised a great deal of political influence. The problem was that the price differential between British and French West Indian molasses was so great that American rum distillers still came out ahead bribing customs officials a penny per gallon and continuing to buy from the French. Under the new Sugar Act, the molasses duty was halved to threepence a gallon, making its payment cost-competitive with bribery. That was the good news for the Americans. The bad news was that Grenville actually expected them to pay the tax, and he included in the Sugar Act specific mechanisms to ensure that they would. One required colonial merchants to document each and every shipment leaving or entering an American port; another transferred the cases of accused smugglers to special admiralty courts, whose judges were much less sympathetic to violations of the law than colonial juries had been. (In smuggling cases, especially in Boston, American juries usually acquitted even the obviously guilty.)

These new tactics appalled the colonists, who deeply resented Parliament's heavy-handedness. Yet even more important was the Americans' objection to the very idea that Parliament could pass a *revenue* act. The colonies recognized Parliament's right to regulate imperial trade; and if import duties happened to generate some additional funds for the Crown, this revenue was incidental to the goal of regulation. Yet direct revenue generation, the acknowledged purpose of the Revenue Act, was another matter entirely. According to the Americans, Parliament did *not* have the right to tax them as it did other royal subjects (i.e., those living in Great Britain), whatever the costs of the French and Indian War had been, because American colonists had no representation in Parliament. As the Virginia House of Burgesses pointed out, "Laws imposing taxes on the People ought not to be made without the Consent of Representatives chosen by themselves." Other colonial assemblies agreed that only they had the right to levy taxes within their borders.

The Stamp Act

THE MOST EMPHATIC OBJECTIONS to the Sugar Act were voiced in commercial cities such as Boston and New York, but even rural Americans realized that a Parliament able to tax commerce was a Parliament able to tax land and other property as well. Meanwhile, the smuggling continued, limiting revenues collected under the Sugar Act to an insignificant twenty thousand pounds and prompting Grenville to devise another means of extracting the necessary revenue from the colonies. The Stamp Act— approved by Parliament on March 22, 1765—required Americans to purchase tax stamps for most forms of printed matter, from legal papers and customs documents to marriage licenses and even newspapers. Grenville was certain that this measure would work because Englishmen already paid a similar tax at home; however, just to make sure that the colonists didn't object to what seemed (at least to Grenville) fair and equal

RIGHT:
Although new to the colonies, revenue stamps of the sort shown here had been required in Britain since 1694.

treatment, he had language inserted into the bill specifically allocating all revenue from the tax to "the Defense of the Colonies."

Two days later, Parliament passed another law sponsored by Grenville relating to the American colonies. The Quartering Act obliged colonial assemblies to furnish British troops with adequate housing and provisions. Again, Grenville considered the measure absolutely reasonable: The troops had been sent for the benefit of the colonies; why shouldn't the colonies at least give them room and board? Most colonists, however, considered the timing rather strange: Why should the Crown station troops in America now when, after more than a century of conflict with the Indians and the French, the colonies were finally safe? The explanation seemed to be that the British government intended to use the troops against the Americans themselves in order to exercise its will and suppress freedoms previously enjoyed by the colonists.

Printing this parody of a revenue stamp in its final issue, the Pennsylvania Journal *shut down rather than consent to the hated stamps.*

GRENVILLE WOULD NOT HAVE DENIED that the British government meant to change its previously permissive ways. Yet he would certainly have challenged any characterization of that shift as a usurpation of colonial rights, and he would have argued instead that he was merely reestablishing the legitimate primacy of the mother country. Whatever the merit of such arguments, in practice Parliament's efforts to tighten the political screws on the colonies sparked protests even worse than those occasioned by the Sugar Act. In fact, the Stamp Act initiated the first organized intercolonial opposition to British policy. Throughout the colonies and especially in the commercial centers (where most of the stamps and tax collectors had been sent), resistance to the Stamp Act was nearly universal.

Taking the lead, the Massachusetts General Court proposed in June 1765 that an intercolonial meeting be held to organize unified opposition to the Stamp Act. Representatives from nine colonies took part in the Stamp Act Congress, which convened in October in New York City and drafted a petition to Parliament calling for repeal of the Sugar and Stamp Acts and asserting the colonists' right to be taxed only by their elected representatives. Meanwhile, street mobs, many organized by the Sons of Liberty, sacked the homes of royal officials in Boston, New York City, and elsewhere, intimidating every single stamp agent into resigning his post. Therefore, when the law went into effect on November 1, there were no agents left to sell the stamps, and the requirement was completely ignored. At the same time, American merchants increasingly subscribed to nonimportation agreements, which caused British merchants and manufacturers to petition Parliament themselves for repeal of the Stamp Act because their businesses were suffering.

THE SONS OF LIBERTY

THE SONS OF LIBERTY was a loosely organized federation of patriot groups that came together during the Stamp Act crisis because of their shared dislike of British rule. In many cities, the Sons of Liberty chapter was simply an old club or association with a new name. The movement largely melted away after Parliament's repeal of the Stamp Act in 1766, but it was revived two years later following passage of the Townshend Acts. British authorities suspected the Sons of Liberty of agitating for independence, but most members remained genuinely loyal to the Crown and emphasized that they were only defending their rights against the usurpation of royal officials.

A handbill from January 1770. It was one of many distributed by the Sons of Liberty to police nonimportation.

Colonial militants such as Samuel Adams even began clamoring for independence, arguing that colonists had the right to overthrow a government that systematically exceeded its authority and violated their rights. This last development troubled William Pitt, who added his own voice to the calls for Stamp Act repeal. "If we repeal the Act," Pitt said, "we shall have all the sober part of America on our side, and we shall easily be able to chastise the few hot-headed republicans among them." Furthermore, Pitt pointed out rather pragmatically, no Americans could be found to collect the tax. So in March 1766, the Stamp Act was repealed. Yet, at the same time, perhaps to save face, Parliament passed the Declaratory Act, which reaffirmed its right to pass any law it wished binding the colonies and people of America.

The Townshend Acts

THEN THERE WAS STILL the revenue problem. Britain's war debt hadn't gone away, and Chancellor of the Exchequer Charles Townshend was determined that the colonies should pay a fair share. He knew that levying a direct tax would reignite the Stamp Act protests, so he chose instead to propose in May 1767 a new series of tariffs, or the Sugar Act revisited. Approved by Parliament in late June, the Townshend Acts placed new import duties on just a few commodities—glass, lead, paints, paper, and tea—but all were in high demand. The Townshend Acts also revived the writs of assistance, made the Crown directly responsible for the payment of colonial governors' salaries (so they couldn't be held hostage by colonial assemblies), and reduced North American troop deployments while simultaneously shifting the financial burden of supplying the soldiers who remained entirely onto the colonists.

This portrait of Thomas Gage was painted by John Singleton Copley shortly after Gage's arrival in Boston in 1768. Generally considered the finest artist produced by colonial America, Copley (like Benjamin West before him) eventually succumbed to the lure of London and moved there in 1774.

Once more, intercolonial resistance was led by the Massachusetts General Court, which issued a Circular Letter advocating resumption of the nonimportation agreements. An irate Francis Bernard, royal governor of Massachusetts, ordered the assembly dissolved and began sending secret messages to Parliament, asking for the immediate dispatch of British troops to Boston. During 1768 and 1769, the royal authorities in Boston competed bitterly with the Sons of Liberty for control of the city's economic and political life. Patriot leaders, notably Samuel Adams, used street mobs to coerce even Tory merchants—that is, merchants loyal to the Crown—into respecting nonimportation. Meanwhile, Governor Bernard begged Maj. Gen. Thomas Gage, the supreme British army commander in North America, to send troops from his large garrison in Halifax to restore royal authority in Boston. The problem was that Bernard did not have the authority to request troops himself. Only the governor's council (the upper house of the Massachusetts legislature) could do that, and the governor's council, which was popularly elected in Massachusetts, had no intention of making such a request. Bernard outlined his dilemma in this July 1768 letter to a superior in London:

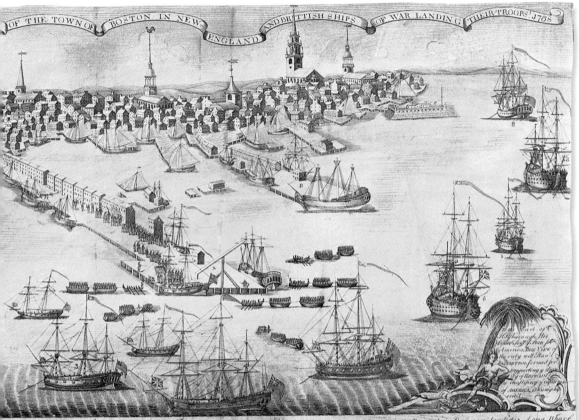

OF THE TOWN OF BOSTON IN NEW ENGLAND AND BRITTISH SHIPS OF WAR LANDING THEIR TROOPS! 1768

Sept.d 30th 1768. the Ships of War armed Schooners, Transports, &c. Came up the Harbour and Anchored round the Town; their Cannon loaded. a Long Wharf
their Cables, as for a regular Siege. At noon on Saturday October the 1st the fourteenth & twentyninth Regiments, a detachment from the 59th Regt, b Hancock's Wharf
of Artillery with two pieces of Cannon, landed on the Long Wharf; there Formed and Marched with insolent Parade, Drums beating & Fifes &c. c North-Battery
and Colours flying, up King Street. Each Soldier having received 16 rounds of Powder and Ball.

Engrav'd Printed & Sold by PAUL REVERE BOSTON

General Gage has now informed me that his orders to Halifax are that the Troops shall be collected & kept in readiness, but are not to move till I require them. I answer that then they will never move: for I shall not make such a requisition without the Advice of Council; & I never expect to obtain that: neither their popular Constitution nor the present intimidation will permit it.... In short, my Lord, Troops are not wanted here to quell a Riot or a Tumult, but to rescue the Government Out of the hands of a trained mob & to restore the activity of the Civil Power, which is now entirely obstructed. And if an open Defiance of the Authority of Great Britain...[is] not sufficient to show the Expedience of quartering Troops at Boston, we must wait till it becomes more apparent.

Two years before he published The Bloody Massacre perpetrated in King Street, *Paul Revere issued this inflammatory engraving showing the September 1768 arrival of British troops at Boston's Long Wharf.*

In late September 1768, pursuant to orders from London, two regiments of Gage's infantry were finally sent to Boston. After a tussle with local officials regarding their quartering (one regiment had to spend its first night in Faneuil Hall), the soldiers began regular patrols, and Boston became an occupied town. The presence of six hundred British troops, however, bound the various patriot factions together as never before, and the result was a political stalemate: Bernard and Lt. Gov. Thomas Hutchinson were reluctant to enforce the customs laws rigorously, lest such action lead to a general uprising. Nor were the radical patriots themselves yet ready for open rebellion. So the royal government in Boston

George III sat for this portrait in the studio of court painter Allan Ramsay during the late 1760s. "The New England governments are in a state of Rebellion," the king observed in November 1774. "Blows must decide whether they are to be subject to this country or independent."

continued to prosecute smugglers selectively, and the merchants continued their boycott of British goods. By March 2, 1770, the day that British soldier Thomas Walker walked into John Gray's ropewalk, both sides agreed that a single major incident could produce a mass uprising against the British.

WHEN WALKER ENTERED THE ropewalk that Friday, Bostonian William Green asked him the obvious question, "Soldier, do you want work?" Walker answered yes, to which Green replied with an amused smirk, "Well, then go and clean my outhouse." The other ropewalkers roared with laughter, but Walker was not amused, and a fight began. The locals quickly chased him from the factory and had nearly as easy a time when Walker returned a short while later with eight or nine friends. Of course, when Walker showed up a third time with nearly thirty soldiers—by which time the number of Bostonians had also grown—the fighting became much more intense. Yet the outcome was the same, and the soldiers were driven from the ropewalk.

That weekend, Boston seemed peaceful, but rumors were spreading from house to house and barracks to barracks that a large, dramatic gesture was being planned—either by the redcoats or by the Sons of Liberty, depending on which rumor you heard. One British private testified later that he had heard some ropewalkers asking where the redcoats planned to bury their dead. A local ropewalker swore that he had heard four soldiers declaring that "there were a great many townspeople who would eat their dinners on Monday next [March 5], who would not eat any on Tuesday."

Most of that Monday passed without incident. A foot of snow had fallen, and locals who braved the cold walked cautiously over the ice sheets that covered the streets. That night at the corner of King Street and Shrimton's Lane, Pvt. Hugh White stood guard duty at a sentry box located near both the Custom House and British military headquarters, known as the Main Guard. About eight o'clock in the evening, a young barber's apprentice named Edward Garrick spotted a British officer of the Twenty-ninth Regiment named John Goldfinch and shouted within earshot of White, "There goes the fellow that won't pay my master for dressing his hair." Later, joined by another apprentice, Garrick returned to the vicinity of White's sentry box and resumed his criticism of Goldfinch. When White defended the officer's reputation as a gentleman, Garrick sneered, "There are no gentlemen in the Twenty-ninth Regiment," whereupon White left his post and joined Garrick in the street. "Let me see your face," White ordered. When Garrick complied, White smashed his musket into the young man's skull. Garrick cried out, and within minutes a mob of some fifty belligerent Bostonians had formed. Loading his musket, White retreated to the steps of the Custom House, where he fixed his bayonet and faced the angry crowd.

THE MOB BEGAN THROWING large chunks of ice at White and shouting, "Kill him! Knock him down! Fire, damn you, fire! You dare not fire!" The sentry shouted for assistance: "Turn out, Main Guard!" Meanwhile, on nearby Brattle Street, a solitary Bostonian ran up and down the road shouting, "Town born, turn out! Town born, turn out!" (This was the usual call for a street mob to gather.) Quickly, another crowd formed at Murray's Barracks, a regimental encampment just off Brattle Street, and it began pelting the soldiers there with snowballs and shouted insults. Several British officers, John Goldfinch among them, ordered the soldiers back to their barracks, and more than once an officer had to knock down a private to stop him from disgorging his musket into the crowd.

That night, the cry of "Fire!" sounded repeatedly through the dark streets. In addition to having no street lamps, colonial Boston depended entirely upon volunteer firefighters, so these shouts attracted a number of sleepy townspeople carrying buckets. With no actual fire to put out, many found their way on King Street and became part of the mob surrounding White, which swelled to perhaps four hundred people. Meanwhile, summoned from his dinner table by White's cry for reinforcements, the captain of the guard that evening, Thomas Preston, ordered up a relief party of six privates and a corporal, which he led himself into the emotional crowd.

After reaching the steps of the Custom House and ordering the beleaguered sentry to fall in, Preston tried to march his party back to the Main Guard. But the press of bodies blocked his path. Now trapped himself, the captain ordered his men to form a defensive arc with their backs to the Custom House, and he shouted for the crowd to disperse. But the Bostonians responded only with hoots and snowballs, taunting the soldiers and daring them to fire. Soon, Tory justice of the peace James Murray arrived on King Street to read the Riot Act, but this law took effect only after it had been read out loud, and the crowd was not about to let Murray do so. Knowing that Preston and his men would be on questionable legal ground if they acted before the Riot Act had been read, the townspeople sent Murray on his way with a volley of snowballs and ice. The emotional level of the crowd then climbed several more notches when someone recognized two of Preston's men, Pvts. Matthew Killroy and William Warren, as participants in the fight at John Gray's ropewalk three days earlier.

The Bloody Massacre

INDIVIDUALS PUSHED AGAINST Preston's troops, denouncing them as cowards and daring them to fire. Townsmen carrying clubs beat them against the guardsmen's musket barrels and bayonets, while Preston continued to shout his demand that the crowd disperse. On several occasions, the captain was approached by members of the crowd, who asked him whether he intended to fire. Each time he responded, "By no means, by no means." But the din was escalating, and Preston was losing control of his men. Indicating his desire to prevent bloodshed, the captain placed himself in front of the musket barrels, and the crowd cheered at his predicament. It seemed almost to match the condition of the British overall in Boston: incapable of either maintaining public order or withdrawing gracefully.

> "It is difficult, for so many separate Communities as there are in all the colonies, to agree in one consistent plan of Opposition."
>
> — *Samuel Adams, letter, April 1771*

This headdress belonged to a British grenadier stationed in America during the 1770s. Known more generally as "redcoats," British soldiers were also called "lobsters" because of their bright red uniform jackets.

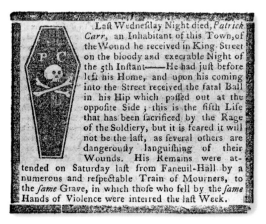

Laſt Wedneſday Night died, *Patrick Carr*, an Inhabitant of this Town, of the Wound he received in King-Street on the bloody and execrable Night of the 5th Inſtant——He had juſt before left his Home, and upon his coming into the Street received the fatal Ball in his Hip which paſſed out at the oppoſite Side ; this is the fifth Life that has been ſacrificed by the Rage of the Soldiery, but it is feared it will not be the laſt, as ſeveral others are dangerouſly languiſhing of their Wounds. His Remains were attended on Saturday laſt from Faneuil-Hall by a numerous and reſpectable Train of Mourners, to the *ſame* Grave, in which thoſe who fell by the *ſame* Hands of Violence were interred the laſt Week.

On the night of March 5, Preston's men killed three Americans: Samuel Gray, son of ropewalk proprietor John Gray; sailor James Caldwell; and Crispus Attucks, who was either a free black, a runaway slave, or an Indian of the Natick tribe (accounts differ). Two others died later from their wounds: seventeen-year-old apprentice Samuel Maverick, who lasted a few hours; and Irish immigrant Patrick Carr, who survived for days. This notice of Carr's death appeared in the March 19 Boston Gazette.

No more than a foot or two separated the line of soldiers from the nearest rioters when a club suddenly went sailing into Pvt. Hugh Montgomery. The impact knocked Montgomery to the ground, and as he staggered to his feet, he picked up his musket and fired. Hearing the shot, members of the crowd lunged at Preston and his men, swinging their clubs wildly. The soldiers managed to fend off these blows, but during the next minute or two (the exact interval remains unclear), others among Preston's men also fired their weapons. The stunned captain neither ordered the shooting, nor halted it immediately once it had begun. When the first round of shooting stopped, the crowd continued to advance, and the soldiers parried blows while reloading their muskets. Then a second round of shooting began, single shots again being fired sporadically over a period of minutes. Finally, the crowd dispersed, although it did regroup later to recover the bodies of those who had fallen. Fearing another attack, the soldiers raised their muskets to fire a third round, but Preston, having regained some of his composure, pushed down their gun barrels and shouted, "Stop firing! Do not fire!"

While emergency hospitals were being set up in nearby homes, Preston marched his squad back to the Main Guard. He then turned out the entire guard and formed a firing line on King Street between the Main Guard and the Old State House. At the same time (and it took less than an hour), more than a thousand Bostonians had massed nearby as rumors spread that the soldiers planned a general slaughter. Moderate patriot leaders pleaded with Thomas Hutchinson, then Boston's leading royal official (Francis Bernard had retired), to remove the troops from King Street before they provoked retaliation. Hutchinson refused. He did exchange some harsh words with Preston, but then he turned his attention to the crowd, which he addressed from a balcony of the Old State House. Hutchinson urged the townspeople to disperse peacefully, promising them that he would order a full and fair inquiry into the shooting. "The law shall have its course," Hutchinson shouted. "I will live and die by the law." Apparently, this course of action seemed acceptable to most of the Bostonians, who subsequently retired to their homes. Only a few hundred radicals remained behind to demand immediate action that never came.

AT 2 A.M. ON MARCH 6, the town sheriff served an arrest warrant on Captain Preston, who surrendered an hour later. The eight soldiers in his party were also imprisoned that night. All nine were charged with murder. At a town meeting the next day, Samuel Adams and other patriots demanded that Hutchinson remove all British troops from Boston, and the acting governor partly complied, ordering Preston's Twenty-ninth Regiment to Castle William, an island fort in Boston Harbor. When that proved insufficient to placate the town meeting, Hutchinson capitulated and ordered the other British regiment in Boston, the Fourteenth, to Castle William as well.

Attention then shifted to the trial of the imprisoned soldiers. On March 19, the Boston town meeting petitioned Hutchinson for an immediate trial, but the governor resisted, fearing that the city's aroused state would dictate a guilty verdict. Considering what had only recently happened to Ebenezer Richardson, Hutchinson had a point: On April 21, a Boston jury had found Richardson guilty of murder despite instructions from the trial judge that the death of Christopher Seider had been justifiable because Richardson had acted in self-defense. In the end, six months passed before the soldiers were formally arraigned on September 7, each pleading not guilty. Preston's trial began on October 24. Ironically, one of his prosecutors was Massachusetts solicitor general Samuel Quincy, a well-known Tory; and among those defending Preston were two accomplished patriot lawyers, Josiah Quincy (Samuel's brother) and John Adams. All wanted to be satisfied that Preston's trial was conducted fairly and honestly.

A parade of prosecution witnesses gave the Bostonian version of events, then the defense team called witnesses to give the soldiers' version. In his closing argument, prosecutor Robert Treat Paine, a patriot, attempted to absolve the mob of blame by pointing out that not every member could be held "answerable for the rude speech of every person that happens to be near them." In other words, Paine thundered, Preston's men had no lawful right to fire generally into the crowd and were therefore guilty of murder. John Adams countered that the shooting was surely justified because the soldiers had indeed been attacked by a mob—although, as Adams carefully pointed out, it had *not* been a mob characterized by patriotic Bostonians:

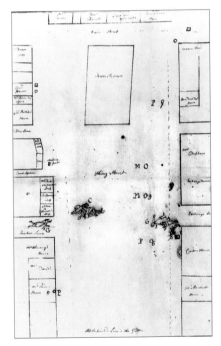

John Adams about 1766, as portrayed by Benjamin Blyth.

> *The plain English is, gentlemen, most [of the mob was] probably a motley rabble of saucy boys, negroes and molattoes, Irish teagues, and outlandish jack tarrs…. The sun is not about to stand still or go out, nor the rivers to dry up, because there was a mob in* Boston *on the 5th of* March *that attacked a party of soldiers. Such things are not new in the world, nor in the British dominions, although they are, comparatively, rareties and novelties in this town. [The late Patrick]* Carr, *a native of* Ireland, *had often been concerned in such attacks, and indeed, from the nature of things, soldiers quartered in a populous town will always occasion two mobs where they prevent one. They are wretched conservators of the peace!*

At the end of the trial, Judge Edmund Trowbridge of the Superior Court of Judicature instructed the jurors that if they were satisfied "that the sentinel was insulted and that Captain Preston and his party went to assist him, it was doubtless excusable homicide, if not justifiable." Under these circum-stances, Trowbridge continued, "any little spark would kindle a great fire, and five lives were sacrificed to a squabble between the sentry and Piemont's barber's boy." On October 30, the jury returned a verdict of not guilty. Josiah Quincy and John Adams had performed well, but the presence of five acknowledged Tories on the jury suggests that the Boston patriots were less concerned with a conviction than with the trial as propaganda. A month later, the eight other soldiers were tried as a group. Six were acquitted, and the other two, Killroy and Montgomery, had their prison sentences reduced to branding of the right thumb.

This map of the scene of the Boston Massacre was drawn by Paul Revere for use at Preston's trial. It shows where four of the dead men fell.

This portrait of Frederick, Lord North, accompanied an article about the prime minister in the March 1778 issue of The Town and Country Magazine.

IN THE MEANTIME, Parliament repealed all of the Townshend duties except one: the duty on tea. (The king's new prime minister—Frederick, Lord North—insisted that the duty on tea remain as a symbol of the "supremacy of Parliament" in America.) With the duties gone, the nonimportation agreements also passed away, and colonists resumed their trade with Great Britain. Even in Boston, where outrage at the "massacre" was still deeply felt, merchants bought and sold British goods rather than lose the business to their competitors in other colonies. As a result, by the time the massacre trials ended in December 1770, the cause of the patriots had lost nearly all its heady momentum.

To revive the opposition, Samuel Adams and other Sons of Liberty persuaded the Boston town meeting in November 1772 to create a Committee of Correspondence designed to articulate and publicize patriotic complaints against the British. Similar committees were established in other Massachusetts towns and in Connecticut, New Hampshire, Rhode Island, South Carolina, and Virginia (where their formation was particularly encouraged by Patrick Henry and Thomas Jefferson). The committees' frequent exchanges of views and information helped revive intercolonial cooperation, and their members became important shapers of public opinion. But it was the British, as always, who did the most to invigorate the patriot cause.

Although tranquility generally prevailed in America during the early 1770s, there were still indications of the tension beneath the surface. In June 1772, for example, a group of Rhode Islanders boarded the British customs vessel *Gaspée* and burned it to the waterline. A royal commission was sent from London to investigate, but the perpetrators were never identified. The import duty on tea, the most popular beverage in the colonies, also remained an irritation to the colonists.

The Boston Tea Party

EVEN WORSE, IN MAY 1773, Parliament passed the Tea Act, granting the financially strapped East India Company a monopoly on the colonial tea trade. Under the Tea Act, the East India Company could sell its tea directly through colonial agents, thereby eliminating British and American middlemen. The elimination of these middlemen allowed the East India Company to charge much less for its tea and still make a sizable profit, but Americans quickly grasped the long-term implications of this arrangement: If Parliament could eliminate one long-standing, profitable trade, why not any other? No aspect of American commerce would be safe from British interference.

During the prerevolutionary period, Boston was governed by a town meeting, consisting mostly of voters, that met in Faneuil Hall (shown here in 1789) as the need arose. Town meetings could attract three thousand people, who could become a mob simply by stepping outside.

Encouraged by the Committees of Correspondence and most colonial newspapers, public protests against the Tea Act spread throughout the colonies. Fearing violence, royal authorities in New York City and Philadelphia turned around the first ships carrying East India Company tea and sent them back to Britain without permitting them to unload. In Charleston, South Carolina, East India Company tea was unloaded but kept locked in a warehouse and not offered for sale. On December 16 in Boston, Sons of Liberty dressed as Indians boarded the *Dartmouth* as it lay dockside and dumped its cargo of East India Company tea overboard. This was the Boston Tea Party.

This engraving of the Boston Tea Party *illustrated a history of North America published in London in 1789.*

PARLIAMENT RESPONDED WITH a quartet of laws designed to punish Boston and tighten its hold on the American colonies generally. The Coercive Acts included the Boston Port Bill, which closed Boston Harbor to all commercial traffic until restitution was made for the spoiled tea; the Administration of Justice Act, which authorized the transfer of legal cases involving royal officials charged with capital crimes to Great Britain (so the defendants wouldn't have to face hostile colonial juries); the Massachusetts Government Act, which made most high elective offices subject to royal appointment, virtually ending self-rule in the colony; and an amended version of the 1765 Quartering Act, which applied to all of the American colonies and required civilians to open their homes to British soldiers when existing barracks proved inadequate. Parliament also passed the Quebec Act at this time, extending the Canadian border south into the Ohio River Valley and giving that province land previously claimed by Massachusetts, Connecticut, and Virginia. These five laws the American colonists grouped together and called the Intolerable Acts.

On September 5, fifty-six delegates from twelve colonies (all but Georgia, whose governor blocked the sending of representatives) met at Carpenters' Hall in Philadelphia to discuss what common action they might take in response to the Intolerable Acts. The underlying point of the new laws, everyone realized, was

The first and last pages of the Olive Branch Petition— *which the First Continental Congress sent to King George in December 1774, importuning him to restrain Parliament.*

Parliament's assertion of its absolute authority over the entire British empire. (The phrase used in the 1766 Declaratory Act had been "in all cases whatsoever.") One aspect of the delegates' response turned out to be the Declaration of Rights, drafted by John Adams, which denied that the colonies had any obligation to respect parliamentary decisions with regard to domestic colonial affairs and acknowledged only Parliament's authority to regulate imperial trade. In addition, the delegates agreed to suspend the importation and consumption of British goods until the Intolerable Acts were repealed.

During its nearly two months of deliberation, the First Continental Congress also debated the volatile situation in Massachusetts, where General Gage had replaced Thomas Hutchinson as royal governor. Gage's authority was supported by the return of British soldiers to Boston, but his situation was nonetheless delicate: He had enough troops to occupy Boston but not nearly enough to control the outlying countryside, which was densely populated and politically aroused. Although the delegates in Philadelphia were reluctant to have the national agenda unduly influenced by violence on the part of zealots in Boston, they could hardly deny the people of Massachusetts the right to defend themselves. So it was decided that, should Gage attempt to rule by force, the residents of Massachusetts could respond in kind, and the other colonists would come to their aid. Finally, before adjourning, the delegates agreed to reconvene for further discussion in early May 1775.

PAUL REVERE'S RIDE

DURING THE SPRING of 1775, Boston was full of spies, British and American. With more than four thousand redcoats in the city now, the climate there had become too hot for men such as Sam Adams and John Hancock—the most important patriot leaders—who had relocated to the countryside. Even so, there were still plenty of Sons of Liberty left in Boston to observe and report on British troop movements.

On the night of April 18, Joseph Warren, the leader of the patriots in Boston, learned that 750 British soldiers had quietly crossed the Charles River by longboat. Immediately, he sent William Dawes by land over Boston Neck to warn the people of nearby Lexington and Concord that the British were coming. Meanwhile, Warren found Paul Revere and sent him on the same mission by the much quicker "sea" route that the British had taken.

Pausing long enough to arrange for the hanging of two lanterns in the North Church steeple—a prearranged signal—Revere crossed Boston Harbor in a rowboat and was met on the

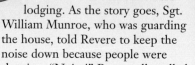

Charlestown side about eleven o'clock by several patriots who had seen the North Church signal. Given a horse, he set off for Lexington, alarming nearly every house he passed along the way. It was nearly midnight when he reached the residence of the Rev. Jonas Clark, where Adams and Hancock were lodging. As the story goes, Sgt. William Munroe, who was guarding the house, told Revere to keep the noise down because people were sleeping. "Noise!" Revere allegedly barked. "You'll have noise enough before long. The regulars are coming out!"

Beyond his notoriety as the hard-riding hero of Longfellow's famous 1863 poem, Paul Revere (shown here in a 1768 John Singleton Copley portrait) is also remembered as one of America's finest silversmiths. His bowls and flatware, in particular, are museum pieces.

THE SHOT HEARD 'ROUND THE WORLD

THOMAS GAGE'S FIRST YEAR as royal governor of Massachusetts sobered him considerably. To subdue the provincial militia, he informed Lord North, would require an additional twenty thousand troops. When only thirty-five hundred of these men were forthcoming, Gage fortified Boston Neck, the only land approach to the city, and kept his adventuring in the countryside to a minimum. On April 14, 1775, however, the general received a letter from Lord Dartmouth, the minister for colonial affairs, instructing him to move preemptively against the colonists' military buildup. Learning of a large store of arms and ammunition eighteen miles away in Concord, Gage made preparations for its seizure. He tried to keep his plans secret, but the shift in regular duty schedules alerted patriots in Boston that something was afoot.

sometimes called Minute Men because of their ability to muster quickly. Pitcairn ordered the defiant but not necessarily threatening Americans to disperse. Before they did, however, someone fired a shot—whether a redcoat or an American will never be known—and this shot led to others. A few minutes later, the outgunned militiamen withdrew, leaving behind eight dead and ten wounded. Only one redcoat was injured.

Later, when the British finally arrived at Concord, they discovered that nearly all the colonial weaponry had been moved elsewhere. Smith's men destroyed whatever supplies they could find and skirmished with another group of Minute Men at North Bridge. Then the British began their long march back to Boston, during which American snipers hiding behind buildings, stone walls, fences, and trees picked off scores of the easily visible redcoats. At Lexington, some nine hundred reinforcements joined Smith's column for the last leg of the march, but the Americans had also gained strength during the afternoon and now outnumbered the British two to one. Had the British not brought some cannon with them, they might not have made it back to Boston at all.

Allegedly, John Hancock (shown here in a Copley work from 1765) heard the first shots of the Revolutionary War as he and Samuel Adams rode away from Lexington in a carriage at dawn on April 19. It was at this moment that Adams supposedly exclaimed, "What a glorious morning for America!"

About 750 British grenadiers and light infantry under the command of Lt. Col. Francis Smith left Boston on the night of April 18. Near dawn the next morning, an advance party under Maj. John Pitcairn reached Lexington Green. There, waiting for the redcoats but neither confronting them nor blocking their path, stood about seventy Massachusetts militiamen,

The American Revolution

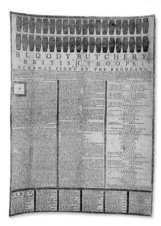

This April 21, 1775, broadside announcing the battles at Lexington and Concord lists the names of forty colonials killed and twenty more wounded.

BY THAT TIME, THE FIRST SHOTS of the American Revolution had already been fired on Lexington Green, and a force of some sixteen thousand militiamen from all over New England already surrounded the besieged British garrison in Boston. In Philadelphia, delegates to the Second Continental Congress, confronted now with the reality of armed conflict, considered what to do. At first, they debated what Silas Deane of Connecticut called "the old affair of the right of regulating Trade"—that is, whether or not the Americans should seek reconciliation through a reaffirmation of Parliament's right to regulate imperial trade. Cautious representatives from the Middle Colonies—notably John Dickinson of Pennsylvania, who knew that public opinion in his colony was mixed— worried that radicals from New England and Virginia were forcing rebellion on the rest of America, when accommodation might still be the wisest course. However, the urgent necessity to plan a military defense propelled the delegates past talk of compromise and into active preparation for war.

On June 15, the Second Continental Congress unanimously appointed George Washington of Virginia, one of the few Americans with any genuine military leadership experience, commander in chief of the Continental Army. Washington made immediate plans to travel to Boston, a trip that would take him twelve days. On June 17, however, even before Washington left Philadelphia, General Gage attacked the colonial lines ringing Boston. The sector he chose was in Charlestown, across the harbor from Boston, where colonial militiamen were fortifying Breed's and Bunker Hills. The British plan called for Maj. Gen. William Howe to attack these strategic elevations from the front, utilizing the beautiful

COMMON SENSE

HUMAN BEINGS DO NOT NORMALLY surrender their traditional loyalties easily. That's why so many delegates to the First and Second Continental Congresses were reluctant to defy the king. Thomas Paine, however, had no such reluctance. A failure in most of his previous pursuits, Paine had left England in 1774 for Philadelphia, hoping to reverse his fortunes. An ardent republican and egalitarian, he began associating with the leading advocates of political change in America and soon became one himself. In January 1776, he published anonymously a pamphlet, titled *Common Sense*, in which he condemned monarchy and empha- sized the world historical significance of the American Revolution. The pamphlet sold an astonishing 150,000 copies and had an incalculable effect on the American political scene during the critical months leading up to independence. "The cause of America," Paine pointed out, "is in a great measure the cause of all mankind."

"I know not whether any man in the world," John Adams wrote in 1805, *"has had more influence on its inhabitants or affairs for the last thirty years than Tom Paine."* This 1793 engraving of Paine by William Sharp follows a 1792 painting by George Romney.

In Congress

The ...... To George Washington Esquire ...... General and Commander in Chief ......

firing lines so admired by military leaders of the eighteenth century. However, this tactic left the British soldiers (who had to carry sixty-pound packs uphill through long grass) vulnerable to substantial musket fire from the entrenched Americans. Howe's troops assaulted the militia positions three times, finally exhausting the colonists' ammunition and driving them from Charlestown. Yet in doing so, Howe lost a great many men: Half of the twenty-two hundred redcoats who fought that day were injured, and more than two hundred were killed, compared to only four hundred Americans killed or wounded. Afterward, King George III relieved Gage of his command and, on August 23, declared the colonies to be "in open rebellion" against the Crown. On December 23, he issued a royal proclamation closing all American ports to trade.

M EANWHILE, THE FIGHTING CONTINUED. During the winter of 1775–1776, while George Washington worked to create a coherent army outside Boston, other American forces invaded Canada. Two small but optimistic armies— one led by Brig. Gen. Richard Montgomery, the other by Brig. Gen. Benedict Arnold—converged on the city of Quebec, one of the most heavily fortified in all of North America. Sometime after 4 A.M. on New Year's Day, they attacked. Having the advantage of surprise—a blizzard was raging at the time—some American units gained access to the city, and had Montgomery not died and Arnold not been wounded, they might have overcome the British defenders. Instead, by 9 A.M., the last of the Americans still inside the city had surrendered, and the rest limped away in defeat.

George Washington (shown below in a 1790 portrait by John Trumbull) received this formal commission as commander in chief of the Continental Army on June 19, 1775.

*The **narrowness of Boston Neck** at the time of the Revolution (it was later filled in) can easily be seen in this British army map, created by an engineering officer in 1775. As long as the American army occupied Dorchester Heights, the British garrison was essentially trapped in the city.*

The other notable military activity that winter was no less arduous but much more successful. In May 1775, Ethan Allen and his Green Mountain Boys had captured lightly guarded Fort Ticonderoga on Lake Champlain. The fort occupied a strategic position at the southern tip of the lake, which was then a major thoroughfare linking the colonies with Canada. Even more important was its assortment of bronze and cast-iron cannon, which Washington needed to accomplish his basic task of chasing the British from Boston. In February 1776, after learning of their existence, Washington sent bookseller and amateur artillery expert Henry Knox to retrieve them.

Knox's mission was no easily accomplished feat. The cannon were extremely heavy, requiring teams of oxen to haul them; and even with the oxen, eighteenth-century transportation technology was not really up to the job of ferrying such bulky, unforgiving objects over mountains (the Berkshires) during the coldest part of the winter. Yet Knox managed to drag those cannon all the way from Ticonderoga to Dorchester Heights, and when the spring thaw came, the British in Boston found themselves within range of some powerful artillery. Recognizing that he had no choice but to evacuate, General Howe proposed a deal: If Washington would allow the British to board their ships unmolested, he would not burn Boston. Washington agreed, and on March 17, 1776, nine thousand British soldiers boarded 125 ships and left for Halifax. Meanwhile, Washington sent his own army south to New York City.

LEFT: *A powder horn once owned by a soldier in the Continental Army.*

Independence

ON THE POLITICAL FRONT, delegates to the Second Continental Congress had spent most of 1775 advancing their preparations for war while still contemplating the possibility of compromise. By the spring of 1776, however, that possibility had become sufficiently remote that the delegates adopted on May 10 John Adams's resolution authorizing colonies to create new, independent, constitutional governments based on the principle of popular consent. Meanwhile, the Second Continental Congress had already begun acting as a provisional national government, seeking diplomatic and military alliances abroad and authorizing privateers to operate against British shipping. It also opened American ports to all foreign commerce, thus ending any pretense that Parliament had the right to regulate American trade.

On May 15, the new Virginia legislature instructed its delegates in Philadelphia to propose independence for the colonies from Great Britain and the creation of a new intercolonial federation. On June 7, Richard Henry Lee of Virginia introduced just such a resolution, and the Congress responded by creating a five-man committee to prepare a suitable document. The members of the committee were John Adams, Benjamin Franklin, Thomas Jefferson, Robert Livingston of New York, and Roger Sherman of Connecticut. Adams and Franklin made suggestions regarding how such a declaration of independence might defend the colonists' action in breaking with Britain, but the final draft was largely the work of Jefferson. On July 2, the full Congress voted to approve Richard Henry Lee's earlier motion calling for a statement "that these united colonies are, and of right ought to be, free and independent states." Two days later, the delegates approved the text of the Declaration of Independence itself.

Jefferson's rough first draft of the Declaration of Independence.

THE DECLARATION OF INDEPENDENCE

THE PURPOSE OF THE DECLARATION of Independence was to explain to the world why the colonists' decision to separate from Great Britain was reasonable and just. To accomplish this, Thomas Jefferson emphasized in his text the right of a people to change their form of government should that government become oppressive. His principal argument was that all governments derive their legitimacy from "the consent of the governed" and that, therefore, a government without such consent had no authority to rule. John Adams later said that there was "nothing new" in the Declaration of Independence, and Jefferson would probably have agreed. Most of the ideas he set forth so eloquently in the declaration had already been articulated in one form or another during the many previous airings of colonial grievances.

As president of the Continental Congress, John Hancock was given the honor of being the first to sign the engrossed document. According to one story, Hancock, as he signed the declaration, said, "We must be unanimous; there must be no pulling different ways; we must all hang together." To which Benjamin Franklin supposedly replied, "Yes, we must indeed all hang together, or most assuredly we shall all hang separately." This story is most likely apocryphal, but it contains a measure of truth: Some of the colonists—at least those making continental policy—were finally beginning to apprehend the emergence of a national entity. Of course, the Declaration of Independence made abundantly clear that the former colonies would henceforth be "free and independent states." Yet many of the delegates at Philadelphia were indisputably coming to see themselves less as New Yorkers, Virginians, and Pennsylvanians and more as Americans.

Although the delegates softened Jefferson's language here and there, the only substantive change they made in the final declaration was to delete a questionably argued passage blaming King George for the existence of slavery in America. The striking of this passage became the price that southern delegates (especially those from South Carolina) exacted for their support. John Trumbull's 1818 painting (at left) re-creates the scene inside the Pennsylvania State House on July 4, 1776, when the Second Continental Congress approved the document's final form.

THE REVOLUTIONARY WAR LASTED another five years. The campaign of 1776 saw Washington's army pushed—actually, shoved—out of New York City and then chased by Howe all the way across New Jersey before reaching relative safety on the Pennsylvania side of the Delaware River. On Christmas night, Washington secretly recrossed the Delaware and surprised a sleeping, slightly hungover garrison of mercenary Hessians at Trenton. But his victory there was little more than a morale booster, and it had no lasting strategic significance.

The following year, the British command approved a plan developed by Maj. Gen. John Burgoyne to isolate New England from the rest of the colonies. Burgoyne's plan called for a three-force campaign: Gentleman Johnny himself would lead one army from Quebec southward on Lake Champlain to recapture Ticonderoga; Col. Barry St. Leger would command another, which would travel up the St. Lawrence River to Lake Ontario and from there make its way eastward along the Mohawk River Valley; finally, Howe would move his army north up the Hudson River from New York City, rendezvousing with Burgoyne and St. Leger at Albany. As commander in chief of British forces in North America, however, Howe had a great deal of discretion in the use of his forces, and he chose instead to move them south to attack the rebel congress at Philadelphia. This proved to be a serious misstep. Howe was indeed able to rout Washington at the battle of Brandywine Creek on September 11, 1777, and occupy Philadelphia two weeks later, but his absence from the northern campaign proved much more significant. In August, colonial militia turned back St. Leger's command at Fort Stanwix (near present-day Rome, New York);

"Gentleman Johnny" Burgoyne, as painted by Joshua Reynolds in 1776.

and on October 17, following a decisive loss at Saratoga, Burgoyne was forced to surrender his army of nearly six thousand soldiers to American commander Horatio Gates. The Continentals' victory at Saratoga was particularly important because it persuaded the French that the time had come to recognize American independence and join the war on the colonists' side.

The British military leadership always thought that its soldiers were superior to the Americans in every conceivable way. Therefore, its strategy during the Revolutionary War emphasized forcing a showdown with Washington that would end the Revolution by wiping out the Continental Army. On the other side, because he largely agreed with the British high command, Washington did all he could to avoid such a decisive confrontation. He couldn't avoid battles entirely, but his most practiced and useful tactic came to be the orderly retreat. Disengaging in this way allowed Washington to keep both an army in the field and "the glorious cause" alive. As his officers often remarked, "The Army is the Revolution."

A button from the uniform coat of a Continental.

Yorktown

BEGINNING IN 1778, as political developments in Europe further engaged the Crown's attention, British tactics became noticeably more defensive. In May of that year, Henry Clinton replaced William Howe as commander in chief of British forces in North America, and a month later Clinton evacuated Philadelphia, returning his army to New York City (where it would sit for much of the rest of the war). The next year was quieter still and nearly over before Clinton launched a major campaign. On December 26, 1779, however, the British commander sent a large armada south to capture Charleston, South Carolina. On February 11, 1780, the British fleet landed eight thousand troops thirty miles below Charleston, and six weeks later Clinton's forces began formal siege operations. On May 12, after weeks of thunderous bombardment from British warships in Charleston Harbor, the fifty-four hundred Americans holding Charleston surrendered. Soon, Clinton returned to New York City, leaving Charles, Lord Cornwallis, in command of his southern expeditionary force.

At first, the British enjoyed a great deal of success in the southern theater. On August 16, General Cornwallis overwhelmed an American army poorly led by Horatio Gates (suggesting that his underling, Benedict Arnold, had been the true hero of Saratoga). In early September, Cornwallis invaded North Carolina, but the defeat of a thousand Loyalists at King's Mountain on October 7 persuaded him to rethink the wisdom of operating in the Carolina interior. On the following March 15, Cornwallis's own army suffered heavy losses while winning a Pyrrhic victory at Guilford Court House. Afterward, the general decided to abandon the Carolinas altogether and march north to Virginia. At Yorktown, he awaited reinforcements from Clinton in New York City, but the only troops that arrived were five thousand Continentals under the command of Washington and a

This drum was carried by an American soldier during the action at Guilford Court House in March 1781.

similar number under Jean de Vimeur, comte de Rochambeau. These troops joined the French and American forces already besieging Yorktown and created a combined army of some eighteen thousand soldiers, compared to the ten thousand that Cornwallis had available.

Even more important was the presence off the Virginia coast of the French fleet under Adm. François de Grasse, which had sailed up from the West Indies earlier that summer. British admiral Thomas Graves, sent to relieve Cornwallis, engaged Grasse's fleet on September 5, 1781. The fighting ended inconclusively, though, and Graves sailed back to New York City while Cornwallis remained trapped on the Yorktown peninsula. After an unsuccessful breakout attempt, the British commander surrendered on October 19. When Lord North heard the news, carried by fast packet boat to London, he exclaimed, "Oh God! It's all over." The mother country still had thousands of troops in New York, South Carolina, and Georgia, but it no longer had the will to fight. The military phase of the Revolutionary War was over. The colonists had weaned themselves.

John Trumbull fought in the Revolutionary War before traveling to London to study painting under Benjamin West. In 1817, Congress commission him to paint four works for the new Capitol. One was Declaration of Independence; *another, the* Surrender of Lord Cornwallis at Yorktown, *shown here.*

AMERICAN PROFILE

Samuel Adams
1722–1803

by Jack N. Rakove

O F ALL THE LEADING PATRIOTS, Samuel Adams best fits the modern image of a revolutionary. Other influential colonists tended to consider their political activity something of an avocation and thus had to learn to accept the demands it placed on their time and resources; Adams, however, lived most of his life for politics. The son of a prominent Boston brewer, he entered Harvard College at age fourteen and, after his graduation in 1740, founded a newspaper. It fared poorly, so when his father died in 1748, Adams took over the family brewery, managing it not very well either. Meanwhile, his interests ran increasingly to politics, especially to the welfare of his native Boston. The policies and ambitions of the royal officials who governed Massachusetts, Adams believed, were eroding the basic liberties to which all Englishmen were entitled, no matter which side of the Atlantic they favored.

Adams became particularly suspicious of fellow colonist Thomas Hutchinson, a rising star in Massachusetts politics who pursued high office relentlessly. Adams knew Hutchinson's type well because, like most patriots, he was well versed in the literature of Britain's eighteenth-century political opposition—which described caustically how the Crown's expanding influence was subverting British liberty. Using patronage and other forms of corruption, the royal government was undermining parliamentary independence at home while appointing men such as Hutchinson to follow a similar course in the colonies.

Adams served as Boston's tax collector for eight years during the late 1750s and early 1760s before joining the Massachusetts General Court in 1765, the year that Parliament passed the Stamp Act. From the start of that controversy, Adams was among the small knot of leaders organizing resistance to the act in Boston, and with each passing year he became more and more influential—not because he wanted to consolidate his power, but because he knew how to get people into the streets. Through it all, Adams made a particular point of targeting Hutchinson (who became acting governor of Massachusetts in 1770) as an archconspirator eager to betray the freedom of his countrymen.

By 1774, Adams could be fairly described as the colonial radical most committed to the cause of intercolonial union. He was fittingly elected that year to the First Continental Congress, which was called in response to the Coercive Acts—themselves intended to punish Boston for the Tea Party Adams had organized. By the time the First Congress disbanded in October 1774, Adams was no longer welcome in occupied Boston, so he took up residence in Lexington. (It was in part to capture Adams and his wealthy ally, Hancock, that Gage organized the April 1775 raid that triggered the outbreak of war.) Exactly when Adams decided that the American colonies should form an independent country remains uncertain, but during the Second Continental Congress he certainly worked toward that end. He remained an active member of the Continental Congress until 1780, when he returned to Massachusetts to serve first as a state legislator and then as lieutenant governor before finally becoming governor in 1794, thereby occupying the same office that Hutchinson had once held.

Earlier historians often portrayed Samuel Adams as a fiery agitator and propagandist, but more recent writers have moderated this image. "We cannot make events," the patriot leader wrote in April 1776. "Our business is wisely to improve them." For Adams, who

This early 1770s portrait by John Singleton Copley shows Adams on March 6, 1770, demanding the removal of British troops from Boston. In his right hand is a petition; with his left, he points to the 1691 charter granted to Massachusetts by William and Mary.

remained always faithful to his Puritan heritage, this meant emphasizing diligence, organization, and preparation. As a result, America's foremost revolutionary looked as much backward to the religious virtue of the past as he did forward to the democratic promise of the future.

5

THE NEW REPUBLIC

The Constitutional Convention

O N SUNDAY, MAY 13, 1787, George Washington entered Philadelphia to the sounds of chiming bells and artillery salutes. There was also the incessant crunch of gravel underfoot as lines of soldiers paraded for his pleasure through the cobblestoned streets of the city. Although the day's celebration was raucous and joyful, the former general had come to town for a decidedly more sober purpose: He had been selected by the Virginia legislature to serve as a delegate to a convention of the states scheduled to begin the next day. The Philadelphia Convention had been called to overhaul the failing national government; most delegates, including Washington, believed that the Revolution itself was at stake.

Following this grand entrance, Washington immediately called on eighty-one-year-old Benjamin Franklin, who lived—when not abroad—in a fashionable town house off Market Street. Although Dr. Franklin's position as president of the Pennsylvania commonwealth was largely honorary, his international reputation (which rivaled that of Washington) was such that the task of hosting the arriving delegates fell naturally to him. More important, Franklin and Washington shared a belief that the solution to America's present woes lay in a central government much stronger than the one currently provided for by the Articles of Confederation.

Washington was particularly worried about what he and many of his fellow delegates, similarly rich and powerful, called an "excess of

AT LEFT: *This lithograph showing Washington's arrival at New York City in November 1783 gives some indication of what his May 1787 reception in Philadelphia might have looked like.*

democracy." Increasingly, majorities in the state legislatures had taken to usurping the rights of minorities, especially creditor minorities. In fact, to most of the delegates in Philadelphia, the word *democracy* meant more nearly "tyranny," so concerned were they with uneducated and unruly masses of common people threatening their property (with high taxes) and their capital (with inflation and other forms of debt relief).

T HE ROOT OF THE TROUBLES seemed to be state sovereignty. In the aftermath of the Declaration of Independence, necessity required that some sort of federal framework be established, hence the drafting of the Articles of Confederation. But few Americans considered this document more than a temporary arrangement—which would, with peace, simply fall away. The creative energies of the country's political elite went instead into designing the new state constitutions, which Thomas Jefferson called "the whole object" of the Revolution. Even John Adams admitted later that no one at the time considered "consolidating this vast Continent under one national government."

Yet the state governments, in which Jefferson and many others placed so much faith, had by the mid-1780s become objects of concern. The extralegal activities of patriots during the Revolution had understandably led to greater popular participation in government. In defiance of the Crown, or in its absence, mobs had taken to patrolling local streets and enforcing the will of the community on wrongdoers. (Although independence reduced the need for such vigilante behavior, many Americans continued to view all official institutions—even their own—with deep distrust.) In the meantime, older conceptions of the public good based on aristocratic or monarchical premises gave way to the idea that government should be responsive and accountable to popular demands.

At the end of the Revolutionary War, nearly every American expected some sort of reward. Debtor farmers wanted lower taxes, court-ordered delays in the repayment of their notes, and more paper money so that inflation would reduce the cost of their debt service. Artisans wanted price regulation of farm produce, the abolition of trade monopolies, and new tariffs on foreign imports that competed with domestic production. Merchant creditors demanded a shift of the tax burden onto landowners as well as greater legal protections for private contracts. Other businessmen sought their own special economic privileges. However, because debtors considerably outnumbered creditors, this group was in a much stronger position to coerce the state legislatures, many of which proceeded to issue bales of paper money and delay legal proceedings against debtor farmers. These and other actions incurred the wrath of creditors, merchants, and wealthy landholders, who began to explore ways in which they might check such an "excess of democracy." They discovered that the national government established under the Articles of Confederation was pitifully inadequate to the task.

The Articles of Confederation

DURING THE FIRST THREE YEARS of its existence, the Continental Congress operated quite independently of state or popular control. Its members raised a national army, issued currency, and conducted foreign relations without any established set of procedures or obligations to constituents. After independence from Great Britain was declared in July 1776, however, the Congress realized that the time had come for a more formal (and thus legitimate) alliance among the states. Therefore, a new entity called the United States of America was established under the Articles of Confederation, which Congress adopted in November 1777 and the states had ratified by March 1781. Unfortunately, the central government created under the Articles was so weak that, beyond responding to the war emergency, little else was accomplished.

The new national government consisted of a single legislative body, the Confederation Congress, in which each state had a single vote. There was no executive, no judiciary, and no mechanism for the enforcement of national laws. The Confederation Congress had no power to raise revenue directly, instead having to request funds from the states. It also had no authority over individual American citizens. Even worse, amendments to the Articles required the unanimous consent of all thirteen states.

At the same time, the country's economic and political elites felt an emerging sense of nationalism. Their experiences in the Continental Congress, the Revolutionary War, and the Confederation government—combined with their personal and class backgrounds—increasingly persuaded

This portrait of Benjamin Franklin was painted in Paris about 1785, while Franklin was serving as the American minister plenipotentiary to King Louis XVI.

The Articles of Confederation were first proposed by Benjamin Franklin in 1775. This early copy bears annotation by Thomas Jefferson.

them that enshrining state sovereignty in the Articles of Confederation had not been a good idea. Also, they were understandably alarmed at the refusal of several states to pay their allotted shares of the federal budget, by the consequent threat of mutiny among unpaid soldiers in the Continental Army, and at the gradual emasculation of the Confederation Congress, which by 1787 was an institution hardly worthy of much respect.

DURING THE MID-1780S, the nationalists developed a proposal to save the United States from collapse. The key to their plan was an amendment to the Articles permitting the Confederation Congress to enact a 5 percent tax on imports. This would have provided the national government with an independent source of revenue, relieving its reliance on what individual states saw fit to contribute. The Confederation Congress, it was argued, could use the money to repay war debt, which would enhance the reputation of the United States both domestically and among international creditors. Presumably, the value of bonds issued by the Confederation treasury would also rise, lowering the cost of government borrowing. Twelve states agreed, but when Rhode Island, alone among the states, refused, the effort failed.

Frustrated nationalist merchants and landowners in Maryland and Virginia—James Madison and George Washington among them—next organized the Mount Vernon Conference of March 1785. Its stated purpose was to resolve a dispute between the two states concerning navigation on the Potomac River, the hope being that trade with the hinterland could be expanded if the two states could enact coordinated commercial legislation. (It was not uncommon during this period for a state to tax all goods as foreign imports, even though they had come from other states; some even resorted to armed force in resolving boundary disputes with their neighbors.)

The meeting went well—so well, in fact, that the Maryland legislature suggested a second conference to consider broader commercial arrangements, with Delaware and Pennsylvania also invited to attend. The Virginia legislature agreed and adopted James Madison's recommendation that all thirteen states be invited to the conference, to be held in Annapolis the following year. When the Annapolis Convention met in September 1786, however, only five states sent delegations. This disappointing turnout caused the delegates present to forgo discussion of the nation's commercial problems and instead urge that action be taken to correct the country's political shortcomings. The Annapolis delegates, spurred on by an eager Alexander Hamilton of New York, asked specifically that a meeting be held in Philadelphia the following May. The Confederation Congress itself promptly seconded the proposal, and thus the Constitutional Convention was called.

The Philadelphia Convention

THE FIFTY-FIVE MEN (only men) who eventually took part in the Philadelphia Convention were thoroughly experienced in colonial (and, lately, state) government. Thirty-nine had served in the Continental Congress, the Confederation Congress, or both, and eight had participated in constitutional conventions at the state level. Seven had been, or were, governors of states. A third were veterans of the Continental Army. All were now being called upon to safeguard with political skill the Revolution they had earlier won with arms.

Portraits of George Washington were among the most common engravings in late eighteenth-century America. Charles Willson Peale published this one of the former general in September 1787 at the close of the Constitutional Convention.

Because heavy spring rains had turned America's dirt roads into mud, making travel slow and uncertain, George Washington was one of the few delegates to arrive on time. On May 14, the day the convention had been scheduled to begin, only the Pennsylvanians and Virginians were present. Not until May 25 were there enough other delegates on hand to constitute a quorum. These twenty-nine men represented seven states, a number that would eventually grow to twelve as, for weeks to come, delegates straggled in. The number never rose above twelve, however, because Rhode Island, obsessively jealous of its independence, refused to take part.

Although none guarded its prerogatives quite so zealously as Rhode Island, America's other small states were similarly wary of the influence of Pennsylvania, Virginia, and Massachusetts, which together accounted for nearly half the U.S. population. As early as 1754, when Benjamin Franklin proposed at the Albany Congress the creation of a continental assembly with representation from each

colony proportional to its tax payments, the small states had opposed any diminishment of their sovereign authority. On a popular level as well, the primary political loyalties of Americans were typically to their individual states: Except perhaps among veterans of the Continental Army, Americans who spoke of their "country" usually meant their state, and they referred to their delegation to the Confederation Congress as their "embassy."

Charles Willson Peale produced this engraving of the Pennsylvania State House (now Independence Hall) to coincide with the opening of the Philadelphia Convention. At the time, Philadelphia was the largest city in the nation with a population of some forty-three thousand.

AS THEY BEGAN DELIBERATIONS, the delegates certainly had the advantage of a setting historically appropriate to their work. They sat in the east room of the Pennsylvania State House (now known as Independence Hall), where the Second Continental Congress had met and the Declaration of Independence had been signed. On May 25, when the presence of a quorum finally allowed the convention to begin, the delegates first went about the business of organization. The Pennsylvania delegation proposed that George Washington preside, and after the formality of balloting his uncontested nomination, the Virginian was escorted to the high-backed speaker's chair. He modestly protested his lack of experience but thereafter served with distinction and (all agreed) impartiality.

The delegates then agreed to give each state a single vote, determined by the majority of delegates from that state. Gouverneur Morris had led other Pennsylvania delegates in making the case that states with larger populations should have greater say. But the Virginia delegation quickly intervened to end the debate, realizing that it might produce rancor between the large and small states.

The Virginia Plan

NEXT, THE VIRGINIANS, whose state was the largest in both size and population, offered a set of proposals for the convention to consider. Presented by Gov. Edmund Randolph on May 29, they were called by some the Randolph Resolutions, but the ideas were mainly the work of James Madison, who had spent much of the previous year—*years*, actually—studying all the texts he could find on political theory and the history of government. (Madison even wrote to his friend Thomas Jefferson, then U.S. minister to France, asking him for more books on "the general constitution and *droit public* of the several confederacies which have existed." Jefferson complied with more than a hundred additional volumes on the subject.) The resolutions that comprised the Virginia Plan pinpointed crucial weaknesses of the Confederation government and offered not merely a revision of the Articles (what most delegates had expected) but an entirely new form of government.

Virginia governor Edmund Randolph

Much of the Virginia Plan is easily recognizable in the Constitution today. Randolph proposed that the new government, for instance, have three branches: legislative, executive, and judicial. The legislative branch, consisting of two houses, would make the nation's laws; the executive branch would carry them out, and the judicial branch would enforce them. Also under the Virginia Plan, representation in both houses of the legislature would be proportional—according to population, tax payments, or a combination of both. The members of the lower house (later the House of Representatives) would be elected by the people, and in turn these men would elect the members of the upper house (later the Senate). Finally, the members of both houses would jointly elect a three-member executive council and commission the nation's judiciary.

In these respects, the Virginia Plan proposed adopting on a national scale structures already utilized by many state governments. The genuinely radical element of the plan was its attitude toward state sovereignty. In Randolph's words,

SECRECY

AT THE FIRST MEETING of the Philadelphia Convention, soon after Washington was made president, the delegates voted overwhelmingly to conduct their deliberations in secret. They already knew that they would likely exceed their mandate by scrapping the Articles of Confederation entirely; and many were concerned that, should this become public knowledge, the pressure of public scrutiny would make delicate negotiation impossible. On the other hand, shielding their deliberations would give them greater freedom to compromise before a public outcry on a particular issue could develop.

Outside their chamber in the Pennsylvania State House, the delegates were remarkably circumspect. Yet the aging Benjamin Franklin could no longer be trusted to watch his words carefully. Once the convention began, it became necessary for another delegate always to be present at the doctor's lively dinner parties so that the conversation could be redirected if Franklin seemed tempted to reveal details of the proceedings.

Because even the convention secretary avoided taking notes, the only detailed source we have for the debates at Philadelphia is the journal of James Madison—which was published (in the edition shown here) in 1840, four years after Madison's death.

"The idea of the states should be nearly annihilated." To achieve this, the Virginia Plan granted the new government direct authority over American citizens, unmediated by the states, as well as the unprecedented power "to negative all laws passed by the several states contravening, in the opinion of the National Legislature, the articles of Union." At the conclusion of Randolph's long and detailed presentation—delivered with his loose, dark, unpowdered hair brushed back from his forehead—the convention adjourned. The next day, it voted six states to one (Connecticut being the only state opposed) to make the Virginia Plan the basis for its deliberations. Then began the great debate.

Financier and land speculator Robert Morris was among the most powerful behind-the-scenes operators in Philadelphia. He had served as superintendent of finance under the Articles of Confederation and may well have been the richest man in America. At the convention, he played an important role in mustering support among his fellow creditors for a strong central government.

DELEGATES FROM THE SMALLER STATES, initially swept along by the fervency of Randolph's nationalism, soon began to reconsider the wisdom of creating a strong national government that might ignore their interests in favor of those of the larger states. Led by delegates from Delaware and New Jersey (lately with a quorum), the small-state caucus made its presence felt. As matters developed, the critical question came to be whether representation in the new national legislature should be equal, as it was in the Confederation Congress, or proportional, as the Virginia Plan proposed. On Saturday, June 9, William Paterson of New Jersey, that state's longtime attorney general, warned that New Jersey would never agree to unite on the basis of proportional representation because it would consolidate power among the most populous states. "Shall New Jersey have the same right or influence in the councils of the nation as Pennsylvania?" demanded James Wilson, a delegate from that state and a close ally of Madison. "I say no. It is unjust." The tension in the room rose perceptibly, and after Wilson sat down, the delegates adjourned for the day—deciding, for the time being, to postpone consideration of the matter.

Another contentious issue was who would elect the new congressmen. Roger Sherman of Connecticut, the mayor of New Haven, insisted that state legislatures, rather than citizens of particular districts, elect representatives to the lower house. The people, Sherman argued, "should have as little to do as may be about the [national] government. They [lack] information and are constantly liable to be misled." Charles Cotesworth Pinckney of South Carolina supported Sherman's view, arguing that election by the state legislatures rather than by popular vote would protect the interests of property holders from assault by the masses and thus present "a better guard against bad measures." Elbridge Gerry of Massachusetts, a signer of the Declaration of Independence who had lately prospered as a merchant and financier in Boston, favored popular elections, but not through love of the people: He simply feared the radicalism of state legislatures more. "The evils we experience," Gerry warned, "flow from the excess of democracy."

When the debate turned to representation in the upper house, however, small-state delegates again moved for election by state legislatures, and this time Gerry went along. He had evidently been profoundly effected by events in western Massachusetts the previous year and was so frightened by Shays's Rebellion that he agreed to accept some limitations on the popular franchise. In the hands of the state legislatures, Gerry reluctantly admitted, "the commercial and monied interest would be more secure than in the hands of the people at large." Support for an elite upper house was, in fact, widespread among the delegates, and it reflected a common perception that the Virginia Plan's bicameral legislature was a wise American adaptation of the much-admired British Parliament, with our own "House of Commons" and "House of Lords."

This portrait of Roger Sherman was based on a 1775 work by Ralph Earl. That same year, Earl also supplied engraver Amos Doolittle with the sketches upon which Doolittle's famous scenes of Lexington and Concord were based.

T HERE WERE THUS substantial class grounds on which the delegates could come together; but in early June, their division along state lines threatened to end the convention. When the delegates reassembled on the morning of Monday, June 11, they were still bitterly split on the question of equal versus proportional representation. At the start of the session, Roger Sherman rose from his chair. Although physically awkward, he was a shrewd and able politician, and he offered a prescient compromise: proportional representation in the lower house and equal representation in the upper. Even though this was the deal eventually accepted, at the time Sherman's proposal attracted neither comment nor second, each side apparently unwilling to modify its stance.

SHAYS'S REBELLION

BETWEEN THE END OF THE Annapolis Convention and the start of the Philadelphia Convention, the case of those who wanted to replace the Articles of Confederation entirely was substantially strengthened by events in western Massachusetts, where Daniel Shays led an uprising of debtor farmers against the Massachusetts General Court. Elsewhere, state legislatures had succumbed to the widespread pressure to issue nearly worthless paper money so that impoverished farmers could pay off their debt at pennies on the dollar. In Massachusetts, however, debts still had to be paid in specie; and when the Massachusetts state legislature adjourned for six months in July 1786 to avoid hearing any more protests, the farmers of western Massachusetts took the law into their own hands.

Aroused by Lexington and Concord and enlisting in time to see action at Bunker Hill, Daniel Shays (at left above) waited a decade for overdue army pay that never came.

Although the economic plight of farmers was a national issue, and debtors took up arms in states from South Carolina to New Hampshire, the rebellion in Massachusetts was the most serious. Led by the thirty-nine-year-old Shays, who had been a captain in the Continental Army, the rebels prevented local civil courts (the ones that handled foreclosures) from sitting and later tried to seize the federal arsenal at Springfield. Beginning in mid-January 1787, hastily mustered state troops under Benjamin Lincoln crushed the rebellion, but the specter of armed insurrection lingered. Perhaps more than any other single factor, Shays's Rebellion persuaded the delegates at Philadelphia to overstep their mandate and create a new, more powerful central government.

The debate continued. John Rutledge and Pierce Butler of South Carolina asked that representation in the lower house be made proportional to "quotas of contribution," as the original Virginia Plan had suggested. This would have had the additional benefit of obviating another difficult question: whether slaves should be counted as citizens for the purpose of representation. But more support existed for representation proportional to population, so James Wilson, whose interests in western land speculation may have reinforced his nationalistic beliefs, moved that a slave be counted as three-fifths of a person, a figure adopted by the Confederation Congress four years earlier during one of its several frustrating attempt to collect taxes. Even more important, however, a majority favoring proportional representation now seemed to be at hand, and this realization galvanized the small-state delegations into unified action.

This illustration of George Washington presiding at the Philadelphia Convention was originally published in an 1823 U.S. history textbook. Because the windows in the East Room of the statehouse were usually kept shut to prevent eavesdropping, the delegates, especially the New Englanders dressed in woolen suits, suffered greatly from the heat and humidity.

The New Jersey Plan

ON JUNE 15, WILLIAM PATERSON introduced the nine resolutions of the so-called New Jersey Plan, which sought not to replace but merely to amend the Articles of Confederation. Under the New Jersey Plan, the Confederation Congress would remain structured as it was—a single house with equal representation—but with additional powers. It would be authorized to raise funds directly through import duties, stamp taxes, and postal fees, and its ability to regulate national commerce would also be expanded. All congressional acts and treaties would be binding on the states, and coercion would be permitted should enforcement of these laws be required. The New Jersey Plan also provided for an executive council composed of several members elected by the Congress. Such an executive would have no veto power over state laws. However, it would appoint members to a federal supreme court that would hear impeachment cases and rule on matters concerning maritime law, international treaties, interstate trade regulation, and the collection of federal taxes.

Had the provisions of the New Jersey Plan been adopted by the states as late as the previous year, the Philadelphia Convention might never have met. But now, having proceeded so far beyond merely amending the Articles, few delegates were inclined to turn back, even if they believed that the Virginia Plan went too far in annihilating the states. Before he sat down, Paterson warned the delegates that they had neither the legal authority nor the popular support to create a new national government, but few heeded his words or the implied threat of a walk-out. As Madison liked to remind the small states, they would be particularly hurt by a dissolution of the federal union because then they would be hard pressed to defend their interests against those of foreign powers, not to mention their larger neighbors.

WHEN THE DELEGATES reassembled on Monday morning, June 18, thirty-year-old Alexander Hamilton spoke for six consecutive hours, during which time he repeated his concerns that the Virginia Plan failed to safeguard adequately the government against democracy. Hamilton, an aloof young intellectual who overshadowed his older colleagues in the New York delegation, wanted a single chief executive, chosen for life and possessing an absolute veto over Congress that it could not override. He wanted life terms for members of the upper house as well and appointment of all state governors by the central government. The people, Hamilton argued, were starting to tire "of an excess of democracy." "What even is the Virginia plan," he asked, "but pork still with a little change of the sauce?"

The next morning, worried that Hamilton's ultra-nationalism might drive some moderates into the small-state camp, Madison intervened. He pointed out that amending the Articles of Confederation, as the New Jersey Plan proposed, would do little to prevent internal rebellions such as the one recently led by Daniel Shays and not much more to protect the states against foreign powers, economically or militarily. Reassured by Madison's eloquent rhetoric, the convention voted that day, seven states to three (with New Jersey, New York, and Delaware opposed and Maryland divided), to reaffirm the Virginia Plan as the basis for its deliberations.

It was now clear that the delegates wanted the new national government to be radically different from the existing loose confederation, but the shape that government would take was still undecided. Unable yet to agree on its fundamentals, the already weary delegates wisely turned to lesser issues that might be more easily resolved. Meanwhile, as the heat and humidity of the Philadelphia summer set in, most worried that the coming debate over representation might deadlock the convention. The discomfort grew as delegates rose in turn to repeat views already familiar to their colleagues—making few, if any, concessions. Madison predicted that, as a practical matter, the larger states would not conspire to further their own interests because those interests were divergent. Virginia's economy depended on tobacco, Pennsylvania's on flour, and Massachusetts's on fish, Madison said. What had they in common? The larger states, he continued, were more likely to become rivals than allies against their smaller neighbors. On the other side, Roger Sherman and others continued to insist that the larger states simply should not have more votes.

Fearing the strong possibility that negotiations would break down, Benjamin Franklin rose to urge greater tolerance and patience. "The small progress we have made after four or five weeks," he said, "is methinks a melancholy proof of the imperfection of human understanding." Franklin then proposed that a member of the Philadelphia clergy be brought in each morning to lead the delegates in prayer. Alexander Hamilton opposed this idea, arguing that it might reveal to the public the extent of dissension within the convention. Franklin responded placidly that such a revelation might do the convention more good than harm. Finally, Hugh Williamson of North Carolina pointed out that, whatever the idea's merits, the convention had no money with which to hire a chaplain.

Alexander Hamilton was born on the West Indian island of Nevis in 1755. In 1772, he emigrated to New York City, where—overcoming his illegitimate birth—he married into one of the colony's wealthiest families.

James Madison was born in Port Conway, Virginia, in 1751 and raised in what he once described as "independent and comfortable circumstances."

This engraving of Chestnut Street appeared as Plate 20 in The City of Philadelphia As It Appeared in the Year 1800, *published that same year by William Russell Birch. During the convention, Philadelphia city officials spread dirt on the cobblestones of Chestnut Street outside the state house to quiet the din from passing horses and carriages.*

RIGHT:
More than once, Gouverneur Morris bitterly chided delegates from the smaller states, insisting that the New Jersey Plan would never work. His comments so angered New York Anti-Federalists Robert Yates and John Lansing that they packed their bags and left. As a result, New York lost its quorum and could no longer cast a vote.

THIS WAS THE STATE of affairs as the first month of the convention came to a close. The delegates, Luther Martin of Maryland later recalled, "were on the verge of dissolution, scarce held together by the strength of a hair." And with the small states, particularly Connecticut, refusing to budge on representation, more delegates began seeking a settlement in the compromise initially suggested by Roger Sherman on June 11: that representation be proportional in one house and equal in the other. However, when Oliver Ellsworth of Connecticut reintroduced Sherman's compromise plan, a furious Madison summarily rejected it, in the process insulting Ellsworth's delegation with the charge that Connecticut had not paid its full share of the cost of the Revolutionary War. Predictably, Ellsworth jumped to his feet, shouting that "the muster rolls will show she had more troops in the field than Virginia!"

Gouverneur Morris took Madison's side. "State attachments and state importance have been the bane of this country," the Pennsylvanian said. "We cannot annihilate; but we may perhaps take the teeth out of the serpent." Yet neither he nor Madison was able to persuade a majority of the delegates to overcome their state loyalties completely. As Gunning Bedford of Delaware made clear, approval of the Virginia Plan was not the only option available to the smaller states. "The large states dare not dissolve the confederation," Bedford said. "If they do, the small ones will find some foreign ally of more honor and good faith who will take them by the hand and do them justice." The possibility of a recourse to foreign patronage Morris countered with his own veiled threat: "This country must be united. If persuasion does not unite it, the sword will." On July 2, a vote was taken on equal representation in the upper house. When Georgia, the final state to be called, divided its vote, the tally stood at five states for and five against. All convention business then came to a standstill.

The Great Compromise

TO RESOLVE THIS DEAD-LOCK, a special committee was formed with one representative from each state. It met while the rest of the convention celebrated the Fourth of July holiday. On July 5, it reported a plan under which the lower house would contain one representative for every forty thousand citizens (including three-fifths of the slaves) and the upper house would have equal representation.

The convention's decisive moment came on July 16, when the delegations voted five states to four to accept equal representation in the upper house of the legislature. Connecticut, Delaware, Maryland, New Jersey, and North Carolina voted in favor of what became the Great Compromise; Pennsylvania, Virginia, Georgia, and South Carolina were opposed; the Massachusetts delegation divided; and New York was unable to vote because it lacked a quorum (its two Anti-Federalist delegates had decided to go home). The vote was a victory for the small states, and thereafter their delegations no longer feared in the same way the encroachments of a strong central government.

Immediately, the disappointed Virginia delegation asked for an adjournment, which was granted. The next morning, the Virginians caucused to consider their options, among them the calling of a separate convention. Eventually, they yielded to the committee's (in Madison's words) "imperfect & exceptionable" plan. What Madison later discovered, much to his relief, was that the smaller states, having made their point on equal representation, were now willing to acquiesce on most other issues. "The whole comes down to this," Charles Pinckney of South Carolina observed. "Give N. Jersey an equal vote, and she will dismiss her scruples, and concur in the National system."

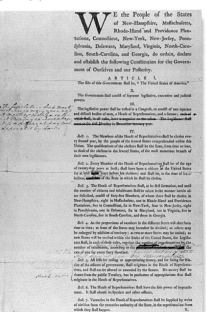

O N JULY 26, the convention appointed Randolph of Virginia, Wilson of Pennsylvania, Ellsworth of Connecticut, Rutledge of South Carolina, and Nathaniel Gorham of Massachusetts to a Committee of Detail charged with organizing the various measures, amendments, and proposals already approved by the delegates into a coherent, workable system of government. The committee was given eleven days to complete the task—during which time the remaining delegates, most in a jovial mood, retired to Philadelphia's many taverns for some relaxation. George Washington, meanwhile, rode off into the countryside to fish for trout with some friends.

When the convention reassembled on August 6, the Committee of Detail presented a preliminary document. Wilson had apparently taken portions of a draft written by Randolph, which he augmented with ideas from the New Jersey Plan and a separate plan drawn up by Charles Pinckney. Elements of the Articles of Confederation and various state constitutions were also present. After copies were distributed, the convention passed out of session again so that delegates could study and reflect on the plan.

Faced with an incomplete and somewhat confusing mandate, the Committee of Detail had thought, in some cases, to leave questions open for the new government to decide once formed. In others, it had arrived at a solution not previously contemplated by the delegates. Thus, citizenship and residence requirements for members of Congress were included, while property qualifications for voting were omitted pending further debate. Some of these details were adopted by the convention without debate, but others generated prolonged discussion. Eventually, for example, the delegates voted against the committee's recommendation that members of Congress be paid by the state legislatures, lest they be too dependent on the states.

This copy of an early draft of the Constitution shows handwritten notes made by George Washington concerning some proposed changes. One change later made was the rewriting of the Preamble after a few delegates realized that one or more of the listed states might not ratify the document.

OVERALL, THE DEGREE to which the delegates, despite their heated disagreements, shared common economic and political interests emerged clearly in the draft. Many delegates, for example, speculated in western land and were personally concerned with the future admission of western states. Some went so far as proposing that the original thirteen states retain permanent control over potential western states, even after their admission. This brazen suggestion was voted down, but the convention did grant Congress the power "to dispose of and make all needful rules and regulations respecting the territory or other property belonging to the United States." Similarly, most members of the convention were creditors. As a matter of course, they held numerous bonds and securities that had been issued by governmental agencies during the Revolutionary War to fund the Continental Army and state militias. Some delegates wanted the new government to have a constitutional responsibility to repay these debts—a plan also voted down—but the convention did find numerous ways to block the rising power of debtor farmers in the state legislatures.

Finally, with the hard business of the convention concluded, a Committee of Style and Arrangement was formed to write a final draft of the Constitution. Its work took four days. The Articles of Confederation had begun, "We the under-signed delegates of the States...." In contrast, the preamble to the new Constitution (written by Gouverneur Morris) began, "We the people of the United States...." George Mason of Virginia suggested that a bill of rights be added as a preface to the Constitution, but the convention rejected the idea, ten states to none, agreeing with Roger Sherman that existing state bills of rights were sufficient.

This map shows how the various state claims to western land were resolved during the early Federal period.

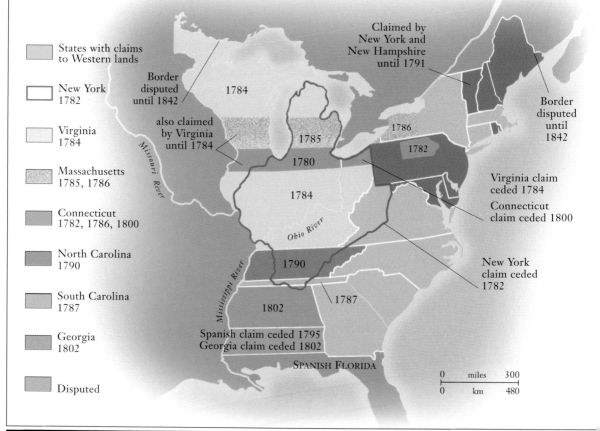

States with claims to Western lands

New York 1782

Virginia 1784

Massachusetts 1785, 1786

Connecticut 1782, 1786, 1800

North Carolina 1790

South Carolina 1787

Georgia 1802

Disputed

Claimed by New York and New Hampshire until 1791

Border disputed until 1842

1784

also claimed by Virginia until 1784

1785

1780

1786

1782

1784

Border disputed until 1842

Virginia claim ceded 1784

Connecticut claim ceded 1800

Ohio River

Missouri River

Mississippi River

1790

1787

New York claim ceded 1782

1802

Spanish claim ceded 1795
Georgia claim ceded 1802

SPANISH FLORIDA

0 miles 300
0 km 480

THE WESTERN LANDS

THE PRINCIPAL LEGACY of the Confederation Congress was its western land policy, especially the precedent-setting Northwest Ordinance of July 1787. This law concerned the Northwest Territory, the region between the Appalachian Mountains and the Mississippi River bounded by the Great Lakes on the north and the Ohio River to the south. At the time of the Declaration of Independence, by virtue of their original royal charters, seven states claimed territories extending either to the Mississippi River or all the way to the Pacific Ocean. The six "landless" states considered this territorial windfall unfair; one of them, Maryland, even refused to ratify the Articles of Confederation until the "landed" states transferred their western claims to the new federal government. In 1780, Virginia, the oldest state with the largest land claim, agreed, and New York and Connecticut soon followed suit. Massachusetts, Georgia, and the two Carolinas held on to their claims substantially longer, but the point had been made well enough for Maryland, the last holdout, to ratify the Articles on February 27, 1781. Two days later, Congress declared the new government to be in effect.

Three years after that, Thomas Jefferson headed a congressional committee that considered how the Northwest Territory should be settled and governed. A year later, Jefferson revised and extended the plan, which became the Land Ordinance of 1785. It called for surveyors to draw north–south and east–west lines dividing the Northwest Territory into square townships, six miles on a side. Each township would then be subdivided into thirty-six sections, each section encompassing a square mile. Once surveyed, the land would be sold to the public at auction, one section at a time, for no less than a dollar an acre, or $640 per section. However, four sections within each township were to be reserved for the federal government, and another set aside for the support of local public education. (This aspect of the ordinance reversed the old colonial policy of giving land away to encourage settlement. Instead, it favored wealthy land speculators over small farmers, who neither needed 640 acres nor could afford $640.)

The Northwest Ordinance of 1787 reaffirmed much of Jefferson's plan and organized the territory into a single political unit with a governor and three judges to run its courts. When the territory's free male population reached five thousand, it could establish a bicameral legislature and send a nonvoting member to Congress. When a district within the territory reached a free male population of sixty thousand, it could apply for statehood "on an equal footing with the original States in all respects whatever." Additionally, in all of these new states, slavery would be prohibited. The Northwest Ordinance was thus the first national legislation to set limits on the expansion of slavery.

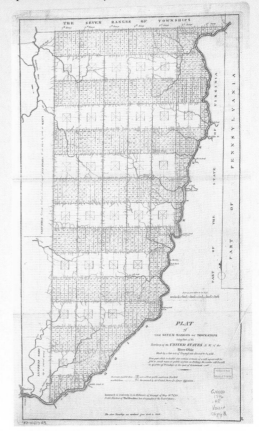

This original plat *shows the result of federal surveys conducted along the Ohio River under the Land Ordinance of 1785. Such work helped speed statehood for Ohio, Indiana, Michigan, Illinois, and Wisconsin under the 1787 Northwest Ordinance. The procedure that this latter law established set an important precedent regarding the admission of new states on an equal basis with established ones.*

This work commemorating the signing of the Constitution was painted by Thomas Rossiter during the course of the Civil War.

Of the fifty-five delegates who took part in the convention at one time or another, only forty-two were present in Philadelphia on September 17, the day of the signing. Benjamin Franklin urged unanimous approval of the document, pleading with the delegates to avoid discussing their differences in public. George Washington also urged all to sign the document. Even so, three delegates refused. Before committing himself to the plan, a politically wary Edmund Randolph wanted to gauge the public reaction in Virginia, which he feared would be largely negative. Elbridge Gerry worried that popular opposition to the power of the new central government would lead to civil war during the ratification debate. And George Mason, still unhappy with the convention's refusal to insert a bill of rights, returned to Virginia to oppose ratification. The remaining thirty-nine men affixed their signatures to the proffered parchment. They dined together that evening at the City Tavern, packed their bags the next day, and returned home after four months of deliberation to take part in the ratification process in their various states.

The signers of the Constitution, despite some specific objections, were generally satisfied that they had created a stronger and more workable form of government. The men who would come to be called the Founding Fathers had authorized a new national government to collect taxes, coin and borrow money, make treaties with foreign countries, and regulate commerce among the states and with other nations. The Constitution would be "the law of the land" and therefore binding on all federal and state courts. As they left Philadelphia, therefore, nearly all the delegates could identify with the sentiment that Madison's notes ascribe to Benjamin Franklin, who watched with evident pleasure as the last of the convention's members signed the new plan of government:

Doctor Franklin looking toward the Presidents chair, at the back of which a rising sun happened to be painted, observed to a few members near him, that painters had found it difficult to distinguish in their art a rising from a setting sun. I have, he said, often in the course of the session, and the vicissitudes of my hopes and fears as to its issue, looked at that behind the President without being able to tell whether it was rising or setting. But now at length I have the happiness to know that it is a rising and not a setting sun.

Ratifying the Constitution

ONE OF THE LAST DEBATES at the Philadelphia Convention concerned how best to win public approval of the Constitution. In the final report of the Committee of Style and Arrangement, the number of states necessary for ratification was left blank. The Articles of Confederation had required unanimous consent for any revision, but the delegates knew already that Rhode Island would not approve the new document. This was a problem because accepting less than unanimous consent meant acknowledging that the Philadelphia Convention had thoroughly transformed the existing framework of government—which, of course, it had.

With his steel-rimmed spectacles hooked onto his powdered wig, James Wilson suggested that a simple majority of seven states be sufficient for ratification. Pierce Butler of South Carolina rose in support of Wilson, asserting that the delegates were obedient to a higher law, which permitted a change in government should the country be poorly governed. After extensive debate, the delegates finally agreed that the approval of three-quarters of the states, or nine, would be sufficient for ratification.

The final question before the convention, then, was whether the state legislatures or special conventions elected by the people should decide the fate of the Constitution. With Shays's Rebellion obviously in his mind, Elbridge Gerry wanted the state legislatures to decide because the people had "the wildest ideas of government in the world." Yet many other delegates observed that self-interested members of the state legislatures, sworn to uphold their local governments, would be unlikely to support a strong national government whose creation the states had never authorized. Eventually, in a decision as important as any previously taken, the convention decided nine votes to one for popular ratification by special convention.

This engraving of Elbridge Gerry follows a portrait painted by John Vanderlyn.

THE AMERICANS who most actively backed the Constitution were those most nearly allied to the country's mercantile and commercial interests. Such people generally believed that the new government's power to regulate commerce would lead to uniform procedures that would in turn end interstate bickering, stabilize trade routes, and create a climate more suitable to increased foreign trade. This segment of the population included not only merchants but also skilled workers and independent artisans with small shops. Coopers (barrel makers) and sail makers, for example, were among those who depended directly on the prosperity of the shipping industry. Some sold their products to merchants for export. Many hoped for protective tariffs to shield their trades. Even farmers who produced surpluses for export thought ratification would lead to a beneficial upsurge in commerce. Newspapers, moreover—reflecting the self-interest of urban printers, who depended for their revenues on merchant readers and commercial advertisers— overwhelmingly supported ratification.

Constituting the ranks of the Anti-Federalists were many subsistence and debtor farmers, especially those on the western frontier who were farthest from interstate and foreign markets. These farmers, like the ones who had marched with Daniel Shays, were suspicious of any new government that might restrain the

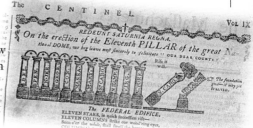

A woodcut from the August 2, 1788, edition of the Massachusetts Centinel. *The cartoon was part of a series charting the ongoing process of ratification; this installment shows New York's recent endorsement of the Constitution.*

ability of state legislatures to print currency and revise contractual obligations. To the Anti-Federalists, such restraints smacked of the British abuses that had sparked the Revolution. Yet their cause was harmed by their own internal disarray: They disagreed among themselves on how the Articles of Confederation should be revised, and they offered no legitimate alternative.

In contrast, the Federalist supporters of the Constitution worked closely across state lines to promote ratification, and personal endorsements from the most prestigious Revolutionary leaders (men such as Washington and Franklin) added enormous symbolic strength to their voluminous political arguments. These were made most forcefully in eighty-five essays written by James Madison, Alexander Hamilton, and John Jay under the pseudonym Publius. Originally published in newspapers in New York (and later in Virginia) to influence ratification debates, these essays were later collected and published in 1788 as *The Federalist*.

The crucial ratification battles were fought in Virginia, Pennsylvania, Massachusetts, and New York. Citizens of these wealthy states were confident that their prosperity would continue even without a new central government. Also, many

THE BILL OF RIGHTS

SUPPORTERS OF THE NEW CONSTITUTION had enormous advantages. They were better organized than their opponents, and their arguments were more cohesive. Those who advocated ratification generally offered the same reasoning, while opponents of the Constitution, because they came from many different political backgrounds, offered divergent and often contradictory points of view. There was one criticism, however, that the Federalists who supported ratification could not ignore: The American people wanted their Constitution to include a specific statement of their personal freedoms, and this turned out to be the price of ratification.

James Madison was not alone in considering a bill of individual rights unnecessary for a government based on popular consent, especially when the various state constitutions already guaranteed many of those rights. Madison also feared that any declaration of rights in the new Constitution would prove too narrow, therefore encouraging the violation of other rights not specified. But when

the First Congress met in New York in April 1789, it became clear that most of its members, having promised their constituents that constitutional guarantees would be enacted, intended to do just that. Unable to change their minds, Madison himself guided the amendments through Congress.

In all, twelve amendments were submitted to the states in September 1789—of which only the first ten were ratified. (The other two proposed amendments concerned the number of representatives and compensation for congressmen.) Probably the most important of these to Madison were the Ninth Amendment, which made clear that the enumeration of certain rights in the Constitution did not preclude the retention of others by the people, and the Tenth Amendment, which explicitly reserved for the states or the people all powers not specifically granted to the federal government.

Madison used these notes to deliver a speech in Congress on June 8, 1789, in which he synthesized public demands for specific individual rights to be included in the Constitution. Later, he used the notes to draft the Bill of Rights.

influential local officials in these states and elsewhere were still reluctant to give up any power by agreeing to the changes incorporated into the Constitution. As a result, the ratification votes in some states were cliffhangers. On December 12, 1787, Pennsylvania became the second state to ratify the Constitution, following Delaware's approval five days earlier. Within the next month, New Jersey, Georgia, and Connecticut also ratified; and on February 6, 1788, Massachusetts brought the total number to six. Maryland and South Carolina voted yes in the spring, and on June 21, 1788, New Hampshire became the ninth state to ratify, thereby establishing the new government. With subsequent approvals from Virginia and New York, North Carolina and Rhode Island remained the only holdouts. Another year passed before North Carolina ratified the Constitution on November 21, 1789, leaving only Rhode Island. That state stubbornly withheld its approval for six more months until finally joining the Union on May 29, 1790.

The Washington Presidency

THE STABILITY OF THE NEW GOVERNMENT was greatly enhanced when George Washington, the unanimous choice of the electoral college, accepted the presidency in 1789. Washington had a well-deserved reputation for personal integrity, and most Americans were confident that he wouldn't abuse his power to subvert their liberties. Washington's selection of cabinet officers from differing geographic regions and political interest groups also suggested that he would govern inclusively. His secretary of state, Thomas Jefferson, and attorney general, Edmund Randolph, were two fellow Virginians. For his secretary of the treasury, Washington chose Alexander Hamilton of New York, who had served on his personal staff during the Revolutionary War. Another Continental Army veteran, Henry Knox of Massachusetts, became the nation's first secretary of war. John Adams, who received the second highest number of electoral votes, became vice president. (Until ratification of the Twelfth Amendment in September 1804, each elector voted twice, and the top two vote getters became president and vice president, respectively.)

This engraving of the first presidential cabinet shows (from left to right) Secretary of War Henry Knox, Attorney General Edmund Randolph, Secretary of State Thomas Jefferson, Treasury Secretary Alexander Hamilton, and President George Washington.

At the Constitutional Convention and afterward in *The Federalist*, Hamilton had championed the cause of a strong central government. Although somewhat disappointed with the result, he was determined to use his position as treasury secretary to enlarge and strengthen the new government's powers. His plan was to increase dramatically the role the government played in the national economy by consolidating American debt, then creating a national bank to manage the debt and enacting federal taxes to service it. The new government had inherited a national debt of about fifty million dollars from its previous incarnation, most of it in the form of notes issued during the Revolutionary War to Continental Army soldiers in lieu of pay. Because few soldiers believed the government would ever pay off these notes, most of them were sold in the years after the war to speculators for a small fraction of their face value. Hamilton now proposed to pay off the notes at par. He also wanted the federal government to assume responsibility for the states' Revolutionary War debt, valued at about twenty-five million dollars, and pay it off as well.

MADISON, THEN SERVING in the first House of Representatives, led the congressional opposition to Hamilton's financial plan. He didn't like the idea that speculators who had preyed on hard-pressed army veterans would be rewarded, nor did he favor the assumption of state debt. Most southern states, including Madison's own Virginia, had already raised taxes to pay their Revolutionary War debt, and they saw federal assumption as merely a bailout for northerners. Yet Madison had something else on his mind: the new federal capital, which he wanted built in Virginia. This issue, too, was being held up in Congress. So, at a private June 1790 dinner party hosted by Thomas Jefferson, Hamilton and Madison made a deal. Hamilton agreed to locate the new federal capital on the Potomac River in exchange for Madison's promise not to block assumption. Within a month, both bills were passed by the House and later approved by the Senate.

THE NATION'S CAPITAL

ON DECEMBER 23, 1784, the Confederation Congress voted to make New York City its tenth meeting place pending construction of a new federal capital on the banks of the Delaware near Philadelphia. Along with the Confederation government, however, that plan was shelved, and the residency question (as it was called) lingered until September 1789, when it finally came before the new Congress.

The struggle over residency was both fierce and frustrating, because each time a winner emerged in one house, advocates of the various other locations banded together to block its approval in the other. By the time Madison and Hamilton had their fateful dinner party at Jefferson's house in June 1790, no fewer than sixteen different sites had been proposed and stalled. "The business of the seat of Government is become a labyrinth," Madison reported to a Virginia assemblyman; and the *New York Daily Advertiser* mocked the futility of the process by suggesting that President Washington point his finger at a map and say, "Here."

The deal that Madison and Hamilton made to locate the federal capital on the banks of the Potomac ended the stalemate, but only because Pennsylvania agreed to support the plan in exchange for Philadelphia's designation as interim capital (until the permanent capital could be built). The Pennsylvanians believed—incorrectly, as it turned out—that once the capital was moved from New York, it would never be moved again.

Jefferson was particularly pleased with the choice of a southern location because he considered the atmosphere in the commercially minded North degrading. Washington, D.C., on the other hand, embodied his vision of America because, at least during his lifetime, it was hardly a city at all. Bankers were nowhere to be found, and the only people who disturbed Congress regularly were the turkey hunters who blazed away in the vicinity of rural Capitol Hill.

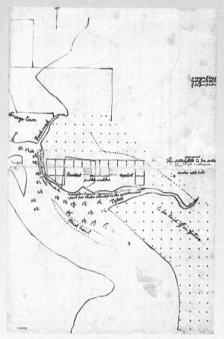

To create the District of Columbia (shown here in a 1791 map drawn by Jefferson), the states of Virginia and Maryland ceded one hundred square miles of land on both banks of the Potomac. In 1846, however, the federal government returned to Virginia its land on the western bank.

THE WHISKEY REBELLION

ONCE THE ASSUMPTION BILL PASSED, Congress had to raise funds to pay off the newly enlarged federal debt. The import duties it had approved in July 1789 weren't producing nearly enough revenue to do this; so at Hamilton's suggestion, the House and Senate in March 1791 approved a new excise tax on distilled liquor.

The liquor tax was a particularly upsetting burden for farmers on the western frontier, who were already struggling to make ends meet. Transporting their surplus crops to eastern markets was impractical because the shipping costs nearly matched the value of the crops. So the westerners typically distilled their extra grain into whiskey, which they shipped much more easily and cheaply. Still, they made so little profit on the whiskey that Hamilton's excise tax reduced their take to practically nothing. So they ignored the law, and when federal marshals came to western Pennsylvania in July 1794 to enforce it, the farmers attacked the marshals.

This defiance of national authority horrified Hamilton, who prevailed upon Washington to mobilize thirteen thousand militiamen to suppress the "rebellion." The treasury secretary himself led this army across the Appalachians, where it arrested more than a hundred men. Of those, only twenty-five ever had their cases come to trial, and just two were convicted. Those two were sentenced to death but later pardoned by Washington, so the only lasting effect of the Whiskey Rebellion was that western Pennsylvania became strongly anti-Federalist.

This turn-of-the-eighteenth-century painting by Frederick Kemmelmeyer shows Washington at Fort Cumberland reviewing the army that Hamilton had raised to put down the Whiskey Rebellion.

For a time, both sides were happy; but as the years passed, Jefferson came to realize that he and Madison had made a terrible mistake. Assumption, he discovered, had been merely an opening wedge that Hamilton used to achieve his broader goal of transforming the United States into a modern capitalistic nation. In taking on the state debt and repaying the federal debt at par, the treasury secretary had aligned the interests of the government with those of the note holders, who were largely the country's commercial elite. From that point on, the note holders joined Hamilton in advocating a strong central government because a strong government was the one most capable of levying taxes and repaying the debt. More than any other aspect of Washington's administration, Hamilton's economic policy made possible the growth of federal power and ensured that the United States would be, fundamentally, a commercial rather than an agricultural nation.

Implied Powers

THE NEXT STEP in Hamilton's master plan was the creation of a national bank. Madison and other opponents tried to block the bank's charter, arguing that it was an unconstitutional extension of congressional authority. In what clause, they asked, did the Constitution give Congress the power to charter a bank? Hamilton responded that, in addition to the powers directly granted by the Constitution,

there also existed "implied powers" derived from Article I, Section 8, which gave Congress the power to "make all laws which shall be necessary and proper for carrying into execution the foregoing powers, and all other powers vested by the Constitution in the government of the United States."

This 1861 painting by Daniel Huntington, entitled The Republican Court, *re-creates a specific levee that the Washingtons held on February 26, 1790, four days after the president's fifty-eighth birthday.*

Hamilton's position, called "loose construction," encouraged a rather broad interpretation of the Constitution, while Madison's "strict construction" promoted a narrower, more literal reading.

This argument notwithstanding, Hamilton was able to push the bank bill through Congress in February 1791, but the president still had to sign it. Before doing so, Washington asked Jefferson, Hamilton, and Attorney General Randolph for their opinions on the constitutionality of the law. Although Jefferson strongly supported strict construction, Randolph equivocated, and in the end Washington accepted Hamilton's argument that the government possessed the implied power to establish the bank. On February 25, he signed the bill chartering the First Bank of the United States for twenty years. Capitalized at far more than all existing state banks combined, the First Bank was a semiprivate institution. The government owned 20 percent of its stock and was entitled to appoint a fifth of its directors. The rest of the stock was publicly bought and sold, mostly by recently enriched government note holders. The federal government used the First Bank to hold and disburse funds as it saw fit, but the private-sector majority that controlled the bank's board set its loan policies and directed the First Bank's other commercial activities, which were many and diverse.

This print by William Russell Birch shows the Philadelphia headquarters of the First Bank of the United States nine years after the bank's founding in 1791.

THE FOREIGN POLICY of the Washington administration also set many important precedents. Inspired by John Winthrop's vision of "a Citty upon a Hill" and Tom Paine's insistence that their cause was "the cause of all mankind," most Americans of the Federal period felt that they were building a new (and better) society that would eventually transform the corruption of the Old World. Within this context, President Washington attempted to devise a foreign policy that treated all nations evenhandedly, especially with regard to trade, while simultaneously distancing the United States from dangerous foreign entanglements. The young nation was still much too weak to allow itself to become involved in European political and military conflicts. Yet maintaining American neutrality proved difficult.

Substantially complicating matters was the French Revolution, which was getting under way just as Washington became president in April 1789. The overthrow of the French king rocked monarchical Europe, and by February 1793 the British and French were at war again. As the American minister to France during the late 1780s, Jefferson had personally experienced the social inequities there; and as secretary of state, he openly sympathized with the revolutionaries (even though his enthusiasm was later tempered by the January 1793 execution of Louis XVI and the ensuing two-year Reign of Terror). Hamilton, on the other hand, sided with the British—who had become, once again, America's strongest trading partners.

Hamilton wanted the United States to declare neutrality in the European War of the First Coalition (1793–1797). Washington, however, was concerned that America's treaty of alliance with France, signed in February 1778, required the United States to side with the French. Hamilton countered that, because the French king had been overthrown, the treaty no longer obtained. Jefferson advised Washington that the 1778 treaty was, in fact, still binding, but he also recognized that the United States needed, for its own sake, to stay out of the fighting. Therefore, he reluctantly backed neutrality while also advising Washington to keep U.S. intentions secret. This way, the French would not be offended, and the British might be persuaded to remove their troops from the Northwest Territory, rather than risk a renewal of the Franco-American alliance.

CITIZEN GENET

IN THEIR 1778 TREATY OF ALLIANCE, the French and the Americans agreed that an attack on France would oblige the United States to defend the French West Indies and accept into its ports prizes seized by French privateers. Assuming that this agreement was still in effect, the moderate Girondins who ruled revolutionary France in early 1793 sent Edmond Genet to America to make the necessary arrangements. Known by his modest revolutionary title Citizen, Genet landed at Charleston on April 8 and spent the next ten days in that strongly pro-French town commissioning privateers and organizing military expeditions against the Spanish in Louisiana and Florida (because Spain was an ally of Great Britain).

On April 18, the French envoy left Charleston for Philadelphia; during his monthlong overland journey, he was greeted warmly all along the way. In the meantime, however, President Washington issued his proclamation of neutrality; and when the charming thirty-year-old Genet arrived at the national capital in mid-May, he was received rather coldly. Washington made it clear that the United States would not be taking part in his war, nor would it tolerate his adventuring. Genet, however, believed that the American people were with him, so he ignored Washington and continued rallying military and financial support for his country. This infuriated even Jefferson, who joined the rest of the cabinet in requesting Genet's recall. By the time that decision was taken in August 1793, however, the radical Montagnards had ousted the Girondins, and Genet decided it would be in his own best interest to remain in the United States as a political refugee. He later married the daughter of New York governor George Clinton and became a U.S. citizen.

This oil-on-wood portrait of Edmond Genet was painted about 1809 by Ezra Ames.

On April 22, 1793, disregarding Jefferson's advice, Washington issued a public proclamation of neutrality in which he affirmed the right of the United States to trade freely with all belligerent parties. The British navy, however, ignored U.S. neutrality and began to stop, search, and confiscate American ships caught trading with France and its West Indian possessions. The Royal Navy's abuse of U.S shipping moved popular opinion toward war, but Washington instead sent Supreme Court chief justice John Jay to negotiate a settlement. Because the United States had essentially no navy, however, Jay was in a poor position to bargain, and the treaty he concluded in November 1794 was so one-sided that Washington considered rejecting it. Jay's Treaty did provide for British evacuation of the Northwest Territory and offered favorable trade status to American merchants, but it also allowed the British to continue boarding and seizing U.S. ships, which most Americans considered an insult to their national honor. The Senate reluctantly approved Jay's Treaty in June 1795, but ratification of the deal only exacerbated domestic political tensions.

This etching shows the last meeting of Louis XVI and his family on January 20, 1793. The next day, the French king was guillotined.

The Development of Political Parties

THE DELEGATES TO THE Philadelphia Convention had been keenly aware of the dangers of factionalism, but they hadn't really anticipated the creation of political parties. During George Washington's first term in office, coalition politics prevailed. But as Washington's second term began in 1793, the coalition that the president had put together began to disintegrate. Frustrated by his lack of influence, Thomas Jefferson resigned at the end of 1793 so that he could more effectively organize a political opposition. Jefferson's inspiration was the French Revolution—which, despite its terror, Jefferson considered an extension of the American Revolution. He enthusiastically championed the French revolutionary ideals of "liberty, equality, fraternity" and helped promote the formation of democratic clubs in imitation of the French Jacobins. Jefferson's supporters also started scores of partisan newspapers in which they freely aired their often virulent objections to government policy.

At this point, there were just two national parties: Hamilton's Federalists and Jefferson's Democratic-Republicans. Although Washington's reelection in 1792 had not been challenged, elements of what would become the Democratic-Republican party did attempt to replace Vice Pres. John Adams with New Yorker George Clinton. Four years later, Washington's decision to retire set the stage for the first contested presidential election. In his farewell address, Washington warned of the dangers of political partisanship (as well as those of foreign entanglement), but the two parties largely ignored his advice, organizing campaigns on the local, state, and national levels. The competition was typically vicious: The Federalists accused the Democratic-Republicans of attempting to bring down the government in the manner of the French Jacobins, while the Democratic-Republicans denounced Federalist elitism as a threat to American liberties. The election was a squeaker, with Adams edging out Jefferson in the electoral college, 71–68. By virtue of his second-place finish, however, Jefferson became Adams's vice president.

John Adams was appalled by the political strife that had dominated the 1796 campaign, yet there was little he could do to end it. He may have been the pro forma head of the Federalist party, but the party membership was loyal to Hamilton, who considered Adams weak and too moderate. As a result, during his presidency Adams faced strong political challenges from both his own party and the opposition. The influence of the retired treasury secretary could be easily seen in Adams's cabinet, whose members were all holdovers from the Washington administration (and all mediocrities). Whatever Adams might have accomplished under different circumstances was severely undermined by his inability to order his own house.

A contemporary portrait of French foreign minister Charles Talleyrand.

T HE GREAT ISSUE OF the Adams administration was the Quasi-War with France. The French had been angered by ratification of Jay's Treaty, which they believed violated the 1778 Franco-American alliance. Moreover, Napoléon's successful conclusion of the War of the First Coalition had left the First Republic feeling rather cocksure. In 1798, therefore, the French navy began interdicting American shipping, much as the British had done several years earlier. To pacify the French and resolve other issues, Adams sent three negotiators to Paris. Upon their arrival, Elbridge Gerry, John Marshall, and Charles C. Pinckney met with three deputies of French foreign minister Charles Talleyrand. These men informed the Americans that Talleyrand required a $250,000 bribe before he would even agree to meet them. The Americans refused to pay, and negotiations ended there. Writing to inform Adams of what had happened, the commissioners referred to the Frenchmen pseudonymously as X, Y, and Z. As a result, when the president made the correspondence public in April 1798, the incident became known as the XYZ affair. Public opinion turned even more aggressively against the French, and soon

This British satire of the XYZ affair was published in London in June 1798. It shows Frenchmen plundering the female "America," as John Bull (the British Uncle Sam) sits laughing atop "Shakespeare's Cliff."

PROPERTY PROTECTED. a la Françoise.

Fifth Congress of the United States :
At the Second Session,

Begun and held at the city of Philadelphia, in the State of Pennsylvania, on Monday, the thirteenth of November, one thousand seven hundred and ninety-seven.

AN ACT CONCERNING ALIENS.

The official printed copy of the Alien Friends Act, enacted in Philadelphia on June 22, 1798.

the United States found itself in an undeclared naval war to protect its commercial shipping.

Hamilton seized upon this opportunity to pressure Adams into arming merchant ships and establishing a standing army (which could also be used to suppress domestic political opposition, as in the case of the Whiskey Rebellion). In Hamilton's view, anti-French sentiment was helpful because it promoted closer ties with Great Britain, which in turned served U.S. commercial interests. Despite pressure from his cabinet, however, President Adams refused to declare war on France. Instead, he sent another mission to Paris two years later, which produced the Convention of 1800. This agreement annulled the 1778 treaty of alliance, established new diplomatic relations between the two countries, and ended the Quasi-War. It also split the Federalist party, because the Hamiltonians wanted no part of peace with France.

The Alien and Sedition Acts

AS THE ELECTION OF 1800 NEARED, even though he had achieved peace with France, Adams found himself in a most difficult political position. His own party rejected his policies, and the Democratic-Republicans, who might have otherwise been assuaged by the Convention of 1800, hated him for another reason: the Alien and Sedition Acts of 1798. These laws, passed by the Federalist-controlled Congress during June and July of that year, were intended to silence domestic (that is, Democratic-Republican) opposition to federal (that is, Federalist) policies. The first was the Naturalization Act, which increased from five to fourteen years the residency requirement for citizenship. (Immigrants were believed to favor

This crude satire depicts a February 1798 fight in Philadelphia's Congress Hall between Matthew Lyon, a Democratic-Republican from Vermont, and Connecticut Federalist Roger Griswold.

the Democratic-Republicans disproportionately; to keep them from voting served Federalist interests.) The next was the Alien Friends Act, which authorized the president to deport foreigners whom he considered dangerous (presumably those with Democratic-Republican opinions). The third was the Alien Enemies Act, which permitted the wartime arrest and expulsion of subjects of an enemy power (such as France); and the last was the Sedition Act, which outlawed antigovernment activity, including the publication of "any false, scandalous and malicious writing against the government of the United States or either house of the Congress or the President." Perhaps because he believed that he knew what was best for the country, Adams signed these bills into law and permitted their enforcement.

The Federalists used the Sedition Act, in particular, to quash Democratic-Republican opposition. The first of those convicted and sentences under the Sedition Act was Vermont congressman Matthew Lyon, who was fined and kept four months in a filthy jail cell for voicing his passionate opposition to the policies of the Adams administration. "I know not which mortifies me most," Jefferson observed of Lyon's situation, "that I should fear to write what I think, or my country should bear such a state of things." In the end, however, Federalist abuse of the Sedition Act backfired, and Democratic-Republican opposition grew, with Jefferson and Madison leading the way.

In November 1798, the Kentucky state legislature adopted a set of resolutions, drafted by Jefferson, that called into question the federal government's authority to pass the Alien and Sedition Acts; a month later, Madison persuaded the Virginia state legislature to go even farther. The Virginia Resolutions clearly asserted the right of all states to review federal laws and invalidate those considered unconstitutional. Although no other states joined in these protests, the precedent established would later figure prominently in the nullification crisis of 1832 and in the political maneuverings that led up to the Civil War.

This portrait of John Adams was painted by Charles Willson Peale during Adams's vice presidency, probably between 1791 and 1794.

DURING THE 1800 CAMPAIGN, although eighteenth-century standards of political behavior compelled the candidates to remain silent and above the partisan fray, Federalist and Democratic-Republican surrogates used newspapers, pamphlets, and public meetings to tar their opponents with both real and contrived failings. The Federalists accused Jefferson of atheism and said that he intended to overturn religion and property, as his beloved French had done. The Democratic-Republicans countered that Adams was little more than a British lackey with strong monarchical tendencies. Both sides were equally scurrilous, yet only the Democratic-Republican newspapermen were prosecuted under the Sedition Act.

Even so, the Democratic-Republicans won the election, which Jefferson later called "the revolution of 1800" because of the change in the country's governing philosophy. He and running mate Aaron Burr each received seventy-three electoral votes to sixty-five for Adams and sixty-four for Charles C. Pinckney. By arrangement, one Federalist elector had voted for John Jay so that Adams could finish just ahead of Pinckney and become president in the event of a Federalist victory. The Democratic-Republicans, however, made no such arrangement, so the election ended in a tie. Even though all Americans understood that Jefferson had been the party's presidential candidate, the ambitious Burr declined to withdraw, so the election was sent to the House of Representatives for a final determination. The Federalists still controlled the balance of power in the House, and many Federalist congressmen wanted to elect Burr out of spite. But Hamilton despised Burr, his longtime rival in New York politics, and he eventually prevailed upon enough of his supporters to give the election on the thirty-sixth ballot to Jefferson.

This hand-painted linen banner was used to promote Thomas Jefferson's presidential campaign in 1800.

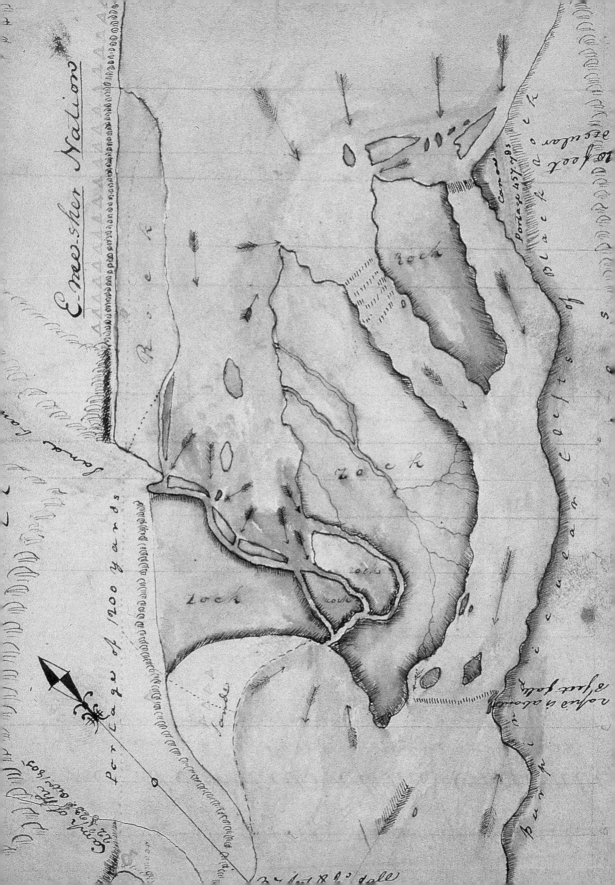

6

JEFFERSONIAN AMERICA

The Lewis and Clark Expedition

THOMAS JEFFERSON was spending the summer of 1802 at Monticello—his home near Charlottesville, Virginia—when a book he had ordered several months earlier finally arrived. Published in London the previous year, it was written by Alexander Mackenzie, a Scot who had immigrated to Canada during the late 1770s to become a fur trader. In 1788, on behalf of the British-owned North West Company, Mackenzie had established Fort Chipewyan, a trading post on Lake Athabasca at about sixty degrees north latitude. Like so many European adventurers before him, Mackenzie believed that he could find an easy passage to the Pacific and thus make his fortune trading with the Orient. In 1789, he led an expedition from Lake Athabasca over to the Great Slave Lake and all the way down the river that today bears his name. When he reached the delta of the Mackenzie River, however, he found not the Pacific but the Arctic Ocean.

Four years later, the intrepid Mackenzie tried again. This time, he and his party of French-Canadian voyageurs (men employed by the fur companies to transport goods to and from remote northern trading posts) ascended the east-flowing Peace River to its headwaters near the Continental Divide. With a short portage only "eight hundred and seventeen paces in length over a ridge of 3000 ft. elevation,"

AT LEFT: *This map of the Great Falls of the Columbia River appears in William Clark's journal between the entries for October 22 and October 23, 1805.*

Mackenzie crossed the northern Rockies into the Pacific Ocean watershed. With the help of some Indian guides, he traveled down the Fraser River and made a final overland march to the shores of the Pacific at present-day Bella Coola, where he used a mixture of vermilion and grease to write on the face of a large rock, "Alexander Mackenzie, from Canada, by land, the twenty-second of July, one thousand seven hundred and ninety-three." Mackenzie thus became the first European, crossing north of Mexico, to reach the Pacific Ocean traveling overland from the East. After returning to Great Britain in 1801, he published his story in *Voyages from Montreal, on the River St. Lawrence, Through the Continent of North America, to the Frozen and Pacific Oceans, in the Years 1789 and 1793*. Mackenzie was knighted in 1802 and subsequently used his influence to urge Great Britain to take greater commercial and political control of the Pacific Northwest.

BOTH JEFFERSON and his private secretary, Meriwether Lewis, read Mackenzie's book with great excitement and some alarm. The president had long been a student of North American geography, and his personal library on the subject was one of the most extensive in the world. He knew better than anyone else that the North American continent west of the Mississippi River was nearly all terra incognita. Between the Mandan Indian villages at the Great Bend of the Missouri River (above present-day Bismarck, North Dakota) and the mouth of the Columbia River a thousand miles away,

One of the most important sources used by Thomas Jefferson and Meriwether Lewis in planning Lewis's expedition was Aaron Arrowsmith's A Map Exhibiting All the New Discoveries in the Interior Parts of North America, *published in London in 1802.*

Jefferson sat for this portrait in 1804 at the request of his daughters. It was painted by Charles de Saint-Mémin, who was famous at the time for his elegance and attention to detail.

contemporary maps showed merely cartographic speculation, because no European had ever explored the southern Rockies. Like everyone else in 1802, Jefferson and his young friend could only guess at what might be waiting for them there.

Nineteen years earlier, shortly after the end of the Revolutionary War, Jefferson had written to George Rogers Clark proposing that Clark lead a group of explorers west of the Mississippi River into Spanish Louisiana. A Virginian like Jefferson, Clark had recently won fame in the Ohio Valley country, where his success against the British and their Indian allies had saved the Old Northwest (later the Northwest Territory) for the United States and especially for Virginia, which until 1780 claimed the land. Jefferson had heard rumors that some wealthy British merchants were planning to explore the trans-Mississippi West in order to colonize it. "Some of us," Jefferson wrote Clark, "have been talking here in a feeble way of making the attempt to search that country [ourselves].... How would you like to lead such a party?" Clark responded that exploring the West "is what I think we ought to do." But business commitments precluded him from undertaking the journey personally. The experienced frontiersman did offer Jefferson some advice: "Large parties will never answer the purpose. They will allarm the Indian Nations they pass through. Three or four young Men well qualified for the Task might perhaps compleat your wishes at a very Trifling Expence."

In 1790, while Jefferson was serving as secretary of state, Secretary of War Henry Knox tried to organize a secret reconnaissance of the Missouri River territory. All the government knew of this country was what it had learned from British fur traders, who were not the most reliable informants. Knox wanted some data of his own because the future strategic importance of the Missouri River system was already becoming quite clear. According to Knox, "An enterprising Officer with a noncommissioned Officer well acquainted with living in the woods, and perfectly capable of describing rivers and countries, accompanied by four or five hardy indians would in my opinion be the best mode of obtaining the information requested." Against the advice of several military leaders, who considered the mission (in the words of one) "too adventurous," Knox commissioned Lt. John Armstrong to lead such a party. But as Armstrong himself realized upon reaching the Mississippi, Knox had dramatically underestimated the equipment and funds necessary to attempt such a trip. Armstrong wrote the secretary requesting another $110, but this never came; so Armstrong never reached the western bank of the Mississippi.

Jefferson himself tried again in 1792, persuading the American Philosophical Society (of which he was a member) to raise a subscription for the funding of a private overland expedition to the Pacific. The project generated a great deal of interest. George Washington, Alexander Hamilton, and Robert Morris all made substantial contributions, and the subscription raised a thousand pounds. (At the time, currency in America was still quite a jumble.) Meriwether Lewis, then just eighteen years old, begged his Albemarle County neighbor for the commission, but Jefferson chose instead French botanist André Michaux. Unlike Lewis, Michaux possessed a scientific background that would allow him to carry out the stated purpose of the expedition: the mapping of the trans-Mississippi West and the study of its natural history. Michaux departed Philadelphia in June 1793, but he had barely reached Kentucky when Jefferson recalled him. The secretary of state had learned that Michaux was actually a French spy who planned to use the expedition as cover for the raising of an army to attack Spanish Louisiana. (Spain was then allied with Great Britain in its war against revolutionary France.)

MERIWETHER LEWIS
1774–1809

MERIWETHER LEWIS WAS MANAGING his late father's Albemarle County plantation in 1794 when the Whiskey Rebellion broke out. Without hesitation, he enlisted in the Virginia militia, and though he never did see any action, he found that military life suited him. Once the rebellion was crushed, he chose to remain in western Pennsylvania with the small army of occupation bivouacked near Pittsburgh, and in May 1795 he joined the regular army with the rank of ensign. Six months later, he was transferred to a company of sharpshooters under the command of William Clark. In 1796, Lewis was assigned to the First U.S. Infantry Regiment, and three years later he became regimental paymaster, a position that required him to travel all over the Northwest. He was still regimental paymaster in February 1801 when Jefferson offered him the post of private secretary to the president. According to Jefferson's letter to Lewis, "Your knowledge of the Western Country, of the Army, and of all of its interests and relations has rendered it desirable for public as well as private purposes that you should be engaged in that office."

On February 28, 1807, after Lewis had returned from the Pacific Ocean, Jefferson nominated him to become governor of the new Louisiana Territory. The Senate immediately confirmed the appointment, and on March 2 Lewis resigned his army commission. It wasn't until late the following winter, however, that Lewis set out once again for St. Louis, and he didn't arrive there until March 8, 1808. His tenure as governor was difficult. He was under pressure from Jefferson to prepare his and Clark's journals for publication, and his private efforts on behalf of the St. Louis Missouri River Fur Company (of which he was a founding investor) also cut into the time he had available for his public duties. As a result, he executed none of them well, if at all, and soon the specters of financial and political ruin loomed. His emotional state, never the best (leading some historians to suspect manic depression), deteriorated; and on October 11, 1809, Lewis shot himself in the head. The ball only grazed his skull, so the governor picked up a second pistol and shot himself again, this time in the chest. The wound eventually killed him, but not until a full day later. "I am no coward," he told his servant, "but I am so strong, [it is] hard to die."

This watercolor of Lewis was painted by Charles de Saint-Mémin in 1807. It shows Lewis dressed in a tippet (short fur cloak) given to him by the Shoshone chief Cameahwait.

The Corps of Discovery

GIVEN THIS CONTEXT, one can easily imagine how the geographic knowledge contained in Mackenzie's *Voyages from Montreal* stimulated Jefferson's curiosity—not to mention that of Meriwether Lewis, now twenty-eight. Mackenzie's book revealed that, at least far north, the Rocky Mountains were easily traversable. This encouraged Jefferson in his long-standing hope that a practical water route might be found between the United States and the Pacific Ocean. Mackenzie's book suggested that there might indeed be a short portage over low mountains connecting a tributary of the Missouri River with one of the Columbia, the major river of the Pacific Northwest. Yet Jefferson also learned from Mackenzie that British fur traders might soon be coming south from Canada to monopolize the fur trade if the United States didn't act quickly.

Shortly after reading and rereading Mackenzie's book, the president decided to send Lewis on a journey of exploration to the Pacific as soon as arrangements could be made. No one knows by what process, or exactly when, Jefferson came to this decision, because there is no documentary record of it. But letters written by Jefferson in the late fall already refer to its as a fait accompli. Apparently, Jefferson consulted no one, except possibly Lewis, and considered no one else to lead the expedition. In one of those subsequent letters, Jefferson explained his choice of Lewis in this way:

It was impossible to find a character who to a compleat science in botany, natural history, mineralogy & astronomy, joined the firmness of constitution & character, prudence, habits adapted to the woods, & a familiarity with the Indian manners & character, required for this undertaking. All the latter qualifications Capt. Lewis has.

This engraving, entitled The Discovery of the Rocks in Queen Charlotte's Sound, *appeared in George Vancouver's account of his 1792–1794 exploration of North America's Pacific Coast. Already, however, Robert Gray had fixed the latitude and longitude of the mouth of the Columbia River in May 1792.*

During the late fall and winter of 1802–1803, Jefferson and Lewis spent considerable time in the President's Mansion (a building not yet known as the White House), planning the minutiae of the trip. Lewis, in particular, spent many hours compiling a highly detailed list of necessary equipment and expenses. He based his estimates on the need to equip a single officer plus ten or twelve enlisted men. (These calculations reflected a decision he and Jefferson must have made early on regarding the ideal number of men in the exploration party.) The largest expense Lewis listed was $696 for "Indian presents," and the total came to a neat $2,500. This amount Jefferson secretly requested from Congress on January 18, 1803, in an intentionally confusing message that focused on Indian problems but did hint rather broadly that the expedition might help Americans swipe the extremely lucrative western fur trade from Great Britain. Despite objections from the Federalist opposition, which didn't like spending money on the West, Congress acquiesced, and the Corps of Discovery was formed.

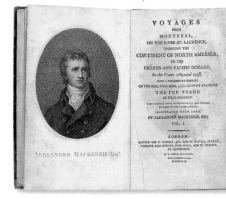

This two-volume edition of Alexander Mackenzie's Voyages from Montreal *appeared in 1802.*

ONE REASON THAT JEFFERSON wanted to keep his intentions secret was that the politics of the trans-Mississippi West had become highly volatile of late. Less than a week earlier, in fact, the president had sent another secret message to Congress requesting funds for the purchase of New Orleans from the French. Specifically, Jefferson's message of January 12, 1803, had asked Congress to make available $9.375 million for the purchase of that crucial Mississippi River port from Napoléon, the new French emperor. Following congressional approval of this request as well, Jefferson named James Monroe his minister plenipotentiary (meaning that Monroe had the power to negotiate on his own) and sent him to Paris to make a deal.

Since the end of the French and Indian War, Spain had controlled New Orleans and the rest of formerly French Louisiana; but in October 1800, during the War of the Second Coalition (1799–1802), Napoléon had pressured King Charles IV into secretly retroceding Louisiana to the French. News of this development, when it leaked, alarmed the United States. A weak, waning Spain had little hope of holding Louisiana much longer, but a powerful, expansionist nation such as Napoleonic France posed a much more significant threat to U.S. plans for its own expansion across the continent. Like most Americans, Jefferson wanted to see the political principles he had

asserted in the Declaration of Independence spread throughout the West. The last thing he wanted was a patchwork of competing nation-states dismembering the continent.

Jefferson was particularly concerned that the half million Americans living west of the Appalachian Mountains in 1802 retain their right to use the Mississippi River to transport their goods. The Treaty of San Lorenzo, negotiated by Thomas Pinckney in October 1795 (and sometimes called Pinckney's Treaty), granted Americans free navigation on the Mississippi and the right of deposit (the right to transfer goods to oceangoing vessels without the payment of duty) at New Orleans. But Jefferson was worried that the rumored retrocession would invalidate Pinckney's Treaty. So in April 1802, he instructed minister to France Robert R. Livingston to negotiate for a parcel of land on the lower Mississippi that Americans could use as a port in lieu of New Orleans.

A landscape of New Orleans painted in 1803 to celebrate the city's purchase by the United States.

THE BURR CONSPIRACY

THE WHISKEY REBELLION had taught Jefferson that the growing number of Americans living west of the Appalachian Mountains thought occasionally about becoming an independent nation. Certainly westerners had much more interest in New Orleans than in New England; and Jefferson, aware of how much rivers meant to early-nineteenth-century communications and commerce, knew that the Ohio-Mississippi River system was vital to their interests. If shipping on the Mississippi were threatened in any way, westerners wouldn't hesitate to leave the Union.

The attention of Vice Pres. Aaron Burr was also focused on secessionist sentiment in the West. Brilliant and thoroughly ambitious, Burr thought he could detach the West from the United States and rule it as an independent empire. After Jefferson chose George Clinton to replace Burr on the 1804 Democratic-Republican ticket, the New Yorker conspired with Gen. James

Wilkinson, military governor of Louisiana (and a paid Spanish agent), to make this fantasy a reality. Soon, however, Wilkinson had second thoughts, and he turned Burr in.

In February 1807, the former vice president was arrested on charges of treason, and Chief Justice John Marshall presided at his trial. Burr acted ably as his own defense counsel, and when the government failed to produce the two witnesses required for a treason conviction, he was acquitted. Afterward, Burr lived for several years in France before returning in 1812 to New York City, where he practiced law until his death in 1836.

On September 3, 1806, at the mouth of the Vermilion River, Lewis and Clark met a trading party heading upstream. The traders gave the members of the Corps of Discovery their first "news" in more than two years. Among the information passed along was that in July 1804, Burr (shown here in a Saint-Mémin drawing) had killed Alexander Hamilton in a duel after Hamilton blocked Burr's election to the governorship of New York.

> "Law is whatever is boldly asserted and plausibly maintained."
>
> —
>
> Aaron Burr, quoted in James Parton's The Life and Times of Aaron Burr (1857)

Livingston's efforts went nowhere, however, and on October 16, Spanish officials at New Orleans (the French had not yet taken control there) revoked the American right of deposit. It seemed to Livingston (and Jefferson) that Napoléon himself had ordered this and that the French emperor would soon close the Mississippi as well. Having little other leverage, the U.S. minister pointed out that, if the French continued to act unresponsively, the United States would have no choice but to seek a rapprochement with Great Britain. In his April 18, 1802, letter of instructions to Livingston, Jefferson himself had written:

There is on the globe one single spot, the possessor of which is our natural and habitual enemy. It is New Orleans, through which the produce of three eighths of our territory must pass to market.... France placing herself in that door assumes to us the attitude of defiance. Spain might have retained it quietly for years. Her pacific dispositions, her feeble state, would induce her to increase our facilities there, so that her possession of the place would be hardly felt by us, and it would not perhaps be very long before some circumstance might arise which might make the cession of it to us the price of something of more worth to her. Not so can it be in the hands of France.... The day that France takes possession of N. Orleans fixes the sentence which is to restrain her forever within her low water mark. It seals the union of two nations who in conjunction can maintain exclusive possession of the ocean. From that moment we must marry ourselves to the British fleet and nation.

The Louisiana Purchase

ALTHOUGH FRANCE AND GREAT BRITAIN were temporarily at peace in April 1803, Napoléon knew well that another European war was imminent and that he was already having trouble holding the rebellious French West Indian colony of St. Domingue. (Now known by its original Arawak name, Haiti, St. Domingue was transferred to France from Spain under the 1697 Treaty of Rijswijk.) The wisdom of spreading his military forces and his dwindling treasury so thinly must have given the emperor pause, because on April 11, the day before Monroe's arrival, Napoléon had Foreign Minister Charles Talleyrand suggest to Livingston that the Americans buy all of Louisiana.

Neither Livingston nor even Monroe had the authority to make such a purchase, but they both knew a good deal when they saw one. Negotiations with French finance minister François de Barbé-Marbois moved ahead swiftly, and on May 2 the parties signed an agreement (antedated to April 30) setting the price for Louisiana at $11.25 million in cash plus another $3.75 million in debt owed by the French to American citizens. The resulting acquisition roughly doubled the territory of the United States.

News of the treaty reached Jefferson in July 1803, at which time he took immediate and personal charge of its ratification, gently displacing Secretary of State James Madison. The $15 million cost of Louisiana would make it nearly impossible for Jefferson to fulfill his campaign pledge to eliminate the national debt, Albert Gallatin complained, but the president paid his treasury secretary little mind. According to historian Joseph J. Ellis, "Jefferson told him to look up from his accountant's ledgers long enough to see the boundless western skies this purchase made possible."

Much more important were the constitutional questions that the Louisiana Purchase raised. Where, it was asked, did the Constitution grant the federal government the power to buy foreign land? Even Jefferson was forced to admit that, according to his own strict construction of the document, a constitutional amendment was required. But the process of enacting and ratifying such an amendment would take too much time. Meanwhile, Napoléon might easily change his mind and withdraw the offer. So Jefferson chose to ignore his constitutional scruples and make the deal anyway. "The less that is said about my constitutional difficulties, the better," he wrote to a friend. "...It will be desirable for Congress to do what is necessary *in silence*." On October 20, with remarkably little fuss, the Senate approved the Louisiana Purchase treaty, 24–7.

The agreement with France was detailed in many respects, but exactly what territory the United States was buying was left vague. This was in part because no detailed maps of the region existed and also because both the United States and France understood that, as a practical matter, specific boundaries would have to be agreed with Spain and Great Britain, whose land claims abutted (and, in some cases, overlapped) Louisiana. Jefferson, predictably, put forth the broadest possible interpretation, asserting that the Louisiana Territory included not only the Missouri River watershed but also West Florida (the disputed Gulf Coast territory between the Perdido River and New Orleans) and all of present-day Texas.

The French colony of Saint-Domingue occupied the western third of Hispaniola. During the late 1790s, freed slave Toussaint-Louverture led an insurrection that won control of the entire island. He is shown here in 1801 proclaiming a new constitution for the Haitian republic.

The Louisiana Purchase treaty, signed personally by Napoléon.

LEWIS'S EDUCATION

ALTHOUGH THE scientific goals of the Lewis and Clark expedition disguised its political and economic aspirations, Meriwether Lewis did undertake and complete much important primary research. He had always been interested in natural history but received little, if any, formal training before Jefferson began preparing him for the expedition in the fall of 1802. That winter, huddled with Lewis in his President's Mansion study, Jefferson instructed his protégé personally in the fundamentals of geography, botany, mineralogy, astronomy, and ethnology.

In March 1803, Lewis left Washington for the federal arsenal at Harpers Ferry to obtain arms and ammunition for the trip. Afterward, he traveled on to Philadelphia, where he spent nearly two months studying with some of the nation's foremost scientific minds, including astronomer Andrew Ellicott, physician Benjamin Rush, and botanist Benjamin Smith Barton. Also with their help, he purchased the scientific instruments he and Clark would need to map the continent's considerable interior.

The botanical specimens collected by Lewis and Clark were carefully dried and preserved on herbarium sheets (such as this one) and donated to the American Philosophical Society.

From the collected specimens, paintings were made, such as this one of Lewisia rediviva.

O N OCTOBER 20, 1803, the day the treaty was ratified, Meriwether Lewis was already in Clarksville, Indiana Territory, meeting with his old friend Lt. William Clark, brother of George Rogers Clark. While making preparatory trips to Harpers Ferry and Philadelphia that spring, Lewis had come to the conclusion that the Corps of Discovery needed not one but two officers; after returning to Washington for the last time in June, he persuaded Jefferson of the same. On June 19, he wrote to Clark, offering him joint command. Clark, who had once been Lewis's superior officer, quickly accepted.

William Clark provided an ideal complement to Meriwether Lewis: He was a better surveyor and mapmaker, a more accomplished frontiersman, and much more comfortable with watercraft. Between October 15 and October 26, the two of them chose from the enlisted men available at Clarksville the first members of their party. Volunteers for the adventure were numerous, and the two officers rated each on hardiness, shooting and hunting ability, physical strength, and character before selecting two sergeants and seven privates. This original group also included Clark's slave, York, a strong and agile man who had been Clark's companion since their mutual boyhoods.

Clark included this sketch of the keelboat in his field notes for January 21, 1804. The waterline sketched along the hull shows its shallow four-foot draft.

From Clarksville, the expedition traveled down the Ohio River, reaching the Mississippi on November 13. Camping at the junction of the two rivers (the site of present-day Cairo, Illinois), Lewis and Clark practiced calculating the latitude and longitude of their location. The coordinates of this junction were well known, enabling them to check their results—a convenience that wouldn't obtain much longer. A week later, they returned to the water, paddling their keelboat and two pirogues (large flat-bottomed rowboats) upstream toward St. Louis. Immediately they realized that they would need more men.

For the past month, they had been drifting easily down the Ohio, but beginning with their entry into the Mississippi and continuing until they reached the Continental Divide, the members of the Corps of Discovery would have to paddle upstream against difficult and tricky currents. Both of the expedition's pirogues needed extra hands, and their custom-made keelboat was even more egregiously undermanned. Jefferson's secretary of war, Henry Dearborn, had approved only a dozen enlisted men (plus an interpreter) for the trip, but Jefferson had anticipated Lewis's need and given him permission to recruit more hands. Stopping at a nearby army post, Lewis and Clark added another dozen men before completing the last sixty miles to St. Louis.

The Spanish governor there refused Lewis permission to ascend the Missouri until the formal transfer of Louisiana sovereignty had taken place. This wasn't scheduled to occur until March 9, 1804, but Lewis was unconcerned. It was already December 8, much too late in the season to begin the eighteen-hundred-mile trip to the Mandan villages located at the river's Great Bend, and the men of the Corps of Discovery had much to do before that trip could begin. While Clark supervised construction of a winter camp on the U.S. side of the Mississippi River directly across from the mouth of the Missouri, Lewis collected in St. Louis what geographic and ethnographic information he could about the territory in which they would be traveling.

George Catlin painted this view of St. Louis between 1832 and 1833. During the 1830s, the confident inhabitants of St. Louis called their home "The Future Great City of the World." Under Lewis's scheme as well, St. Louis was to become a national hub because of its control of the Upper Missouri fur trade.

St. Louis to Fort Mandan

ON MARCH 31, 1804, Lewis and Clark ceremoniously inducted twenty-five of the soldiers into their permanent company, which also included York and civilian interpreter George Drouillard, son of a French father and Shawnee mother. Another five soldiers were chosen to accompany the Corps of Discovery as far as the Mandan villages, where the captains expected to spent the winter of 1804–1805. (These men would return to St. Louis in the spring with the keelboat, a report, and the specimens of flora and fauna Lewis had thus far collected.) Later, additional civilians of mixed French and Indian ancestry joined the party, which in mid-May began its ascent of the Missouri. Capt. Amos Stoddard, the ranking U.S. Army officer in St. Louis, saw the group off. He later described the sight in a

This skin of Melanerpes lewis *(Lewis's woodpecker) is the only zoological specimen collected by Lewis that is known to have survived.*

letter to Secretary of War Dearborn: "All of [the boats] were deeply laden, and well manned. [Lewis's] men possess great resolution and they are in the best health and spirits." The captains expected to be gone at least two years.

During its first two months on the Missouri, the Corps of Discovery covered nearly seven hundred miles and saw nary an Indian. (Nearly all the Missouri tribes were off hunting buffalo on the Great Plains.) The expedition's first contact with Native Americans came on the night of August 2, when a party of Otos appeared at their campsite not far above the Platte River. The next day, a council was held at which Lewis addressed the local chiefs. As recorded by Clark, Lewis delivered a long speech in which he told the Otos that "your old fathers the French and Spaniards" had gone "beyond the great lake towards the rising Sun, from whence they never intend returning to visit their former red children." That was why, Lewis said, "the great Chief of the Seventeen great nations of America" had sent the Corps of Discovery "to undertake this long journey, which we have so far accomplished with great labour and much expence, in order to council with yourselves and his other red children on the troubled waters, to give you his good advice; to point out to you the road in which you must walk to obtain happiness." Lewis was following Jefferson's instructions to promote peace among the Missouri tribes so that they could join together in a vast American-run trading empire. When the captain was finished, one of the Oto chiefs spoke. He thanked Lewis for his good advice and expressed his pleasure at learning that the new father was so kind and dependable. Then he asked for some powder and whiskey—which Lewis, eager to please, provided. After that, the Otos left, and the expedition continued on its way. Similar councils were held farther up the Missouri with the Yankton Sioux in late August, the Teton Sioux in late September, and the Arikaras in early October.

INDIAN POLICY

AN IMPORTANT GOAL OF LEWIS AND CLARK'S mission was to promote peace among the various Indian tribes, who were often at war with one another, so that commercial development of Upper Louisiana and the Pacific Northwest could proceed safely. Intertribal peace was important because the Sioux and the Blackfeet were both powerful enough to block trade on large section of the upper Missouri.

Jefferson considered the Native Americans "noble savages" of the sort depicted by James Fenimore Cooper in his Leatherstocking novels of the 1820s. Lewis, however, disagreed that whites could live harmoniously with "uncivilized" Indians. In one journal entry penned at Fort Clatsop in February 1806, Lewis wrote, "Notwithstanding their apparently friendly

disposition, their great averice and hope of plunder might induce them to be treacherous.... We well know that the treachery of the aborigenes of America and the too great confidence of our countrymen in their sincerity and friendship has caused the distruction of many hundreds of us."

One can certainly date the beginning of the subjugation of the Great Plains tribes to the arrival of Lewis and Clark, but given the history of Indian-white relations on the Atlantic seaboard during the seventeenth and eighteenth centuries, one can also conclude quite reasonably that the fate of the Plains tribes was already fixed well before Lewis and Clark appeared. As it had been on the East Coast, the conquest of these natives would be bloody, costly, time-consuming, and never in doubt.

This view of one of the Mandan villages visited by Lewis and Clark was painted in the late 1830s by Karl Bodmer, a young Swiss artist who accompanied Prince Maximilian of Wied-Neuwied on the naturalist's 1832–1834 expedition up the Missouri.

I N LATE OCTOBER, the expedition reached the Mandan villages located at the Great Bend of the Missouri, about sixty miles above present-day Bismarck. The Mandans were the premier Indian traders of the northern Plains. Their villages were important distribution points at which Indians from distant tribes—including Crows, Kiowas, Cheyennes, and Arapahos—exchanged pelts for manufactured goods provided by agents of the North West and Hudson's Bay Companies. In fact, at the time the Corps of Discovery arrived, North West Company agent Hugh McCracken happened to be visiting the Mandans, and Lewis took this opportunity to write a short letter to McCracken's superiors at the company's Assiniboine River trading post. Lewis began the letter with his usual pretense that "We have been sent by the government for the purpose of exploring the river Missouri, and the western parts of the continent, with a view to the promotion of general science." Then he moved on to the main point: For the time being, the Corps of Discovery had no desire to disrupt existing trade relationships so long as the British acknowledged U.S. sovereignty. Also, knowing that he would be spending the next five months surrounded by thousands of Indians with whom communication was limited, he invited the British traders to come visit him at Fort Mandan, the winter camp that the Americans were building across the river from the Mandan villages. Several traders, in fact, took him up on this offer.

Meanwhile, Lewis and Clark made the acquaintance of Toussaint Charbonneau, a forty-five-year-old French Canadian who had once been a roving North West Company agent but lately had settled among the Hidatsas (neighbors of the Mandans), with whom he worked as an independent trader. When Charbonneau offered his services as an interpreter, the captains promptly hired him because his two wives were Shoshones from a band that lived near the headwaters of the Missouri. Before Charbonneau made his offer, Lewis and Clark were unsure how they would communicate with that mountain tribe. Now, the

Bodmer painted this watercolor of the leader of a Mandan warrior society in April 1834.

Shoshones could speak to Charbonneau's wives in their native language, the wives could speak Hidatsa to Charbonneau, Charbonneau could speak French to Drouillard, and Drouillard could speak English to the Americans. As it turned out, only one of Charbonneau's wives made the trip, but Sacagawea's presence was sufficient, and it did permit communication with the Shoshones.

In early April 1805, after sending the keelboat back to St. Louis, the Corps of Discovery left Fort Mandan and continued up the Missouri in the two large pirogues plus six additional canoes that had been hollowed out from cottonwood trees during the winter. (The three-man canoes would be more maneuverable in the Missouri's shallow, swift headwaters.) On June 3, the captains, the enlisted men, York, Drouillard, Charbonneau, Sacagawea, and Sacagawea's baby (born February 11) camped at the junction of two large rivers. "An interesting question was now to be determined," Lewis wrote in his journal. "Which of these rivers was the Missouri?" Several days of scouting persuaded the captains that the south fork was the true Missouri, and they followed it southwest to the Great Falls. (Meanwhile, Lewis named the north fork Maria's River, or the Marias, after his cousin Maria Wood.) Once they had explored the falls, the men hid their pirogues for the return trip and portaged their baggage to a camp above the falls, where they made new canoes (replacements for the pirogues) out of two large cottonwood trees.

The first member of the Corps of Discovery to publish an account of the expedition was Sgt. Patrick Gass. His original 1807 text was unillustrated, but the edition published in 1810 contained several woodcuts such as this one, "Captain Lewis shooting at an Indian."

Across the Continental Divide

WITH ALL THAT HAD TO BE DONE, the eighteen-mile portage took a full month to complete, and it wasn't until mid-July that the expedition was back on the water. About two weeks later, on July 27, Lewis and Clark reached the Three Forks, where three lesser rivers converge to form the Missouri. Lewis named these principal tributaries after Secretary of State Madison, Secretary of the Treasury Gallatin, and President Jefferson. Up the Jefferson the party proceeded, increasingly eager to find the Shoshones, who were said to be rich in horses.

Certainly the Americans would need more than a few to carry their baggage over the Rocky Mountains, and they also needed help from the Shoshones in finding their way. (Already the captains could see that the portage would not be nearly as easy as the one Mackenzie had described.) Finally, on the afternoon of August 8, Sacagawea recognized a high plain as not very far from the summer home of her people. The next day, Lewis set off overland with Drouillard and two enlisted men to find the Shoshones. "In short," Lewis wrote in his August 8 journal entry, "it is my resolution to find them or some others, who have horses if it should cause me a trip of one month." He made for the Continental Divide.

After four days of hiking, Lewis contacted a band of Shoshones from whose chief, Cameahwait, he learned something of the local geography. Several days later, he persuaded Cameahwait to return with him to rendezvous with Clark at the upper navigational limit of the Jefferson River. Thoughtfully, Cameahwait and his warriors brought with them thirty horses to carry the explorers and their baggage back through Lemhi Pass and down into the Shoshone camp on the Lemhi River. According to Lewis's journal, the plan was then to "remain sometime among them and trade with them for horses."

Among the "Indian presents" that Lewis and Clark brought with them were peace medals bearing Jefferson's likeness. One of these was presented to Cameahwait. Lesser chiefs were given smaller medals with George Washington's likeness.

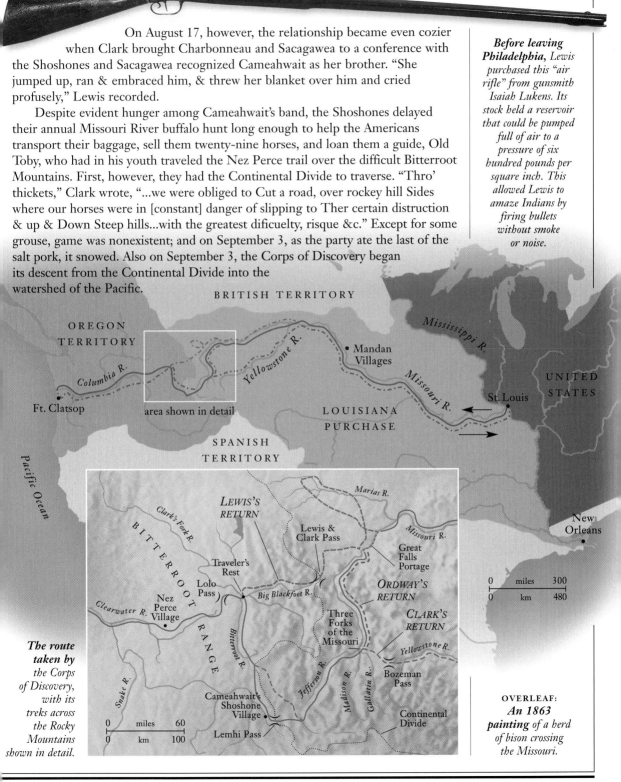

On August 17, however, the relationship became even cozier when Clark brought Charbonneau and Sacagawea to a conference with the Shoshones and Sacagawea recognized Cameahwait as her brother. "She jumped up, ran & embraced him, & threw her blanket over him and cried profusely," Lewis recorded.

Despite evident hunger among Cameahwait's band, the Shoshones delayed their annual Missouri River buffalo hunt long enough to help the Americans transport their baggage, sell them twenty-nine horses, and loan them a guide, Old Toby, who had in his youth traveled the Nez Perce trail over the difficult Bitterroot Mountains. First, however, they had the Continental Divide to traverse. "Thro' thickets," Clark wrote, "...we were obliged to Cut a road, over rockey hill Sides where our horses were in [constant] danger of slipping to Ther certain distruction & up & Down Steep hills...with the greatest dificuelty, risque &c." Except for some grouse, game was nonexistent; and on September 3, as the party ate the last of the salt pork, it snowed. Also on September 3, the Corps of Discovery began its descent from the Continental Divide into the watershed of the Pacific.

Before leaving Philadelphia, Lewis purchased this "air rifle" from gunsmith Isaiah Lukens. Its stock held a reservoir that could be pumped full of air to a pressure of six hundred pounds per square inch. This allowed Lewis to amaze Indians by firing bullets without smoke or noise.

BRITISH TERRITORY

OREGON TERRITORY

Mississippi R.

Columbia R.

Mandan Villages

Yellowstone R.

Missouri R.

UNITED STATES

Ft. Clatsop

area shown in detail

St. Louis

LOUISIANA PURCHASE

Pacific Ocean

SPANISH TERRITORY

New Orleans

Marias R.

LEWIS'S RETURN

Lewis & Clark Pass

Missouri R.

CLARK'S FORK R.

BITTERROOT RANGE

Traveler's Rest

Great Falls Portage

Lolo Pass

Big Blackfoot R.

ORDWAY'S RETURN

Nez Perce Village

Clearwater R.

Bitterroot R.

Three Forks of the Missouri

CLARK'S RETURN

Yellowstone R.

| 0 | miles | 300 |
| 0 | km | 480 |

Snake R.

Jefferson R.

Madison R.

Gallatin R.

Bozeman Pass

Cameahwait's Shoshone Village

Continental Divide

| 0 | miles | 60 |
| 0 | km | 100 |

Lemhi Pass

The route taken by the Corps of Discovery, with its treks across the Rocky Mountains shown in detail.

OVERLEAF: *An 1863 painting* of a herd of bison crossing the Missouri.

Jefferson wrote for Lewis this letter of unlimited credit, which obligated the government to reimburse any merchant who provided supplies to the expedition.

These portraits of Lewis (top) and Clark were both painted by Charles Willson Peale. The illustrious Philadelphia artist painted Lewis in 1807 and Clark in 1810.

DURING THE NEXT WEEK, the expedition marched down into the valley of the Bitterroot River, where it met a band of friendly Salish Indians, who sold Lewis and Clark some additional horses. At the Bitterroot River's junction with Lolo Creek, the party spent the night at a campsite Lewis named Traveler's Rest. The next morning, September 10, he sent out all the hunters, who returned later that day with four deer, a beaver, three grouse, and three Nez Perces, one of whom agreed to accompany the whites over the Bitterroots. "His relations...he informed us were numerous and resided in the plain below the mountains on the Columbia river, from whence he said the water was good and capable of being navigated to the sea," Lewis wrote enthusiastically in his journal.

That night, however, two horses strayed, and it wasn't until midafternoon that they were found. By then, the impatient Nez Perce had set out on his own. The captains still had Old Toby, but it had been many years since the Shoshone had last crossed the Bitterroots, and he became temporarily lost in the snowy mountains, costing the party the better part of two days. Meanwhile, it rained, hailed, and finally snowed, obscuring the rough Nez Perce trail all the more. On September 16, another eight inches of snow fell, slowing the group's progress still further. The nearly starving horses, looking for grass, strayed again, and it took all morning on September 17 to round them up. The men, too, were nearing the limits of their physical endurance, which they had already demonstrated to be substantial. The last of the colts they had bought was killed and cooked for supper while Lewis and Clark talked. The captains would probably have chosen death before retreat, but with their food supply nearly gone and game not available, they knew they couldn't go on that way much longer. What they decided to do was send Clark and several hunters ahead to the plains, where they could presumably find game and send some back to the main party. For four days, Lewis's group plodded along with the cumbersome baggage, waiting for one of Clark's hunters to return with food. Finally, on September 22, they met a member of Clark's party hurrying back to them with dried fish and roots obtained by Clark at a nearby Nez Perce village. That evening, the expedition reunited.

On a white elk skin, a Nez Perce chief named Twisted Hair drew for Clark a map of the country to the west. It showed the creek that ran beside Twisted Hair's village flowing into a river (the Clearwater) that flowed into the Snake, which itself flowed into the Columbia. According to the chief, it was a ten-day trip from his village to the falls of the Columbia River—where, he said, many Indians lived and there were even some white trading posts. (Twisted Hair's information worried Lewis, who feared that British traders were already established along the Columbia, but this turned out not to be the case.) While most of the party recovered from the crossing of the Bitterroots (and from the dysentery that the shift in diet from all meat to fish and roots brought on), Clark supervised the construction of canoes. Because the captain was short on manpower, Twisted Hair showed him how to make canoes Indian fashion by placing each tree trunk over a slow-burning fire, which burned out its interior. Twisted Hair also agreed to look after the expedition's horses until it returned the following spring. On October 7, a rejuvenated Corps of Discovery again took to the water. But now, for the first time since leaving the Ohio River in November 1803, they would be riding downstream with the current all the way to the Pacific.

To the Pacific

EAGER TO COMPLETE THE LAST LEG of their journey, the captains chose to run some challenging rapids that were probably better portaged. In the process, they lost some of their supplies. Overall, however, the journey was remarkably swift and efficient. At the Short Narrows of The Dalles, where high rock walls forced the Columbia into dangerous rapids, the men who couldn't swim disembarked and portaged the most valuable items—the journals, field notes, rifles, and scientific instruments—while Lewis, Clark, and the rest of the expedition shot the rapids. Local Indians gathered on the high banks

to witness the attempt (and claim the belongings of the whites once they drowned), but the canoes made it all the way through without capsizing.

Two weeks later, on November 7, 1805, Clark wrote the following entry in his journal:

Great joy in camp we are in view of the Ocian, *this great Pacific Ocean which we been So long anxious to See, and the roreing or noise made by the waves brakeing on the rockey shores (as I suppose) may be heard distinctly.*

Actually, Clark was a little premature. What he had seen was the Columbia estuary, and for the next week he saw nothing else. Bad weather and swells trapped the Corps of Discovery at Point Ellice, where overhanging rocks made it impossible for them to climb out and hunt the interior. They might have starved had it not been for the local Clatsop Indians, who crossed the estuary in their heavier coastal canoes and sold the Americans roots and fish. On November 15, after the weather broke, Clark moved the camp to a more suitable location beside a neighboring bay, while Lewis scouted the coastline and, in the manner of Alexander Mackenzie, carved his name on a tree at the end of Cape Disappoint-ment, a small peninsula jutting out into the Pacific Ocean.

THAT MOMENT must have been supremely satisfying for Lewis, yet tempered by the irony of his achievement. The very difficulties he and his men could take such justifiable pride in having overcome meant also that their mission had, in an important respect, failed: They had found no water route across the continent; even worse, having survived the Bitterroots and run the many perilous rapids of the Columbia, they knew for certain that no commercial route existed.

Originally written on loose pages, Clark bound these field notes for the last quarter of 1805 with elkskin during his winter at Fort Clatsop. The entries cover the arduous period from September 11 to December 31, 1805, and include Clark's first sighting of the Pacific.

And Lewis likely had other worries on his mind: Finding so little game about, he must have been concerned with provisioning his men for the winter. He could buy some food from the Clatsops, but after two years of traveling, his supply of trade goods was low and wouldn't sustain the expedition long. He and Clark had reached the Pacific, but if they couldn't survive the winter there and make their way back to St. Louis the following year, all they had learned and accomplished would be lost.

Some relief came when the party found a greater supply of elk on the southern shores of the Columbia estuary, but conditions that winter remained mostly miserable. Under Clark's direction, the men worked in nearly constant rain building Fort Clatsop, their winter home. Living in two rough cabins within the palisaded walls of the fifty-foot-square stockade, the Corps of Discovery spent a depressing, rainy four months hunting, scraping hides (with which to make clothing and moccasins), tending the fire in the smoke-house (a difficult chore with always damp wood), and carrying out other monotonous tasks. The weather was so bad that, for the entire first month at the fort, Lewis was unable to take a single astronomical reading. He did, however, compile extensive notes on the region's animal and plant life and on the ethnology of the Clatsop Indians.

The Return

WHILE LEWIS KEPT HIMSELF busy observing the natural history and Indian culture of the Pacific Northwest, Clark worked on his map of the territory they had traveled from Fort Mandan. He finished it on February 11, after which he and Lewis spent three days reviewing it. "We now discover," Lewis wrote in his journal, "that we have found the most practicable and navigable passage across the Continent of North America." What he meant was that, with all that they had learned from various Indian sources since leaving the Shoshones, their journey home would be easier and more direct, even if far short of the route he and Jefferson had imagined.

It was March 23 when the party left Fort Clatsop and began paddling back up the Columbia. This time, they had no choice but to portage the rapids; and by the time they reached The Dalles, the captains were so frustrated with the strong current that they decided to abandon their canoes, purchase a few pack animals, and continue their journey marching overland to the base of the Bitterroots, where Twisted Hair was holding their horses. The Nez Perce chief had informed Lewis and Clark the previous fall that he and his band would be leaving for the Missouri buffalo country in early May; as it turned out, unusually heavy winter snows blocked passage of the Bitterroots until late June.

On June 25, ahead of the main body of Indians, the expedition set out on the Lolo Trail with five Nez Perce guides. The snow was still seven feet deep but firm enough to support the horses, which the guides led quickly along the fastest route.

This sketch of a eulachon appears in Clark's journal accompanying the entry for February 25, 1806. Of the small smeltlike fish, Lewis wrote, "I find them best when cooked in Indian stile, which is by roasting a number of them together on a wooden spit."

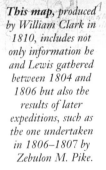

A MAP

B Y JUNE 30, THE CORPS OF DISCOVERY was back at Traveler's Rest, and at this point the expedition divided. Sometime during the winter, as a result of Clark's careful mapmaking, the two captains had decided to explore different routes back to the Missouri. Lewis would follow the overland route that the Nez Perce annually took to their hunting grounds. This trail led directly to the Great Falls of the Missouri and would save days over the circuitous water route the Corps of Discovery had taken the previous year. From the Great Falls, Lewis would take three men and explore up the Marias River, the large tributary of the Missouri that had confused the captains on their outward journey. Meanwhile, Clark would retrace the previous year's path, moving up the Bitterroot and down the Jefferson River to the Three Forks, retrieving their canoes and cached supplies as he went. At the Three Forks, Clark's group would itself divide, with Sgt. John Ordway leading a squad down the Missouri to join the men Lewis (scouting the Marias) had left behind at the Great Falls portage. This would leave Clark—along with Charbonneau, Sacagawea, her seventeen-month-old child, and the rest of the men—to cross over into the valley of the Yellowstone River, which they would follow down to the Missouri. The plan was to rendezvous with Lewis and the others at the junction of the two rivers.

It was an ambitious itinerary and risky in its division of the expedition into small, relatively defenseless groups. In fact, it nearly doomed Lewis during his Marias River reconnaissance. On July 26, the captain, Drouillard, and two privates encountered a party of eight young Blackfoot warriors. The Blackfeet were the most dangerous tribe on the Plains because their trading relationship with the British provided them, alone among Plains tribes, with nearly unlimited access to arms and

This map, produced by William Clark in 1810, includes not only information he and Lewis gathered between 1804 and 1806 but also the results of later expeditions, such as the one undertaken in 1806–1807 by Zebulon M. Pike.

Clark used this compass *to plot and record the expedition's headings. These headings, along with Clark's notes on the distances traveled in each direction, allowed him to reconstruct the expedition's route and make his maps.*

ammunition. These eight Blackfeet warily agreed to share a camp that night with the Americans, and they listened apparently with interest to Lewis's well-rehearsed speech about intertribal peace and the coming American trade empire. But at first light, they tried to steal the Americans' rifles, and this led to the most serious violence of the entire expedition. One of the Blackfeet was stabbed to death by one of the privates, and Lewis himself shot a second in the stomach. Even more important, others raced away to alert the much larger bands of Blackfeet nearby. Soon, Lewis was sure, these Blackfeet would be coming after the whites, almost certainly prepared to kill any they found.

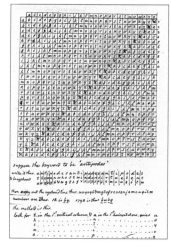

Karl Bodmer painted this Blackfoot chief in August 1833 while at Fort Mackenzie, a trading post at the junction of the Missouri and Marias Rivers built in 1832 for the American Fur Company.

L EWIS AND HIS MEN RODE all that day and much of the night, covering more than a hundred miles. They slept for two hours and then rode on, not only to escape the Blackfeet but also to warn their comrades coming down the river. By midmorning, they had reached the bluffs above the Missouri and ridden downriver eight miles. At that point, they heard rifle volleys and, according to Lewis, "had the unspeakable satisfaction to see our canoes coming down." The men reunited and hurried down the river—rendezvousing with Clark, who had traveled farther downstream in search of game, on August 12, 1806. Two days later, they reached the Mandan villages, where they learned to their disappointment that their peacemaking efforts had failed. The Hidatsas had sent a war party to the Rockies, where they killed some Shoshones (possibly members of Cameahwait's band); the Arikaras were at war with the Mandans; and the Sioux were also causing trouble. The only good news was that the Mandan chief Big White had agreed to accompany them back down the Missouri and on to Washington for a meeting with the Great Father. The Corps of Discovery arrived back in St. Louis without further incident on September 23, 1806, and Lewis's first question was, When does the post leave?

The letter Lewis wrote to Jefferson that day made clear no practical all-water route to the Pacific had been found, and it described the difficulties of the portage plainly. But once the bad news was reported, Lewis went on to describe his vision of an American trading empire in the trans-Mississippi West. He proposed that pelts trapped on the upper Missouri, in the Rockies, and across the Pacific Northwest be collected at the mouth of the Columbia River and shipped from there to the fur market at Canton, China, where they could be exchanged for Asian trade goods. The Nez Perces and Shoshones could provide plenty of horses, Lewis explained, and "the cheep rate at which horses are to be obtained...reduces the expences of transportation over this portage to a mere trifle." Lewis also pointed out that the British, whose mercantile laws still compelled them to ship all their goods through London, would have difficulty competing with such a streamlined American system.

Making this trade route safe, however, would require a substantial commitment of federal arms and money. For example, Lewis envisioned a series of forts along the Missouri that would double as trading posts (while keeping the hostile Sioux and Blackfeet in line); but they would be expensive to build and garrison. Aggressive government intervention and spending on this scale was antithetical to Jefferson's strict constructionism; but when it came to the West, as we have seen, the president's principles were usually observed only in their denial.

Jeffersonian Democracy

PERSONALLY, JEFFERSON WAS the owner of a substantial plantation, but he identified both his party and his presidency with the interests of the small subsistence farmers who made up three-quarters of the American population at the turn of the nineteenth century. In fact, Jefferson fairly idealized those farmers. He despised cities, which he considered sores on the body politic, and instead cherished the uncrowded agrarian society of his native Albemarle County, which he believed was the ideal medium for nurturing healthful republican values. This is why he chose to ignore his constitutional scruples and buy Louisiana: He believed its purchase would provide enough fertile land to extend the agrarian way of life in the United States for at least another two or three generations and perhaps even longer.

The Lewis and Clark expedition had similarly challenged Jefferson's ethics. In sending the Corps of Discovery to the Pacific Ocean—through land claimed variously by Spain, Great Britain, and Russia, but *not* the United States—the president had knowingly violated international law as it was then understood. But the subterfuge had paid off, and now Lewis was back and describing in his September 23 letter, amid details of water routes and the fur trade, exactly what Jefferson had been longing to hear: the enunciation, in practical terms, of a United States stretching from sea to sea across the entire North American continent.

This 1801 engraving of the Federal City shows its serene, rural character at the time the U.S. government moved there in 1800. Pennsylvania Avenue between Capitol Hill and the White House had been fairly well cleared, but one still came across stumps and bushes in the road.

Specifically, Jefferson's vision encompassed an American empire of equals—that is, a nation of small, economically independent farmers living in a decentralized multiplicity of states, whose own equality with the original thirteen had already been assured by the Northwest Ordinance of 1787. Farmers of this sort would be the perfect citizens for such a republic because their self-sufficiency would make them nearly invulnerable to political coercion. In a city, perhaps, the temptations and pitfalls of industrial society might allow a resumption of political tyranny. But farmers who tilled the land, Jefferson believed, had a measure of virtue sufficient to sustain a democratic society. "Those who labor in the earth," he wrote in 1784, "are the chosen people of God."

Lewis's report to Jefferson of plentiful beaver and otter in the Rockies set off a rush to the mountains. This depiction of beaver, the fur trader's sine qua non, appeared in John James Audubon's The Viviparous Quadrupeds of North America *(1845–1848).*

WITHOUT QUESTION, Jefferson allowed his utopian agrarian fantasies to influence his administration's management of the West—a failing from which the United States has, equally without question, benefited. Otherwise, in most respects, the president did keep his 1800 campaign pledge to reduce the size and influence of the federal government. Working closely with Treasury Secretary Gallatin, Jefferson reduced the number of federal employees by half and cut other expenditures sharply. This allowed the administration to eliminate many federal taxes and still cut the national debt, despite the fifteen million dollars spent on Louisiana, from eighty-three million dollars in 1801 to fifty-seven million dollars in 1809.

With regard to this and other matters, Jefferson's attention to detail was extraordinary, especially when it came to dislodging zealous Federalists from civilian and military office. According to historian Joyce Appleby, "Not a symbol, a civil servant, or a presidential initiative escaped his consideration as a tool in dismantling the 'energetic' and elitist government of his predecessor." During Jefferson's second term, however, it was foreign policy that increasingly came to occupy the president's attention. The May 1803 resumption of Napoléon's war with Great Britain brought renewed harassment of American shipping, and Jefferson was even less effective than John Adams had been at halting the violations. The situation was serious because, then as now, the United States depended on its international trade for a large measure of its prosperity; any interruption of that trade portended not only economic dislocation but also social turmoil.

In 1811, New York City merchant John Jacob Astor established the first U.S. presence on the Pacific Coast. He called his fur-trading post at the mouth of the Columbia River Astoria.

The worst abuse was British impressment. Under the informal theory "once an Englishman, always an Englishman," the Royal Navy began impressing American sailors at the rate of more than a thousand a year between 1804 and 1812. British naval officers never formally claimed the legal right to impress, or force into service, native-born Americans, but desertions were making it difficult to keep their ships at fighting strength, and they tended to ignore the niceties of nationality when it came to recovering alleged deserters. (It was during this frustrating period that Lewis first presented Jefferson with his plan to displace British fur traders in the Pacific Northwest.) France also seized U.S. ships, but only half as many, and impressment wasn't an issue.

THE BARBARY PIRATES

BEGINNING IN THE SIXTEENTH CENTURY and continuing for more than two hundred years, the Barbary states of Morocco, Algiers, Tunis, and Tripoli sheltered pirates who preyed successfully on European shipping entering and leaving the Mediterranean Sea. These small but influential kingdoms collected tribute from European nations wishing to safeguard their commerce, and similar payments were demanded from the United States once independence removed the protection offered by Great Britain's unique (because of the Royal Navy) exemption from piracy. Under a treaty signed in June 1786, the United States agreed to pay an annual tribute to Morocco; similar treaties were eventually signed with the other Barbary states.

In 1801, however, the pasha of Tripoli increased his demands, and when the Americans refused to pay more, Tripoli declared war. President Jefferson dispatched warships to the Mediterranean, but the force he sent proved too weak to defeat the pirates, who captured the U.S. frigate *Philadelphia* in October 1803. The most memorable action of the war came in February 1804, when Lt. Stephen Decatur led a nighttime raid to recapture and burn the *Philadelphia* so that its guns could not be used against Americans.

This hand-colored 1846 lithograph by Nathaniel Currier depicts the bombardment of Tripoli by U.S. warships in August 1804.

A subsequent blockade punished Tripoli, forcing the pasha to sign a June 1805 peace treaty that ended the payment of tribute.

During the War of 1812, the dey of Algiers sought to take advantage of American preoccupation, demanding more tribute as the pasha had. Again the Americans refused; and in May 1815, six months after the signing of the Treaty of Ghent, another U.S. naval expedition led by Stephen Decatur (now a captain) defeated the Algerians and ended tribute payments to them. Tunis and Morocco were soon forced to give up tribute payments as well, and the reign of the Barbary pirates ended.

The Embargo Act

THE CONFLICT ESCALATED ON JUNE 22, 1807, when the British frigate *Leopard* stopped the smaller U.S. frigate *Chesapeake* off the coast of Virginia and demanded permission to board and search it for deserters. When the American captain refused, the British warship fired, killing three American sailors, wounding eighteen, and impressing four alleged deserters, only one of whom turned out to be British. After learning of this engagement, Jefferson demanded on July 2 that all British warships leave U.S. territorial waters. The British countered by announcing their intention to search U.S. ships even more aggressively. Believing that he had no alternative, the president asked Congress to pass a nonimportation law of the sort that had chastened Great Britain during the 1760s. The resulting Embargo Act of December 1807 halted all foreign exports and, therefore, nearly all imports as well. The point of the hugely unpopular law was to deny Britain and France American matériel until they agreed to behave more respectfully. The actual victims of the law, however, were American merchants, especially those in New England, and smuggling activity surged.

The happy *Effects of that* Grand *System* of shutting Ports against the English !!

This British cartoon from October 1808 shows Jefferson defending the Embargo Act as Napoléon peeks out from behind his chair. The act (and the war that followed it) greatly stimulated American manufacturing—completely unintentionally, of course, because Jefferson believed that industrialization would bind employees to factory owners and undermine the nation's democracy, not unreasonable prospects in an age before modern labor unions and the secret ballot.

RIGHT: *This portrait of James Madison, following an earlier work by Gilbert Stuart, hangs now in Independence Hall.*

By early 1809, even Jefferson had to admit that the Embargo Act had failed. Therefore, on March 1, three days before leaving office, he reluctantly signed the Non-Intercourse Act, which repealed the Embargo Act and reopened trade with all countries except Britain and France. (Under the terms of the new law, each of these belligerent nations would continue to be excluded from commerce with the United States until the president determined, by proclamation, that its behavior had sufficiently improved.)

However, the Non-Intercourse Act proved impossible to enforce, and in May 1810 Congress replaced it with Macon's Bill No. 2, which allowed trade with all nations. If, however, either Britain or France subsequently agreed to respect U.S. neutrality, then the president (now James Madison) was empowered to reimpose nonintercourse with the remaining offender.

Learning of Macon's Bill No. 2, Napoléon disingenuously informed the Americans that he would begin respecting U.S. neutrality if nonintercourse with Britain was reimposed. This deception led Madison to issue an unwise November 1810 proclamation prematurely halting trade with Great Britain. Meanwhile, many of the young Democratic-Republicans from the South and West who had won seats in Congress during 1810 elections began clamoring for war with Great Britain. Led by Henry Clay of Kentucky and John C. Calhoun of South Carolina, these War Hawks, as they were called, denounced Madison's policy of "peaceful coercion" and pressured the president into calling up one hundred thousand militiamen for six months' service. Two months later, a frustrated President Madison, who was additionally upset by British encouragement of Indian attacks along the western frontier, reluctantly asked Congress for a declaration of war. The Senate deliberated seventeen days before approving the declaration on June 18. In the meantime, responding to the economic hardship that the various American embargoes had finally created, the British government rescinded its orders in council permitting the harassment of U.S. shipping. By the time the Americans learned of this development, however, Mr. Madison's War was already under way.

The War of 1812

THE UNITED STATES ENTERED THE WAR OF 1812 poorly prepared and divided. Every Federalist congressman and senator had voted against declaring the war, their constituents in New England hated waging it, and all blamed Madison for conducting it so ineptly. The Madison administration, itself somewhat reluctant to engage in hostilities, had waited too long to begin building up the nation's military establishment, especially its navy, which the penny-pinching Jefferson administration had substantially downsized. The army's resulting dependence on state militias was particularly a problem in the Northeast, where Federalist state governments usually ignored federal requests for troops.

For this reason, as well as because of poor planning by Secretaries of War William Eustis (1809–1812) and John Armstrong (1813–1814), the British easily repulsed three separate U.S. Army invasions of Canada, which was never seriously threatened. Fortunately for the Americans, the U.S. Navy performed better. On August 19, 1812, three days after the surrender of Detroit to a combined British-Indian expedition, the USS *Constitution* decisively defeated the HMS *Guerrière* off Nova Scotia. The victory cheered an otherwise discouraged nation but did nothing to ease the Royal Navy blockade that was smothering the middle and southern Atlantic coasts. (To encourage internal dissension, and keep some American goods flowing indirectly into British markets, the Royal Navy exempted the ports of New England from its blockade until April 1814.)

On September 10, 1813, twenty-eight-year-old Oliver Hazard Perry won a much more significant victory when his makeshift ten-ship fleet defeated the Royal Navy's six-ship squadron on Lake Erie. Thus deprived of free navigation on the lake, the British recalled their advance forces, evacuating Detroit. This presented Gen. William Henry Harrison with an opportunity, which he seized. Catching up with the retreating British and Indian column on October 5 at the Thames River,

An 1813 engraving showing the fighting along the Thames River in Ontario, published not long after the American victory there.

Harrison won a decisive victory marked by the death of the Shawnee chief Tecumseh. Even with this success, however, Britain's own triumph in its war with Napoléon, capped by the emperor's abdication in April 1814, suddenly made available large numbers of troops and large supplies of munitions previously committed to Europe. In August 1814, a well-armed British fleet sailed up the Chesapeake Bay and landed four thousand experienced soldiers on the Maryland shore. This veteran army easily pushed aside the American defenders at the August 24 battle of Bladensburg, Maryland, and that night captured the U.S. capital.

THE OCCUPATION AND BURNING OF WASHINGTON, D.C., on August 24–25 was the low point of the war for the Americans. Yet Baltimore held, and on September 11 Capt. Thomas Macdonough won the naval battle of Lake Champlain. Macdonough's victory halted a British offensive launched from Canada and persuaded the authorities in London that the time might be right for peace. Having defeated Napoléon, the British government no longer cared much about stopping U.S. trade with the French, and the British public was tired of war. On December 24, 1814, therefore, British and U.S. negotiators signed the Treaty of Ghent, whose specific provisions included British pledges to forswear impressment and surrender its forts along the northwest frontier. The peace treaty also established a boundary commission to fix the vague U.S.-Canadian border, but these codicils were quite modest given the fighting, which had lasted more than two years. Decisions on the most contentious issues, such as the militarization of the Great Lakes and ownership of the Oregon Territory, were postponed, and little of lasting significance was resolved.

TECUMSEH'S CONFEDERACY

IN 1808, FROM HIS HOME IN OHIO, the Shawnee chief Tecumseh began traveling up and down the Mississippi River Valley, organizing a confederacy of tribes to resist the increasing white encroachment onto Indian land. With the help of his brother, Tenskwatawa, a religious mystic known as the Prophet, Tecumseh became the chief spokesman for the Native Americans living in the trans-Appalachian West. In November 1811, during one of Tecumseh's many absences, Gen. William Henry Harrison marched on Prophetstown, which he burned to the ground after defeating the Shawnees at the battle of Tippecanoe Creek. Thereafter, Tecumseh allied himself with Great Britain. During the War of 1812, he helped the British capture Detroit but lost his life in October 1813 during the battle of the Thames.

Tenskwatawa survived the battle of Tippecanoe Creek, but because his magic had failed to defeat the whites, he lost all his credibility. The Shawnee Prophet lived until 1834, most of that time on a British pension, and was living in Kansas when he sat for this portrait by George Catlin in 1830.

ALTHOUGH THE INTERNATIONAL SITUATION of the United States remained largely unchanged, the War of 1812 did have a considerable effect on domestic circumstances. Politically, for example, it marked the end of Federalist influence. The Federalist party, whose base was New England, had ridiculed Mr. Madison's War from the start, and its criticism only intensified after the British extended their coastal blockade to New England in the spring of 1814. On December 15 of that year, representatives from Massachusetts, Rhode Island, and Connecticut met secretly at Hartford to devise a regional strategy. Secession was discussed, and the New England state legislatures were invited to nullify a conscription bill presently before Congress—an expression of states' rights that Madison himself had advocated sixteen years earlier with regard to the Alien and Sedition Acts. But the signing of the Ghent peace treaty and word of Andrew Jackson's heroic January 8 victory at New Orleans (news of the peace didn't reach him until after the battle) ended all such talk and made the Hartford Convention, which disbanded on January 5, seem treasonous. It was a debacle from which the Federalist party, already in decline, never recovered.

Meanwhile, although they ruined many U.S. shipping companies, Jefferson's embargo policy and the British blockade had the unanticipated benefit of stimulating the growth of U.S. domestic industry. Soon American factories, especially in New England, began producing manufactured goods of the sort once imported from Britain, and interstate trade boomed. In other respects as well, the War of 1812 brought the country much closer together. Even the most remote frontiersman seemed eager to defend his country against foreign attack, and the ascendancy of the Democratic-Republican party created such a political consensus, known as the Era of Good Feeling, that Pres. James Monroe ran for reelection in 1820 unopposed. Whatever the country's future held, it seemed clear by then that the young American republic had withstood successfully its first major political and foreign challenges. The next ones, of course, would involve spreading the American republic across the continent and thus fulfilling, for better or worse, the destiny of Lewis and Clark.

This 1814 British cartoon, entitled The Fall of Washington—or Maddy in Full Flight, *shows the president and his incompetent secretary of war, John Armstrong, fleeing the burning capital.*

AMERICAN PROFILE

John Marshall
1755–1835

by Joseph J. Ellis

BETWEEN 1801 AND 1835, five U.S. presidents came and went, while Chief Justice John Marshall came and stayed. He was one of the "midnight judges" appointed by John Adams during the last weeks of Adams's lame-duck presidency, and he held his Supreme Court post until the final years of Andrew Jackson's second term. Marshall's longevity was unprecedented; his timing, perfect. "He hit the Constitution much as the Lord hit the chaos," one admirer wrote, "at a time when everything needed creating."

Although the fourth chief justice overall, Marshall was the first to define and establish the enduring powers of the office. Almost single-handedly he transformed the Court from a peripheral branch of the federal government into an equal partner with the Congress and the president. At the core of Marshall's vision were two seminal convictions: first, that the Constitution was a binding contract among the American people (rather than a compact made by sovereign states); and second, that the Supreme Court should be the Constitution's ultimate arbiter. Because of Marshall, these convictions have now achieved the status of self-evident truths.

In a series of landmark decisions—beginning with *Marbury v. Madison* (1803) and continuing with *Fletcher v. Peck* (1810) and *McCulloch v. Maryland* (1819)—Marshall established both the authority of the Court to define the law and the power of the federal government to impose its will on the states. If Washington can be said to have founded our nation, then Marshall was the person who defined it. His legacy is beyond dispute.

Born in the foothills of Virginia's Blue Ridge Mountains in 1755, Marshall had his life shaped early on by the American Revolution, through which he led an elite company of backwoods riflemen that took part in most of the major battles. He was at Valley Forge with Washington, who became his lifelong hero. Much like the commander in chief himself, Marshall learned from his experience in the Continental Army to be skeptical of state and local governments, which often failed to provide promised support once the fighting moved beyond their borders. Also like Washington, Marshall believed that the American Revolution was not merely a war for independence from England, but also a movement to create a sovereign American nation.

This interpretation put him somewhat at odds with his distant cousin Thomas Jefferson, whom Marshall slyly described as "the great lama of the mountains." Jefferson had much worse things to say about Marshall, whom he called "a man of lax, lounging manners" and whose judicial decisions he described as "twistifications" because they tended to contort Jefferson's own fond convictions regarding state sovereignty. Yet even Jefferson had to admit that Marshall was truly formidable: "So great is his sophistry you must never give him an affirmative answer or you will be forced to grant his conclusion. Why if he were to ask me if it were daylight or not, I'd reply 'Sir, I don't know. I can't tell.'" Jefferson went so far as to call the Marshall Court "a subtle corps of sappers and miners constantly working underground to undermine the foundations of our confederated republic." The trouble, of course, was that Marshall considered the United States not a "confederated republic" but a republican nation.

Jefferson eventually came to regard Marshall as a diabolical wizard because newly appointed justices invariably came under his spell. When the Court was in session, the justices lived and boarded together, so they often deliberated as Marshall presided over meals and postprandial

Madeira. The decisions they reached under his prodding were then announced to the world with a single voice, usually Marshall's.

The Marshall magic was as much a matter of temperament as intelligence. Even the chief justice's enemies—apart from Jefferson—found him difficult to dislike. His laugh, one colleague wrote, was "too hearty for an intriguer." He clearly manipulated the constitutional views of his fellow justices, and yet Marshall still struck most observers as a man so comfortable with himself that he lacked any personal agenda at all.

This 1880 portrait of Marshall by Richard N. Brooke was based on an earlier likeness by W. D. Washington.

7

JACKSONIAN AMERICA

The People's Inauguration

ON SUNDAY, JANUARY 18, 1829, the steamboat *Pennsylvania* arrived at bustling Nashville, Tennessee. The *Pennsylvania* had been engaged to carry President-elect Andrew Jackson from his nearby home at the Hermitage down the Cumberland River and up the Ohio to Pittsburgh, where he would transfer to a stagecoach for the final leg of his journey to Washington. The trip was expected to take about three weeks. Initially, Jackson wanted to leave on the same afternoon that the *Pennsylvania* arrived, but he chose instead to wait a day because during the recent presidential campaign, Jackson's Democratic surrogates had flogged outgoing president John Quincy Adams for routinely traveling on the Sabbath.

Through the Democratic party press, Jackson had let it be known that he wished "no public shows or receptions" on his way to the capital because he was still deeply mourning his late wife, Rachel, who had died only four weeks earlier. Even so, Jackson's admirers couldn't resist gathering along his route to greet the man they had just elected to the White House. Whenever the *Pennsylvania* docked or the stagecoach carrying Jackson stopped to change horses, ordinary Americans would mob the president-elect, approaching him without any self-consciousness to shake his hand and speak to him. One female member of Jackson's entourage described this behavior, which offended her class sensibilities, as "brutal familiarity." Nevertheless, Jackson shook each hand offered and gave each citizen his due. In Pittsburgh, he spent more than

an hour satisfying the crowd that had gathered at the dock.

After his February 11 arrival in Washington, Jackson announced through the *United States Telegraph* that he would make himself available to greet well-wishers from noon to 3 P.M. each day at his hotel. But the callers proved so numerous (and the small talk so tiring) that the general suspended the receptions in order to concentrate on selecting his cabinet. In the meantime, visitors who had come to town for the inauguration filled every hotel room and boardinghouse in the district, as well as more than a few tavern and barn floors. "I never saw such a crowd here before," Massachusetts senator Daniel Webster wrote in a letter dated February 19. "Persons have come five hundred miles to see General Jackson, *and they really seem to think that the country is rescued from some dreadful danger!*"

The danger that these Americans perceived was nothing less than the loss of their right to govern themselves, especially their right to choose their own president. Pres. John Quincy Adams may have been *for* the people, but he was certainly not *of* them, and his aloofness had made him vulnerable to Democratic charges that he was an autocrat, an aristocrat, or both. For his part, Andrew Jackson was no less arrogant than Adams, but his personal history— that of a self-made man, not the European-educated son of a president—enabled the folksy Jackson to present himself as a true representative of the people, elevated not to administer congressional laws but to lead the country as he had led armies at Horseshoe Bend and New Orleans.

AT LEFT: *Andrew Jackson posed for this 1830 lithograph at the Hermitage, his estate outside Nashville, Tennessee.*

Dawn on March 4 (inauguration day) broke clear and bright. The ceremony, scheduled to begin at noon, was set for the Capitol's East Portico. "Like a mighty, agitated sea," historian Robert V. Remini wrote, "the masses pushed and shoved to get closer to the place where Jackson would appear. They even swarmed up the steps leading to the Portico so that a ship's cable had to be stretched about two-thirds of the way up the flight of stairs to hold them back. Francis Scott Key stared in wonder at the incredible spectacle of this surging, pulsating mass of humanity. 'It is beautiful,' he gasped, 'it is sublime!'"

After disembarking in Pittsburgh, Jackson traveled to the capital along the National (Cumberland) Road. This contemporary illustration shows well-wishers greeting him along the way. The extension of the National Road from Wheeling, Virginia, to Columbus, Ohio, was the only land transportation project that Jackson approved while president.

ANDREW JACKSON WAS BORN in South Carolina on March 15, 1767, to parents who had recently emigrated from Carrickfergus, Ireland. By the time he was fourteen, however, Jackson was an orphan. His father died shortly before his birth, and his mother passed away in 1781 from cholera that she contracted while nursing American prisoners of war in British-held Charleston. Jackson's two older brothers also died during the Revolution, and Jackson himself was slashed while a prisoner of the British, leaving a permanent scar.

After the Revolution, Jackson studied law for three years in North Carolina before receiving his license to practice in September 1787. He had difficulty finding work, however, and in early 1788, he crossed the Appalachians and settled in Nashville. Founded just nine years earlier, Nashville was perched on the edge of the wilderness and still very much threatened by Indian attack. Jackson arrived with a horse, a slave, and a friend's promise of work. His old gambling buddy John McNairy had just been appointed superior court judge for the Western District of North Carolina; and McNairy could, by virtue of his appointment, make Jackson public prosecutor for the district. The twenty-one-year-old's legal knowledge was rather limited, but the task of imposing law and order on the frontier required at least as much determination and physical courage as it did forensic expertise.

Typically, Jackson made his rounds with a knife and rifle close at hand; if at times a suspect had to be subdued before he could be prosecuted, Jackson could handle that as well.

Jackson's tall, lanky silhouette; his shock of red hair; and his blazing blue eyes soon became well known in the Western District, which became the state of Tennessee in 1796. Neighbors feared his temper but respected his courage and honesty. He helped draft the state's

This map of North Carolina's Western District was published in 1795, just months before Tennessee formally became the seventeenth state.

new constitution in January 1796 and was sent to the House of Representatives in the fall as Tennessee's first member. In Philadelphia, then the nation's capital, Jackson passionately supported Thomas Jefferson's Democratic-Republican party and shunned the Federalists. Almost immediately, he voted against a resolution praising the outgoing administration and wishing President Washington well in his retirement. Jackson opposed this courtesy because he believed that Jay's Treaty had been a disgrace to the nation and that Washington's support for it was indefensible.

Throughout his brief service in Congress, Jackson refused to conform. Rather than wear a powdered wig (then the fashion), he wrapped his long hair in an eel skin, a practice that caused one Democratic-Republican leader to describe him as

RACHEL JACKSON

WHEN ANDREW JACKSON reached Nashville in 1788, he found a frontier town with a courthouse, two stores, two taverns, and a distillery. Accommodations were not plentiful, so Jackson was lucky to find room in a boardinghouse run by the widow Donelson. There he met the widow's twenty-one-year-old daughter, Rachel. From the start, Jackson found Rachel enchanting—and also married, but this didn't stop Jackson. Rachel and her husband, Kentuckian Lewis Robards, had already been separated once before, and it wasn't long before (with some help from Jackson) they parted ways again.

During the fall of 1790, however, a rumor reached Rachel that Robards planned to return from Kentucky to reclaim her. Wanting no part of Robards, Rachel decided to leave Nashville and travel with some relatives to Spanish-held Natchez. Jackson volunteered to accompany the party, in part because of the danger from hostile Indians but also because he likely wanted his offer, morally questionable according to the standards of the day, to provoke Robards into suing for divorce and thus freeing Rachel to marry Jackson. Upon returning to Nashville in the spring of 1791, Jackson heard that Robards had indeed obtained a divorce from the Virginia state legislature, which still had jurisdiction over the territory of Kentucky. Yet Jackson never sought confirmation—which, for a lawyer, seems a suspicious omission. Instead, he hurried back to Natchez and married Rachel.

Or so Jackson's friends later claimed. In fact, no record of the Natchez marriage has ever been found despite Spanish precision in such matters. What Spanish records do show is that the Donelson party arrived in Natchez during the winter of 1789–1790, a full year before the date given in the defense prepared for the Democratic party in 1827. Almost certainly Jackson knew that Rachel was still legally bound to Robards when he began living with her in 1791. Upon returning to Nashville that fall, the Jacksons took up respectable residence as man and wife and were accepted as such until late 1793, when Andrew and Rachel learned that the document Robards had obtained in 1791 was not a divorce but merely an enabling act permitting him to sue for divorce. A final divorce wasn't granted until September 27, 1793; therefore, Rachel and Andrew had been committing adultery for at least two years. Another marriage ceremony held in Nashville in January 1794 seemed to resolve the matter permanently; but three decades later, Rachel's legally declared adultery became the central character issue of the 1828 presidential campaign.

Whatever the circumstances in 1790 might have been, it is undeniable that in 1828 Andrew Jackson dearly loved his wife and took great umbrage at the mockery the National Republicans were making of her character. Unable to control his rage, he called Secretary of State Henry Clay, the man whom he believed responsible for the attacks, "the basest, meanest scoundrel that ever disgraced the image of his God." Only with difficulty could his advisers dissuade Jackson from challenging Clay to a duel. Then, less than three weeks after Jackson's victory, Rachel died. Refusing to accept her passing, Jackson spent an entire night sitting beside her lifeless body; for the rest of his life, he blamed her death on the slanders from which he had tried but failed to protect her. "May God forgive her traducers," he told a friend. "I know that I never shall."

According to one contemporary, Rachel Jackson (shown here in an early 1830s portrait) was "irresistible to men." They especially admired her dark eyes and overlooked her fondness for smoking a corncob pipe.

This early 1830s portrait of Jackson by Ralph W. Earl was entitled Tennessee Gentleman. *It shows the president far removed from his youth as an impoverished orphan.*

an "uncouth-looking personage, with manners of a rough backwoodsman." When the second session of the Fourth Congress finally adjourned in March 1797, Jackson left Philadelphia with no plans to return. When the Tennessee legislature elected him to the Senate in the fall, Jackson did return to Philadelphia, but he served only five months before resigning. All the talk and paperwork seemed to him simply a painful waste of time and money.

In addition to the tedium, Jackson also left Congress because his personal affairs required his attention. He had made a fortune speculating in western land during the early 1790s, but the financial panic of 1795 had wiped out all his gains and left him deeply in debt. It took Jackson nearly nineteen years to become solvent again, and during that time he came to blame banks and their paper money for his troubles.

Jackson the General

WHEN CONGRESS DECLARED WAR on Great Britain in 1812, the forty-five-year-old Jackson eagerly offered to raise and lead an army of twenty-five hundred Tennessee volunteers. President Madison responded to his proposal with a polite note thanking Jackson but not calling him to duty. Jackson was mystified and outraged, but then he realized why Madison had been keeping him at arm's length: During 1806, when Jackson had been Tennessee's major general of militia, Aaron Burr had involved Jackson, albeit unwittingly, in his conspiracy to create an independent western empire. Now the War Department was reluctant to give Burr's erstwhile friend, well known as a hothead, an active command.

It wasn't until October 1812, two months after the fall of Detroit, that Madison finally asked Tennessee governor Willie Blount to raise fifteen hundred volunteers for the defense of New Orleans. To lead these troops, Blount chose Jackson, a close political ally. The expeditionary force left Nashville in January 1813, but travel was particularly slow. Ice clogged the Ohio River, and the immense New Madrid earthquakes of 1811–1812 had sufficiently changed the course of the Mississippi River to make navigation difficult in some places. It took more than a month for Jackson to reach Natchez; and when he did, he found waiting for him a series of dispatches from James Wilkinson, the commanding general in New Orleans, ordering him to stay away. Wilkinson wrote that he hadn't yet received orders from the War Department concerning Jackson and he didn't have enough food on hand to feed Jackson's men.

Weeks passed while Jackson remained at Natchez, awaiting further orders. Finally, on March 15, he received a letter from the new secretary of war, John Armstrong, dismissing his troops from service. "The causes [for] marching to New Orleans the Corps under your command having ceased to exist," Armstrong wrote in a February 5 dispatch, "you will on receipt of this letter, consider it as dismissed from public service and take measures to have delivered over to Major General Wilkinson all articles of public property which may have been put into it's [sic] possession." The order was clear, but obeying it would have meant abandoning his still-unpaid troops in hostile Indian country with no food, no medicine, and no transportation home. The only possible reason for Armstrong to strand his troops

Andrew Jackson's pocket watch.

in this way, Jackson concluded, was to force them to enlist with Wilkinson's army as regulars. Actually, the War Department had been considering ordering Jackson's army to invade Spanish Florida—even though Spain was officially neutral in the war—but diplomatic concerns had put the invasion on hold and Armstrong was merely responding to this change in strategy. All Jackson knew, however, was that he wasn't going to obey Armstrong's order. Instead, he decided to march his army back to Nashville—at his own expense, if necessary.

During the long walk back from Natchez to Nashville, Jackson displayed resolution; courage; fortitude; and, most of all, willpower. "Not the ordinary kind," according to Robert V. Remini. "Nothing normal or even natural. This was superhuman. This was virtually demonic. This was sheer, total, concentrated determination to achieve his ends. So if he determined to get his men back to Nashville he would get them there even if it meant carrying every one of them on his back." Giving up all three of his horses to soldiers unable to walk, Jackson marched the entire route alongside his men, personally overseeing the distribution of rations and ranging up and down the line to offer encouragement as he could. Jackson was tough, his men decided, as tough as hickory, which was the toughest thing most of them knew. So they called the general Hickory at first and then Old Hickory to show even greater respect. "Long will the General live in the memory of his volunteers of West Tennessee for his benevolent, humane, and fatherly treatment," the *Nashville Whig* rejoiced soon after the army's return. "If gratitude and love can reward him, General Jackson has them." Later would come their votes as well.

This illustration from an early Jackson biography shows the general in his camp at Natchez persuading his soldiers not to mutiny but rather to accompany him on a march back home to Nashville.

Jackson's second campaign of the 1812 War began in the aftermath of the Fort Mims massacre. On August 30, 1813, a band of Creeks known as the Red Sticks had massacred a group of white settlers at Fort Mims in Alabama, then a part of the Mississippi Territory. The Red Sticks had long been hostile to whites, and in October 1811, Tecumseh had visited them, offering British guns for use against the Americans. (Tecumseh was away on this trip when William Henry Harrison

The Hermitage, as it appeared in 1856. Jackson bought the property in 1804.

attacked Prophetstown.) "Let the white race perish!" Tecumseh told the Red Sticks. "They seize your land; they corrupt your women; they trample on the bones of your dead! Back whence they came, upon a trail of blood, they must be driven!"

Only two months later, the first of the three immense New Madrid earthquakes, each estimated at greater than 8.0 on the Richter scale, shook the Mississippi Valley and persuaded many of the Creeks, who lived along the Gulf Coast, that their gods favored Tecumseh's call to war. For the next two years, the result was mainly border raiding, in which the whites gave at least as good as they got. The attack on Samuel Mims's fortified residence forty miles north of Mobile, however, was a notable escalation. Nearly 250 whites had holed up with Mims, and the Creeks killed nearly all of them in the most brutal fashion: Men were burned alive, women were scalped, pregnant women were eviscerated while still alive, and children were swung by their legs against the walls of the fort until their heads cracked open and their brains poured out.

Once news of the massacre reached Nashville, Governor Blount ordered Jackson, who was by no means fond of Indians, to "call out, organize, rendezvous, and march without delay" twenty-five hundred men against the Creeks. (At the same time, Blount ordered Maj. Gen. John Cocke to raise another twenty-five hundred men in eastern Tennessee.) Jackson's plan was to build a road through the Alabama wilderness to Mobile, literally paving the way for future expansion and dispersing the Creeks as he went. After reaching Mobile, he would then invade Spanish Florida, which he called "the root of the disseas," and take Pensacola.

This portrait is believed to be the only true likeness of Tecumseh ever created. Painted by an unknown artist, it was passed down in the family of brothers George Rogers Clark and William Clark until the late nineteenth century, when it became part of the collection of the Chicago Natural History Museum.

THE WAR DEPARTMENT had a different strategy in mind. It wanted Jackson to merge his force with Cocke's, then march the combined army south to the junction of the Tallapoosa and Coosa Rivers (at the site of present-day Montgomery), where it would rendezvous with Georgia volunteers under John Floyd and Mississippi volunteers under Ferdinand L. Claiborne. But this never happened. After taking command on October 7, Jackson marched his West Tennessee army over the Lookout Mountains into Alabama, where he eventually joined up with Cocke, but Floyd and Claiborne never appeared. Each had fared poorly in early encounters with the Indians, and both had withdrawn, leaving Jackson and the Tennesseans to fight the Creek War alone.

The decisive moment in that war came on March 27, 1814, when Jackson, reinforced by the Thirty-ninth U.S. Infantry Regiment, attacked the Creek stronghold at Horseshoe Bend on the Tallapoosa River. Jackson led some four thousand men (including warriors from a number of friendly Creek bands) against a thousand hostile Creek warriors who were encamped with nearly three hundred women and children on a wooded peninsula bordered on three sides by the Tallapoosa. The hostile Creeks felt secure because the peninsula's 350-yard-wide neck was protected by a wooden breastwork of large tree trunks six to eight feet high. According to Jackson's March 31 letter to Blount, Horseshoe Bend was "a place well formed by Nature for defence & rendered more so by Art." Nevertheless, Jackson's men defied the withering Indian fire, stormed the breastwork, and systematically slaughtered the Creeks until nightfall ended the carnage. Jackson's victory at Horseshoe Bend was particularly important because it crushed the power of the Creek Nation at a time when the British were just about to begin regular military operations in the South.

After Horseshoe Bend, the Madison administration could no longer ignore Jackson's merit, especially given the notorious failures of Secretary of War Armstrong's choices for command. So Old Hickory was offered a brigadier generalship in the regular army with the brevet rank of major general and command of the Seventh Military District, which encompassed Tennessee, Louisiana, the Mississippi Territory, and the Creek Nation. Jackson expected more—a major general's commission at least—but Armstrong said the offer was the best he could do, and Jackson accepted on June 18. At the same time, the British were completing their preparations for a Gulf Coast expedition designed to push the Americans out of Louisiana and West Florida, which the United States had taken rather easily from Spain in early 1813. The original British plan called for a landing at Mobile, where Spanish and Indian allies could assemble for an overland march to Natchez, thus isolating New Orleans. Occupying Natchez would also leave the British army well placed to move up the Mississippi Valley to Canada and reinforce the troops fighting there. But when the British high command learned that Jackson had moved his army to Mobile, it shifted the invasion target to New Orleans, which it correctly believed to be undefended.

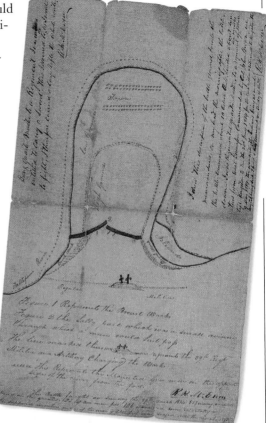

The Hero of New Orleans

ALTHOUGH JACKSON'S VICTORY at Horseshoe Bend made him a legend in Tennessee, it was victory over the British at New Orleans that made him America's first bona fide national hero. After capturing Pensacola in early November and thus electrifying the West with his unauthorized invasion of Spanish territory, Jackson had returned to Mobile to assure himself that it was suitably defended. Then he hurried on to New Orleans, arriving on December 1. Several weeks later, he received an urgent letter from James Monroe, who had replaced Armstrong at the War Department while continuing on as secretary of state. Monroe's letter informed Jackson that a large British invasion force had recently departed Cuba and was believed headed for New Orleans. "Mobile is comparatively a trifling object with the British government," Monroe wrote. "...All the boasted preparation, which the British government had been making thro' the year, with veteran troops from France and Spain, after having been gloriously foiled, in attacks on other parts of our Union, is about to terminate in a final blow against New Orleans. It will, I hope, close there its inglorious career, in such a repulse as will reflect new honor on the American arms." At the time, Jackson had only two thousand troops with him in New Orleans, compared to the fourteen thousand whom Monroe thought made up the British complement. Fortunately for the Americans, a thousand reinforcements soon became available from an unexpected quarter.

The morning after Horseshoe Bend, one of Jackson's officers, quartermaster Robert McEwen, drew this map of the battle. McEwen's young cousin, Sam Houston, also took part in the fighting, leading some of the first men over the breastwork before a Creek arrow pierced his thigh and hobbled him.

This lithograph honoring the Hero of New Orleans was issued by Nathaniel Currier in 1837.

Early in September, the British had sent a sloop to Barataria Bay, an inlet seventy miles southwest of New Orleans out of which pirates led by Jean Lafitte had been operating. The British offered Lafitte's men, who preyed mostly on Spanish shipping, land in exchange for their aid and their promise to harass neither British nor Spanish shipping. Asking for time to ponder the arrangement, Lafitte immediately reported its particulars to his American friends at New Orleans, with whom he hoped to strike an even better deal. The city's Creole leadership regarded Lafitte rather tolerantly and had for many years accepted his stolen goods in trade. But Jackson loathed the Baratarians, considered them dishonorable, and more than once described them as "hellish banditti." On numerous occasions in the past, Jackson had lectured the governor of Florida on Spain's responsibility as a neutral to curb Indian raids launched from within Spanish territory, only to have the governor point out rather caustically the hypocrisy of American toleration of Baratarian piracy.

Once Jackson arrived in New Orleans, however, local leaders pressed Lafitte's case, and Jackson eventually relented, agreeing to accept the pirates' help in exchange for a general grant of amnesty. Lafitte brought with him badly needed powder, shot, and men. Around the same time, Jackson also accepted the services of two battalions of free blacks, despite the protests of some Louisianians, who objected to arming African Americans. The black soldiers were given the same pay, rations, and clothing as white volunteers; and although white officers were appointed to lead them, the men were allowed to choose their own noncommissioned officers.

THIRTY-SEVEN-YEAR-OLD Lt. Gen. Edward Pakenham, having served most ably in the recently concluded Napoleonic Wars, was given command of the invasion force that arrived at the entrance to Lake Borgne on December 13. Pakenham carried with him a royal commission naming him governor of Louisiana. After displacing the Americans, he was to rule that territory—"fraudulently conveyed by [Napoléon] Bonaparte to the United States," according to the commission—in trust for Spain. But New Orleans had to be captured first, and the tangled swamps and bayous of the Mississippi Delta were proving especially difficult to negotiate. It wasn't until ten days later, on December 23, that an advance column of Pakenham's army went into camp just nine miles below New Orleans.

Because these eighteen hundred soldiers had moved up through Bayou Bienvenue and Bayou Mazant with complete secrecy, the surprise attack they could have launched against New Orleans would probably have taken the town. Yet captured American soldiers and sailors had been consistently lying to their interrogators about the strength of Jackson's army, causing the British to overestimate its size by a factor of four. So Maj. Gen. John Keane, in charge of the advance column, chose to be cautious.

Not so Andrew Jackson. Another general might have focused on strengthening his fortifications, but Jackson decided instead to attack. He quickly assembled the regulars he had brought with him to New Orleans and added to them the city militia and free black battalions—all told, about three thousand men. (Another three thousand Tennessee volunteers, who had arrived two days earlier, were left behind with the Louisiana state militia to guard the town.) The ensuing night-time battle produced a standoff with similar casualties on both sides. The British claimed victory because the Americans had failed to drive them back, but Jackson's aggressiveness had, more importantly, halted the British column and gained him precious time to prepare for the main attack. Reasoning that Jackson must indeed command a force of fifteen thousand men if he could risk such an attack, Keane decided to remain where he was until all of Pakenham's army could be brought up. This took several days.

On December 28, Pakenham ordered a slow advance along the eastern bank of the Mississippi, only to be pushed back by American crossfire from the USS *Louisiana* and artillery placed along an old millrace called the Rodriguez Canal. Moving up artillery of his own to counter the American firepower, Pakenham tried again on New Year's Day to breach the American fortifications. Once again, he failed, largely because of the skill of a pirate artillery battery commanded by Lafitte's brother, Dominique You. A somewhat chastened Pakenham went back into camp to wait for some expected reinforcements. Meanwhile, on January 4, 1815, more than two thousand militiamen from Kentucky arrived to bolster Jackson's lines.

OVERLEAF:

This 1815 engraving of Jackson's victory at New Orleans was based on drawings made by Hyancinthe Laclotte, an assistant engineer with the Louisiana militia who witnessed the battle.

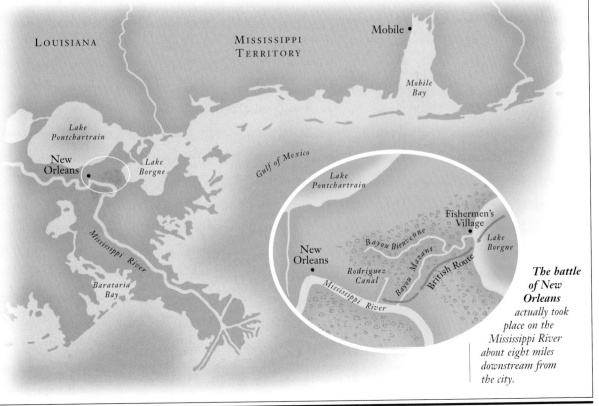

The battle of New Orleans actually took place on the Mississippi River about eight miles downstream from the city.

of the *British Army* 12,000 strong, under the Command of *Sir* Edward Packenham
of the *American* Lines defended by 3,600 Militia commanded by Major General
Jackson. January 8th 1815, on Chalmette plain, five miles below New Orleans, on the left bank of the Mississipi
Drawn on the Field of Battle and painted by H the Laclotte arch.t and Lt E

Défaite de l'Armée *Anglaise*, forte de 12,000 homme, Commandée par Sir *Edward Packenham*

du 8 Janvier 1815 de la ligne de retranchement de l'Armée *Américaine* défendue par 3,600 miliciens sous les

Général *Andrew Jackson* dans la plaine de l'habitation Chalmette, rive gauche du Mississipi, a 5 milles Est de la Nouv

JUST AFTER DAWN on the morning of January 8, two Congreve rockets streaked up from the British lines, signaling the start of the final attack. As the Americans waited for the British to move closer, the Battalion d'Orleans band struck up "Yankee Doodle." Only when Jackson was sure that the redcoats were within range did he give the command to fire. He had deployed his troops into four lines, and as one line moved to the rear to reload, another stepped up to discharge its muskets. Simultaneously, the Baratarian artillery helped blow great holes in the orderly enemy lines. In the face of this "leaden torrent no man on earth could face" (according to one British account), Pakenham's army buckled and broke. The British showed no lack of valor; rather, Jackson's defenses, with the river on one side and a swamp on the other, were simply too strong. Pakenham had ordered a predawn flanking maneuver on the Mississippi's western bank, but the failure of the flanking force to accomplish its goal in a timely manner made the rest of the army's frontal attack suicidal. While desperately trying to rally his men, Pakenham himself took two pieces of grapeshot and died on the field. His army retreated, and the commander of the British reserves, Maj. Gen. John Lambert, seeing no point in fighting on, ordered an end to the attack.

By eight in the morning, when the action ended, British casualties numbered more than two thousand. In contrast, the Americans lost just seventy-one men. Four were black soldiers, who had been so eager to fight that they left their lines to chase retreating redcoats. Ten days later, after burying their dead, the shattered British left their camp on the Mississippi and marched back to the shores of Lake Borgne, where their transport ships had been waiting. The Royal Navy then carried the survivors on to Mobile, where Lambert expected to implement the original invasion plan. On February 11, in due course, the British invested Fort Bowyer at the entrance to Mobile Bay, but before an invasion of the mainland could be mounted, news arrived that the war had ended on December 24 with the signing of the Treaty of Ghent.

When Jackson received word in mid-February, he was still governing New Orleans under martial law. In the years since 1815, it has been suggested on occasion that Jackson's victory there was meaningless because the war had already been over for two weeks. Yet this perspective is naive. Pakenham's commission as royal governor of Louisiana makes clear that, had the British captured New Orleans, they would not have surrendered it— Treaty of Ghent or no.

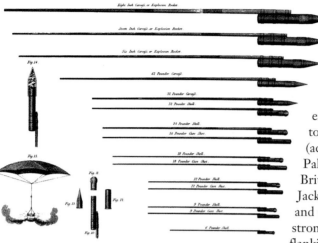

William Congreve's The Rocket System *(1814) includes this plate showing "rocket sticks" of the sort he invented in 1808. Made separately for ease of transportation, the explosive heads were later attached to wooden sticks with iron ferrules. The assembled weapons were then fired from half-pipe launchers.*

RIGHT:
A broadside announcing Jackson's victory to the people of Boston. Given the largely pitiful performance of the U.S. military during the War of 1812, the news that Jackson had won at New Orleans made Americans ecstatic. All eighteen state legislatures passed resolutions expressing their gratitude.

The American System

WITH THE WAR NOW OVER, Jackson returned to the Hermitage, where he relaxed and adjusted once again to plantation life. Meanwhile in Washington, Speaker of the House Henry Clay and his chief ally, John C. Calhoun, reshaped the politics of the now all-powerful Democratic-Republican party. Clay believed strongly that, in the aftermath of the War of 1812, the United States needed to reduce its economic dependence on Europe substantially. To accomplish this, he developed a set of policies that he called the American System. The key elements were encouragement of northeastern factory construction (to spur domestic demand for southern and western raw materials, especially cotton), enactment of protective tariffs (to discourage competition from foreign imports), and the federal funding of internal improvements (such as roads and canals). Clay also wanted Congress to charter a new national bank so that more money could be made available for business expansion.

Early success came in March 1816, when the House and Senate each voted by narrow margins to approve a twenty-year charter for the Second Bank of the United States (the charter of the First Bank had expired in 1811). The Second Bank's mandate was clear: Manage the substantial federal war debt while actively promoting U.S. economic growth. Reluctantly, President Madison went along, despite the suspiciously Hamiltonian cast of the plan. Then, a month later, Congress passed the Tariff Act of 1816, which kept in place high wartime tariffs for the protection of U.S. firms. On its face, the 1816 tariff appeared to injure the financial interests of southern plantation owners (Calhoun's primary constituency), but many southerners supported the tariff because of the revenue it promised to provide for internal improvements as well as national security. (The Indians and the Spanish in Florida were still threats on the southern frontier.)

With regard to internal improvements, however, Clay and Calhoun's momentum broke. In February 1817, Congress passed legislation setting aside $1.5 million for public works projects, but in his last official act before leaving office, Madison vetoed the bill. Although he had already signed both the bank legislation and the tariff, Jefferson's chief protégé could brook no more. He rejected Clay's argument that the federal government had the implied power to build roads and canals and in his March 3 veto message insisted that a constitutional amendment was required. The defeat was so profound that for the next two generations, states had to develop all public works on their own.

This factory in Methuen, Massachusetts, harnessed the falls of the Spigot River for power half a century before electricity became commercially available.

The First Seminole War

DURING THE END of Madison's presidency and the beginning of James Monroe's, Andrew Jackson occupied himself on the southern frontier, attempting to enforce the treaty he had imposed on the Creeks in the aftermath of Horseshoe Bend. Yet the core problem, Jackson believed, was Florida; as long as the Spanish remained there, supporting and encouraging the Indians, hostilities would continue, and the frontier would remain unsafe.

The most significant threat came from the Seminole tribe, which periodically raided settlements in Georgia from the safety of their villages on the Spanish side of the border. The First Seminole War began in November 1817, when the army burned a small Seminole village just north of the Florida border and the Seminoles responded by ambushing a large open boat carrying forty soldiers and some women and children. (The killings on both sides were similarly brutal.) After the ambush, the War Department authorized the garrison at nearby Fort Scott to pursue the Seminoles into Florida, if necessary. Ten days later Secretary of War John C. Calhoun ordered Andrew Jackson to take command of the expedition.

There were two primary reasons that Calhoun sent Jackson to Fort Scott. One was that Jackson had already proven his ability as a general and leader of men. The other was that Calhoun (and the president) knew of Jackson's personal determination to wrest Florida from the Spanish by whatever means might be available. Calhoun specifically authorized Jackson to conduct the war as he thought best, and to Jackson that meant nothing less than taking Florida from the Spanish. By late May 1818, he had swept through northern Florida, captured Pensacola, and put the Spanish governor on a boat for Cuba with instructions not to return until he could guarantee an end to future "criminal" attacks on the United States—which was, given the condition of the Spanish empire, never. In fact, had it not been for the general's poor health, Jackson would probably have followed the poor governor to Cuba and seized that Spanish colony as well.

Jackson was famous for his dueling. The last of his three major pistol fights took place in Nashville on September 4, 1813, when he fought brothers Jesse and Thomas Hart Benton (later an influential Missouri senator). Jackson was shot in the shoulder, and the bullet remained with him until 1832, when it was surgically removed.

YET ALL WAS NOT WELL in Washington. At the start of the war, President Monroe had believed, along with Calhoun, that the judicious application of military pressure was all that was needed to persuade Spain to give up Florida. Jackson, however, had applied so much pressure that Monroe now found himself at the center of an international incident. Spain alone did not pose a significant threat to the United States; but in the course of his campaign Jackson had executed two British subjects for encouraging the Seminoles, and now London was involved. At a mid-July meeting of his cabinet, Monroe asked for opinions, and Calhoun, angry at Jackson for slighting him, blamed the general for the cock-up and demanded his censure. Fearing Jackson as a potential presidential rival,

Treasury Secretary William H. Crawford backed Calhoun, as did Attorney General William Wirt, and all three urged the return of Florida to Spain. Only Secretary of State John Quincy Adams defended Jackson's conduct and insisted that the United States keep Florida. Because he was an authority on international law (among many other things), Adams was able to persuade the president that he could justify Jackson's activities and successfully defend the U.S. diplomatic position. Even so, Monroe hedged his bets, retaining Florida but also accusing Jackson of exceeding his instructions.

For his part, Adams told an irate Spanish minister Luis de Onís that Jackson had acted justifiably out of military necessity and a reasonable concern that the Seminole attacks would continue. "Spain must immediately make her election," Adams told Onís in a July 23, 1818, letter, "either to place a force in Florida adequate at once to the protection of her territory...or cede to the United States a province, of which she retains nothing but the nominal possession, but which is, in fact, a derelict, open to the occupancy of every enemy, civilized or savage, of the United States, and serving no other earthly purpose than as a post of annoyance to them." Negotiations for the sale of Florida soon commenced; and in February 1819, the United States and Spain concluded the Adams-Onís Treaty, which ceded Florida in exchange for up to five million dollars in assumed debt and U.S. abandonment of its claim to Texas.

One of the social highlights of the Monroe administration was this ball for Sen. Andrew Jackson, given by Secretary of State John Quincy Adams.

THE MONROE DOCTRINE

THE BRILLIANT DIPLOMACY of John Quincy Adams found no greater outlet than the message he wrote for Pres. James Monroe to deliver to Congress on December 2, 1823. At the time, Adams was fearful of Russian designs on the Oregon Country and Spain's efforts to reconquer its former South American colonies, which had lately declared independence. With regard especially to South America, British foreign secretary George Canning pressed Adams in August 1823 to join him in issuing a statement warning the Spanish and their French allies against recolonization, which would surely lead to a reimposition of the Spanish trade monopoly.

Adams, however, feared that such a joint declaration would make the United States seem "a cockboat in the wake of the British man-of-

Spain's humiliation during the Napoleonic Wars gave South American liberators such as Simon Bolívar (left) and José de San Martín the opportunity to free their countrymen from Spanish colonial rule.

war" and lead to demands by Britain that America restrict its continental expansion as the price for British support. So he proposed to Monroe an independent course of action. In his annual message to Congress that year, the president declared, "The American continents...are henceforth not to be considered as subjects for future colonization by any European powers." Along with Washington's Farewell Address warning against foreign entanglement and John Hay's Open Door policy concerning China, the Monroe Doctrine remains one of the cornerstones of American foreign policy.

Meanwhile—motivated, as Crawford had been, by the obvious growth in Jackson's political stature—Henry Clay scheduled hearings in the House to investigate the general's actions. Different congressional factions supported the hearings for different reasons. Political rivals wanted to embarrass both the general and the president; strict constructionists were outraged by the usurpation of Congress's power to declare war; others believed that, as Thomas Jefferson had once suggested, Jackson was a "dangerous" man whose passion, vanity, and military prowess posed a threat to the republic. The ensuing House debate began on January 12, 1819, and lasted twenty-seven days. Never before had the House spent nearly so much time on a single issue. On January 23, having galloped hastily from Nashville through the winter snow, the general himself arrived in Washington to safeguard his interests and defend himself, if necessary.

On January 20, Clay had delivered a widely anticipated speech condemning the Monroe administration's conduct of the Seminole War and warning of the danger military heroes such as Alexander the Great, Caesar, and Napoléon posed to democracies. Because Jackson believed deeply in the Constitution and democratic civil government, Clay's implication that he was a potential tyrant infuriated him all the more. After reading the text of Clay's speech, he focused his enmity on the representative from Kentucky: "The hypocracy & baseness of Clay," Jackson told a friend, "in pretending friendship to me, & endeavouring to crush the executive through me, make me despise the Villain." Such emotional outbursts notwithstanding, Jackson's presence in the capital overall strengthened his hand and enabled his many loyal friends in the House (with the help of the administration) to defeat the censure motion, 107–63.

Jackson the Politician

THUS VINDICATED, Jackson returned to Tennessee, where he would likely have resigned his army commission had it not been for the financial panic then weighing down the country. The panic of 1819, the latest in a series of economic downturns that would recur approximately every twenty years until 1929, began when the three-year-old Second Bank started calling in loans and clamping down on credit. The directors of the Second Bank acted because postwar speculation in western lands had gotten out of hand, leading to alarming inflation and too much paper money. When the Second Bank suddenly reversed its easy credit policies in January 1819, the shock to the nation's financial system was devastating. Overextended banks failed, personal bankruptcies mounted, most paper money became worthless, and prices collapsed. Like many other Americans, especially westerners, Jackson blamed the Second Bank, and several state legislatures even tried to tax its branches out of existence. But on March 6, the Marshall Court ruled in *McCulloch v. Maryland* that such laws were unconstitutional because states could not legally limit any power granted to the federal government by the Constitution.

This engraving published just a few months after the battle of New Orleans shows Andrew Jackson looking particularly Napoleonic. According to Thomas Jefferson, who worked with Jackson in the Senate during 1797 and 1798, "His passions are, no doubt, cooler now; he has been much tried since I knew him, but he is a dangerous man."

THE MISSOURI COMPROMISE

IN 1819, AS THE FINANCIAL PANIC ROILED the nation's economy, the issue of statehood for Missouri brought the U.S. Congress to a standstill. In February, as part of its routine business, the House passed a bill giving the Missouri Territory permission to draft a constitution and prepare for statehood. New York congressman James Tallmadge introduced two antislavery amendments to this bill, neither of which passed. Nevertheless, Tallmadge's attempt ended the uneasy sectional truce that had existed on the question of slavery since 1787. For the next year, the admission of Missouri remained stalled, and the rancor intensified.

The crux of the problem was the balance of power in the Senate. Because of their larger population, free states in the North controlled the House; but in the Senate, the eleven free states shared power with the eleven slave states. Admitting Missouri as either a free state or a slave state would upset that balance, so the Congress did neither. Antislavery members argued that the government could and should prohibit slavery in new states, while slaveholding southerners countered that all states, old or new, were sovereign and therefore entitled to decide the matter for themselves.

Finally, Maine's application for statehood in early 1820 made compromise possible. According to the final deal engineered by Henry Clay, the South agreed to allow the admission of Maine, which would obviously be a free state, in exchange for the admission of Missouri as a slave state. Furthermore, it was agreed that slavery would henceforth be banned in all Louisiana Purchase lands north of latitude 36°30' N.

The Missouri crisis quickly subsided, as did the issue of the compromise's constitutionality; but not so its implications for the country's future. This "momentous question, like a fire-bell in the night, awakened and filled me with terror," Thomas Jefferson wrote from his retirement at Monticello. "I considered it once as the knell of the Union.... This is a reprieve only, not a final sentence."

In early 1821, however, Jackson did resign his commission to become the first territorial governor of Florida. He stayed on long enough to establish a permanent territorial government there and then resigned in November 1821. Thus ended the military phase of Andrew Jackson's career, during which he became one of the foremost expansionists in U.S. history, rivaled only by Jefferson and perhaps James K. Polk. His military victories over the British and Spanish ended international threats to U.S. territorial integrity, and his repeated suppressions of the Creeks, Cherokees, Chickasaws, Choctaws, and Seminoles resulted in the cession between 1814 and 1820 of enormous tracts of Indian land in the Southeast.

The next phase of Jackson's career began in December 1823, when he appeared again in Washington, this time as both a senator from Tennessee and a candidate for president. His four rivals for the White House, all with much more experience in politics than he, were Treasury Secretary Crawford of Georgia, who claimed the support of the old Jeffersonians (and the former president himself); Secretary of State Adams of Massachusetts, backed by the united vote of New England; Secretary of War Calhoun, a native of South Carolina who enjoyed similar bloc support from the South; and Speaker of the House Clay of Kentucky, who drew much of his political strength from the frontier West. The dynamics of the campaign shifted considerably when Crawford, considered the front-runner, suffered a stroke that left him at least temporarily unable to move or speak. Several months later, a Pennsylvania meeting supposedly called to back Calhoun overruled its chairman to endorse Jackson. Jackson's strength throughout the country soon became clear, leading Calhoun to give up his presidential ambitions and run for office as Jackson's vice president. Even so, the field remained crowded, and sectional loyalties conspired against Old Hickory.

John Quincy Adams was—like his father, the second president— crusty and inflexible. He believed in government only by the most able and, therefore, had been preparing for the presidency his entire life.

IN 1824, THERE WAS NOT YET a national election day, so the states chose their electors in various ways on different days. Early on in the process, however, it became clear that no candidate was going to win a majority of the electors; therefore, according to the Constitution, the House of Representatives would have to decide among the top three vote getters. This had been the situation following the 1800 election, and it seemed to favor Clay, who controlled the House—except that Clay had finished fourth with thirty-seven electoral votes, compared to ninety-nine for Jackson, eighty-four for Adams, and forty-one for the only somewhat recovered Crawford. So Clay played the role of kingmaker, and he chose Adams, whose political program most closely resembled his own American System. (Jackson's intentions remained unclear throughout the campaign because his handlers emphasized his military heroism to the exclusion of nearly all else.) Later, President-elect Adams named Clay his secretary of state.

Jackson's supporters were livid. They already felt cheated because their candidate had received the most popular and electoral votes, even if he had fallen short of the required majority. Now they knew the reason: Adams and Clay had evidently made a "corrupt bargain," exchanging the State Department for the presidency. "The Judas of the West has closed the contract," Jackson raged in reference to Clay, "and will receive the thirty pieces of silver." Soon after Adams's inauguration, Jackson resigned his seat in the Senate and began the 1828 campaign. Meanwhile, his friends in Congress, notably Sen. Martin Van Buren of New York, worked to block every bill that the Adams administration put forth,

PARTY POLITICS

AS THE FEDERALIST PARTY WITHERED during the Era of Good Feeling, many Americans came to believe that the country might have finally done away with partisan politics. Quickly enough, though, Andrew Jackson brought the two-party system back. During his campaigns for president in 1824, 1828, and 1832, his supporters organized the Democratic party, while his opponents, to counter his efforts, formed first the National Republican party and then the Whigs.

Unlike their Jeffersonian forebears, the Jacksonian Democrats reveled in partisanship. They believed, in fact, that political parties presented the best means available for resolving the legitimate conflicts that inevitably arise in a democracy. Though not themselves the first to

hold nominating conventions or draft party platforms, the Democrats did foster a political culture that emphasized democratic processes.

Prior to 1828, most presidential candidates were chosen by congressional caucus. That is, the members of a particular party in Congress would meet in private to select their party's candidate. Not surprisingly, this method of nominating candidates came under attack as "undemocratic," and after William Crawford's failure in 1824—he was the last candidate chosen by congressional caucus—the practice was abandoned. Its eventual replacement was the much more democratic, at least in appearance, nominating convention. The Anti-Masons held first national nominating convention in September 1831, choosing William Wirt for president, and the National Republicans followed three months later with their own convention, at which Henry Clay was chosen.

Andrew Jackson *was the undisputed leader of both his party and the government. His power in one role strengthened his authority in the other and enabled him to enforce his will upon others. Democrats who wanted to remain in favor, for example, knew that they had to follow the party line as it appeared daily in the pages of Francis P. Blair's* Washington Globe.

regardless of its merit. Then the Democrats attacked Adams for accomplishing almost nothing while in office. But the principal charge against Adams, that he had made a corrupt bargain with Clay, would likely have been enough in any case. Organizing themselves well, the Jacksonians established partisan newspapers across the country and denounced Adams and Clay at every opportunity, sometimes slanderously. The National Republicans (but not Adams himself) responded with similarly scurrilous comments concerning the virtue of Jackson's wife. It was the first national campaign to emphasize gutter politics.

The People's President

AFTER JACKSON'S VICTORY in the 1828 election, official Washington nervously awaited the coming of the new president.

Henry Clay's March 7, 1825, appointment as secretary of state.

The capital had known the six previous presidents well: All had spent years at the seat of government and held many numerous political offices. On the other hand, the people of Washington knew Jackson primarily through rumor. As one uneasy Washingtonian wrote, "General Jackson will be here [about] 15 of Feb—Nobody knows what he will do. My opinion is that when he comes he will bring a breeze with him. Which way it will blow I cannot tell."

Jackson brought more than a breeze with him. "Never can I forget the spectacle, nor the electrifying moment when the eager, expectant eyes of that vast and motley multitude caught sight of their adored leader," wrote one audience member at his 1829 inauguration. As Old Hickory appeared on the East Portico, he bowed low to the crowd and then delivered his inaugural address, which opened with the sentence, "Fellow-Citizens: About to undertake the arduous duties that I have been appointed to perform by the choice of a free people, I avail myself of this customary and solemn occasion to express the gratitude which their confidence inspires and to acknowledge the accountability which my situation enjoins." Jackson's sentence was a paraphrase of the first sentence of Thomas Jefferson's 1801 inaugural address, and the audience roared its approval of the gesture.

Following the speech and oath taking, the crowd, unable to control itself any longer, broke through the ship's cable and mobbed Jackson. After the marshals on duty applied no little effort in freeing the president from the exuberant throng, Jackson found temporary refuge inside the Capitol. But a public reception was scheduled to begin soon at the White House, and the new president, as host, had to be there. Along with most of those who had witnessed his inauguration, Jackson slowly made his way down Pennsylvania Avenue on a handsome white horse. "Such a cortege as followed him!" Margaret Bayard Smith, the wife of a Maryland senator, observed. "Country men, farmers, gentlemen, mounted and dismounted, boys, women and children, black and white. Carriages, wagons and carts all pursuing him to the President's house."

A Democratic party ticket circulated in Ohio during the election of 1828.

The best estimates place the number of people attending the inaugural reception at twenty thousand. Even after Jackson escaped, most of the well-wishers continued celebrating in the overcrowded residence, causing the White House staff to become concerned for the building's structural integrity. Finally, the remaining refreshments were placed outside—a gambit that worked. Thousands followed the liquor out onto the lawn, climbing through the open windows that provided the most direct means of egress.

AFTER HIS OWN 1801 INAUGURATION, Thomas Jefferson had walked back to the boardinghouse where he had been staying to join his fellow lodgers for noon lunch. Jackson, however, couldn't escape the mob of well-wishers who were determined to express their enthusiasm and goodwill, even to the point of following him *inside* the executive mansion. "Public" receptions at the White House were normally restricted to the members of polite society, but Jackson was a new sort of president—a man of the people—and the people wanted to celebrate with him. Supreme Court justice Joseph Story described the crowd that soon jammed the public rooms of the White House as "the highest and most polished down to the most vulgar and gross in the nation.... The reign of King Mob seemed triumphant. I was glad to escape from the scene as soon as possible."

Orange punch had been prepared, but before the waiters could serve anyone, the thirsty crowd helped itself. Pails of punch were spilled on the floor, and amid the commotion several thousand dollars' worth of glass and china was broken. Meanwhile, more than a few men with muddy boots stood on satin-covered chairs to get a better look at Jackson, who finally extricated himself about 4 P.M., returning to his hotel. No one recorded when the last of the "guests" departed and the White House gates were finally locked, but it took six days of picking up before the White House was clean and orderly enough for Jackson to move in.

Jacksonian Democracy

DURING THE EIGHT YEARS that Old Hickory spent in the White House, he permanently strengthened the office of the presidency and dramatically recast what Americans believed they could expect from government. Before the 1820s, politics in the United States had been relatively genteel. Most states limited the franchise to male property owners; as a result, wealthy merchants in the North and large landowners in the South tended to dominate public affairs. Many states came to be so thoroughly controlled by these groups and their parties that competition hardly existed. Jackson's personal popularity broke the lock.

One of the first things Jackson did upon entering office was rearrange the furniture. Previously, presidents had been reluctant to turn out officeholders appointed by their predecessors for fear of appearing embarrassingly partisan. As a result, a man such as Postmaster General John McLean, appointed by Monroe, was allowed by John Quincy Adams to stay in office despite his repeated and obvious exertions on behalf of Andrew Jackson. Jackson, however, didn't share his predecessors' view regarding partisanship. Instead, during his first year in office, he dismissed about 10 percent of the federal workforce and filled their jobs with Democrats loyal to him. (Of course, Jefferson had replaced a similar number of Federalists, but Jackson made much greater noise in doing so.) Some Democrats argued that Jackson's "rotation" policy reduced elitism and privilege in the operation of government, but the president himself saw no need to defend the principle that, in the words of New York senator William L. Marcy, "to the victors belong the spoils." Thereafter, the practice of rewarding one's political supporters with government jobs came to be known as the spoils system.

As it turned out, with regard to public policy, Old Hickory was basically an old Republican. He hated the national bank; resisted federal funding for internal improvements; and rejected the use of protective tariffs (though he didn't deny their constitutionality). So his politics weren't all that different from Jefferson's, Madison's, or Monroe's—but his tenacity in office was. Jackson was by far the strongest and most assertive chief executive the country had ever had; Congress, ascendant since the close of Jefferson's first term, was no match for him.

This early 1850s daguerreotype shows Supreme Court justice John McLean in his judicial robes. McLean, who was Jackson's first appointment to the Court, served from 1829 until 1861. In 1857, he distinguished himself by dissenting from Chief Justice Roger B. Taney's majority decision in the Dred Scott *case.*

SENATORS AND REPRESENTATIVES who failed to support Jackson's viewpoint found themselves promptly cut off from federal patronage. If they passed bills not to the president's liking, he showed no hesitation in vetoing them. Between 1789 and 1829, six presidents had vetoed a total of ten bills; Jackson alone rejected twelve. His favorite method was the pocket veto (withholding his signature until Congress adjourned and the bill lapsed). Even more important, previous presidents had reserved their vetoes for bills they deemed unconstitutional; Jackson simply vetoed anything he didn't like, constitutional or not.

Another innovation introduced by Jackson was the "kitchen cabinet." Before 1829, presidents had taken advice mainly from their official cabinets, but this posed a problem, as department heads sometimes served the interests of their own political careers first. Therefore, Jackson supplemented his own cabinet with a group of informal advisers, mostly newspapermen such as Amos Kendall and Francis P. Blair, who met with him privately in the White House kitchen. They discussed public and party affairs and helped the president draft his messages to Congress.

Nullification

JACKSON'S MOST FORCEFUL EPISODE in office involved the nullification of 1832–1833. The trouble over protective tariffs had been escalating since the day of his election. On May 19, 1828, President Adams had signed a new law establishing exceptionally high tariffs on imported manufactured goods. Southern planters called the law the Tariff of Abominations, and on December 19, the South Carolina state legislature issued an *Exposition and Protest* condemning the tariff as unjust and unconstitutional. This document was published anonymously but written by Vice President Calhoun, who had once strongly supported protective tariffs but now aligned his views with those of his most powerful constituents. Most important, the *Exposition and Protest* argued, in the spirit of the Kentucky and Virginia Resolutions, that a state could nullify (refuse to enforce) any unendurable federal law. (The aging Madison denied that his and Jefferson's work carried Calhoun's interpretation, but no one in South Carolina seemed to care.) With the Missouri statehood crisis less than a decade in the past, few Americans missed the implication of Calhoun's doctrine with regard to slavery. As the vice president himself explained, "I consider the Tariff but as the occasion, rather than the real cause, of the present state of things."

During his first term, Jackson attempted at times to fashion a compromise tariff bill but never made it a priority, probably because he resented South Carolina's

THE EATON AFFAIR

IF THE INAUGURAL MESS wasn't enough to turn Washington society against Jackson, then the Peggy Eaton affair certainly was. John H. Eaton was one of Jackson's closest friends, and when Old Hickory became president, he appointed the Tennessee senator to head the War Department. Several months earlier, Eaton had married Margaret O'Neal Timberlake, the widowed daughter of the family that ran his boarding-house. The problem was that Eaton may have begun sleeping with the charming Peggy long before her husband's death. (Her late husband, navy purser John Timberlake, was often away at sea.) "Eaton has just married his mistress, and the mistress of eleven doz. others!" reported one Washington gossip.

The ensuing scandal ostracized the Eatons socially but became a matter of national policy only when Jackson himself became involved. Because of the president's fierce personal loyalty to Eaton, he raged at the treatment Peggy Eaton received and even called a September 1829 cabinet meeting to upbraid the secretaries and through

This image of John Eaton dates to the time of his service as secretary of war. The portrait of his wife shows her at a more advanced age.

them their wives. Still, the Eaton Malaria, as Secretary of State Martin Van Buren called it, continued.

Nothing in the aftermath of his own wife's death could have guaranteed Jackson's anger more than similar rumors about a close friend's spouse. Typically, he turned the matter into a test of political loyalty. Van Buren, whose status as a widower made him more flexible socially, used the flap to press his advantage, conspicuously befriending the Eatons and thus ingratiating himself even further with the president. Meanwhile, Vice Pres. John C. Calhoun—whose wife, Floride, was considered the ringleader of the gossips—found himself increasingly alienated from Jackson's trust. The Eaton affair finally ended in April 1831, when John Eaton resigned his position at the War Department in an overall reorganization of the cabinet.

threat to act unilaterally. At a memorable April 1830 dinner party celebrating the anniversary of Jefferson's birth, the president offered a toast that deliberately challenged Calhoun's doctrine of nullification. "Our federal Union—it must be preserved!" Jackson proclaimed, to which Calhoun responded with "The Union—next to our liberty, the most dear." A new tariff bill finally passed Congress in July 1832, reducing many rates—but not enough to satisfy South Carolina. On

November 24, a special state convention called by the legislature adopted an ordinance nullifying the tariffs of 1828 and 1832 and forbidding the collection of duties within the state. If the federal government attempted to enforce its tariffs, the ordinance continued, South Carolina would leave the Union. Meanwhile, plans were made for South Carolina's military defense.

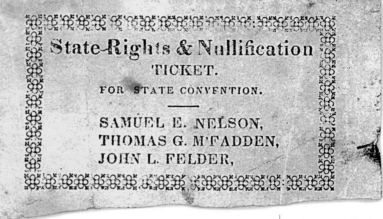

On December 10, five days after the declaration of his reelection victory over Henry Clay, the president issued a proclamation to the people of South Carolina insisting that all federal laws be obeyed. "Disunion by armed force is treason," he declared. Jackson also sent Gen. Winfield Scott to Charleston with a warship and several revenue cutters to reinforce the federal garrison there. Because military confrontation seemed likely, Jackson asked Congress to pass a force bill giving him the specific authority to use federal troops to enforce the tariffs. At the same time, Henry Clay, now a senator but always eager to work out a compromise, introduced another tariff law gradually reducing the rates on manufactured goods over ten years. Both bills passed the Congress on March 1 and were signed by the president within twenty-four hours. The Compromise Tariff of 1833 indeed ended the nullification crisis. On March 15, South Carolina (which had received little support from the rest of the South) recalled its Ordinance of Nullification. Then three days later, perhaps merely to save face, the state convention nullified the Force Act. Jackson chose to ignore the gesture; he could afford to, having emerged from the crisis with more power and prestige than ever.

This 1832 election ticket identifies which of the candidates running for seats at South Carolina's special state convention favored nullification.

YET AS SOON AS the nullification crisis passed, another imbroglio consumed the presidency: Jackson's "war" against the Second Bank. Since taking office, Old Hickory had complained that bank president Nicholas Biddle's tight credit policies were obstructing expansion in the West. As the years passed, the criticism escalated until the rechartering of the Second Bank became the central issue of the 1832 presidential campaign. Biddle's bank, Jackson charged, made "the rich richer and the potent more powerful." Why did Jackson hate the national bank so? In part because of his own unpleasant experiences with banks during the panics of 1795 and 1819, but also because his Jeffersonian values led him to distrust the concentrated institutional power of a large national bank. In Jackson's mind, just

In his July 1832 message vetoing a Second Bank recharter bill, Jackson referred to the bank as a "hydra of corruption." This 1836 cartoon shows the president "slaying the many-headed monster" with help from Vice Pres. Martin Van Buren (center).

because the Supreme Court had declared the Second Bank constitutional in *McCulloch v. Maryland*, that didn't make it so.

Quite reasonably, the president considered his reelection a mandate to crush the bank, and that's precisely what he did. "The Bank, Mr. Van Buren, is trying to kill me," he announced during the campaign, *"but I will kill it."* On September 23, 1833, he ordered Treasury Secretary William Duane to remove all federal deposits from the Second Bank. But Duane refused to carry out the order because federal law required him to inform Congress before taking such an action and Congress wasn't in session. So Jackson sacked Duane and replaced him with Attorney General Roger B. Taney. Three days later, without waiting for the recessed Senate to confirm the nomination, Taney began the lengthy and tiresome process of withdrawing the funds. The task ended up taking the entire fall and winter of 1833 to accomplish. Following Jackson's orders, Taney transferred the funds to specially chosen state banks, called the "pet banks" because many were owned by Democrats. In December, when the Senate came back into session, Clay introduced a resolution censuring both Taney and the president. Jackson responded to its passage with a "protest" asserting his right as the sole representative of all the people to direct national policy. In the meantime, Taney (whom Jackson later rewarded with a Supreme Court nomination) continued the transfers.

A man of considerable talent and arrogance, Nicholas Biddle liked to boast that he wielded, as president of the Second Bank, more power than the president of the country.

Biddle counterattacked. He stopped issuing new loans and called in many that were outstanding. This produced an immediate economic downturn, which Biddle monitored with apparent satisfaction. "Nothing but the evidence of suffering," he wrote, "will produce any effect on Congress." Feeling that Jackson may have finally gone too far, anxious businessmen (including many prominent Democrats) flooded Congress with petitions calling for the rechartering of the Second Bank. Responding to those who pleaded with him personally, Jackson said, "What do you come to me for? Go to Nicholas Biddle. We have no money here, gentlemen. Biddle has all the money." It was, of course, foolish for Biddle to believe that he could break Jackson's will—and in the end, he didn't.

Supporters of the bank felt that their best strategy was to build a veto-proof coalition in Congress by backing like-minded candidates in the 1834 midterm elections. (They already had majorities in both the House and Senate, but Jackson had vetoed one bank bill in July 1832 and would undoubtedly veto others.) With the National Republican party in disarray, the probank

JACKSON'S INDIAN POLICY

AS A GENERAL, Jackson subjugated the tribes of the Southeast; as president, he evicted them. The Indian Removal Act of May 1830 authorized the government to exchange Indian lands in the East for unsettled lands west of the Mississippi. Jackson, however, went far beyond the law in forcing the Five Civilized Tribes (Cherokees, Chickasaws, Choctaws, Creeks, and Seminoles) to resettle in the West.

Resistance to Jackson's Indian policy took two forms: legal and military. During the early nineteenth century, the Cherokees living in Georgia had developed a modern farming society with a written language and an independently elected government. State officials, however, ignored the tribe's 1827 constitution and tried to seize its land for distribution to white settlers. The Cherokees brought suit in federal court, claiming that Georgia had no right to supersede treaties made with the federal government. The Marshall Court agreed and in *Worcester v. Georgia* (1832) declared that state law "can have no force" within Indian boundaries. However, with the complicity of the Jackson administration, Georgia defied the court's ruling and seized the lands anyway. "John Marshall has made his decision," Jackson declared, "now let him enforce it!"

In December 1835, a handful of Cherokees signed the Treaty of New Echota, which purported to exchange the Cherokee land in northwestern Georgia for a five-million-dollar settlement and infertile tracts of the new Indian Territory (later Oklahoma), which Congress had specifically created for the purpose of Indian removal eighteen months earlier. Fifteen

This 1837 portrait of Sequoyah shows the Cherokee holding the alphabet he invented so that his people could write their own spoken language and impress whites with their literacy.

thousand of the sixteen thousand Cherokees signed a petition denouncing the treaty, but the Senate ratified it regardless, and in 1838 federal troops removed the Cherokees to the Indian Territory under armed guard. Because thousands died of starvation, disease, and exposure along the twelve-hundred-mile route, the Cherokees' lamentable winter journey has become known as the Trail of Tears.

The Seminoles in Florida did not submit so easily, however. Led by Osceola and supported by more than a few runaway slaves, the Seminoles actively resisted removal for more than six years. Using Florida's swamps as cover, they waged a guerrilla-style war against the federal troops sent by Jackson to subdue them. In October 1837, however, Osceola was taken prisoner at St. Augustine, where he had been invited to negotiate under a flag of truce. Thereafter, Seminole morale slowly deteriorated, and by early 1842, the war was over.

During the 1830s, the U.S. Army also purged Indians from the states carved out of the old Northwest Territory. The Black Hawk War of 1832 began when displaced Sauks and Foxes tried to reclaim their land in northern Illinois. The war ended in August at a bend in the Bad Axe River, where most of Black Hawk's followers were massacred. This 1833 portrait shows a defeated Black Hawk (right) with his son Whirling Thunder.

consortium founded the Whig party to take its place. The Whigs were primarily former National Republicans, Democrats who had split with the president on one issue or another, southerners alienated by his stance on nullification, and others who personally resented his arrogant conduct of government. When they failed to gain any seats despite the economic hardships of the winter and spring (they even lost a few), even Biddle knew that the Bank War was over.

Money that would have been in circulation at the time the Specie Circular was issued.

The Panic of 1837

THE PRESIDENT'S VICTORY, however, made credit so easy to obtain that the national economy went into overdrive. The government took in so much revenue that the national debt essentially disappeared for the first and only time since the passage of Hamilton's Assumption Bill in 1790. Yet even Jackson realized before too long that the financial system in general and western land speculation in particular were spiraling way out of control. (Between 1832 and 1836, for example, government land sales— mostly to large speculators—shot up from $2.6 million to $24.9 million.) New capital was flowing into the country from Europe, where investors correctly saw the United States as an undeveloped market, but not nearly enough had been invested to sustain the expansion then taking place in the money supply.

To check the excesses in land speculation, Jackson had Treasury Secretary Levi Woodbury issue on July 11, 1836, the Specie Circular. Henceforth, government land could be purchased only with gold or silver coins (specie). This slowed the speculation mania considerably— a little bit too much, in fact—producing a deflationary shock of the sort caused by the Second Bank's credit tightening in 1819. A similar result followed.

Jackson's popularity in 1836 was such that Martin Van Buren, his handpicked successor, had little trouble defeating three regional Whig candidates for the presidency. From nearly the moment he took office in March, however, Van Buren found his administration held hostage to the worst financial panic yet. By May, banks all over the country were suspending specie payments—that is, refusing to exchange hard cash for paper money. Meanwhile, bankruptcy and unemployment rates soared. Believing that the crisis had been caused by banks loaning more money than their reserves justified, Van Buren responded with a bill establishing an independent treasury system to hold and distribute government funds. (Van Buren's system differed from the First and Second Banks in that the new government-managed "subtreasuries" would not conduct private business.) With Whigs and conservative Democrats opposed, however, Van Buren couldn't win congressional approval of the bill until 1840, by which time the worst of the depression was already over.

RIGHT:
This portrait of Martin Van Buren by Daniel Huntington hangs in the New York State Capitol, where Van Buren rose to national prominence as the leader of the Albany Regency.

Remarking on Van Buren's *troubled subtreasury plan, this 1838 cartoon lampoons his political reliance on the retired Andrew Jackson.*

A S VAN BUREN'S FIRST TERM drew to a close, the Whigs marshaled their forces to unseat the Democrats. They had the support of wealthy Americans; Democrats who had abandoned Van Buren now that Jackson was gone from Washington; and nativists, who feared the increasing influx of Catholic immigrants (most of whom voted Democratic). Led by Henry Clay and Daniel Webster, the Whigs argued that the country needed the sort of economic development that only a strong national bank and activist government could provide. They wanted more turnpikes, more canals, more railroads, and more credit. Uniting behind the Hero of Tippecanoe, William Henry Harrison, the Whigs blamed the Democrats for the recent depression and ridiculed President Van Buren for his dandiness in manner and dress. Their own candidate they marketed as a Jacksonian clone: westerner, military hero, man of the people.

In a campaign that marked the birth of modern electioneering, Harrison won rather handily, and it seemed as though the Whig party might finally have arrived. Even those Whig leaders who had been bypassed for the presidency had cause for satisfaction: Webster became secretary of state, Clay expected to run the country from the Senate, and Harrison was reluctant to make trouble. Then, just a month after his inauguration, President Harrison died, the first to expire while in office. Vice Pres. John Tyler, once a Democratic senator from Virginia, became the tenth president. Tyler had been placed on the ticket with Harrison merely to attract the votes of southern states' righters. As a result, he had no particular loyalty either to Webster or Clay. Almost immediately, he made trouble.

This photograph of John Tyler was taken during the early 1850s, a decade after his term in the White House.

ECAUSE NO PRESIDENT HAD EVER DIED in office before, Tyler's legitimacy was in question. Furthermore, the Whig leadership had an interest in keeping his status low, so they began addressing him as "Vice President Tyler, Acting as President." A much shrewder man than Harrison, Tyler resisted and from the start demanded that he be "President," even to the point of refusing to open mail addressed to "Acting President Tyler." At the first cabinet meeting following Harrison's death, the Whig appointees pressed him to agree not to take any significant actions without obtaining their consent first—a proposal that Tyler immediately dismissed. "I am very glad to have in my Cabinet such able statesmen as you," he said. "But I can never consent to being dictated to as to what I shall or shall not do.... I am the President.... When you think otherwise, your resignations will be accepted." On September 11, 1841, two days after Tyler's veto of the Whig banking bill, the cabinet did resign (all but Daniel Webster, who delayed resigning until he had completed the negotiations with Great Britain that resulted in the 1842 Webster-Ashburton Treaty settling the eastern Canadian border and leaving only the Oregon Country in dispute).

Wᴹ H. HARRISON, OUR BRAVE DEFENDER.

J. PIERSON.

The songs, rallies, and torchlight parades that dominated the populist Harrison campaign largely drowned out the political issues. "We have taught them to beat us," a veteran Democratic politician remarked bleakly. Because of all the electioneering, an unprecedented number of Americans cast ballots in 1840— slightly more than 80 percent of those eligible to vote.

AT RIGHT:

Jackson's personal servant Alfred poses in front of his late master's tomb.

The Slavery Question

ONE OF THE THINGS that made Tyler's presidency so unusual was that, after September 1841, he operated without the backing of a major political party. The Whigs formally expelled him, and the Democrats didn't want him back, either. So he had little domestic influence. In foreign affairs, however, the president has much greater freedom to act unilaterally, and Tyler concentrated his efforts there. He devoted what remained of his "accidental" presidency to annexing Texas, a goal he accomplished in late February 1845, just a week before leaving office. Tyler's achievement showed what a president could do, even a president without a party, but it came at a cost: the fragile sectional truce with regard to slavery.

Back in 1827, acting as an agent of Andrew Jackson, Martin Van Buren had traveled to Virginia to meet with the so-called Richmond Junto, the political machine that controlled the state much as Van Buren's own Albany Regency controlled New York. What Van Buren proposed was that New York and Virginia form a North-South alliance to defeat not only John Quincy Adams but also his (and Clay's) activist ambitions for the federal government. The election of Jackson, Van Buren pointed out, would accomplish both these goals because Old Hickory, though not a states' rights extremist, favored a limited national government and owned nearly a hundred slaves himself. Furthermore, Van Buren endorsed the idea of keeping slavery out of national politics.

That agreement held for nearly two decades, but as the Age of Jackson ended, the Democratic coalition began to disintegrate. Southern Democrats, angered by the party's opposition to Texas annexation, became more introverted, while northerners began to complain that the party's leadership was much too tolerant of the slave trade, especially the buying and selling of human beings in the nation's capital. This divisiveness cost Van Buren the 1840 election, and that was only the beginning.

8

SLAVERY IN THE ANTEBELLUM SOUTH

Nat Turner's Revolt

IN THE DEEP WOODS of Southampton County, Virginia, six black men sat around a campfire, roasting a pig and drinking stolen apple brandy. The year was 1831, and the men were all slaves. They had arrived at the meeting place near Cabin Pond about noon on Sunday, August 21, and waited. Toward midafternoon, another slave emerged suddenly from the surrounding trees and entered the clearing. Thirty-year-old Nat Turner was not a large man—he stood just five feet seven inches tall and weighed only 150 pounds—but his work as a field hand for Joseph Travis had made him strong, and his fierce, deep-set eyes gave him an imposing, brooding countenance.

Nat's mother, Nancy, had been enslaved in Africa during the mid-1790s, then shipped to the United States aboard a European slave transport and sold to Benjamin Turner of Southampton County in 1799. About a year later—on October 2, 1800—she gave birth to a son, Nathaniel. Immediately, Nat also became the property of Benjamin Turner and took Turner's last name. (Slaves throughout the South were generally known by the surnames of their masters; when they changed masters, they changed surnames as well.)

As a boy, Nat Turner showed himself to be an exceptionally quick learner, and he easily stood out among the other children, both black

AT LEFT: *This 1862 photograph taken on Smith's Plantation in Beaufort, South Carolina, shows five generations of a single slave family—an unusual occurrence because slaveholders rarely kept slave families together.*

and white. By age three or four, he later recalled, he already felt as though God had singled him out "for some great purpose." He thought he would surely "be a prophet," and his parents encouraged this self-esteem, remarkable in a slave child, by offering him great praise and affection. So did his master, Benjamin Turner, who must have helped young Nat learn to read and write because his own parents almost certainly did not know how. Nat's literacy, also apparent at an early age, made him "a source of wonder," he said, in the local community.

IMPRESSED BY and proud of the boy's accomplishments, Benjamin Turner encouraged him to study the Bible, took him along to Methodist prayer meetings, and often showed off Nat's abilities to his guests. In October 1810, however, Benjamin Turner died, and Nat became the property of Turner's oldest son, Samuel, who had little interest in developing the slave's obvious intellectual gifts. Two years later, when Nat turned twelve (the age when slave children were typically put to work), Samuel Turner sent Nat into the cotton fields.

Although he had much less time now for study and prayer, Nat still maintained the religious focus that Benjamin Turner had given him; in 1825, he began having apocalyptic visions in which black and white spirits engaged in battle "and blood flowed in streams." Certain that Judgment Day was soon approaching, Nat began preaching at "praise meetings," which local slaves held on the Sabbath with the consent of their white masters. According to the few accounts that have survived, Nat Turner seems to have been as mesmerizing as he was mysterious.

Nat's fellow slaves considered him aloof and puzzling, and whites knew even less what to make of him. Most regarded him with a mixture of humor, curiosity, disdain, and respect. He was known around the county as "the smart nigger," and many whites in Southampton even knew his name. After Samuel Turner's death in 1822, Nat became the chattel first of Thomas Moore and then of Joseph Travis, yet he was allowed in both instances to keep the surname Turner—a rare privilege for a slave. Not one of the men waiting for Nat in the woods that Sunday in 1831, for example, had his own last name.

THE ROLE OF RELIGION

IN THE ANTEBELLUM SOUTH, religion—and the Bible, in particular—played important roles in the ideologies of both master and slave. According to the whites' rather selective interpretation of the Scripture, God wanted slaves to accept their lot and be meek and faithful, even should their masters be cruel to them (in which case it was still the Lord's place to punish the masters). At the slaves' praise meetings, however, Nat Turner and other black preachers presented a different version of Christianity. They typically cast the slaves as Israelites, and their sermons emphasized both the evils of enslavement and the certainty of a future deliverance from bondage. It was faith in this righteous Old Testament God that gave many slaves the strength they needed to endure their suffering. Some slaves, of course, were unwilling to wait for a heavenly reward, and they transformed their religious zeal into a motivation for resistance.

Mrs. Juliann Jane Tillman, *a minister of the African Methodist Episcopal Church in Philadelphia, exhorts her congregation to prepare for the Second Coming in this 1844 portrait from life.*

Nat's Millennial Vision

NAT TURNER HAD CALLED SAM, Nelson, Hark, Henry, Jack, and Will together so that they could share a last meal while planning the final details of the great deed that God intended Nat to accomplish: the destruction of the whites. The turning point for Nat had come on May 12, 1828, when he experienced his most apocalyptic vision yet. "I heard a loud noise in the heavens," he said later, at which point God appeared and told Nat that "the time was fast approaching when the first should be last and the last should be first." Signs would follow, God promised him, whereupon "I should arise and prepare myself, and slay my enemies with their own weapons." And such a sign did eventually come: In February 1831, the moon eclipsed the sun. That same month, Turner revealed his purpose to the Chosen Four—Hark, Henry, Nelson, and Sam. With their help, he began spreading disaffection as best he could throughout Southampton's slave community. Toward the local whites, however, he appeared just as he always had: submissive and uncomplaining, if a bit eccentric.

During the next six months, Turner and the Chosen Four gathered easily at praise meetings to make plans for their revolt. (By keeping his group small, Nat avoided the leaks that had exposed earlier slave conspiracies led by Gabriel Prosser and Denmark Vesey.) Nat's plans remained vague, however, and he later admitted to having had some second thoughts. He'd always been an extremely pious man, eschewing even petty thievery, and he wasn't altogether sure that he could go through with the killings. The whites he had marked for execution weren't faceless strangers but people he'd known all his life, many of whom had shown him kindness. Even Joseph Travis was, according to Nat, "a kind master [who] placed the greatest confidence in me; in fact, I had no cause to complain of his treatment to me."

SLAVE UPRISINGS

SLAVEHOLDERS HAD ALWAYS been aware of the potential for rebellion, but it wasn't until the successful 1791 revolt on St. Domingue (Haiti) that southerners really began to take seriously the possibility that uprisings could happen to them. Whites were particularly unnerved when, in August 1800, they uncovered a plot in Richmond possibly including up to eleven hundred slaves. Eager to save their master, two of those slaves (house servants) had betrayed the plot, which had been organized primarily by skilled urban slaves politicized by the rhetoric of the American Revolution and inspired by the example of Toussaint-Louverture. Their leader, Gabriel Prosser, a slave blacksmith and self-taught preacher, spread the word through praise meetings and other religious functions. He planned to burn down Richmond and take Gov. James Monroe prisoner while sparing Quakers, Methodists, and others who had opposed slavery.

The second major insurrection conspiracy that Nat Turner would have known about through the slave grapevine was the Denmark Vesey plot of May 1822. A free black carpenter living in Charleston, South Carolina, Vesey was a former slave who had bought his freedom by working odd jobs and keeping a portion of the proceeds. (He still had several wives and many children in bondage, however.) Like Prosser, Vesey was a compulsive reader, and he became particularly obsessed with the transcripts of Congress's debate over the Missouri Compromise, especially the portions relating to slavery. His scheme—which involved perhaps nine thousand blacks, slave and free, from both city and countryside—also used religious meetings as cover and was revealed by a frightened house slave.

Insurrection plots were especially feared in the South Carolina low country, where slaves substantially outnumbered whites. Thus the response to the Vesey plot was swift and persuasive. The white authorities immediately arrested 135 people, of whom 36 (including Vesey) were hanged. Moreover, the state legislature passed laws criminalizing the education of slaves and requiring all free blacks to have "respectable" white guardians.

But on Saturday, August 13, 1831, Nat received another sign. Along the eastern seaboard from Charleston to New York City, Americans watched in awe as an atmospheric disturbance caused the sun to dim and change hue from yellow to green to blue to white. Finally, a black spot crossed the sun's surface. From his vantage point on the Travis farm, Nat thought the spot looked like a black hand. Later, he told his four lieutenants that "as the black spot passed over the sun, so shall the blacks pass over the earth."

During the next week, a specific plan emerged in Nat's mind. His group would strike on the coming Sunday night, because whites in Southampton County typically spent their summer Sundays visiting, eating, and drinking, so they would be sluggish. Furthermore, because slaves were also relieved from their work on the Sabbath, he and his men wouldn't be missed until Monday morning. Although his cabal remained quite small, Nat was confident that, once the insurrection began, other slaves and free blacks would rally to his cause. With blacks outnumbering whites in Southampton County by two to one, the local demographics certainly favored him, but his planning seemed to begin and end with the seizure of Jerusalem, the county seat. Some historians have speculated that Turner may have intended to fight his way into the Great Dismal Swamp, some twenty miles to the east and long a haven for fugitive slaves. Once safely inside, he could perhaps have established a base from which to conduct raids into Virginia and North Carolina in imitation of the Florida Seminoles. Others believe that Nat expected God to guide him once the insurrection began. No one knows for sure.

WHEN NAT TURNER SAT down beside the campfire on that late August midafternoon, he began staring at Jack and Will, the two new recruits. Nat knew and trusted Jack because he was Hark's brother-in-law, but Will was another matter because of his obvious penchant for brutality. "How come you here?" Turner demanded. Will replied that his life was worth no more than the others' and that his liberty was just as dear to him. "I asked him if he thought to obtain his freedom," Turner went on. "He said he would, or lose his life." Brutality not being unwelcome in a revolt, Nat let him stay.

Then, at sunset, after reviewing their plans and finishing their meal, the seven slaves left the woods and passed through several tobacco fields before entering the clearing in which stood the large frame house belonging to Joseph Travis. At this point, according to Turner's account, an eighth slave named Austin joined them, and "they all went to the cider press and drank, except myself."

Sometime after midnight, the group gathered again before the Travis home. Nat climbed in through a window, unbarred the doors, and gave his men the guns he found inside. The others then insisted that Nat "spill the first blood." Accompanied by Will, he entered Joseph Travis's bedroom and swung a hatchet at his sleeping master. The blade, however, merely grazed Travis's skull, causing him to jump out of bed calling for his wife. "It was his last word," according to Turner. "Will laid him dead with a blow of his axe, and Mrs. Travis shared the same fate, as she lay in bed." A fourteen-year-old apprentice and the family's two children were also killed as they slept. With these murders began the bloodiest slave revolt in the history of the United States.

This crude sketch of Nat Turner accompanied an early edition of his Confessions.

Southampton County

A detail from an 1826 map of Virginia showing Southampton County and its environs. During the early nineteenth century, southeastern Virginia was an important agricultural region with several large cotton plantations and numerous smaller farms employing slave labor.

The Origin of Slavery in the South

WITH THE WISDOM OF HINDSIGHT, we can see that legislative negotiations were never going to solve the many complex social and economic problems caused by slavery in the antebellum (pre–Civil War) South. After all, whites had already been wrestling with the question of how best to incorporate black people into American society for more than two hundred years, with little measurable progress.

It's difficult to date the exact beginning of black slavery in English North America because the first "20 negars" who arrived in Jamestown in 1619, sold to the Virginians by Dutch sailors, may not have been slaves at all but merely indentured servants. After 1660, however, the House of Burgesses ended whatever brief period of legal equality may have existed for blacks with a series of laws that degraded them and imposed a policy of permanent enslavement. In 1662, for example, the Virginia colonial legislature discarded an English common-law precedent that granted children the status of their fathers and, in light of the increasing number of children being born to slave mothers and white fathers, declared that all children born in Virginia would henceforth take on the status of their mothers. Seven years later, "An Act About the Casuall Killing of Slaves" made it legal for either masters or overseers to kill slaves for resisting punishment "since it cannot be presumed that...malice should induce any man to destroy his own estate."

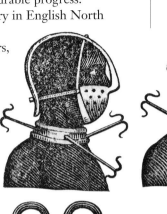

In addition to whatever racism existed, there were more important economic forces promoting African slavery in late-seventeenth-century Virginia. Early in the colony's history, when mortality rates were high, few planters saw much economic sense in buying a slave who would probably die sooner rather than later when a poor white could be hired as an indentured servant with much less risk. However, several factors gradually changed the terms of this equation: Public health stabilized, the English economy improved (reducing the number of unemployed whites willing to emigrate), and increased trade lowered the price of slaves considerably. By 1700, it was foolish for planters *not* to buy African slaves, whose labor they would own for life. The tobacco, rice, and cotton crops being grown in the plantation colonies required vast amounts of toil, and the white landowners were themselves certainly not willing to perform the backbreaking work, which is why the seemingly inexhaustible supply of enslaved Africans seemed a godsend.

Meanwhile, the same rhetoric that wealthy Englishmen once used to disparage the "natural" inferiority of the peasantry was now applied to blacks by white Virginians of all classes. Even poor tenant farmers who had no hope of ever owning a slave themselves came to feel that they had a stake in the South's "peculiar institution" because of the psychological comfort it gave them to know that at least they were superior to blacks. Chief Justice Roger B. Taney gave voice to this attitude when he declared famously in his 1857 *Dred Scott* decision that blacks had "no rights which the white man was bound to respect." In other words, even the basest, least worthy white ranked higher in southern society than the brightest, most noble black.

Slaveholders used *Iron masks and shackles of the type shown in this 1807 book illustration to restrict the movements of disobedient slaves. Because nearly all southern (and most northern) whites believed unquestionably in the inferiority of blacks, it seemed reasonable to employ these items of hardware despite their brutality.*

THE TRIANGULAR TRADE

TRIANGULAR TRADE IS THE SIMPLIFIED name that historians have given the trading patterns that prevailed among the American colonies, the British West Indies, Great Britain, and the African coast during the seventeenth and eighteenth centuries. There were, in fact, many profitable trade "triangles." One important route began in New England, where American ships loaded their holds with foodstuffs bound for the West Indies. These provisions were exchanged for sugar, which the New Englanders carried on to Britain and exchanged for manufactured goods, which were then carried home. Another triangle originating in New England involved the shipment of simple, domestically manufactured goods to West Africa, where they were exchanged for slaves that were traded in the West Indies for molasses, which was later sold at home to make rum. Additional commodities involved in other aspects of the triangular trade included ivory and silver from West Africa, coffee and cacao from the West

*The **hold** of a mid-eighteenth-century Spanish slave ship, as depicted by a British naval officer.*

Indies, firearms and furniture from Great Britain, and tobacco and timber from the colonies.

The voyage from Africa to the West Indies was known as the Middle Passage. Most of the early ships that made this trip had three decks, the lower two of which were used to hold slaves. On the lowest deck, usually no more than five feet high, slaves were forced to lie prone, side by side, to maximize the available space. On the middle deck, slaves (often shackled in pairs) were stacked vertically on shelves that extended from the sides of the boat. The mortality rate of slaves making the Middle Passage has been estimated at 15 to 20 percent. During the 1700s, some English merchants began building ships specifically designed to carry slaves (as part of yet another triangle) from Africa to the American colonies. These ships were long, narrow, and fast, and they could hold four hundred slaves, or twice the number of an ordinary cargo ship.

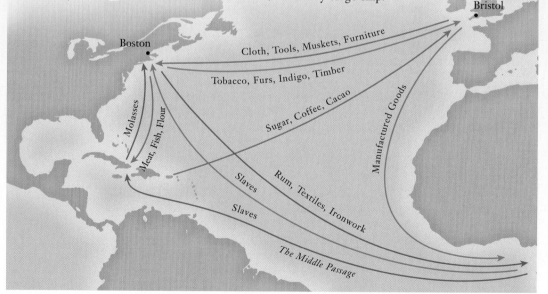

*With **Pres. Thomas Jefferson's** encouragement, Congress banned the foreign slave trade beginning January 1, 1808, the earliest date permissible under the Constitution.*

SLAVES WERE UNDERSTANDABLY of a different mind, especially after 1776. The Declaration of Independence had proudly asserted that "all men are created equal," yet slaves found it equally "self-evident" that all men were not treated so. Thus the egalitarian values of the American Revolution stimulated the first significant antislavery activism. As early as 1774, Connecticut, Rhode Island, and Massachusetts passed laws prohibiting the importation of slaves, and the First Continental Congress included a similar ban in its proposed boycott of British commerce. Then, on April 14, 1775, just a week before the battles of Lexington and Concord, a group of Quakers in Philadelphia founded the Pennsylvania Society for the Abolition of Slavery, the first antislavery society in North America. Later, states such as New York and Rhode Island compensated masters who freed their slaves to fight with the Continental Army, and many others (including Virginia) simply offered all slaves who enlisted their freedom.

At the height of the Revolution, the United States contained about half a million slaves. Every colony had at least some, but the great majority were held in the tidewater. Nearly 40 percent lived in Virginia alone, and about 85 percent lived in either Virginia, the Carolinas, or Maryland. In comparison, New York, the largest slave state in the North, had just about twenty-five thousand slaves, or 5 percent of the total; Pennsylvanians held only six thousand slaves. With so few slaves, it was relatively easy for northern states to end slavery within their borders. In March 1780, Pennsylvania passed a gradual emancipation law that freed the offspring of slaves once they reached their twenty-eighth birthday; three years later, the Massachusetts Supreme Court declared slavery illegal under the state's 1780 Declaration of Rights; and before the Constitutional Convention met in Philadelphia in 1787, Connecticut, Rhode Island, New York, and New Jersey all passed laws either abolishing slavery outright or providing for its gradual elimination. Even the Northwest Ordinance of 1787 prohibited, at Thomas Jefferson's direction, slavery in the Northwest Territory.

In this engraving from The American Slave Trade *(1822), a runaway slave jumps from a high window rather than be recaptured.*

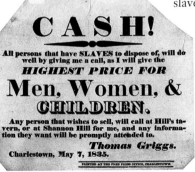

CASH!

All persons that have **SLAVES** to dispose of, will do well by giving me a call, as I will give the

HIGHEST PRICE FOR

Men, Women, & CHILDREN.

Any person that wishes to sell, will call at Hill's tavern, or at Shannon Hill for me, and any information they want will be promptly attended to.

Thomas Griggs.

Charlestown, May 7, 1835.

PRINTED AT THE FREE PRESS OFFICE, CHARLESTOWN.

King Cotton

IN THE SOUTH, however, the situation was radically different: The overall population was 35 percent black (as compared to 4 percent in the North), and nearly all of these people were slaves (whereas in the North, nearly half were free blacks). What would happen to southern society if all of those slaves were freed? Southerners shuddered at the thought. Even moderate whites who favored gradual emancipation were not prepared to accept a large free black population living among them and assumed that freed slaves would have to be "colonized" elsewhere. The other issue affecting emancipation, of course, was that, at the turn of the nineteenth century, slavery became much more profitable.

During the colonial period, the major southern cash crops were tobacco, rice, indigo, and (to a much lesser extent) cotton. The problem with cotton was its seeds, which had to be picked out by hand—a costly process, even when

LEFT: *With the end of the foreign slave trade in 1808, domestic trafficking in slaves picked up considerably.*

This Currier & Ives lithograph shows a cotton plantation on the Mississippi River. During the nineteenth century, the prosperity that cotton brought to the states of the Deep South drew population away from the older seaboard states of Virginia, Georgia, and the Carolinas.

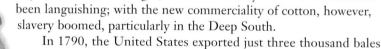

performed by slaves. In 1793, however, Eli Whitney patented the cotton gin (short for *engine*), which removed the seeds mechanically, thus permitting one slave to do the work of fifty. Before the cotton gin, the slave-labor system in the South had been languishing; with the new commerciality of cotton, however, slavery boomed, particularly in the Deep South.

In 1790, the United States exported just three thousand bales of cotton. By 1831, the year of Nat Turner's Revolt, that number had surged to eight hundred thousand bales. In 1860, U.S. cotton exports exceeded five million bales, and cotton accounted for nearly two-thirds of all U.S. foreign trade. During this period, the American South became the world's leading cotton producer.

Even more important than the old cotton states of Georgia and South Carolina were the new cotton lands in Alabama, Mississippi, Louisiana, Texas, and Arkansas. Between 1810 and 1850, even though Congress had banned foreign imports beginning in 1808, the number of slaves in the United States jumped from 1.2 million to 3.2 million. Slavery's center of gravity also shifted during this same period from Virginia, where tobacco production had leveled off, to the Deep South, where the demand for slaves to work on new cotton plantations was great and growing. Of the 3.2 million slaves counted in the 1850 census, 1.8 million were engaged in cotton production, while just 350,000 grew tobacco.

The original patent drawing for Eli Whitney's cotton gin.

THE CONDITIONS UNDER which these slaves lived varied considerably. In Virginia, for example, slavery was rather genteel compared to the oppressive conditions that existed on cotton plantations in the Deep South. Because slaves were valuable property, masters seldom abused them so cruelly that they died; yet for all practical purposes, a master could treat his slaves as poorly as he pleased with little to fear from the law or his neighbors. Some masters subjected their slaves to horrific degradation; even so, as southern politicians were quick to point out, the lot of many slaves compared favorably with that of common laborers in the urban industrial Northeast. Almost every plantation slave received a weekly day of rest, for example, and occasionally other holidays as well.

In return—whether out of loyalty, fear, or a combination of reasons—many slaves accepted their servitude. For example, slaves themselves often provided whites with the best information regarding planned uprisings. Both the Prosser and Vesey conspiracies were exposed by slave informants; and trusted, indulged slaves, particularly house servants and skilled artisans, often guarded their relatively privileged status at the expense of other blacks. On the other hand, history has shown time and again that, within an oppressed group, it is often those with privileged status who become the most acutely aware of their oppression and act to end it. So it was with the slave preachers, artisans, house servants, and freed blacks who risked their privileges to join the Prosser, Vesey, and Turner conspiracies.

The Course of the Insurrection

FROM THE TRAVIS FARM, Nat and the others began walking toward Jerusalem, some fifteen miles away. At each house they passed, they took the occupants by surprise, dispatching the whites with blades (because noisy firearms might have alarmed the neighborhood) and recruiting the slaves to their "army." By sunrise on Monday morning, General Nat's band had increased to fifteen, with Turner and eight others mounted on horses.

Sometime after daybreak, Hark led the infantry to the farm of a slaveholding family named Bryant, while Nat and the cavalry rode on to the Whitehead plantation. As the other whites had been, the members of the Whitehead family were slashed repeatedly with various knives and hatchets until they were dead and often decapitated as well. Richard Whitehead was overseeing some slaves in a cotton patch when Nat's horsemen called him over for a chat. What did they want? Whitehead asked suspiciously. Will answered with a windmill of ax blows. Here, too, Nat killed Richard's sister Margaret, who had attempted to conceal herself under a cellar cap between two chimneys. It was the only murder that Turner ever admitted to committing personally. "On my approach," he remembered, "she fled, but was soon overtaken, and after repeated blows with a sword, I killed her by a blow on the head, with a fence rail."

When Hark later returned with the footmen, having slain the family of Henry Bryant, the mutinous slaves resumed their march toward Jerusalem. Several more times Turner divided his soldiers to assault the homes of slaveholding families scattered before them. When Nat reached the home of Richard Porter, however, he found that the Porter family had fled. "I understood there," he later explained, "that the alarm had already spread."

Jerusalem had indeed been roused, and express riders were already on their way to neighboring counties with requests for help. One such rider carried a letter to the governor at Richmond, seventy miles away. Wild rumors spread nearly as fast, one claiming that well-armed rebels, supplied by northern abolitionists, were

The southern judicial system rarely imposed more than minor penalties on masters who deliberately injured or killed their slaves. Even had slaves been permitted to testify in court (not even free blacks could), the law still allowed slaveholders in most cases to whip and beat their property as they saw fit.

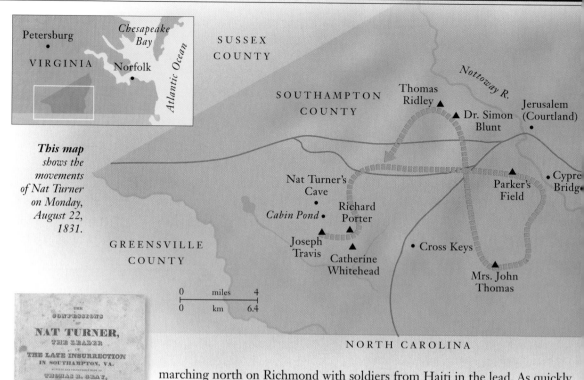

VIRGINIA
Petersburg
Chesapeake Bay
Norfolk
Atlantic Ocean

SUSSEX COUNTY

Nottoway R.

SOUTHAMPTON COUNTY

Thomas Ridley ▲

▲ Dr. Simon Blunt

Jerusalem (Courtland) •

This map shows the movements of Nat Turner on Monday, August 22, 1831.

Nat Turner's Cave •

Cabin Pond •

Richard Porter •

Parker's Field ▲

• Cypre Bridg

Joseph Travis ▲

Catherine Whitehead ▲

• Cross Keys

GREENSVILLE COUNTY

Mrs. John Thomas ▲

| 0 | miles | 4 |
| 0 | km | 6.4 |

NORTH CAROLINA

The primary source for all quotations attributed to Nat Turner is The Confessions of Nat Turner *(1831), a transcript of Turner's discussions with lawyer Thomas R. Gray, who was sufficiently impressed by his client's eloquence to record what he said. "For natural intelligence and quickness of apprehension," Gray wrote, Turner "is surpassed by few men I have ever seen."*

marching north on Richmond with soldiers from Haiti in the lead. As quickly as he could, Gov. John Floyd called up the state militia, but by the time the first companies arrived in Southampton County, the uprising was largely over, crushed by local whites.

WHEN HE FOUND Porter's family missing, Nat Turner realized the importance of moving as quickly as possible to seize Jerusalem. He ordered the men on horseback to ride ahead, killing whomever they met, while Turner himself remained in the rear, directing the foot soldiers. While his advance party murdered all the whites it could find, Nat concentrated on recruiting more slaves to his force, which eventually grew to about seventy, including several free blacks. According to Turner, by the time the rebels reached the Barrow Road, they were "all mounted and armed with guns, axes, swords, and clubs."

About noon, Turner's army, moving along the Barrow Road, reached its intersection with the Jerusalem highway, about three miles from the town. So far, the insurgents had sacked fifteen homes and killed about sixty whites. Now Nat Turner returned to the head of the column and ordered it on to Jerusalem. However, about half a mile down the road, he reluctantly allowed some of his men to stop by the farm of James Parker, where they had relatives who might join the uprising. When these men failed to return promptly, Turner went down to the Parker place himself and found them boozing it up in the main house. He ordered the men back to the road, but before they could reach Jerusalem, they were attacked by a party of eighteen armed whites under the command of Alexander Peete, a local militia captain.

At the first shot, Peete's horse stampeded, giving the more numerous blacks an advantage. But the poor quality of the firearms they had stolen, their lack of discipline, and the generally drunken condition of many of Nat's men allowed Peete's equally hapless band to hold out long enough for militia reinforcements to arrive. These truly well-armed units drove the insurgents back in disorder, and Turner's band scattered into the woods. Nat himself escaped on horseback with some sixteen others, many of whom were wounded. Undaunted, he led this group back along a little-known trail to Cypress Bridge, which he planned to cross so that he could take Jerusalem by surprise from the rear. Nat was forced to give up this plan when he found the bridge well guarded by whites.

Instead, he headed south to Cross Keys, where he hoped to gather new recruits. After reaching the abandoned farm of Mrs. John Thomas, however, he turned north again and headed for the plantation of Thomas Ridley, one of the largest in the county with 145 slaves. Arriving at dusk, Turner found the main buildings bristling with militia, so he camped for the night in the woods with about forty men. In the middle of the night, some of his pickets panicked and raised a false alarm. The resulting confusion caused about half of the slaves to desert.

The next morning, Turner and the twenty followers he had left proceeded to the nearby plantation of Dr. Simon Blunt, where they were ambushed. More of Turner's men were killed, and the rest fled in complete disarray. Nat spent Tuesday night in the woods while parties of militiamen patrolled the roads and better-traveled forest paths, rounding up rebels. Two days after the Turner Revolt began, it was over, though Nat himself remained at large for nearly two months.

The Reaction

THE SLAVES AND FREE BLACKS who joined Nat Turner killed fewer than five dozen whites, but they could have killed five thousand for all the psychological damage they caused. Fearful that Turner's example would inspire rebellious slaves elsewhere, whites took their revenge in a conspicuously barbaric manner. A century and a half earlier, Nathaniel Bacon's men, having failed to find any marauding Indians, consoled themselves with the slaughter of peaceful ones. Now, Bacon's heirs in Southampton County behaved just as wantonly: They slaughtered dozens of blacks, apparently without bothering to determine whether or not their victims had actually participated in the insurrection. The indiscriminate killing became so offensive to Brig. Gen. Richard Eppes, leader of the state militia forces sent by Floyd to Southampton County, that he issued an order on August 28 threatening to shoot any soldier caught committing "acts of barbarity and cruelty" against local blacks.

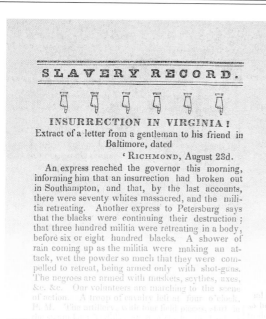

SLAVERY RECORD.

INSURRECTION IN VIRGINIA!
Extract of a letter from a gentleman to his friend in Baltimore, dated

'RICHMOND, August 23d.

An express reached the governor this morning, informing him that an insurrection had broken out in Southampton, and that, by the last accounts, there were seventy whites massacred, and the militia retreating. Another express to Petersburg says that the blacks were continuing their destruction: that three hundred militia were retreating in a body, before six or eight hundred blacks. A shower of rain coming up as the militia were making an attack, wet the powder so much that they were compelled to retreat, being armed only with shot-guns. The negroes are armed with muskets, scythes, axes, &c. &c. Our volunteers are marching to the scene of action. A troop of cavalry left at four o'clock, P. M. The artillery, with four field pieces, start in an hour

William Lloyd Garrison published this account of Nat Turner's Revolt in The Liberator.

Gov. John Floyd became so obsessed with the Jerusalem trials and various rumors of other slave conspiracies that his diary entries for late 1831 mention little else.

Southern state legislators responded to the revolt by further limiting the already restricted condition of slaves. The Virginia legislature showed that it had learned what the *Richmond Enquirer* called the "lesson" of Southampton County—that "no black man ought to be permitted to become a preacher"—by passing a law banning "any assembly or meeting, for religious or other purposes" held by slaves or free blacks. Henceforth, all preachers would be white, and slaves could attend church services only in the company of their masters. Other new laws prohibited free blacks from carrying weapons, increased the criminal penalties for black-on-white violence, prohibited the sale of liquor to slaves, and permitted the whipping of any black who expressed "seditious" thoughts. Similar laws were passed in other southern states as well. All southern whites were worried.

While Nat Turner remained free, hiding in a hole he dug for himself not far from Cabin Pond, forty-nine others, including five free blacks, were brought to trial in Jerusalem. Thirty of these defendants (including one of the free blacks) were sentenced to be hanged, although ten later had their sentences commuted by Governor Floyd from death to banishment, presumably to cotton plantations in the Deep South (where Virginians typically sent their defiant slaves as punishment). The rest of those accused were acquitted, which may seem remarkable until one considers that the state of Virginia was legally obligated to compensate masters for any slaves put to death. The wholesale hanging of forty-four slaves would have been a costly proposition indeed. The court valued Hark alone at $450.

THE FIRST DEFENDANT was put on trial September 8, and by October 1, the last of the hangings (with the exception of Nat's and one other) was over. Throughout this period, recognizing that his political future was at stake, Governor Floyd remained actively involved in the resolution of the uprising. He insisted that each court transcript be certified by the county sheriff and sent to him in Richmond so that he could study it personally and assure himself that the trials were being conducted fairly.

Why would a southern governor show such concern for blacks who might have been unjustly accused? The answer is that Floyd, although an admirer and political ally of John C. Calhoun, disagreed with Calhoun when it came to slavery. Along with a significant number of whites in 1831 Virginia—enough to get him elected governor—Floyd opposed slavery on economic grounds, considering it wasteful, and favored gradual emancipation for the good of white Virginia. (Yet Floyd, at the same time, had trouble containing his fury at the northern abolitionists whose pamphlets, he believed, provoked slave rebellions such as Turner's in the South.) As for Nat Turner, he was finally captured on October 30, tried on November 5, and hanged on November 11 from the gnarled old tree that served as the county's gallows. A large crowd gathered to witness the execution. The county sheriff offered Turner a chance to address the crowd if he wanted, but Nat said only, "I'm ready." As the sheriff placed the noose around his neck, Turner remained silent and composed; and as several whites hoisted him off the ground, "Not a limb nor a muscle was observed to move," reported one eyewitness.

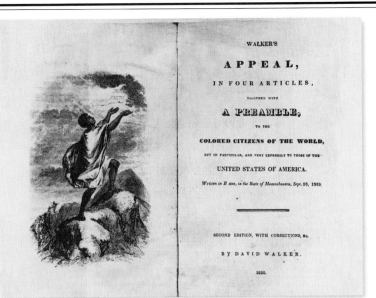

WALKER'S

APPEAL,

IN FOUR ARTICLES,

TOGETHER WITH

A PREAMBLE,

TO THE

COLORED CITIZENS OF THE WORLD,

BUT IN PARTICULAR, AND VERY EXPRESSLY TO THOSE OF THE

UNITED STATES OF AMERICA.

Written in B ston, in the State of Massachusetts, Sept. 28, 1829.

SECOND EDITION, WITH CORRECTIONS, &c.

BY DAVID WALKER.

1830.

The Aftermath

AFTER TURNER'S DEATH, southerners shifted their attention from his capture to his motivation. Why had there been a Southampton insurrection in the first place, and how could similar revolts be prevented in the future? Many southerners, John Floyd among them, found their explanation in the growing vitriol of northern abolitionists, which they believed was roiling otherwise placid southern waters. Had not David Walker, a militant free black living in Boston, published a widely distributed 1829 pamphlet calling for exactly the sort of uprising that Turner had led? Earlier in 1831, in response to Walker's *Appeal…to the Colored Citizens of the World*, Virginia and several other states had made it illegal to teach slaves how to read and write. Now that these laws had been shown to be inadequate, more extreme measures seemed to be in order.

Floyd and his allies argued vigorously that the best way to prevent slave revolts in the future was to eliminate slavery altogether and rid Virginia of its blacks. "Before I leave this government," Floyd write in his diary, "I will have contrived to have a law passed gradually abolishing slavery in this state, or at all events to begin the work by prohibiting slavery on the west side of the Blue Ridge Mountains." What Floyd specifically had in mind was freeing slaves after paying their masters compensation and resettling them outside the state so that Virginia could become a whites-only paradise. (Like the proslavery advocates, he had no intention of sharing the state with a large free black population.)

A free black who was well read in history, David Walker traveled widely before writing his Appeal. *The militant pamphlet he produced contained both blazing religious imagery and sincere revolutionary zeal. It explicitly encouraged African Americans to resist slavery and was the abolitionist work most despised by southern whites of the 1830s.*

WHO OWNED SLAVES

THE MASTER-SLAVE RELATIONSHIP certainly had a determinative effect on social and economic structures in the South, yet the reality was that most southerners didn't own slaves—and most of those who did, owned just a few and worked beside them in the fields. In 1860, the total white population of the South was 7 million people, grouped into approximately 1.4 million households. Yet there were just 383,635 slaveholders. In other words, nearly three out of every four white families in the South owned no slaves at all. Of the remainder, only forty-eight thousand slaveholders owned more than twenty slaves (the number widely considered to be the minimum necessary for "planter" status).

COLONIZATION

MOST SOUTHERN SUPPORTERS of gradual emancipation, from Thomas Jefferson to John Floyd, believed also in colonization, which was the name given to the policy of deporting blacks from America for resettlement elsewhere. Many nineteenth-century Americans who were sincerely opposed to slavery nevertheless believed that the two races were indeed incompatible. Therefore, they considered colonization to be the most humane solution to the problem of what to do with the freed slaves. The most famous colonization group, the American Colonization Society, was founded in 1817 by Robert Finley, a Presbyterian minister from New Jersey. Five years later, the group established Monrovia on the west coast of Africa; and over the next four decades, some twelve thousand African Americans were relocated there. (The colony was originally named after President Monroe but later rechristened Liberia.) For many white Americans, colonization was a first step on the path to becoming an active abolitionist; but radicals such as William Lloyd Garrison, after initially embracing the idea, rejected it as a slaveholders' trick to avoid equality for blacks.

This 1830 map shows the colony of Liberia on Africa's west coast. Twelve thousand former slaves were transported there between 1822 and 1861, but the colonization movement never took off, lacking both popular appeal and consistent leadership.

This idealized portrayal of American slavery is one half of an 1841 diptych; the other panel shows the plight of abused "white slaves" working in British factories.

In December 1831, Floyd personally urged the Virginia legislature to end slavery through gradual emancipation; a month later, formal debate began. For three weeks, legislators grappled with the problem of slavery and engaged in the most open and frank dialogue ever conducted on the subject of manumission in the antebellum South. Floyd's allies in the western half of the state, where few whites owned slaves and most resented the fractiousness that slaveholding caused, lobbied hard on his behalf. But the tidewater gentry—in whom most of the state's wealth, power, and prestige were concentrated—chose to block Floyd's plan because they feared it would restructure Virginian society to their disadvantage. Instead, to ensure public safety, the legislature further increased the legal restrictions on blacks.

AFTER 1832, the subject of emancipation was never again raised in Virginia or elsewhere in the South. The nullification crisis of late 1832 and early 1833 grabbed people's attention away from lingering moderate arguments, and most white southerners concerned themselves thereafter with defending slavery against northern attacks. Similarly, before 1832 (and even during the Virginia debate), many southern legislators were willing to accept the description of slavery as a "necessary evil," one that the South had inherited unintentionally, along with its economic system. After 1832, however, proslavery advocates, led by Calhoun, began referring to the institution of slavery as a "positive good"; and moderate whites, feeling themselves oppressed by the Turner Revolt and the growing stridency of abolitionist attacks, simply went along.

Calhoun explained the new morality this way: "Where two races of different origin, and distinguished by color and other physical differences, as well as intellectual, are brought together," he wrote in 1832, "the relation now existing in the slaveholding states between the two is, instead of an evil, a good—a positive good." What Calhoun meant was that blacks, as a race, were suited for bondage because they were intellectually and morally inferior. Therefore, masters were actually *helping* blacks by enslaving them and thereby taking responsibility for their welfare. Moreover, Calhoun pointed out, class distinctions had always existed in human society, and these distinctions—by making the formation of wealth possible—had also enabled human progress and intellectual growth, making slavery a boon to whites as well.

During the 1830s, Calhoun's arguments came to dominate the ideology of the white South, and they persisted through the Civil War and beyond. According to James Henry Hammond, who served as governor of South Carolina during the early 1840s, "In all social systems there must be a class to do the menial duties, to perform the drudgery of life." Otherwise, Hammond continued, "you would not have that other class which leads progress, civilization, and refinement." Around the same time, slavery propagandist George Fitzhugh made the point this way: "Some are born with saddles on their backs, and others booted and spurred to ride them—and the riding does them good." Of course, such attitudes deviated enormously from the basically optimistic, democratic point of view shared by the rest of the country.

The city of Charleston, South Carolina, as it appeared in 1838. A prosperous seaport since colonial times, Charleston was the cultural center of the Old South. Its planters supported concerts, lectures, plays, and libraries when such refinements were unknown elsewhere in the colonies.

The End of Moderation

ALSO DURING THE 1830S, the level of militancy rose dramatically in the South, as whites armed themselves and established slave patrols to police the countryside. By the 1840s, moderates such as John Floyd were no longer viable candidates for public office, and their like was gradually driven from leadership positions with churches, universities, and newspapers. No longer was compensated emancipation considered a fit topic for political discussion.

Although Floyd (who died in 1837) never supported Calhoun's positive-good ideology, the generation of southerners that followed him embraced it wholeheartedly—among them the governor's son, John Buchanan Floyd, who also led Virginia for a time before Pres. James Buchanan made him secretary of war in 1857. Floyd the younger believed so thoroughly in the benevolence of slavery that, before resigning from the Buchanan cabinet in December 1860, he took pains to ensure its persistence by surreptitiously transferring arms from the North to federal arsenals in the South.

William Lloyd Garrison
1805–1879

by Ira Berlin

WILLIAM LLOYD GARRISON hardly seemed a likely choice to become the radical voice of racial equality in nineteenth-century America. Born in 1805 in a provincial Massachusetts seaport more than two decades after the state had abolished human bondage, Garrison had no direct knowledge of slavery and little contact with black people. As a young man, he had leaned heavily toward the Federalist party, known more for its commitment to order and hierarchy than for any endorsement of freedom and equality. Yet on January 1, 1831, with the debut of his radical antislavery newspaper *The Liberator*, Garrison became slavery's most implacable foe. In an inaugural editorial, he declared, "I will be as harsh as truth, and as uncompromising as justice. On this subject, I do not wish to think, or speak, or write with moderation…. I am in earnest—I will not equivocate—I will not excuse—I will not retreat a single inch—AND I WILL BE HEARD."

Garrison became an abolitionist at a time when the antislavery movement had few friends, other than the slaves themselves. Emancipation in the North, begun during the 1780s, remained incomplete nearly half a century later, and the number of slaves in southern states was rapidly growing. Of the few white men and women who did evince an interest in emancipation, nearly all believed that freedom for the slaves could be achieved only through their physical removal to Africa.

During the heyday of colonization, Garrison worked alongside Benjamin Lundy, the Quaker publisher of an irregular antislavery sheet grandly entitled *The Genius of Universal Emancipation*. Traveling with Lundy during the 1820s, Garrison met with numerous influential black leaders who persuaded him that colonization was a slaveholders' trick designed to remove free blacks from the United States and weaken the opposition to slavery. The intense aversion of these men to colonization and their passionate commitment to the nation's founding egalitarian principles touched Garrison deeply. If black people could be free and equal in Africa, he thought, why not in the United States?

The Liberator drew much of its antislavery philosophy from the protests of these black leaders. Apologizing for his previous support of the "pernicious doctrine of gradual abolition"—a belief he now acknowledged to be "full of timidity, injustice, and absurdity"— Garrison demanded instead an immediate end to slavery and the resurrection of the principles of the Declaration of Independence. Condemning slavery as a sin, he unsheathed the moralistic weapons that he would subsequently use in his assault on chattel bondage. There would be no groveling for political favor, with its implicit willingness to compromise—because the immoral nature of slavery did not permit compromise. There would be no call for slaves to rise up and throw off their chains, with its explicit threat of bloodshed— because violence only begot more violence. Instead, there would be a relentless reassertion of the principle of human equality, and a limitless denunciation of the evil that slaveholding represented. Thus Garrison began his crusade against slavery.

The spark that he set in 1831 grew during the next three decades into a blaze that only civil war could extinguish. Yet Garrison's influence did not end with Appomattox. His crusading inspired a tradition of moral agitation that

Garrison posed *for this studio portrait sometime during 1857.*

social activists, from Frederick Douglass to Martin Luther King Jr., have felt proud to continue. Moreover, as the first American to elevate the work of social reform into a viable profession, Garrison made possible the altruistic careers of such men and women as Susan B. Anthony, Jane Addams, and Ralph Nader. William Lloyd Garrison has indeed been heard.

9

SOCIAL REFORM IN ANTEBELLUM AMERICA

The Seneca Falls Convention

A MIDSUMMER AFTERNOON TEA in the upstate village of Waterloo, New York, might ordinarily have been a quiet social occasion—even in 1848, the "year of revolution" in Europe and growing antislavery insurgency in the United States. Yet on this particular Thursday afternoon, July 13, the five women gathered around Jane Hunt's parlor table had the sense they were making history.

Hunt's guests included Lucretia Mott, probably the best-known woman in the American abolitionist movement; Mott's sister Martha Wright; Mary Ann M'Clintock, a Waterloo neighbor; and Elizabeth Cady Stanton, an old friend of Mott's from nearby Seneca Falls. Although Mott's permanent home was in Philadelphia, she traveled often and had been spending the last few weeks visiting fellow Quakers in upstate New York. Earlier that summer, Mott had taken part in a local schism relating to Quaker involvement in nonsectarian antislavery organizations, and she was currently helping Hunt and M'Clintock establish a new meeting of Progressive Friends more committed to abolitionism.

Elizabeth Cady Stanton wasn't a Quaker, but her connection to Mott was equally strong. Eight years earlier, Stanton and her husband, Henry, had traveled on their honeymoon to

AT LEFT: *Lucretia Mott (shown here in a daguerreotype from the early 1850s) helped found the Philadelphia Female Anti-Slavery Society in December 1833 because, at the time, women were excluded from all the major antislavery societies.*

London to attend the 1840 World Anti-Slavery Convention. The Stantons sailed on a ship carrying the bulk of the American delegation, which included Henry Stanton as well as James and Lucretia Mott. During the voyage, the exuberance of the young Mrs. Stanton charmed the middle-aged Mrs. Mott, and the two became fast friends. Later, Mott wrote a letter complimenting the twenty-four-year-old on her "open generous confiding spirit." Meanwhile, Stanton was awed by Mott's self-confidence. Meeting Mott, Stanton later wrote, "seemed to me like meeting a being from some larger planet, to find a woman who dared to question the opinion of Popes, Kings, Synods, Parliaments, with the same freedom that she would criticize an editorial in the *London Times.*"

I NITIALLY DRAWN TO ONE ANOTHER by temperament, the pair later formed what proved to be an historic political alliance. At the time of the London convention, the abolitionist movement was split into two camps on the question of whether women should be allowed to take part on an equal basis with men. This quarrel, of course, reflected the restrictions that society imposed on women in other spheres as well. Although active in almost every progressive cause in antebellum America, women were nevertheless deprived of the same rights that they pursued so diligently for others. For example, American women in 1840 had no political rights to speak of and, except for those living in Mississippi, few civil rights, either.

Although taken in 1869, this photograph of downtown Waterloo, New York, shows a Main Street relatively unchanged since 1848.

Until 1839, when Mississippi passed an unprecedented law granting property rights to married women, no married woman in the United States could own property (even property she had inherited) beyond the control of her husband. American women were also severely limited in their professional and social lives. Although Oberlin College began admitting women in 1837, U.S. graduate schools continued to bar them, and practically all female careers outside the home ended with marriage. Women were expected to keep house and raise children while their husbands interacted with the world on their behalf.

In the late 1830s, however, women active in the antislavery movement began demanding a larger, more active role. This, in turn, forced many men and women to reconsider the wisdom of preventing women from speaking in public before mixed-race and mixed-gender audiences. (Permitting such public scrutiny was a rather revolutionary notion for a society that considered public exposure of any kind tantamount to prostitution.) One faction, led by Lewis Tappan, held that women were more properly suited to the gentler work of prayer and private persuasion, and most of the clergymen in the abolitionist movement agreed. Yet William Lloyd Garrison, Wendell Phillips, Gerrit Smith, Samuel Gridley Howe, and other radical abolitionists countered that denying equal status to women was just as wrong as denying equal status to blacks. In London, the controversy entered a new phase when a floor fight developed over whether or not the American women delegates should be seated. A bitter exchange of views followed, the Tappanites prevailed, and Mrs. Mott was forced to observe the rest of the convention from behind a curtained grille in the upstairs spectators' gallery.

Mott knew from her long experience with social reform movements that even genuinely high-minded men could excuse the most egregious behavior if the victims happened to be women. Yet Stanton's visible anger and disappointment penetrated Mott's jaded perspective; and as the two walked back to their hotel in the evening, reviewing the events of the day, they decided (according to Stanton) that, once they returned to the United States, they would organize a meeting devoted exclusively to the promotion of women's rights. Back home, however, the routine of each woman's life reasserted itself and their enthusiasm flagged until, eventually, the project was forgotten. Mott returned to Philadelphia, where she resumed her enervating speaking and preaching schedule, while Stanton began her married life in Boston, giving birth to the first of her seven children in 1842.

At the time of the 1840 World Anti-Slavery Convention (one of whose sessions is shown here), social activism was just beginning to emerge as a distinct, full-time vocation.

EVEN THOUGH SHE NEGLECTED to pursue the cause of women's rights, Elizabeth Cady Stanton nevertheless found the intellectual life of 1840s Boston exhilarating. With skilled servants to help her run the household, she had plenty of time available for the remarkable goings-on in town. During the 1840s, Boston was a singular hub of intellectual and reform activity, where the likes of Garrison, Ralph Waldo Emerson, Frederick Douglass, Horace Mann, Dorothea Dix, and others routinely held forth. Inspired by their examples, Stanton became active in temperance and antislavery organizations. In 1847, however, Henry moved the family to Seneca Falls, closer to Elizabeth's relatives but far from her sophisticated, cosmopolitan life in Boston. Competent servants were hard to find, and more children demanded more of her attention. Henry was away on business much of the time, leaving Elizabeth feeling generally oppressed. Her status as one of the few educated women in America had largely protected her until now, but in Seneca Falls she finally began to comprehend on a visceral level the plight of the ordinary overworked female majority. In early 1848, Stanton did make time to circulate petitions advocating passage of the New York State Married Women's Property Act—similar to the Mississippi law, it passed in April of that year—but she arrived at Jane Hunt's house as dissatisfied as ever with her lot and eager to experience more.

Elizabeth Cady Stanton, posing here with her sons in 1848, knew many of the legal reformers in Albany because her father was an upstate New York judge.

DOROTHEA DIX
1802–1887

ONE ASPECT OF AMERICAN society that received its first widespread attention during the 1840s was the manner in which Americans treated the mentally ill. In 1841, Boston schoolteacher Dorothea Dix began teaching a Sunday school class in a local jail. What she found was that many mentally ill people were being imprisoned there along with the criminals. Deeply disturbed by their treatment, Dix spent the next eighteen months visiting institutions in Massachusetts supposedly dedicated to the treatment of the mentally ill. She encountered conditions just as deplorable as those in the jails. Inmates, Dix wrote, were "confined in cages, closets, cellars, stalls, and pens, where they were chained naked, beaten with rods, and lashed into obedience." Her 1843 report to the Massachusetts state legislature documented these abuses and more. With the support of Horace Mann and Charles Sumner, Dix fought for public recognition of the problem, and her persistence eventually led to the construction of dedicated mental hospitals in fifteen states where none had existed previously.

Evidently, the reunion with Mott released Stanton's bottled-up emotion. According to her memoirs, "I poured out that day the torrent of my long accumulating discontent, with such vehemence and indignation that I stirred myself, as well as the rest of the party, to do and dare anything." Impulsively, the five women decided to organize at once a women's rights convention of the sort Mott and Stanton had envisioned eight years earlier. That very afternoon, they composed a notice, which they placed in the next day's *Seneca County Courier* and several other regional newspapers. It read:

Martha Wright

Jane Hunt

Mary M'Clintock

> WOMAN'S RIGHTS CONVENTION
>
> *A Convention to discuss the social, civil and religious condition and rights of Woman, will be held in the Wesleyan Chapel, at Seneca Falls, N.Y., on Wednesday and Thursday, the 19th and 20th of July current; commencing at 10 o'clock A.M.*
>
> *During the first day, the meeting will be exclusively for Women, which all are earnestly invited to attend. The public generally are invited to be present on the second day, when* LUCRETIA MOTT, *of Philadelphia, and others both ladies and gentlemen, will address the convention.*

The Declaration of Sentiments

IN AN ACCOUNT THAT Stanton later prepared for the *History of Woman Suffrage* (1881–1886), she emphasized (writing in the third person) how politically naive she and the other women had been: "Having no experience in the *modus operandi* of getting up conventions, they felt as helpless and hopeless as if they had been suddenly asked to construct a steam engine." But this characterization was a bit disingenuous. In fact, all of the women had superior organizing skills, developed and honed over the course of many years of church and social activism. Mott's credentials in this regard were particularly impressive, and the recent Quaker schism had demonstrated that Wright, Hunt, and M'Clintock were also far from shy. How could five timid women have even attempted to put together such a controversial meeting in just six days' time?

After placing the newspaper notices and composing some flyers to be circulated locally, the five organizers met again on Sunday, July 16, to plan the convention's agenda. Gathering this time in the M'Clintock home, they decided to draft a statement of purpose and an accompanying set of resolutions that those attending the convention could debate and adopt—if anyone showed up, that is. Because so little had yet been written on the subject of women's rights, Mott, Stanton, and the others looked over pamphlets issued by other reform groups that M'Clintock happened to have on hand—among them, the proceedings of antislavery, peace, and temperance conventions. The women were searching for

PACIFISM

WILLIAM LADD OF MAINE worked as a sea captain and then as a farmer before devoting his life after 1819 to the cause of world peace. Like many other perfection-oriented causes, the peace movement gained a great deal of strength during the antebellum period, especially after Ladd founded the American Peace Society in 1828. But several years later, the question of whether nations could legitimately use force to defend themselves produced a schism within the group, weakening it considerably. Among the leaders of the faction that condemned the use of force under any circumstances was abolitionist William Lloyd Garrison, under whose auspices the much smaller New England Non-Resistance Society was established. Pacifism lost more momentum as the slavery controversy heated up, and the onset of the Civil War, widely considered to be a "just war," caused the movement to implode. Most pacifist leaders were also abolitionists, and when forced to choose, even Garrison decided that putting an end to slavery was more important than peace.

The records of William Ladd's American Peace Society are currently housed at Swarthmore College.

examples after which they could pattern their own manifesto describing the present situation and future aspirations of American women such as themselves.

In the end, however, they chose not a recent political pamphlet but an old one—the Declaration of Independence—as the model for their document, which they called the Declaration of Sentiments. "When, in the course of human events, it becomes necessary for one portion of the family of man to assume among the people of the earth a position different from that which they have hitherto occupied, but one to which the laws of nature and of nature's God entitle them," the declaration began, "a decent respect to the opinions of mankind requires that they should declare the causes that impel them to such a course."

IN ITS USE OF WORDS SUCH AS *tyranny, despotism,* and *usurpation,* the Declaration of Sentiments echoed the rhetoric of the republican uprisings in Paris, Vienna, and Berlin earlier that year; but its content was altogether new, focusing on man's injustice to woman. "The history of mankind," the declaration asserted, "is a history of repeated injuries and usurpations on the part of man toward woman, having in direct object the establishment of an absolute tyranny over her."

A specific example was coverture, a principle of English common law inherited during colonial times and left unchanged by the men of the founding generation. According to this principle, a woman was legally "covered" by her father (or husband) to the extent that she had no rights of her own. As a result, no woman could retain her own earnings or hold property in her own name (hence the need for a Married Women's Property Act). The obvious analogy that married women were to their husbands as slaves were to their masters found its place in the Declaration of Sentiments in a section decrying the injustice that a married woman must

This Currier & Ives lithograph, issued during the 1848 U.S. presidential campaign, shows Parisians burning the French throne on February 25 of that year.

"promise obedience to her husband, he becoming, to all intents and purposes, her master—the law giving him power to deprive her of her liberty, and to administer chastisement."

However, beyond its vigorous call for an end to coverture, the Declaration of Sentiments was mostly vague in the remedies it sought for women. Of the twelve resolutions appended to the declaration, the first three called (each in a slightly different way) for the nullification of all laws "contrary to the great precept of nature" that "woman is man's equal." The next two urged greater gender consciousness among women; and the sixth and seventh resolutions argued, respectively, that men should be held to the same standards of social refinement as women and that women should be permitted the same active public lives as men. Resolution Eight criticized "the circumscribed limits which corrupt customs and a perverted application of the Scriptures have marked out" for woman and encouraged her to "move in the enlarged sphere which her great Creator has assigned her." The ninth resolution proclaimed that "it is the duty of the women of this country to secure to themselves their sacred right to the elective franchise."

The right to vote! Now that made people sit up. Resolution Eleven went on to demand "the overthrow of the monopoly of the pulpit" (an important goal for these churchgoing women) as well as "equal participation with men in the various trades, professions, and commerce," but Resolution Nine was the nervy one, and it was Elizabeth Cady Stanton's special contribution. Never before had female suffrage been a topic of candid public discussion in the United States. In a petition to the New York state legislature advocating enactment of the Married Women's Property Act, a few women had complained that they were victims of taxation without representation; yet they had gone no farther because, even to women, female disenfranchisement seemed routine and normal. According to historian Christine Stansell, "Women seemed to fall so entirely outside the boundaries of the political community, that no one even thought to comment on it."

When the Motts arrived in Seneca Falls on the eve of the convention, Lucretia asked that Resolution Nine be struck from the agenda. Henry Stanton had already suggested this, but Mrs. Mott's reasons were strategic rather than sexist. She urged caution, lest this one proposal distract public attention from the declaration's other points, especially those relating to coverture. "Lizzie," she said, "thee will make us ridiculous. We must go slowly." But Stanton insisted, and the next day at what she correctly described as "the first women's rights convention that has ever assembled," all twelve resolutions were presented.

The Second Great Awakening

THE TOWN OF SENECA FALLS, where the convention was held, lay within that region of western New York known as the "burned-over district" because of the flames of religious revivalism that blazed there during the early decades of the nineteenth century. Beginning in the 1790s, following a rather drowsy period in American religious history, and peaking during the 1830s in towns such as Rochester and Buffalo, evangelical Protestantism enjoyed a second golden age reminiscent of the 1740s, when the Great Awakening shook the land. As before,

After the Seneca Falls convention, many conservative newspapers printed the full text of the Declaration of Sentiments to ridicule the proceedings and embarrass the delegates. The strategy largely backfired. Twenty-eight-year-old Susan B. Anthony, for instance, clipped this newspaper transcript of the declaration for her scrapbook. Twenty-one years later, she helped Stanton found the National Woman Suffrage Association.

submitted.

When, in the course of human events, it becomes necessary for one portion of the family of man to assume among the people of the earth a position different from that which they have hitherto occupied, but one to which the laws of nature and of nature's God entitle them, a decent respect to the opinions of mankind requires that they should declare the causes that impel them to such a course.

We hold these truths to be self-evident: that all men and women are created equal; that they are endowed by their Creator with certain inalienable rights; that among these are life, liberty, and the pursuit of happiness; that to secure those rights governments are instituted, deriving their just powers from the consent of the governed. Whenever any form of Government becomes destructive of these ends, it is the right of those who suffer from it to refuse allegiance to it, and to insist upon the institution of a new government, laying its foundation on such principles, and organizing its powers in such form as to them shall seem most likely to effect their safety and happiness. Prudence, indeed, will dictate that governments long established should not denominational allegiances were largely set aside, with older, more established doctrines giving way to an exuberant new religiosity. Again, itinerant clergymen swept up believers in a sideshow of spirituality, preaching an emotionally powerful gospel of conversion and salvation. The greatest of these preachers was Charles Grandison Finney, an erstwhile lawyer who began his ministerial career in 1826, riding circuit through the small towns and villages of central New York, attracting larger and larger crowds, and winning more and more converts. Along with other evangelists of the Second Great Awakening (or Great Revival), Finney emphasized the importance of good works in obtaining salvation, and he was himself an abolitionist.

The relationship between Finney's theology and his antislavery politics was quite similar to that between the religious beliefs of the four Quaker ladies—Mott, Wright, Hunt, and M'Clintock—and their promotion of women's rights. In fact, during the decades immediately preceding the Civil War, religion and reform in America were inseparably linked. The American reformers who took part in the antislavery, women's rights, temperance, and peace movements—among many others—were more often than not motivated by religious beliefs, and they regularly cited Scripture as their justification for the social changes they sought. Nor could it have been otherwise in a society that nearly universally considered the Bible to be the ultimate moral guide. Between the American Revolution and the Civil War, a period of some eighty years during which U.S. nationality came into being, Americans (which meant primarily Protestants) paid more attention to religion than at any other time in their history, except perhaps for the height of Puritan orthodoxy and possibly today.

The Second Great Awakening profoundly altered the viewpoint of most American Protestants by doing away with the terrible Calvinist uncertainties that had so burdened the Puritans. According to Finney and his colleagues, God did *not* control the destiny of human beings, whom Finney characterized as "moral free agents." Rather than being marked at birth for membership in the "company of saints," believers could become at any time instruments of their own salvation by making a positive commitment to God and performing good works.

As the eighteenth century ended, American religiosity seemed on the wane. Many of the nation's leaders (Jefferson and Franklin among them) had publicly embraced the religion of reason, known as deism. During the early nineteenth century, however, hundreds of thousands of Americans rediscovered the appeal of spirituality at Methodist camp meetings such as this one, held in 1819.

LEFT:
After serving as pastor of the Broadway Tabernacle in New York City from 1834, Charles Grandison Finney (shown here in 1850) joined the Oberlin College faculty as a theology professor in 1837.

MORMONISM

A LESS CONVENTIONAL PRODUCT of the burned-over district was the Church of Jesus Christ of Latter-day Saints, founded by Joseph Smith in 1830. Born in Vermont in 1805, Smith was an energetic if not particularly successful man. Beginning in 1820, however, he learned from visions he received that God had chosen him to restore the church of Christ on earth. Seven years later, according to Smith's account, the angel Moroni revealed to him the location of a book, written in strange hieroglyphics on golden plates, that described the history of the true church in America. With miraculous aid, Smith translated the document and published it as *The Book of Mormon* (1830). It became the sacred text of the church Smith established that same year in Fayette, New York, just a few miles south of Seneca Falls.

In 1831, scorned by disbelieving neighbors, Smith and his "community of saints" left New York, traveling west in search of both economic opportunity and freedom from persecution. They paused in Kirkland, Ohio, and Independence, Missouri, but each time their efforts to establish a "New Jerusalem" were undermined by antagonistic locals made suspicious by the Mormons' intense secrecy as well as their practice of polygamy. In 1839, Smith resettled his followers in the Mississippi River town of Commerce, Illinois, which the Mormons took over and renamed Nauvoo.

During the next five years, the small town became, under Smith's leadership, a prosperous community of twenty thousand, making it the largest city in the state.

Even so, as before, Smith's claim to divine instruction, despotic leadership style, and fierce exclusivity gradually riled his Protestant neighbors and even some church members, who objected to several new Mormon policies recently put forth by Smith as belated "revelations." Once Smith announced his candidacy for U.S. president in February 1844, a dissenting Mormon newspaper made him the subject of vicious editorials denouncing his political ambition. Smith's response was to order the newspaper's press destroyed, which only exacerbated the situation.

Joseph Smith

With Smith's death, leadership of the church fell to Brigham Young, who assumed similar dictatorial powers and led the Mormons to the Great Salt Lake Valley, where they settled in 1847 and built this tabernacle.

After Smith called out troops to preserve his rule, he was arrested, charged with treason, and imprisoned outside Nauvoo in the (non-Mormon) Carthage city jail. On June 27, a mob, fearful of Mormon influence and envious of the sect's economic success, broke into the jail and killed Smith along with his brother.

The Mormon temple at Nauvoo stood high on a hill above the city until a tornado gutted it in May 1850.

ANOTHER IMPORTANT ASPECT of Great Revival theology was its replacement of the hellfire-and-damnation Puritan God with a gentler divinity of love, around which several new denominations were formed. One of the most influential of these was Unitarianism, which took hold in Congregationalist churches in and around Boston during the late eighteenth century and won many followers among the educated middle class. The beliefs that set Unitarians apart from more orthodox Protestants included their rejection of both the Trinity (they believed Jesus to be great but not divine) and the doctrine of original sin (they believed, to the contrary, that humanity was innately good). Accordingly, Unitarians emphasized humanity's capacity for moral improvement. The sect's most prominent minister, the Rev. William Ellery Channing, valued moderation and reason above revivalist enthusiasm, and the clarity and benevolence with which he espoused his message propelled him to national stardom.

Later, out of Unitarianism came Transcendentalism, whose central figure, Ralph Waldo Emerson, actually trained as a Unitarian cleric. (Emerson served briefly as minister of Boston's Second Church before resigning in 1832 over his refusal to administer Communion.) As a leader of the Transcendental Club, a group of Romantic writers and reformers (including Henry David Thoreau, Amos Bronson Alcott, Margaret Fuller, and George Ripley) that flourished in New England between 1830 and 1850, Emerson attempted to replace the reified aspects of organized religion with a more personal, intuitive spirituality based on self-reliance and "the god within." The Transcendentalists were particularly concerned that Americans were idolizing historical Christianity rather than concentrating on the truths it conveyed—in other words, they were deferring their own authority to powers outside themselves, which is the classic definition of alienation. As expressed by Emerson and others, the Transcendentalist viewpoint influenced an entire generation of American writers—including Herman Melville, Nathaniel Hawthorne, Walt Whitman, and Emily Dickinson—while making Emerson the most popular American philosopher of the nineteenth century.

The philosophy of Transcendentalism also influenced mass opinion with its emphasis on human progress. Like their Puritan forebears, the Transcendentalists aspired to create "a City upon a Hill." The difference was that Emerson and the others saw little to be gained from hierarchically imposed social regulation and instead encouraged people to find their own "original relation to the universe."

During the early 1840s, the Transcendentalists published a journal of literature, art, and ideas called The Dial. *Its editor from 1840 until 1842 was Margaret Fuller (above).*

LEFT: *The most notable works of Ralph Waldo Emerson included* Nature *(1836) and two volumes of essays that he published in 1841 and 1844.*

THE DIAL.

VOL. III.   JULY, 1842.   No. I.

LECTURES ON THE TIMES.

BY R. W. EMERSON.

Introductory Lecture read at the Masonic Temple in Boston, Thursday Evening, December 2, 1841.

THE TIMES, as we say—or the present aspects of our social state, the Laws, Divinity, Natural Science, Agriculture, Art, Trade, Letters, have their root in an invisible spiritual reality. To appear in these aspects, they must first exist, or have some necessary foundation. Beside all the small reasons we assign, there is a great reason for the existence of every extant fact; a reason which lies grand and immovable, often

ADVENTISM

To promote conversion experiences, many preachers of the Great Revival emphasized the imminence of Christ's Second Coming. Even Charles Grandison Finney, who taught his followers that they could obtain salvation through individual effort, warned that they should hurry because time was growing short. Yet Finney's admonitions were mild compared to those of the Adventists, whose millennialist viewpoint was deeply rooted in the biblical book of Revelation.

The most influential Adventist minister was William Miller. As an army officer during the War of 1812, Miller had become skeptical of religion, but after the war he had a conversion experience and began preaching the Baptist faith of his father. Studying closely the books of Daniel and Revelation, he came to the conclusion that the Second Coming would occur soon; and although most of his contemporaries avoided assigning precise dates, Mill announced that Christ would come sometime between March 21, 1843, and March 21, 1844. As the first date neared, Miller's followers soared in number to perhaps one hundred thousand, concentrated in upstate New York but influential throughout New England. After March 21, 1844, of course, the failure of Miller's prophecy enervated his sect; yet Adventism persisted and remains today an important millennialist movement, sometimes called Seventh-day Adventism because of its doctrine that the religious observance of Saturday (the seventh day) rather than Sunday will expedite the Second Coming.

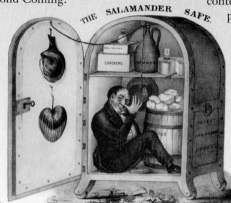

This 1843 caricature shows a Millerite hiding inside a well-stocked safe, awaiting the end of the world.

Social Reform Movements

This new emphasis on personal responsibility, working in tandem with Finney's good-works theology, promoted an efflorescence of social reform movements in the United States during the 1830s and especially the 1840s. (It was this energy that so captivated Elizabeth Cady Stanton during her years in Boston.)

The shared goal of the people who took part in these movements, however, was less salvation for themselves in the afterlife than the perfection of American society in the here and now, specifically through the correction of human as well as societal defects.

The temperance crusade that began to gather momentum during the 1840s illustrates this pattern well. Americans of the colonial and early national periods were a hard-drinking lot, and liquor made from excess western crops was both plentiful and cheap. (The still was as much a part of the well-run nineteenth-century farm as the gristmill.) Limiting the production and consumption of alcohol in the United States in 1820 would have been just as difficult as limiting the ability of Americans to own slaves. Nevertheless, inspired by revivalist preachers and their own religious conversions, members of the American Society for the Promotion of Temperance (founded in 1826) urged churchgoing Americans to take pledges of abstinence, and many did; by the mid-1830s, the society claimed more than one million people on its rolls. Still, the evils of drunkenness remained everywhere apparent; it seemed that the alcoholics were not among the pledge takers.

The antislavery scene that decorated Lucretia Mott's work bag demonstrated the multiplicity of her commitments to social reform.

CHRISTIAN SCIENCE

MARY BAKER EDDY, her able biographer Gillian Gill informs us, "was recognized in her day as the most influential and controversial woman in America." Eddy's role as the founder of the Church of Christ Scientist and its leader for nearly half a century made her the most prominent woman leader within the lively complex of nineteenth-century American religious movements. She alone developed the major doctrines and ideas of Christian Science during an era when the subordination of women in all walks of American life was virtually complete.

Few could have predicted at Mary Morse Baker's birth in 1821 the success she would achieve in the second half of her life. Raised in rural New Hampshire by strict Congregationalist parents of modest means, she began the first of her three marriages in 1843, when she wed building contractor George Washington Glover. Glover took her to North Carolina, then died a year later, leaving his new wife penniless and pregnant. Having little choice, Mary Baker returned to her parents' home, where she gave birth to a son, who was sent to live with relatives better able to care for him.

Mary Baker Eddy (shown here in 1850) pioneered the field known today as mind/body medicine.

(Mary was both in poor health and impoverished at the time.) In 1853, she married dentist Daniel Patterson, who shared her growing preoccupation with physical health; but their relationship failed in 1866, when Patterson ran off with a married woman. For other reasons as well, 1866 proved to be a critical year in Mary Baker's life.

She had been living in a procession of boardinghouses, often dependent on the charity of friends and in pain much of the time from a variety of ailments. During this period, she had become a student and patient of Phineas Quimby—a practitioner of "mental healing" in Portland, Maine. Two weeks after Quimby's death in January 1866, Mary Baker (then living in Lynn, Massachusetts) slipped on some ice and fell hard, apparently becoming paralyzed. Although given little chance of recovery, soon thereafter, Gill writes, "to the astonishment of friends, she gets up unaided and resumes normal life. [She] dates [the] discovery of Christian Science to this event."

In her seminal work *Science and Health*, published nine years later and still in print today, Baker explained that illness and death were illusions and that all healing came from God through prayer and by living in accordance with His teachings.

In 1877, Mary Baker married one of her students, Asa Gilbert Eddy; that same decade, she founded the Church of Christ Scientist. Administering its affairs, however, proved more troublesome than she expected, with numerous internal divisions straining her flock. Her greatest consolation during this period was likely her marriage to Asa Eddy, which ended with Eddy's death in 1882.

Meanwhile, despite an ongoing series of conflicts with the medical establishment and controversies involving former disciples, the Christian Science movement continued to gather many more supporters than adversaries during the late nineteenth and early twentieth centuries.

In 1906, four years before her death, the *New York World* published an article alleging that Eddy was senile and incapable of managing her own—or the church's—affairs. Subsequently, a court-appointed master visited Eddy and found her to be fully alert and competent. But Eddy didn't let the matter rest. In August 1908, she wrote to the trustees of the Christian Science Publishing Society, requesting that they "start a daily newspaper at once" with a greater adherence to truth. The result was the now internationally respected *Christian Science Monitor.*

UTOPIAN COMMUNITIES

THE IDEALISM OF ANTEBELLUM America was perhaps best expressed in the dozens of utopian communities that sprang up between 1800 and 1850. The most impressive in scale and duration were generally those organized around religious worship. There had been a long history of such communities in North America, dating back to the Dutch Mennonites who settled near Lewes, Delaware, in 1663. The Shakers, established in America by Mother Ann Lee in 1774, were a notable success of the eighteenth century. In 1824, however, utopianism, or the desire to create a perfect society on earth, took a different turn when British visionary Robert Owen arrived in America. Already, Owen had used his vast industrial fortune to transform the New Lanark textile mills in Manchester into model factories with improved working conditions, sick pay, old-age insurance, and even recreational facilities.

In America, Owen put even more radical socialist theories into practice when he purchased a ready-to-occupy settlement in Indiana (from a German communitarian sect eager to move to Pennsylvania) and created in 1825 the town of New Harmony. Its purpose, according to Owen, was "to introduce an entire new system of society" that would transform property and labor relationships, but the experiment failed dismally, lasting until 1828 merely on the strength of Owen's formidable personal resources. Owen's ideas, however, remained influential throughout the 1830s and 1840s, when—along with those of French social theorist Charles Fourier—they prompted George Ripley, another former Unitarian minister, to establish Brook Farm, a Transcendentalist experiment in communal living that operated a few miles west of Boston from 1841 until 1847.

The members of the prosperous Oneida Community, shown here during the 1860s, owed a great deal of their success to the vision of John Humphrey Noyes (left).

One of the few utopian settlements ever to achieve self-sufficiency was the Oneida Community started by John Humphrey Noyes in 1848. Located in central New York, it initially provided a haven for Noyes, whose advocacy of "free love" had prompted his arrest in 1846. Noyes and his "Bible communist" followers practiced "complex marriage," a system according to which every member of the group was simultaneously married to every other member. Generally, the Oneidans sought a return to the practices of the early Christian church, including joint ownership of property. More important, though, were Noyes's views on community organization. He believed that light industry provided a much more favorable economic base than agriculture, so he established factories to produce and market animal traps, furniture, and other consumer goods. The prosperity that this strategy produced greatly enhanced the settlement's longevity; it wasn't until 1881, two years after outside pressures forced the abandonment of complex marriage, that the Oneida Community transformed itself into a joint-stock company specializing in the manufacture of silverware.

New Harmony in 1832.

During the late 1830s, businessman Neal Dow observed in his own hometown of Portland, Maine, how drunkenness led to a variety of other social problems, from family violence to crime to declining productivity among workers. At first, he went the persuasion route, establishing the Maine Temperance Union in 1838 to promote voluntary abstinence. But when his efforts failed to improve the situation in Portland, Dow became politically active. In 1851, he became the mayor of Portland and that same year wrote a statewide temperance law, enacted by the Maine legislature on June 2. The so-called Maine Law, the first of its kind in the nation, prohibited the manufacture and sale of intoxicating liquor; by 1855, thirteen other states (of the thirty-one then in the Union) had similar laws on the books. Dow's victory was rather short-lived, however; the South ignored the temperance crusade, and a counterreformation began in 1856, when New York courts declared that state's prohibition law unconstitutional because it deprived New Yorkers of property (their liquor) without due process of law.

The Drunkard's Progress (1846) shows the nine steps from "a glass with a friend" to "death by suicide."

O N THE OTHER HAND, the various movements promoting human progress through education, especially tax-supported primary education, were much less a product of Protestant evangelism. Their fundamental target was illiteracy, a scourge as destructive as alcoholism according to those reformers who viewed schooling as a superb agency for social control. Although literacy rates were higher in the United States than in many European countries during the first half of the nineteenth century, estimates are that a majority of U.S. citizens could neither read nor write. To teach more people how to read and write, reformers pursued a variety of strategies. Their greatest success came in persuading states (except those in the South) to establish free public primary schools for the education of every child. In the antebellum South, it was generally only the children of wealthy parents who were educated, either at private academies or at home through instruction provided by private tutors.

The leader of the public school movement in the North was Horace Mann of Massachusetts, ably seconded by Henry Barnard in neighboring Connecticut and Rhode Island. During colonial times, some New England communities had established publicly funded "common schools," but their availability was far from universal and by the 1830s the inadequacies of the system had become unmistakable. Many impoverished or parsimonious towns had no schools at all, and others had merely ramshackle establishments with poorly paid teachers and poorly equipped students. Beginning in 1837, when he became the first secretary of the new Massachusetts Board of Education, Mann reorganized the state's school system, doubled teachers' salaries, lengthened the school year, and upgraded the curriculum and teacher training. (Although secondary schools also gained in importance during this period, they remained far out of reach for the vast majority of Americans until after World War I.)

Horace Mann resigned as secretary of the Massachusetts Board of Education in 1848 after his election to Congress as an antislavery Whig.

EDUCATING WOMEN

UNTIL LATE IN THE NINETEENTH century, women had far less access to education than did men of comparable means. The improvements that took place after the Civil War, however, had their origins in the work of several important antebellum reformers. During the early nineteenth century, most well-bred ladies received elementary-level schooling but were discouraged from proceeding farther with their studies. In fact, they were barred from U.S colleges and universities until 1837, when Oberlin College in Ohio became the first to admit women to its degree program. The trustees allowed four young ladies to enroll in the school's new "female department" despite protests that equated coeducation with free love. Also that year, Mary Lyon opened a female seminary in South Hadley, Massachusetts, which soon became Mount Holyoke College. Even so, women's colleges remained extremely few in number—and coeducation even rarer—until the founding of Vassar (1865), Wellesley (1875), Smith (1875), and Bryn Mawr (1884) after the Civil War. Even education reformers such as Horace Mann and Henry Barnard saw little urgency in the need to improve postsecondary instruction for women.

Improvements in the primary education of women during the late eighteenth century led to demands in the early nineteenth for more secondary education. These were answered by the establishment of boarding schools at which the daughters of the emerging middle class were given both religious and academic instruction. Among the most famous of these "female seminaries" was the one founded in 1821 in Troy, New York, by Emma Willard (left)—and attended several years later by a young Elizabeth Cady.

This daguerreotype *shows the female members of the Oberlin College class of 1855. Seated among them is Mrs. Charles Grandison Finney, wife of the Oberlin president. (The Reverend Finney was elevated from the theology department in 1851.)*

At the same time, higher education was also expanding. Several southern and midwestern states (strongly encouraged by John Quincy Adams) established public universities, and influential private educators founded scores of new colleges as well. Between 1831 and 1850, the number of U.S. colleges rose from 46 to 119. Even so, because only 5 percent of the antebellum population ever attended college, the education of adults during this period was conducted largely through the lyceum movement. Lyceums were local auditoriums with small libraries attached that offered readings and discussion groups in history, literature, science, art, and philosophy. They were best known, however, for their lectures, delivered often by eminent Americans making well-paid regional and even national tours. Emerson was a regular on the lyceum circuit, as was Daniel Webster. The first lyceum opened in Millbury, Massachusetts, in 1826; by 1836, more than three thousand were operating in the North and Midwest. Like many other social crusades of the period, the lyceum movement encouraged personal growth, and it was within this context that Mott, Stanton, and the others planned their women's rights convention.

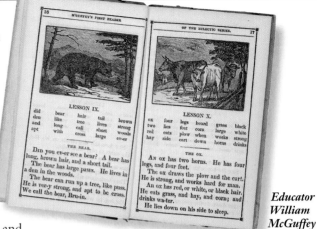

Educator William McGuffey sold more than 120 million copies of his popular Readers *during the mid–nineteenth century.*

The Proceedings of the Convention

THE ORGANIZERS DIDN'T KNOW what to expect, but they had reason to believe, given the popularity of lyceums and the fervent intellectual climate of the burned-over district, that their call would be answered. In fact, when Stanton arrived at the Wesleyan Chapel on the morning of July 19, she found dozens of carriages parked beside the church, some genteel and others simple farm wagons. Outside the church was a crowd of people waiting patiently for admission. These "delegates," mostly women but also some men, had come from all over western New York to hear what the ladies of Seneca Falls had to say. "At first we travelled quite alone," a young seamstress named Charlotte Woodward recalled, "…but before we had gone many miles we came on other waggon-loads of women, bound in the same direction. As we reached different cross-roads we saw waggons coming from every part of the county, and long before we reached Seneca Falls we were a procession."

It had been the organizers' original intention to exclude men from the first day of proceedings, but this plan was abandoned when none of the women proved willing to preside. After a brief caucus, James Mott was appointed convention chair; and for the next two days, more than 250 women and at least 40 men

THE PENNY PRESS

A MUCH LESS FORMAL (though nonetheless important) boost to literacy during this period came from the "penny press," which benefited from new printing technologies (especially the steam-powered rotary press). These new technologies dramatically reduced the cost of publishing newspapers, magazines, and other printed materials. In September 1833, the *New York Sun* famously demonstrated the economic possibilities of mass circulation by selling its copies for just one penny, compared to the six cents typically charged by other New York City newspapers. Within two years, the *Sun*'s circulation had reached nineteen thousand, making it the most widely read newspaper in the world. (Also recommending the *Sun* to a mass audience was its sensational coverage of crime, scandal, and other "human interest" stories.) Later, periodicals such as *Godey's Lady's Book* and *Harper's Weekly* emerged to satisfy an increasingly literate American audience hungry for new reading material.

(including thirty-one-year-old Frederick Douglass) filled every seat in the Wesleyan Chapel to listen and discuss. Lucretia Mott delivered a well-received keynote address, but the most impressive speaker of the day turned out to be the inexperienced Elizabeth Cady Stanton, whose presentation included a reading of the Declaration of Sentiments and its twelve appended resolutions.

For the most part, the audience responded enthusiastically to the speeches demanding equal rights and fair treatment for women. The Declaration of Sentiments was embraced by the delegates without reservation, and the various resolutions were approved unanimously—except for the ninth resolution, which called for female enfranchisement. Some delegates argued hotly, as Mott had, that endorsement of such an excessive demand would invite public ridicule and undermine all that the convention might otherwise accomplish. It was a persuasive argument and would likely have killed the suffrage resolution had not Frederick Douglass (whom Stanton had met in Boston) placed his considerable weight behind her proposal. According to Douglass, the right to vote was key, because it alone provided the sort of political leverage that women would need in order to achieve their other goals. Even so, when the vote finally came, the controversial resolution passed by only a narrow margin. Yet in the weeks, years, and decades ahead, it was Resolution Nine that came to be seen as the convention's greatest and most remarkable achievement.

According to historian Stansell, "Had Stanton not presented this resolution, the sentiments of Seneca Falls would most likely have melted into what had been, up to that point in the Atlantic world, a halting, episodic tradition of women's protest." Instead, "the call for suffrage came to galvanize women's politics in the United States; and during the next fifty years, the fight for woman suffrage would become the centerpiece of a popular, powerful, and innovative movement."

Frederick Douglass escaped from slavery in 1838. When this photograph was taken a decade later, he was living in Rochester, New York, and publishing The North Star, *a regional anti-slavery newspaper.*

THUS WAS LAUNCHED the suffrage crusade—after abolitionism, the most controversial of the antebellum reform movements. Ironically, its troublesome nature was an important factor in its early growth. The enormous volume of negative publicity that the Seneca Falls convention generated made knowledge of its demands far more widespread than anything western New York's regional newspapers or the abolitionist press could have accomplished. Daily newspaper editors all over the country, notably James Gordon Bennett of the *New York Herald*, denounced the conduct of the Seneca Falls delegates as "unwomanly" and warned that such behavior would lead to a breakdown of morality and the destruction of the family. To ridicule the convention further, Bennett's newspaper printed the entire text of the Declaration of Sentiments—but this was "just what I wanted," Stanton wrote in a contemporary letter. "Imagine the publicity given to our ideas by thus appearing in a widely circulated sheet like the *Herald*. It will start women thinking, and men too; and when men and women think about a new question, the first step in progress is taken."

New York Herald *founder James Gordon Bennett in 1851 or 1852.*

SOJOURNER TRUTH
1797?–1883

FEW REFORMERS PROVED so adept at stirring audiences as Sojourner Truth, who stumped the country during the 1840s and 1850s preaching both emancipation and women's rights. Born into bondage in Ulster County, New York, about 1797 but freed when New York State abolished slavery in 1827, Truth went by her slave name Isabella until 1843, when she rechristened herself and became a traveling preacher. Her greatest asset was her rich, powerful voice, with which she often turned angry audiences into receptive ones. She gradually became associated with the Garrisonian abolitionists and, after 1850, the women's rights

I Sell the Shadow to Support the Substance.
SOJOURNER TRUTH.

Sojourner Truth stood six feet tall and spoke English with a Dutch accent (because her first master spoke Low Dutch). To fund her travels, she sold carte-de-visite images of herself such as this one.

movement as well. One of her best-remembered presentations took place at the May 1851 women's rights convention in Akron, where she declared:

That man over there says that women need to be helped into carriages, and lifted over ditches, and to have the best place everywhere. Nobody helps me any best place! And ain't I a woman? Look at me! Look at my arm! [She bared her right arm and flexed its powerful muscles.] I have ploughed, I have planted and I have gathered into barns. And no man could head me. And ain't I a woman? I could work as much, and eat as much as a man—when I could get it— and bear the lash as well! And ain't I a woman? I have borne children and seen most of them sold into slavery, and when I cried out with a mother's grief, none but Jesus heard me. And ain't I a woman? …If the first woman God ever made was strong enough to turn the world upside down all alone, these women together ought to be able to turn it back and get it right-side up again. And now that they are asking to do it the men better let them.

During the next several years, activists in Massachusetts, Ohio, Indiana, and Pennsylvania organized regional women's rights gatherings, and two national conventions were held, the first in Worcester in October 1850 and the second in Akron seven months later. Even so, seventy-two years would pass before women were granted the right to vote. Of all the women at the 1848 Seneca Falls convention, only Charlotte Woodward lived to witness the triumph of Resolution Nine. The nineteen-year-old seamstress had sat unnoticed in the rear of the Wesleyan Chapel, attracted to the convention by its promise of liberation. "Every fibre of my being rebelled, although silently, all the hours that I sat and sewed gloves for a miserable pittance which, after it was earned, could never be mine," she wrote later. "I wanted to work, but I wanted to choose my task and I wanted to collect my wages [rather than have them controlled by her father or husband]."

Woodward never rose to speak, but at the convention's end, she ventured forward to sign the Declaration of Sentiments and its accompanying resolutions—one of only five score people (sixty-eight women and thirty-two men) to do so. Pressure from hostile family members, ministers, and neighbors later persuaded a number of these signers to withdraw their names, but not Woodward. She remained committed to the cause of women's rights her entire life, and in November 1920, following ratification of the Nineteenth Amendment, she cast her first vote for president.

> "If women want any rights more'n they've got, why don't they just take 'em and not be talking about it?"
>
> —
>
> *Sojourner Truth, speech at the National Women's Rights Convention, October 1850*

Harriet Beecher Stowe

1811–1896

by Joan Hedrick

WHEN HARRIET BEECHER STOWE met Abraham Lincoln at the White House in November 1862, the president reportedly greeted her with the words, "So you're the little woman who wrote the book that started this great war!" The book to which Lincoln was referring, *Uncle Tom's Cabin* (1851–1852), had made a nation already in tumult over the 1850 Fugitive Slave Law exquisitely aware of the contradiction that slavery posed to a purportedly democratic society.

Born in 1811 into a ministerial household where she watched her brothers train in the art of polemic and saw her famous father, Lyman Beecher, triumph in three heresy trials, Harriet Beecher Stowe learned early on how to wield the pen as a social and political weapon. Of his precocious daughter, Lyman Beecher once said that he would give a hundred dollars if Harriet could have been born a boy and his son Henry Ward Beecher a girl.

In 1851, believing that Christianity should be a force for transformation in this world, Stowe found herself infuriated by the tepid response of Protestant ministers to the obviously un-Christian Fugitive Slave Act, whose inhumanity had moved Stowe herself to tears. Resolving to use "women's weapons" to fight the law's injustice, she drew upon her own emotional experience as the mother of a recently deceased child to evoke with rich detail the legal separation of families brought about by the domestic slave trade. Stowe's dramatic tale of bondage and escape encouraged Americans to commit acts of civil disobedience—which Stowe justified by invoking both a higher law and the ideals of liberty on which the nation had been founded.

Initially serialized in an antislavery weekly, *Uncle Tom's Cabin* had readers alternately laughing and crying over the adventures of a cast of characters who would become stock figures in the national lexicon. Upon its publication in book form in 1852, the novel became a runaway best-seller and the most widely read text of its time, after the Bible. It was adapted for the stage, translated into dozens of foreign languages, and transmogrified into decorated cups, candlesticks, wallpapers, and every other form of kitsch that nineteenth-century merchandisers could imagine.

More important, though, was the effect the novel had in swelling the ranks of the antislavery movement. Recognizing its political value, Frederick Douglass praised the book's "keen and quiet wit, powers of argumentation, exalted sense of justice, and enlightened and comprehensive philosophy." At the same time, southerners denounced *Uncle Tom's Cabin*, complaining that Stowe's representation of slavery was too highly colored by her abolitionist politics. Novelistic ripostes such as Mary Eastman's *Aunt Phyllis's Cabin* (1852) expressed the proslavery view, while other books attacked Stowe and her credibility. Understanding that her book was being judged not as fiction but as historical truth, Stowe responded by publishing *A Key to Uncle Tom's Cabin* (1853), which contained voluminous documentation relating to her novel's characters and scenes.

Invited to Great Britain, where *Uncle Tom's Cabin* sold a million and a half copies during its first year in print, Stowe was showered with money and feted at large gatherings. Upon her return to Connecticut, she used this money to finance a petition campaign opposing the Kansas-Nebraska Act, which permitted the extension of slavery into federal territories north of the Missouri Compromise line. She also published a second antislavery novel, *Dred*

(1856), which featured as its hero a character supposed to be the son of Denmark Vesey, leader of the 1822 slave insurrection in South Carolina.

The success of *Uncle Tom's Cabin* assured Stowe a large audience for her work, which eventually encompassed thirty books in numerous genres. She also wrote influential political columns for such journals of opinion as the *Independent* and the *Atlantic Monthly*. After the Civil War, however, her reputation declined as "high culture" journals established aesthetic standards against which her passionate cries for social justice were deemed overly senti-mental and not worthy of the appellation "art." Yet *Uncle Tom's Cabin* continues to be read around the world and appreciated as a powerful story of oppression and liberation. It may be as close as our culture has come to producing a national epic.

Even northerners who distrusted abolitionists and endorsed the Compromise of 1850 wept at the end of Uncle Tom's Cabin *as they read of Tom's martyrdom. The slave's death distressed many readers but represented for Stowe (shown here in an 1853 engraving) the ultimate triumph of Christian good in an evil society.*

10

THE DEEPENING SECTIONAL CONFLICT

The Compromise of 1850

POTOMAC RIVER BREEZES chilled the air as legislators gathered in Washington, D.C., for the December 3, 1849, opening of the Thirty-first Congress. To reach Capitol Hill, senators and representatives had to tramp through muddy streets, passing the city's many boardinghouses, hotels, and half-finished public buildings. On the Mall, the beginnings of a colossal stone tower stood out like a silo foreshortened by a violent summer hailstorm. There was even remodeling work going on at the Capitol itself (still crowned by a temporary dome), where room was being made for all the new congressmen needed to govern the ever-expanding nation.

Washington when a new Congress convenes is ordinarily a town charged with excitement, but there was even greater cause for gossip than usual in December 1849 because of the remarkable 1848 presidential election. For the first time in American history, a presidential campaign had turned on the issue of slavery, and now the nation waited to see how Congress would react. Many politicians preached calm, but pessimists feared that the crucial issue of slavery's expansion into the western territories recently acquired from Mexico would lead to a collapse of the Union itself.

America's first two generations of political leadership had deliberately suppressed the slavery

issue because they were personally aware of the divisive emotions that discussions of slavery inevitably aroused. The Missouri Compromise (1819–1820) and the subsequent nullification crisis (1832–1833) notwithstanding, presidents and congressmen were remarkably successful in sparing the fledgling nation this trauma. But the annexation of slaveholding Texas in 1845, as well as escalating abolitionism in the North, brought the issue back into national focus. By 1848, there was no way that a presidential candidate could avoid it.

The Whigs in 1848 nominated Mexican War hero Zachary Taylor, a native of Kentucky (and therefore something of a southerner) who currently owned plantations worked by slaves in Louisiana. To replace the retiring James Knox Polk, the Democrats chose Sen. Lewis Cass, a rather colorless expansionist from Michigan. A third player in 1848 was former president Martin Van Buren, who ran as the nominee of the new antislavery Free Soil party. Both Taylor and Cass understood that winning the election required some coalition building between North and South, so they worked hard to develop positions that might appeal to both sides without actually taking on the central question of whether slavery should be permitted in territories controlled by the federal government.

Although he generally said as little as possible, Taylor did promise, if elected, to restrict his use of the presidential veto to measures that he deemed unconstitutional (rather than simply inexpedient). This pledge

AT LEFT: *This 1850 lithograph shows the U.S. Capitol shortly before construction began on the wings that today hold the House and Senate chambers.*

CONGRESSIONAL SCALES.
A TRUE BALANCE.

This 1850 satire shows Pres. Zachary Taylor attempting to balance southern and northern interests. Henry Clay is among the congressmen pictured in the tray on the left, marked "Wilmot Proviso." John Calhoun can be seen in the tray on the right, marked "Southern Rights."

RIGHT: *Not long after losing the battle for the Speaker's chair, Robert C. Winthrop was elevated to the Senate by the Massachusetts state legislature.*

appealed primarily to northern voters who hoped that Congress would soon pass the Wilmot Proviso banning slavery in the former Mexican lands. (The proviso had already passed the House twice, and if it ever got through the Senate, northern supporters certainly didn't want the president vetoing it.) Taylor could afford the political cost of such a pledge because his ownership of more than a hundred slaves seemed to make him a safe bet for southern voters.

Cass, on the other hand, was much more vocal in his campaign, which advocated "squatter sovereignty." According to this doctrine, the residents of a territory (and not Congress) should decide for themselves the question of whether to permit slavery. Among the three leading candidates, only Van Buren, who had no chance at all of winning, explicitly opposed the extension of slavery into the West. In the end, however, it was Van Buren's 26.4 percent of the New York vote, taken primarily from Cass, that gave Taylor the state and elected the only slaveholder in the race.

THE RESULTS OF the 1848 congressional elections were also confused. So went the election of 1848, during which Democratic margins in both houses of Congress were also eroded. In the Senate, where most of the first session's pyrotechnics would take place, there was no doubt that Democrats retained organizational control. Even had the two Free Soilers voted routinely with the Whig minority, the Democrats still had a 33–27 advantage. But the increasing importance of sectional loyalties made party discipline difficult to maintain, and voting patterns became much less predictable.

In the House, the situation was even more complicated because there was no majority party. Instead, there were 112 Democrats and 109 Whigs—along with 9 Free Soilers, who controlled the balance of power. The first order of business for any new House is the election of a Speaker, a task usually handled by the majority party. It meets in caucus to agree on a candidate and then votes as a bloc to ensure that member's election. In December 1849, however, neither party had enough votes to guarantee the election of its standard-bearer, and the first month of the session was turmoil, confirming for many their fears concerning the future of sectional political warfare.

The House Whigs renominated Robert C. Winthrop of Massachusetts, a descendant of that state's original Puritan governor who had served as Speaker of the House during the two previous sessions and now ran as Taylor's man. Winthrop opposed the extension of slavery into the new territories but didn't support abolition. In general, he was well liked by his colleagues, but the Free Soilers thought him too moderate and six southern "cotton" Whigs bolted their party's caucus when Winthrop refused to guarantee slaveholders' rights in the

West. During the next three weeks, sixty-two separate ballots for Speaker were held. Winthrop never received more than 102 votes.

The Democrats put forth Howell Cobb of Georgia, their thirty-four-year-old floor leader. Cobb was devoted to southern rights but also to the doctrine that all problems relating to slavery should be settled on the basis of national (rather than sectional) principles. His reluctance to join John C. Calhoun in lambasting the North for its "interference" with slavery won him the support of many northern representatives, but his best total in those first sixty-two ballots was only 103 votes. Throughout, the Free Soil and rebel Whig blocs refused to support either major-party candidate, denying both the majority needed for victory and paralyzing the House, which couldn't get down to business until a Speaker was elected.

Even the withdrawal of Cobb's and Winthrop's names at various points failed to break the stalemate. Finally, both sides agreed to a rule change that permitted election by plurality rather than majority; and on December 22, voting for the sixty-third time, the House elected Cobb Speaker over Winthrop, 102–99. The new Speaker was a genial man with an excellent sense of humor, and his desire to heal led him to parcel out committee chairmanships to members from all sections of the country. But the House's continuing inability to form a stable voting majority kept it on the legislative sidelines throughout most of the 1849–1850 session.

Manifest Destiny

YET THE ROOTS OF THIS edgy political situation extended much farther back than the 1848 election and concerned nothing less than America's view of itself as a nation. Since colonial times, Americans had felt generally entitled to the continent's unsettled land (unsettled, that is, by whites). Thomas Jefferson and Meriwether Lewis are two obvious examples of political leaders who asserted the nation's North American birthright. But never before had so many Americans felt that birthright so strongly as during the 1840s, when whites began moving much more rapidly across the Mississippi River and even the Rocky Mountains. Some were bound for Mexican California; others for Oregon, which the United States occupied jointly with Great Britain.

Sensing the momentum, nationalist politicians and their newspaper allies began promoting expansion at every

*LEFT: **After completing** his fourth congressional term in 1851, Howell Cobb left Washington, only to return in 1857 to serve in James Buchanan's cabinet as secretary of the treasury.*

A pioneer family pausing on the Oregon Trail in 1870.

THE OREGON TRAIL

THE MOMENT THAT most determined the course of western settlement came in mid-February 1824, when some Crow Indians showed a small band of fur trappers a relatively easy way to cross the Rocky Mountains. This route, which intersected the Continental Divide at South Pass, gradually became the focus of nearly all overland immigration to Oregon and California.

From its start in Independence, Missouri, the famous Oregon Trail cut through Kansas to follow the Platte and North Platte Rivers into Wyoming. After crossing the Rockies at South Pass, it forked at Fort Bridger. Travelers could either turn south to follow the California Trail or continue northwest toward the Snake River. From the Snake, the Oregon Trail made a difficult climb through the Blue Mountains to Fort Walla Walla, then turned due west and followed the Columbia River to the trail's terminus at Fort Vancouver, which guarded the northern end of the Willamette Valley.

The first major party of settlers infected with "Oregon fever" set out from Independence in 1843, covering the two thousand miles to Fort Vancouver in about six months. For the next three decades, traffic on the trail remained steady. In open country, pioneer wagons would wander, but along rivers and through mountain passes they converged to follow a single rutted path that still scars the land today.

Independence (shown here in 1855) was no stranger to wagon trains. Even before Oregon-bound pioneers began arriving there in 1843, the town served as the jumping-off point for the Santa Fe Trail, which William Becknell opened in 1822 following Mexican independence. (Previously, Spain had barred U.S. trade with New Mexico.) The Santa Fe Trail quickly became the principal route to and from the Southwest, and it remained so until after the Civil War, when construction of the Atchison, Topeka & Santa Fe Railroad put the wagoners out of business.

opportunity. The phrase that has since come to represent their efforts is *manifest destiny*. It was coined by Democratic magazine editor John L. O'Sullivan, who wrote in the July 1845 issue of *United States Magazine and Democratic Review* that God specifically intended the United States to export its Protestant religion, democratic politics, and capitalist economics all the way to the Pacific. It was, O'Sullivan claimed, "our manifest destiny to overspread the continent allotted by Providence for the free development of our yearly multiplying millions."

Most of the enthusiasm focused on the Oregon Country, which at the time encompassed all of the land west of the Rockies from Spanish California to Russian Alaska. Initially, four nations sought title to all or part of Oregon; by 1825, however, Spain and Russia had withdrawn their claims, leaving only the United States and Great Britain (and their respective fur companies) to compete for control. In 1818, the Rush-Bagot Treaty that fixed the Canadian border at the forty-ninth parallel from the Great Lakes to the Continental Divide also provided for a ten-year joint occupation of Oregon. In 1827, the joint occupation was extended indefinitely.

THE GREAT AMERICAN rush to Oregon, which began in 1843, was stimulated by missionaries who moved there during the 1830s to convert the local Indians. In 1834, Methodists Jason and Daniel Lee crossed the Rockies with Nat Wyeth's trading party so that they might minister to the Flathead Indians. When the Lees arrived at the Columbia River trading post of Fort Vancouver, however, they reconsidered. Judging the Flatheads to be irredeemably savage, they chose instead to colonize the Willamette Valley and farm its attractively fertile soil. Their homestead became the first permanent American settlement in Oregon.

The first whites to populate the central Rockies were solitary trappers, known as mountain men, who went there to find the plentiful beaver reported by Meriwether Lewis. Once a year, they held a "rendezvous," at which they traded their pelts for supplies. This rendezvous was held in 1837.

A year later, Marcus Whitman made the same overland journey but stuck to his original purpose, establishing a Presbyterian mission near present-day Walla Walla. Then he returned east; took a wife, Narcissa; and in 1836 brought her back to Oregon with him. Accompanied by fellow missionary Henry Harmon Spalding and his wife, Eliza, the Whitmans crossed the Rockies with Tom Fitzpatrick's supply caravan, making it the first wagon train to ferry white women into the Pacific Northwest. In 1843, it was Whitman himself who led the first large group of settlers into Oregon. That same year, Americans already in Oregon began the work of organizing a provisional government so that they could petition Congress for annexation and statehood. With the permanent American population now far exceeding the resident Canadian fur traders, even the British began to realize that joint occupation was no longer viable.

Not surprisingly, the annexations of Oregon and Texas became the dominant issues of the 1844 presidential campaign. While Whig nominee Henry Clay temporized, Democrat James K. Polk made expansion the centerpiece of his campaign. Polk's slogan "Fifty-four Forty or Fight!" referred to his demand that Britain relinquish the entire Oregon Country to north latitude 54°40' (the southern border of Russian Alaska). After his election, however, with war to the south imminent, Polk chose to compromise with London and acceded to the reasonable British demand that Oregon be partitioned at the forty-ninth parallel, the same border that separated the United States from Canada east of the Rockies.

A map of the West from 1846.

Stephen F. Austin, as he appeared in a miniature portrait painted on ivory in 1833.

Texas

TEXAS WAS ANOTHER MATTER. As part of the 1819 Adams-Onís Treaty, under which Spain ceded Florida, the United States gave up its claim to Texas (dubiously asserted by Jefferson to be part of the Louisiana Purchase). Yet Spain exerted little influence there, leaving Texas subject to only the most cursory supervision of provincial officials. Even after Mexico declared independence from Spain in February 1821, Texas remained an overlooked backwater. Mexico's new republican government had neither the means nor the inclination to police the few thousand souls living there, and after reauthorizing a Spanish policy designed to encourage white settlement, it gave the region a rather wide berth.

Prior to Mexican independence, Missourian Moses Austin had negotiated with the Spanish authorities for a large land grant in the Brazos River Valley. He died during the shift in governments, but his son pursued the grant, which the new Mexican government soon confirmed. Stephen F. Austin then set about colonizing the land and building up the local economy, which was his (and Mexico's) ultimate goal. By 1830, there were at least twenty-five thousand Americans living in Texas; and because many of them were southerners who intended to grow cotton, there were two thousand slaves as well.

Around the same time, a more confident Mexican government attempted to exert greater control over the province, and problems inevitably developed. The terms of the original Austin land grant had required American settlers (nearly all of whom were Protestant) to convert to Roman Catholicism, the religion of the Mexican state. Widespread defiance of this requirement, among other behaviors that reflected a reluctance to assimilate, persuaded Mexican leaders that the arrogant Americans in the Brazos Valley needed greater discipline. The central government tried to limit further white immigration by forbidding the importation of slaves (Mexico had already abolished slavery) and placing high import duties on U.S. goods, but poor enforcement meant that these actions served only to anger the colonists without affecting their behavior.

The situation escalated in 1833, when Austin himself was jailed in Mexico City for urging that Texas become a self-governing state within the Mexican federation.

In early 1836, Gen. Antonio López de Santa Anna, who had recently assumed dictatorial powers, marched an army of six thousand professional soldiers north to subdue the recalcitrant Texans. Aware of Santa Anna's advance, a group of settlers met on March 2 at Washington-on-the-Brazos to declare Texan independence. They also adopted a constitution legalizing slavery, formed a provisional government, and placed Sam Houston in charge of their armed forces. Meanwhile, on February 23, Santa Anna had already

An early photograph of the ruins of the Alamo.

besieged the Alamo, an abandoned mission in the heart of San Antonio, Texas's largest city. Col. William Barret Travis, commanding fewer than two hundred Texans, responded to Santa Anna's demand for the Alamo's surrender with a defiant cannon shot. The siege lasted until March 6, when the Mexican army overran the mission and, honoring Santa Anna's earlier pledge, killed every Texan who had resisted. Yet the stand made by Travis and the others (including Davy Crockett and Jim Bowie) gave Houston two additional weeks to complete his preparations, and the time proved decisive. At San Jacinto on April 21, Houston's eight hundred Texans defeated an army composed of twice as many Mexicans. Their victory, highlighted by the capture of Santa Anna, guaranteed Texan independence. Of course, the matter didn't end there.

SAM HOUSTON
1793–1863

STATELY SIX-FOOT-THREE-INCH Sam Houston was flamboyant in his speech, manner, and dress. One of his favorite ensembles included a gold-headed cane, a panther-skin waistcoat, a large sombrero, and a Mexican blanket. Ten years after San Jacinto, when he arrived in Washington to represent the new state of Texas in the U.S. Senate, a contemporary described the fifty-two-year-old Houston as "a magnificent barbarian, somewhat tempered by civilization" with "a lion-like countenance capable of expressing the fiercest passions."

As a runaway youth on the Tennessee frontier, Houston lived for nearly three years with the Cherokees, who called him Black Raven. The rapport he developed with them later made Houston useful to the federal government, which employed him in 1817 to help manage the removal of the Cherokees to a reservation in the Arkansas Territory. (In the meantime, Houston had served in the War of 1812, studied, and taught school.) Later, in Nashville, he became a lawyer and a protégé of Andrew Jackson, who helped Houston become governor of Tennessee in 1827. Two years later, however, with the failure of his marriage, Houston resigned the post and returned to live with the Cherokees, who formally adopted him into their tribe. Twice during the next three years, he traveled to Washington to expose frauds being perpetrated against the Cherokees by government agents. In 1832,

President Jackson sent Houston to Texas (still a Mexican province) to negotiate Indian treaties for the protection of border traders. Houston ended up relocating to Texas, where he became deeply involved in the settlers' power struggle with the Mexican government. After Texan independence, he served twice as president of the republic before winning election in 1846 to the U.S. Senate, where he legislated as a Democrat.

Texas was a slave state, and Houston was himself a slaveholder, but he refused to be bound in the Senate by any sectional ties. "I know neither North nor South," he once said; "I know only the Union." He voted for all five of the Senate bills that made up the Compromise of 1850 (the only southerner to do so), and he cast one of only two southern votes in the Senate against the 1854 Kansas-Nebraska Act. (The latter resulted in his formal censure by the Texas legislature.) Such staunch unionism cost Houston presidential nominations in 1852 and 1856 and also his Senate seat in 1859. Still vigorous at sixty-six, he made a comeback, winning the race for governor of Texas that fall, but his efforts to block secession and his refusal to swear allegiance to the Confederacy resulted in his removal from office in March 1861.

This portrait of Sam Houston was taken not long before the secession of South Carolina in December 1860.

Later in 1836, the Texans indicated their desire to join the United States, but annexation was delayed while Congress debated its merits. Proslavery southerners favored annexation because they expected Texas to seek admission as a slave state; northern abolitionists opposed annexation for the same reason. The moderates who held the balance of power did what they could to keep the issue off the table because they knew it was political dynamite. They were abetted in this by Presidents Jackson and Van Buren, neither of whom wanted to see disputes over slavery increase sectional divisions.

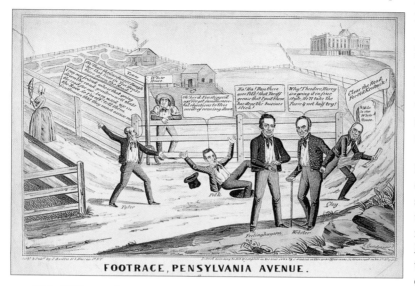

FOOTRACE, PENSYLVANIA AVENUE.

This 1844 presidential campaign cartoon appeared before Tyler's formal withdrawal on August 20.

By 1844, however, the leadership situation had changed: President Tyler strongly favored annexation, as did the Democrats running the Polk campaign. Moreover, recent efforts by the Republic of Texas to court European recognition and aid worried many congressmen, who feared that cotton-hungry Great Britain might become too close an ally of cotton-producing Texas. In early March 1844, Tyler made John C. Calhoun his new secretary of state, and just six weeks later the president submitted to the Senate the annexation treaty Calhoun had quickly negotiated with the Texans. It was rejected overwhelmingly on June 8, but Polk's victory in the 1844 election so energized the forces of expansion that Congress reversed itself, passing a joint resolution on February 28, 1845, authorizing the annexation. (The joint-resolution strategy was a slick parliamentary maneuver on Tyler's part because congressional resolutions require only simply majorities, whereas treaty ratification demands a two-thirds vote.) Four days later, Polk became president and made clear in his inaugural address that he would complete the annexation of Texas. Two days after that, Mexico angrily broke off diplomatic relations with the United States. Nevertheless, on December 29, 1845, Texas became the twenty-eighth state.

This January 1838 poster described the annexation of Texas as "a scheme fraught with...ruin."

Several times during his first year in office, Polk attempted to mollify the Mexican government so that he could proceed with another of his expansionist goals: the purchase of California. The Mexicans, however, spurned his envoys. Warned in early January 1846 by his latest emissary, John Slidell, of growing agitation in Mexico for the reconquest of Texas, Polk ordered Gen. Zachary Taylor and a thirty-five-hundred-man "army of observation" into the disputed border area between the Nueces River and the Rio Grande. In early May, Mexican troops crossed the Rio Grande, ambushing a cavalry patrol and killing sixteen Americans. Learning of the raid, Polk immediately asked for a declaration of war, which Congress approved on May 13.

The Mexican War

POLK WAS TAKING a rather large risk. The Mexican army in 1846 included thirty-two thousand soldiers hardened by a decade of civil war. In comparison, the U.S. Army, which numbered just seven thousand, had spend most of the last three decades fighting only hopelessly overmatched Indians (and those not very often). The House authorized the recruitment of fifty thousand volunteers, but a similar reliance on raw recruits during the War of 1812 had substantially undermined the military's competency. Polk soon showed himself to be a shrewd commander in chief when he chose to blend the glory-hungry volunteer regiments with battalions of more experienced professional soldiers. But even so, the American war effort began precariously. Only later did the U.S. superiority in arms and supplies become obvious.

"A LITTLE MORE GRAPE CAPT BRAGG"

Zachary Taylor directs artillery fire during the February 1847 battle of Buena Vista. It was the Americans' superior artillery that proved decisive at Buena Vista and elsewhere.

In fact, the Americans never lost a battle. Taylor won early engagements at Palo Alto (May 8) and Resaca de la Palma (May 9) north of the Rio Grande. Then he moved south to capture the northern Mexican stronghold of Monterrey on September 25. However, despite these battlefield accomplishments, Taylor's independence and disrespectful attitude angered the president, who transferred most of Taylor's command after Monterrey to the army Gen. Winfield Scott was organizing for an assault on Mexico City. On March 9, 1847, leading about ten thousand men, Scott attacked the fortified city of Veracruz in the U.S. military's first large-scale amphibious operation. From Veracruz, which fell on March 29, Scott followed in the footsteps of Cortés, advancing inland toward the Mexican capital. On April 18, his army stormed a mountain pass at Cerro Gordo, thrashing Santa Anna's army badly. At Contreras on August 19 and the next day at Churubusco, the Americans again routed the Mexican army, which subsequently asked for an armistice. There were some peace talks, but these failed, and the fighting resumed on September 7. A week later, Scott smashed his way through the Mexico City's last defensive line and entered the capital, effectively ending the war.

MEANWHILE, and more importantly, American soldiers had already captured New Mexico and California. At the same time that he sent Taylor to the Nueces River (the summer of 1845), Polk also sent secret instructions to the commander of the U.S. Pacific fleet (actually just a naval squadron) ordering him to seize the ports of California should he learn that Mexico had declared war. The president also wrote to the American consul in Monterey, Thomas O. Larkin, asking him to arrange a "spontaneous" revolt among the American settlers and pro-American Mexicans.

Winfield Scott's entrance into Mexico City on September 14, 1847, is depicted in this 1851 painting by Carl Nebel.

CENTER:
This flag was carried by the founders of the Bear Flag Republic in 1846.

Larkin might well have arranged such an uprising had the flamboyant John C. Frémont not arrived unexpectedly in California in January 1846. Frémont had spent most of the past several years mapping the West for the U.S. Army Corps of Topographical Engineers—using exploration as a diplomatic weapon, much as Lewis and Clark had—and his appearance put the Mexicans on their guard, forcing the abandonment of Larkin's plan. The provincial government eventually asked Frémont and his men to leave—which they did, withdrawing to the Oregon border in March. On June 14, however, Americans settlers meeting at Sonoma declared independence for California during what came to be called the Bear Flag Revolt, and Frémont immediately moved south to join the rebels, who accepted his leadership on July 5. At about the same time, U.S. warships commanded by Commo. John Sloat captured Monterey (July 7) and San Francisco (July 9). On August 13, Frémont joined forces with Commo. Robert F. Stockton, who had replaced the ailing Sloat, to conquer Los Angeles. Four days later, Stockton proclaimed the annexation of California.

Such freebooting by Stockton and Frémont deeply concerned the cautious Polk, who quickly sent Col. Stephen W. Kearny to take command of the ramshackle U.S. forces in California. Kearny, who had recently captured Santa Fe and annexed New Mexico without a fight, arrived to find most of California back under Mexican control. The Mexican Californians who had earlier fought beside the Americans had lately reconciled with their provincial government and helped it recapture San Diego and Los Angeles. Kearny subsequently reconquered California and on January 13, 1847, accepted the surrender of the last Mexican troops. The entire Southwest was now in American hands, a situation that became permanent on February 2, 1848, with the signing of the Treaty of Guadalupe Hidalgo. This agreement forced Mexico to give up 529,000 square miles of occupied territory in New Mexico and California, as well as recognize the annexation of

John C. Frémont, as photographed by Mathew Brady in 1856.

Stephen Kearny's troops repulse Mexican lancers at the decisive battle of the Plains of Mesa on January 9, 1847.

Texas and accept the Rio Grande boundary in exchange for fifteen million dollars in cash plus assumption by the United States of all private claims against Mexico.

The Politics of the Mexican Cession

THE MEXICAN CESSION, however, brought with it major political headaches—the unwanted but hardly unforeseen consequences of manifest destiny. Texas, for example, now claimed a large chunk of New Mexico (about half of the present-day state). A much more important question, however, was whether the new territories carved out of the Mexican Cession would be slave or free. Already, on August 8, 1846, Pennsylvania congressman David Wilmot, a member of Polk's own party, had introduced an amendment to a Mexican War spending bill prohibiting slavery in any land acquired from Mexico. The House approved the measure in late 1846 and again in early 1847, but both times it was blocked by the Senate. Nevertheless, many northerners, including most of the "conscience" Whigs, remained committed to and hopeful of its passage.

During 1848, many nonaffiliated abolitionists joined with conscience Whigs and antislavery Democrats (including David Wilmot) to form the Free Soil party, whose platform cleverly included planks unrelated to slavery that were intended to broaden the new party's appeal. For example, the Free Soilers endorsed Whig demands for greater national control of the economy, as well as a Democratic-style plan to grant free public land to homesteaders willing to settle the trans-Mississippi West. "Free Soil, Free Speech, Free Labor, and Free Men" was the party's motto. At the same time, southerners in Congress formed their own bloc, nominally retaining their respective party affiliations but voting without regard to party when it came to regional issues, especially slavery.

This was the situation as Zachary Taylor took up residence in the White House in March 1849. The new president hadn't said much about California or New Mexico during the campaign, but he knew his own mind: He wanted immediate statehood for both. The situation in California was especially urgent, because the discovery of gold there in January 1848 had produced a stampede of '49ers eager to find their fortune. Some sort of civilian government (to replace the makeshift military rule) had to be established soon, and Taylor knew that proposing territorial status for California would inevitably lead to a congressional battle over the legalization of slavery there. However, if California and New Mexico were permitted to bypass the territorial stage and join the Union immediately as states, they could decide the slavery question for themselves, as all states had the right to do. The trouble was that neither California nor New Mexico was likely to seek slave status on its own (economic conditions there were simply not conducive to slave labor), and the South knew this quite well.

The U.S. Army benefited during the Mexican War from an outstanding corps of junior officers recently trained at West Point. They included Ulysses S. Grant (shown here participating in the capture of Mexico City), George B. McClellan, Thomas J. Jackson, and Robert E. Lee.

Abolitionists opposed the Mexican War because they feared the creation of new slave states in the conquered territory. A few, such as Henry David Thoreau (shown here in 1856), refused to pay their taxes and went to jail.

THE CALIFORNIA GOLD RUSH

DURING THE FIRST HALF of the nineteenth century, Spanish (and later Mexican) California attracted very few American settlers. In fact, there were just about eight hundred Americans living there—and only about fourteen thousand people overall—when the Mexican War broke out in 1846. By 1852, however, the state's population had jumped to nearly three hundred thousand.

The difference was James Marshall's discovery of gold along the American River in January 1848.

It took about nine months for the California gold rush to begin. The news of Marshall's find didn't reach the East until August 19, when it was published for the first time in the *New York Herald*. And even after that, many future gold seekers waited until December 5, when President Polk confirmed the report, before setting out for California. The first boatload of prospectors reached San Francisco on February 28, 1849—hence the nickname '*49er*. Their ship, the *California*, had left New York six months earlier nearly empty. In the meantime, fifteen hundred '49ers had taken fast clipper ships to Panama and crossed the isthmus by rail so they could board the northbound *California* on Panama's Pacific coast in January.

San Francisco and its harbor about 1855.

Taking advantage of the fact that the new Congress wouldn't convene until early December (as was standard practice), Taylor quietly sent Georgia representative T. Butler King to California to inform the political leaders there of his preference should they be inclined to draft a constitution and apply for immediate statehood. This, of course, is precisely what the Californians did, holding a constitutional convention at Monterey in September 1849 and ratifying the resulting anti-slavery document on November 11. (The president also used several intermediaries to send an identical message to the political oligarchy in Santa Fe, but the confused state of New Mexico's boundaries made the calling of a constitutional convention there problematic.)

On December 4, in a special message to Congress delivered while the Speaker fight in the House still raged, Taylor formally backed the admission of California as a free state. The southerners who had voted for him couldn't believe what they heard.

William Seward's election as governor of New York in 1838 broke the two-decade-old hold of the Albany Regency on state politics.

MEANWHILE, THERE WAS TROUBLE in Congress over fugitive slaves. The law currently on the books was a 1793 statue that most northerners either ignored or flouted. Early in January 1850, Virginia senator James M. Mason introduced a bill designed to make the recapture of runaway slaves easier and more certain. In response, William H. Seward, an antislavery Whig from New York, threatened to amend Mason's bill so that alleged runaways would be guaranteed local jury trials—at which point the chamber exploded into a predictable outpouring of sectional invective. Mississippi senator Henry S. Foote, for example, branded Seward a fanatic who wanted only to punish the South. The situation was ripe for Henry Clay.

After failing in his 1844 bid for the presidency, the seventy-two-year-old Clay had been in semiretirement, but he returned to the Senate in 1849 just in time to initiate the third major compromise of his long congressional career. (In 1820, while Speaker of the House, the Kentuckian had helped pass the Missouri Compromise; in 1833, he had introduced the Compromise Tariff.) Known as the Great Pacificator, Clay gloried in his reputation as a peacemaker and knew that this conflict would be his last great political battle. On January 29, eight days after President Taylor once again called for congressional action on California, Clay rose in the Senate to deliver a much-anticipated speech in which he introduced the eight resolutions that made up his compromise:

1. *California should be admitted immediately as a state.*
2. *Congress ought to establish "appropriate" territorial governments in New Mexico without including any provisions either introducing or limiting slavery.*
3. *The boundary dispute between Texas and New Mexico should be resolved in New Mexico's favor.*
4. *In exchange for relinquishing its claim, Texas should be paid an (intentionally unspecified) sum toward the debt the state incurred prior to its admission.*
5. *Ownership of slaves within the District of Columbia should not be restricted.*
6. *The slave trade within the District of Columbia should be banned.*
7. *A more effective fugitive slave law should be enacted.*
8. *Congress should acknowledge its lack of authority to regulate slave trading within the slaveholding states.*

The engraving above shows Henry Clay presenting his eight-resolution compromise to the Senate on January 29, 1850. The official text of those resolutions is also shown here.

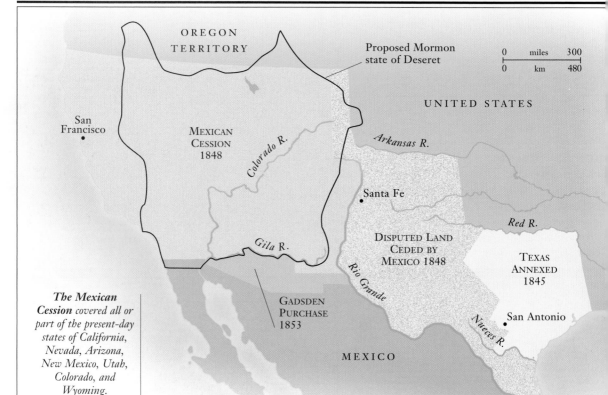

OREGON
TERRITORY

Proposed Mormon
state of Deseret

0 — miles — 300
0 — km — 480

UNITED STATES

San
Francisco

MEXICAN
CESSION
1848

Colorado R.

Arkansas R.

Santa Fe

Red R.

DISPUTED LAND
CEDED BY
MEXICO 1848

TEXAS
ANNEXED
1845

*The Mexican
Cession* covered all or
part of the present-day
states of California,
Nevada, Arizona,
New Mexico, Utah,
Colorado, and
Wyoming.

Gila R.

Rio Grande

GADSDEN
PURCHASE
1853

Nueces R.

San Antonio

MEXICO

THE NORTH STOOD to gain a great deal from Clay's
proposals: California's admission would alter the delicate free–slave
equilibrium in Senate, currently balanced at fifteen states apiece, to the North's
advantage. It would also increase free-state representation in the House, which was
already dominated by northerners because of that section's much larger population.
Even the significant enticement that Clay offered the South in return, a new
fugitive slave law, depended (as Mississippi senator Jefferson Davis
caustically pointed out) on the willingness of northerners to
cooperate with its enforcement.

Davis's vocal opposition came as no surprise to Clay, who
expected nothing less from the "fire-eaters," as the South's
proslavery extremists were called. Yet while Clay canvassed
for votes among the Senate's moderates, his old ally John C.
Calhoun prepared a response. In March 1850, Calhoun was
dying, and he knew it. Several times already he had fainted
in the Senate lobby, and on at least one occasion he had to
be carried out. Although the senator's feeble health now
prevented him from delivering his March 4 speech person-

*Jefferson Davis
married Varina Howell
(right) in February
1845. Earlier, he had
been married to
Zachary Taylor's
daughter Knox,
who died in 1835.*

ally, its text, read in his presence by Senator Mason, demonstrated that Calhoun's
mind was as firm and uncompromising as ever.

In contrast to the emotionalism shown by Davis and the younger generation
of southern politicians, Calhoun used logic to demand specific concessions for the
South. He argued that a temporary patchwork solution would not do. (Chanting
"Union!" over the body of Clay's resolutions, he warned in a memorable phrase,
would be about as useful as crying "Health!" over the body of a dying man.)

Instead, he demanded that the political balance between North and South be guaranteed with a constitutional amendment, even though northern whites now outnumbered southern whites by more than two to one. With regard to statehood for California and New Mexico, Calhoun refused to compromise, asserting that southern slaveholders had just as much right to settle the West as any Americans. If northerners thought otherwise, Calhoun concluded, then "tell us so, and let the states we both represent agree to separate and part in peace. If you are unwilling we should part in peace, tell us so, and we shall know what to do when you reduce the question to submission or resistance."

The Seventh of March Oration

CALHOUN'S STEELY DEFIANCE derailed, at least temporarily, the momentum Clay had built for compromise and challenged the North to respond. The man who took up this challenge was Sen. Daniel Webster of Massachusetts, who scheduled a major Senate speech for March 7. During the nineteenth century, important congressional addresses of the sort Webster was expected to deliver carried considerably more weight than they do today and were treated as significant public occasions. Congress-men worked for days or weeks on their remarks, and their colleagues listened attentively for as long as four or five hours. Members of the public were no less interested, and they usually scrambled for seats in the gallery once notice was given in the congressional calendar. Often, people who couldn't find a seat stood in the aisles for the duration.

On March 7, 1850, the portly Webster stood up beside his desk, pulled his vest down over his paunch, raised his head, and struck a theatrical pose. "I wish to speak to-day," he began, "not as a Massachusetts man, nor as a northern man, but as an American, and a member of the Senate of the United States.... I speak to-day for the preservation of the Union. Hear me for my cause." Webster then traced the history of North–South differences, denouncing both northern abolitionists and southern secessionists for their dangerous extremism. Antislavery legislation such as the Wilmot Proviso, he asserted, was both offensive to the South and utterly unnecessary because slavery would never, under any circumstances, take root in the West, where the land and the economic conditions were "naturally" hostile to slave labor. "I would not take pains to reaffirm an ordinance of nature, nor to reenact the will of God," the senator said in an often-quoted line.

Webster even went so far as endorsing, with some reservations, Mason's fugitive slave bill and insisting that the North respect southern political rights,

Daniel Webster in a portrait taken at Mathew Brady's studio between 1845 and 1849.

SPEECH

HON. DANIEL WEBSTER,

Mr. Clay's Resolutions,

IN THE SENATE OF THE UNITED STATES.

MARCH 7, 1850.

WASHINGTON:
PRINTED BY GIDEON & CO.
1850.

More than 120,000 copies of Webster's March 7 speech were rushed into print. This one eventually found its way into the collection of John F. Kennedy. Even the Charleston Mercury noted that "with such a spirit as Mr. Webster has shown, it no longer seems impossible to bring this sectional contest to a close."

no matter how repugnant northerners might consider the slave system to be. In his conclusion, however, Webster castigated Calhoun for suggesting that secession might be peaceable. "Secession! Peaceable secession!" Webster roared. "Your eyes and mine are never destined to see that miracle." He would not specify what might produce "a disruption of the States," but he did offer this: "I see it as plainly as I see the sun in heaven—I see that disruption must produce such a war as I will not describe." Calhoun, who had earlier (and with great difficulty) taken his Senate seat, responded, "I cannot agree that this Union cannot be dissolved. Am I to understand that no degree of oppression, no outrage, no broken faith, can produce the destruction of this Union? The Union can be broken." These were Calhoun's last words on the Senate floor. By the end of March, he was dead.

By all accounts, John Calhoun was brilliant, ambitious, and nearly totally humorless.

DURING THE WEEK that followed, two other northern senators gave influential addresses. As Jefferson Davis had done for the fire-eaters, William Seward rose on March 11 to speak for the younger northern politicians who considered slavery a barbarous relic of less enlightened times. Most of Seward's speech, as expected, followed the northern hard line, but the senator did add one noteworthy twist: God Himself opposed slavery. "There is a higher law than the Constitution," Seward said, and the assertion lingered, much to the displeasure of his more expedient colleagues, who considered the statement irresponsible. The mood of the Senate changed two days later, however, when Democrat Stephen A. Douglas of Illinois reiterated his own party's intention to cooperate fully with Clay. Despite efforts already under way to reorganize the national political parties along geographic lines, Douglas said, the people "will not sanction any such movement. They know its tendencies and its dangers." Combined with the favorable press coverage that Webster's March 7 speech was receiving—it was generally hailed both North and South as an eloquent statement of the need for conciliation—Douglas's restatement of Democratic support for Clay resurrected the mood of compromise, and the Great Pacificator went back to work.

As a career military officer, Zachary Taylor was purposefully nonpartisan. Before 1848, in fact, he had never voted in a presidential election.

Then, as now, the real work of Congress went on in committee. In this case, the Senate formed in mid-April a select Committee of Thirteen, chaired by Clay, to work out the details of the compromise. During the next three weeks, Clay retired to the Maryland estate of Charles B. Calvert to compose a report while most of his fellow senators took advantage of the lull to return home and court their constituents. On May 8, before a packed chamber, Clay read his seven-point report, which strongly resembled his January 29 plan. (The last of Clay's original resolutions was dropped, and the others folded into an omnibus bill.) On May 13, formal debate on the report began, with nearly every senator heard at least once and some several times. The most compelling comments, however, came from President Taylor, who made it clear that, pledge or no, he would veto any omnibus bill that linked statehood for California and New Mexico to such inflammatory issues as fugitive slaves and the Texas debt. Taylor's veto threat stalled the omnibus bill, as opponents spent the majority of June attacking the report of the Committee of Thirteen and offering one hostile amendment after another. "We shall have a warm summer," Webster predicted. "The political atmosphere will be hot, however the natural may be. I am for it and shall fight it out."

Then, on July 9, Zachary Taylor died. Attending lengthy Independence Day ceremonies under a broiling sun at the base of the unfinished Washington Monument, the president had become weak. Back at the White House, he had refreshed himself with iced liquids and a variety of fresh fruits and vegetables. (He consumed "cucumbers and cherries with mush and milk," according to one of the many varying accounts of his menu.) Five days later, Taylor died of acute gastroenteritis. Vice Pres. Millard Fillmore succeeded him. Fillmore was a rather nondescript New Yorker who had climbed the ladder of Anti-Mason and Whig politics along with Seward but always a few rungs behind. Southerners tended to distrust him because he came from western New York, one of the most antislavery regions in the state. But few congressmen knew for a fact where Fillmore stood on the compromise; and, as Taylor had shown, assuming that a president would act according to his geography was risky.

The Great Compromise

AS LATE AS APRIL 1850, Fillmore had indicated his support for the Taylor administration line, but sometime after that he changed his mind. He later claimed that, just prior to Taylor's death, he had told the president that should the Senate split evenly, he would cast his tiebreaking vote in favor of the compromise. Later, as president, Fillmore did dedicate himself passage of the compromise, praising the Committee of Thirteen's report as "a means of healing sectional differences." Yet compromise still proved elusive. On July 31, during a complicated series of votes, the Senate stripped away, one by one, various provisions of the omnibus bill until all that remained was territorial status for Utah, which had heretofore been part of New Mexico. The Utah bill passed easily, because everyone in Congress was eager to reassert federal authority over the Mormon settlers; but the nation was no closer to statehood for California or a resolution of the slavery question.

Clay was humiliated. When the Senate adjourned for the weekend on Friday, August 2, the Great Pacificator left the capital for the resort town of Newport, Rhode Island, probably in a huff and surely exhausted—as, it seemed, was his generation's leadership. Clay didn't return to Washington until August 27. In the

LEFT:
***This account** of Taylor's death appeared in the* Boston Cultivator *of July 13, 1850.*

***Ironically,** it was the choice of vice-presidential candidate Millard Fillmore (and not the selection of Taylor) that most concerned southerners at the 1848 Whigs convention.*

The publisher of this 1852 group portrait hoped to take advantage of the optimism that followed enactment of the Great Compromise. Entitled simply Union, *it shows the principal players, most of whom had already died.*

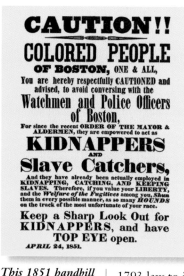

CAUTION!!
COLORED PEOPLE
OF BOSTON, ONE & ALL,
You are hereby respectfully CAUTIONED and advised, to avoid conversing with the
Watchmen and Police Officers
of Boston,
For since the recent ORDER OF THE MAYOR & ALDERMEN, they are empowered to act as
KIDNAPPERS
AND
Slave Catchers,
And they have already been actually employed in
KIDNAPPING, CATCHING, AND KEEPING
SLAVES. Therefore, if you value your LIBERTY,
and the *Welfare of the Fugitives* among you, Shun
them in every possible manner, as so many HOUNDS
on the track of the most unfortunate of your race.
Keep a Sharp Look Out for
KIDNAPPERS, and have
TOP EYE open.
APRIL 24, 1851.

This 1851 handbill warned blacks in Boston to beware enforcement of the new Fugitive Slave Law.

meantime, the confident and resourceful Stephen Douglas put his compromise through the Senate piecemeal. Douglas accomplished this by persuading different combinations of senators to support different bills. When California statehood passed on August 13, for example, the senators who voted for it included seventeen Democrats, fifteen Whigs, and two Free Soilers (twenty-eight northerners and six southerners). Fourteen Democrats and four Whigs (all southerners) opposed the measure, while two southern Democrats, four southern Whigs, and two northern Whigs did not vote. The fugitive slave bill that passed on August 23 had fifteen southern Democratic supporters, along with nine southern Whigs and three northern Democrats. Three northern Democrats, eight northern Whigs, and one Free Soiler voted against the bill; twenty-one other senators ominously did not record a preference. These results showed clearly that, while Clay (a Whig) may have initiated the compromise, it was Douglas and the Democrats who made it law.

In the end, five separate acts made up the Great Compromise. In addition to the two already cited, the Texas–New Mexico law settled the Texas border and debt issues, as well as the slavery question for New Mexico. It established the present western border of Texas, thus resolving the boundary dispute in New Mexico's favor. For this and other considerations, Texas was paid ten million dollars. The act also created the enormous territory of New Mexico, which included present-day New Mexico and Arizona as well as parts of Colorado and Nevada, and provided that "when admitted as a State, the said territory, or any portion of the same, shall be received into the Union, with or without slavery, as their constitution may prescribe at the time of their admission." This last provision represented Douglas's guiding principle in the debate: that the people of a territory, rather than the federal government, should decide the slavery question. He called this doctrine "popular sovereignty," but it was really just a restatement of the squatter sovereignty that Lewis Cass had espoused during the 1848 presidential campaign. The fourth act organized the territory of Utah (using the same language regarding slavery as that applied to New Mexico), and the final law outlawed the slave trade in the District of Columbia beginning January 1, 1851.

The most controversial element of the compromise was undoubtedly the Fugitive Slave Act, which amended the existing 1793 law to include the appointment of federal commissioners to facilitate the return of runaway slaves. What outraged northerners most were the ways in which this system was biased against alleged runaways: To begin with, the commissioners were paid ten dollars for each slave they returned and only five dollars for each wrongfully accused black whom they freed. Even worse, accused runaways were denied jury trials and the right to testify on their own behalf. Instead, northern blacks could be arrested and sent south merely on the basis of affidavits sworn out by southerners who claimed to be their masters.

EVEN WITH THE FUGITIVE SLAVE controversy, passage of the Compromise of 1850 did cool tempers for a time, as public opinion in both the North and the South rallied to the moderate position. During the 1852 presidential campaign, which Democrat Franklin Pierce of New Hampshire won rather easily, both parties endorsed the compromise, which was hailed (at least publicly) as a final settlement of the slavery issue. Pierce was himself a compromise choice, nominated because he was a "doughface"—that is, a northerner sympathetic to the southern position on slavery. But more than anything else, his campaign showed clearly that a majority of the country simply wanted to bury the slavery issue and exclude it from political debate. Despite the Democrats' best efforts, however, that proved impossible.

During the 1852 campaign, Franklin Pierce, a Mexican War veteran, was accused of drunkenness and ridiculed as "the hero of many well-fought bottles."

Even after the 1852 election, antislavery northerners continued to agitate for the exclusion of slavery from the western territories. They believed, as Seward had said, that a higher law demanded free labor; and their cause was aided by anger in the North generated by rough enforcement of the new fugitive slave law. Even though the abuses were more symbolic than real—only one in five thousand slaves escaped annually, and few masters showed much interest in recovering those who did—the activities of "slave catchers" operating in New England and the Middle West stirred up a hornets' nest of antisouthern fervor. Despite the region's otherwise racist treatment of blacks, northerners made heroes of defiant runaways and the abolitionists who aided them. On occasion, mobs in Boston and elsewhere physically prevented the return of runaway slaves.

President Pierce tried to divert the nation's attention by pursuing an aggressive foreign policy. In late 1853, U.S. minister to Mexico James Gadsden negotiated the purchase of a strip of land from the Gila River (then the U.S.-Mexico boundary) south to the present-day borders of Arizona and New Mexico. The ten million dollars he paid—an enormously high sum—was considered by many Whigs who had opposed the war to be "conscience money," but the amount seemed reasonable to Gadsden and other southerners who had ambitious plans for the land. The next great sectional struggle was shaping up to be one over where the first transcontinental railroad would be built. Gadsden and his fellow entrepreneurs wanted the line to run through the South, and they persuaded Pierce to approve the Gadsden Purchase because it contained the only feasible southern route to the Pacific. Meanwhile, Stephen Douglas was scheming to ensure that the first transcontinental line passed through his own state of Illinois.

THE OSTEND MANIFESTO

AN IMPORTANT ASPECT of Pierce's foreign policy was his agitation for American expansion into Cuba and Central America, but these efforts also foundered on the shoals of sectionalism. Early in his administration, Pierce directed U.S. minister to Spain Pierre Soulé to negotiate the purchase of Cuba. When Spain refused to sell, Secretary of State William L. Marcy requested that the U.S. ministers to Great Britain (James Buchanan) and France (John Y. Mason) meet with Soulé in Ostend, Belgium, in order to consider together alternate policies. On October 18, 1854, the three diplomats sent a confidential memorandum to the State Department recommending that, if Spain's recalcitrance continued, the United States should simply seize the island. Soon, the contents of the Ostend Manifesto were leaked to the press, and the issue became swallowed up in controversy. Antislavery northerners denounced the document (especially its intemperate language) as a southern plot to extend slavery, and their objections ended any possibility that Pierce might acquire Cuba, peacefully or otherwise.

The Kansas-Nebraska Act

IT WAS, IN FACT, the railroad issue that prompted Douglas to introduce in January 1854 a bill creating the territories of Kansas and Nebraska (a prerequisite for any railroad construction on the sparsely settled Plains). Douglas hoped to win over proponents of a southern route (led by Jefferson Davis, now Pierce's secretary of war) by applying his doctrine of popular sovereignty to these Louisiana Purchase lands. Specifically, Douglas proposed that the region be divided into two territories, with the slavery question to be decided in each by a vote of its residents. The assumption was that Nebraska would become a free territory, but Kansas—influenced by neighboring Missouri—might well permit slavery. This was the same treatment that Congress had given the new territories of Utah and New Mexico, but Kansas and Nebraska were different because they were Louisiana Purchase lands and therefore subject to the terms of the 1820 Missouri Compromise. What Douglas was really proposing was a repeal of the Missouri Compromise banning slavery north of latitude 36°30'. With the support of President Pierce, the Kansas-Nebraska Act became law in late May.

This early 1850s photograph shows the first railroad train to cross the Allegheny Mountains.

The fierce debate that preceded enactment, however, broke the uneasy truce that had existed, more or less, since 1850. It also led directly to the formation of the Republican party, which brought together conscience Whigs, anti-Douglas Democrats, and, of course, Free Soilers. The new party demanded the complete exclusion of slavery from all federal territories and took an equally hard line on other related issues. Meanwhile, the situation in Kansas became a national crisis.

Once the Kansas-Nebraska Act became law, activists on both sides encouraged their followers to move to Kansas in order to control the slavery vote there. Abolitionists organized the New England Emigrant Aid Society and other such

NATIVISM

By the early 1850s, the Whig party was obviously dying, and its members began to seek political homes elsewhere. While many became Republicans, others (including former president Millard Fillmore) joined the new American party, whose members were called Know-Nothings because their platform was secret and when asked about it, they answered, "I know nothing of it." The Know-Nothings were nativists—that is, they opposed immigration (which had surged during the 1840s) because they believed that it threatened the status of the "native Americans." (By this phrase of course, the Know-Nothings meant themselves and other descendants of the original white colonists, not the Indians.)

This 1854 soap label attempted *to capitalize on the "purity" sought by the Know-Nothings.*

Know-Nothings especially scorned Catholics, hundreds of thousands of whom had recently arrived in the United States. Some had left Germany because of economic distress there; even more fled Ireland after 1845 to escape the famous potato famine. As a result, the relatively minor U.S. Catholic population of three hundred thousand in 1830 soared by 1860 to more than three million people. Although the Constitution guaranteed them freedom of religion, tolerance did not produce acceptance, and the fear of a grand papist conspiracy strained even toleration at times, leading to fierce discrimination and even some violence against the working-class Catholic populations of the urban Northeast.

groups to finance free-soil migration to Kansas, while "border ruffians" from Missouri crossed the border to swell the proslavery ranks. (One of those who came to Kansas to cleanse the territory of slavery was an ardent free-stater named John Brown.) The result Horace Greeley's *New York Tribune* dubbed "Bleeding Kansas." It was a war zone in which armed factions clashed frequently, and none proved able to form a stable territorial government. Competing conventions were called, and several constitutions approved in tainted elections; but violence ruled the territory, and Pierce was blamed, deservedly, for the carnage.

The red line on this 1849 map shows the proposed route of a railroad between St. Louis and San Francisco. The path closely follows John C. Frémont's 1843 route, shown in green.

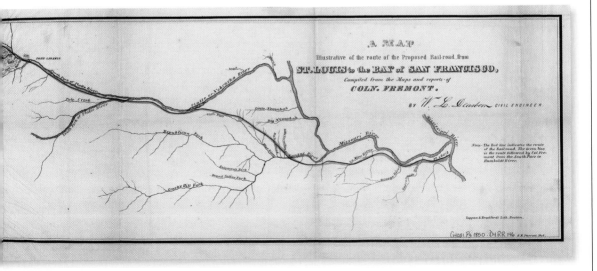

AMERICAN PROFILE

Matthew C. Perry
1794–1858

by John W. Dower

ON JULY 8, 1853, residents of Uraga on the outskirts of Edo, the sprawling capital of feudal Japan, beheld an astonishing sight: four foreign warships entering the harbor under a cloud of black smoke, with not a sail visible among them. They were, the Japanese quickly learned, two coal-burning steamships towing two sloops—all under the command of a dour and imperious American, Matthew Calbraith Perry, who intended to force the long-secluded Japanese to open their doors to the outside world.

Commodore Perry was the younger brother of Oliver Hazard Perry, the naval hero who had defeated the British in the 1813 battle of Lake Erie. His own reputation as a wartime leader had been established recently in Mexico, where he commanded a squadron that captured several ports and supported Winfield Scott's siege of Veracruz. Victory in that war had given the United States not merely California (and the rest of the Mexican Cession) but also a vista of new frontiers extending even farther west—to the markets and heathen souls of near-mythic "Asia."

U.S. merchant firms had been involved in the China trade centering on Canton since the previous century. Following Great Britain's victory in the Opium War of 1839–1842, the United States joined the system of "unequal treaties" that opened additional Chinese ports to

foreign commerce. Thus, tall, fast, elegant clipper ships were already carrying Oriental luxuries such as silk, porcelain, and tea to America's thriving eastern ports. Now, as Perry ponderously conveyed to the Japanese, ports on America's new west coast (notably San Francisco) were also opening up, and in this dawning age of steam-driven vessels, the distance between California and Japan had been reduced to just eighteen days. Given such new realities of time and space, the commodore believed, his demands upon Japan were relatively modest. For the Japanese, however, the intrusion was traumatic and rang the death knell to centuries of insular security and self-sufficiency.

The United States in midcentury was still the America of Herman Melville's *Moby-Dick*—a time when whale-oil lamps illuminated homes, baleen whale bones gave body to women's skirts, and the leviathan's grease lubricated industrial machinery. One of Perry's primary objectives was thus to arrange access to coal and provisions for whalers and other sailors plying the waters around Japan. The message that he brought from Pres. Millard Fillmore also sought humane treatment for shipwrecked Americans and looked forward, in general terms, to the establishment of trade relations.

Perry's visit was short. While persuading the Japanese to accept Fillmore's letter, he blithely surveyed local waters—including Edo Bay, as Japanese officials looked on in horror—and then took his leave, warning that he would return shortly with a larger squadron for the government's answer. Some six months later, he was indeed back—with nine vessels, more than 120 cannon, and a crew of eighteen hundred. The resulting Treaty of Kanagawa met all of Perry's requests. It opened two ports (Shimoda and Hakodate) to American ships and laid the groundwork for Japan's reluctant acceptance of an American "consul," who later broke down the remaining barriers to Japan's incorporation into the global marketplace.

The samurai-led feudal regime that had dominated Japan for seven centuries collapsed under this pressure in 1868, while the harsh lessons the Japanese learned from Perry lived on. As it turned out, the Japanese grasped more adroitly than any other non-Western, non-Christian people what Perry's "gunboat diplomacy" portended: inescapable immersion into an international order governed by realpolitik and social Darwinism.

At the same time, however, Perry also introduced to these quick learners the technologies essential for their survival in such a challenging new world. He invited them aboard his "black ships" to examine the vessels' awesome engines and gunnery. His officers demonstrated how the revolving chambers of their Colt pistols allowed the handguns to fire multiple bullets. Official gifts to the Japanese included a model telegraph and a quarter-scale railroad, complete with locomotive, tender, passenger car, and 370 yards of track.

Nine decades later, the United States would destroy two Japanese cities with nuclear weapons, and another American military hero, Gen. Douglas MacArthur, would enter the same harbor that Perry had used (now called Tokyo Bay) to accept Japan's surrender following a horrendous war. A huge armada of U.S. warships accompanied the American general, and glistening military aircraft filled the sky. In ways that Matthew Perry and his generation could never in their wildest imaginations have dreamed possible, the world had been transformed.

LEFT: *This woodcut of Matthew Perry by an unidentified Japanese artist was published in Edo (Tokyo) shortly after the commodore's 1853 visit.*

RIGHT: *A carte-de-visite portrait of Perry taken during the mid-1850s.*

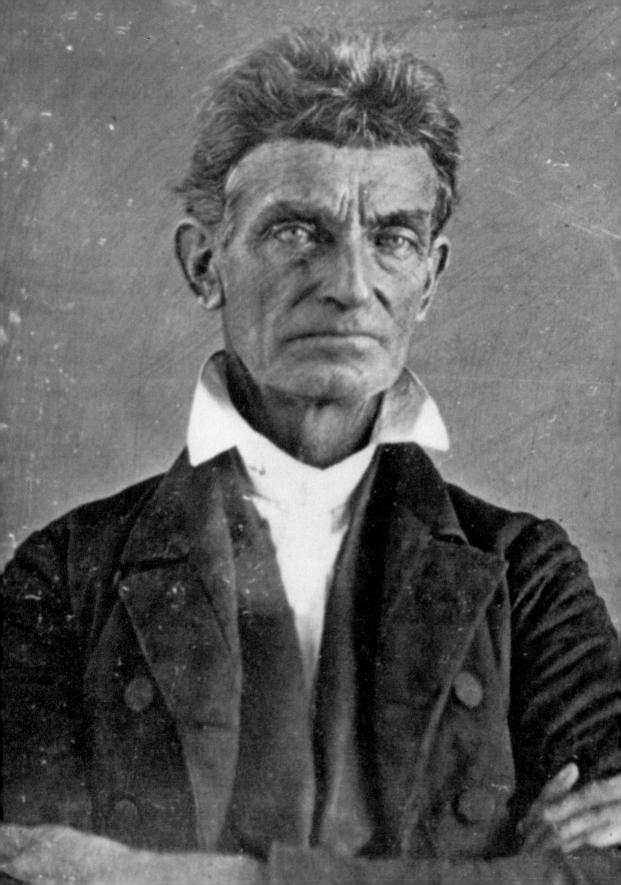

11

THE ROAD TO CIVIL WAR

John Brown's Raid

IT BEGAN WITH AN EMBARRASSING intelligence failure. In late August 1859, Secretary of War John B. Floyd was vacationing at the Virginia resort of Red Sweet Springs when he received an anonymous letter warning him that "'old John Brown,' late of Kansas," was organizing "a secret association" to incite a slave uprising in the South. Dated August 20, the letter went on to detail Brown's accumulation of arms at a hideout in Maryland and his intention to cross the Potomac in a few weeks' time. The letter's author—later revealed to be David J. Gue, a Quaker from Springdale, Iowa—even specified Brown's crossing point: Harpers Ferry, Virginia, the site of an important federal armory. Gue wrote Floyd because he sympathized with Brown and considered the operation suicidal. He urged Floyd to send troops to Harpers Ferry immediately so that Brown, observing the move, would have to abandon his plans.

The plot, however, seemed so incredible to Floyd that he refused to believe it. To begin with, he didn't recognize Brown's name (even though Pres. James Buchanan had recently put a $250 bounty on Brown's head), and a few small inaccuracies in Gue's letter made the secretary of war even more dubious. One such error was Gue's reference to a secret agent Brown had recruited to spy on a federal armory in Maryland. Floyd knew this was impossible because there were no federal armories in Maryland. (Of course, Gue meant Harpers Ferry, but this didn't occur to Floyd.)

AT LEFT: *John Brown sat for this* ambrotype in early *1856, while living in Osawatomie, Kansas.*

Yet, according to his testimony before a Senate committee in March 1860, the primary reason that Floyd "laid [the letter] away in my trunk" was that he thought "a scheme of such wickedness and outrage could not be entertained by any citizens of the United States." As Floyd knew quite well, there hadn't been a significant slave uprising since 1831, the year of Nat Turner's Revolt, during which Floyd's father had been governor of Virginia. Three decades later, the younger Floyd simply couldn't believe that another revolt was imminent. So he took no action. Slavery was a political issue, he must have thought to himself, not a military one.

Meanwhile, at a rented farmhouse in western Maryland, fifty-nine-year-old John Brown was indeed planning an insurrection. Already, on July 3, he had visited Harpers Ferry and met with John E. Cook, his secret agent there. Next, accompanied by his sons Owen and Oliver, Brown had scouted the nearby Maryland countryside for a suitable property at which his followers could assemble. With funds provided by supporters in the North, Brown had leased the Kennedy farm about seven miles away. He used the name Isaac Smith and told his new neighbors he was a cattle buyer from New York.

DURING THE MONTH of August, while Floyd vacationed and Brown studied his maps, small groups of mostly young men made their way to the Kennedy farm. So as not to arouse suspicion among the neighbors, they hid upstairs in the farmhouse's attic. By the end of August, there were fifteen recruits living there—including a third Brown son, Watson; several young free-staters Brown had met while fighting

Oliver Brown and his wife, Martha, posed for this photograph only months before Oliver's death in the Harpers Ferry raid.

in Kansas; and a couple of brothers from Springdale, Iowa, the Quaker community that had sheltered some of Brown's band the previous winter. The oldest conspirator, apart from Brown himself, was forty-eight-year-old Dangerfield Newby, a freed slave who had joined the conspiracy hoping to liberate his wife and seven children, who were still enslaved on a Virginia plantation. To make life on the farm appear more normal, Brown sent for his seventeen-year-old daughter-in-law Martha (Oliver's wife) as well as his own fifteen-year-old daughter Annie. These young women cooked for the men, cleaned, tended the garden, and diverted the attention of nosy neighbors.

In the meantime, Brown sent a steady stream of letters north, pleading with the radical abolitionist community for more money and additional men. He was concerned because much had been promised him and, so far, little had been delivered. On August 19, he traveled to Chambersburg, Pennsylvania, for a discussion with his friend Frederick Douglass. At that meeting, Brown revealed to Douglass his scheme to raid Harpers Ferry, and Douglass was shocked. He warned Brown that such a plan was madness; that Brown would likely die; and that, by attacking federal property, he would surely turn the entire country against him. Apparently not listening, Brown beseeched Douglass to join him, but Douglass refused. (After the raid, once the closeness of the Brown–Douglass relationship became known, the state of Virginia charged Douglass with "murder, robbery and inciting to servile insurrection." When he was told that the governor of New York was preparing to surrender him, Douglass fled to Canada.)

Through the late summer and early fall, Brown's soldiers waited restlessly in Maryland. The cramped nature of their attic quarters precluded much physical exercise, and the constant fear of discovery gnawed at their minds. At times, the tension became unbearable. One night, while a passing thunderstorm concealed the sound, the dozen-plus recruits ran up and down the farmhouse stairs, shouting

John Brown leased the Kennedy farm in Maryland as a staging area for his raid into Virginia. At the time, Maryland was also a slave state.

and hooting to relieve their stress. Yet they remained both committed and determined. On September 8, Watson Brown wrote to his wife, "I think of you all day and dream of you at night. I would gladly come home and stay with you always but for the cause which brought me here— a desire to do something for others, and not live wholly for my own happiness."

During this period, numerous crates of weapons arrived at the Kennedy farmhouse. They contained 198 Sharps rifles and 200 Maynard revolvers, purchased originally for use in Kansas, as well as 950 iron-tipped pikes that Brown had ordered for his anticipated slave army. (The revolvers turned out to be useless because Brown had ineptly bought ordinary percussion caps for them instead of the special tape primings they required.) Brown also revealed to his men at this time the fundamentals of his plan. Most had thought they would be participating in raids of the sort Brown had conducted a year earlier in Missouri. These had rescued small groups of slaves, who were then led to safety in Canada. Brown's sons had heard their father speak of a more ambitious plan involving the armory at Harpers Ferry, but they had little idea of its scope.

LEFT: *John Edwin Cook* was the well-educated son of a well-to-do Connecticut family.

Brown's Plan

ENCOURAGED BY COOK, who had been living in Harpers Ferry while studying the armory for the past year, Brown had grown ambitious. At first, he had envisioned a quick raid on the armory followed by a hasty retreat into the mountains of western Virginia. Now he wanted to capture the entire town and hold it while slaves, free blacks, and dissident whites from the surrounding counties rallied to his cause. The Harpers Ferry raid, Brown explained, would spark an immediate, massive uprising, and the weapons the raiders obtained at the armory would equip the arriving volunteers long before any federal or state soldiers appeared. Brown would then march this new insurgent army through the South, freeing the rest of the slaves as he went.

To emphasize the calculated nature of his plans, Brown showed his men maps of seven different southern states. Each had been mounted on sturdy cambric and annotated meticulously with slave statistics obtained from the 1850 census. Counties with extremely high slave populations were marked with crosses. Brown's intention was to lead his anticipated army on a zigzag course through each of the marked counties until he reached the Gulf Coast. Even if he failed to get there, Brown reasoned, the hysteria his actions would produce in the South would lead to a major sectional crisis and probably a civil war, which would be just as good.

Oliver Brown was among those who objected strongly to the fantastic notion that fewer than two dozen men could take and hold a town of twenty-five hundred people. However, when his father threatened to resign as "commander in chief"—a strategic psychological ploy—the quarrel ended. "If I could conquer Virginia," Brown explained later, "the balance of the Southern states would nearly conquer themselves, there being such a large number of slaves in them."

One of the 950 pikes ordered by Brown with which he planned to equip his slave army.

Brown had doubts of his own concerning the timing of his raid—he still wasn't sure why the abolitionist community hadn't been more forthcoming in its support—but the arrival of three more volunteers on Saturday, October 15, raised his spirits considerably. Two of the new recruits were Oberlin Rescuers (college students who had been active in the Underground Railroad); and the third, Francis Jackson Meriam, was a young abolitionist from Boston who had heard about the plot from a free black and inquired into Brown's whereabouts until he learned of the Kennedy farm. (According to some estimates, more than a hundred people knew in advance of Brown's plans, in addition to the secretary of war.) Also contributing to Brown's sense of relief was the six hundred dollars in gold that Meriam had brought with him. Having already sent Martha and Annie home to North Elba, New York, two weeks earlier, Brown now announced that it was finally time to move. Because God had not provided more, the commander in chief concluded, He must want Brown to strike with what he had.

In 1835, two years before admitting women, the trustees of Oberlin College voted to enroll blacks, making Oberlin one of the nation's first racially integrated colleges. The school's long association with abolitionism continued into the 1850s, when these Oberlin Rescuers helped conduct fugitive slaves to freedom in Canada as members of the Underground Railroad.

THE ROLE THAT God's will played in Brown's thinking was paramount. A devout Bible-quoting Christian who aspired to the ministry, Brown believed that God wanted him personally to cleanse the land of slavery. Therefore, Brown didn't worry about the details, leaving most of them to the Lord, who would supply divine guidance as necessary. This explains why Brown did such a poor job reconnoitering the area around Harpers Ferry. He never scouted access roads for hiding places; nor did he make any contingency plans for escape should the raid fail. Instead, as in all things, he trusted to the Almighty, who would provide. He and his men knew that they might be killed, but their devotion to the antislavery cause sustained them. "We have here only one life to live, and once to die," Brown said; "and if we lose our lives it will perhaps do more for the cause than our lives would be worth in any other way."

Counting the three late arrivals, there were now twenty-one soldiers in Brown's Provisional Army—five blacks and sixteen whites. On Sunday morning, Brown gathered all of them together for a final prayer service. In the afternoon, he handed out their assignments. Eighteen of the men, grouped into four platoons, would accompany Brown into Harpers Ferry, while Owen Brown, Meriam, and one of the Springdale brothers remained at the farm as a rear guard. It was their job to haul the guns and pikes to a schoolhouse near the Potomac River that Brown had designated as a gathering point for runaway Maryland slaves and dissident whites arriving from Pennsylvania.

There was a light rain falling at eight o'clock when Brown walked out of the farmhouse and climbed into his wagon. The night was cool and moonless. With rifles on their shoulders, Brown's army (all but two of them under the age of thirty) assembled behind the wagon. By the time the insurrectionists reached Harpers Ferry, the town was mostly asleep.

This cross, found in John Brown's Osawatomie cabin, presumably belonged to him.

Harpers Ferry

HARPERS FERRY SAT at the strategic junction of the Potomac and Shenandoah Rivers. Baltimore lay eighty miles to the east along the B&O railroad line; Washington was fifty-seven miles away by turnpike. The principal industry in Harpers Ferry was arms manufacture. In addition to the federal armory, there was also Hall's Rifle Works, a private firm located on an island in the Shenandoah River that performed contract work for the army. In this and other parts of western Virginia, because mountains dominated the topography, there was no large-scale agriculture and therefore few slaves. Most of those who did live in the area were well-treated house servants.

The first thing that Brown did as he approached Harpers Ferry was order the telegraph lines cut. Then his men subdued a night watchman and seized the two bridges leading into town. Leaving Oliver Brown, Dangerfield Newby, and two others to guard the river crossings, Brown guided the remaining fourteen raiders quietly past the well-lit Wager House hotel and onto the grounds of the armory, where they took the single government watchman completely by surprise. "I came here from Kansas, and this is a slave State; I want to free all the negroes in this State," Brown told him. "I have possession now of the United States armory, and if the citizens interfere with me I must only burn the town and have blood."

After securing the armory, Brown himself led a party to capture Hall's Rifle Works—which he did, garrisoning the island with three of his men. Meanwhile, other raiders rounded up several people they found on the street and took them back to the armory to serve as hostages.

Dangerfield Newby was the mulatto son of a Virginia plantation master.

*The **main entrance** to the Harpers Ferry armory in 1862. The engine house can be seen on the left.*

Returning to the armory himself, Brown, now highly confident, sent out a detachment to seize more hostages in the countryside. The hostage takers' primary target was a local slaveholder named Lewis W. Washington, who happened to be the first president's great-grandnephew. Brown wanted Washington "for the moral effect it would give our cause having one of [his] name as a prisoner." The group returned not long after midnight with Washington and two other prisoners, as well as ten freed slaves.

About this time, a whistle signaled the approach of an express train from Wheeling en route to Baltimore. When the train found the railroad bridge barricaded, it came to a stop, and two B&O employees walked down the track to investigate. The raiders drove them off with just a few rifle shots, but the gunfire aroused the town. People gathered on the streets with whatever weapons they had handy. At first, when rumors of a large-scale slave revolt spread, the townspeople panicked and fled, gathering on Bolivar Heights in back of Harpers Ferry. (Ironically, many local blacks fled with them.) But as morning dawned, church bells began ringing—the signal that an uprising was under way—and residents of nearby Charlestown, Shepherdstown, and Martinsburg all mobilized. Meanwhile, John Brown decided to let the express train through so that it could carry news of his insurrection to Monocacy. From there, the telegraph operator would send word to Baltimore, Richmond, Washington, and elsewhere in the country.

John Brown in May 1859, near the end of a life marked by nearly complete business failure. Brown worked hard for decades to support his twenty children, yet various turns as a tanner, sheep drover, wool merchant, and land speculator produced nothing but debt.

The Abolitionists

HAD JOHN BROWN LAUNCHED his raid thirty years earlier, nearly the entire North would have joined the South in expressing its shock and outrage. Even though, by that time, every northern state had abolished slavery, and many northerners had come to view slave labor with hostility, few thought it appropriate in 1829 to interfere with slavery's operation in the South. Most northerners supported the Missouri Compromise and accepted slavery in the South as a political necessity that made Union possible.

Between the 1820s and the 1850s, however, northern attitudes underwent a significant transformation, for which a small cadre of antislavery activists—stubborn, committed, and intensely religious men and women—deserve a large portion of the credit. In Massachusetts, the best known of these activists were *Liberator* editor William Lloyd Garrison; Garrison's principal lieutenant, Wendell Phillips; and Frederick Douglass, who moved to Rochester in the late 1840s. In New York,

RIGHT: This 1837 handbill urged citizens to "silence by peaceful means" an abolitionist lecturer, whom it described as a "tool of evil and fanaticism." Often, however, the means used to obstruct antislavery meetings were quite violent indeed.

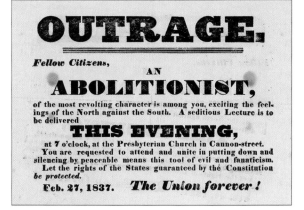

OUTRAGE.

Fellow Citizens,

AN

ABOLITIONIST,

of the most revolting character is among you, exciting the feelings of the North against the South. A seditious Lecture is to be delivered

THIS EVENING,

at 7 o'clock, at the Presbyterian Church in Cannon-street. You are requested to attend and unite in putting down and silencing by peaceable means this tool of evil and fanaticism. Let the rights of the States guaranteed by the Constitution be protected.

Feb. 27, 1837. *The Union forever!*

THE GAG RULE

IN GENERAL, GAG RULES are parliamentary devices used to shorten or eliminate debate on a particular subject. The famous gag rule that the House of Representatives adopted in May 1836, however, related specifically to slavery. During the mid-1830s, as the result of a campaign organized by the American Anti-Slavery Society, northern congressmen began receiving a deluge of antislavery petitions. Because southern congressmen perceived any debate on slavery as an attack against their section, they sought a way to stifle debate on these petitions, and they came up with the gag rule, which automatically tabled all petitions related to slavery without discussion. Many northern congressmen went along, either because they didn't believe Congress had the right to regulate slavery or simply out of political expediency.

In this 1839 cartoon, John Quincy Adams cowers on a pile of antislavery petitions before South Carolina representative Waddy Thompson Jr., a cotton Whig.

From its inception, former president John Quincy Adams (who served in the House from 1831 until his death in 1848) fought against the gag rule, which he considered an indefensible limitation of citizens' rights. He contested each annual renewal of the rule and gradually gathered support. Finally, in December 1844, the gag rule was lifted. While it remained in effect, however, the abolitionists made excellent use of it as propaganda: The gag rule was persuasive evidence that the Slave Power had indeed usurped control of the federal government, and it helped persuade many northerners with no particular opinion regarding slavery that efforts to appease the South were threatening everyone's constitutional rights.

the most prominent abolitionists were the Tappan brothers, Lewis and Arthur; and Gerrit Smith. In Ohio, there was Theodore Weld, whose wife (Angelina Grimké Weld) and sister-in-law (Sarah Grimké) traveled the lyceum circuit extensively, lecturing against slavery and later for women's rights. Initially, these antislavery radicals were ostracized, but slowly they gained acceptance for themselves and their view that slavery was wrong and deserved to be eliminated, not merely restrained.

During the 1830s, the stubborn, humorless Garrison used *The Liberator* to set an ambitious agenda for the abolitionist movement, firmly rejecting colonization and advocating instead immediate, uncompensated emancipation. In January 1832, he established the New England Anti-Slavery Society. Only a dozen men signed that group's constitution, yet less than two years later, Garrison was able to start a corresponding national organization, the American Anti-Slavery Society. The Tappan brothers, Theodore Weld, and sixty other delegates attended the American Anti-Slavery Society's first convention, held in Philadelphia in December 1833, and the group's following swelled from there. It became the main activist arm of the abolitionist movement and by 1839 had close to two hundred thousand members. That year, however, the abolitionist movement split along ideological, personal, and geographic lines.

A black Philadelphian shops for stockings in this prejudiced 1829 view of African-American life in the North, where free blacks were subject to widespread abuse and discrimination.

ARRISON'S FAVORITE TARGETS included the American republic, which he attacked for not living up to its ideals, and the Constitution, which he criticized for its discriminatory treatment of blacks. (In 1854, Garrison publicly burned a copy of the Constitution, exclaiming, "So perish all compromises with tyranny!") This approach discomfited many in the antislavery movement, especially those who had drifted over from other reform causes, because they, unlike Garrison, approved of the American political system. They also regretted Garrison's attacks on Protestant denominations (most of which still refused to endorse black emancipation); disagreed with him regarding equality for women (they were against it); and disliked his personal style, which was overbearing.

After the split, the Garrisonians remained centered in Boston, where they continued publishing *The Liberator*, writing pamphlets, and staging public meetings to focus attention on the moral atrocity that was slavery.

The principal objection that William Lloyd Garrison (shown here at age thirty) and other abolitionists had to slavery was moral. Therefore, they believed, if they could only persuade others of their view, the American people would demand slavery's end.

The movement's other wing, the "political abolitionists," pursued similar strategies from their headquarters in New York City, but they organized politically as well, embracing the American political system and working within it to build coalitions that might overturn slavery through legislative means. At first, they questioned major-party candidates regarding slavery and voted for those whose answers were the least unsatisfactory. Occasionally, when elections were close and their voting bloc mattered, their cause was paid some lip service, but the results were hardly encouraging.

Yearning for bolder action, the political abolitionists decided in late 1839 to form their own political party, which they called the Liberty party. Its two-time presidential candidate, former Kentucky slaveholder James G. Birney, had been converted to the antislavery cause by Theodore Weld. In 1840, Birney won only 6,797 votes, or just 0.3 percent of the popular total. Four years later, however, he

THE REACTION TO THE ABOLITIONISTS

DURING THE 1830s, anyone calling for the abolition of slavery knew that he or she was risking not merely social censure but legal sanction and physical violence as well. Southern states routinely offered rewards for the extradition of northern activists. The state of Georgia, for example, offered five thousand dollars to anyone arresting William Lloyd Garrison and delivering him to a state court to stand trial on charges of libel.

Even in the North, many conservatives feared and despised abolitionists

for the threat they posed to national unit, and reactionary mobs often threatened their lives and property. During a famous October 1835 incident, one such mob in Boston kidnapped Garrison and nearly lynched him before the police took him into protective custody. Abolitionist often had their meetings disrupted and their printing presses smashed. Elizabeth Cady Stanton's husband, Henry, an abolitionist orator, claimed to have been attacked himself over two hundred times.

This 1838 woodcut *depicts the November 1837 Alton, Illinois, riot in which abolitionist publisher Elijah P. Lovejoy was murdered.*

received 62,103 votes, or 2.3 percent of the popular tally. Included in this number were 15,812 votes in New York State that Birney stripped away from Henry Clay, the Whig nominee. In the end, Clay lost New York to Democrat James K. Polk by fewer than six thousand votes. Had it not been for Birney's presence in the race, Clay would have won New York, that state's thirty-six electoral votes, and the presidency. This was heady stuff for the political abolitionists.

Emergence of the Republican Party

DESPITE GARRISON'S FREQUENT warnings against accommodation, Birney's showing in the 1844 election inspired Liberty party members to become even more ambitious in their efforts to build antislavery coalitions. In 1846, the New Hampshire Liberty party joined with antislavery Democrats to elect John P. Hale to the U.S. Senate. Two years after that, the national Liberty party decided to give up its independence and become part of the new Free Soil party, founded in New York in 1848 with the support of Barnburner Democrats and conscience Whigs. (The Barnburners got their name from Democratic party regulars, who claimed that the Barnburners were acting like the proverbial Dutch farmer who burned down his barn to rid it of rats.) At the August 1848 Free Soil convention held in Buffalo, party delegates nominated Martin Van Buren for president and adopted a platform (ridiculed by Garrison) that opposed the admission of new slave states but remained silent regarding slavery's continuation in the South.

Afterward, even political abolitionists felt too much had been conceded; and in 1852, after both major parties endorsed the Great Compromise and the Barnburners returned to the Democratic fold, the contracting Free Soil party ran a decidedly more radical campaign. Senator Hale, who had opposed the Compromise of 1850, became the party's presidential nominee, and its 1852 platform declared "that slavery is a sin against God and a crime against man…and that Christianity, humanity, and patriotism alike demand its abolition." Not surprisingly, Hale received only half of Van Buren's 1848 total. Yet the 1852 election revealed a hard core of 150,000 antislavery votes, and these became Republican votes in February 1854, when that party emerged in response to the introduction of Stephen A. Douglas's Kansas-Nebraska bill.

The various factions that came together under the Republican banner united behind the principle that slavery must not be allowed to expand into the West. Beyond that, viewpoints and degrees of commitment to emancipation varied

This daguerreotype, the earliest known photograph of John Brown, was taken in Springfield, Massachusetts, about 1847, when Brown was in the wool business there.

Martin Van Buren's inability to bridge the gap between conscience Whigs and conservative Democrats is mocked in this 1848 cartoon.

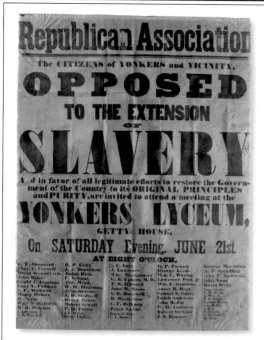

widely. As Horace Greeley's *New York Tribune* explained, "There are Republicans who are Abolitionists, there are others who anxiously desire and labor for the good of the slave, but there are many more whose main impulse is a desire to secure the territories for Free White Labor, with little or no regard for the interests of negroes, free or slave." Even so, the enthusiasm for emancipation generated by this new party scared the South.

THE REPUBLICANS' FIRST presidential candidate, John C. Frémont, proved to be something of a disappointment. In his 1856 race against Democratic nominee James Buchanan, Frémont swept New England and ran competitively in the Middle West, but he received not a single popular vote in twelve southern states where former president Millard Fillmore, the Know-Nothing candidate, was Buchanan's only competition. Fillmore won one state (Maryland); Frémont won eleven states; and Buchanan, a doughface in the mold of Pierce, won the presidency. "We are beaten," conceded a leading Republican, "but we frightened the rascals awfully."

The first U.S. national party system pitted the Federalists against the Democratic-Republicans. In the second, which lasted from the late 1820s until the early 1850s, the Whigs contested the Democrats. After 1854, however, the Democrats had to contend with a new rival: the Republican party.

Given the situation—with southerners voting one way, Republicans voting another, and only northern Democrats still trying to bridge the gap—it would have taken an extraordinary, nationalist president skilled in the political arts of bullying and compromise to bring the country together. James Buchanan—an aging fussy bachelor, quick to please and slow to offend—was no such man. His first stab at sectional reconciliation came in his March 4, 1857, inaugural address, when he made reference to the *Dred Scott* case currently pending before the Supreme Court. This case had important implications regarding the expansion of slavery into the western territories, and Buchanan urged the nation to accept the Court's decision, whatever it might be. What Buchanan didn't say was that he'd already been informed secretly by Associate Justice Robert C. Grier, a fellow Pennsylvanian, that the Court had decided to uphold the southern position on slavery in the case.

A year later, Stephen Douglas ran for reelection to the Senate from Illinois. His Republican opponent, Abraham Lincoln, was a lawyer from Springfield who had served as a Whig in the House during the Mexican War. (Elected in 1846, Lincoln lasted only a single term because his opposition to the war proved unpopular back home.) Like most moderate Republicans, Lincoln believed that slavery was legal but wrong, and that it couldn't be

RIGHT: *The Republican slogan for the 1856 presidential campaign was "Free Soil, Free Speech, Frémont."*

eliminated (at least not yet) but should be kept out of the West so that it could expire gradually and naturally. (Even southerners agreed that, if restricted permanently to the South, slavery would eventually die out.)

DRED SCOTT

In April 1846, an illiterate Missouri slave named Dred Scott filed a petition in St. Louis County Court demanding his freedom. He claimed, truthfully, that he had been taken by his master, an army surgeon, to live for a time in Illinois, a free state. Under prevailing Missouri law, any slave residing for even a short time on free soil became automatically free. Yet numerous technicalities and delays held up Scott's case until January 1850, when a jury finally found in his favor. Scott's owner appealed, and several more years passed before the appeal was heard. In the meantime, Congress passed the Compromise of 1850, and southerners began demanding more positive legal protections for slavery. Scott's case got caught up in this political maelstrom, and in March 1852, the Missouri Supreme Court, ignoring its own precedents, reversed the lower court and declared Scott still a slave. "Times are not now what they were when the former decisions on this subject were made," Chief Justice William Scott explained.

A year later, Dred Scott's supporters brought a new suit in federal district court, charging unlawful imprisonment. The trial went against Scott when the judge instructed the jury that it had no choice but to ratify the Missouri court's decision. This time, Scott appealed, and on March 6, 1857, the Supreme Court offered its opinion on the matter. Writing for the 7–2 majority was Chief Justice Roger B. Taney of Maryland, who sought to resolve much more than Scott's status. The seventy-nine-year-old Taney declared that blacks, free or

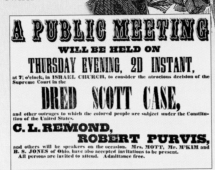

Lucretia Mott was among those who spoke at the meeting announced by this poster— called to protest the continued enslavement of Dred Scott (above).

slave, had no standing to sue in federal court because they were not, and had never been, citizens of the United States. Pushing this logic still farther, Taney asserted that Congress was powerless to ban slavery from the federal territories because slaves were property and thus protected by the Constitution.

The implications of Taney's decision were mind-boggling. During his 1858 U.S. Senate campaign, Abraham Lincoln spoke often of the ruling's questionable legality. In his famous "House Divided" speech, Lincoln pointed out that, by permitting Scott to remain enslaved despite his residence in a free state, the Supreme Court was legalizing slavery everywhere. "What Dred Scott's master might lawfully do with Dred Scott, in the free sate of Illinois," Lincoln said, "every other master may lawfully do with any other one, or one thousand slaves, in Illinois, or in any other free state."

That *Dred Scott* was bad law was obvious, even in March 1857; that it was bad politics soon became clear as well. According to historian Sean Wilentz, "Taney supposed that, with a single emphatic stroke, he and his colleagues could suppress the slavery question once and for all. Instead, he rendered a decision so one-sided that it was denounced the next day by the *New York Tribune*…as 'entitled to just so much moral weight as would be the judgment of a majority of those congregated in any Washington bar-room.'" To this day, Taney's reputation has never escaped the disgrace.

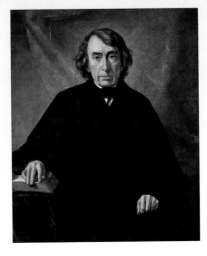

Chief Justice Roger B. Taney

During a series of campaign debates held at various locations around the state, Lincoln peppered Douglas with awkward questions about the *Dred Scott* decision. Specifically, how could territorial residents ban slavery—which was their right, according to Douglas's own doctrine of popular sovereignty—now that the Supreme Court had legalized slavery everywhere? With little else he could say, Douglas was forced to reply that antislavery legislatures could prohibit human bondage by refusing to enact laws protecting the rights of slaveholders. This weak counterargument gave Douglas just enough credibility to keep his Senate seat, but its suggestion that *Dred Scott* could be ignored antagonized southerners and dramatically undermined Douglas's national ambitions. Lincoln, meanwhile, emerged as a major contender for the Republican party's 1860 presidential nomination.

ABRAHAM LINCOLN
1809–1865

BORN ON THE KENTUCKY FRONTIER to poor, illiterate parents, Abraham Lincoln moved with his family first to Indiana and later to Illinois. As a young man, he educated himself by reading extensively on his own. In 1830, he left his family and moved to the village of New Salem, where he spent six years working at a variety of jobs, including store clerk, mill hand, and postmaster. He also became politically active in the Whig party. In 1832, he ran unsuccessfully for the state legislature but won two years later and served four consecutive terms. He idolized Henry Clay and supported Clay's American System, largely because of the opportunity for upward mobility it offered. In the meantime, Lincoln began studying for the bar because he knew that a legal practice, then as now, would promote both his income and his political career. He was admitted to the Illinois bar in 1836, and the next year he moved to Springfield, where he began a successful law practice. Lincoln said little in public about slavery before the Kansas-Nebraska Act became law in 1854. Then—aroused, he said, as he had never been before—he began delivering numerous speeches, 175 in all over the next six years, whose chief theme was the need to ban slavery in the western territories. Lincoln helped found the Illinois Republican party in 1856 and two years later accepted its nomination for the U.S. Senate with his "House Divided" speech. "A house divided against itself cannot stand," Lincoln said. "I believe this government cannot endure, permanently, half *slave* and half *free*."

A sheet from a small mathematical "sum book" that Lincoln kept as a teenager during the mid-1820s.

Lincoln posed for this portrait on June 3, 1860.

John Brown in Kansas

AT THE TIME OF his October 1859 Harpers Ferry raid, John Brown was a fugitive from justice, wanted for antislavery raids he had conducted while living in the Kansas Territory. After failing in one business after another for most of his adult life, Brown had decided in early 1855 to join five of his sons who had recently moved to Osawatomie, about thirty miles from the free-state stronghold of Lawrence, Kansas. Brown had always been an abolitionist. His home in Ohio had been a station on the Underground Railroad, and he lived for a time in North Elba, a free black community in northern New York founded on land donated by Gerrit Smith. In Kansas, however, where proslavery and free-state forces were struggling violently for the right to establish a territorial government, Brown became a paramilitary leader in what was essentially a guerrilla war.

In late May 1856, a proslavery army of some eight hundred Missouri militiamen (called "border ruffians") sacked Lawrence, looting stores, burning the Free-State Hotel, and destroying the town's printing press. Much to Brown's disgust, the residents of Lawrence refused to defend themselves. Two days later, Brown personally led a group of Osawatomie volunteers into the valley of the Pottawatomie Creek, where they murdered and mutilated five proslavery men (sparing their wives and children). For most of the next three years, Brown moved clandestinely between Kansas and the East, leading raids into Missouri one month and courting wealthy benefactors in Boston the next. During this time, Brown's ambitions escalated, and by early 1858 he was talking about a new plan "to overthrow slavery in a large part of the country."

Brown's most consistent support came from a group of northeastern abolitionists later known as the Secret Six. They included New Yorker Gerrit Smith and five residents of Massachusetts: Concord schoolteacher Franklin B. Sanborn; Unitarian ministers Theodore Parker and Thomas Wentworth Higginson; philanthropist George Luther Stearns, who chaired the Massachusetts Kansas Committee; and Dr. Samuel Gridley Howe. These men intentionally avoided learning too much about Brown's plan but understood that whatever happened would be violent. And why not? Did any American still believe that there could be a peaceful resolution to the slavery issue?

After the Harpers Ferry raid, *most of the Secret Six fled to Canada to escape prosecution. Gerrit Smith, however, broke down and was institutionalized.*

On May 19, 1856, *during a Senate debate on Kansas, Charles Sumner of Massachusetts excoriated Andrew P. Butler of South Carolina for defending slavery in his state. Three days later, Butler's cousin, Rep. Preston Brooks, entered the Senate chamber and beat Sumner so savagely with a cane that Sumner's recovery took three and a half years.*

BLEEDING KANSAS

IN 1854, CONGRESS FORMALLY organized the territory of Kansas. Until that year, the land there was undeniably free soil because Kansas sat north of the 36°30' Missouri Compromise line. The Kansas-Nebraska Act, however, repealed the Missouri Compromise, substituting in its place Stephen Douglas's doctrine of popular sovereignty. It was Douglas's idea that the Kansans themselves should decide whether or not to permit slavery. This may have sounded like a fine idea, but in practice it was a disaster.

Once Kansas came into play, outsiders poured into the territory (or sent money and guns) with the aim of influencing its decision regarding slavery. The first territorial elections were held in March 1855. Thousands of border ruffians rode over from Missouri to cast illegal ballots, often at gunpoint, for proslavery candidates. The free-state forces complained bitterly that six thousand votes had been cast in a territory with only fifteen hundred eligible voters, but President Pierce allowed the proslavery results to stand. So the free-staters held their own election and formed a competing territorial government. On January 24, 1856, Pierce condemned the antislavery election, called it an act of "rebellion," and committed his administration to the territory's proslavery government.

Northerners in Congress were outraged by the president's blatant bias, and on July 3 they pushed through the House a bill approving statehood for Kansas under its antislavery constitution—a move soon blocked by the southern-dominated Senate.

The increasingly violent state of affairs in Kansas, combined with the disclosure of the Ostend Manifesto, ended whatever possibility Pierce may have had of winning a second term. Yet President Buchanan fared no better. In February 1858, he asked Congress to admit Kansas under the proslavery Lecompton Constitution, approved the previous December in yet another tainted election. This time, the Senate went along, but the House balked. By the time Kansas was finally admitted as a free state on January 29, 1861, South Carolina had already left the Union.

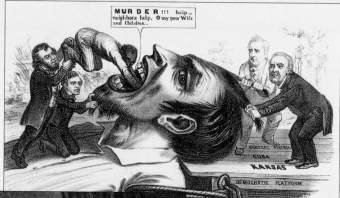

This 1856 cartoon blamed prominent Democrats for the violence in Kansas.

When Buchanan (shown here with his proslavery cabinet) embraced the Lecompton Constitution, even Stephen Douglas, a fellow northern Democrat, attacked him. "If this constitution is to be forced down our throats," Douglas raged, "...I will resist it to the last." The sectional split in the Democratic party was growing.

IN ADDITION TO the armory building itself, the federal compound at Harpers Ferry included a storehouse (the arsenal), a machine shop, a forge, and a fire-engine house. It was to the engine house that the hostages were taken, and Brown regrouped there as he waited for the anticipated arrival of so many runaway slaves and sympathetic whites.

At this point, dawn on Monday morning, the Virginians who had so far learned of the uprising believed it was a slave insurrection of the same sort organized in 1831 by Nat Turner. As the daylight strengthened, however, two things happened: The townspeople realized that the raiders were white, and Brown's men lost their initiative. Instead of either taking more hostages or retreating quickly into the mountains, Brown simply dawdled away the morning, talking with his prisoners and even ordering breakfast for them from the Wager House. Then, dividing his already small band further, he sent three raiders and several of the liberated slaves across the Potomac to join Owen and the rear guard at the schoolhouse.

This revolver, believed to have been the property of John Brown, now belongs to the Kansas State Historical Society.

By eleven o'clock, Brown was trapped. Townspeople, along with farmers from the countryside who had answered the call of the church bells, had assembled on the streets of Harpers Ferry and begun firing into the armory compound. Their rifles kept the raiders pinned down and would have prevented allies from reaching them, had any appeared. About this time, Maryland militiamen retook the river bridges, cutting Brown off from his rear guard. During the assault on one of the bridges, a sniper shot and killed Dangerfield Newby, who became the first of Brown's men to die in the raid. As it lay in the street, drunken militiamen beat and mutilated Newby's body and allowed hogs to root on it. In Newby's pocket was a letter from his wife. "Oh dear Dangerfield," it read, "come this fall without fail monny or no Monney I want to see you so much that is the one bright hope I have before me."

FINALLY, BROWN BEGAN looking for a way out. He offered to free his thirty-odd hostages in exchange for safe passage out of Harpers Ferry, but the emissary he sent to the townspeople was taken prisoner by the excited, already half-drunken crowd. Becoming more desperate, Brown sent his son Watson and another raider into the street under a white flag. This time, the mob gunned them both down, a wounded Watson somehow managing to crawl back to the armory before collapsing at his father's feet. Later that evening, Brown attempted a third time to negotiate, sending out a note offering the same deal and signed "John Brown." The raiders' leader had already been recognized by locals as the mysterious "Isaac Smith." Now, his real name was known, and dispatches leaving Harpers Ferry thereafter identified him as the notorious John Brown of Kansas.

Brown and the men he had left spent that Monday night barricaded in the engine house, which they chose for its brick construction and heavy oaken doors. There

This article about the Harpers Ferry raid appeared in the weekly edition of Horace Greeley's New York Tribune.

The Weekly Tribune.

INSURRECTION IN VIRGINIA.

OLD JOHN BROWN SHOT.

TERROR THROUGH THE SOUTH.

QUIET RESTORED.

Old John Brown, of Kansas fame, has excited an insurrection at Harper's Ferry. With 21 men he took possession of the United States Arsenal, at that place, last Sunday evening, and held it against the forces of Maryland and Virginia, until Tuesday morning, when it was stormed by United States marines. His object is not quite clear; it is said that he made his first appearance in Harper's Ferry more than a year ago, accompanied by his two sons—all three of them assuming the name of S...land in the w...

The demand for surrender that Robert E. Lee wrote and Jeb Stuart carried to John Brown inside the engine house.

was no light and no heat but a good deal of noise coming from Watson and Oliver Brown, who lay on the floor crying with pain from their fatal bullet wounds. Only four of the seven surviving raiders (plus Brown) were still able to defend themselves, and they took turns guarding the eleven prisoners left inside the engine house. During the night, Oliver Brown repeatedly begged his father to shoot him and thereby end his agony. "If you must die, die like a man," Brown said. Then he addressed the prisoners: "Gentlemen, if you knew of my past history you would not blame me for being here. I went to Kansas a peaceable man, and the proslavery people hunted me down like a wolf."

At dawn on Tuesday, October 18, 1859, when Brown looked out the windows of the engine house, he saw not the scruffy, drunken militiamen of the previous day but a company of smartly dressed U.S. Marines that had arrived sometime during the night. When President Buchanan first learned of the insurrection on Monday (he was told that it involved "700 whites and Negroes"), he had called up three artillery companies. But artillery companies take time to muster, so he also ordered ninety marines from the Washington Barracks to set out immediately for Harpers Ferry. These soldiers, armed with bayoneted rifles and sledgehammers, were commanded by Col. Robert E. Lee and Lt. J. E. B. Stuart, both natives of Virginia.

Lee watched from about forty feet away as Stuart approached the engine house carrying a white flag. With Brown's rifle pointed at his head, Stuart delivered a note from Lee demanding Brown's unconditional surrender but promising marine protection from any mob violence. (Having served in Kansas in 1856, Stuart at once recognized Osawatomie Brown, "who had given us so much trouble.") When Brown refused to surrender, some of the prisoners pleaded with Stuart to have Lee come himself to reason with Brown. Stuart replied that Lee would offer only those terms outlined in the note. Then, suddenly, Stuart jumped aside, waving his cap. It was a signal for the marines to rush the engine house. Two thousand spectators lining Potomac Street cheered them on.

CENTER: **Frank Leslie's Illustrated Newspaper** *used this art to accompany its October 29, 1859, article on the raid. The engraving, which shows marines storming the engine house, was based, according to the original caption, on "a sketch made on the spot by our special artist."*

The storming parties quickly captured two of the able-bodied raiders and bayoneted two others to death. As for Brown, Lt. Israel Green knocked away his rifle with a sword blow and tried to run him through, except that Brown's belt buckle (or perhaps a bone) parried the blow. As Brown collapsed, Green beat him unconscious with the hilt of his sword. Soon after the armory was secured, Baltimore militiamen investigated reports of insurrectionists gathered at a Maryland schoolhouse. Warned by John Cook, the rear guard had already fled by the time the militiamen arrived, but Brown's men left behind a chilling sight: cases and cases of weapons intended for use by mutinous slaves. Later that morning, Stuart led a marine detachment to the Kennedy farm, where he found an inventory of documents incriminating not only Brown but also the Secret Six and other conspirators.

The **Harper's Weekly** *artist known as Porte Crayon sketched this portrait of Brown during his interrogation in the paymaster's office by various officials, including Virginia governor Henry Wise. At the time— it was late Tuesday afternoon—the fate of all the raiders wasn't yet known, but it soon would be. In all, seventeen people died: Ten of them Brown's men, plus three townspeople, one slaveholder, two of the liberated slaves, and one marine. Along with Brown, six other raiders were (or soon would be) captured; the rest (including Owen Brown) escaped.*

John Brown on Trial

AFTER HE REGAINED consciousness and his wounds were dressed, Brown was taken to the armory paymaster's office, where he was interrogated later that afternoon by Virginia governor Henry A. Wise and a delegation of congressmen, including Virginia senator James M. Mason. Lee offered to remove the visitors (who also included a few reporters) if the prone, bandaged prisoner objected to the questioning, but Brown asked that they be allowed to remain so that he could "make himself and his motives clearly understood."

Actually, Brown obfuscated a great deal. He tried to hide the involvement of the Secret Six, telling Mason that he had provided most of the money for the raid himself. He also attempted to conceal the scope of his plan, advising the senator, "We came to free the slaves, and only that." Rep. Clement L. Vallandigham of Ohio, a conservative Democrat whose sympathies for the Confederacy would later lead to his 1863 imprisonment for treason, followed up

with a more specific question: "Did you expect a general rising of the slaves in case of your success?" "No, sir," Brown lied, "nor did I wish it. I expected to gather them up from time to time, and set them free." The interview concluded with a reporter telling Brown, "I do not wish to annoy you; but if you have anything further you would like to say, I will report it." Brown paused for a moment and gathered himself up before replying:

I have nothing to say, only that I claim to be here in carrying out a measure I believe perfectly justifiable, and not to act the part of an incendiary or ruffian, but to aid those suffering great wrong. I wish to say, furthermore, that you had better—all of you people of the South—prepare yourselves for a settlement of this question, that must come up for settlement sooner than you are prepared for it…. You may dispose of me very easily— I am nearly disposed of now; but this question is still to be settled—this negro question, I mean; the end of that is not yet.

The engine house was disassembled in 1891 and shipped to Chicago for the Columbian Exposition. It attracted only eleven visitors in ten days, however, and was abandoned on a vacant lot until a Washington, D.C., journalist raised funds for its return to Harpers Ferry.

FROM THAT TUESDAY afternoon until his death by hanging on December 2, John Brown labored ceaselessly to convey to his fellow northerners the vision that had led him to Harpers Ferry. Of course, the evidence that he left behind at the Kennedy farmhouse undermined much of what he had told Mason and Vallandigham, but it turned out to be neither the identity of his backers nor the reach of his ambitions that really mattered. Rather, it was Brown's conviction that opposition to slavery could no longer be peaceful. The time had come to take up arms.

Seeking to minimize the raid's importance, moderates in the North characterized Brown as a fanatic whose use of violence could find no support among respectable Americans. Republican party leaders particularly distanced themselves from Brown's extremism. "John Brown was no Republican," Abraham Lincoln insisted, pointing out that not "a single Republican [has been implicated] in his Harpers Ferry enterprise." But southerners believed otherwise. They were convinced that Brown's actions were merely a predictable extension of Republican antislavery agitation. Even Stephen Douglas, eager to repair his relationship with the South, called the Harpers Ferry raid a "natural, logical, inevitable result of the doctrines and teachings of the Republican party."

At Governor Wise's insistence, it was agreed that the raiders would be tried in state (rather than federal) court. On October 26, a grand jury in Charlestown indicted Brown and the other surviving, captured raiders for murder, conspiracy, and treason against the state of Virginia. Each of the five defendants pled not guilty, and their lawyers asked for separate trials. Judge Richard Parker agreed, and the trial of John Brown began the next day, with the injured defendant lying on a cot. His court-appointed lawyer, Lawson Botts, offered a surprise insanity defense, introducing into evidence a telegram from an Akron man who declared that "Insanity is hereditary in that family" and went on to list the various Brown relations currently residing in asylums. Clearly, Botts thought that the only way he could save Brown's life was to arrange for his commitment, but Brown would have none of it. In fact, Brown welcomed martyrdom. As Secret Six member Thomas Higginson wrote at the time, Brown's "acquittal or rescue would not do half as

The key to the Charlestown jail cell in which John Brown was imprisoned prior to his execution.

Mrs. John Brown + two of her children, from daguerreotype —

much good as his being executed, so strong is the personal sympathy with him." The Rev. Henry Ward Beecher offered a similar view: "Let no man pray that Brown be spared! Let Virginia make him a martyr!"

Brown's trial lasted just four days, and the jury deliberated only forty-five minutes before finding him guilty on all counts. On November 2, Judge Parker pronounced the anticipated death sentence, but not before Brown was given the opportunity to speak. He talked for five minutes, knowing that the text of his remarks would appear the following day in newspapers all over the country. Brown spoke slowly and eloquently, defending his actions at Harpers Ferry and appealing directly to the antislavery North:

I see a book kissed, which I suppose to be the Bible, or at least the New Testament, which teaches me that all things whatsoever I would that men should do to me, I should do to them. It teaches me further to remember them that are in bonds, as bound with them. I endeavored to act up to that instruction. I say I am yet too young to understand that God is any respecter of persons. I believe that to have interfered as I have done in behalf of His despised poor, is no wrong, but right. Now, if it is deemed necessary that I should forfeit my life for the furtherance of the ends of justice, and mingle my blood with the blood of millions in this slave country whose rights are disregarded by wicked, cruel, and unjust enactments, I say let it be done.

Brown's second wife, Mary Ann, posed for this portrait around 1851 with her daughters Annie (left) and Sarah. She and the younger children were living at the family's farm in North Elba at the time of the Harpers Ferry raid.

The Death of John Brown

BROWN SPENT THE LAST month of his life continuing the renovation of his public image, further distancing himself from the vengeful perpetrator of the Pottawatomie Massacre while embracing a much more forgiving, Christian persona. He endured his final days with simple dignity, welcoming to his cell a steady procession of sympathetic visitors and conducting a remarkably prolific correspondence with family members and friends, as well as many opinion makers in the North. These letters, which boosted Brown's popularity considerably, emphasized his "cheerful" resignation to death and his belief that his own suffering would somehow speed the liberation of the slaves.

On December 2, the day of Brown's much-anticipated hanging, the condemned man rose at dawn to read the Bible briefly before writing a final note to his wife, Mary, who had come south to bring his body (as well as those of her sons Watson and Oliver) back home to North Elba. Soon afterward, his jailers opened his cell and led him out of the prison to the wagon that would carry him to the gallows. Because the wagon was rather small, Brown had to sit atop his own coffin. Before stepping up, he handed a last message to one of the guards: "I John Brown am now quite *certain* that the crimes of this *guilty, land: will* never be purged *away*; but with Blood. I had *as I now think: vainly* flattered myself that without *very much* bloodshed; it might be done."

Based on a New York Tribune *account published three days after Brown's death,* Thomas Hovenden's *highly romanticized* The Last Moments of John Brown *(1884) shows the doomed raider kissing a slave child on his way from jail to the gallows. In fact, this incident never happened.*

At the gallows site, an open field outside Charlestown, fifteen hundred federal and state troops stood guard in case the attempt to save Brown's life that had been rumored materialized. The county sheriff covered the prisoner's head with a white linen hood, then guided him into place over the trapdoor. For the next ten minutes, however, Brown had to wait while confused soldiers found their designated places. Among the hundreds of spectators who had gathered to witness the execution was Thomas J. Jackson, then a professor at the Virginia Military Institute, who described Brown's manner (with some appreciation) as "unflinching firmness." However, John Wilkes Booth, who was there serving as a member of the First Virginia Regiment out of Richmond, despised Brown too much to record anything positive about him. During the execution itself, the crowd was silent, and it remained quiet for a short time afterward until one of Jackson's VMI colleagues, Col. J. T. L. Preston, broke the stillness with a shout: "So perish all such enemies of Virginia! All such enemies of the Union! All such foes of the human race!"

WHAT WAS LEFT for legislators to negotiate? For a time, the election of doughface presidents had assured southerners of their political invincibility. But Brown's raid caused many in the South to rethink whether such arrangements indeed protected them adequately from abolitionist aggressors. A large number concluded that they did not, and as a result, preparations began in many southern states for secession, if not war. Meanwhile, the northern view of slavery had itself changed considerably since 1831, when Garrison first published *The Liberator*. Typical were the views of George Templeton Strong, a New York City lawyer and Democrat who had until recently considered himself a conservative on the slavery question:

> *Old Brown's demeanor has undoubtedly made a great impression—his simplicity and consistency, the absence of fuss, parade and bravado, the strength and clearness of his letters, all indicate a depth of conviction that one does not expect in an abolitionist (who is apt to be a mere talker). Slavery has received no such blow in my time as Brown's strangulation. The supporters of any institution are apt to be staggered and startled when they find that any one man, wise or foolish, is so convinced of its wrong and injustices as to acquiesce in being hanged by way of protest against it. One's faith in anything is terribly shaken by anybody who is ready to go to the gallows condemning and denouncing it.*

Brown's raid came at the end of a decade characterized by bitter and often violent conflict over the spread of slavery. No longer would it be possible to avoid the issue simply by not talking about it, and northern agitation had eroded any basis for compromise. Both abolitionists and slaveholders agreed that, if kept out of the West, slavery would ultimately perish in the South as well. Therefore, how could either side compromise the point? With his actions at Harpers Ferry, Brown accelerated the political collapse, but it was coming regardless.

John Bell's 1860 running mate, Edward Everett, was considered the finest orator of his day. On November 19, 1863, he spoke for two hours at Gettysburg before yielding the platform to President Lincoln for some brief remarks.

Secession

IN LATE APRIL 1860, the Democratic party held its national convention in Charleston, South Carolina. On April 30, when northern delegates defeated a platform plank endorsing federal protection of slavery in the territories, the party's southern wing walked out, and the convention adjourned. Northern Democrats reconvened in mid-June to nominate Stephen Douglas; a week later, southern Democrats met separately to nominate Vice Pres. John C. Breckinridge of Kentucky. In the meantime, the new Constitutional Union party—a hodge-podge of conservative Whigs, border-state moderates, and remnants of the Know-Nothings—chose former senator John Bell of Tennessee as their presidential candidate. The Republicans opted for Abraham Lincoln, who narrowly beat out New York senator William H. Seward. On Election Day, Douglas and Breckinridge split the Democratic vote, while Bell carried three border states. Like Frémont four years earlier, Lincoln failed to receive a single popular vote in nine southern states (and only 1 percent of the vote in Virginia and Kentucky), but his sweep of the populous North earned him an electoral majority nonetheless.

Southern extremists had promised that a Lincoln victory would mean secession, and the fact that the Republicans had been able to secure the presidency without any electoral support from the South alarmed even temperate southerners, who feared northern political and economic domination. In the aftermath of the election, talk of dissolving the Union was everywhere, and South Carolina, that bastion of southern sectionalism, soon took the first step. Just as it had during the nullification crisis of 1832, the state legislature called a special

This special edition of the Charleston Mercury *announced South Carolina's secession.*

SOUTH CAROLINA'S "ULTIMATUM."

"Oh don't! Governor Pickens, don't fire! till I get out of office," President Buchanan (right) exclaims in this early 1861 Currier & Ives print. The cannon that Pickens threatens to fire, however, is pointed at his own midsection.

After Sumter's fall, Stephen Douglas (above) visited President Lincoln at the White House to pledge his support for restoration of the Union. He died two months later, however, exhausted in mind and broken in spirit.

convention, and on December 20, delegates to that convention voted for secession. The reason they gave was the president-elect's stated opposition to slavery's expansion.

During the four critical months that separated Lincoln's victory from his inauguration, the lame-duck Buchanan administration did little—what could it do?—to impede the course of secession. Although the outgoing president belatedly condemned southern disunionism, he was by this time so discredited that his words had no effect. Yet, as southerners took control of federal property throughout the region, Buchanan refused to abandon Fort Sumter in Charleston Harbor. Eventually, this led to the problem of resupplying the Sumter garrison. Because the arrival of a U.S. Navy warship in Charleston Harbor would surely provoke a violent response from the already excited South Carolinians, the War Department decided to send a civilian ship, the *Star of the West*, to resupply the island fort. However, on January 9, 1861, the day that Mississippi became the second state to vote for secession, a group of cadets from the Citadel stationed on Morris Island just outside Charleston Harbor fired on the *Star of the West*, causing no damage but forcing the ship to withdraw before reaching Fort Sumter.

AT THE SAME TIME, IN CONGRESS, various proposals were being circulated in the hope that one might placate the South. The most promising of these was the constitutional amendment introduced on December 18 by Kentucky senator John Crittenden. The Crittenden Compromise, as it was called, extended the Missouri Compromise line across the entire country, outlawing slavery in all federal territories north of that line and expressly permitting it in territories to its south. The amendment also permanently prohibited Congress from outlawing slavery in any states where it currently existed (or might exist in the future). But in the end, southerners were no longer prepared to accept any limitations on slavery, and few northerners wanted a compromise. In the North, public opinion generally broke down into two camps: the unionists, who wanted to impose their will on the South, and the "Let them go" crowd, led by *New York Tribune* editor Horace Greeley, who argued that the North couldn't block southern secession without violating Jefferson's principle that governments derive their legitimacy from the consent of the governed.

Between January 10 and January 26, Florida, Alabama, Georgia, and Louisiana followed South Carolina and Mississippi out of the Union. On February 4, delegates from these six states met in Montgomery, Alabama, to form the Confederate States of America. On February 9, after preparing a draft constitution, they elected Jefferson Davis of Mississippi president of the new southern nation. On February 23, Texas left the Union to join the Confederacy.

On March 4, cannon guarded strategic points in Washington and sharpshooters monitored the crowd at the Capitol as fifty-two-year-old Abraham Lincoln delivered his first inaugural address. Lincoln tried to ameliorate the situation by appealing to the common national heritage shared by all Americans: "Though passion may have strained it must not break our bonds of affection. The mystic chords of memory, stretching from every battlefield and patriot grave to every living heart and hearthstone all over this broad land, will yet swell the chorus of the Union, when again touched, as surely they will be, by the better angels of our nature." The new president restated his intention to contain slavery's growth but also made it clear that he didn't believe slavery could be outlawed in the states where it already existed. In the end, however, Lincoln confronted the South: "In your hands, my dissatisfied fellow-countrymen, and not in mine, is the momentous issue of civil war. The Government will not assail you. You can have no conflict without being yourselves the aggressors."

The Civil War Begins

LINCOLN'S PROMISE TO retain control of all federal property in the South made the issue of Fort Sumter a priority for the new administration. But Lincoln had to move cautiously in order to maintain the allegiance of the Upper South. There were more unionists in Virginia, North Carolina, Kentucky, and Tennessee than in the Deep South, but John Brown's raid had affected public opinion there in antifederal ways, and no one knew what would happen if and when a shooting war began in South Carolina. For a month, Lincoln considered how he might maintain the authority of the federal government in the seceded states without provoking a war that might cause even more states to secede.

Finally, on April 6, the president dispatched a messenger to inform South Carolina governor F. W. Pickens that the federal government intended to provision the troops holding Fort Sumter with food and water. (The fort's commanding officer, Maj. Robert Anderson, had estimated that his supply of rations would run out about April 15.) If no resistance was made to this resupply mission, which would be conducted in a peaceful manner, then no troop reinforcements would follow, Lincoln promised. Pickens received Lincoln's message on April 8 and communicated it immediately to the commander of the Confederate forces in Charleston, Brig. Gen. P. G. T. Beauregard, who informed the Confederate War Department. Beauregard was ordered to demand Sumter's surrender "at once…and if this is refused proceed, in such manner as you may determine, to reduce it." On April 11, a landing party of three Confederate officers insisted on the fort's surrender. Major Anderson refused. At half past four the next morning, Beauregard's batteries opened fire. "Both parties deprecated war," Lincoln recalled in his brief second inaugural address, "but one of them would make war rather than let the nation survive; and the other would accept war rather than let it perish. And the war came."

Lincoln's March 4, 1861, inauguration was a somber affair. As shown here, the crowd was small and not at all celebratory. It was suggested at the time that work on the Capitol's new wings and half-completed dome be suspended, but the president ordered the expansion to continue, primarily for its symbolic value.

AMERICAN PROFILE

Harriet Tubman
1820?–1913

by Catherine Clinton

OUTSIDE THE TROY, NEW YORK, courthouse on April 27, 1860, a crowd circled restlessly, awaiting news of the fate of runaway slave Charles Nalle. The presiding judge in Nalle's case had already indicated his inclination to enforce the 1850 Fugitive Slave Act, which meant that Nalle would be turned over to a slave catcher for transport back to his master in Virginia. At the back of the courtroom, a short black woman, dressed in a shawl, held a basket of baked goods that she appeared to be selling. When Nalle was brought forth, however, this woman wrenched him free from his guards and pulled him down the courthouse stairs toward a group of waiting accomplices—no easy feat because "she was repeatedly beaten over the head with policeman's clubs," according to one eyewitness. A hair-raising chase across the Hudson River followed before Nalle was finally tucked safely away into a wagon bound for Canada. He thus became one of several hundred slaves who owed their freedom to Harriet Tubman.

The Troy courthouse raid notwithstanding, Tubman generally carried out her clandestine work far from the public eye. Before the Civil War, she was one of the most famous and successful "conductors" on the

Underground Railroad, reportedly making nineteen trips and spiriting away more than three hundred slaves. After Fort Sumter, she went to work for the Union army, spying behind enemy lines and otherwise acting as an intermediary with black informants. In June 1863, she took part in the Union raid up

Harriet Tubman is shown here with a group of runaway slaves whom she personally conducted to freedom. Although some early abolitionists helped fugitive slaves reach places of safety as early as the 1780s, it wasn't until the 1830s that the Underground Railroad emerged. Its purpose was to conduct runaways from the South to the North—or, even better yet, to the "promised land" of Canada, beyond the reach of the slave catchers. Frequently traveled routes were called "lines"; safe houses were "stations"; guides, "conductors"; and the fugitives themselves were either "packages" or "freight."

the Combahee River, which helped liberate nearly six hundred South Carolinian slaves.

Tubman was born a slave herself in Dorchester County, Maryland, about 1820. In 1849, when it was rumored that she would be sold to a cotton plantation in the Deep South, she ran away. (Years earlier, three of her siblings had been "sold down the river," and Tubman had promised herself that she would never share their fate.) With the help of some Quakers, she made it to Philadelphia, where she got a job in a hotel and met the African-American abolitionist William Still, who recruited her for the Underground Railroad. Risking her freedom again and again, Tubman began returning to Maryland in December 1850, first to rescue her family and then to help others in need. Later, she began slipping into neighboring slave states as well.

Most of the slaves she freed were taken to upstate New York and hidden there until safe passage to Canada could be arranged. After 1859, when

John Brown's Harpers Ferry raid severely darkened the political climate, abolitionist friends urged her to slow her pace and not tempt the southern authorities who had placed bounties totaling nearly forty thousand dollars on her head. Yet "General" Tubman (as Brown had called her) never let up and, once the Civil War started, only redoubled her efforts.

After the war, Tubman continued crusading for reform, supporting suffrage for women in addition to civil rights for African Americans. She also championed philanthropy, using all of her income and savings to support widows, orphans, and impoverished veterans in her adopted hometown of Auburn, New York. She even established a home for the aged and indigent, which continued her charitable work even after her greatly mourned death in 1913.

12

CIVIL WAR AND RECONSTRUCTION

Sherman's March to the Sea

EARLY ON THE MORNING OF
November 16, 1864, sixty-two thousand
Union troops, moving in four columns,
left Atlanta, Georgia, where they had been
encamped for the past two months. Their
destination was a secret, but it soon became
obvious that they were headed for the coastal
city of Savannah, three hundred miles away.
As he reached a prominent hilltop outside the
city, Maj. Gen. William Tecumseh Sherman,
the commander of the Union forces, turned
back to look at the city, still smoking from
fires set by his men the previous night. In his
memoirs, Sherman recalled what he saw:

*Behind us lay Atlanta, smouldering and in
ruins, the black smoke rising high in the air, a
nd hanging like a pall over the ruined city.
Away off in the distance, on the McDonough
road, was the rear of [Maj. Gen. Oliver O.]
Howard's column, the gun-barrels glistening in
the sun, the white-topped wagons stretching
away to the south; and right before us the
Fourteenth Corps, marching steadily and
rapidly, with a cheery look and a swinging
pace, that made light of the thousand miles that
lay between us and Richmond. Some band, by
accident, struck up the anthem of "John Brown's
soul goes marching on;" the men caught up the*

AT LEFT: *One of the Northern photographers who
journeyed to Charleston to record the ceremonial flag raising
at Fort Sumter on April 14, 1865, took this photograph of
central Charleston, through which Sherman's army had
passed two months earlier.*

*strain, and never before or since have I heard
the chorus of "Glory, glory, hallelujah!" done
with more spirit, or in better harmony of time
and place. Then we turned our horses' heads to
the east; Atlanta was soon lost behind the screen
of trees, and became a thing of the past.*

Thus, on a day memorable for its "clear
sunlight" and "bracing air," Sherman began his
March to the Sea. The general's plan called for
his army to abandon its supply line (the Chattanooga-to-Atlanta railroad), already stretched to
the limit, and operate independently until it
reached the Atlantic coast, where the Union
navy would provide fresh supplies. Sherman's
soldiers brought enough ammunition with them
for a long campaign but little in the way of
rations or fodder for their animals. These
provisions, Sherman explained in his Special
Field Orders, No. 120, would be obtained along
the way by foraging. "The army will forage
liberally on the country during the march,"
Sherman wrote. "To this end, each brigade
commander will organize a good and sufficient
foraging party, under the command of one or
more discreet officers, who will gather, near the
route traveled, corn or forage of any kind, meat
of any kind, vegetables, corn-meal, or whatever is
needed by the command." Furthermore, cavalry
and artillery units were permitted to appropriate
"horses, mules, wagons, etc., belonging to the
inhabitants…freely and without limit."

Each morning at 7 A.M., as the four
columns moved out on their daily fifteen-

This highly accurate field map, *created specifically for Sherman's Atlanta campaign, made use of intelligence provided by refugees, spies, and prisoners. It was printed on durable cloth to stand up under battlefield conditions.*

mile march, the foraging parties would overspread the countryside, ranging as far as necessary in search of provisions. The army's timing was perfect. It set out from Atlanta just as the fall harvest was being collected, and data from the 1860 census allowed Sherman to steer his men through the state's most productive counties. Foragers were instructed to seize the stores of wealthy planters, if possible, ahead of those belonging to the poor farmers Sherman described as "industrious, usually neutral or friendly." Yet such distinctions were typically overlooked by foragers, or "bummers," who took whatever they could find wherever they found it. They collected so much, in fact, that a great deal of food was left to rot each day beside abandoned Union campsites.

Although Sherman's Order No. 120 specifically prohibited soldiers from entering private homes and reserved to corps commanders "the power to destroy mills, houses, cotton-gins, etc.," the army knew its purpose was to lay waste to the state of Georgia, and it did so without much regard to the niceties of regulations. The Union troops under Sherman's command weren't chasing Confederate soldiers. After evacuating Atlanta, Lt. Gen. John Bell Hood's Rebel army had moved north into Tennessee, leaving behind only token resistance. Sherman, therefore, intended all along to target the Georgia economy, and it's this insightful, remarkably innovative strategy that has made his March to the Sea so significant and memorable. Sherman understood—as did his commanding officer, Lt. Gen. Ulysses S. Grant—that war extended well beyond the occasional clash of competing armies. Rather, it was a competition between rival societies, with victory going to the side that first eliminated its opponent's ability (or willingness) to fight.

Sherman's success in Georgia implementing this "total war" strategy has persuaded many military historians that he was the first commander of the modern military era. The general himself explained his thinking in this December 24, 1864, letter, written from Savannah to army chief of staff Henry W. Halleck:

I attach more importance to these deep incisions into the enemy's territory, because this war differs from European wars in this particular: we are not only fighting hostile armies, but a hostile people, and must make old and young, rich and poor, feel the hard hand of war, as well as their organized armies. I know that this recent movement of mine through Georgia has had a wonderful effect in this respect. Thousands who had been deceived by their lying newspapers to believe that we were being whipped all the time now realize the truth, and have no appetite for a repetition of the same experience. To be sure, Jeff. Davis has his people under pretty good discipline, but I think faith in him is much shaken in Georgia, and before we have done with her South Carolina will not be quite so tempestuous.

Sherman in September or **October 1864,** *while still resting his troops in Atlanta.*

THE DESTRUCTION WROUGHT by Sherman's scorched-earth policy focused on railroads, factories, foundries, warehouses, and other buildings that had been or could be used in the Confederate war effort. Yet all of Georgia suffered. Stories of Union brutality circulated for generations, and whether or not the Northerners murdered and raped Georgians—Sherman adamantly denied this—arson and looting were certainly common. Small Confederate cavalry units appeared from time to time to harass isolated Union columns, but these raids had little effect on Sherman's conduct, and Georgia remained essentially defenseless.

Union troops, whether in sanctioned foraging parties or not, set out each morning on foot, but when opportunity presented itself, many soldiers seized wagons and loaded them with anything movable and valuable they could find. One of Sherman's aides, Maj. Henry Hitchcock, described in his diary one typical day along the route of the march:

> Plenty of forage along road: corn, fodder, finest sweet potatoes, pigs, chickens, etc. Passed troops all day, some on march, some destroying railroad thoroughly. Two cotton gins on roadside burned, and pile of cotton with one, also burned. Houses in Conyers look comfortable for Georgia village, and sundry good ones along road. Soldiers foraging all along, but only for forage—no violence as far as I saw or heard. Laughable to see pigs in feed troughs behind wagons, chickens swinging in knapsacks. Saw some few men—Whites look sullen—darkies pleased.

During November and December, Sherman's army cut a path forty to sixty miles wide through the heart of Georgia, and every family along that path experienced its own particular ordeal. Houses were sacked and burned, food and valuables taken, treasured family possessions tossed onto the flames, cotton gins and public buildings put to the torch. "Everything has been swept as with a storm of fire," wrote one Macon newspaper. "The whole country around is one wide waste of destruction." In her journal, Mary Jones Mallard recounted the arrival of Union "marauders" at her mother's plantation in Liberty County. The first foragers arrived on December 15. They searched the house and took some family keepsakes. During the next two weeks, on an almost daily basis, more bummers

THE FIRST MODERN WAR

THE CIVIL WAR IS OFTEN DESCRIBED as the first modern war. In part, this label refers to the innovative strategies that Grant and Sherman developed to conduct the latter stages of the fighting. Yet it also acknowledges the many advances in weapons technology first employed in the war. During the mid–nineteenth century, the same American ingenuity that had earlier produced the cotton gin and the rotary printing press turned out the first repeating rifles, the first machine guns, the first ironclad warships, and some of the earliest submarines (although these generally sank before reaching their targets). Even the basic infantry weapon, the single-shot musket, was improved with rifling to increase its range and accuracy well beyond that of earlier smoothbore guns.

Telegraph lines revolutionized military communications. According to one estimate, the Union Signal Corps strung more than fifteen thousand miles of wire, over which six million messages were sent.

arrived—sometimes in large detachments; at other times, only a few stragglers—to search the house again and take whatever hadn't already been carted away. On December 17, Mrs. Mallard wrote:

A Union forage cap.

> *The Yankees made the Negroes bring up the oxen and carts, and took off all the chickens and turkeys they could find. They carried off all the syrup from the smokehouse. We had one small pig, which was all the meat we had left; they took the whole of it. Mother saw everything like food stripped from her premises, without the power of uttering one word. Finally they rolled out the carriage and took that to carry off a load of chickens. They took everything they possibly could…carriages, wagons, carts, horses, mules and servants, with food and provisions of every kind—and, so far as they were concerned, leaving us to starvation.*

The Early Course of the War

THE POWER OF THE UNION ARMY was not always so. For three and a half years, in fact, the Northern military had floundered. In 1861, when the Civil War began, there were just eighteen thousand soldiers in the regular army, and many of those soon left to join the Confederacy. So the first order of business for both sides after the surrender of Fort Sumter on April 13, 1861, was mobilization. On April 15, President Lincoln issued a proclamation calling up seventy-five thousand state militiamen for three months' service. The term was so short because neither the North nor the South expected the war to last very long (or be especially painful). The South didn't believe the North had the stomach to fight, while the North considered the South no match for its superior resources. Both sides were dismally wrong.

Forced by the events at Sumter to make a choice, Virginia on April 17 chose secession and joined the Confederacy. Arkansas followed on May 6, North Carolina on May 20, and on June 8, Tennessee became the eleventh and last state to leave the Union. At the same time, the secession of Virginia produced a host of

The attack on Fort Sumter (shown here in an 1861 Currier & Ives lithograph) outraged Northerners of every political persuasion. The president's call to arms was hailed, and eager volunteers rushed to join the regiments being organized in nearly every Northern community.

resignations from the U.S. Army, whose officer corps boasted more than its share of Virginians. During the next several weeks, 286 officers (out of about 1,000 on active duty) resigned their commissions to join the Confederate army. Brig. Gen. Joseph E. Johnston, the highest-ranking officer to defect, resigned as quartermaster general of the army on April 18. Two days later, after reportedly being offered the command of all Union forces, Col. Robert E. Lee wrote this regretful letter to Union general in chief Winfield Scott: "Since my interview with you on the 18th inst., I have felt that I ought no longer to retain my commission in the Army. I therefore tender my resignation, which I request you will recommend for acceptance. It would have been presented at once but for the struggle it has cost me to separate myself from a service to which I have devoted the best years of my life, and all the ability I possessed."

Volunteers were relatively easy to come by during the early months of the war, when patriotic emotions ran high on both sides. As the fighting dragged on, however, it became apparent that voluntary enlistment would not provide enough manpower, even with the added inducement of cash bounties to those who signed up. When casualty lists began to lengthen in early 1862, the undermanned Confederacy moved first to institute compulsory service. On April 16, 1862, the Confederate Congress passed a military conscription act that created the first general draft in American history. (Five days later, however, the first of many, many exceptions was added to the law, sparing government officials, postal workers, ferrymen, ironworkers, academics, and pharmacists, among others.) On July 17, 1862, the Union instituted its own limited draft. In later years, when manpower needs became more severe, conscription rules were extended and tightened; yet throughout the war, wealthy and influential men on both sides were able to avoid military service by paying for substitutes. Future president Grover Cleveland, for example, paid $150 for a thirty-two-year-old Polish immigrant to fight in his place.

On April 19, six days after the fall of Sumter, Lincoln declared a Union blockade of the entire Confederate coast. At first, this order was more wishful than real. The South possessed more than a thousand miles of irregular coastline with numerous natural hideouts out of which speedy blockade runners could operate with impunity. It was also unclear whether a Union blockade was legal. According to international law, blockades could be enforced only against sovereign nations, and the Lincoln administration had no intention of awarding any such status to the Confederacy. Yet a blockade made such excellent military sense that Lincoln went ahead with it anyway. Because the South's industrial base was too small to support a sizable war effort, the Confederacy had to trade. Therefore, if the Union could prevent Southern cotton from reaching markets in Britain and elsewhere, the rebellion would crumble. During 1861 and 1862, Confederate shipping persevered, with five out of every six blockade runners successfully eluding Union patrols. Yet after 1863, the blockade tightened and proved instrumental in choking the vulnerable Confederate economy, ending exports of cotton as well as imports of arms and other war supplies.

The Civil War divided many families along sectional lines—including the Lincolns. Most of Mary Todd Lincoln's family lived in Kentucky, where the first lady herself had been raised. Her brother-in-law Ben Hardin Helm (pictured above) spent several days at the White House early in Lincoln's term. The president offered him a major's commission in the Union army. Instead, Helm, a West Point graduate, chose the Confederacy. He died at Chickamauga.

Members of a recently formed company of Georgia volunteers, assigned to Fort Sumter, display their new uniforms in April 1861.

FOLLOWING THESE EARLY MOVES, not much happened as both sides prepared and organized their armies. In late May 1861, the Confederate government decided to move its capital from Montgomery, Alabama, to Richmond, Virginia. A larger city with superior rail connections, Richmond was a more suitable location for the expanding Confederate bureaucracy. The shift also had undeniable political overtones: It emphasized the Confederacy's commitment to defend the Upper South and suggested the importance of Virginia to the rest of

the region. From the North's point of view, the significance of the relocation was simple: Richmond now became the Union's primary military target, and the hundred miles between Northern and Southern capitals, the war's principal theater of operations.

The first major battle of the Civil War took place on July 21, 1861, just as the term of the Union's original "three-months' men" was about to expire. After several days of maneuvering, thirty-seven thousand Union troops under Maj. Gen. Irvin McDowell attacked thirty-five thousand Confederates in the first battle of Bull Run (known as Manassas in the South). At 9 A.M., McDowell

The Civil War involved a great deal of waiting. This cartoon appeared in Frank Leslie's Illustrated Newspaper *on February 1, 1862, above the title,* "Masterly inactivity," or Six Months on the Potomac.

led thirteen thousand Federals across Bull Run creek, driving Rebel defenders back over the fields and low hills north of the town of Manassas, Virginia. The Confederates regrouped, however, and turned the Federal line, precipitating first an orderly Union retreat and then a full-scale rout. Raw, terrified Northern soldiers ran headlong into Union dignitaries and other civilians who had come out for the day from nearby Washington to picnic and watch what they expected to be the first and only battle of the Civil War. Fortunately for the Union, the Confederate troops were themselves too exhausted and inexperienced to mount much of a pursuit. The casualty numbers—2,896 for the North, 1,982 for the South—were considered extremely high at the time but proved later to be rather modest.

Following the Union army's embarrassment at Bull Run, Lincoln made the first of many command changes that would mark his early conduct of the war. Six days after the battle, he named thirty-four-year-old George B. McClellan (promoted to major general just two months earlier) to replace McDowell as commander of the Division of the Potomac. In November, McClellan rose even farther, replacing the aging Winfield Scott as general in chief of the army. A naturally cautious and well-disciplined man, McClellan clearly understood that the war would not end soon, so he spent the fall and winter of 1861 instituting examination boards to weed out incompetent junior officers and developing rigorous training programs to prepare the army's many inexperienced recruits. During this time, he also developed a grand plan for the capture of Richmond. The ensuing Peninsular Campaign began in earnest in mid-March 1862, when McClellan's soldiers began boarding troop carriers at Alexandria.

RIGHT: *Thomas J. Jackson received his nickname, Stonewall, at the first battle of Bull Run. As he held his line atop Henry House Hill, a significant turning point in the fighting, Confederate brigadier Barnard Bee exclaimed, "Look, there is Jackson with his Virginians, standing like a stone wall!"*

The Monitor and the Merrimack

An important technological milestone of the Civil War (and of naval history in general) was the March 9, 1862, battle between the USS *Monitor* and the CSS *Virginia* (more commonly known by its original name, the *Merrimack*). Fought in the Hampton Roads channel off Norfolk, Virginia, it marked the first time that two fully ironclad ships fought one another.

The *Monitor*, designed by Swedish naval engineer John Ericsson, had a shallow draft and a small rotating turret located amidships. According to one contemporary description, it looked like "a tin set upon a shingle." The *Virginia* was a converted U.S. Navy frigate that had been burned to the waterline by Federal sailors retreating from the soon-to-be-overrun Norfolk Navy Yard in late April 1861. The ship was then raised and refitted with armor plating.

The mission of the *Virginia* was to break the Union blockade. On March 8, it battered four Union warships during a battle that lasted about four hours. That evening, the *Monitor* reached Hampton Roads. Its mission was to stop the *Virginia*. On the morning of March 9, the two

The deck and turret *of the USS* Monitor, *photographed on July 9,1862. Six months later, the* Monitor *was lost in a storm off Cape Hatteras.*

ships exchanged fire for more than three hours, with the *Virginia* eventually returning to Norfolk in "a sinking condition," according to the *Monitor*'s chief engineer. The Union blockade remained intact.

The Peninsular Campaign

There has never been any doubt that McClellan was an excellent organizer of men, but as a battlefield commander he left much to be desired. His campaign plan called for a massive landing at Fort Monroe, the Union's precious foothold on the Virginia peninsula formed by the James and York Rivers, from which Richmond lay just upstream on the James. Yet McClellan, despite an enormous advantage in numbers, crept forward so slowly that it seemed he believed his was the lesser force. On April 9, a frustrated President Lincoln urged the general to attack: "Once more, let me tell you, it is indispensable to *you* that you strike a blow…. The country will not fail to note—is now noting—that the present hesitation to move upon an intrenched enemy is but the story of Manassas repeated." Nevertheless, McClellan kept to his ultraslow pace, requiring an additional two months to eject the Confederates from Yorktown and move his own army, numbering ninety thousand men, along the Chickahominy River to within six miles of Richmond.

The first major engagement of the Peninsular Campaign came at Seven Pines (also known as Fair Oaks) on May 31. Recognizing the obvious threat that McClellan's army posed to Richmond, Joseph E. Johnston, one of the Confederacy's five full generals, attacked two Union corps moving up the south bank of the Chickahominy. Because of poor communication, the Confederate offensive resulted in nothing better than a standoff; importantly, however, Johnston was wounded, necessitating his replacement as field commander of the Confederate forces in Virginia. For this crucial position, Confederate president Jefferson Davis chose his senior military adviser, Robert E. Lee.

"If McClellan is not using the army, I should like to borrow it for a while."

—
Abraham Lincoln, comment, April 9, 1862

George McClellan's service revolver.

The Fifth New Hampshire Infantry *built this bridge over the Chickahominy River in late May 1862 during the Peninsular Campaign.*

Already familiar with McClellan and his methods, Lee knew that the Union commander would not likely blunder out of incompetence or haste; however, Lee also recognized that McClellan tended to overestimate the strength of his enemy. On June 12, the Confederate commander sent his most daring cavalry officer, Brig. Gen. J. E. B. Stuart (the same officer who had accompanied Lee to Harpers Ferry), on what came to be known as Stuart's Ride Around McClellan. Engaged primarily in scouting the disposition of the Union forces, but also skirmishing at times, Stuart led his cavalry entirely around the Army of the Potomac. During the next four days, his men seemed to be everywhere, putting Federal commanders on the defensive and seriously undermining Union morale. Meanwhile, Confederate newspapers hailed the feat as the epitome of Southern martial prowess.

Making use of the valuable intelligence obtained by Stuart, Lee attacked McClellan's army on June 25, beginning what came to be known as the Seven Days' Campaign. Taken all together, the Union forces slightly outnumbered Lee's Confederates, but McClellan, upon learning of the first preliminary fighting at Oak Grove, became irrationally concerned with the safety of his army. He immediately requested reinforcements from Washington, to which an exasperated Lincoln replied the next day, "[Your dispatch] suggesting the probability of your being overwhelmed by 200,000, and talking of where the responsibility will belong, pains me very much. I give you all I can, and act on the presumption that you will do the best with what you have, while you continue, ungenerously I think, to assume that I could give you more if I would." Meanwhile, on June 26, the bulk of Lee's army attacked the Federal position at Mechanicsville, producing a hasty but orderly retreat. On the following day, June 27, pursuing Rebels broke through the new Union lines at Gaines' Mill, forcing Maj. Gen. Fitz John Porter's command to retreat all the way across the Chickahominy River in order to seek safety with the main wing of McClellan's army. While these movements were taking place, several Union generals urged McClellan to advance quickly on Richmond, arguing (correctly) that Lee had left only a thin defensive line guarding the city. But McClellan quailed at the risk and instead ordered a general retreat to the James River. It would be two years before the Union army again came so close to Richmond.

WITH THE FAILURE OF THE PENINSULAR CAMPAIGN, the Union high command ordered McClellan's Army of the Potomac (now reinforced to 120,000) to evacuate the peninsula and join forces near Alexandria with Maj. Gen. John Pope's 63,000-man Army of Virginia. The order was issued August 16. Eager to win a decisive victory that might force peace talks, Lee knew that he would have to strike before the two Union armies merged, thereby giving the Federals a three-to-one advantage in manpower over his diminutive Army of Northern Virginia. The plan that Lee developed called for Maj. Gen. Thomas J. "Stonewall" Jackson to maneuver a Confederate corps around Pope's army on the Rappahannock River and attack (on August 26) the huge Federal supply depot at Manassas Junction, where First Bull Run had been fought thirteen months earlier. As Lee expected, Pope moved (on August 29) against Jackson, while Lee secretly sent a second corps under Maj. Gen. James P. Longstreet across the Bull Run Mountains to attack Pope's left flank. Longstreet's surprise assault on August 30 precipitated another rout of the Federals, who fled once again in disarray across Bull Run. Pope was quickly banished to the Department of the Northwest and McClellan restored to command of the Union forces in Virginia, including those defending the capital.

Many residents of Washington feared that Lee would soon be at their doors, but the Confederate commander moved north instead, crossing the Potomac River into Maryland with momentum clearly on his side. On September 13, however, two Union soldiers—stopping to rest in a meadow just east of Frederick, Maryland—found by chance a mislaid copy of Lee's September 9 orders detailing the current disposition of his forces. The discovery of this Lost Order initiated a chain of events that resulted four days later in the battle of Antietam, the single bloodiest event in American history.

As historian James M. McPherson has observed, "Two of Lee's hallmarks as a commander were his ability to judge an opponent's qualities and his willingness to take risks." In September 1862, the risk that Lee decided to take was to divide his army in the face of the enemy. While keeping a third of his forces in Maryland, Lee sent the remainder, under the overall command of Stonewall Jackson, to capture Harpers Ferry. Lee felt that this risk was justified because of McClellan's predictable caution. "His army is in a very demoralized and chaotic condition," Lee wrote at the time, "and will not be prepared for offensive operations—or he will not think it so—for three or four weeks. Before that time I hope to be on the Susquehanna." This would likely have been the case—until the discovery of the Lost Order changed everything. Although McClellan still proceeded slowly, even with Lee's battle plans in hand, he certainly moved much faster than he would have otherwise.

On September 14, three Union corps moved against the rear of one of the Confederate divisions besieging Harpers Ferry. The next day, after Harpers Ferry fell to Jackson, Lee issued orders for the Army of Northern Virginia to regroup immediately. Typically, McClellan failed to attack in strength before this reunification occurred, but on September 17 he ordered the seventy-five thousand Federals he had mobilized to attack forty thousand Rebels Lee had deployed along Antietam Creek, just east of the Maryland village of Sharpsburg.

Few military historians have questioned George McClellan's superior organizational skills, but many have blamed him (especially his hesitancy) for not ending the war in 1862.

(Characteristically, McClellan began the battle believing once again that his army was outnumbered, despite its nearly two-to-one advantage.) The Union attack plan called for coordinated assaults on the Confederate left and right, but poor timing allowed Lee to move his forces from quiet sectors in the line to potential breaking points as he needed them. Vicious fighting in the Cornfield, along Bloody Lane, in the West Woods, and at Dunkard Church resulted in horrific casualties, including six thousand dead and another sixteen thousand wounded. The next day, after McClellan failed to renew the attack, Lee's exhausted army retreated into Virginia.

EMERSON ON LINCOLN

ON JANUARY 31, 1862, during a visit to Washington, Ralph Waldo Emerson recorded this assessment of Pres. Abraham Lincoln:

The President impressed me more favorably than I had hoped. A frank, sincere, well-meaning man, with a lawyer's habit of mind, good clear statement of his fact, correct enough, not vulgar, as described; but with a sort of boyish cheerfulness, or that kind of sincerity & jolly good meaning that our class meetings on Commencement Days show, in telling our old stories over. When he has made his remark, he looks up at you with great satisfaction, & shows all his white teeth, & laughs.

This Lincoln portrait *was taken by Alexander Gardner on November 8, 1863.*

The Emancipation Proclamation

ALTHOUGH IT WAS NOT ALL that he had hoped for, President Lincoln quickly declared Antietam a significant Union victory. He had a variety of motives for making this questionable assertion. In the aftermath of the Seven Days' Campaign, Northern morale had plummeted. One day, Richmond seemed within the Federals' grasp; a week later, victory seemed more distant than ever. During early 1862, the Union had won numerous victories in Missouri, Tennessee, Kentucky, and elsewhere in the western theater of the war, but its failure in Virginia was the most newsworthy. "It seems unreasonable," Lincoln complained, "that a series of successes, extending through half a year, and clearing more than a hundred thousand square miles of country, should help us so little, while a single half-defeat [the Seven Days' Campaign] should hurt us so much." Yet that was the case.

At the same time, the disappointment of the Peninsular Campaign encouraged Peace Democrats in the North, led by Clement L. Vallandigham, to step up their criticism of Lincoln's war policy. Known pejoratively as Copperheads, the Peace Democrats advocated a negotiated settlement. They ridiculed Lincoln's insistence on restoring the Union by force and pointed to the army's recent shortcomings as proof that their position was the more credible. Unwilling to contemplate dissolution of the Union under any circumstances, Lincoln decided instead to press the North's obvious advantages in population and industrial capacity, calling on July 1 for three hundred

LEFT: *This reprinting* of the president's August 22 letter appeared in the August 26 edition of the Tribune's semiweekly newspaper.

thousand more volunteers and approving the first federal income tax ever implemented to pay for them. Meanwhile, the president set about reconsidering and revising the Union's war aims. From the start, Northern abolitionists had urged him to include among them emancipation of the slaves among them, but Lincoln had refused to do this because his emphatic focus on preserving the Union made the abolition of slavery seem nearly irrelevant.

On August 19, 1862, *New York Tribune* editor Horace Greeley published another call for Lincoln to free the slaves. It was entitled "The Prayer of Twenty Millions," and three days later, Lincoln responded:

My paramount object in this struggle is to save the Union, and is not either to save or to destroy slavery. If I could save the Union without freeing any slave I would do it, and if I could save it by freeing all the slaves I would do it; and if I could save it by freeing some and leaving others alone I would also do that. What I do about slavery and the colored race, I do because I believe it helps to save the Union; and what I forbear, I forbear because I do not believe it would help to save the Union.

BLACKS IN THE UNION ARMY

IMMEDIATELY AFTER THE FALL of Fort Sumter, free blacks in the North began pressing for the opportunity to enlist in the Union army. Before the war began, blacks had been excluded from army service, and this policy continued for more than a year afterward. Not until July 17, 1862, did Congress repeal the ban, which had been in force since 1792. (Interestingly, there was no similar ban on black service in the navy, which began accepting African-American enlistments in September 1861 to ease its severe manpower shortage.)

With the issuance of the Emancipation Proclamation in January 1863, the Union began actively recruiting blacks, and eventually 386,000 served in the Union army: 186,000 in combat regiments and another 200,000 in support units. One of the first of the all-black regiments, and certainly the most famous, was the Fifty-fourth Massachusetts Volunteer Infantry. On July 18, 1863, the Fifty-fourth Massachusetts stormed heavily defended Fort Wagner, which sat on Morris Island defending the entrance to Charleston Harbor. Nearly half of its six hundred men died that day while failing to capture the fort; but the valiance of their nearly suicidal effort, reported widely in the press, persuaded many Northerners that blacks indeed deserved the opportunity to fight.

ABOVE: *An unidentified* Union private. Soldiers often had inexpensive ambrotypes such as this one made for loved ones.

LEFT: *As evidenced by this recruiting poster,* published by Philadelphia's Supervisory Committee for Recruiting Colored Regiments *in 1863, black regiments were universally led by white officers.*

WHAT LINCOLN DIDN'T SAY was that he had already decided privately that freeing the slaves would indeed help save the Union. A month earlier, on July 22, he had surprised his cabinet by presenting to it a preliminary draft of the Emancipation Proclamation. Most of the cabinet members agreed with Lincoln that "the slaves [are] undoubtedly an element of strength to those who [have] their service, and we must decide whether that element should be with us or against us." Furthermore, making emancipation a principal Union war aim would please the many Northerners who considered slavery a sin.

Yet Secretary of State William H. Seward strongly advised the president to postpone his announcement of the proclamation "until you can give it to the country supported by military success." Without such a victory, Seward shrewdly predicted, the nation would likely view the proclamation "as the last measure of an exhausted government, a cry for help...our last *shriek* on the retreat."

So Lincoln waited for a Union victory that many Northerners worried might never come. "The nation is rapidly sinking just now," New York City lawyer George Templeton Strong recorded in his diary during the late summer of 1862. "Stonewall Jackson (our national bugaboo) about to invade Maryland, 40,000 strong. General advance of the rebel line threatening our hold on Missouri and Kentucky.... Disgust with our present government is certainly universal." But then came Antietam. Although not the sort of persuasive victory that either Seward or Lincoln had in mind, it was the best the Union might enjoy for some time, and Lincoln was determined to move ahead. Five days after the battle, he issued a preliminary Emancipation Proclamation that announced his intention to free all the slaves held in Rebel-controlled territory as of January 1, 1863, if the Confederacy had not surrendered by then. Lincoln knew that his announcement would be hailed by grateful abolitionists, but he feared the possibly severe reaction of border-state slaveholders and rank-and-file Northerners, to whom racism was no stranger. This concern explains why the president emphasized, in both the preliminary draft and the final version of the Emancipation Proclamation, the point that he was freeing *only* those slaves in Confederate-held territory and

The Confederacy, of course, printed its own money—more and more as the war went on.

Fugitive slaves, bound for the Union lines, ford the Rappahannock River in northern Virginia during the summer of 1862. Before the Emancipation Proclamation settled the matter, Union officers who didn't know what to do with these "contrabands" often returned them to their owners.

specifically *not* those slaves in the loyal border states and other Union-controlled areas. He left universal emancipation to Congress, which passed the Thirteenth Amendment abolishing slavery in January 1865.

In the meantime, Lincoln once again became increasingly unhappy with McClellan's reluctance to pursue and engage the enemy. On October 25, he sent the general this note in response to a request for more horses: "I have just read your despatch about sore-tongued and fatigued horses. Will you pardon me for asking what the horses of your army have done since the Battle of Antietam that fatigues them anything?" Two weeks later, he once again relieved McClellan of command and replaced him with a reluctant Maj. Gen. Ambrose Burnside.

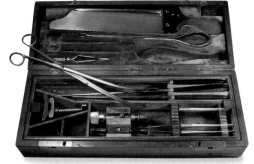

Civil War surgeons used instruments such as these to perform hundreds of amputations a day during heavy fighting. An experienced sawbones could relieve a soldier of a limb in as little as two minutes.

A month after that—on December 13, 1862—Burnside's reluctance proved prescient when he engaged Lee's army in an unusual winter battle at Fredericksburg, Virginia. After using a pontoon bridge to cross the Rappahannock River, Burnside set his 130,000-man Army of the Potomac against the town's 75,000 entrenched defenders—and lost badly. In January 1863, Lincoln relieved Burnside, literally and figuratively, of the command he never wanted and gave it to Maj. Gen. Joseph Hooker, who proved himself nearly as unworthy during the May 1–4, 1863, battle of Chancellorsville, Virginia, where Stonewall Jackson executed one of the most impressive military maneuvers of the war, only to fall victim on May 2 to the misaimed fire of his own troops. The bullet wound that he suffered in his arm that day required its amputation, yet even this surgery failed to save Jackson's life. (He died on May 10.) Meanwhile, Hooker's failure meant that Lincoln had to keep looking for a general who knew how to fight.

The War in the West

THROUGHOUT THIS PERIOD, the Southern war strategy remained simple. Well aware of the Northern political situation, Jefferson Davis and Robert E. Lee had agreed that the best course of action was to take the war into the North and cause enough discomfort there that public opinion would turn against Lincoln and force him to adopt a peace policy. "The present posture of affairs places it in [our] power…to propose the recognition of our independence," Lee wrote to Davis on September 8, 1862, as he prepared to invade Maryland. Such a "proposal of peace," he continued, "would enable the people of the United States to determine at their coming [November 1862 congressional] elections whether they will support those who favor a prolongation of the war, or those who wish to bring it to a termination."

Holes in this raincoat, worn by Stonewall Jackson at Chancellorsville, indicate where three rounds entered his body.

The Northern war strategy, on the other hand, had three primary targets, all pursued simultaneously. One was the Confederate economy, against which the Union naval blockade was directed. Another was Richmond, the elusive goal of the Army of the Potomac. The third was control of the Mississippi Valley and especially navigation on the Mississippi and Tennessee Rivers. If those waterways could be captured and held, the Union would have split the Confederacy in half and brought it that much closer to submission.

The first fighting in the West took place during the summer of 1861 in Missouri, where Federal troops under Capt. Nathaniel Lyon overcame an ad hoc army of secessionists to establish Union control over the state. The fighting then shifted to another slave state, Kentucky, which had initially declared its neutrality in the war. On September 3, 1861, however, Brig. Gen. Gideon Pillow of the Confederacy seized the Mississippi River towns of Hickman and Columbus, violating that neutrality. Pillow and his commanding officer, Maj. Gen. Leonidas Polk, claimed that the invasion of Kentucky was necessary because Union troops were planning to occupy those same towns in order to threaten western Tennessee. The Kentucky state legislature demanded the Confederate troops' immediate withdrawal; when Polk refused, Kentucky joined the Union. More than seventy-five thousand Kentuckians would don Union blue during the next four years, while about twenty-five thousand others chose instead Confederate gray. As was often the case during the Civil War, families were often split along these lines.

In early January 1862, Union Brigadier General Ulysses S. Grant, already recognized as one of the more aggressive commanders on the western front, prepared a reconnaissance-in-force into Rebel-held Kentucky. His successful mission served as a prelude to the Tennessee River campaign that he began in early February. Grant's first important objectives were Forts Henry and Donelson, guarding the Tennessee and Cumberland Rivers, respectively. The forts sat across from one another on a well-defended peninsula just south of the point at which the two rivers converged on the Kentucky-Tennessee border. Grant's army was able to reduce Fort Henry rather easily on February 6, but Donelson proved much more stubborn. On February 14, Grant sent four ironclads against it without success. The next day, the fifteen-thousand-man Confederate garrison under Gideon Pillow, Simon Bolivar Buckner, and former secretary of war John Buchanan Floyd punched a hole in Grant's encircling lines, temporarily opening an escape route to Nashville. However, a Union counterattack closed the gap before the indecisive Rebels pressed their advantage. That night, Floyd and Pillow snuck ignominiously out of the fort (neither would command troops again), leaving Buckner alone to offer a truce the next morning to Grant, his former West Point classmate. To Buckner's note, Grant replied, "Yours of this date, proposing armistice and appointment of Commissioners to settle terms of capitulation, is just received. No terms except unconditional and immediate surrender can be accepted. I propose to move immediately upon your works." As it turned out, Grant's demand of Buckner begat a new nickname for him: "Unconditional Surrender" Grant. It also made him a hero in the Northern press and a major general as well. Meanwhile, the capture of Fort Donelson allowed Grant to secure western Kentucky and made possible his army's subsequent passage into the Deep South.

After the Civil War, Simon Bolivar Buckner *edited the* Louisville Courier *and served as governor of Kentucky from 1887 until 1891.*

I N EARLY MARCH 1862, Grant received orders to move up the north-flowing Tennessee River into Mississippi. Although he understood that the Confederate armies of Albert Sidney Johnston and P. G. T. Beauregard would have to engage his invasion force at some point, he expected them to make a stand near Corinth, Mississippi, a strategic road and rail center in the northeast corner of the state. Instead, Johnston and Beauregard took Grant completely by surprise, attacking his army on April 6 at the small Tennessee River hamlet of Pittsburg Landing, just north of the Mississippi-Tennessee border. The two-day battle of Shiloh (named after the church about which Grant's army was encamped) turned out to be the war's bloodiest yet. Of sixty-two thousand Union troops, more than thirteen thousand were killed, wounded, or reported missing. Confederate casualties were equally horrible, amounting to fully one-quarter of the forty thousand Rebels engaged. Grant was later faulted for his egregious lack of precaution, yet his quick recovery deprived Beauregard and Johnston (who was fatally wounded in the battle) of the decisive victory they had anticipated. Nevertheless, on April 11, Maj. Gen. Henry W. Halleck, overall commander of Federal forces in the West, arrived in Pittsburg Landing to take personal command of the troops, relegating Grant to second in command. Several months would pass before Grant again led a Union army of his own.

In the meantime, the Union's joint naval and land campaign against Rebel strongholds on the Mississippi River produced two important successes. On April 8, 1862, Maj. Gen. John Pope received the surrender of Island No. 10, an important choke point in the river about forty miles south of Cairo at New Madrid Bend. (This well-publicized victory led to Pope's promotion and short-lived tenure as commander of the Army of Virginia.) Sixteen days later, Flag Officer David G. Farragut led an equally successful amphibious invasion of New Orleans. The next major objective in the West would be Vicksburg, Mississippi, the heavily fortified linchpin of the Confederacy's Mississippi River defenses. Grant began the campaign's preliminary troop movements in late October 1862. He ordered Sherman, then commanding a corps of thirty-two thousand men, to transport his troops by riverboat from Memphis to a rendezvous point north of Vicksburg, where Grant's army—marching overland from Corinth—would meet him. The plan fell apart, however, when Rebel cavalry under Nathan Bedford Forrest forced Grant's temporary retreat into Tennessee.

Railroads served a variety of military purposes during the Civil War. In addition to transporting troops and supplies faster than ever before, they hauled weapons as well—such as this mortar, nicknamed the Dictator, which Union forces used to assault the Confederate lines at Petersburg.

In April 1863, Grant moved once again aggressively toward Vicksburg, sending Col. Benjamin Grierson on a destructive sixteen-day cavalry raid behind enemy lines while joining forces himself with Rear Adm. David Dixon Porter's Mississippi Squadron downstream of the Vicksburg guns. During late April and early May, Grant moved his forces ever closer to the city, launching his first direct assault on May 19. When this attack and another one on May 22 failed to penetrate sufficiently the sturdy Confederate works, Grant switched tactics and instead ordered a siege. Six weeks later, on July 4, Vicksburg capitulated; and with the July 8 surrender of Louisiana's Port Hudson, the last Confederate garrisons on the Mississippi River fell. Union control was complete.

LEFT: *Adm. David Dixon Porter's Mississippi Squadron runs the Vicksburg guns on April 16, 1863, in this Currier & Ives lithograph.*

Gettysburg

THE OTHER WEIGHTY EVENT OF JULY 1863 was, of course, the battle of Gettysburg. With Lee's army returning to the offensive, Lincoln discharged Hooker and ordered Halleck to appoint Maj. Gen. George Gordon Meade in his place. (Halleck had himself been promoted by Lincoln to general in chief in July 1862.) The order placing Meade in command of the Army of the Potomac was executed on June 28, 1863; by that time, Lee's advance troops were already in southern Pennsylvania.

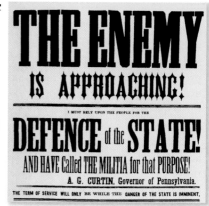

Still convinced that the South's only hope was to bring the war into the North and force a negotiated settlement, Lee had maneuvered his army around Hooker's on the Rappahannock and then marched it quickly north through the Shenandoah Valley before crossing the Potomac River into western Maryland. When Lee learned later on June 28 that Meade had immediately put the Army of the Potomac into motion, he ordered his dangerously scattered troops to regroup in the Gettysburg-Cashtown area. The climactic three-day battle of Gettysburg began on July 1, when a division of Confederates under the command of Lt. Gen. A. P. Hill attacked some troops they thought to be lightly armed militiamen. Instead, Hill's men had engaged the dismounted cavalry of Union brigadier general John Buford, who were armed with powerful breech-loading rifles. It was a crucial mistake. As the day progressed, more and more units from both sides became drawn into the fighting; by evening, there were so many troops involved— upward of 170,000—that Lee found himself committed to a major battle on terrain and under circumstances that he would not otherwise have chosen.

This map, created shortly after the battle, shows the various troop positions at Gettysburg. The Rebel positions are shown in red.

For example, as the battle of Gettysburg began, Lee's cavalry chief, the flamboyant Jeb Stuart, was off on the far side of the Army of the Potomac, unable to rejoin Lee's main army until late on July 2, the battle's second day. By this time, Meade had already positioned his troops in a strong defensive line that took advantage of the available high ground—a broken, fishhook-shaped ridge that ran from Culp's Hill on the Union right through Cemetery Ridge to the Round Tops on Meade's left. Costly Confederate assaults had failed to dislodge the Federals from these positions on July 2, and repeated failures on July 3, including George Pickett's famous charge, determined Lee's fate. Once again, he pulled his army back onto Southern soil.

The dual Union victories at Vicksburg and Gettysburg proved, as one might expect, a remarkable tonic for sagging Northern morale. Which one of these accomplishment marked the genuine turning point of the war remains a matter of contention among Civil War historians; undoubtedly, though, the Confederate war effort (along with Southern morale) went inevitably downhill after July 1863. "Vicksburg is gone and as a consequence Mississippi is gone and in the opinion of all most every one here the Confederacy is gone," one Mississippi planter wrote to Confederate president Jefferson Davis in late July. After two years of fighting, the North's superior resources were finally producing a noticeable advantage, forcing the South into a slide from which it would never recover. The manpower and supply problems it faced became increasingly severe during late 1863 and 1864, while a booming Northern economy churned out ships, guns, ammunition, clothing, and food in ever-increasing quantities.

A crowd gathers in Gettysburg on November 19, 1863, the day that President Lincoln spoke briefly at the dedication ceremony for a new battlefield cemetery there.

THE NEW YORK CITY DRAFT RIOTS

ALTHOUGH A STEADY FLOW of volunteers meant that the Union army had little trouble meeting most of its manpower needs, there were occasions when unwilling conscripts made their displeasure known. Typically, these violent outbursts were directed against blacks.

The worst of these incidents took place during the summer of 1863. On Saturday, July 11, just a week after Lee's defeat at Gettysburg and the simultaneous fall of Vicksburg, a new federal draft law, signed by Lincoln in March, took effect in New York City. The names of the first men conscripted appeared in that Sunday's newspapers. Yet before the draft lottery could resume on Monday morning, a resentful mob stormed the city's central recruiting station, while other New Yorkers rioted elsewhere, temporarily overpowering the police and even fighting pitched battles with the military. Most of the rioters were impoverished Irish immigrants who felt unfairly targeted because, unlike their rich neighbors, they couldn't afford to pay for exemptions. (A widely resented provision of the new law allowed conscripts to pay three hundred dollars in lieu of service.)

These poor, prejudiced whites also worried that their jobs would soon be taken by freed slaves, who were moving north in ever-greater numbers. During the four days of rioting, they targeted the city's black population, beating many African Americans severely and lynching others from lampposts before desecrating their bodies. (In all, approximately 120 people were killed, including police, rioters, and black victims.) White abolitionists and wealthy New Yorkers were also attacked, but to a much lesser extent. Meanwhile, other Northern cities, especially in the Middle West, experienced similar race riots, as antagonism toward blacks ran high during (and after) the war years.

AFTER THE FALL OF VICKSBURG, Grant's forces in the western theater targeted Chattanooga, Tennessee, through which a great deal of vital Confederate rail traffic passed. In mid-August 1863, after displacing Braxton Bragg's Army of Tennessee from Tullahoma, Union major general William S. Rosecrans marched his own Army of the Cumberland southeast rather slowly in pursuit of Bragg, who had predictably retreated to Chattanooga. Bragg pleaded for reinforcements, but none arrived; when Rosecrans finally showed up, Bragg was forced to evacuate the city, which Rosecrans occupied without resistance on September 9. That same day, however, Jefferson Davis decided to detach James Longstreet's corps from Lee's army and send it to Bragg's aid. Because Union control of the Cumberland Gap made a direct march impossible, Longstreet's corps was transported to the vicinity of Chattanooga by rail along a circuitous route through northwestern Georgia. This unusual troop movement took ten days to accomplish, near the end of which Rosecrans began probing south out of Chattanooga, hoping to locate Bragg. On September 19, some of Rosecrans's advance forces under Maj. Gen. George H. Thomas encountered the dismounted cavalry of Maj. Gen. Nathan Bedford Forrest along a three-mile stretch of Chickamauga Creek. Unaware of Longstreet's arrival, Thomas chose to engage Forrest; as at Gettysburg, other units quickly became involved.

In the language of the native Cherokees, *chickamauga* meant "river of blood," and the two-day battle fought alongside Chickamauga Creek produced some of the war's bloodiest casualties. The Union suffered 16,170 men killed, wounded, or missing, while Confederate losses totaled 18,454. Yet Bragg and Longstreet won an important victory. On the second day of the fighting, September 20, Longstreet found a gap in the Federal center (caused by miscommunication), which he exploited, creating panic and flight. Only Thomas's corps held its ground, blocking Rebel pursuit and preventing a Union slaughter. In the aftermath of the battle, Rosecrans lost his command, Thomas won fame as the Rock of Chickamauga, and Bragg laid siege to Chattanooga, establishing strong positions atop Lookout Mountain and Missionary Ridge. On October 16, 1863, Lincoln named Grant to command the newly formed Military Division of the Mississippi, which included the Armies of the Ohio and the Tennessee, as well as Rosecrans's Army of the Cumberland, whose command would soon pass to George Thomas.

Grant traveled immediately to Chattanooga, arriving there on October 23 to take personal command of the situation. Within a week, he had opened up a badly needed supply line (called the Cracker Line) and begun regular artillery bombardments of the Confederate positions. Meanwhile, he ordered Sherman's Army of the Tennessee to join him at Chattanooga. On November 23, he attacked the Rebels in force, breaking the Confederate siege and chasing Bragg's army off into Georgia. The key battle took place on November 25 along Missionary Ridge. Weakened by the November 4 transfer of Longstreet's corps, Bragg was unable to withstand the strength of Grant's combined armies. The decisive blow was struck by Thomas's men, who charged across the valley floor to capture the Confederate rifle pits at the base of Missionary Ridge, only to find themselves subject to such withering fire from above that they had no choice but to keep going. At first, Grant was angered by their unauthorized advance up the mountain, but he watched with increasing amazement and admiration as this disorganized charge—actually, a "backward retreat"—dislodged the Confederates from Missionary Ridge and dismantled their lines.

Nathan Bedford Forrest

Grant Takes Command

FOR THREE YEARS, Lincoln had been searching desperately for a Union commander who was both willing to fight and able to do so competently. In Grant, he finally found the man who could end the stalemate in the East. On March 9, 1864, in a White House ceremony, Grant was promoted to the rank of lieutenant general; three days later, Lincoln gave him command of all Union armies. (At the same time, Sherman took over Grant's duties as head of the Military Division of the Mississippi, and Halleck became army chief of staff.) Grant immediately began organizing a spring campaign against Richmond and,

---

NORTHERN PROSPERITY

INDUSTRIALIZATION OF THE NORTH began in earnest well before the Civil War with the introduction of "the Lowell system," named after the textile mills of Lowell, Massachusetts, which began hiring unmarried young women— a previously untapped labor pool—during the 1820s. This process, however, was vastly accelerated by the demands of the North's wartime economy. For instance, between 1860 and 1870, the number of Northern factories nearly doubled (from fewer than 140,000 to more than 250,000). Railroad mileage also doubled during this period, with huge government subsidies supporting most of the new construction.

Before the war, Southern Democrats had blocked nearly all federal legislation designed to promote economic growth, including bills backing protective tariffs, a national banking system, and most internal improvements. With the South's secession, however, Northern Republicans found themselves able to pass a wide range of economic development measures. The Morrill Tariff of March 1861 introduced the first protective tariff rates, while the National Currency Act of February 1863 established a uniform national banking system. Meanwhile, the May 1862 Homestead Act made available free public land in the West to families willing to farm it. (Southerners had stubbornly opposed this plan because they believed it would hamper the western expansion of slavery.)

The North's ability to manufacture goods, especially armaments, in much greater quantities than the South could either produce or import played a crucial role in its victory.

in the meantime, took an equally important step: On April 17, he ordered an end to all prisoner exchanges with the South. Although Grant's decision was criticized as inhumane by the Northern as well as the Southern press, its impact on the military situation was substantial because the Union army could replace its captured soldiers much more easily than the already shorthanded South. As with many of Grant's decisions, this one resulted in thousands of deaths (in this case, among POWs in overcrowded, undersupplied prison camps) but also a significantly shorter war.

Working closely with Meade, who remained in direct command of the Army of the Potomac, Grant crossed the Rapidan River on May 3, 1864, and marched around Lee's right flank, headed straight for Richmond. Grant's forces numbered 122,000, or nearly twice the number (66,000) Lee had available, but the region's densely forested terrain, known as the Wilderness, served as a force equalizer—as Hooker had found out at nearby Chancellorsville exactly one year earlier. The ensuing Battle of the Wilderness began with some desperate but inconclusive fighting on May 5, after which the two sides spent the night entrenching. The next morning, fighting resumed with much the same result. Over the two days, the Union lost seventeen thousand men (compared to seven thousand Confederate casualties), yet Grant showed no sign of pulling back. Instead, he pushed ahead, trying to outflank Lee once again. "That man will fight us every day and every hour till the end of the war," Longstreet warned.

After the slugfest in the Wilderness, Grant headed for the strategic crossroads at Spotsylvania Court House, but the always deft Lee used a nighttime march to beat Grant there on May 8. Over the next two weeks, operating in the same general area, the two armies struck repeatedly at one another until Grant shifted his forces south and east on May 21. Again, casualties were astronomical: Out of 110,000 Federals engaged at Spotsylvania, 17,500 were killed or wounded. (There are no reliable Confederate casualty figures for this period, as became increasingly the case during the later stages of the war.) On June 1, Lee blocked Grant's advance once more at Cold Harbor, near the battlefields of the Seven Days' Campaign. Bad weather, ammunition problems, and fatigue delayed the major Federal assault until June 3, and afterward Grant must have wished that he had waited still longer or never launched it at all. Being so close to Richmond, Grant was especially determined to force his way through the Confederate line, but thickly defended Rebel positions (which Grant hadn't sufficiently inspected) proved impenetrable despite the best efforts of three Union corps. (Unlike their commanding officers, the soldiers of these corps looked over the Confederate breastworks the day before the battle and were motivated by the sight to pin crude tags to their uniforms, noting their names and home addresses, so that they might be properly buried.) Seven thousand Federals died in the main assault, which lasted less than ten minutes. Cold Harbor, however, turned out to be Lee's last victory of the war.

African Americans attached to the Union army collect the remains of soldiers killed at Cold Harbor. During the first month of Grant's 1864 Wilderness Campaign, the Union army lost forty-five thousand men, or about two-thirds of the strength of Lee's entire army. Yet the North could replace such losses in men and equipment, while the South lacked adequate reserves of both.

On June 12, nine days after the disastrous Cold Harbor charge, Grant began quietly moving elements of his enormous army across the James River to join Benjamin Butler's Army of the James in a surprise attack on Petersburg, which guarded the southern approach to Richmond. In all likelihood, Petersburg would have fallen that day (June 15) to Butler's sixteen thousand Federals had it not been for a combination of Union timidity and tardiness that gave P. G. T. Beauregard time to reinforce his token three-thousand-man Rebel garrison. As a result, the quick assault on Petersburg became instead an extended siege. As additional elements of the Army of the Potomac arrived on the Petersburg line, a number of frontal assaults were finally attempted, but the Confederate lines held, and by June 18, the two sides had settled into a routine that remained relatively stable until April 1865. In the meantime, while he sat outside Richmond, Grant sent Sherman to capture Atlanta.

O N MAY 7, 1864, while Grant and Lee raced one another to the Spotsylvania crossroads, Sherman began moving his hundred-thousand-man army out of Chattanooga. Sherman's command included Thomas's Army of the Cumberland, the Army of the Tennessee under James B. McPherson, and the Army of the Ohio commanded by John M. Schofield. Sherman's mission was to capture Atlanta and, in doing so, destroy the Confederate Army of Tennessee, now led by a recovered Joseph E. Johnston. Over the course of the next three weeks, Sherman probed, while Johnston, always aware of Sherman's superior strength, fell back in a series of planned retreats. At New Hope Church, twenty-five miles northeast of Atlanta, the Rebels held Sherman's army at bay for nearly two weeks; on June 4, however, Johnston again pulled back to yet another prepared, fortified position. The next major action came on June 27, when Sherman ordered an unusual (for him) frontal assault on the Confederate lines at Kennesaw Mountain, which he mistakenly judged to be overextended. Military historians have since speculated that he had in mind the successful assault on Missionary Ridge, which he had witnessed personally seven months earlier. But Johnston's force was more poised than Bragg's had been, and the Federals were routed.

Sherman recovered, of course, and kept inching his way closer to Atlanta. Aware of Sherman's efforts to turn his flanks, Johnston continued his orderly retreats. In Richmond, however, Jefferson Davis became so displeased with this demoralizing, if prudent, strategy that he could brook no more. On July 17, he replaced the cautious fifty-seven-year-old Johnston with the brash thirty-three-year-old Lt. Gen. John Bell Hood, who had a reputation for aggressiveness that Davis hoped would prove contagious now that the fighting had reached the suburbs of Atlanta. It was Hood's idea to confront each of Sherman's three armies separately, and on July 20 he attacked Thomas's Army of the Cumberland at Peachtree Creek. Unfortunately, even Thomas's single army proved too much for the Rebels, who retired after two hours of frantic, ineffective charges with nearly five thousand casualties (compared to two thousand for the Union), out of approximately twenty thousand engaged on each side.

After Cold Harbor, some of Lincoln's advisers urged him to get rid of Grant (shown here in June 1864) because of Grant's astronomically high casualty figures. "I cannot spare this man," Lincoln had told them earlier. "He fights."

John Bell Hood earned his reputation for bravery by surviving serious wounds at both Gettysburg and Chickamauga.

The next day, unshaken by his losses, Hood sent Lt. Gen. William J. Hardee's corps on a fifteen-mile nighttime march to a position behind McPherson's Army of the Tennessee. On July 22, Hardee attacked and suffered an even greater defeat, losing perhaps as many as ten thousand of his forty thousand troops. After the war, Hood judged this particular battle to be "a partial success" because, "notwithstanding the nonfulfillment of the brilliant result anticipated," Hardee's attack "defeated the movement of McPherson [who died in the battle] and Schofield upon our communications" and "greatly improved the *morale* of the troops."

Democratic candidate George McClellan acts as an intermediary between Lincoln and Davis in this presidential campaign cartoon from 1864. As late as September of that year, Lincoln believed that the Democrats' peace platform would persuade a war-weary public to turn him out of office.

August was mostly taken up with harassing cavalry raids until Sherman shifted a large portion of his command to the southern end of Atlanta, where it severed one of the two remaining Confederate supply lines (on August 30) and threatened to cut the other one off as well. The next day, in the final battle of the Atlanta Campaign, an understandably concerned Hood sent two corps under Hardee to attack the Army of the Tennessee (now, with McPherson's death, under the command of Maj. Gen. Oliver O. Howard). The heavy losses Hardee took that day at Jonesboro—while failing, once again, to dislodge the Federals—finally persuaded Hood that he could no longer hold Atlanta. During the late afternoon of September 1, the Confederate army began to evacuate the city. The next day, Sherman's troops entered Atlanta.

Sherman in Atlanta

NOT YET THE STATE CAPITAL, Atlanta was a city of just twelve thousand residents when the war began in 1861. By the time Sherman besieged the city in late July 1864, many of those people had left, and still more fled with Hood's army at the end of August. Yet there remained enough civilians in Atlanta in early September to concern Sherman, who wanted to turn the town into an armed Union camp. "The use of Atlanta for warlike purposes is inconsistent with its character as a home for families," the Union commander declared on September 7, the day he ordered all remaining civilians to leave Atlanta. When the mayor and the city council protested, the general replied:

War is cruelty, and you cannot refine it; and those who brought war on the country deserve all the curses and maledictions a people can pour out.... You might as well appeal against the thunderstorm as against these terrible hardships of war. They are inevitable, and the only way the people of Atlanta can hope once more to live in peace and quiet at home is to stop this war which can alone be done by admitting that it began in error and is perpetuated in pride. We don't want your negroes or your horses, or your houses or your land, or anything you have; but we do want and will have a just obedience to the laws of the United States. That we will have, and if it involves the destruction of your improvements, we cannot help it.

A segment of the Confederate breastworks that ringed Atlanta.

For the next month, Sherman rested his troops. In early October, however, he began to take greater notice of Hood, who had wheeled his Army of Tennessee northwest to threaten Sherman's primary supply line, the Chattanooga-to-Atlanta railroad. Hood reasoned that, without adequate supplies, Sherman would have to retreat. As it turned out, Hood's raids were not particularly successful, but the attempt must have in some way influenced Sherman's subsequent decision to give up his supply line and march to Savannah on his own. After sending Thomas to Nashville to keep Hood's army at bay, Sherman prepared the rest of his army for its virtually unopposed March to the Sea. Grant wired his approval on November 2: "I do not really see that you can withdraw from where you are to follow Hood [into Tennessee], without giving up all we have gained in territory. I say, then, go on as you propose."

On November 15, suggesting what was to come, Sherman's army set fire to Atlanta's railroad depot and machine shops; not surprisingly, the flames spread into the residential areas, destroying much of the city. The next morning, Sherman moved out.

The Savannah waterfront after the city was captured by Sherman's troops.

Sherman's troops never faced any substantial Confederate opposition, but they did strain under the deluge of tens of thousands of runaway slaves, known as contrabands, who attached themselves to the Union army as it passed through rural Georgia. Sherman ordered some organized into "pioneer battalions," whose job it was to repair and improve the roads. Otherwise, he did his best to discourage their presence because he didn't want to feed, shelter, or take responsibility for them in any way. They were not his problem and didn't merit his sympathy. "I would not if I could abolish or modify slavery," Sherman had written before the war while serving as superintendent of a Louisiana military academy. "I don't know that I would materially change the actual political relation of master and slave. Negroes in the great numbers that exist here must of necessity be slaves. Theoretical notions of humanity and religion cannot shake the commercial fact that their labor is of great value and cannot be dispensed with…. All the congresses on earth can't make the Negro anything else than what he is."

Nevertheless, more than thirty thousand blacks joined Sherman's march at one time or another. Because most of these were chased away, only ten thousand remained when the army reached Savannah on December 10. The methods used to discourage runaways were various and at times heartless. On one occasion, Union corps commander Jefferson C. Davis decided to relieve his column of some contrabands by forcing them to remain behind at a river crossing, then burning the bridge behind him. Panic-stricken at the thought of having to return to their masters, many of the runaways attempted to swim the river, drowning in the process.

WILLIAM T. SHERMAN
1820–1891

Although born and raised in Ohio, William T. Sherman knew the South well. After his graduation from West Point in 1840, he served in Florida and South Carolina before spending the Mexican War as an administrative officer in California. In September 1853, he left the army to become a banker in gold-crazy San Francisco but failed to cash in, instead accruing a thirteen-thousand-dollar debt. When the army refused to reinstate him, old friends P. G. T. Beauregard and Braxton Bragg helped him find work as the superintendent of the Louisiana State Seminary of Learning and Military Academy. Sherman enjoyed his new role as a schoolmaster but resigned in January 1861 when Louisiana seceded from the Union. Returned to the North, he used the connections of his brother, Sen. John Sherman, to obtain in May 1861 a colonel's commission in the army.

When Ulysses Grant became president in 1869, Sherman succeeded Grant as general in chief of the army, serving in that capacity until his retirement in 1884. During those fifteen years, Sherman applied the same total-war strategy he had developed in Georgia to the subjugation of the Indian tribes of the Plains and the Southwest. The U.S. Army's many victories during the Indian wars of the 1870s made Sherman an even more popular figure, yet he refused to be drawn into politics, as Grant had been. When Republicans opposed to the nomination of James G. Blaine began a Sherman boomlet at the party's 1884 national convention, the general put a stop to it at once with this terse message: "If nominated, I will not accept. If elected, I will not serve."

The telegram *that Sherman sent to Lincoln on December 22, 1864.*

Sherman's first move upon arriving at Savannah was to reduce Fort McAllister on the Ogeechee River. The fort's December 13 fall made possible the opening of a marine supply line to Rear Adm. John Dahlgren's Union fleet waiting offshore. Next, on December 17, Sherman wrote a note to Hardee, who had been sent to command the Savannah garrison after Hood requested his transfer from the Army of Tennessee. Sherman directed Hardee's attention to the numerous well-laden ships currently resupplying his army and informed him that "I have already received guns that can cast heavy and destructive shot as far as the heart of your city; also, I have for some days held and controlled every avenue by which the people and garrison of Savannah can be supplied, and I am therefore justified in demanding the surrender of the city." In his response, Hardee disputed both of these claims and refused to capitulate. On December 20, however, while Sherman prepared to attack, Hardee slipped out of Savannah using a route that Sherman had carelessly left unguarded. Crossing the Savannah River on a pontoon bridge made of rice flats, the ten-thousand-man Confederate garrison retreated quietly into South Carolina. Two days later, Sherman sent President Lincoln a well-publicized telegram offering him the city "as a Christmas gift." The March to the Sea was over. In his official report, Sherman estimated that it had caused more than one hundred million dollars' worth of damage to the Georgia economy. Of that figure, an astronomical sum in 1864, he supposed that 20 percent had gone to the army's use, while the rest had simply been destroyed.

The Problem of the Freed People

YET THE CAPTURE OF SAVANNAH, while itself
a major military accomplishment, did little to resolve
the problem of what to do with all the runaway slaves.
In fact, the pressure on Sherman only increased. On
December 30, writing to the general "in a private and
friendly way," Henry Halleck warned Sherman of
growing disgruntlement in Washington with his
treatment of the slaves:

A slave family arrives behind Sherman's lines.

> *While almost every one is praising your*
> *great march through Georgia, and the capture of*
> *Savannah, there is a certain class having now great influence with the President,*
> *and very probably anticipating still more on a change of cabinet, who are decidedly*
> *disposed to make a point against you. I mean in regard to "inevitable Sambo." They*
> *say that you have manifested an almost criminal dislike to the negro, and that you*
> *are not willing to carry out the wishes of the Government in regard to him, but*
> *repulse him with contempt! They say you might have brought with you to Savannah*
> *more than fifty thousand, thus stripping Georgia of that number of laborers, and*
> *opening a road by which as many more could have escaped from their masters; but*
> *that, instead of this, you drove them from your ranks, prevented their following you*
> *by cutting the bridges in your rear, and thus caused the massacre of large numbers by*
> *[Joseph] Wheeler's cavalry.*

Sherman defended himself as one might expect, pointing out that his job was
to subdue the Rebels, not to settle "this negro question." But with the countryside
around Savannah pacified, such a rationale no longer obtained, and Sherman found
himself in the position of having to do *something*. Following a visit from Secretary
of War Edwin M. Stanton, Sherman issued on January 16, 1865, Special Field
Orders, No. 15, which outlined his new policy regarding the freed people.
Henceforth, "the [Sea Islands] from Charleston south, the abandoned rice-
fields along the rivers for thirty miles back from the sea, and the country
bordering the St. John's River, Florida, are reserved and set apart for the
settlement of the negroes now made free by the acts of war and the
proclamation of the President of the United States." Whites were
specifically excluded from the new communities, which were to be
governed by the black residents themselves, subject only to U.S. military
authority and the acts of Congress. Each Negro family that applied was
to be given "a plot of not more than forty acres of tillable ground" and
"[military] protection until such time as they can protect themselves."

By now impatient to begin his march northward, Sherman
appointed Brig. Gen. Rufus Saxton to supervise this arrangement, which
Stanton had obviously forced upon him. Saxton, however, undertook
his new duties with great energy, arranging transportation for homeless
blacks to the set-aside lands and writing urgent letters to sympathetic
Northerners requesting food and other supplies to sustain the freed people
until their first crops could be planted and harvested. During the first six months
of 1865, Saxton and his aides managed to resettle successfully more than forty
thousand former slaves. These people faced numerous hardships—neglected soil,

Brig. Gen. Rufus Saxton

inadequate equipment, a shortage of good seed—but they worked industriously, eventually producing decent crops of cotton and various foodstuffs. Meanwhile, Northern volunteers, especially teachers and missionaries, traveled south to see what they could do to help.

The impressive success of this pilot program put pressure on Congress to enact more general land reform so that freed people elsewhere could benefit. Landless former slaves came to believe that, because forty thousand of their number had already been quickly and effectively resettled, they would soon themselves be given a similar opportunity. Such expectations did not seem unreasonable at the time, yet matters ultimately took a different path.

When Johnston surrendered to Sherman on April 26, it was the second time that the two generals had met for this purpose. On April 18, they had signed a memorandum that, among other things, recognized existing Rebel state governments and provided for a general amnesty. Rejecting this deal, President Johnson insisted that Johnston accept the same terms given Lee.

On January 21, 1865, Sherman left Savannah to begin his enormously destructive Carolinas Campaign, highlighted by his army's February 17 capture (and burning) of Columbia, the South Carolina capital. Meanwhile, outside Petersburg, Grant prepared his entrenched forces for a final push against the deteriorating Confederate lines. On March 31, Maj. Gen. Philip H. Sheridan led twelve thousand Federal cavalrymen, closely followed by two additional corps of infantry, south to Dinwiddie Court House, where he threatened both Lee's right flank and the crossroads known as Five Forks. "Hold Five Forks at all hazards," Lee ordered Maj. Gen. George Pickett on the morning of April 1, but that afternoon Pickett's defenses caved before Sheridan's assault. The overextended Rebel lines snapped, and Lee began evacuating Petersburg and Richmond so that he might continue fighting with Joseph E. Johnston's army in North Carolina.

At 4:40 A.M. on April 2, 1865, Grant began an attack along the entire Petersburg front that was everywhere successful. With the few troops he had left, Lee escaped across the Appomattox River and headed west. Meanwhile, President Davis and his cabinet left the capital on a special train bound for the southern Virginia town of Danville, where they briefly established a temporary capital. On April 3, Richmond fell. On April 6, taking a roundabout route to Danville, Lee encountered the first of Grant's pursuing troops along Sayler's Creek. That day, Lee lost eight thousand men, or about a third of his army, which was rapidly melting away. On April 7, he and Grant began exchanging notes that eventually led to Lee's April 9 surrender. On April 26—the same day that Lincoln assassin John Wilkes Booth was discovered and killed—Johnston yielded to Sherman. And a month after that—on May 26, 1865— Lt. Gen. E. Kirby Smith, commander of the Confederacy's Trans-Mississippi Department, surrendered the last Rebel army, ending the Civil War.

Reconstruction

COMPARED WITH THE RETRIBUTIVE VIOLENCE that followed twentieth-century civil wars in Russia, Spain, China, and Cambodia, the aftermath of the American Civil War was remarkably mild. Confederate leaders were neither shot nor driven into exile. Instead, most resumed their antebellum careers. Only a few, such as Jefferson Davis, were ever imprisoned, and even Davis—who was finally captured on May 10 in Georgia, reportedly disguised as a woman—was released in May 1867. No property was permanently confiscated, no wealth redistributed.

The peace took this course largely because, beginning in 1863, President Lincoln made it his policy to reintegrate the South on the most forgiving of terms. On December 8 of that year, he issued the Proclamation of Amnesty and Reconstruction, which offered pardons to most Confederates who had participated in the rebellion but would now swear an oath of loyalty to the United States. Furthermore, Lincoln declared that seceded states could rejoin the Union once 10 percent of their voters (according to 1860 registration records) elected new, loyal state governments. Lincoln's plan was considered at the time a moderate, if somewhat lenient, course between the demands of extremist Republicans, who wanted the South treated as subjugated territory, and the desires of conservative Democrats, a good number of whom advocated rescinding emancipation and resurrecting the antebellum South.

During early 1864, Union-held Louisiana and Arkansas both met Lincoln's criteria for restoration, yet Radical Republicans in Congress blocked the seating of their delegations because they objected to Lincoln's generous peace terms. Instead, Congress passed the Wade-Davis Bill, which embraced a much tougher standard for reunification, based on the "state suicide" theory that the Confederate states had dissolved their bonds with the Union and therefore had to be readmitted (as Congress saw fit) rather than simply restored by presidential fiat. Under the terms of the bill, sponsored by Ohio senator Benjamin F. Wade and Maryland representative Henry Winter Davis, seceded states could gain readmission only after 50 percent of their enrolled white male populations swore a much more stringent oath and adopted constitutions acceptable to both Congress and the president. In addition, while Lincoln had excluded from this process mainly high-ranking Confederate officials and Rebel officers who had once held U.S. Army commissions, the Wade-Davis Bill excluded any Southerner who had voluntarily taken up arms against the Union, whether he now took the "ironclad" oath or not. Already committed to the legal theory that the Confederate states had never truly left the Union, Lincoln opposed the bill, which he pocket-vetoed in July 1864 despite enormous last-minute pressure to sign it.

The basic dispute was that Lincoln thought the executive branch should manage Reconstruction, while Congress, having lately put up with a vast expansion of presidential authority (because of the wartime emergency), wanted control of Reconstruction for itself. The outcome of this struggle would determine whether the South was restored quickly under former Confederates with minimum federal interference, or whether it had to undergo fundamental political change (such as extending the franchise to blacks) before readmission became possible. Even with Lincoln's death, this dynamic persisted.

Pursuing Federal cavalry finally caught up with Jefferson Davis, his wife Varina, and their dwindling retinue outside Irwinsville, Georgia. According to a New York Tribune *reporter, Davis was clothed in petticoats and a morning dress, with a hood closely drawn over his head. This wood engraving originally appeared in* Frank Leslie's Illustrated Newspaper.

LINCOLN'S ASSASSINATION

ON THE EVENING OF April 14, 1865, President and Mrs. Lincoln attended a performance at Ford's Theatre of the popular comedy *Our American Cousin*, starring Laura Keene. Shortly after ten o'clock, John Wilkes Booth, a twenty-seven-year-old actor who had access to the theater, shot Lincoln as he sat in a lightly guarded box. (Lincoln's sole bodyguard had briefly stepped away from his post.) Booth then jumped onto the stage, shouting "Sic semper tyrannus! The South is avenged!" In the process, he caught his right foot on the flag decorating the presidential box, causing him to break his leg in the fall. Still, he managed to hobble offstage while the stunned performers stood motionless. He escaped on a horse that he had stashed in the alley.

The dying Lincoln, whom Booth had shot in the back of the head using a .44-caliber single-bullet derringer, was carried across the street to the Peterson boardinghouse. His six-foot-four-inch frame, unable to fit otherwise, was draped diagonally across a bed in one of the unoccupied rooms. The president died at 7:22 the next morning without once regaining consciousness. "Now he belongs to the ages," offered Secretary of War Edwin Stanton, one of the many government officials who had gathered at Lincoln's bedside during the night. Later, it became clear that the Lincoln assassination had been part of a much larger plot to murder several important Union leaders: General Grant and Vice President Johnson had also been stalked, while Secretary of State Seward was stabbed in his bed, nearly dying from his wound.

John Wilkes Booth (left) waited to strike until the third act, when the character Asa Trenchard delivers the play's biggest laugh line: "Well, I guess I knew enough to turn you inside out, you sockdologizing old man trap!" These were the last words Lincoln heard.

THE MAN WHO SUCCEEDED LINCOLN, Andrew Johnson, was a staunch unionist from the mountains of eastern Tennessee who loved the South but not as much as he hated the plantation aristocracy. When Tennessee left the Union in June 1861, Johnson became the only senator from a seceding state to remain loyal to the Union. Lincoln rewarded this loyalty in March 1862, when he appointed Johnson military governor of Tennessee, and again in June 1864, when he persuaded delegates at the National Union (Republican) convention to expand the party's base by nominating Johnson, an erstwhile Democrat, as his running mate. After Lincoln's death, Johnson adopted his predecessor's lenient approach to Reconstruction, yet Johnson's nearly total lack of sympathy for the freed slaves—he had never seen anything wrong with slavery—gave his Reconstruction policy a mean-spirited edge that caused many Northerners to worry that the Civil War had been fought for nothing.

Because the first session of the Thirty-ninth Congress wasn't scheduled to begin until early December 1865, Johnson used the eight months following Lincoln's assassination to inaugurate the era of presidential Reconstruction. In late May 1865, he announced a plan that would permit white Southerners to form new state governments without black participation as long as they repudiated secession, abolished slavery, and disavowed the Confederate war debt—at which point, federal military rule would be lifted and the states could once again send representatives to Congress. Given these easy terms, it wasn't long before nearly all of the former Confederate states met them. The major problem was that these "Johnson state governments" also enacted, at the same time, Black Codes designed, in the words of one observer, to "restore all of slavery but its name." In addition to denying former slaves the right to vote, the Black Codes variously restricted the movements of freed people, outlawed their ownership of land, excluded them from certain jobs, made them subject to a separate draconian penal code, and forbade their possession of weapons. This last provision made Southern blacks especially vulnerable to the white paramilitary groups that many former Confederate soldiers were then busily organizing.

Southern whites insisted that political, social, and economic controls were necessary to prevent social disorder in the wake of emancipation; but most Northerners saw the Black Codes for what they were, denouncing them and calling for strict federal management of the "conquered provinces," to use Pennsylvania congressman Thaddeus Stevens's phrase—at least until the emergence of suitably repentant governments.

Thomas Nast's 1868 caricature of "the white man's government" in the South indicates the oppression of freed people even under congressional Reconstruction.

The Freedmen's Bureau

ALTHOUGH ITS RATIFICATION in December 1865 abolished slavery in the United States, the Thirteenth Amendment spoke not at all to the uncertain future of the newly freed people. The former slaves were free—but free to do what? What could freedom mean to people, raised in slavery, who had no resources and faced a social system prejudiced against them? The answer for many was "all of

THE KU KLUX KLAN

THE MOST NOTORIOUS of the South's white paramilitary groups was the Ku Klux Klan, organized in December 1865 by Confederate veterans in Pulaski, Tennessee. The purpose of the Klan was to resist Reconstruction, which it did through the use of violence and intimidation against newly enfranchised black voters. Prominent among the Klan's founders was Nathan Bedford Forrest, the indomitable Rebel cavalry commander who had led the April 1864 Confederate assault on Fort Pillow in western Tennessee. Although the exact course of events at Fort Pillow remains unclear, it was reported that Forrest's men slaughtered hundreds of black Union soldiers even after they had surrendered.

Klan members often (but not always) dressed in hooded white robes, which they thought would frighten superstitious blacks while simultaneously concealing their own identities from occupying federal troops. The nineteenth-century Klan reached its peak about 1870, after which federal suppression of the group, beginning with the 1871 Ku Klux Klan Act, reduced its numbers significantly—but so did the fact that the Klan had already largely achieved its goal: white supremacy in the South.

Although most active in the South, the Ku Klux Klan was, even in its nineteenth-century incarnation, a national organization. This photograph shows Klan members in Watertown, New York, about 1870.

slavery but its name." Most former slaves simply remained with their former masters, toiling in the same fields for either a portion of the harvest (sharecropping) or a near-subsistence wage. Meanwhile, those who left their homes faced even more precarious futures.

Believing that the federal government had a duty to help these people, the Thirty-eighth Congress had passed on March 3, 1865—the final day of its final session—a bill authorizing the creation of a Bureau of Refugees, Freedmen, and Abandoned Lands within the War Department. The Freedmen's Bureau, as it was more commonly known, was intended to act as the legal guardian of the freed slaves, protecting their long-term interests as well as helping them meet their immediate needs for food, clothing, shelter, education, and jobs. The law's sponsors argued that white society owed the freed people at least this much. In practice, however, the bureau came under near-constant attack from Southerners, who thought it was doing too much, and from Northerners, who complained it was doing to little.

The officer whom President Johnson appointed to head the Freedmen's Bureau was Maj. Gen. Oliver O. Howard, former commander of the Army of the Tennessee, who had accompanied Sherman to Savannah and fought with him during the subsequent Carolinas Campaign. A man genuinely concerned for the welfare of the freed slaves, Howard directed his underlings to establish schools, build hospitals, negotiate labor contracts, and feed hundreds of thousands of hungry blacks. Even so, the Freedmen's Bureau was never adequately staffed or funded, and it struggled until July 1872, when it was finally disbanded.

A MONG THE FOUR MILLION freed people placed under Howard's aegis were the former slaves who had been resettled by Rufus Saxton under Sherman's Special Field Orders, No. 15. Their situation changed dramatically after May 1865 because Johnson's new Reconstruction plan restored to most white Southerners their real property along with their political and civil rights. Specifically, Johnson directed that all land confiscated under wartime orders such as Sherman's be returned to its original owners. Although the president couldn't return the blacks themselves to bondage, he nevertheless made it plain that he expected blacks to surrender all newly acquired land immediately.

Maj. Gen. Oliver O. Howard lost his right arm at Seven Pines (Fair Oaks) during the Peninsular Campaign. After the war, he helped found Howard University, which was named for him in 1867.

Former slaves at a school set up by the Freedmen's Bureau in Virginia.

With the help of Secretary of War Stanton, both Howard and Saxton (now assistant director of the Freedmen's Bureau) delayed and otherwise resisted Johnson's decision. Nevertheless, in June 1865, Sherman's field order was revoked; and three months later, the former owners of Edisto Island, one of the Sea Islands off the coast of South Carolina, petitioned Johnson for the return of their land. Howard was subsequently ordered to visit the island and persuade the freedmen who had settled there to accept a "mutually satisfactory solution," by which Johnson meant they should pack up and leave. Caught between his duty and his sympathies, Howard sat down with the black residents of Edisto in late October in a local church. Furious with the course of events, former slaves crowded into the church and refused to quiet down until one woman began singing, "Nobody Knows the Trouble I've Seen."

The freed people listened to Howard as he urged them to surrender their farms and agree to work for the island's once and future owners. Interrupted from time to time by cries of dismay and exasperation, Howard patiently explained that the "possessory titles" the settlers had been granted under Sherman's order were not absolute and had been rescinded. Afterward, he received permission to appoint a commission made up of three freed people, three former owners, and three Freedmen's Bureau officials to adjudicate the matter further. This was, in part, another delaying tactic; Howard hoped that once the new Congress convened in December 1865, Johnson's order would be overridden. It wasn't.

In January 1866, the president replaced Saxton, who was still blocking the dispossession of black landholders, with Davis Tillson, another Freedmen's Bureau official but one much more sympathetic to the president's policy. Tillson immediately issued an order restoring white ownership of the confiscated land and even went so far as to charter a boat so that he could accompany the former owners on their inspection tour, thereby assuring black compliance with his order. Freed people willing to work for the whites were generally allowed to remain on the land; the rest were driven off the Sea Islands, either by Union troops or white vigilante groups.

The Fourteenth Amendment

As expected, the Thirty-ninth Congress convened on December 4, 1865. Unexpected, however, were the identities of the Southerners sent by the new Johnson state governments to take seats in the House and Senate. To the shock and outrage of most Northerners, these delegates included more than a few high-ranking Rebels. Georgia had even sent Alexander H. Stephens, who eight months earlier had been vice president of the Confederacy! Along with Johnson's obvious and inveterate racism, the brazenness with which Stephens and other former secessionists had retained control of their states' political machinery produced an uprising in Congress. The Radical Republicans, who would dominate

In addition to former Confederate vice president Alexander H. Stephens (pictured here), the Southern congressmen sent to Washington in December 1865 included six members of Jefferson Davis's cabinet, fifty-eight former Confederate congressmen, and four Rebel generals.

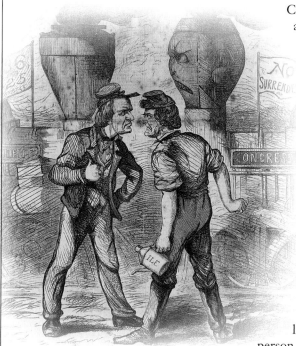

This November 1866 cartoon depicts the impasse that had developed between President Johnson and the Radical Republicans led by Thaddeus Stevens. After the 1866 midterm elections, however, the Radicals had enough votes in Congress to pass their own Reconstruction laws and override Johnson's numerous vetoes. The Fortieth Congress even convened in March 1867 (rather than the usual December) so that the president wouldn't have nine months on his own to govern as he wished.

Congress after the 1866 elections, did not yet enjoy a majority; but the conduct of the Johnson state governments so offended Republican moderates that they joined the Radicals in refusing to seat the new Southern congressmen. Moreover, Johnson's intransigent refusal to compromise on this or any other issue augured poorly for the future.

As floor leader of the Radicals, Thaddeus Stevens set the congressional agenda, calling for dissolution of the Johnson state governments and their replacement by new ones based on the principles of universal manhood suffrage and equality before the law. This latter principle underpinned both the Civil Rights Act of April 1866 and the Fourteenth Amendment, which Congress approved two months later. The Civil Rights Act, passed to counter the Black Codes, outlined rights that all Americans possessed, regardless of their race. These included the rights to make contracts and bring lawsuits, as well as others related to the security of person and property. (The bill even included a provision allowing freedmen deprived of their land by Johnson's May 1865 proclamation to lease twenty acres of government-owned Sea Island property with an inexpensive option to buy.) Johnson vetoed the bill, but Congress immediately passed it again, making the 1866 Civil Rights Act the first significant piece of legislation ever passed over a presidential veto. The veto also cost the president whatever residual goodwill he might have had among the moderates and persuaded the Radicals that the rights outlined in the new law needed to be permanently written into the Constitution.

The Fourteenth Amendment's purpose, according to historian Eric Foner, was nothing less than "to secure the fruits of Union victory in the Civil War by guaranteeing equal civil rights for the freed slaves and loyal governments in the South." In addition to prohibiting any state from abridging the equality of its citizens before the law, the Fourteenth Amendment excluded Confederates who had taken a constitutional oath from holding state or federal office, prohibited repayment of the Confederate debt, and reduced a state's representation in Congress should it deprive any male citizens of the right to vote. (It did not, however, otherwise prevent Southern states from denying blacks the right to vote, nor was this last provision ever enforced.) The Fourteenth Amendment, therefore, embodied an entirely new approach to the protection of personal liberty: A century earlier, Jefferson had warned that the federal government posed a threat to personal liberty; now, according to Massachusetts senator Charles Sumner, that same government had become "the custodian of freedom."

H OPING TO REVIVE HIS POLITICAL FORTUNES, President Johnson spent the fall of 1866 traveling the country on a whistle-stop speaking tour known as "the swing around the circle." His intention was to rally support for like-minded congressional candidates, mostly Northern Democrats associated with his National Union party; meanwhile, he called for reconciliation between North and South on the basis of a mutual respect for states' rights. Few Northerners were persuaded. Instead, the 1866 midterm elections produced a clear mandate for the Radicals, who won a voting majority in both houses of the Fortieth Congress. During the next two years, through the Joint Congressional Committee on Reconstruction, Stevens and his colleagues replaced presidential Reconstruction with a congressional version.

When every former Confederate state (except Tennessee, which had already been readmitted) refused—at Johnson's urging—to ratify the Fourteenth Amendment, Congress began Reconstruction anew. The First Reconstruction Act, passed over Johnson's veto in March 1867, divided the South into five military districts, each governed by a federal commander with broad powers to remove local officials, initiate constitutional conventions, determine voter eligibility, impose martial law, and guarantee the rights of blacks. The act also established much more stringent requirements for readmission, notably enfranchisement of the freed people. Other significant legislation passed over Johnson's veto included the March 1867 Tenure of Office Act, which limited the president's ability to replace executive branch officials who had been confirmed by the Senate, and the Fifteenth Amendment, the last of the Reconstruction amendments, which barred states from denying citizens the right to vote because of their race.

According to the terms of the First Reconstruction Act, to rejoin the Union each state under military rule had to draft a new constitution guaranteeing universal manhood suffrage, elect a state government under this new constitution, and ratify the Reconstruction amendments. (When most Southern states continued to balk, two additional Reconstruction Acts were passed to force their compliance.) In five states—Alabama, Florida, Louisiana, Mississippi, and South Carolina—where former slaves were numerous and many whites were disqualified because of their Rebel histories, the new rules created black voting majorities. So when new elections were held under federal auspices—the first in which the freed people could participate—hundreds of blacks won election to local, state, and even national office. Elsewhere in the South, black voters joined with eligible (and therefore mostly Unionist) whites to elect sympathetic Radical Republicans. Once these Radical governments, supported by federal troops, were firmly in place, Congress finally began the process of readmitting the Southern states. By June 1868, when an omnibus bill readmitted Alabama, Florida, Georgia, Louisiana, North Carolina, and South Carolina, the only state remaining out of compliance was Texas, which wasn't readmitted until March 1870.

In February 1870, Hiram R. Revels of Mississippi became the first African American to serve in Congress when occupied the Senate seat previously held (until 1861) by Jefferson Davis. In all, during the period of Radical Reconstruction, there were two black senators and fourteen black representatives.

THE IMPEACHMENT OF ANDREW JOHNSON

THE FINAL BATTLE IN THE WAR between Andrew Johnson and the Congress began in February 1868, when the House voted to impeach the president for violating of the Tenure of Office Act, among a few other alleged high crimes and misdemeanors. In August 1867, Johnson had tried to fire his insubordinate secretary of war, Edwin Stanton, only to be informed by the Senate Committee on Military Affairs that the Tenure of Office Act precluded him from doing so. In February 1868, outraged by Stanton's continuing sabotage of his Reconstruction policy, Johnson decided to try again and dismissed Stanton a second time.

The president's lengthy Senate trial began on March 13. Because all of the important facts were acknowledged by both sides, the trial came down to whether Johnson's actions genuinely amounted to a violation of his constitutional oath.

On May 16, the Senate took a decisive vote on the last of the eleven impeachment articles, the catchall. The tally was 35–19 against Johnson, or one vote short of the two-thirds majority necessary for his removal. In part, Johnson escaped conviction by cutting a few deals and promising privately to end his active interference with congressional Reconstruction. Yet most of the senators who voted for his acquittal would likely have done so anyway because they didn't want the Senate to set an unfortunate precedent: They considered Johnson and his inept, insensitive leadership expendable but were loath to see the presidency tarnished in any more permanent way.

Andrew Johnson, though honest, was a dogmatic, tactless man upon whom circumstances forced a uniquely difficult episode in American history. According to Jefferson Davis, he had "the pride of having no pride."

Carpetbaggers and Scalawags

WHO WERE THE RADICALS running these Southern state governments? Many were footloose Northerners, known as "carpetbaggers" because their few belongings fit easily into one of the common satchels of the day. Tens of thousands of these political adventurers migrated south after the war—some genuinely concerned with the plight of the freed people, others motivated purely by personal gain. Because of the broad and generous powers Congress had granted the military governors in the Reconstruction South, corruption there was both easily undertaken and unfailingly profitable.

The Southerners who cooperated with the carpetbaggers were known as "scalawags." Before the war, most of these people had been either cotton Whigs opposed to secession or tenant farmers who disliked blacks but hated the planters more for leading them into "a rich man's war and a poor man's fight." After the Confederacy's collapse, many of these people quite naturally joined the Radical governments, eager to encourage Northern investment and rebuild the South's shattered economy. Others, however, simply joined to share in the looting.

Of course, governmental corruption during the 1870s was widespread in the North and West as well.

This fine example of a mid-nineteenth-century carpetbag once belonged to Pres. Franklin Pierce.

Because of his much-admired wartime record, Ulysses S. Grant was elected president in 1868 and again in 1872, yet his skill as a general did not transfer well to the executive branch. His administration was routinely beset by ever-worsening scandals involving close personal friends or relatives or wartime associates of the president who had conspicuously absconded with public funds. Even when the evidence was indisputable, Grant still stood by these crooks, naively accepting their explanations and often blocking their prosecution. Among the most egregious incidents were Jay Gould and James Fisk's September 1869 attempt to corner the gold market (it was the job of Grant's brother-in-law to keep him from releasing federal gold), the June 1874 resignation of Treasury Secretary William A. Richardson (for conspiring with tax collector John D. Sanborn to permit Sanborn keep half the funds he collected), the Whiskey Ring (a group of 110 government officials who stole millions of dollars in liquor taxes), and the Indian Ring (a similar group of officials, led by Secretary of War William W. Belknap and involving the president's brother, who received kickbacks in exchange for the awarding of Indian post trading rights).

REGARDING RECONSTRUCTION POLICY, the Grant administration initially went along with the Radicals in Congress, who in May 1870 passed the first of the Force Acts designed to protect the rights granted blacks by the Fourteenth and Fifteenth Amendments. (Organized white violence had recently kept blacks from the polls in Georgia, North Carolina, and Tennessee, helping to elect white Democratic governments there.) The Force Acts empowered the federal government to supervise elections in cities with more than twenty thousand people while using troops as necessary to put down terrorist organizations such as the Ku Klux Klan. In October 1871, President Grant used the third of these acts (the April 1871 Ku Klux Klan Act) to impose martial law in South Carolina, where Klan violence had become particularly intense.

This acerbic cartoon was published in February 1880 as New York senator Roscoe Conkling and his Stalwart faction of the Republican party promoted Grant for a third term. It depicts the many corrupt "rings" that had disgraced two previous Grant administrations. Among the other acrobats pictured is former secretary of war William Belknap.

Beginning with passage of the Amnesty Act in May 1872, however, Northern fatigue regarding Reconstruction became increasingly apparent. The new law restored the civil rights of most white Southerners, permitting all but a very few of the top Confederate leaders to vote as well as hold public office. As a result, hundreds of thousands of former Rebels were returned to the voting rolls, enabling them to vote out the Radicals and take control of nearly every Southern state government. Three years later, Congress passed the Civil Rights Act of 1875, the last of the Force Acts, which forbade the exclusion of blacks from juries and outlawed racial discrimination in public places, such as hotels and restaurants. But the act contained no enforcement mechanism and was universally ignored. In this way, growing Northern indifference combined with intensifying Southern hostility to produce a rolling back of all the political and economic gains the freed people had made. "The whole public," explained President Grant, "is tired of these outbreaks in the South."

As a result, the federal presence there diminished, and white terror groups filled the power vacuum, ending enforcement of all congressional civil rights legislation. Meanwhile, the failure of Jay Cooke's New York City brokerage firm in September 1873 set off a panic that evolved into a five-year depression. Not surprisingly, the bad economic news helped the opposition Democrats immensely; during the 1874 midterm elections, the party took eighty-five House seats away from the Republicans—more than enough to win control of the House for the first time since James Buchanan was president. Apparently, a decade after Lee's surrender and the death of Lincoln, very few Americans still cared terribly much about the problems of the freed people in the South.

The Compromise of 1877

THE PRESIDENTIAL CAMPAIGN of 1876 began with Grant's apology to the nation for the scandals his administration had caused. Hoping to capitalize on the corruption issue, the Democrats nominated the cleanest candidate *they* could find, New York governor Samuel J. Tilden, who had successfully brought down William Marcy Tweed, the corrupt political boss of New York City's Tammany Hall machine. To compete with Tilden, the Republicans passed over James G. Blaine, the tainted Speaker of the House, and chose instead Ohio governor Rutherford B. Hayes, who was the cleanest candidate they could find. Tilden campaigned effectively on the corruption issue, while the Republicans praised Hayes for his brave Civil War service. (This successful tactic, known as "waving the bloody shirt," was a staple of Republican campaigning during the late nineteenth century. It was intended to—and did—remind Northern voters of the Democratic party's previous association with secession.)

The race remained too close to call—even after Election Day. Tilden had clearly won the popular vote, but the electoral vote was confused. The day after the election, Tilden led Hayes in the electoral college, 184–165, but returns from four states were being challenged, leaving twenty votes still undecided. Nineteen of these votes came from three Southern states (Florida, Louisiana, and South Carolina) still under Radical rule. Electors chosen by each of the carpetbag governments were being contested by slates representing the white, former Confederate opposition. The legitimacy of one of Oregon's electors was also being challenged.

To resolve the dispute, Congress created a special electoral commission, whose fifteen members included five senators, five representatives, and five Supreme Court justices. More importantly, the party breakdown was supposed to be seven Democrats, seven Republicans, and one independent (Justice David Davis). Davis, however, disqualified himself when the Illinois legislature elected him to the Senate. His spot was taken by Justice Joseph P. Bradley, a Republican. The Democrats on the Court went along with Bradley's selection because he seemed to be the most nonpartisan of the remaining four justices, all of whom were Republicans. Even so, Bradley voted consistently with his party colleagues. As a result, the commission slowly awarded each of the disputed electors to Hayes by an 8–7 margin.

As the outcome of the process became apparent, Democrats in the House threatened to launch a filibuster that would have halted the electoral count and blocked indefinitely the election of Hayes. This threat was never carried out, however, because the Hayes forces made a deal with the Southern Democrats:

The cover of this October 4, 1873, issue of Frank Leslie's Illustrated Newspaper *shows the New York Stock Exchange closing its doors during the worst of the financial panic.*

The Southerners agreed to oppose the filibuster in exchange for Hayes's promise that his administration would immediately remove all federal troops from the South and make a few other concessions. From the Southerners, Hayes extracted a corresponding promise, never kept and never meant to be, that the states of the former Confederacy would respect the constitutional rights of blacks. So ended the era of Reconstruction.

AT 4 A.M. ON MARCH 2, 1877, the Senate announced Hayes's election to the presidency; later that day, Hayes arrived in Washington. Because March 4 fell on a Sunday, the new president took the oath of office privately on Saturday night, with his inauguration following on Monday morning. The country went along with Hayes's election, as it did with his removal of federal troops from the South, because it had other, more pressing concerns: There was a depression going on, there were hostile Indians on the Plains, and Custer had yet to be avenged. With the federal troops gone, Democratic state governments in the South moved quickly to disenfranchise black voters, and with each passing year, black electoral participation declined. For nearly a century, conservative whites used violence—from beatings to murder— to keep the freed people in a ruthlessly subordinated position. They weren't reenslaved, perhaps, yet neither were they fully free.

This highly detailed rendering of an electoral commission hearing on the legitimacy of the Florida vote was painted by C. A. Fassett in 1879. The fifteen members of the commission are seated on the raised platform on the left.

Thaddeus Stevens

1792–1868

by Eric Foner

THADDEUS STEVENS WAS THE MOST radical of the Radical Republicans during the Civil War and Reconstruction, and he remains one of the most controversial figures in American history. In traditional accounts of Reconstruction, he is typically portrayed as an evil genius who—motivated by hatred of the South—torpedoed Andrew Johnson's lenient plans for reuniting the nation. Yet recent historians have written much more sympathetically of Stevens, citing his lifelong defense of African-American rights and his support for land redistribution, which would have provided at least some economic foundation on which the freed people could build.

A native of Vermont, where he was born in 1792, Stevens moved as a young man to Lancaster, Pennsylvania, where he practiced law and worked as an iron manufacturer. In 1833, he entered the Pennsylvania state legislature, serving for eight years as an Anti-Mason and becoming a leading advocate of free public education. His sympathy for the plight of blacks was also conspicuous, and as a member of the convention that drafted a new state constitution in 1838, Stevens refused to sign the final document because it rescinded the voting rights the state's blacks had enjoyed.

Stevens served his first tour of duty in Congress (1849–1853) as a Whig; during his second tenure (1859–1868), he legislated as a Republican, having helped found that party in 1854. He was known in the House as a blunt speaker and master of debate. Even his opponents respected his honesty, and everyone feared his quick wit. "I would sooner get into difficulty with a porcupine," one colleague remarked. Caring not a whit about his public image, the unmarried Stevens lived for years with a black housekeeper, neither confirming nor denying the many rumors about their relationship.

During his antebellum years in Congress, Stevens fought against the expansion of slavery; when the secession crisis came, he opposed compromise with the South; and in wartime, he was an early advocate of both emancipation and the enlistment of blacks into the Union army. After the war—in the words of future French prime minister Georges Clemenceau, then reporting American events for a Parisian newspaper—Stevens became the "Robespierre" of "the second American Revolution." As the Republicans' floor leader in the House, he oversaw passage of the key legislation that established the principle of equality before the law—the Civil Rights Act of 1866, the Fourteenth Amendment, the Reconstruction Act of 1867. Even though none of these bills was as radical as he desired, he voted for them anyway because, he said, "I live among men, not among angels." Stevens was also a prime mover in the failed 1868 attempt to remove President Johnson from office through impeachment.

Reconstruction, Stevens believed, offered the possibility of creating a "perfect republic" without racial inequality, but only if the economic underpinnings necessary for black freedom could be created as well. Tirelessly but ultimately unsuccessfully, he promoted a plan to divide among the former slaves the land of former slaveholders. "The whole fabric of southern society," he declared, "*must* be changed, and never can it be done if this opportunity is lost." Yet Stevens's plan proved too radical for most Republicans to support, and it was never enacted.

Following Stevens's death in office in August 1868, he was buried in one of Pennsylvania's few racially integrated cemeteries. His epitaph, which he composed himself, read: "I have chosen this that I might illustrate in my death the principles which I advocated through a long life, Equality of Man before his Creator."

Thaddeus Stevens, photographed in 1858.

13

THE AMERICAN WEST

The Battle of the Little Bighorn

THE SIOUX CALLED THE LAND *Paha Sapa;* to the whites, it was the Black Hills. The Sioux considered it sacred; the whites, not surprisingly, wanted to exploit the region. The problem for the whites was that, according to the 1868 Treaty of Fort Laramie, the Black Hills were reserved to the Sioux exclusively and forever.

Despite the clear language of the Fort Laramie treaty, the federal government decided in March 1874 to send a team of surveyors into the Black Hills. Chosen to command this expedition was Lt. Col. George Armstrong Custer of the Seventh Cavalry, who had taken part in a similar expedition the previous summer, during which a Northern Pacific Railroad crew had scouted possible routes along the Yellowstone River, which the government (but not the Indians) considered the northern boundary of Sioux land.

During the spring and early summer of 1874, as word of the army's intent to explore the Black Hills spread, scores of civilians besieged Custer with requests to tag along. Except perhaps for a few mountain men, no whites had ever seen the Black Hills—which made the trip especially appealing to scientists, newspaper reporters, and prospectors eager to confirm rumors of gold in the hills. Custer personally invited along Othniel C. Marsh, but Marsh wasn't available; instead, the renowned Yale paleontologist sent a young colleague, George Bird Grinnell, who discovered more dinosaur

AT LEFT: *This Brulé Sioux camp near Pine Ridge, South Dakota, was photographed in mid-January 1891 by John C. H. Grabill—not far from, and not long after, the massacre at Wounded Knee.*

bones than he could carry. In addition, Custer brought with him ten companies of the Seventh Cavalry, two companies of infantry, several dozen Indian scouts, a three-inch Rodman artillery piece, and three Gatling guns. In all, the column boasted a thousand men, two thousand animals, and more than a hundred wagons.

Custer collected this armada at Fort Abraham Lincoln, one of several recently built army posts on the upper Missouri River. Home to the Seventh Cavalry for only a year, the fort stood just south of the railhead at Bismarck in the Dakota Territory. Because Custer's preparations took longer than expected, it wasn't until July 2 that he rode out of Fort Lincoln. To make up some time, he marched his men hard across the hot dusty Plains, typically rousing them at 3 A.M. so that they could be on the move by 4 A.M. At this pace—on some nights, the Seventh Cavalry didn't make camp until midnight—it took just three weeks for the regiment and its guests to reach the Black Hills. On July 22, Custer made camp at the northwestern edge of Paha Sapa—at which point his mostly Arikara scouts, fearful of Sioux retaliation, told him he had gone far enough. When Custer made it clear that he was going to enter the Black Hills regardless, they refused to lead him and many left.

Although on his own, Custer found his way well enough through valleys of incomparable loveliness. "One of the most beautiful spots on God's green earth," *Bismarck Tribune* reporter Nathan Knappen declared. "No wonder the Indians regard this as the home of the Great Spirit and guard it with jealous care." Meanwhile, on July 27, just two days after Custer's

> "If I were
> an Indian,
> I often think
> that I would
> greatly prefer
> to cast my
> lot among
> those…who
> adhere to the
> free open
> plains."
>
> —
> *George Armstrong
> Custer*

This photograph by W. H. Illingworth *shows Custer's 1874 expedition crossing the Dakota plains during mid-July, a week or so prior to its arrival at the Black Hills.*

entry into the Black Hills, the miners found gold. The first discovery came along French Creek (near present-day Custer, South Dakota), and it was soon followed by numerous other strikes. "On some of the water courses almost every panful of earth produced gold," Custer wrote exultingly in a dispatch. "The miners report that they found gold among the grass roots."

JUST AS CUSTER DID, the federal government knew that, with the country in depression following the panic of 1873, reports of gold in the Black Hills would inevitably produce a rush of prospectors to the region that no power on earth could stop—not that the government wanted to stop them, for seizure of the Black Hills was the government's plan all along, if only to divert attention from the economic situation. This was why Custer had taken along a geologist, Newton Winchell, to authenticate gold samples and why he highlighted the gold discoveries in his preliminary report. By the time the Seventh Cavalry returned to Fort Abraham Lincoln in late August, the eastern newspapers were already full of stories about the Dakota gold, and Sioux City, Iowa, was advertising itself as an excellent jumping-off point for enthusiastic prospectors.

During the fall of 1874 and the spring of 1875, thousands of reckless gold hunters flooded the Sioux homeland. The government issued pro forma warnings reminding Americans that the Black Hills belonged to the Sioux, but army efforts to enforce the Indians' treaty rights were halfhearted at best. Even those members of the bureaucracy sympathetic to the Sioux found it difficult to support their interests in this matter. The U.S. economy was in an awful state, and most of the prospectors were otherwise jobless. Few whites were therefore prepared to deny them access to the precious metals of the Black Hills, which the nomadic Sioux didn't even want. "It is a mistaken idea that the Indian occupies any portion of the Black Hills," Custer wrote in a September 1874 message, which he sent to the War Department and also made available to reporters. "They neither occupy nor make use of the Black Hills, nor are they willing that others should."

The arrival of so many miners, of course, angered the Sioux and their allies, the Northern Cheyennes. In a letter to his wife, Elizabeth, written during the Seventh Cavalry's march back to Fort Lincoln, Custer reported that the "hostiles" had given him a new nickname: Thief. Similarly, the trail his column had left for other whites to follow became known among the Indians as the Thieves' Road. Although the Sioux never threatened Custer's column directly—it was simply too strong—they did set grass fires along its path, hoping to immobilize the whites. Yet Custer always found enough forage for the horses to continue his march. The peace still held as 1874 ended, but not by much.

The Sioux Nation

THE NAME *SIOUX*, WHICH WHITE Americans gave to the confederation of peoples sharing the Siouan language, came from *Nadouessioux*, the Ojibwa word for "enemies." Prior to the eighteenth century, most Sioux lived in and around the Great Lakes region; then the Ojibwas, their traditional enemies, drove them west. The Santee Sioux, one of the three main Siouan divisions, moved into present-day Minnesota, where they displaced their linguistic cousins, the Yanktons and the Tetons—who were forced to move farther west onto the Great Plains. (The Siouan names for the Santee, Yankton, and Teton peoples are *Dakota*, *Nakota*, and *Lakota*, respectively.) Previously, the Yanktons and Tetons had lived in forests, speared fish from canoes, and gathered wild rice and beans. On the Plains, however, they gave up even the most limited forms of agriculture and became mounted nomadic hunters, surviving nearly entirely on the huge buffalo herds that covered the northern grasslands.

Most of the Teton Sioux settled along the Missouri River, where Lewis and Clark found and avoided them in 1804. (It's not known precisely when the first Tetons entered the Black Hills, but best estimates place this event sometime about 1770.) Later, the combative Tetons became friendlier with the whites who began traveling up and down the Missouri in the 1820s, even going into business with some of the fur-trading mountain men. Yet they continued fighting other tribes and by the 1840s came to dominate the central Plains.

To protect the huge number of immigrants who took to the Oregon Trail beginning in 1843, the federal government purchased a trading post along the route that the declining American Fur Company no longed needed. The post, Fort Laramie, located on the North Platte River about a third of the way from Independence to Oregon, gave the pioneers a chance to relax before undertaking the crossing of the Rocky Mountains. It also gave the army a well-placed base from which to monitor the Teton Sioux, who were not at all pleased with the government's unilateral deployment of soldiers into their territory.

BEFORE THE OPENING OF THE OREGON TRAIL, the federal government cared not a whit for the comings and goings of the Indians in the expansive trans-Mississippi West. During the 1830s, empowered by the Indian Removal Act, Pres. Andrew Jackson had forced the Five Civilized Tribes out of the Southeast and relocated them at gunpoint to the desolate Indian Territory, where they could do as they pleased—or die, for all Jackson cared. In this sense, the Indian Territory

Tall, slim, and powerfully built, George Custer was, in every respect, a physically distinctive figure. He typically wore his blond hair long and, while campaigning, dressed in buckskin. The Sioux had a variety of nicknames for him—including Pahuska, or Long Hair.

After attending the 1851 treaty conference at Fort Laramie, Jesuit missionary Pierre-Jean De Smet drew this map to show the new boundaries of the Indian lands. Later, after his tribe had been moved several times from land "guaranteed" to it by such treaties, one Indian chief remarked that whites should simply put Indians on wheels to make them easier to transport from one reservation to another.

was an early "reservation"—that is, a geographically defined area set aside for the use of a Native American people. Supervising this and other reservations established by the government was the Bureau of Indian Affairs—a federal agency created within the War Department in 1824, then transferred to the new Interior Department in 1849.

Yet the California gold rush, along with Oregon fever, attracted so many whites to the Oregon Trail that the Indians through whose land they passed felt compelled to react. Unrest spread, and to forestall more, the federal government called for a council, which met at Fort Laramie in September 1851. Among the estimated ten thousand Indians attending were representatives of the Sioux, Cheyennes, Arapahoes, Crows, Assiniboins, Gros Ventres, Mandans, and Arikaras. Conducting the negotiations for the government was Superintendent of Indian affairs D. D. Mitchell, who had traveled all the way from Washington, where the Great Father lived. On hand to assist Mitchell was Thomas Fitzpatrick, one of the first mountain men and now a reservation agent for Mitchell's bureau.

From the various tribes, Mitchell and Fitzpatrick extracted permission to build more roads and military posts on Indian land. In exchange, they agreed to provide fifty-thousand-dollar annuities (paid to each tribe in provisions and trade goods), as well as army protection from "the commission of all depredations by the people of the United States, after the ratification of this treaty." Furthermore, perhaps as a sop to the federal bureaucracy (which found the roaming habits of the Plains tribes incomprehensible), the 1851 treaty allocated to each tribe a specific "tract" of land, or reservation. The Sioux, for example, were assigned land between the North Platte and Yellowstone Rivers specifically including "the range of mountains known as the Black Hills."

The Sand Creek Massacre

THE PEACE MADE AT FORT LARAMIE held for more than a decade, but it ended abruptly in November 1864, when Col. John M. Chivington led a force of twelve hundred Colorado volunteers against a surrendered, partially disarmed Southern Cheyenne village on Sand Creek. The Pikes Peak gold rush of 1859 had brought more than a hundred thousand miners to the central Rockies, at that time a part of Kansas. At first, the Arapahoes and Southern Cheyennes who owned the land found the miners' search for the yellow metal amusing. Shortly after the founding of Denver City in 1859, the Arapaho chief Little Raven visited the boomtown, where he learned how to smoke cigars and use cutlery. He told the miners that they could have all the gold they wanted but then expressed his hope that they would soon be satisfied and leave. Of course, the whites never left; instead, more and more arrived, prompting the organization of a separate Colorado Territory in February 1861. Meanwhile, the whites began maneuvering to force the Indians off their land.

At Fort Wise on February 18, 1861, Southern Cheyenne and Arapaho chiefs agreed to a new treaty allegedly designed to preserve their land rights and protect their freedom of movement. The document to which they affixed their marks, however, actually ceded most of their 1851 land to the whites and required them to live within much smaller defined boundaries. Because none of the chiefs could read the English in which the treaty was written, they had to rely on interpreters who misled them—certainly not the first time, nor the last, that Native Americans experienced this sort of trouble in their dealings with whites. Prominent Indian signatories to the Fort Wise treaty included Little Raven of the Arapahoes and Black Kettle of the Southern Cheyennes; among the army officers who signed the treaty as witnesses was Lt. J. E. B. Stuart of the First Cavalry, who would resign his commission two months later when the Civil War broke out.

Although the language of the Fort Wise treaty confined the Southern Cheyennes to a modest triangular reservation along the Arkansas River, members of the tribe continued to frequent their usual hunting grounds because that's where the game was. In their minds, the land still belonged to them, yet their presence raised the ire of local whites. Matters escalated during the summer of 1864, when several cavalrymen died in an army-provoked skirmish near Ash Creek. Fearful of white retaliation, Black Kettle moved his followers to a campsite near Fort Lyon, site of their reservation agency, where they were repeatedly promised safety. On November 29, however, with the connivance of the Fort Lyon commander, Colonel Chivington led a surprise attack on Black Kettle's village. The chief desperately waved a U.S. flag that he had been given years earlier by representatives of the Great Father as a token of the president's appreciation for Black Kettle's commitment to peace. He also waved a white flag, but to no avail. Under Chivington's brutal leadership, the Colorado men slaughtered and mutilated four hundred Southern Cheyennes, including numerous women and children. The massacre began an all-out war with the whites on one side, and the Southern Cheyennes and Arapahoes on the other. The fighting continued in fits and starts for a year until Lee's surrender at Appomattox permitted the transfer of army troops out west—at which point the Indians were beaten into submission. The Sand Creek massacre, meanwhile, had a profound effect on the disposition of the watchful Sioux.

After the Sand Creek massacre, Col. John M. Chivington resigned from the militia and returned to Denver, where he displayed before theater audiences more than a hundred scalps taken from Indians at Sand Creek.

Black Kettle arrives at Camp Weld (near Denver) with other Southern Cheyenne and Arapaho chiefs in September 1864 to take part in new peace talks. His large American flag, blurred by the camera's slow shutter, can be seen in the lead wagon.

THE MINING FRONTIER

ONCE GOLD WAS DISCOVERED near Pikes Peak in 1858, almost as many prospectors raced to the region as had descended on California a decade earlier. Boomtowns sprang up seemingly overnight wherever large deposits were found, and they were quickly populated by business owners—restaurant and saloon keepers, retailers, assayers, prostitutes, and gamblers—who catered to the mining trade.

In each case, sparsely populated regions, where Indians had been able to move about freely, suddenly became inhospitable. The teeming whites demanded that the Indians leave even those lands guaranteed to them by treaty. When the U.S. Army failed to respond satisfactorily, local militias (as at Sand Creek) took a more active role. The armed encounters that resulted were a primary cause of the Indian wars of the 1860s and 1870s.

The first major U.S. silver strike took place in 1859 in Nevada (then part of the Utah Territory) on land owned by Henry Comstock. Until the 1880s, the fabulous Comstock Lode generated more than half of the nation's annual silver output. This photograph shows mine cars emerging from the Comstock shaft in 1867 or 1868.

IN LATE 1865, the Teton Sioux were themselves disturbed by the recent handiwork of miner John M. Bozeman. In 1861, Bozeman had left his home in Georgia to make a fortune in the Colorado gold fields; a year later, however, the gold rush shifted to Montana, and Bozeman followed it there. It was during his time in Montana that Bozeman became aware of the need that eastern prospectors had for a direct route to the Montana mining country. To meet this need, he and a partner in late 1862 blazed a trail from Bannack, Montana, east across the Rockies and south through the Bighorn Mountains to Fort Laramie. They were apparently unconcerned, or perhaps unaware, that nearly all of the land through which the new trail passed belonged by treaty to the Sioux, who were not at all pleased. In 1863, when Bozeman tried to lead a wagon train back over this route, Sioux warriors blocked his path and forced him to retreat. In 1864, however, Bozeman tried again, and this time he succeeded in reaching Montana. The next year, federal troops began guarding travelers along the Bozeman Trail.

Unwilling to tolerate such a brazen land grab, the Teton Sioux fought a war over the Bozeman Trail and won. Leading the fight was the Oglala chief Red Cloud. (Other large branches of the Teton Sioux included the Brulés, Hunkpapas, Miniconjous, and Sans Arcs.) Throughout the summer of 1866, the Sioux carried out a relentless guerrilla campaign against civilian and military wagon trains using the Bozeman Trail. Then, in December, a decisive engagement took place at Fort Phil Kearny, an army post located at the foot of the Bighorn Mountains and one of three built that summer to protect the Bozeman Trail. Soldiers assigned to cut firewood at Fort Phil Kearny already knew that working outside its walls was dangerous, because woodcutting details were attacked often. On the morning of December 21, another of these details was beset by Indian warriors.

Red Cloud's name in his native Siouan language was Mahpiua Luta.

At the first sound of gunfire, a relief party hurried out of the fort to rescue the woodcutters—at which point several Indian decoys, including the Oglala warrior Crazy Horse, appeared outside the fort and began daring the soldiers left inside to come out and chase them, which the soldiers did. Leading this second party was Capt. William J. Fetterman, who had explicit orders not to pursue the Indians beyond Lodge Trail Ridge. But Fetterman's blood was up, and Crazy Horse's tauntings angered him sufficiently that he became reckless. Believing that there were no more Indians than the ten he could see, Fetterman crossed Lodge Trail Ridge and fell right into a trap. In fact, there were hundreds of Arapaho, Northern Cheyenne, and Sioux warriors hidden among the trees on the far side of the ridge; and once Fetterman decided to charge down the hill, he and his eighty men were dead. The defeat was the worst the U.S. Army had ever suffered in a century of fighting Indians.

The Fort Laramie Treaty

RED CLOUD'S WAR continued for another year, during which the federal government gradually softened its position. Finally, in the spring of 1868, Lt. Gen. William T. Sherman, then commanding the Military Division of the Missouri, accompanied a delegation of peace commissioners to Fort Laramie with orders to abandon the Powder River forts in exchange for peace with the Sioux. Yet Red Cloud wasn't interested in Sherman's assurances, and he refused to talk peace until he had personally witnessed the army withdraw. "We are on the mountains looking down on the soldiers and the forts," he communicated by messenger. "When we see the soldiers moving away and the forts abandoned, then I will come down and talk." Understandably humiliated by Red Cloud's attitude, the War Department stewed for several months before finally issuing orders in July for the garrisons to give up the forts. On July 29, the regiment holding Fort C. F. Smith packed its bags and left; the next morning, Red Cloud's Oglalas burned the fort to the ground. A month later, when Fort Phil Kearny was evacuated, the honor of razing that structure went to the Northern Cheyennes. A few days after that, Fort Reno was deserted, and the Bozeman Road closed. Red Cloud had won his war.

Not until November 6, however, did the victorious Oglala belatedly appear at Fort Laramie to make peace. The treaty he signed that day began with a statement of intent: "From this day forward all war between the parties to this agreement shall forever cease. The Government of the United States desires peace, and its honor is hereby pledged to keep it. The Indians desire peace, and they now pledge their honor to maintain it." To achieve this peace, the government promised that "if bad men among the whites…shall commit any wrong upon the person or property of the Indians," the offender would be swiftly arrested and punished.

The Fort Laramie treaty also drew some new reservation lines (having nothing to do with the Black Hills) and promised to set these lands "apart for the absolute and undisturbed use and occupation of the Indians herein named,…and the United States now solemnly agrees that no persons except those herein designated and authorized so to do, and except such officers, agents, and employees of the Government as may be authorized to enter upon the Indian reservations in

The Indian signature page from the 1868 Treaty of Fort Laramie. Because the chiefs were illiterate and couldn't sign their names, they instead affixed their marks next to names written by the white commissioners.

discharge of duties enjoined by law, shall ever be permitted to pass over, settle upon, or reside in the territory described." Custer's Black Hills expedition of 1874, therefore, clearly violated this article of the Fort Laramie treaty, and the encroachment of white prospectors during 1874 and 1875 represented an even more egregious breach.

A pile of buffalo skulls heaped trackside in Detroit, bound for the Michigan Carbon Works. On a tour of western army posts in 1866, Maj. Gen. Philip H. Sheridan had estimated that there were a hundred million buffalo south of the Platte River. Other officers reported seeing herds ten miles long and fifty miles wide blackening the Plains. An expedition in 1883, however, found only two hundred buffalo left.

YET EVEN BEFORE CUSTER'S Black Hills expedition, there were problems with the Fort Laramie treaty. As was often the case—take the 1861 Fort Wise treaty, for example—the agreement that the Indians thought they had made at Fort Laramie and the text of the treaty they marked were two different things. The Sioux believed that they had reserved their right to follow game as they pleased; the language of the treaty, however, limited their hunts to the territory above the North Platte River and only "so long as the buffalo may range thereon in such numbers as to justify the chase."

Ultimately, the government wanted the Sioux to settle down and farm under the close supervision of reservation agents. It knew, however, that the nomadic Sioux would never voluntarily go along, so the government went after the Indians' primary food supply: the buffalo. In support of this policy, the federal bureaucracy encouraged the work of professional hunters who began exterminating the buffalo during the late 1860s. Some worked for railroads, supplying meat to the construction crews building the new transcontinental lines; others left the meat to rot but sold the hides to tanneries in the East, who turned them into leather. Between 1872 and 1874, at the height of the slaughter, white hunters killed as many as 3,000,000 head of buffalo a year, compared to 150,000 killed by Indians. As a result, by late 1874, the great herds upon which the Plains Indians had depended for generations were largely gone, along with most of the other wild game. In other words, there no longer were "such numbers as to justify the chase."

The dearth of game dramatically restricted the Sioux's independence and forced more and more of them onto reservations, where they could at least get occasional handouts of food and supplies. Yet in most other respects, agency life was torture for the Plains tribes because little in their cultures prepared them for life as bourgeois farmers. Instead, the agency Indians spent most of their time sitting around, drinking whiskey, and feeling sorry for themselves.

There were some Plains Indians, however, who continued to resist the humiliation of reservation life even after the buffalo had gone. Sustaining themselves as best they could on what little wild game remained, they kept to the most remote valleys and avoided whites whenever possible. These "roamers" accounted for about 20 percent of the total Teton Sioux population, but they gradually became the entire focus of the government's effort to pacify the northern Plains.

The Sioux War

AFTER CUSTER'S VIOLATION of the Black Hills, Red Cloud once again took the lead in negotiating with the whites. In the spring of 1875, he traveled to Washington for a meeting with President Grant. It was actually Red Cloud's second trip to Washington; he had already visited there in 1870 at the government's request. This time, however, his reception was not nearly so friendly. Shortly after his arrival, the president told Red Cloud and the other members of his delegation that the government intended to purchase the Black Hills. For many days afterward, lesser officials pressured the Indians to agree to the sale. Finally, Red Cloud persuaded the Bureau of Indian Affairs that the matter was too important to be decided except by a council of all the Sioux chiefs. Such a council was scheduled for the fall, at which time the government would send out another peace commission from Washington to negotiate the purchase. The plan suited the government well enough because Article 12 of the 1868 Fort Laramie treaty provided that no cession of reservation land could be made "unless executed and signed by at least three-fourths of all the adult male Indians." What the government didn't count on was the outrage of the Sioux.

The accelerating penetration of Paha Sapa by miners that summer had gotten even the reservation Indians up in arms, and a number of Sioux bands had already begun raiding white mining settlements in the Black Hills. By September 1875, when the government commission arrived at Fort Laramie, more than twenty thousand Indians had gathered nearby to express their great displeasure. Although Red Cloud urged moderation, his authority had already been undermined by younger, more militant Oglalas, especially Crazy Horse, and by the powerful Hunkpapa medicine man Sitting Bull, who wanted no part of any treaty with whites. Several council sessions produced only rising tensions among the Sioux, at which point the commissioners wisely withdrew and returned to Washington. In their report, they recommended to President Grant that he adopt a much sterner policy. Implicit in their advice was the assumption that, if the roamers could be forced to submit to reservation

The Sioux War of 1876 was fought on the same landscape as Red Cloud's War a decade earlier.

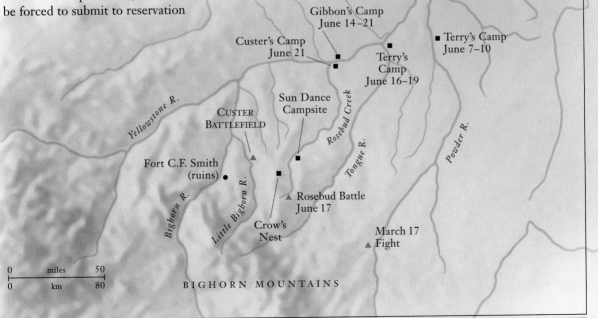

In 1870, the U.S. government invited Red Cloud, Spotted Tail, and other Sioux chiefs to Washington to meet with President Grant. During the visit, officials attempted to impress the Sioux with displays of white military power, but Red Cloud remained intransigent in his discussions with Interior Department and army bureaucrats concerning the removal of the Sioux to reservations. This photograph of the Indian delegation was taken in Washington in June 1870. Red Cloud, seated on the left, is shown in profile.

life, the rest of the Sioux would become much more docile and compliant.

Of course, Grant *could* have sent the army to arrest the lawbreaking prospectors, as the Treaty of 1868 compelled him to do. But in the world of 1875, this was not a realistic alternative. Instead, he sent the army against the Indians—but not until his aides had initiated a dishonest propaganda campaign designed to undermine public support for the Indians. At a secret White House meeting in November 1875, it was decided that the Bureau of Indian Affairs would order all of the roamers to return to their reservations by January 31, 1876. The plotters knew, of course, that even should the scattered off-agency Sioux wish to comply, they would have great trouble doing so during the coldest months of an already severe winter. But it didn't matter whether the Indians showed up or not. The order produced a win-win situation for the government: Either the roamers would become fearful and return to their agencies, or the government would have a perfectly credible excuse for sending the army out after them.

THE GREAT SIOUX WAR OF 1876 thus followed the pattern established by the Pequot War of 1637 and repeated many times over as white America pushed west. The first white settlers arriving in a new region typically depended on the Indian bands already living there for food, advice, and goodwill. Consider, for example, the case of the Pilgrims and the Wampanoags. Had it not been for the generosity of the Wampanoag sachem Massasoit, the Pilgrims would probably not have survived. Even had he continued to supply much-needed provisions and counsel to the Plymouth Colony, Massasoit could easily have used his people's superior military strength to wipe out the colony completely at any time during its early years. Therefore, during this first stage of settlement, white settlers tolerated the Indians, even courting them in many instances. However, once the white population grew strong enough that its military power exceeded the might of the local Indians, the oppression of the tribes began and expanded until the Indians could brook no more. When the tribes eventually fought back, the whites typically exterminated them, justifying the slaughter on the grounds that the Indians had initiated the violence.

Once the frontier began moving west, this pattern repeated itself again and again—the Black Hawk War of 1832 being merely one memorable example. By 1876, the army had finally amassed enough strength on the northern Plains to enforce the government's will there. Manifest destiny demanded the removal of the Sioux, who could perhaps delay but not elude their fate. Americans hadn't accepted Spanish rule in Florida, Mexican rule in California, or British rule in Oregon; how could anyone have believed that they would leave to the Sioux the richest land in Dakota?

GEORGE ARMSTRONG CUSTER

1839–1876

AS A YOUNG MAN OF MODEST MEANS growing up in Monroe, Michigan, sixteen-year-old "Autie" Custer craved an appointment to the U.S. Military Academy at West Point. He was ambitious, his parents couldn't afford a higher education for him, and at West Point he could get one for free while simultaneously raising his social standing. Custer was also in love, though the girl's father objected. Fortunately, the father was well connected, and he used his influence to get Autie the appointment—and a ticket out of town.

Although Custer placed last in his West Point Class of 1861, the need for Union officers was great that summer, and he was soon assigned to McClellan's staff. It was only after he received command of his own cavalry regiment, however, that Custer's boldness in battle became clear. His natural instinct was to charge, and his numerous successes brought him rapid promotion. In June 1863, after a particularly noteworthy victory at Brandy Station, Virginia, Custer won promotion to brigadier general of volunteers. Although just an impermanent brevet rank, it nevertheless made him the youngest army general in U.S. history.

After the Civil War, Custer gained even more notoriety as an Indian fighter and promoter of the western life. Recommissioned as a captain once the Union had dismantled its massive volunteer army, he was promoted to lieutenant colonel in July 1866 (after a brief stint in Texas) and given command of the Seventh Cavalry, one of the new regiments organized that year to fight in the Indian wars. In early 1867, he and his wife, Elizabeth, joined the new unit at Fort Riley, Kansas, where the regiment took part in several campaigns against the Southern Cheyennes, Oglalas, and Arapahoes.

The Seventh Cavalry's most significant battle during its years at Fort Riley took place in late November 1868 on the banks of the Washita River, where Custer divided his command for a daring four-pronged attack on an Indian village.

It should be noted, however, that at the time Custer ordered the attack, he had no idea which Indians lived in that village or how numerous they were. (The village turned out to be an encampment of Southern Cheyennes led by Black Kettle.) Yet the risk paid off for the Seventh Cavalry, as surprise permitted the regiment to crush all resistance within an hour. Black Kettle was among the first to die, and scores of women and children followed, along with many warriors. But the battle was no Sand Creek because Custer

Captain Custer of the Fifth Cavalry *poses at Fair Oaks, Virginia, in May 1862 with Confederate lieutenant James B. Washington, his prisoner and former West Point classmate.*

found in many tipis daguerreotypes, letters, and other evidence proving that more than a few young braves had taken part in the recent raiding of white settlements in Kansas. The ensuing press coverage boosted Custer's reputation enormously, as did his own self-promoting articles for eastern magazines. He also wrote the memoir *My Life on the Plains*, published in 1874.

In mid-February 1876, about the time that the last messengers returned from notifying the various bands of roamers of its November order, the Bureau of Indian Affairs estimated that three thousand Sioux, among them several hundred warriors, remained off the reservations. Meanwhile, Lt. Gen. Philip H. Sheridan, Sherman's replacement as head of the Military Division of the Missouri, developed a plan to bring them in. It involved a two-pronged campaign: George Crook, commanding the Department of the Platte, would lead one column northeast from Fort Fetterman in Wyoming, while Department of Dakota commander Alfred H. Terry sent another under Custer westward from Fort Abraham Lincoln. Sheridan wanted both armies to leave at once, but the same cold and snow that restricted the movement of the roamers also trapped the soldiers, particularly Custer's men, at their frontier forts. Crook wasn't able to leave Wyoming until March 1; the Dakota column had to wait even longer, until May 17.

Yet the delays gave Terry enough time to have Col. John Gibbon, commander of the District of Montana, and his Seventh Infantry join the campaign. Terry ordered Colonel Gibbon to march the Seventh Infantry from Fort Ellis down the valley of the Yellowstone until it rendezvoused with Custer's column somewhere near the mouth of the Bighorn River.

P ART OF THE REASON for the Dakota column's delay was that Custer had been called to testify before Congress in the unfolding Indian Ring scandal. During the winter of 1875–1876, Custer had spent a leave of absence in New York City, hobnobbing with some old Democratic party friends, whom he told about the corruption then plaguing most Indian agencies and army trading posts in the West. Not at all wealthy himself, Custer was angered by the prices being charged by the Fort Lincoln post trader, which were often double those charged by the Bismarck merchants just across the river. (Army regulations required all soldiers to shop with the post trader.) Custer told his friends the open secret—at least it was open in the West—that Secretary of War William W. Belknap received illegal kickbacks for awarding the trading rights to politically connected businessmen. He also described the active role that the president's brother, Orvil Grant, had played in the scheme. On February 10, 1876, Custer confidant James Gordon Bennett, publisher of the anti-Grant *New York Herald*, broke the story with an inflammatory editorial suggesting that the president ask his brother how much money he had made "in the Sioux country starving the squaws and children."

In March, Custer was summoned to Washington to testify before the House committee investigating Bennett's allegations. He laid out the details of the conspiracy, then prepared to return to Fort Lincoln to lead his regiment against the Sioux. But President Grant personally withheld Custer's permission to leave Washington; and when Custer—fearing that the Seventh Cavalry would ride off without him—left two weeks later without Grant's permission, the president had Custer arrested in Chicago for disobeying orders. Additionally, Grant directed that Custer not be allowed to take part in the upcoming expedition against the Sioux. For Custer, this was the worst punishment possible.

Although Brig. Gen. George Crook fared poorly against the Sioux, he later redeemed himself and revived his career with several effective campaigns against Geronimo's Chiricahua Apaches. He was promoted to major general in 1888.

Fortunately—or not so fortunately, given the eventual result—Custer's friends in the Democratic press made his arrest a cause célèbre, attacking Grant for "high-handed abuse of his official power" and creating a great deal of public pressure for the lieutenant colonel's reinstatement. Meanwhile, Custer received permission to travel on to St. Paul, where he met with General Terry. Although Terry was no particular friend of Custer, he wanted his subordinate back also so that he wouldn't have to lead the Dakota column himself. Terry felt much more comfortable behind a desk than he did in a saddle, and he had come to rely on Custer's experience, courage, and energy. Whether Custer was aware of this or not, he apparently had tears in his eyes when he begged Terry to intercede on his behalf with Grant. Of course, Terry did intervene (as, cautiously, did Sheridan), and Grant's order was reversed, returning Custer to command of the Seventh Cavalry—but not to overall command of the Dakota column, which Grant insisted remain Terry's responsibility. Nevertheless, Terry was satisfied because Custer would be coming along, and Custer was ecstatic. It didn't faze him at all that Terry would have overall command in the field. As he told Col. William Ludlow, the expedition's engineer, "[I expect] to cut loose from and make my operations independent of General Terry." A week later, the Dakota column left Fort Lincoln.

Sitting Bull, whose Siouan name was *Tatanka Iyotake,* sat for this portrait during the 1880s. On his lap, he holds a calumet, or ceremonial tobacco pipe.

Sitting Bull's Vision

A PRELIMINARY ATTACK launched by Crook's advance forces on March 17 warned the Sioux of the Wyoming column's approach. After Oglala warriors beat back six companies of cavalry under Col. Joseph J. Reynolds, Crazy Horse ordered messengers sent to the other roaming bands—as well as to the Sioux and Northern Cheyenne reservations—inviting all to join him for a summer war against the *wasichu,* or whites. (Sitting Bull had already sent a similar message in February.) More than five thousand Indians responded, reducing agency populations by half. "Most of them seemed to have no illusions about the long-term future," historian Stephen E. Ambrose wrote. "The army certainly made no attempt to hide its preparations for the campaign, which was common gossip among whites at the Red Cloud and Spotted Tail agencies, and the agency Indians knew enough about the white man and his power to realize that the end had come…. It was almost as if the entire Sioux nation (or at least a goodly portion of it) had decided to have one last, great summer before giving in to the whites."

The hostiles made their camp in eastern Montana on the banks of Rosebud Creek, which flowed north into the Yellowstone.

Estimates of its size range from one thousand to two thousand lodges, inhabited by perhaps two thousand to four thousand warriors. The Teton Sioux were the most numerous group, with separate lodge circles for the Oglalas, Hunkpapas, Brulés, Miniconjous, and Sans Arcs. The Northern Cheyennes were another large contingent, but there were also Santee and Yankton Sioux, Blackfeet, and Arapahoes present. The principal war chiefs were the Oglala Crazy Horse, Gall of the Hunkpapas, and Two Moons of the Northern Cheyennes.

In early June 1876, aware that soldiers even then were marching toward them from the east (Terry-Custer), west (Gibbon), *and* south (Crook), the Indians decided to hold a Sun Dance to reaffirm their faith in the spiritual meaning of the universe. A sacred ritual of many Plains tribes, the Sun Dance included self-mutilation and often evoked in participants the sensation of being guided by supernatural forces. This particular Sun Dance began with its sponsor, Sitting Bull, seated placidly before the ceremony's central pole, which had been cut from a sacred tree. Carefully, his brother Jumping Bull used an awl to lift bits of flesh from Sitting Bull's arm, which Jumping Bull then cut away with a sharp knife. When fifty pieces of flesh had been cut from each arm, Sitting Bull rose, blood streaming down his body, and began to dance. For the rest of that day and all through the night, Sitting Bull danced around the sacred pole, collapsing finally after eighteen hours. When other Sioux revived him, the Hunkpapa chief described the vision he had experienced: It began with a voice from above announcing, "I give you these because they have no ears." Then Sitting Bull looked up to see soldiers on horseback "coming down like grasshoppers, with their heads down and their hats falling off. They were falling right into our camp." The assembled Indians understood without further explanation that Sitting Bull's vision meant the whites would soon be attacking their village and that the Indians would kill them all. After the Sun Dance, the hostiles moved their camp into the valley of the Little Bighorn River, which the Sioux called the Greasy Grass.

Sitting Bull's tomahawk.

O N J UNE 16, some Northern Cheyenne scouts discovered Crook's column camped near the headwaters of the Rosebud. Crook had about a thousand men with him, plus several hundred Crow and Shoshone scouts. (The Crows and Shoshones were traditional enemies of the Sioux.) That same day, the hostile chiefs held a council, after which Crazy Horse led perhaps fifteen hundred warriors, or about half of those available, on a thirty-mile nighttime march over the divide between the two valleys. The point was to attack Crook before Crook attacked the village, which held many women and children. Reaching Crook's column the next morning, Crazy Horse hid his men behind a hill while he observed the movements of the general's scattered troops. Before he could formulate a battle plan, however, some Crow scouts discovered his presence, and the battle of the Rosebud began.

Never before had such a large Indian force attacked a white army, and Crook was surprised by its unprecedented coordination. Previously when battling whites, Plains Indians had generally circled and hovered, believing that the worst punish-

Crook's field headquarters near Whitewood in the Dakota Territory. Taken after the Rosebud fight, this photograph shows tents that his men improvised from dismantled wagon frames.

ment they could inflict on their enemies was to humiliate them. Therefore, they tended to place more emphasis on "counting coup," or touching an enemy during battle, than on killing him. On this day, however, the Sioux and Cheyennes charged Crook's men repeatedly, pressing their attacks much as white cavalry would have. The fighting continued for several hours until the appearance of Col. Anson Mills's cavalry on their flank disconcerted the Indians and caused them to break off the engagement. Crook lost eighty-four men; the Sioux and Cheyennes, ninety-nine. Because the Indians withdrew first, Crook claimed victory; but after a day or so, he pulled his army back southward and stayed in camp for a month until reinforcements arrived. Crazy Horse's attack, therefore, put the Wyoming column out of commission, and because the hostiles remained between Crook and the Yellowstone, the general had no way of informing Custer, Terry, and Gibbon of the Indians' location or how numerous they were.

Custer's Orders

BY THE SECOND WEEK OF JUNE, about the time of Sitting Bull's Sun Dance, the Terry and Gibbon columns had converged sufficiently for Terry to arrange a conference. Using the steamer *Far West*, he traveled upstream on June 9 to Gibbon's camp on the Yellowstone midway between the Tongue and Powder Rivers. Because neither Terry nor Gibbon had seen any signs that the hostiles had crossed the Yellowstone, they reasoned that Crazy Horse and Sitting Bull must still be camped along one of its southern tributaries. On June 10, Terry sent half of the Seventh Cavalry under Maj. Marcus A. Reno, Custer's second in command, to scout the valleys of the Tongue and the Powder. Custer objected, reportedly shouting at Terry that the Indians were just two days' march away on the Rosebud or the Little Bighorn; but Terry insisted, and Custer had to wait.

Finally, on June 20, three days after Crook's Rosebud fight, Custer received Terry's Special Field Orders No. 14 directing him to rejoin the returning Reno, who had found a sizable Indian trail leading in the direction of the Little Bighorn. It was Terry's plan (communicated to Custer in detailed orders written on the morning of June 22) that the Seventh Cavalry should move up the Rosebud and across the divide into the valley of the upper Little Bighorn. Meanwhile, accompanied by Gibbon's Montana column, Terry and the rest of the Dakota column would move up the Yellowstone to the mouth of the Bighorn, then up the Bighorn to the Little Bighorn, which they expected to reach sometime on June 26. In this way, Terry hoped to trap the Indians between Custer and himself. Custer's 647 men (including Indian scouts, a reporter from Bennett's *New York Herald*, and Custer's young nephew Autie Reed) started up the Rosebud on the afternoon of June 22.

After two days of hard marching, Custer found the wide Indian trail late on June 24. Terry's instructions had been specific: From this point, he was to follow the Rosebud south to the headwaters of the Tongue and only then turn toward the Little Bighorn. But Terry's order had also contained language that gave Custer permission to act otherwise should he "see sufficient reason." When Custer came

Through the magazine articles he wrote and other publicity, Custer promoted his own identification with frontier life in the public mind. Yet his prowess as a hunter was greatly exaggerated. In fact, he was a poor shot. Although he claimed to have brought down this bear during the 1874 Black Hills expedition, it was actually his scout Bloody Knife who finished the animal off.

upon the trail, he could tell from its direction and freshness that the Indians who made it were nearby on the Little Bighorn, not on the Tongue, and he decided to head the Seventh Cavalry straight for them. (For Terry to permit Custer this sort of leeway was appropriate, given Custer's experience and past success, yet it later became the source of much controversy when some critics blamed Custer's defeat on disobedience of Terry's orders.)

That said, Custer, Terry, and Gibbon all knew that this would probably be the last great campaign of the Indian wars, and each wanted to reserve for himself and his men the fame and honor that would accompany the defeat of the last hostile Sioux. None believed that any accumulation of Indians, no matter how numerous, could withstand the concentrated firepower of a U.S. Army regiment, and this conviction made at least Custer impudent. He declined, for example, four Second Cavalry companies offered by Terry, even though they would have increased his fighting strength by 30 percent, because he apparently didn't want to share the glory with them.

AFTER RESTING HIS TIRED MEN briefly on the evening of June 24—they had already ridden twenty-seven miles that day—Custer marched them all night up the divide separating the valleys of the Rosebud and the Little Bighorn. About 9 A.M. on June 25, after they had covered another dozen miles, the men of the Seventh Cavalry reached the Crow's Nest, a lookout on the ridge from which Custer's scouts could see much of the terrain below. Standing beside his favorite scout, Bloody Knife, Custer used a spyglass to scan the Indian village that spread out for several miles along the river's western bank. According to Bloody Knife, there were so many white tipis that the valley appeared snowbound. At this point, shots were fired when a sergeant discovered several Northern Cheyennes lurking about. Previously, Custer had considered hiding his regiment for the day so that the Terry-Gibbon column could move into position; now—fearing that the Indians, once warned, would escape—he ordered an expedited attack on the village.

Bloody Knife is shown here during Custer's 1873 Yellowstone expedition. The Arikara scout was killed just before 3 P.M. on June 25, 1876, when he was shot through the head during the fight in the valley bottom. The bullet splattered his brains over Reno's face, accounting in part for the major's subsequent loss of nerve.

From the Crow's Nest, the men of the Seventh Cavalry could see the huge village, but they were still about a dozen miles away; and by the time they left, it was already noon. At a quick trot, their horses could manage about six miles in an hour, so (with occasional stops) it took them about three hours to reach the village. Along the way, Custer showed his lack of concern for the size of the village by dividing his command into three battalions: Capt. Frederick Benteen, commanding three companies, was ordered to make a wide sweep to the south in case any Indians tried to escape that way. Three more companies were detailed to Major Reno, whom Custer directed to cross the Little Bighorn at the nearest ford and attack the southern end of the village. Meanwhile, Custer himself proceeded with five companies to the north, where he would lead the main assault against the center of the village. The last of the Seventh Cavalry's twelve companies was detailed to guard the pack train.

Exactly when the Indians learned of Custer's approach is difficult to say, but the Seventh Cavalry wasn't a particularly quiet outfit. As Lt. Edward S. Godfrey of K Troop (part of Benteen's battalion) noted in his diary, the clatter of horses' hooves and the banging together of equipment sometimes made it difficult to give and receive orders. Cast-iron skillets, in particular, rang like gongs whenever they knocked together, which was often; and if this noise wasn't enough to warn the watchful Indians, then surely they saw the swirling dust kicked up by more than six hundred trotting mounts. In fact, a number of Indian scouts did see and hear the soldiers approaching, but the village was so large and busy that it took time for the alarm to spread.

The Battle

RENO FORDED THE RIVER and began the charge that Custer had ordered just after 3 P.M., but the Indians responded in such great numbers that he had to halt the attack almost immediately and deploy his men into a defensive skirmish line. As soldiers fell all around him, Reno wavered. Finally, after about twenty minutes of this hell, with more and more Indians joining the battle, Reno chose to abandon the attack entirely and ordered his men to retreat into a nearby stand of timber. During the hastily accomplished maneuver, many soldiers became separated from what remained of Reno's main force and were killed. Those who could managed to recross the river and climb a gully to some high ground later christened Reno Hill. There, the survivors of the charge were quickly surrounded.

Meanwhile, on the Little Bighorn's eastern bank, Custer and his battalion were following a high bluff that paralleled the village. Earlier, as they had passed Reno's position, at least two of the scouts had seen clearly Reno's retreat from the river bottom. These scouts were riding higher up on the bluff than Custer and had a better view, so it isn't known for certain whether the lieutenant colonel himself knew of Reno's predicament at this time. A mixed-blood scout named Mitch Boyer waved his hat excitedly at Reno's men. Later, some of them claimed mistakenly that it had been Custer waving at them. In any case, it was the last time any of Reno's men saw any soldier in Custer's battalion alive.

Carrying the terrible news of Reno's situation, Boyer hurried to catch up with the front of the column, which was by then galloping two-abreast down a gulch called the Medicine Tail Coulee. At the bottom, beside a shallow ford, Custer ordered a charge across the river, but Indians on the far side poured so much rifle fire into the coulee that the cavalrymen leading the charge had to give it up before they even reached the water. By the time Boyer caught up to Custer, the lieutenant colonel had already ordered a retreat; but instead of retracing his steps up Medicine Tail Coulee, Custer wheeled the battalion around to the north and took it up another gulch that led to some tableland above a bend in the river. A number of military

*Mitch Boyer
in 1875.*

About 3:30 P.M., *Custer had his adjutant, W. W. Cooke, send this scrawled note to Benteen, urging him to come up quickly with extra ammunition from the pack train. The ink transcription was probably written by the receiving officer to make the message easier to read.*

historians have since faulted Custer for this action, arguing that he should have led his men back in the direction of Reno, Benteen, and possible survival; yet it's hard to imagine that Custer's men could have escaped no matter what they did. There were simply too few soldiers and too many Indians.

Tourists and souvenir hunters began visiting the Little Bighorn battlefield as soon as the dust had settled. One found this Seventh Cavalry trumpet on the battlefield.

LEAVING THE RIVER, the soldiers had a slight head start on the Indians because the dismounted warriors—primarily Hunkpapas led by Gall and Oglalas under Crazy Horse—first had to collect their ponies, but this delay was minimal. Mitch Boyer's companion that day was a twenty-year-old Crow scout named Curley, and according to Curley, the Indians at this point began to drive the soldiers "like a herd of horses." The highest ground that Custer could see was a ridge delimited by hills at either end. He led his men straight for the nearest hill at a gallop. As Curley later explained through an interpreter, "I do not know whether or not anyone was killed on the way to the ridge, but the firing was so heavy that I do not see how the command made the ridge without some loss. Going up from [the] river, [there were] Sioux on all sides except [the] front."

The 210 men accompanying Custer climbed the hill at the southeastern end of the ridge while thousands of Indians clung to their flanks. The five companies, still together and in fairly good order, moved west along the ridge while Custer and his officers dismounted for a hasty conference. According to Curley, for whom the conversation was translated by Boyer, Custer ordered the soldiers to hold their ground. In time, Custer said, the rest of the regiment— meaning perhaps Benteen's battalion—would come to their aid. Boyer didn't think this was likely, knowing for certain that Reno could offer no help and believing that Benteen had been "scared out." (Actually, Benteen was just then arriving on Reno Hill.)

A studio portrait of the Crow scout Curley.

Boyer advised Custer to attempt a breakout to the south, where a deep ravine led back to the river—and beyond that, to Reno and Benteen. Apparently, Boyer was willing to gamble that the Indian pursuit had emptied the village. When the hostile fire suddenly slackened, Custer indeed ordered the breakout, but before his officers could even remount, hundreds more warriors filled the ravine. There was, in Curley's own rough English, "heap shoot, shoot, shoot." At this point in his 1908 retelling, the Crow scout clapped his hands swiftly to indicate rapid firing.

I T WAS A HOT, DRY DAY, and the Plains dust must have risen in great clouds and mingled with the sweat of the soldiers, staining their faces. With escape to the south impossible and the battalion's position collapsing, Capt. Tom Custer (the lieutenant colonel's brother) turned to Boyer and told him that the scouts should get out now. The Crows had been paid to guide the Seventh Cavalry to the Sioux, he said, not to die with them. Boyer translated Tom Custer's words for Curley, who said he would leave only if Boyer came with him. But Boyer refused, saying that he had been wounded and couldn't make it; he told Curley to go on alone because he felt sure all the soldiers would die. Reconsidering the situation, Curley grabbed a stray pony and, masquerading as a Sioux, slipped away from the battle. He later said that, before he left, he saw the soldiers fleeing in a disorganized mass to the far end of the ridge, now called Last Stand Hill. The men who still had horses were trying to mount them, and the rest were running on foot.

At this point, Curley's account ended. Ever since, courts of inquiry, scholars, and Little Bighorn enthusiasts have debated what happened next: Did Custer's five companies panic, or did they fight to the last man? Sioux and Cheyenne accounts, though helpful in many other respects, disagree and offer little reliable evidence on this point. In 1984, however, a team of archaeologists took advantage of a prairie fire (which exposed soil covered by vegetation since 1876) to excavate the battlefield for the first time. Using metal detectors, they located thousands of artifacts, including bullets, shell casings, gun parts, buckles, buttons, mess kits, and even a cavalry boot with a skeletal foot preserved inside it. Judging by the type of ammunition (Indian or cavalry) and the location where it was found, the researchers were able to conclude that at least some of Custer's men stood their ground, perhaps even enacting a "last stand" of the sort later portrayed on barroom walls and movie screens. Remarkable as it may seem, even with his command breaking down around him and death minutes away, George Armstrong Custer may well have believed that he was still fighting a battle he could win.

Exactly when Custer died, or who killed him, remains unknown. Several warriors later claimed the honor, but it's just as likely that the Indian who killed him never recognized Custer because he had cut his famous long hair short for the 1876 campaign. However Custer's death took place, what is known is that it took less than an hour for the Sioux and Cheyennes to finish off the entire battalion. Afterward, to be certain that not a single soldier remained alive (a few were apparently faking death), the warriors fired more bullets and arrows into their prone bodies. Finally, the women of the village arrived to strip the dead of anything useful and mutilate the corpses in accordance with Plains tradition.

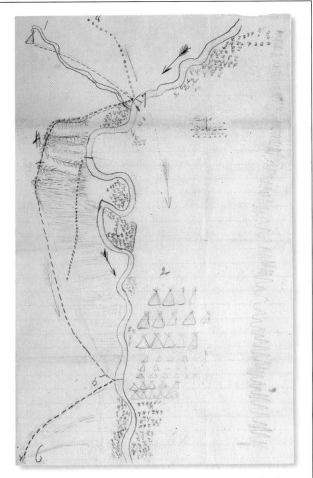

Terry's aide-de-camp, Lt. Robert Patterson Hughes, drew this map of the battle on June 30, 1876. It accompanied an eight-page letter in which Hughes blamed Custer's defeat on his reckless failure to wait for Terry's column to come up. The map shows both Reno's charge (at top) and Custer's route along the bluff (at left).

Unaware of Custer's fate, Reno spent the late afternoon of June 25 improving his defensive position. Shortly after Benteen's 4:20 P.M. arrival, the troops on Reno Hill began hearing the sound of heavy gunfire coming from the north. They all knew that Custer had been heading in that direction, so they immediately concluded that his battalion had now engaged the Indians. Just after 5 P.M., Capt. Thomas B. Weir of D Troop led his company north along the bluff, hoping to reach Custer. His departure began an uncoordinated exodus from Reno Hill—indicative of the nervous Reno's tenuous hold on command. Before long, however, the sound of gunfire dissipated, and the advancing soldiers observed a multitude of Sioux rushing toward them. Weir turned around, and by 6 P.M., the Seventh Cavalry—or what was left of it—had regrouped on Reno Hill, where it remained under steady fire until the following morning, when the approach of Terry and Gibbon caused the Indians to pack up their lodges and move south toward the Bighorn Mountains. Only later did Reno and Benteen learn from Terry's men of Custer's previously unimaginable fate.

This 1877 photograph shows human and animal remains scattered atop Last Stand Hill. Custer's body was among those positively identified by the burial detail. The Sioux, however, probably never recognized him because he had cut his long hair short for the 1876 campaign. His corpse, stripped naked by scavenging Indians, had two bullet wounds, one in the head and another in the body, but was otherwise unmutilated.

RIGHT: *The* **Bismarck Tribune** *published the first news of Custer's defeat eleven days after the battle (on July 6). Because Terry's report had yet to reach Washington, army officials there learned of the massacre from newspaper accounts.*

The Reaction

REVENGE FOR THE ARMY WAS SURE, if not all that swift. Reluctant (like Crook) to pursue the hostiles until reinforced, Terry hurriedly buried Custer's men, then pulled back to his supply depot on the Yellowstone. Meanwhile, reaction in the country was immediate and to the point. The Sioux and Northern Cheyennes had beaten Crook and Custer not simply in a presidential election year but during the nation's centennial (then being celebrated with a spectacular exposition in Philadelphia's Fairmount Park). The public was outraged and wanted an explanation. How could Custer have been defeated by inferior Indians? Because the truth was unacceptable to most people, other analyses were offered. One widely reported account had a young Sitting Bull attending West Point in disguise; how else but with a West Point education could savages have defeated the pride of the Seventh Cavalry?

In Washington, the search for scapegoats began. Congressmen blamed the army for not crushing the Indians sooner. Senior military officials blamed the Indian agents for not properly advising them of the number of warriors who had left the reservations to join the hostile bands. Many officers also blamed Custer for disobeying orders and behaving recklessly to promote his own personal ambition; but even more blamed Reno for failing to move more aggressively in support of Custer's battalion, either by continuing his charge (and thus occupying

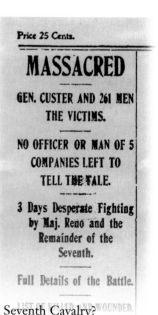

Price 25 Cents.

MASSACRED

GEN. CUSTER AND 261 MEN THE VICTIMS.

NO OFFICER OR MAN OF 5 COMPANIES LEFT TO TELL THE TALE.

3 Days Desperate Fighting by Maj. Reno and the Remainder of the Seventh.

Full Details of the Battle.

LIST OF KILLED AND WOUNDED.

more of the Indian forces) or by moving earlier from Reno Hill to join Custer near Medicine Tail Coulee. General in Chief Sherman laid the blame for the campaign's failure on its "wrong premises," especially Terry's estimation that he would be facing at most a thousand warriors. (At a meeting with Terry and Gibbon on June 21, Custer had estimated there would be fifteen hundred.)

When the fighting resumed in the fall, the army's campaigning was relentless and punitive. The huge hostile village had broken up into smaller winter camps; army harassment, however, quickly undermined their viability. Unable to find game and tired of running, many of the Sioux and Northern Cheyennes returned to their agencies, expecting to be fed and sheltered until spring. They discovered, however, that soldiers had taken over the agencies and were confiscating guns, ammunition, and horses from all those suspected of having spent the summer with Crazy Horse, Sitting Bull, and Gall. In addition, angered by Custer's massacre, Congress had delayed appropriating the funds necessary to feed and clothe the agency Indians, and the bill that finally passed the House and Senate withheld these provisions until the Sioux agreed to a new treaty surrendering not only the Black Hills but also the Powder River and Bighorn Mountain territories.

TRYING TO GET AS FAR AWAY from the whites as possible, Sitting Bull and Gall led their Hunkpapas north to the Yellowstone, where they hoped to find some buffalo. Instead, they found soldiers building a new fort at the mouth of the Tongue River—named Fort Keogh, after Capt. Myles Keogh, who had died with Custer in June. On October 22 and again on October 23, Sitting Bull parlayed with Col. Nelson A. Miles, called Bear Coat by the Indians because his long winter coat was trimmed with bear fur. Sitting Bull said there would be no more fighting if the soldiers would only leave the Indians alone; Miles replied that there would be no peace until all the Indians lived on reservations. At this point, Sitting Bull became angry, declaring that the Great Spirit hadn't intended the Hunkpapas to be agency Indians and he wouldn't become one, either. Then he ended the conference and returned to his warriors, whom he quickly dispersed, fearing an imminent army attack that indeed did come. During the next six months, Sitting Bull and his people moved up and down northern Montana trying in vain to escape the pursuing soldiers. Finally, they chose not to run anymore and crossed the border into Canada. Several hundred Hunkpapas remained there, beyond the reach of American vengeance, until July 1881, when frigid winters, lack of adequate food, and the Canadian government's refusal to grant them land—they were not, after all, British subjects—forced their return and surrender.

Between 1871 and 1886, federal troops fought an on-and-off-again war against various Apache tribes in the Southwest. The conflict finally ended in September 1886 with the surrender of Geronimo (shown here in 1887). The army promised the Chiricahua leader that his people would be allowed to remain in their Arizona home-land. This promise was never kept.

337

THE NEZ PERCE WAR

DURING THE SPRING OF 1877, about the time that Sitting Bull fled to Canada and Crazy Horse surrendered, the Nez Perces held a tribal council to discuss the government's demand that all roaming Nez Perce bands move immediately onto the Lapwai reservation, located along the Clearwater River in present-day Idaho. Chief Joseph, the Nez Perces' most skilled diplomat, was chosen to negotiate with the army officer sent to press this demand: Brig. Gen. Oliver O. Howard. Although one might have expected Howard, formerly director of the Freedmen's Bureau, to sympathize with the Indians' plight, the general gave Joseph a stark ultimatum: Report to the reservation within thirty days or face the unpleasant consequences. (Howard acted so harshly because, as a devout Christian, he despised the messianic Dreamer faith practiced by most of the roaming Nez Perces.)

The off-agency bands began making reluctant preparations to comply. Yet as these preparations were under way, the accumulating stress of the situation provoked a number of young Nez Perce warriors to stage a series of murderous raids. In response, a hastily formed army battalion marched on the main Nez Perce camp. The Nez Perces won the ensuing battle of White Bird Canyon—fought on June 17, 1877—but they knew they couldn't match the strength of Howard's full army, so they fled.

During the next four months, the Nez Perces led Howard (and later Nelson Miles) across fifteen hundred miles of the West's most difficult terrain on an ultimately futile dash for freedom. Elliott West has compared the under-

Chief Joseph's people knew him as Heinmot Tooyalakekt, or Thunder Rising to Loftier Mountain Heights. He is shown here with members of his family sometime after the Nez Perce War.

taking to the men of a small Virginia village leading their wives, children, elderly, and livestock all the way to Denver while being chased by Union troops. Even so, the Nez Perces outmatched the army at every turn along the way—except the last. On September 29, 1877, Joseph's people stopped for a brief rest beside Snake Creek in northern Montana. They were just forty miles south of Canada, where they expected to join Sitting Bull's Hunkpapas shortly. The next morning, however, Miles's scouts found their trail. The Nez Perces fought the soldiers to a stalemate, but the Indians' horses were stampeded and Howard's troops were approaching fast.

The standoff ended on October 5, when Chief Joseph surrendered to Howard and Miles. The speech that accompanied his surrender—recorded in translation (and likely edited) by Howard's aide-de-camp, Lt. C. E. S. Wood—is remembered today as a most poignant farewell to a traditional Indian way of life:

I am tired of fighting. Our chiefs are killed. Looking Glass is dead. Toohoolhoolzote is dead. The old men are all dead. It is the young men who say yes or no. He who led on the young men is dead. It is cold and we have no blankets. The little children are freezing to death. My people, some of them, have run away to the hills, and have no blankets, no food; no one knows where they are—perhaps freezing to death. I want to have time to look for my children and see how many of them I can find. Maybe I shall find them among the dead. Hear me, my chiefs. I am tired; my heart is sick and sad. From where the sun now stands I will fight no more forever.

About the same time that Sitting Bull left for Canada, the last of the defiant Oglalas, led by Crazy Horse, surrendered to the whites at the Red Cloud agency. On April 27, Red Cloud had personally carried a message to Crazy Horse from Crook, promising him a reservation on the Powder River if his people submitted immediately. With nine hundred followers starving and nearly out of ammunition, Crazy Horse had little choice. The promise of a Powder River reservation was all he had needed to hear. The rest of the spring and that summer passed quietly as Crazy Horse waited for Crook to keep his word. On August 31, however, the closely watched Crazy Horse became agitated when he learned that the army was pressuring Oglalas to help it find and subdue the fleeing Nez Perces. He began talking about soon taking his people north to the Powder River country, whether or not Crook gave his permission.

Learning through his Indian spies of Crazy Horse's fulminations, Crook ordered the Oglala's arrest, and Crazy Horse was taken into custody on September 5. As he was being led into the Fort Robinson guardhouse, however, the Oglala chief began to struggle. According to historian Dee Brown, "The windows were barred with iron, and he could see men behind the bars with chains on their legs. It was a trap for an animal, and Crazy Horse lunged away like a trapped animal…. The scuffling went on for only a few seconds. Someone shouted a command, and then the soldier guard, Pvt. William Gentles, thrust his bayonet deep into Crazy Horse's abdomen." Crazy Horse died that night at the age of perhaps thirty-five.

This pouch was made by an Indian woman from a cavalry boot she had removed from a corpse on the Little Bighorn battlefield.

THE SIGNIFICANCE OF THE FRONTIER

AMERICANS OF THE 1890s would have been hard pressed to draw "the West" on a map because it existed, most of all, in their imagination. Yet the region, whatever its boundaries, had dominated the nation's development for the better part of a century, influencing America politically, socially, economically, and culturally. The most persuasive advocate of its influence was an innovative University of Wisconsin history professor named Frederick Jackson Turner. In his 1893 essay "The Significance of the Frontier in American History," Turner first presented his thesis that the recently vanished frontier had been responsible for nurturing the distinctive values of American democracy. "To the frontier," Turner wrote, "the American intellect owes its

Frederick Jackson Turner poses during the 1893–1894 academic year with his University of Wisconsin history seminar class. Turner is seated second from the right.

striking characteristics: That coarseness and strength combined with acuteness and inquisitiveness; that practical, inventive turn of mind, quick to find expedients; that masterful grasp of material things…; that restless, nervous energy, that dominant individualism…and withal that buoyancy and exuberance which comes with freedom.

"American democracy," Turner continued, "was born of no theorist's dream; it was not carried in the *Susan Constant* to Virginia, nor in the *Mayflower* to Plymouth. It came out of the American forest, and it gained new strength each time it touched a new frontier. Not the Constitution, but free land and an abundance of natural resources open to a fit people, made the democratic type of society in America for three centuries."

AFTER THE 1870s, the American frontier disappeared. The censuses of 1850, 1860, 1870, and 1880 had tracked the steady progress of emigrants across the Great Plains and the Rocky Mountains, recording the communities they built and the towns they established. By 1890, however, the situation had changed: "Up to and including 1880," the director of the 1890 census reported, "the country had [an identifiable] frontier…but at present the unsettled area has been so broken into by isolated bodies of settlement that there can hardly be said to be a frontier line."

During this period, U.S. Indian policy also entered a new phase. With the Plains tribes no longer threatening commerce, and eastern liberals rapidly organizing Indian rights groups to protest federal abuse of the Native Americans, the government stopped trying to subjugate the Indians—because this had already been largely accomplished—and instead began encouraging their assimilation into white society. The most difficult obstacle was considered to be the Indians' traditional tribal culture, especially their nomadism and common ownership of land. To change these practices, Congress passed in February 1887 the Dawes Severalty Act, which reversed the federal policy, dating back to Andrew Jackson's time, of isolating Indians on reservations. Instead, the Dawes Act established a process for converting tribal lands to individual ownership. In exchange for relinquishing their tribal affiliations, heads of families were given 160 acres of reservation land for their own; single adults and orphans received 80 acres; and dependent children, 40 acres. In addition, all adult Indian landowners would become U.S. citizens.

It was thought that stripping the tribes of their legal standing and turning their members into landholding farmers would force individual Indians to become more like their white neighbors. Indeed, the Dawes Act did, as intended, weaken the structures of tribal life. Yet it did nothing to increase the acceptance of Indians among whites and failed to end their isolation. Meanwhile, through the sometimes inept, sometimes corrupt administration of this patronizing policy, tribal holdings amounting to 138 million acres in 1887 had shrunk to just 78 million acres by 1900. Not until 1934, when Congress passed the landmark Indian Reorganization Act, did the government begin respecting Native American cultural traditions and protecting the land under tribal ownership.

To encourage assimilation, Indian children were separated from their families and sent to boarding schools, where they were taught to abandon their native ways and accept Christianity. These girls were photographed at the Riverside Indian School in Anadarko, Oklahoma, in 1901. Not surprisingly, few succeeded in making the wrenching transition from tribal collectivity to bourgeois individualism.

RIGHT: *It was the Miniconjou Sioux Kicking Bear who brought the Ghost Dance from Nevada to the Great Plains. Kicking Bear's version, however, was noticeably more militant than Wovoka's original religion.*

The Ghost Dance

ACCORDING TO HISTORIAN Elliott West, "The white invaders had given the Indians three choices: adopt our ways, submit to the reservation system, or be destroyed." Even so, during the late 1880s, the tribes of the Great Plains made one last attempt to retain their dignity and cultural integrity. The vehicle that they chose was the Ghost Dance religion, a messianic faith combining Indian and Christian elements recently created in Nevada by the Paiute prophet Wovoka, who promised that its practice would revive the old ways. "My brothers," Wovoka said,

I bring to you the promise of a day in which there will be no white man to lay his hand on the bridle of the Indians' horse; when the red men of the prairie will rule the world…. I bring you word from your fathers, the ghosts, that they are marching now to join you, led by the Messiah who came once to live on earth with the white man but was killed by them.

The central rite of Wovoka's religion was the Ghost Dance. After purifying themselves by forswearing alcohol and violence, believers were taught to dance in large circles as they chanted to the spirits of their ancestors. Wovoka promised that if their faith was strong, the ghosts of their fathers would return to cleanse the land of the whites and bring the buffalo back to the prairie. It didn't take long for the Ghost Dance to reach the Great Plains, where the humiliated agency Sioux were eager for any offer of hope. As the practice spread, however, Wovoka's message of nonviolence, obviously influenced by the teachings of Christian missionaries, became lost, overshadowed by the Sioux's angry militancy. Some of the younger Sioux, for instance, came to believe that their Ghost Dance shirts would protect them from soldiers' bullets. Older leaders, including Sitting Bull, knew better and saw the risk, but they could do little to stop the dancing. The power of the new faith also concerned the region's army commanders, who put their troops on alert as Indian agents warned of possible trouble on their reservations.

On November 12, 1890, the jittery Pine Ridge agent, Daniel Royer, whom the Sioux called Young Man Afraid of Indians, wired the army to send help: "Indians are dancing in the snow and are wild and crazy…. We need protection and we need it now." In response, Nelson Miles (now a major general) left his Chicago headquarters with five thousand men, among them the reconstituted Seventh Cavalry, to see what the matter was. On December 12, he ordered the arrest of Sitting Bull, who had recently changed his mind and begun supporting the Ghost Dance. Three days later, Lt. Bull Head and his squad of Indian policemen appeared at Sitting Bull's cabin on the Standing Rock reservation to take the aging chief into custody. While Sitting Bull was being led away, one of his followers fired a rifle bullet into Bull Head's side. Bull Head then shot Sitting Bull in the chest, while Sgt. Red Tomahawk put a second bullet through Sitting Bull's brain—after which the cavalry, waiting nearby, rode in to end the skirmish. Sitting Bull was already dead.

This D. F. Barry photograph, taken near the time of Sitting Bull's death, shows three of the reservation policemen who killed the Hunkpapa leader. In the middle is Red Tomahawk, who fired the fatal bullet.

FEARING THAT MILES'S ARMY might soon attack, several hundred members of Sitting Bull's Standing Rock band fled to the Cheyenne River reservation, home to Big Foot's Miniconjous. Soon Red Cloud asked Big Foot to bring all of his people over to Pine Ridge so that further trouble might be avoided; but Miles, misunderstanding the movement of Big Foot's enlarged band, sent the Seventh Cavalry to intercept it. On December 28, the regiment, led by Col. James W. Forsyth, caught up with Big Foot's Miniconjous and the Standing Rock Hunk-papas near Wounded Knee Creek, where the soldiers compelled the 350 Indians (of whom only 120 were adult males) to make camp for the night. Hotchkiss artillery pieces were placed on a rise overlooking the camp in case there was any trouble, but the soldiers felt secure enough to postpone disarming the Indians until the next day.

The next morning, Forsyth demanded that the Sioux turn over whatever weapons they were carrying. When the Indians produced fewer firearms than Forsyth thought reasonable, he ordered his soldiers to search their lodges, where more repeating rifles were found.

During one of these searches, a gun went off. That was all the Seventh Cavalry needed as an excuse to open fire. Well aware of the history of their regiment, the soldiers raked the Indian camp with their rifles and Hotchkiss guns until at least 150 of the 350 Sioux were dead. The equally numerous wounded were taken to Pine Ridge's Holy Cross Episcopal Church, where Christmas decorations still covered the walls. One crudely lettered banner stretched above the pulpit read, "PEACE ON EARTH GOOD WILL TO MEN."

That sign was but a minor irony of the Indian wars—which the United States, a nation ostensibly dedicated to personal liberty, fought in order to cage an independent people and suppress their way of life. Another irony, according to Elliott West, is that

> *white Americans, meanwhile, have come to identify with the same lands, animals, and peoples they once sought to conquer. They have created islands of the wild, starting with Yellowstone [National Park], and promised themselves that these enclaves will be forever free of the same civilization they previously struggled to carry westward. They have also come to identify with the Indians themselves—who, once defeated, were transformed into symbols of a wild nobility said to be at the heart of the national character.*

In American history, of course, such contradictions were nothing new.

Six hundred Oglala Sioux women wait in line for rations at the Pine Ridge agency. Rations typically included flour, cornmeal, sugar, bacon, and coffee, but they were rarely sufficient to sustain the Indians, many of whom died of starvation during the 1880s and 1890s.

AMERICAN PROFILE

Quanah Parker
1845?–1911

by Elliott West

ON MAY 19, 1836, near the Navasota River in East Texas, a party of Comanche and Kiowa warriors swept down on palisaded Fort Parker, killing four settlers and carrying away five women and children. One of those carried away was Cynthia Ann Parker, just nine years old at the time. Of course, Indian kidnappings were nothing new on the frontier. Some captives were ransomed, others adopted into tribes depopulated by warfare and disease. The Comanches kept Cynthia Ann, who subsequently married Chief Peta Nocona and bore three children. In 1861, when Cynthia Ann was thirty-four years old, some Texas Rangers recaptured her, along with her three-year-old daughter. The daughter soon died, and Cynthia Ann, heartbroken by this loss and her separation from her adopted people, passed away herself in 1870.

At the time of Cynthia Ann's recapture, her son Quanah was about sixteen years old. As a seasoned warrior of the Kwahadi band of Comanches, he spent most of the late 1860s and early 1870s raiding the camps of white buffalo hunters who were rapidly annihilating the herds of West Texas, where the Comanches lived. Bison provided the Comanches with food, housing material, clothing, sacred objects, and even toys for their children. Without this economic mainstay, the Indians of the Staked Plain couldn't survive; they would have no choice but to accept reservation life and dependence on white society. (The threat posed by these buffalo hunters became even more severe after 1871, when a Pennsylvania tanner discovered a new curing process that created a nearly bottomless market for bison hides.)

In June 1874, Quanah helped lead a party of seven hundred Kiowas, Comanches, and Southern Cheyennes against about thirty hunters gathered at Adobe Walls, an old supply depot in the Texas Panhandle. Although greatly outnumbered, the hunters (among them a young Bat Masterson) held off the attackers with long-range rifle fire that killed over a dozen Indians and wounded even more, including Quanah. The federal government sent troops to retaliate, of course, and the resulting Red River War (or Buffalo War) became a typical cat-and-mouse affair, with large army columns doing their best to pin down highly mobile bands of warriors. In September 1874, however, the relentless Col. Ranald Mackenzie trapped Quanah's Comanches and most of their Kiowa allies in Palo Duro Canyon.

Although nearly all of the Indians eventually escaped, they had to leave behind their horses—which, as much as the bison, were essential to their independence. Well aware of this, Mackenzie ordered nearly fifteen hundred Indian mounts slaughtered. Later, the screams of the dying horses came to symbolize for Quanah an important realization: His people had lost the Buffalo War not because the whites were stronger, but because they destroyed the foundation of the life that the Comanches wanted to live. Although he was certainly a brave warrior, Quanah became an even greater peacetime leader for his people because he came to understand quickly the new reality in which the Comanches had to live.

On June 2, 1875, three months after the Kiowas surrendered at Fort Sill, Quanah brought in his Kwahadis, who agreed to accept a reservation in the southwestern corner of the Indian Territory (later Oklahoma). Once resettled, Quanah shrewdly negotiated leases that protected Comanche control of reservation land. Later, when the pressure to sell off some of this rangeland to white ranchers became irresistible, he haggled and got a decent price. With skills equaling those of any Gilded Age politician, Quanah became an invaluable cultural broker, balancing tribal and white interests while protecting traditional Comanche practices as best he could.

For example, for twelve years Quanah sat as a judge on the potentially invasive Court of Indian Offenses. Whites had created the court to stamp out "heathenish" practices, such as polygamy; but Judge Quanah, who had no fewer than five wives of his own, used it to settle disputes on the reservation according to a blend of white and Comanche principles. He also became a devotee of the religion later recognized as the Native American Church. Its central ritual involved the ingestion of peyote buttons (hallucinogens produced by the peyote cactus). Some whites wanted to confiscate the buttons and thereby suppress the religion, but Quanah maneuvered successfully against them, at one point even enlisting the support of members of Oklahoma's congressional delegation.

In 1905, Quanah rode in Theodore Roosevelt's inaugural parade and later hunted coyote with the president. Meanwhile, his 19 children and 114 grandchildren (these are conservative estimates) fanned out into different spheres of white and native society to carry on his legacy. In December 1910, a month before he died, Quanah had his mother's remains unearthed in Texas and reburied in Oklahoma. At the ceremony, he spoke in both Comanche and English, telling those who had gathered to "be ready [for death], then we all lie together again."

Quanah Parker stands outside his tipi on the Comanche reservation in Oklahoma during the early 1890s.

14

THE GILDED AGE

The Pullman Strike

THE ESSENCE OF George M. Pullman's business was comfort. As president of the Pullman Palace Car Company, he built and maintained railroad cars designed to make long-distance train travel as pleasurable and leisurely as possible. Throughout the late nineteenth century, his sleeper and dining cars were the most luxurious on the market, and he added new features to them regularly because he believed that his company's success depended on its constant attention to the comfort of its passengers. For much the same reason, Pullman also concerned himself with the comfort of his workers, because he believed that attending to their basic needs promoted the success of his business as well.

After the Civil War, the pace of industrialization in the United States accelerated rapidly, and cities such as Chicago, where the Pullman company had its headquarters, grew at a correspondingly explosive rate—too quickly, in fact, for anyone's good. The poorer urban neighborhoods became pestilent slums; infectious diseases, such as cholera and tuberculosis, spread unchecked; and social maladies, including crime and alcoholism, ravaged the population. With more and more people arriving every day—economically displaced farmers as well as foreign-born immigrants—working-class families had little choice but to accept overcrowded accommodations in shoddy tenements. All of this provoked a great deal of labor unrest in Chicago during the 1870s.

AT LEFT: **This Pullman car,** *one of the company's "parlor" models, ran on the Chicago & Alton Railroad during the late 1890s. Another Pullman innovation, it allowed passengers to ride during the day in plush, swiveling easy chairs.*

Labor trouble was something that Pullman very much wanted to avoid. During the late 1870s, enormous U.S. railroad expansion had created a massive new demand for his cars—whose profitable construction required, in turn, a stable workforce. Early in 1879, the Pullman company realized that it would have to build a new plant to meet the new demand. Several urban sites were considered, but George Pullman rejected them all; either the real estate was too pricey or the neighborhoods in which the workers would have to live were too appalling. Because Pullman recognized that sickness and absenteeism could potentially cost him more than the construction of decent housing would, he decided to build not merely a new factory but an entirely new town, whose benefits would allow the Pullman company to attract the sort of first-class employees who would stay healthy and work hard.

In July 1880, the Pullman Palace Car Company bought four thousand acres in the township of Hyde Park on Chicago's South Side and began constructing its model settlement. Pullman, Illinois, was certainly a social experiment, though perhaps not quite the innovation that its founder thought. In the aftermath of the War of 1812, as New England experienced America's first wave of industrialization, many factory owners had found it advisable to provide housing for the young rural women they were recruiting as workers. Later, in the post–Civil War South, many textile mill operators began compelling their employees to live in company towns, where inflated rents were automatically deducted from their wages; meanwhile, in the mining settlements of

Workmen's houses in Pullman, Illinois, photographed during the 1890s. All had water and gas service, and the better ones had plumbed bathtubs and steam heat as well. By 1894, the town was home to more than twelve thousand people. Its streets were named after famous inventors, and George Pullman himself donated five thousand volumes to launch the municipal library.

Appalachia, some employers stopped paying their workers in cash and instead issued scrip redeemable only at overpriced, company-owned stores. Miners in some of these towns, for example, had to pay $3.25 for kegs of blasting powder that regularly sold for $2.00.

Although arguably as controlling as the economic peonage practiced elsewhere, Pullman's brand of paternalism was a good deal gentler—at least during the 1880s. He built superior single-family homes on wide, tree-lined streets, included parks and athletic fields in his town plan, and priced his rents to return a modest 6 percent on his capital investment. Yet Pullman was no visionary of the Robert Owen variety: He described his namesake town as a "strictly business proposition" and expected it to pay off for him in workingmen of the highest caliber—prompt, dedicated, sober, and indifferent to unionization. On January 1, 1881, the family of a foreman transferred from the company's Detroit shops became the town's first residents; on April 2, Pullman's eleven-year-old daughter Florence started the Corliss engine that would power the new manufacturing equipment. A year later, Pullman, Illinois, had a hotel, a church, a shopping arcade, a library (filled with five thousand volumes donated personally by George Pullman), a theater, a bank, a vegetable farm, and a quickly growing population.

B Y 1885, HOWEVER, GEORGE PULLMAN'S working-class utopia was already showing signs of stress. For one thing, the men in Pullman greatly outnumbered the women, which proved to be a problem because so many of the company's workers were young, single, and eager to be married. Another cause of concern involved the town's ethnic composition: Although the Pullman company had expected to hire (and rent to) primarily native-born Americans, the majority of

GEORGE M. PULLMAN

1831–1897

BORN IN WESTERN NEW YORK, George Mortimer Pullman was raised in a traditional American environment of hard work and devotion to family and religion. He left school at age fourteen to become a clerk in a general store; then, in 1853, he took over his late father's business moving houses away from the banks of the Erie Canal, which was being widened at the time. Six years later, Pullman moved to Chicago, where he found similar work elevating buildings along the shores of the Chicago River and Lake Michigan. Gradually, Pullman accumulated enough capital to begin designing and producing prototypes of his longtime dream: an improved railway sleeping car.

George M. Pullman *sat for this daguerreotype in 1857, when the twenty-six-year-old was still living in New York.*

Between 1850 and 1860, as railroad mileage in the United States more than tripled, it became obvious that coast-to-coast travel would soon be common but arduous. Already, the three-and-a-half-day trip between Chicago and New York was, in Pullman's words, "a nightmare." Having to endure such journeys himself for business reasons focused his mind on the need for greater comfort. Most long-distance trains already had some sort of sleeping accommodations, but these were typically little more than wooden shelves with thin, hard mattresses.

The early sleeping cars also had a conversion problem—that is, they were at best awkward to convert from night to day use. (Sleeping cars needed to be convertible because railroads couldn't afford to haul cars that were empty half the time.)

As late as 1860, sleepers remained clumsy and crowded, with lower berths fashioned out of two day-coach seats and upper berths supported by awkward iron pillars. Pullman's innovation was to eliminate the iron supports and instead suspend roomy upper berths from the car's ceiling. This way, the upper berths could be folded away during the day, transforming the cars into comfortable first-class day coaches. At night, porters simply lowered the berths again for sleeping. Pullman cars also featured polished cherry-wood interiors, plush upholstery, and other deluxe appointments that made them the most fashionable conveyances available. In 1867, Pullman bought out his erstwhile partner, Ben Field, and founded the Pullman Palace Car Company to build and maintain these sleeper cars for various railroads. Later, dining and other "parlor" cars were added to the line. Some Pullman cars were sold outright to the railroads; others were leased for a portion of the ticket sales.

the town's population was, by the mid-1880s, disappointingly (to Pullman) foreign born, which added to the tensions there. For these and other reasons, George Pullman's goal of a stable workforce proved frustratingly elusive. During the late 1880s and early 1890s, for example, even though the company gave employment preference to residents, the average stay in Pullman was just four years.

It didn't help that the Pullman company refused to sell any of its building lots to better-paid workers who wanted to own their own homes. Nor was George Pullman's pervasive personal control of the town's civic life much of an incentive to stay. For years, he appointed all the municipal officials and withheld use of the town's public halls as he saw fit, refusing to rent them to any speakers he considered "radical." Understandably, it wasn't long before resentful residents began moving out of Pullman into other new South Side communities, where rents were much lower, even if the housing wasn't as comfortable. Among those workers who remained in Pullman, the company's overbearing influence undermined whatever pride they might have otherwise had in the town, and morale continued to decline.

Yet much of this discontent remained beneath the town's placid surface until early 1893, when a financial panic led to an economic collapse that seemed to worsen each month. During the late summer of 1893, Pullman company business declined dramatically, as people began to travel less frequently and new car orders were canceled. Reacting decisively, George Pullman closed his shops in Detroit, laying off about eight hundred people. At the same time, he also began lowering the wages of hourly workers in Pullman. Between August 1893 and May 1894, he cut wages an average of 25 percent, arguing that reducing manufacturing costs was the only way he could keep any workers employed. Yet Pullman reduced neither management salaries, nor stockholder dividends, nor the rents he charged workers—which he kept deducting from their pay, leaving some with less than a dollar to show for two weeks' work. After March 1894, despairing Pullman employees, many of them reduced to short hours, began joining the American Railway Union (ARU) in large numbers.

UNIONISM

ALTHOUGH THERE WERE craft guilds as far back as colonial times, modern trade unionism didn't really emerge until a large market for wage labor developed during the Jacksonian era. The most active of the early unionists believed firmly in English economist David Ricardo's labor theory of value, which held that a commodity's worth depended on the amount of labor required to produce it. For obvious reasons, these workers were troubled by the growing subordination of labor to capital, which was not only lowering the perceived value of their contribution but also threatening the social equality for which the American Revolution had only recently been fought.

This emphasis on maintaining the social dignity of labor continued after the Civil War, even when the focus of union organizing activity shifted from skilled artisans to the new unskilled or semiskilled industrial workforce. In

This bilingual handbill announced the May 4, 1886, mass meeting that devolved into the Haymarket Riot when an unknown terrorist threw a bomb into a crowd of policemen.

December 1869, garment cutter Uriah S. Stephens founded the Noble Order of the Knights of Labor "to affirm the nobility of all those who earn their bread through the sweat of their brows." Stephens's organization, the first important national labor group to span all the trades, began as a secret society in order to protect its members from management reprisals. With the election of Grand Master Workman Terence V. Powderly in 1879, however, the Knights of Labor began moving away from the mystical trappings of its early years, and it soon became a public organization committed to a broad program of social reforms, including an eight-hour workday, restrictions on child labor, and the eventual replacement of capitalism with a quasi-socialist economic system based on workers' cooperatives. By 1886, membership in the Knights had expanded to more than seven hundred thousand people, many of them self-employed middle-class Americans who

The American Railway Union

FOR YEARS, SKILLED PULLMAN EMPLOYEES had belonged to craft unions of the sort represented by the American Federation of Labor (AFL). The year-old American Railway Union, however, was something altogether different. To begin with, the union didn't restrict membership to higher-wage skilled workers but opened its doors to white railroad workers at all skill and wage levels. (Blacks were excluded.) The ARU also featured a decentralized constitution that permitted workers to establish local unions as they wished, as long as each contained at least ten workers. The union lobbied for eight-hour workdays, improved workplace safety, and restrictions on Sunday labor; it also offered low-cost life and disability insurance, helped unemployed workers find jobs, and sponsored lectures on industrial economics and other related subjects. The ARU's disposition was noncombative. It counseled against strikes and instead encouraged mediation and arbitration. Each local, for example, was instructed to elect its own board of mediation to negotiate with management concerning worker grievances.

A pivotal test of the ARU's belief in working-class mutuality came in April 1894, just ten months after the union's founding, when it came into conflict with

shared its vision of a nation of factories and stores owned by the people who worked them. Sadly, 1886 also marked the decline of the group's influence. That year, sixteen hundred strikes, many of them violent, disrupted the U.S. economy and produced a great deal of antiunion backlash, most of it directed against the prominent Knights. The most important of these strikes took place in Chicago at the huge McCormick Harvesting Machine Company. On May 1, eighty thousand workers marched peacefully outside the reaper works as part of a broad national effort urging an eight-hour workday. Two days later, when a fight broke out at the McCormick factory between strikers and replacement workers, police fired into the crowd, killing four of the strikers; many others were beaten with billy clubs. On May 4, a small group of anarchist labor leaders, led by August Spies, circulated a notice announcing a protest rally to be held that evening in Haymarket Square. Because of the short notice, only thirteen hundred people showed up, and most of those left when a light rain began to fall. So there were only three hundred protesters remaining in Haymarket Square when about two hundred policemen arrived to break up the rally. At this point, someone threw a

bomb into the phalanx of officers, fatally wounding eight of them. The police responded with wild gunfire that killed seven or eight people and wounded about a hundred more (half of them fellow officers).

Newspaper reports "exposing" anarchist subversion of the labor movement exacerbated the national climate of fear and fired the prosecution of Spies and seven others. None of the Haymarket defendants was ever accused of having thrown the bomb, and no evidence was ever presented at trial linking any of them with the anonymous bomb thrower, but all were convicted of conspiracy to commit murder. Four, Spies among them, were hanged in November 1887. (One defendant had already killed himself in prison, and three others received long prison sentences.) In the meantime, Powderly's refusal to criticize the obviously biased trial produced a deep division within the Knights of Labor that led to the group's precipitous decline and the founding in December 1886 of the American Federation of Labor, which pledged itself to avoid all political entanglements and focus entirely on workers' economic goals.

This lead casing was introduced into evidence at the Haymarket trial to show the type of bomb exploded on May 4.

This billy club belonged to a Chicago police captain, who used it during the Haymarket Riot.

James J. Hill and his Great Northern Railway. The Great Northern ran from Minneapolis to Seattle and employed about nine thousand workers, of whom fewer than half were unionized. Following the 1893 panic, its president, James Hill, slashed wages three times in seven months, dropping them well below the compensation being offered by other intercontinental lines. On behalf of its aggrieved members, the ARU sent Hill a letter requesting a meeting. When Hill contemptuously ignored the letter, the ARU called a strike. Even those workers usually loyal to management (such as station agents and yardmasters) walked out in sympathy, paralyzing Great Northern operations. Some mail trains and a few locals were permitted to run, but all long-distance passenger and freight service was stalled.

Hill tried to import strikebreakers to work the line, but the antagonism this generated among local farmers and businessmen, already resentful of the railroad's monopolistic pricing, persuaded Hill to settle. Just eighteen days after the strike began, Hill and ARU president Eugene V. Debs agreed to arbitrate the matter. A panel of fourteen businessmen from Minneapolis and St. Paul heard the case and found for the workers, awarding them substantial wage increases. The victory greatly expanded the prestige of the ARU and swelled its ranks. In the weeks following the successful conclusion of the strike, new members joined the union at the rate of two thousand a day. Under Debs's leadership, the ARU became, by mid-1894, the largest union in the United States, with 425 locals and more than 150,000 members.

Eugene V. Debs poses with railroad workers in this undated photograph, mostly likely taken during the mid-1890s.

AFTER THE ARU'S TRIUMPH in the Great Northern strike, the flow of Pullman workers into the union became a torrent. By the end of April, the nineteen ARU locals in Pullman boasted a combined membership exceeding four thousand. Recognizing labor's weakness during this period of severe economic depression, ARU officials cautioned the Pullman locals against a strike, instead counseling mediation. Following the national union's advice, a forty-six-member grievance committee met with Pullman vice president Thomas Wickes on May 7. It requested either an across-the-board rent reduction or the restoration of pre-depression wage levels; the committee also complained about shop foremen who were abusing workers in order to increase their productivity. Wickes promised to consider the matter seriously, and a follow-up meeting was scheduled. George Pullman attended this May 9 meeting personally.

Although Pullman hadn't objected much in the past to his employees' membership in specialized craft unions, he now took offense that so many of his workers had joined the ARU. Among George Pullman's many paternalistic beliefs, the one he held most deeply was that he could deal fairly with his workforce. It had been his reason for building the model town of Pullman in the first place, and he considered the presence of the ARU a betrayal of his trust. Even so,

RIGHT: *Railroad workers used this simple form provided by the ARU to charter their own local unions.*

at that May 9 meeting, he expressed his acute concern for the welfare of his workers before informing the grievance committee sadly that business conditions didn't permit wage increases. He did, however, offer to investigate the allegations of worker abuse and assured the members of the grievance committee that their jobs weren't threatened by their union activity.

The workers didn't believe him. They were sure he was lying about the company's financial situation and believed he would doctor the books (if he hadn't already) to prove his point. To make matters worse, on May 10, the very next day, three members of the grievance committee were laid off. The foremen involved claimed that there simply wasn't enough work. Pullman denied any personal involvement in the firings but reminded workers that some layoffs were necessary to keep the shops open. (The Pullman workforce had already been reduced from fifty-five hundred at the start of the depression to thirty-three hundred in May 1894.) That evening, the ARU locals voted to strike.

Industrialization

DURING THEIR LIFETIMES, both Pullman and Debs saw profound changes transform the rural, predominantly Protestant America of their youths. Before the Civil War, when most Americans farmed or otherwise depended on agriculture for their livelihood, the country's chief social dilemma was slavery. After the war, with slavery gone, the nation's focus shifted to the struggle between capital and labor. As large-scale industry expanded during the 1870s and 1880s, millions of semiskilled and unskilled workers, often recent immigrants, found jobs in America's booming manufacturing sector. Yet the factories where they spent their time, like the cities in which they lived, were dangerous, dismal places where too few workers seemed able to get ahead.

George M. Pullman in 1894.

Mills in Lowell, Massachusetts, during the second half of the nineteenth century. At the time, most factory laborers worked ten hours a day, six days a week.

IMMIGRATION

THE INDUSTRIAL EXPANSION of the Gilded Age created an insatiable demand for labor that, in turn, fed a huge new wave of immigration. Excluding slaves and Indians, the American population through the early national period had remained remarkably homogeneous. From colonial times until the 1840s, the vast majority of white Americans claimed either English or Scottish ancestry, with those of German heritage (the next largest group) making up only about 10 percent of the population. In 1845, however, the Irish potato famine began, triggering the first of three large waves of immigration that transformed American society into what would later be termed "the melting pot."

During the first wave, which lasted from the mid-1840s until the Civil War, more than a million Irish (about 15 percent of that country's total prefamine population) crossed the Atlantic.

Most of those people settled in the coastal cities where they landed, notably Boston, New York City, and Philadelphia. They lived in crowded tenements in the poorest neighborhoods and faced substantial prejudice because of their poverty, not to mention their Catholicism. This first wave of immigration also included many Germans fleeing the political turmoil created by the revolutions of 1848 and the hard economic times of the 1850s. Unlike the Irish, however, the Germans tended to move on to the Middle West, where they cleared land for farming, established small towns, and won relatively easy acceptance.

The start of the second great wave of immigration coincided, understandably, with the close of the Civil War. During the next quarter century, another ten million foreigners arrived in the United States, including some 789,000 during the peak year of 1882. As before, this wave was dominated by northern and western Europeans; after 1890, however, when the third wave began, the ethnic pattern changed significantly. Until World War I choked off its flow, the third wave flooded American ports with seventeen million immigrants, most of them from southern and eastern Europe. Marked by their distinctive languages, cultures, and physical appearance, these Italians, Hungarians, Poles, Russians, Greeks, and Turks typically settled in large cities, took low-paying factory jobs, and replaced the Irish as America's despised underclass.

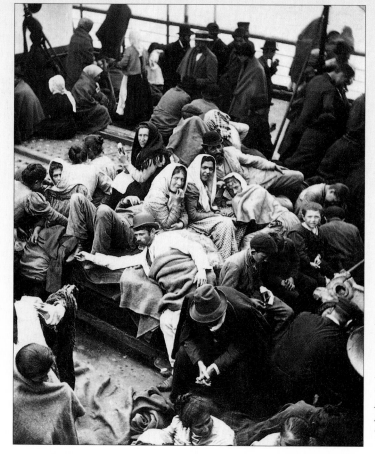

Immigrants on their way to *America, 1902. Most overcame the chief barrier to assimilation— learning English—with remarkable rapidity. Many public schools and settlement houses offered free classes, and private groups (such as political parties and labor unions) also provided language instruction as part of their efforts to "Americanize" new arrivals.*

The Industrial Revolution, both in the United States and abroad, changed the basic relationship that had existed for generations between employer and employee. Prior to industrialization, most American wage earners who worked in manufacturing pursued their craft in small shops, producing goods for customers they knew and with whom they often interacted. These craftsmen nearly always worked closely with the shop owners who employed them, sometimes even sharing lodging and socializing with them. The new technologies of mass production, however, undercut this arrangement and devalued many trades while transforming their skilled practitioners into interchangeable hourly workers— much like the interchangeable parts that Eli Whitney had introduced in 1801 to speed firearms production.

In the preindustrial shop, the workers were the focus; in the industrial factory, machines dominated. Few factory workers ever met their employers, much less socialized with them, and none interacted (except by chance outside the work environment) with any of the thousands or millions of people who bought the products they had helped to create. Few Pullman workers, for example, could afford tickets to ride in one of the company's fashionable sleeper cars; and throughout American industry, laborers increasingly felt alienated from the product of their labor.

Beyond the low wages and impersonal, monotonous work environments, factory life in the United States was also poisoned by ethnic and racial antagonisms that shrewd industrialists exploited to their own advantage and their workers' misery. Some businessmen intentionally juxtaposed hostile nationalities and races on the shop floor, thereby hoping to reduce the likelihood of a demand for collective bargaining. Although generally unable to land factory jobs under ordinary circumstances, black workers were often brought in as strikebreakers or to distract native-born racist whites from union organizing activities; industrialists used foreign immigrants in much the same way. Because most of these immigrants were economic refugees who had never before received decent wages or treatment, they eagerly accepted even the most oppressive jobs as a first step up the American ladder. Consequently, native-born workers tended to treat them with hostility—not merely because they competed for the same jobs, but also because their willingness to accept less drove down everyone's wage.

A first edition of The Gilded Age: A Tale of To-Day, *the 1873 novel by Mark Twain and Charles Dudley Warner that gave its name to this period of infamous political and financial corruption. Many of the book's characters, such as the political boss William M. Weed, are thinly disguised caricatures of well-known Americans of the time.*

THE NATIVIST BACKLASH

THE POSTWAR SURGE in Catholic and Jewish immigration naturally produced a backlash among America's Protestant majority, for political as well as cultural reasons. Nativists objected not only to the alien ways of the new arrivals but also to their politics, which at times tended toward the radical. Of course, only a minuscule percentage of the immigrants engaged in any extremist political activity, but with urban populations becoming predominantly foreign born, one can imagine the economic elite's distress. Much less understandable was the anti-Chinese sentiment that swept the nation, especially the West Coast, during the 1880s—because, comparatively, there were so few Chinese immigrants. In May 1882, when Congress passed the Chinese Exclusion Act suspending immigration from China for ten years, there were only about a hundred thousand Chinese living in the entire country.

When advances in agricultural technology put numerous farmhands out of work after the Civil War and forced them to take low-paying industrial jobs instead, many blamed their troubles on immigration, which they believed was bloating the labor force and driving down wages. Specifically, many Irish laborers in California blamed immigrant Chinese for taking away railroad construction jobs. As a result, during the late 1870s, Irish mobs in San Francisco rioted often against Chinese residents. Meanwhile, in 1879, California adopted a new state constitution that eliminated Chinese voting rights and forbade their employment by corporations.

In this nativist cartoon, published in San Francisco during the late 1860s, Irish and Chinese immigrants together devour Uncle Sam. Then the Chinese immigrant eats the Irishman.

FOR THE POST–CIVIL WAR GENERATION, nothing symbolized the benefits and disadvantages of America's recent industrial expansion quite so much as the railroads. As late as 1865, the United States had only 35,000 miles of track; by 1890, that figure had soared to 164,000 miles, or a third of all the railroad track in the world. European investors, sensing the opportunity for profit, contributed more than a third of the capital that funded this construction boom—which employed, during its peak in the 1880s, more than two hundred thousand workers. Huge government loans and generous land grants made up another important segment of the financing. For example, railroads such as the Central Pacific and the Union Pacific received from Congress allotments of public land adjoining their routes that matched the amount of transcontinental track each company laid. (The ratio was ten square miles of land to each mile of track laid in a state and double that for track laid in a federal territory.) This land was then marketed to settlers, who became freight customers. All told, between 1850 and the end of the land grant policy in 1871, Congress gave the railroads 175 million acres of public land, or one and a half times the amount it distributed to individual settlers under the Homestead Act. As a result, in some of the new western states, railroads and other land speculators owned more than a quarter of the available land.

Yet even with all this financing, the postwar expansion of the U.S. rail system couldn't have taken place without immigrant labor. The original transcontinental companies, in particular, hired tens of thousands of recent arrivals. The Central Pacific used large numbers of Chinese workers, called "coolies," to construct its line moving eastward from California, while the Union Pacific employed mainly Irishmen to lay its track across Nebraska and Wyoming. Completed in May 1869, the first transcontinental railroad reduced long-distance travel times considerably. Cross-country trips now required just seven days—a duration short enough to attract many new passengers, yet still long enough to provide George Pullman with a lively market.

For a time, however, the railroads were their own worst enemies. They overconstructed and then engaged in destructive competition that put many of them out of business. As an economic system, the industry was absurdly inefficient: On most of the competitive routes, railroads offered below-cost rates to lure business away from their rivals. On routes where no competition existed, customers were routinely gouged to recoup losses elsewhere. Following a wave of bankruptcies, a number of chastened companies sought to end the cutthroat competition through the introduction of "pool" agreements. Intended to bring both stability and profitability to the industry, these agreements divided up freight traffic in a rational manner and set uniform prices. Needless to say, they also produced an uproar among western shippers, most of whom already hated the railroads, and led directly to passage of

An 1888 map of the Union Pacific Railroad and its branch lines.

This photograph recorded the historic completion of the first transcontinental railroad. A golden spike driven by a silver sledge was used to join the Central Pacific and Union Pacific lines at Promontory Point, Utah, on May 10, 1869.

RAILROAD CONSOLIDATION

ONCE U.S. CORPORATIONS BEGAN issuing stock to finance their operations, the role of the nation's bankers changed accordingly: from loaning their own money to raising capital from a variety of sources, foreign as well as domestic. That is, bankers became the principal intermediaries between corporations on the one hand and potential individual and institutional investors on the other. One of the most skillful and ambitious of these new investment bankers was J. Pierpont Morgan, the tall and commanding son of a wealthy Connecticut merchant with considerable banking interests in London.

Because arranging financing for the nation's largest corporations was Morgan's specialty, he saw in the numerous railroad bankruptcies of the 1870s and 1880s a magnificent opportunity. The problem

John Pierpont Morgan, photographed in 1902.

of cutthroat competition, he realized, could be solved easily by the consolidation of rival lines, many of which were now selling at bargain prices. All Morgan had to do was raise the necessary capital—child's play for a banker as well connected as he.

In 1885, Morgan intervened to end the ruinous competition between the New York Central and Pennsylvania Railroads. During the next fifteen years, he steadily reorganized more and more lines, reducing their indebtedness and raising their rates to profitable levels (often *very* profitable levels). Meanwhile, Morgan began applying his talents to other industries as well, notably steel. When an 1890s price war sent that industry into a temporary decline, Morgan created U.S. Steel, the world's first billion-dollar corporation, which bought out the assets of Andrew Carnegie's steel company in 1901 and soon controlled 60 percent of U.S. production.

the 1887 Interstate Commerce Act, which set up a federal commission to regulate the railroads and ensure that all rates were "reasonable and just." Meanwhile, the great lines persevered. They made cities of small towns, transported people and products nationwide, and created the first national economic marketplace.

Politics in Transition

AS THE IMPORTANCE OF THE RAILROAD industry grew, its magnates naturally sought to acquire influence with the government in Washington. They wanted favors, such as federal subsidies for new track construction and the appointment of interstate commerce commissioners sympathetic to their interests. The nation's elected officials provided such considerations willingly in exchange for millions of dollars in railroad stock, cash payments, and other forms of bribery. Members of both major parties fed at this trough, but the greater beneficiaries were undoubtedly the Republicans, whose support for government-subsidized economic growth predated the Civil War.

The messiest of the many railroad scandals that besmirched the Gilded Age involved the Crédit Mobilier, a company set up by the major stockholders of the Union Pacific Railroad to carry out its track construction. Numerous influential congressmen were given shares in the Crédit Mobilier to encourage their support for continued extravagant construction subsidies. Despite the Union Pacific's own troubled financial situation, the Crédit Mobilier paid annual dividends whose return on investment (if there even was an actual investment) at times exceeded

300 percent. The *New York Sun* broke the story of the payoffs just before the 1872 election, and subsequent congressional investigations implicated (among others) outgoing vice president Schuyler Colfax, incoming vice president Henry Wilson, and Speaker of the House James G. Blaine. Rep. James A. Garfield was also connected to the scandal, but he denied the charges successfully enough to keep his House seat and eight years later win the presidency.

Of course, during the Gilded Age, political corruption was by no means limited to the national government and the Republican party. In the teeming cities of the North, Democratic machines fleeced the public even more brazenly. In New York City, for instance, the Tammany Hall machine reached unprecedented heights of corruption under "Boss" William Marcy Tweed. During the late 1860s, the Tweed Ring stole as much as two hundred million dollars in city funds—some in payments to Tweed-owned companies for work never performed, some in kickbacks from contractors given sweetheart deals. Tweed's most notorious scam involved construction of a lavish new courthouse. When the *New York Times* began exposing Tweed Ring corruption in July 1871, it reported that Andrew Garvey, dubbed "the Prince of Plasterers," had received $2.8 million in compensation for his work alone.

Although reform lawyer Samuel J. Tilden made a national name for himself leading the successful effort to indict and convict Tweed, the boss blamed his downfall on Thomas Nast, the *Harper's Weekly* cartoonist who began caricaturing Tweed in 1869. At one point, Tweed used an intermediary to offer Nast a ten-thousand-dollar bribe that Nast mischievously negotiated up to five hundred thousand dollars before turning down. When asked why he considered Nast such a problem, Tweed replied that Democratic voters may not know how to read but they can "look at the damn pictures."

Harper's Weekly *published this Thomas Nast cartoon in July 1876, a year after Boss Tweed's release from jail and shortly before his reimprisonment on further charges.*

IMMIGRANT POLITICS

THE POWER OF URBAN POLITICAL parties during the Gilded Age depended on the loyalty of immigrant voters, so the machines routinely courted new arrivals. Operatives known as "ward heelers" (because they wore out pairs of shoes walking the streets of the city wards to which they'd been assigned) provided all manner of support services to recent immigrants—from housing and food to money and jobs—in expectation that the recipients (and their friends and families) would express their gratitude come Election Day by voting for the machine candidates. In the post–Civil War period, the urban political machines were the most important source of Democratic power in the North, and they remained—along with the Solid South—the core of the party for generations to come.

THE APPOMATTOX OF THE THIRD TERMERS—UNCONDITIONAL SURRENDER.

PATRONAGE, OR THE POWER to distribute government jobs, was the main source of machine wealth and influence. Therefore, in the wake of the Tweed Ring revelations and the Grant administration scandals, civil service reform became an increasingly important political issue. As president, Rutherford B. Hayes made civil service reform one of his top domestic priorities. In June 1877, he issued an executive order prohibiting federal employees from taking part in any partisan political activity. A year later, he fired Chester A. Arthur as collector of customs for the Port of New York for accepting kickbacks. (In some years, the "perks" Arthur received amounted to fifty thousand dollars, or what the president was making at the time.) Yet Hayes failed to persuade a recalcitrant Congress to enact any comprehensive civil service legislation. A strong new reform law wouldn't reach the president's desk until 1883, when—in one of the great ironies of American history—*Chester Arthur* signed the Pendleton Civil Service Reform Act.

In 1880, following Hayes's decision not to run again, the Republican party wasn't sure how to proceed. In the midterm elections of 1878, the Democrats—who already controlled the House—had won back the Senate as well. The stakes for the Republicans were thus particularly high. The party's conservative Stalwart faction, led by New York senator Roscoe Conkling (who was, coincidentally, Arthur's patron), wanted to run Ulysses S. Grant for a third term; the more moderate Half-Breeds backed James G. Blaine, now a senator from Maine.

Paraphernalia from the 1880 presidential campaign.

After thirty-five ballots, the Republican convention remained deadlocked; then various anti-Grant voting blocs united behind a dark horse, James Garfield. Conkling's man Arthur was subsequently added to the ticket as a sop to the Stalwarts; promises of federal patronage were also made—perhaps vague, perhaps not so vague. Yet after winning the election, which he couldn't have done without the help of Conkling's machine in New York, Garfield cut the boss off, and a Blaine lieutenant was given Arthur's old job at the New York Custom House. Feeling understandably betrayed, an outraged Conkling tried to get even by blocking the appointment in the Senate. Garfield prevailed.

In the end, however, patronage issues would literally destroy Garfield. A few months after the confrontation with Conkling, as the president was leaving Washington to spend the rest of his summer on the Jersey Shore, he was shot in the back at the Baltimore & Potomac railroad station by Charles J. Guiteau, a deranged Stalwart. Several times during the preceding months, Guiteau had appeared at the White House asking for a patronage appointment, only to have his requests rebuffed. Now, on July 2, 1881, he sought to improve his status by shooting Garfield so that Arthur might become president. The wound itself was not fatal, but doctors were unable to remove the bullet; moreover, their repeated unsanitary probings weakened his condition. Garfield lingered for two months before dying of blood poisoning on September 19.

As Guiteau intended, Garfield's death made Arthur president. No one in Washington believed for a moment that Arthur (or any other Stalwart) had put Guiteau up to the crime, yet there was some expectation that Conkling would soon be running the government. A dead Garfield, however, turned out to be much more valuable to the forces of reform than a living one had been. The American people, aghast at Garfield's murder, interpreted its cause as office-seeking run amok and began clamoring for reform of the civil service. The Pendleton Act was the result. Meanwhile, Arthur experienced a transformation on his elevation to the presidency: Incredibly, he lobbied hard for the Pendleton Act and vetoed several treasury raids, including the flagrantly pork-barrel Rivers and Harbors Act of 1882 (which Congress nevertheless passed over his veto). The Pendleton Act established a bipartisan civil service commission to administer competitive exams for the purpose of making merit (rather than patronage) appointments. The new law also banned the common practice of requiring government jobholders to contribute a portion of their salaries to the political party that had placed them in office.

Y ET THESE REFORMS, though welcomed, did little to relieve the many other inequities pervading Gilded Age life. As had been the case during the age of slavery, American politicians wanted to avoid as best they could the troublesome issues of immigration, urbanization, and industrialization. Their evasions continued from 1865 until the 1890s, when economic depression and the rise of populism forced the nation's political class to address some of the problems it had been ignoring for thirty years.

Why did Gilded Age politicians pay so little attention to the new industrial society? One reason was their preoccupation with the recently concluded war and its intensely emotional aftermath. The Civil War was the central event in all of their lives, and even after Reconstruction ended in 1877, most American politicians found it difficult to turn their psychological focus anywhere else. The same held true for voters. With the exception of Grover Cleveland, every president elected between Abraham Lincoln and Theodore Roosevelt was a Republican with an admirable Union army service record. Rutherford Hayes and James Garfield had both been major generals; Benjamin Harrison, a brigadier general; and William McKinley, a young major. Even Chester Arthur had served for a time as quarter-master general of the New York State militia. Another reason that Gilded Age politicians had so little interest in urban and immigrant issues was that the great majority of them came from small towns and thus had little experience dealing with problems found mostly in large cities.

Garfield's White House desk calendar, which has not been reset since the day he was shot.

William McKinley served from June 1861 until July 1865 with the Twenty-third Ohio Volunteer Infantry. His regimental commander was Col. Rutherford B. Hayes.

URBANIZATION

THE SPECTACULAR GROWTH of U.S. cities after the Civil War certainly reflected increased foreign immigration, but often overlooked are the many domestic migrants who contributed to the process of American urbanization during the late nineteenth century. Displaced by foreclosure, drought, and the growing mechanization of agriculture, so many people left rural America during the postwar years that, by 1900, 40 percent of the country lived in cities, up from 20 percent in 1860. Much of this expansion took place during the 1880s, when 101 cities more than doubled in size. Some growth rates were little short of spectacular: Kansas City increased tenfold in population, while Minneapolis expanded from 47,000 to 164,000 residents and Omaha from 30,000 to 140,000. The lure, of course, was all the factory jobs—and as more workers became available, more factories were built, further undermining the rural economy. In this way, the twin processes of urbanization and industrialization fed on each other.

At the turn of the twentieth century, Chicagoans bragged that South Water Street (shown here in 1899) was the busiest street in the world. Like other American cities, Chicago grew during this period in an uncontrolled, often chaotic manner, promoting both inefficiency and corruption. Sanitation was a common problem, and the construction of new freshwater delivery systems became high priorities for most municipal governments.

Technological innovation also contributed importantly to the urbanization of the 1880s. Without the large-scale production of electricity made possible by men such as Thomas Alva Edison, George Westinghouse, and Nikola Tesla, it's difficult to imagine how cities such as New York and Chicago could have grown as they did. Electric trolleys made it possible for residents to live in outlying neighborhoods yet reach a city's business and shopping districts easily. By replacing horse-drawn cars, they also curbed a significant urban sanitation problem: horse manure. Similarly, advances in steel production made possible the building of skyscrapers, which permitted cities to grow vertically as well as horizontally.

Because many of the most talented men of this period went into business, those who chose careers in government were, more often than not, mediocrities unprepared to handle the challenges posed by rapid industrialization. Most were also too deeply involved with America's entrepreneurial class—that is, on the tycoons' payroll—to regulate business interests effectively. Only when political and economic conditions changed in the 1890s did the nation's politicians finally bring some measure of public accountability to the corporate system.

The Rise of the Corporation

ONE ASPECT OF GILDED AGE business practice that politicians certainly didn't inhibit was the formation of powerful manufacturing corporations. In 1860, the United States ranked fourth in manufacturing among the nations of the world; by 1900, it ranked first, producing more than the *combined* outputs of Great Britain,

France, and Germany (the world's other leading industrial powers). Such meteoric growth could not have been possibly had not the corporation replaced the family-held firm as the primary form of industrial organization.

Corporations, of course, were nothing new. In fact, the joint-stock companies that sponsored the first settlements in Virginia and Massachusetts were themselves corporations of a sort. Those chartered before the Civil War, however, were typically beholden to state legislatures and supported with public funds. In other words, antebellum corporations were usually quasi-public bodies, obligated in numerous ways to serve their local communities. Yet as wealthier Americans began to accumulate private capital, their search for investment opportunities led them to fund certain "mixed" corporations, such as the Second Bank of the United States, which conducted both public and private business. Entrepreneurs took the next step in this developing trend during the 1830s and 1840s, when they lobbied state legislatures to enact more liberal incorporation laws that freed corporations from any obligations to the chartering state or the public. The purpose of these laws was to allow the creation of companies large enough to fund (through the sale of stock to the public) projects of enormous scope—a transcontinental railroad, for example—that no single individual or manageable group of partners could capitalize on its own.

From railroads, this method of financing spread to steel, meatpacking, oil production, and other industries. Among its most attractive features was the limited liability it offered to investors. Never before had Americans funded businesses with which they had so little personal contact. Yet the fact that they could lose no more than their original investment—that they would not be exposed to any of the company's accumulated losses—reassured them. As a result, capital poured into the new corporations, creating the modern stock market and enabling industrialists to establish business entities exponentially larger than any previously imagined. Corporate growth took two main forms: Companies that practiced horizontal integration either merged with or bought out competitors to obtain ever-larger market shares, some becoming near-monopolies. Others that practiced vertical integration sought to acquire not only sources for the raw materials they needed but also distribution outlets through which their products could be sold.

ONE OF THE EARLIEST and most successful of the vertical integrators was Andrew Carnegie, whose steel business dominated the market during the late nineteenth century. At one time a poor Scottish immigrant, Carnegie worked his way up in railroads before concentrating all of his assets into steel. In 1873, he opened a plant outside Pittsburgh, using new technologies—such as the Bessemer process and open-hearth smelting—to produce cheaper, better steel. With the resulting profits and even greater amounts raised from the sale of additional stock, he began acquiring a network of complementary businesses. For example, in addition to buying nearby coal fields to supply

A stock certificate issued by the Pullman Palace Car Company in March 1884.

Andrew Carnegie in 1896. His rags-to-riches story persuaded Americans that wealth lay within the grasp of anyone who had sufficient ability and worked hard enough.

COMMUNICATIONS

THE IMPORTANCE OF RAILROADS to the development of a national marketplace cannot be overestimated, yet Gilded Age corporations also benefited from equally significant advances in communications. To expand beyond a single city, businesses needed an affordable, efficient means of exchanging information among branch offices. The telegraph, developed by Samuel F. B. Morse during the late 1830s, proved highly useful for a time, its reach extended in July 1866 when Cyrus W. Field laid the first durable transatlantic cable. But by the 1870s, it seemed increasingly inadequate.

The next great development was the telephone, invented by Scottish immigrant Alexander Graham Bell. Settling in Boston in 1872, the twenty-five-year-old Bell established a school for the deaf and later became a professor of speech and vocal physiology at Boston University. As part of his efforts to help his deaf students learn to speak, he experimented with telegraphic technology and sound waves. In 1874, he got the idea for a device that could "transmit sound telegraphically" by "mak[ing] a current of electricity vary in intensity precisely as the air varies in density during the production of sound." Bell patented his telephone on March 7, 1876. Three days later in his laboratory, he transmitted the first coherent telephonic sentence: "Mr. Watson, come here; I want you."

Bell's invention became one of the technological "wonders" displayed that summer at the Centennial Exposition in Philadelphia. Two years later, the first citywide telephone exchanges went into operation, changing not only the nation's business practices but its sociocultural patterns as well.

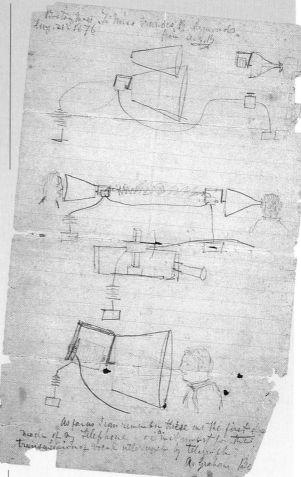

Because many other inventors *had been working along the same lines since before the Civil War, the announcement of Bell's success led to a deluge of patent infringement suits. Some six hundred were filed before Bell's claim was ultimately upheld. These drawings from the summer of 1876 are the first he ever made of his remarkable invention.*

the fuel for his furnaces, he leased large tracts of iron-rich land on Minnesota's Mesabi Range. To carry this ore to his plant on the Monongahela River in Homestead, Carnegie bought a fleet of ships capable of plying the Great Lakes. Meanwhile, he bought railroads not only to transport his product but also to guarantee a market for its use in bridge and track construction.

Carnegie believed, correctly, that he could create at least a continental market for his steel, if not a global one. This would have been inconceivable before the Civil War, given antebellum standards of transportation, communication, and business organization. Yet the increasing sophistication of the corporate model, pioneered by Carnegie and others, made such ambitions genuinely possible.

The rise of a national marketplace created opportunities for economic expansion that, in turn, helped lift standards of living; but expansion also had a downside, because it encouraged greed and its fruits were far from equitably distributed. Giant corporations soon came to control most American industries, and often they banded together to fix prices and limit wages. Sometimes these arrangements resembled the railroad pools; in other cases, they took the form of "trusts." Whatever the type, they all served to restrain competition and further consolidate control.

The Trusts

JOHN D. ROCKEFELLER introduced the trust form of business organization in January 1882. From the time moment he built his first refinery in 1863, Rockefeller had been struggling to tame the oil industry and stabilize its wild price gyrations. His strategy was to manipulate the supply side of the supply–demand equation, so he used his company, Standard Oil of Ohio, to buy up as many refineries as he could. By 1880, he owned 90 percent of the nation's oil-refining capacity. But control of the remaining 10 percent of refineries eluded him until Standard Oil lawyer Samuel C. T. Dodd came up a with an innovative legal strategy. Dodd advised Rockefeller to form a trust, which the law defined as a property interest held by one person for the benefit of another. Previously, the statutes regulating trusts had been applied only to relationships among individuals, but Dodd saw no reason why they couldn't be applied to corporations as well. (Four years later, in the *Santa Clara County v. Southern Pacific Railroad* decision of 1886, the Supreme Court stated as much, ruling in this landmark case that corporations were legally "people" and entitled to the same rights and privileges as any other citizen.)

Dodd's idea was to have the owners of all the competing oil companies turn their stock over to a board of trustees—dominated, in this case, by Rockefeller—which would run the companies jointly and distribute the profits according to each participant's contribution to the whole. Given such extensive market control, profits soared. Eventually, pressured by consumer and small-producer protests,

This 1900 cartoon, entitled The Trust Giant's Point of View, *illustrates the common perception that government was subordinate to industry. It shows John D. Rockefeller holding the White House in his palm as smoke belches from an industrialized U.S. Capitol. Most Gilded Age tycoons treated politics as simply another business expense, like raw materials or labor. In 1880, for example, Rockefeller instructed his salesmen, of whom there were thousands in the Midwest alone, to work actively for the Republican ticket. With this help, Garfield was able to carry the entire region.*

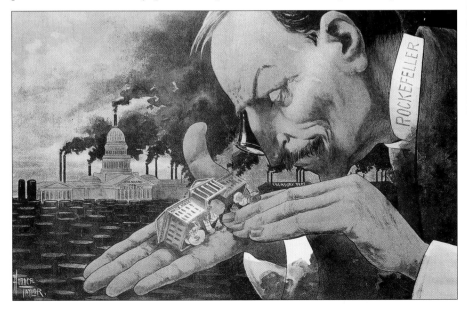

Congress acted reluctantly to limit Rockefeller's new aggregation of power, passing the Sherman Anti-Trust Act in July 1890. The Sherman Act outlawed trusts as illegal restraints of trade, yet its language was vague, its enforcement powers weak, and Benjamin Harrison's Justice Department had no intention of subjecting any "combinations" to prosecution regardless. Five years later, when Grover Cleveland's attorney general finally brought a suit under the Sherman Act, the Supreme Court gutted the law. Ruling in *U.S. v. E. C. Knight*, the Court declared that the Sherman Act couldn't be used to break the sugar trust, even though that trust controlled 98 percent of the market, because manufacturing per se was not interstate commerce. Therefore, manufacturing trusts were more properly a matter for state regulation.

Yet state governments weren't having much success regulating trusts, either. In March 1892, for example, the Ohio Supreme Court dissolved the Standard Oil trust, but Rockefeller was unfazed. He merely moved his operations to New Jersey, where he reestablished the trust as a new form of business entity: the holding company. Rockefeller chose New Jersey because in 1889 that state had enacted innovative incorporation legislation designed to attract new business to the state. A key provision permitted corporations to own stock in other corporations. A holding company, therefore, was a corporation that produced nothing but merely held enough stock in other corporations to control their policies. "The growth of a large corporation," Rockefeller wrote, "is merely a survival of the fittest, the working out of a law of nature and a law of God."

Beginning with one of his first books, Ragged Dick *(1867), Horatio Alger Jr. became America's most popular novelist of success. A Unitarian minister who specialized in stories for youngsters, Alger wrote often of newsboys and bootblacks whose inherent goodness enabled them to rise to positions of wealth and power in the world. The subtitle to this 1888 Alger work, for instance, is* How Phil Brent Won Success. *Between 1867 and his death in 1899, Alger wrote 119 books with sales in excess of twenty million copies.*

THE MAGNATES WHO CONTROLLED these trusts naturally saw themselves as deserving victors in the relentless struggle for economic survival. In this belief they were supported by a new ideology known as social Darwinism. Using English biologist Charles Darwin's theory of natural selection, the social Darwinists—most of whom were, ironically, intensely pious Christians—argued that it was only "natural" for successful companies to purchase, bankrupt, or otherwise subordinate their lesser competitors. Furthermore, it would be not only unwise but also "unnatural" for any governmental body to interfere with the free workings of the marketplace. It was believed that, in such a laissez-faire environment, inefficient producers would be quickly eliminated, leaving the national economy—to everyone's benefit—in the hands of the country's most capable businessmen.

These ideas were not altogether new, having solid roots in the eighteenth-century writings of Adam Smith, but the social Darwinists' charming scientific spin made them seem fresh and compelling. Cleverly, social Darwinists rationalized both the naked greed of the Gilded Age and the stark contrasts of wealth and poverty that postwar industrialization had created. Poverty simply had to be the result of individual shortcomings, social Darwinists such as English philosopher Herbert Spencer and American sociologist William Graham Sumner contended, because each person controlled his or her own economic destiny. Low-born tycoons such as Carnegie were proof of this.

Yet the social Darwinist vogue emerged at a time when America's giant corporations had already eliminated nearly all of the competition in the domestic marketplace. In fact, most large corporations were now actively seeking government intervention on their own behalf, such as the imposition of prohibitively high tariffs on imported manufactured goods. And few factory owners were reluctant to involve government officials (and troops) when they needed striking workers subdued.

The Homestead Strike

STRIKES WERE CERTAINLY a common feature of labor-management relations during the Gilded Age. During the 1880s alone, labor organizations staged more than twenty-four thousand strikes involving over six million workers. One reason for the abundance of strikes was the attitude of many employers. As the tycoons became wealthier and more powerful, they tended to lose touch with the concerns and problems of their employees. In the case of Andrew Carnegie, this contrast was particularly extreme because of his own rags-to-riches personal history. By the early 1890s, however, Carnegie was spending much of his time in a remote Scottish castle he had purchased and leaving the day-to-day operation of the Homestead works in the capable hands of his chief lieutenant, Henry Clay Frick. Carnegie was in Scotland, for example, when the trouble at Homestead began during the early summer of 1892.

In 1889, members of the powerful Amalgamated Association of Iron and Steel Workers (an AFL affiliate) had struck the Homestead plant, winning for themselves a three-year contract and a major pay increase. In the spring of 1892, however, just before that contract was due to expire, a still-angry Carnegie decided to break the union. On June 25, after Carnegie had left for Scotland, Frick announced that the company would not be renewing its Amalgamated contract and would instead negotiate with workers only on an individual basis. Meanwhile, knowing that the union would insist on collective bargaining, Frick prepared for a strike, erecting a twelve-foot-high fence around the Homestead works and topping it off with some sharp barbed wire. On July 2, he shut down the plant, locking out the thirty-eight hundred workers and announcing that he would be reopening later with nonunion

"The problem of our age is the proper administration of wealth, that the ties of brotherhood may still bind together the rich and poor in harmonious relationship."
—
Andrew Carnegie, "The Gospel of Wealth" (1889)

The Carnegie Steel works in Homestead, Pennsylvania, about 1905.

This woodcut from Harper's Weekly *shows the barges of the Pinkerton men burning in the Monongahela River. Factory owners often used such "detectives" and armed guards to impede (or halt entirely) the organizing of their workers.*

(scab) labor. At the same time, Frick hired three hundred armed guards from the Pinkerton Detective Agency (which specialized more in strikebreaking than investigating) to protect the plant and its new nonunion workforce.

Arriving by barge during the predawn hours of July 6, the Pinkertons were met on the banks of the Monongahela by ten thousand strikers and their families, many of whom were armed. A battle ensued, lasting most of the day. Three Pinkertons were killed, along with nine strikers; many more on both sides were injured. Finally, the Pinkertons surrendered, but the war wasn't over. At Frick's request, the governor of Pennsylvania sent in the state militia. More than 150 union members were arrested and charged with murder, though in the end none were convicted. In the meantime, the Amalgamated's strike fund sustained the workers, but it eventually ran out in late November, when most Homestead workers had no choice but to return to work—for longer hours, less pay, and with no union.

LESS THAN TWO YEARS LATER—on June 12, 1894—Eugene V. Debs opened the American Railway Union's first national convention in Chicago. The strike at the Pullman works was, of course, an important topic of discussion. On June 15, a delegation of ARU officials was sent to call on Pullman vice president Thomas Wickes, but Wickes refused to negotiate. A week later, the ARU informed Wickes that unless his company responded to worker complaints immediately, union members would stop handling trains carrying Pullman cars as of June 26. Meanwhile, on June 25, Wickes attended a meeting of the General Managers' Association (GMA), a consortium of the two dozen railroads that terminated in Chicago. Recognizing that the Pullman situation might enable them to break the ARU, the members of the GMA offered their earnest support to Wickes and began holding daily meetings to coordinate their plans.

On June 26, with no concessions forthcoming, Debs ordered his union members to begin sidetracking all trains with Pullman cars attached. At nine o'clock that evening, George Pullman arrived at Chicago's Twelfth Street Station to observe the departure of the Diamond Special for St. Louis and see for himself the extent of the boycott. That train left on time, but a short distance down the track some switchmen refused to let it pass because it had Pullman cars attached. After this incident, the boycott spread rapidly, even though the General Managers' Association announced that its member companies would fire and blacklist any worker who took part. Within days, more than 250,000 railroad workers had joined the labor action—enough to shut down a good deal of the nation's rail traffic and nearly all of the trains passing into or out of Chicago. It seemed to many observers as though the ARU would soon prevail; then Attorney General Richard Olney became involved.

A former railroad lawyer, Olney sided strongly with management. At the railroads' request, he applied for a federal court order enjoining the boycott on the grounds that it was disrupting delivery of the U.S. mail. (This was indeed true, but only because the railroads were intentionally attaching Pullman cars to the mail trains.) The landmark injunction was issued on July 2, and a day later President Cleveland, at Olney's request, ordered federal troops into Chicago to enforce its provisions.

Until this point, there had been minimal violence, but the arrival of the federal troops shortly after midnight on July 4 triggered several days of rioting. First, cars of the Rock Island line were attacked when officials of that railroad attempted to use federal troops to get their trains running again; the next day, forty-eight Illinois Central cars were set on fire; on July 6, strikers burned the Panhandle yards in South Chicago. On July 7, during a skirmish at the Forty-ninth Street and Loomis railroad crossing, state militiamen killed four strikers; that same day, police arrested Debs and everyone else of note at ARU headquarters for violating the federal court order.

> ## "More!"
> —
> *Samuel L. Gompers, when asked at a congressional hearing what the unions wanted*

EUGENE V. DEBS
1855–1926

EUGENE VICTOR DEBS was born and raised in Terre Haute, Indiana, where his grocer father, an Alsatian immigrant, taught him to appreciate not only fine books but also the dignity of human labor. He left school in his teens to help his struggling family and found work scraping paint off railroad cars. Later, he became a locomotive fireman, whose job it was to man the boiler and maintain an adequate supply of steam. Concerned for his safety, Debs's parents persuaded him to leave the railroad in 1874 for a clerking position at a wholesale grocery firm. Yet Debs continued to support railroad workers in their efforts to obtain better pay and working conditions. In February 1875, he was elected secretary of the local lodge of the Brotherhood of Locomotive Firemen; by 1880, he was running the national organization and helping it recover from setbacks caused by the recent depression (in part by donating a year's salary to the union fund). In 1885, with strong support from Terre Haute's working-class neighborhoods, Debs won election to the state assembly. He seemed at age twenty-nine to be embarking on a promising political career, but his disgust with the corruption of the political system led him to quit the legislature after a single term.

The idea of the American Railway Union grew out of Debs's desire to unite all railroad workers under a single banner. He recognized that the present system, under which skilled workers were divided among specialized trade unions while unskilled workers were left out in the cold, promoted rivalry rather than solidarity. To remedy this, he presented the idea of a single large union embracing all railroad workers to the Brotherhood of Locomotive Firemen's national convention in 1892. A year later, he founded the ARU and became its first president.

Striking railroad workers at Blue Island listen to a reading of the injunction obtained on July 2 by Attorney General Olney.

RIGHT: *The reluctance of AFL president Samuel L. Gompers (shown here in 1897) to become involved in the Pullman strike demonstrated dramatically the conservatism of the craft unions that he represented. Spurning the sort of industry-wide organizing that Debs had pioneered, the AFL focused its efforts increasingly on a single goal: improving the economic status of America's skilled workforce.*

In addition to prohibiting any interference with the trains, the order obtained by Olney enjoined Debs and the other ARU leaders from persuading more workers to join the boycott and from coordinating strike activities in any way. With the federal government as well as the General Managers' Association now besetting the union, the pressure became simply too great. With Debs and the rest of the ARU leadership temporarily in jail and more federal troops arriving each day, the boycott collapsed, the rioting ended, and by July 12 most of the nation's trains were again running on schedule.

In Re Debs

ALSO ON JULY 12, AFL president Samuel L. Gompers traveled to Chicago with two dozen union leaders to review the situation and adopt a course of action. Some of the men with Gompers wanted to back Debs's call for a nationwide general strike, but the majority of them preached caution. That evening, Debs, out on ten thousand dollars' bail, met with Gompers and the others to request that the AFL act as an intermediary between the ARU and the General Managers' Association so that the ARU members might end their strike and return peacefully to their jobs. With the strike already lost, however, the increasingly conservative Gompers refused to act as a go-between, proposing only to send an AFL official along with any ARU delegation that Debs sent to the GMA. Well aware that the railroad executives would never agree to meet with ARU representatives under any circumstances, Debs declined the meager offer.

Five days later, Debs and his ARU colleagues were again arrested for continuing violation of the July 2 injunction. (They were apparently still sending telegrams to ARU locals in the western states, which the court considered an unlawful restraint of interstate commerce.) Refusing this time to post bail, Debs remained in jail until his December 1894 trial, at the end of which he was found guilty of contempt of court and sent to prison for six months. His appeal, handled by a defense team that included thirty-seven-year-old Clarence Darrow, reached the Supreme Court in March 1895. In his brief, Darrow contested the trial judge's remarkable assertion that a union such as ARU could be enjoined from striking under the Sherman Anti-Trust Act because unions were combinations and strikes conspiracies in restraint of trade. Unpersuaded, the Court upheld Debs's conviction. Thus, along with *U.S. v. E. C. Knight* (handed down two months earlier), *In Re Debs* declared the Court's (and the government's) clear preference for capital over labor.

The failure of the Pullman strike was now complete: The federal government had acted for the first time in U.S. history to break a strike, and the Supreme Court had upheld its right to do so. On August 2, 1894, the Pullman Palace Car Company reopened for business without having made a single concession to its understandably cowed workforce. Union leaders were blacklisted as the General Managers' Association had promised, and those workers allowed to return to their jobs were forced to sign "yellow dog" contracts prohibiting them from joining any union as long as they remained Pullman employees.

KING DEBS.

Harper's Weekly *published* this caricature of "King Debs" on the cover of its *July 14, 1894,* issue. By that time, there were more than twelve thousand federal troops in Chicago—or about half of the entire U.S. Army.

MEANWHILE, DEBS BECAME a hero to working people everywhere for his courageous resistance to management domination. When he emerged from the McHenry County (Ill.) Jail in November 1895, having completed his sentence, he was met at the local train station by representatives of more than fifty unions, all waiting to accompany him the short distance back to Chicago, where more than a hundred thousand people cheered his return.

While in jail, Debs had pondered his personal situation and reached two conclusions: The first was that trade unions couldn't possibly overcome the entrenched power of the capitalist tycoons as long as the federal government remained on their side; the second was that democratic socialism was the only answer for him.

John Fiske

1842–1901

by David Levering Lewis

URING THE THREE DECADES of national consolidation that followed the end of Reconstruction in the late 1870s, John Fiske bestrode the American intellectual landscape—exhorting, evangelizing, and educating like a one-man university. Possessing a stentorian voice empowered by three hundred pounds of girth, Fiske was "perhaps the most popular lecturer on history America has ever known," according to the entry "Fiske, John" in the 1930 edition of the *Dictionary of American Biography*. From 1879 until his death in 1901— a period aptly called by some intellectual historians "the search for order"—Fiske captivated audiences of genteel Americans from Maine to California, as well as south of the Mason-Dixon Line, with his unique blend of social Darwinism, therapeutic Christianity, and Anglo-Saxon triumphalism. Long before the phrase *American exceptionalism* entered the historical lexicon, Fiske thoroughly articulated his own infectious creed of national uniqueness in such popular writings as the March 1885 *Harper's Weekly* article "Manifest Destiny" and *The Beginnings of New England* (1889).

During an 1873 trip to England, Fiske met with Herbert Spencer, Charles Darwin, Thomas Huxley, and other scientific luminaries, whose friendship helped establish Fiske's own standing as an impressive thinker on both Atlantic shores. Indeed, before returning to the United States in 1874, the thirty-two-year-old Harvard Law School graduate completed his *Outline of Cosmic Philosophy* (1874), a spectacular two-volume interpretation of Spencerian evolutionism. By 1879, the year that he resigned as Harvard College's assistant librarian, Fiske had become Spencer's North American representative and the principal avatar of the social Darwinist ethos

that was currently sweeping the Northeast. As historian Richard Hofstadter has observed, Fiske led the "movement to make evolution respectable."

Unlike Yale sociologist William Graham Sumner, who invoked inexorable Spencerian laws-of the-fittest to defend laissez-faire economics and justify the oppression of striking workers at Andrew Carnegie's Homestead steel works, Fiske put forth a kinder, gentler social Darwinism inflected with Christian meliorism. "He who has mastered the Darwinian theory," Fiske wrote, "[has grasped that] the whole of creation has been groaning and travailing together in order to bring forth…God's handiwork, the Human Soul."

This human soul, Fiske predicted, would find its completeness not in a parliamentary democracy of the British variety but within America's federal system, because the American people had been "equipped as no other nation has ever been" by God to achieve "a millennium of freedom and peace." Such spiritual assertions provoked a fierce theological reaction (enough to compel Harvard University president Charles Eliot to withhold Fiske's appointment to a professorship), yet Fiske's advocacy of Spencerian evolution never countenanced atheism or agnosticism. Indeed, its enormous popularity derived from precisely the opposite: Fiske's ability to persuade lecture halls filled with Rotarians that religion and science were fully compatible and that one need not sacrifice faith for knowledge.

As the decade of the 1890s wound down, however, Fiske's profoundly optimistic belief in the peaceful, inevitable spread of Anglo-Saxon civilization faltered. He had spent twenty years trumpeting manifest destiny yet found himself morally disconcerted in 1898 when the United

States wrenched an empire from Spain by force of arms. At the same time, new and more massive waves of foreign immigration posed another challenge to his *weltanschauung*. In Emma Lazarus's "huddled masses yearning to breathe free," Fiske saw nothing less than the extinction of his cherished white Anglo-Saxon Protestant America.

Following his acceptance of the presidency of the Immigration Restriction League in 1894, Fiske acquired honorary degrees from Harvard and the University of Pennsylvania before receiving the crowning accolade of his career as a tribune of Anglo-American supremacy: a royal invitation to address the millennial celebration honoring King Alfred the Great at Winchester. Unfortunately, writing deadlines and the constant lecturing required to keep his large family in the considerable comfort it enjoyed fatally taxed his enormous frame. Fiske died on July 4, 1901, one month prior to the great occasion, as the United States celebrated its 125th birthday.

In one of his most important works, The Critical Period of American History, 1783–1789 *(1888), John Fiske (shown here in 1878) applied his faith in humanity's inevitable progress through evolutionary change to the history of the United States, in which he saw the embodiment of the latest "segment" in that advancement.*

15

THE CRISIS OF THE 1890s

The 1896 Election

DURING THE SECOND WEEK of July 1896, so many arguments raged in the lobbies and corridors of Chicago's Palmer House hotel that the bellhops stopped looking up. Day and night, longhaired southerners and flat-voiced midwesterners disputed loudly the opinions of well-dressed easterners as reinforcements rushed to join the verbal melees on both sides. Only when the interchanges seemed likely to precipitate fistfights did the hotel management intercede to suggest that the gentlemen take their discussions elsewhere.

The argument was nearly always the same— at its most basic, a dull, technical question of economics. The federal government currently backed its currency with gold; that is, Americans holding paper dollars could take them, if so inclined, to the Treasury and receive gold bullion in return. Democrats from the South and the Middle West, however, preferred bimetallism; that is, they wanted the government to issue additional currency backed by silver. Such an enormous expansion of the money supply, eastern Democrats retorted, would lead to rapid inflation and a devaluation of the dollar. Yes, said the prosilver southerners and midwesterners, inflation was exactly the point. Because most silverites were farmers with large mortgages, they wanted inflation, because "cheaper" money would make their debts easier to pay off. The easterners, who tended to represent banking interests, naturally wanted to keep the dollar's value high.

AT LEFT: *Illinois governor John P. Altgeld told his friend Clarence Darrow in early 1896 that Bryan (shown here in a September 1896 Judge cover) was too superficial a thinker to become the Democratic candidate for president.*

Resembling in their exuberance their Jacksonian forebears, the prosilver delegates were by far the most boisterous faction at the 1896 Democratic national convention in Chicago, having only recently taken control of the party from its astonished former owners. Organizing themselves in schoolhouse meetings and at county conventions, the farmers and their allies had captured state after state in the South and Midwest; now they had come to Chicago with a clear majority of delegates and an equally clear purpose in mind. Filling the downtown streets and sidewalks, they marched and shouted and sang along with the numerous bands hired by various presidential contenders to drum up support. Their spirits were high.

Yet they lacked a strong presidential candidate. The most prominent figure in their movement, Illinois governor John Peter Altgeld, had become a hero to American workers when he opposed Pres. Grover Cleveland's use of federal troops during the 1894 Pullman strike. But Altgeld was German born, which meant that he was disqualified from ever serving as president. With Altgeld out of the running, the shrewder silverites worried whether divisions within their ranks might lead to a deadlock. Because convention rules required a two-thirds majority for nomination, it wouldn't take much dissension among the silverites for the outnumbered "goldbugs" to force a compromise candidate on the divided bimetallists.

The silver men feared one goldbug in particular: former navy secretary William C. Whitney, who was considered in ability and intelligence Altgeld's only equal in Chicago.

Both men were country boys turned big-city lawyers; but unlike Altgeld, who had moved to Chicago for a career in reform politics, Whitney had chosen New York City for its financial opportunities. Indeed, working for the Vanderbilts and other railroad magnates, Whitney had amassed a considerable personal fortune (amounting to some forty million dollars) and only then turned his attention to politics. Making use of the same brilliance and ruthlessness he had shown in business, Whitney masterminded the presidential campaigns of Grover Cleveland in 1884, 1888, and 1892, winning two of them and simultaneously gaining for himself the reputation of being the most effective organizer in American politics.

Whitney rolled into Chicago aboard a "gold train" he had commissioned to carry elite eastern Democrats to the convention. Along with choice foods and wines, the New York Central special was stocked with powerful cabinet officers, senators, and state party leaders. At previous conventions, these men had controlled the platform and chosen the nominee. It was no coincidence that seven of the party's last eight presidential candidates had been New Yorkers (the other being a Pennsylvanian). Yet now the power brokers journeyed nervously, not quite sure whether the fifty-four-year-old Whitney would once again be able to work his magic and save them from humiliation.

Elected by a farmer-labor coalition in 1892, Governor Altgeld pardoned the three Haymarket anarchists still imprisoned in 1893 and later opposed President Cleveland's use of federal troops to break the

THE EVENTUAL OUTCOME of Whitney's efforts remained anyone's guess as the convention opened on July 7. Fifteen thousand people jammed Chicago's Coliseum, the world's largest permanent exhibition hall. Among those in attendance was William Jennings Bryan, a thirty-six-year-old former congressman from Nebraska who owed his allegiance to no one and had his own ideas about whom the party should nominate. On the second night of the convention, before returning to his modest two-dollar-a-day digs at the Clifton House, Bryan confided to his wife and a friend: "So that you both may sleep well tonight, I am going to tell you something. I am the only man who can be nominated. I am what they call the logic of the situation."

William C. Whitney as navy secretary during the late 1880s.

The next day, July 9, the prosilver delegates cheered wildly as Bryan, already famous for his oratory but hardly considered a serious candidate, took the stage at the close of the platform debate. Acknowledging that the gold men had thus far made the more persuasive arguments, the Nebraskan began his speech with a bit of coquettish modesty: "I would be presumptuous, indeed, to present myself against the distinguished gentlemen to whom you have listened if this were a mere measuring of abilities; but this is not a contest between persons. The humblest citizen in all the land, when clad in the armor of a righteous cause, is stronger than all the hosts of error." After this preamble, he reviewed the numerous recent successes of the silver movement, directly challenging the claims made by "those who live upon the Atlantic Coast" that bimetallism would "disturb" the country's business interests. Only then did the insurgence come. "We have petitioned, and our petitions have been scorned," Bryan exclaimed in a rising voice; "we have entreated, and our entreaties have been disregarded; we have begged, and they have mocked when our calamity [the panic of 1893] came. We beg no longer; we entreat no more. We defy them!"

With cheers interrupting him constantly, Bryan thereafter commanded the hall, shaking its rafters as he poured more and more scorn onto the rhetoric of the goldbugs. Finally, as Bryan's speech neared its conclusion and the enthusiasm of the audience reached its peak, the convention took on the feel and emotion of a revival meeting, making Bryan's closing imagery all the more appropriate. "We will answer their demand for a gold standard by saying to them: You shall not press down upon the brow of labor this crown of thorns, you shall not crucify mankind upon a cross of gold!" For the next five seconds, after delivering one of the most famous perorations in American history, Bryan stood silently on the platform, his arms outstretched in the suggestion of a crucifix. Even those delegates most hostile to his ideas were forced later to admit the uncanny skill with which Bryan had transformed the convention, even briefly, into a coronation.

The hall went mad. Usually reserved judges and legislators screamed and danced in the aisles; other admirers carried the Boy Orator of the Platte from the hall on their shoulders as scores of delegates rushed up to him to pledge their support. Bryan's subsequent nomination on a prosilver platform delighted the party's rank and file—though not, for different reasons, its twin kingmakers. Speaking for many of his eastern colleagues, Whitney announced before leaving Chicago that he would not support the ticket financially nor vote for it. Altgeld was pleased, of course, that silver had triumphed, but he also doubted Bryan's suitability. "It takes more than speeches to win victories," the Illinois governor told a friend as the convention dispersed. "I have been thinking over Bryan's speech. What did he say, anyhow?"

This photograph of the interior of the cavernous Chicago Coliseum dates to June 1908, when the Republican party held its national convention there.

A ticket to the 1896 Democratic convention with its stub still attached.

377

Settling the West

ONE THING BRYAN HAD CERTAINLY made clear was his compassion for the plight of America's farmers, who had suffered profoundly since the Civil War from depression and deflation as well as the national trends toward urbanization and industrialization. "You [eastern Democrats] come to us and tell us that the great cities are in favor of the gold standard," Bryan had declared on July 9; "we reply that the great cities rest upon our broad and fertile prairies. Burn down your cities and leave our farms, and your cities will spring up again as if by magic; but destroy our farms and the grass will grow in the streets of every city in the country."

Economic discrimination made up the core of the farmers' discontent, yet its roots ran far deeper. Once described by Thomas Jefferson (in resonant puritanical terms) as the nation's "elect," American farmers had been universally considered the backbone of the country for as long as anyone could remember. Indeed, until the 1870s, more than half of all Americans made their livings from agriculture, most by tending their own small farms. Farming was at the heart of what it meant to be an American, and that perception had seemed unlikely to change.

As Jefferson himself had predicted when he made the Louisiana Purchase, the trans-Mississippi West provided more than enough land to sustain America's agrarian style of life for several generations. At first, not many settlers chose to take on the meteorologic and geologic challenges of farming the Great Plains, a region known for decades as the Great American Desert; yet after the Civil War, as so much else did, the situation changed. The Homestead Act made a great deal of land available for nothing (or next to nothing), technological improvements such as the steel plow made the hard prairie soil easier to farm, and the army began busily "pacifying" the Indians who had previously objected violently to

> "Go west, young man, and grow up with the country."
>
> —
> *Horace Greeley*

THE HOMESTEAD ACT

ALTHOUGH AMERICANS HAD BEEN moving west without assistance from the federal government since the founding of the republic, the passage of the Homestead Act in May 1862 certainly accelerated the process. Under this law, any adult citizen (or immigrant intending to become a citizen) who was also the head of a family could claim 160 acres of public land simply by paying a small registration fee. All he then had to do was live on the property for five years continuously, and the land would be his. Alternatively, homesteaders could buy their land from the government for $1.25 an acre after just six months of residency.

During the Civil War, some fifteen thousand claims were filed under the Homestead Act, and after the war even more families took to the Plains. In all, half a million Americans settled more than eighty million acres of public land under the act. Much of that land was later mortgaged, however, subjecting it to the vagaries of

speculation and the risk of foreclosure, which became all too real during the late 1880s.

Many settlers reacted to the rising price of land by seeking to acquire even more. They funded their purchases using mortgages on their existing holdings underwritten by eastern and European investors eager to profit from the land boom. The expectation, of course, was that the good times would last forever. Well into the 1880s, easy credit and bumper crops put money in almost everyone's pockets, encouraging farmers to go even farther into debt. They borrowed to buy not only more land but also more machinery to farm their larger and larger spreads. On paper, at least, the high land prices made them seem wealthy. In the late 1880s, however, the land bubble burst.

AT RIGHT: *Because of the lack of timber* on the *Plains, settlers had to make do with sod houses (such as this one) and use buffalo or cow chips for fuel.*

white settlement. The railroads, to which so much land was being granted, were another important factor encouraging migration to the Plains. Marketing land soon became as crucial a function of the railroad business as track construction—not merely so that the acreage could be turned into cash, but more importantly to develop new sources of freight and passenger revenue. In cahoots with western newspapers, the railroads conducted publicity campaigns specifically designed to lure easterners to the Plains. The flow of settlers increased accordingly; so did the amount of western land speculation.

THERE WERE TWO PRIMARY CAUSES of this devastating reversal: One was a sudden act of nature; the other, a steady economic process. In 1886 and 1887, the Plains weather, already troublesome in the best of years, turned particularly severe. Dry, blistering summers followed frigid, miserable winters. A prolonged drought hit the grain farmers hard, while harsh winter weather thinned out many a cattle herd. Thousands of settlers, driven by their losses to the brink of bankruptcy, tried to recoup their capital by selling off some of their valuable land. As more and more land went on the market, however, it became less valuable. Soon enough, with the passive investors now looking to get out, the market turned, and the bottom fell out of it.

Many settlers went under, and those who did survive faced difficult economic circumstances even after the rains returned and their crops once again grew high. Increases in farm yields—made possible by mechanization and the development of chemical fertilizers—so lowered crop prices that farming became hardly profitable. In a frantic attempt to remain afloat, many farmers responded by planting even more land, leading to still further drops in farm prices. For

CATTLE

SEVERAL FACTORS COMBINED during the late 1860s to create a major new beef industry in Texas and later on the Great Plains. One was the confinement of the Indians; another was the depletion of the buffalo herds that had previously consumed so much of the forage; a third was the arrival of the railroads, which provided an effective new method for shipping cattle to hungry eastern markets.

The first American cowboys were the Mexican vaqueros who tended the herds of Spanish cattle in Texas. By the 1850s, the Spanish were gone, but millions of longhorns, the descendants of those cattle, still roamed the grasslands of southern and western Texas. Before the Civil War, when there wasn't much of a market for southwestern beef, cattle sold locally for three to five dollars a head. After 1865, however, ranchers learned that they could get perhaps ten times that at the Missouri Pacific railhead in Sedalia. Thus began the era of the "long drive"—the first one taking place during the spring of 1866, when a group of Texans drove 260,000 longhorns up the country to Missouri. The next year, another band of cowboys led by scout Jesse Chisolm headed farther west to the new railhead at Abilene, Kansas. (The route they took became the much-traveled Chisolm Trail.) To manage all the arriving cattle (and to attract more business), entrepreneurs used railroad and meatpacking money to build large stockyards at the railheads, as well as hotels, barns, stables, and loading chutes. Besides Abilene, other Kansas "cow towns" developed in this manner included Ellsworth, Dodge City, and Wichita.

By 1885, an estimated seven million cattle had been driven from Texas to one of the various Kansas railheads. Most of these animals ended up in either Chicago or Kansas City, both towns becoming centers of the nation's meatpacking industry. From there, the beef traveled on in refrigerated railroad cars to markets in the populous cities of the East, where demand for the newly affordable beef kept growing. Developed in 1877 by Chicago meatpacker Gustavus Swift, the improved refrigerator cars used fresh air passing over ice to keep the perishable meat from spoiling.

From the vaquero came the distinctive equipment of the American cowboy, including his chaps, pommeled saddle, and la reata *(lariat).*

example, the same bushel of wheat that sold for $1.19 in 1881 brought only 49¢ in 1894. It seemed that the Plains farmer, whose success with indifferent soil had astounded the world, was now being destroyed by his own achievement. Prices for corn fell so low that some farmers burned their harvests to heat their homes rather than selling them off as food. Many simply gave up and returned east carrying signs that read, for example, "IN GOD WE TRUSTED, IN KANSAS WE

BUSTED."Although many of these farmers failed to make the connection before the early 1890s, the falling crop prices were part of a national deflation that began after the Civil War when Congress passed a number of measures to stabilize the currency. In particular, congressional decisions to stop coining silver and to redeem Civil War–era "greenbacks" at par (face value) decreased the U.S. money supply substantially, thus increasing the value of each dollar that remained in circulation. (The price of wheat, for example, had been falling since 1868, when it was $2.50 a bushel.) To make matters even worse, farmers who had borrowed cheap 1860s dollars to buy their land now had to pay creditors off with much more expensive 1890s dollars.

The farmers who had worked so hard to establish themselves naturally felt cheated; and, like true Jeffersonians, they found their villains in the cities, especially among the owners of the railroads. Because most rural areas were serviced by just one line, the prices being charged by that carrier to transport crops to market were usually outrageous. And even when a farmer lived within traveling distance of two lines, collusion between the railroads usually left him with Hobson's choice. Farmers also denounced the combinations of agricultural machinery companies that had formed to keep equipment prices high. These sorts of arrangements had been outlawed by the Interstate Commerce Act of 1887, yet few governmental authorities seemed likely to intervene. Most were too deeply in the pockets of the railroad interests. So the farmers decided to help themselves.

CURRENCY

THE FAVORITISM THAT THE GOVERNMENT showed eastern financial interests during the 1870s can been seen quite clearly in its monetary policies. To help pay for the Civil War, Congress had passed the Legal Tender Act of 1862, which permitted the federal government to meet its credit needs by printing paper money not backed by gold or silver. In all, the Treasury printed some $450 million worth of "greenbacks," as these unredeemable notes were called.

After the war, the issue of what to do with these notes, whose value fluctuated, became a hot political topic. Western farmers and other debtor constituencies wanted even more greenbacks issued so that they could pay off their loans cheaply; creditors and other "sound money" advocates wanted greenbacks withdrawn from circulation. In the end, the creditor lobby got the next best thing: In January 1875, Congress passed the Specie Resumption Act, which required the Treasury to redeem greenbacks in gold as of January 1, 1879. This and other sound-money policies endorsed by the Republicans produced so much monetary confidence that when the redemption date arrived, few Americans bothered to turn in their greenbacks, which simply remained part of the circulating currency.

Following passage of the Specie Resumption Act, debtors opposed to hard money organized the Greenback party to push for its repeal and the printing of more unredeemable paper money. In 1876, the Greenbackers ran inventor and philanthropist Peter Cooper for president. He fared poorly. The great strikes of 1877, however, substan-*This* tially increased union interest in the Greenback party and led to its reorganization in 1878 as the Greenback Labor party. The new alliance had little effect on government policy, but it did improve marginally the party's electoral performance, laying some of the groundwork for the Populist party to come.

The Grange and the Farmers' Alliances

AS EARLY AS THE 1860S, American farmers began organizing themselves through a cooperative movement known as the Grange. During a tour of the South immediately after the Civil War, Oliver H. Kelley, then a minor official with the U.S. Bureau of Agriculture, had found himself struck by the bleakness and isolation of rural life. After leaving the government in 1867, Kelley and six former Agriculture Bureau colleagues formed the National Grange of the Patrons of Husbandry, which began as little more than a support organization for farm families. Kelley's group sponsored lectures on new agricultural techniques, but more importantly it created a network of local organizations that promoted a sense of community among farmers. Only later did the panic of 1873 transform the Grange from a social organization into an instrument of political change.

After 1873, membership in the Grange grew rapidly in the agricultural heartlands of the South and Midwest until, by 1875, it numbered eight hundred thousand in twenty thousand local lodges. By this time, the organization had grown large enough to sponsor its own marketing cooperatives, which allowed farmers to wholesale their crops directly, cutting out the hated middlemen. From those cooperatives, it wasn't much of a leap for the Grange to establish its own grain elevators, warehouses, creameries, equipment factories, and even insurance companies. At the same time, the Grange became politically active, taking control of several midwestern state legislatures and passing Granger Laws regulating the rates being charged by railroads; not surprisingly, the railroads sued in federal court.

Initially, the Supreme Court upheld the Granger Laws. Specifically, in *Munn v. Illinois* (1877), it ruled that the state of Illinois had the right to regulate Chicago's grain storage industry. However, as the Court's composition changed over the next decade, so did its opinion of the Granger Laws. Beginning with its decision in *Wabash, St. Louis, and Pacific Railway Co. v. Illinois* (1886), the Court began to whittle away at *Munn*, holding that an Illinois law controlling railroad freight rates was an unconstitutional usurpation of Congress's power to regulate interstate commerce. Four years later, in *Chicago, Milwaukee, and St. Paul Railroad v. Minnesota* (1890), the Court went even farther in reversing *Munn*, ruling that states could not set fees that deprived railroads of a "reasonable profit" because doing so would deprive the railroads of their due-process rights as "people" (according to the 1886 *Santa Clara* case) under the Fourteenth Amendment.

While working as a traveling salesman out of St. Louis, Aaron Montgomery Ward learned firsthand of the troubles that rural consumers had obtaining goods. Inspired by their complaints, he founded the nation's first mail-order business. Ward focused his marketing efforts on the Grangers and in August 1872 sent his first single-sheet "catalog" to a mailing list of Grange members.

YET THE OUTCOMES OF THE GRANGER CASES had little effect on the Granger movement, because by 1880 it was already moribund. A combination of political naïveté and rising crop prices had stripped the Grange of its momentum, leading to a rapid decline. At the same time, however, many former Grangers became actively involved in the regional Farmers' Alliances. Like the Grange, the Alliances had initially been formed to solve local problems and only later developed into powerful political organizations. The first and most important was the Southern Farmers' Alliance. Founded in 1877, it grew by 1890 to include more than four million members. The Northwestern Farmers' Alliance, composed overwhelmingly of farmers from states west of the Mississippi, shared many of the goals of the Southern Alliance yet never matched its size. There was also a Colored Farmers' Alliance active in the South, which enrolled a million and a quarter members during the 1880s. While the strength of the Grange had been concentrated in the more prosperous midwestern states of Illinois, Minnesota, Iowa, and Wisconsin, the appeal of the Farmers' Alliances was much deeper and more widespread.

As the Grange had, the Farmers' Alliances sought to benefit members by establishing useful economic institutions, such as cooperative stores and joint marketing companies, while simultaneously educating farmers about their political situation and the reasons for it. In many states, the Alliances used their voting strength to elect legislators who passed laws conducive to Alliance goals—only to find out, as the Grangers had, that state laws were usually inadequate to control the nationally powerful railroads.

Meanwhile, the Alliances' economic ventures weren't faring too well, either. The antagonism of wholesalers and middlemen was taking its toll, as was ordinary mismanagement. So the Alliances found themselves pushed and pulled into adopting a national strategy that emphasized not only their numerical strength but also their ideological fervor. Helped along by the able leadership of several remarkable personalities, the Farmers' Alliances entered national politics in 1890 on an unprecedented scale, winning majorities in one or both houses of twelve state legislatures. Eight of those states were located in the South, where Alliance members seized control of local Democratic machinery and displaced the conservative Bourbons who had previously ruled the party. More than forty southern Democratic congressmen subsequently announced their support for the Alliance's agenda, and two Southern Alliance leaders became important national political figures: one-eyed "Pitchfork Ben" Tillman, the new governor of South Carolina, and the slight but fiery Tom Watson, the new congressman from Georgia's Tenth District.

The mechanization of farming during the 1850s and 1860s dramatically increased U.S. agricultural production. As the number of hours required to cultivate an acre of land fell from sixty-one in 1830 to fewer than three by 1900, the amount of acreage in production expanded commensurately. Among the most important advances was the introduction of the Cyrus H. McCormick reaper shown here.

The Growth of Populism

ON THE PLAINS, members of the Northwestern Farmers' Alliance resolved in many cases to abandon the two major parties and run their own candidates. In a thousand sunbaked courthouse squares, Alliance orators demanded change, describing both the Democrats and the Republicans as nothing more than two sides of the same railroad coin. Lawyer and mother of five Mary Elizabeth Lease was one of the movement's most active personalities, delivering 160 speeches during the 1890 campaign. "What you farmers have to do," she reportedly told one Kansas audience, "is raise less corn and more hell!"

Although the Northwestern Alliance didn't achieve quite the success of its sister organization in the South, its emphasis on political independence proved prescient. Southern Alliance leaders weren't sure they could trust the dozens of congressmen they had helped elect in 1890. As a result, some began meeting in May 1891 with counterparts in the Northwestern Alliance (and also representatives of the declining Knights of Labor) to discuss the possibility of forming a new national farmer-labor party. The outcome of these discussions was the People's party, known more commonly as the Populist party.

Although its base remained always strongly agrarian, the new People's party generated a great deal of immediate interest among existing urban radical reform groups, many of whom quickly joined its ranks. These included, among others, Henry George's Single Taxers, who insisted that only land (and not industry) be taxed; and the Nationalists, who wanted to realize the socialist vision expressed by Edward Bellamy in his 1888 utopian romance *Looking Backward*.

In July 1892, thirteen hundred delegates representing these and other groups came together in Omaha to write a platform and nominate the first Populist candidate for president. "We meet in the midst of a nation brought to the verge of moral, political, and material ruin," the preamble to the Omaha platform warned. "Corruption dominates the ballot-box, the Legislatures, the Congress, and touches even the ermine of the bench." Therefore, profound changes were needed. For example, "the time has come," the platform declared, "when the railroad corporations will either own the people or the people must own the railroads." There were also planks backing the free coinage of silver, a graduated income tax, the prohibition of land speculation by corporations and foreign investors, and the eight-hour workday. Others opposed "the maintenance of a standing army of mercenaries, known as the Pinkerton system, as a menace to our liberties," and wanted to end the present level of immigration, "which opens our ports to the pauper and criminal classes of the world and crowds out our wage-earners."

Because the new party wanted, more than anything, to help farmers overcome the unfair handicaps imposed on them by industrial growth, it strongly supported a plan developed by the Farmers' Alliances several years earlier. Under this scheme, the federal government would establish a national system of warehouses, called "subtreasuries," which would store crops deposited by farmers when market prices were low. Farmers could take out loans worth up to 80 percent of the deposited

Mary Elizabeth Lease was one of many women who played prominent roles in the Farmers' Alliances. From the start, most local alliances made women full voting members.

RIGHT:
Tom Watson was among those who led the movement that historian John D. Hicks once called "the struggle to save agricultural America from the devouring jaws of industrial America."

crops' current market value. When prices rose to acceptable levels, farmers could sell the stored crops and repay whatever loans they had taken.

To promote this subtreasury plan and the rest of the Populist platform, the 1892 convention delegates chose James B. Weaver, a former Civil War general and congressman who had run for president once before as the 1880 Greenback Labor party nominee. Weaver's politics and high name recognition made him a reasonable standard-bearer for the new party, and, as expected, he campaigned vigorously.

The farm of John G. Painter, photographed by Solomon D. Butcher in 1892. Painter was a prominent Populist in Custer County, Nebraska.

T HAT SO MANY SOUTHERN Alliance leaders chose to give up their Democratic affiliations in 1892 reflected the rapidly deteriorating relationship between the agrarians and the national Democratic party leadership, personified by former president Grover Cleveland. Since losing the 1888 election, Cleveland had practiced law on Wall Street in partnership with J. P. Morgan's attorney. Such an association irked farmers, who also abhorred Cleveland's dogged support for "sound" gold-backed money (which Cleveland defended even more resolutely than did his Republican rival, Pres. Benjamin Harrison). When Cleveland was nominated again for president in late June 1892, the leaders of the Southern Alliance faced a decision: Some, led by Ben Tillman, put aside their personal distaste for Cleveland and remained within the Democratic party; others joined Tom Watson in bolting the Democrats and nominating a full slate of Populist candidates to oppose them.

SOUTHERN AGRICULTURE

ALTHOUGH SOUTHERN FARMERS SHARED the economic misery of the Plains homesteaders, the circumstances of their suffering were somewhat different. With the collapse of the plantation system at the end of the Civil War, millions of acres of farmland became available for purchase. Yet few among the region's land-hungry whites and freed slaves had the capital to buy any of this land outright; nor was credit made available to them by the foreign investors who were busily funding the land boom in Kansas and Nebraska.

Instead, poor farmers in the South became sharecroppers, farming someone else's land and turning over to the landlord a share of the resulting crop. As a general rule, sharecroppers kept for themselves no more than half of the harvest—and often much less. Meanwhile, to support themselves during the growing season, they ran up large tabs with local storekeepers, which were secured with further liens against

their fall crops. (Often, landowner and storekeeper were the very same person.) Because harvests rarely provided enough to wipe out a farmer's standing debt, his obligations to landowner and storekeeper kept him tied to a particular patch of land. For poor black farmers, and for many whites as well, the system wasn't much better than indentured servitude or slavery.

Also harmful was the insistence of many southern landowners that their tenant farmers grow cotton, the crop most easily turned into cash. Having to raise cotton exclusively made it hard for sharecroppers to feed their families and also took a heavy toll on the region's soil, which now required large doses of chemical supplements to sustain its fertility. To make matters worse, the nationwide post–Civil War farm-price collapse hit cotton hard, dropping its price per ton from a high of $16.57 in 1871 to just $7.32 in 1878.

Pitchfork Ben Tillman in 1905, by which time he had become an influential U.S. senator.

The situation in the South was further complicated, as always, by the issue of race. The southern Democrats were, above all, "the white man's party," yet the Southern Farmers' Alliance had always been deeply involved with the efforts of the Colored Farmers' Alliance to organize blacks. Because nearly all southern blacks at this time voted solidly Republican, the relationship between the white and black agrarians seemed at first to have little political significance. Then the 1892 Democratic split raised the possibility of a Populist-black-Republican coalition that prompted Tillman's faction to accuse Watson's group of turning traitor to the white race.

Ignoring this charge, at least for the time being, the Populists openly appealed for the votes of African Americans, declaring racism to be just one more tool used by the wealthy to oppress the laboring masses. This sort of talk provoked even more ferocious attacks on the southern Populists; when Weaver campaigned in the South, Democratic vigilante groups often broke up his rallies. (In Georgia, demonstrators made "a walking omelette" out of the Populist nominee, according to the always-evocative Mary Lease.) Some Populist candidates were shot at; others, threatened with economic reprisals. Meanwhile, Democrats terrorized many blacks into staying home on Election Day or forced them to the polls at gunpoint to vote for Democratic candidates. Bravely, many Populists did what they could; in one instance, Tom Watson arranged for dozens of white party members to protect the home of a black leader who had been threatened. But their efforts could never hope to match those of the forces arrayed against them.

WITHOUT THE RACE ISSUE to divert them, Populists on the Great Plains had a much easier time campaigning in 1892. Many enjoyed positive working relationships with local Democrats (Bryan among them), who largely accepted the Populist platform. Even pro-Cleveland hardliners, aware that they had little chance of carrying Kansas or Nebraska, threw their support in those states to Weaver, hoping at least to keep them out of the Republican column.

Gold and silver coinage minted in 1890.

The results were mixed. Cleveland won the election, but Weaver polled more than a million votes (8.5 percent of the popular total) and carried four states, along with parts of two others, for a total of twenty-two electoral votes. At the same time, the Populists elected three governors, five senators, ten congressmen, and nearly fifteen hundred state legislators. On the other hand, these gains came disproportionately in the depressed trans-Mississippi West, with the People's party performing not nearly as well in the South and among workers as many had hoped. One reason for this was the difficulty that all new political organizations have in overcoming existing party loyalties. Yet more significant—at least with regard to the failure to attract workers—was the party's antieastern, antiurban, occasionally anti-Semitic tone. Its call for immigration restrictions, for example, couldn't have been too popular in urban neighborhoods at a time when immigration, especially Jewish immigration, was reaching its peak. Even so, the Populist showing in 1892 startled most of the country and shocked the elite East.

The Silver Question

IN THE AFTERMATH OF THE 1892 ELECTION, some shrewd party leaders recommended that Populist efforts to attract labor voters be not merely continued but substantially increased. This was not done. Instead, the party began focusing even more narrowly on its core constituency: the nation's struggling farmers. And among these voters, thanks to the education programs of the Alliances, one issue was emerging as the sine qua non of the 1896 campaign: the remonetization of silver. For nearly all of the nation's history, silver coins had been legal tender in the United States. The government had established an official exchange rate, called the mint ratio, of sixteen to one—that is, sixteen ounces of silver to one ounce of gold—and for decades coins of both metals had been minted accordingly. During the 1860s, however, silver's market value relative to gold became so high that miners stopped selling their silver to the Treasury and instead sold it to jewelers, who were willing to pay substantially more.

When Congress passed the Coinage Act of 1873 ending the minting of silver, the government seemed to be merely formalizing a reality that had already come to pass. Almost no one objected. Yet as silver prices began to fall rapidly that same year with the mining of sizable deposits in the mountain West, farmers realized that the demonetization of silver had foreclosed a highly useful means of increasing the money supply and reversing deflation. They also suspected treachery. Attacking the Coinage Act as a conspiracy foisted on the country by railroads, grain storage companies, eastern bankers, foreign investors, and other oppressors, the growing prosilver movement demanded repeal of "the Crime of '73" and a return to the unlimited coinage of silver. Bankrolling many of these efforts were silver-mine owners eager to unload their now-depressed ore at the old mint ratio of sixteen to one.

In February 1878, to forestall an even bloodier fight over silver coinage, Congress agreed reluctantly to pass (over President Hayes's veto) the Bland-Allison Act. This law returned to silver money the status of legal tender and required the government to purchase (and coin) not less than two million dollars' but not more than four million dollars' worth of silver each month. (The treasury secretaries of the Hayes, Garfield, Arthur, Cleveland, and Harrison administrations— all "sound money" men—consistently purchased the minimum amount required.) Given that the total value of all currency in circulation in 1878 was about a billion dollars, the impact of this limited coinage of silver was not especially great, and it was more than offset in January 1879 by the resumption of specie payments, which turned even paper greenbacks into "hard" money.

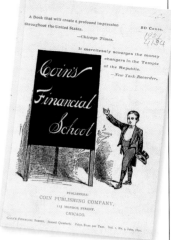

In 1894, William Hope Harvey published a pamphlet reminiscent of Common Sense in its stridency and influence (if not in its humor). Coin's Financial School used simple, accessible prose and plentiful cartoons to explain the causes of the current depression and promote the unlimited coinage of silver. The cartoon below, for example, depicts the West as a cash cow being milked by eastern financial interests.

The Bland-Allison Act remained in effect until July 1890, when it was replaced by the Sherman Silver Purchase Act. This new law, part of a deal that secured western support for higher tariffs, required the government to purchase at market prices 4.5 million ounces of silver each month—estimated to be the entire domestic output. The mine owners were pleased (although they would have been happier at sixteen to one), but the farmers felt cheated because none of the new silver was being minted. Instead, it was merely being hoarded. Meanwhile, the gold-backed notes that the Treasury issued to buy all this silver were being redeemed in gold and then immediately reissued to buy more silver. The resulting gold drain sent the government's reserves plummeting from $190 million in 1890 to just over $100 million at the time Grover Cleveland returned to the White House in March 1893. The $100 million figure was significant because, according to the relevant statute, below that amount the Treasury was no longer obligated to redeem U.S. currency in gold. Six weeks later, with the financial panic of 1893 already under way, Treasury gold reserves fell below the $100 million mark.

Missouri senator Richard P. Bland in summer 1896. As cosponsor of the 1878 Bland-Allison Act and leader of the free-silver bloc in Congress, Bland was the front-runner for the Democratic nomination in 1896 until Bryan stole it.

THE PANIC BEGAN RATHER SLOWLY with the failure in February 1893 of the chronically mismanaged Philadelphia & Reading Railroad. By the time of Cleveland's inauguration, however, the stock market had become much more nervous, and the gold situation was a prime cause of concern. There were other factors as well: six years of regional depression in the West, declines in foreign trade brought on by high tariffs, and abnormally high levels of private debt. But Cleveland focused on the gold drain, certain that the source of the government's financial woes was all the silver it was buying. To stop the hemorrhaging, the president convened a special session of Congress on August 7 so that the Sherman Act could be repealed.

The new Populist congressmen refused to go along, as did many western Democrats who had been elected with Populist support. If the overwhelmingly Democratic Fifty-third Congress had a mandate at all, they insisted, it was to

THE TARIFF

IN ADDITION TO SOUND MONEY, high tariff rates were another government policy that favored big business over other sectors of the American economy during the late nineteenth century. Although as old as the country itself, the tariff debate took on new importance with the coming of the industrial age. During the 1820s, Henry Clay had justified the duties he wanted to impose on imports as part of his American System by citing the need to protect immature U.S. industries from foreign competition. By the 1880s, however, competition from abroad was no longer a threat, yet tariff rates rose higher than ever before. Among those most hurt by the high rates were farmers, who had to sell their goods at prices set by the open world market—yet were forced to pay artificially high prices for manufactured and processed goods protected by the tariffs.

Republicans were by no means the only proponents of protectionism, but they became closely identified with high tariff rates during the presidential campaign of 1888, in which Grover Cleveland ran for reelection on a platform that championed much lower rates. When Cleveland lost that election, in part because of all the big-business money backing Benjamin Harrison, the Republicans seized the opportunity to enact the McKinley Tariff of 1890, which imposed the highest rates yet (rising from an average of 38 percent to 48 percent). As a result, foreign trade dropped precipitously—and so, therefore, did government revenues, exacerbating the gold drain. When Harrison was himself cast out of office in 1892, the resurrected Cleveland induced Congress, over strong Republican objections, to pass the August 1894 Wilson-Gorman Tariff, which reduced the average rate to 41 percent. (To make up for the lost revenue, the Wilson-Gorman Tariff also included a 2 percent tax on incomes over four thousand dollars, which the Supreme Court declared unconstitutional in May 1895.)

Even then, the back-and-forthing wasn't over. In July 1897, now-president William McKinley signed the Dingley Tariff, which raised rates back up to an average of 46 percent. For McKinley, as for most other influential Republicans, bimetallism was an insignificant issue compared to protectionism's importance to the American economy.

repeal the McKinley Tariff, not the Sherman Silver Purchase Act. Yet Cleveland kept pushing and pushing, using the mounting number of business failures and all his powers of patronage to pressure wavering representatives into voting for Sherman Act repeal. It was a testament to his remarkable determination that the president finally won this political battle on November 1. In the process, however, he badly divided his party, damaged his presidency, and failed to halt the gold drain, which continued at a brisk pace. With no reason to remain loyal to the administration and under intense pressure from their constituents, southern and western Democrats rushed to embrace "free" silver.

In February 1895, with U.S. gold reserves down to $41 million, a desperate Cleveland made a deal with J. P. Morgan, who put together a foreign syndicate to loan the Treasury $62 million in gold, or just enough to bring its reserves up over $100 million. The fix was only temporary, however, as another run brought the reserves back down to $61 million within six months of the deal. This depressed Cleveland's political stock even further because the extraordinarily high interest the Treasury was paying Morgan's syndicate made it seem as though the president had completely sold out to the bankers.

Out in the country, Americans were suffering the worst depression yet in their history. During the first six months alone, more than 8,000 businesses failed, including 150 railroads and 400 banks. As a result, unemployment reached new

In 1894, Jacob S. Coxey led a ragged "petition in boots" to Washington to demand federal assistance for the masses of unemployed. Yet Coxey's Army itself (the term was used ironically) was far less numerous, never exceeding

highs, and agricultural prices fell to new lows. In 1894, at the depression's depth, one out of every five U.S. workers was out of a job, and four out of five Americans were living at or below a subsistence level. Some were reportedly starving to death. Meanwhile, employers cut wages, and unions responded angrily with strikes.

The Nomination of McKinley

THIS WAS THE SITUATION that confronted Americans when they went to the polls for the 1894 midterm elections. As expected, the Democrats in power took a beating, losing control of both houses of Congress. Losses in the 356-member House of Representatives were particularly severe, with the Republicans nearly doubling their caucus from 127 to 244 seats. The Democratic party was in a shambles.

Not so the Populists, who became even more energized and committed to ending the suffering in the South and on the Plains, where the depression was being felt most painfully. The obvious cure, they insisted, was free silver. Disbelieving the stern warnings of bankers and industrialists that America's European trading partners would never accept currency backed by silver and that remonetization would only worsen the financial chaos, the Populist leadership saw no reason to support the gold standard when the economy's persistent deflation so obviously demanded an increase in the money supply. Inflation resulting from the unlimited coinage of silver, they believed, would not only ease the farmers' debt burden but also raise the prices being brought by their crops. Therefore, for the Populists, the issue became one of eastern greed versus southern and western sweat. "It is a struggle," explained Populist congressman "Sockless Jerry" Simpson of Kansas, "between the robbers and the robbed."

Meanwhile, the Republicans sat pretty. Their 1896 national convention, held in mid-June in St. Louis, was the dullest anyone could remember, according to one newspaper account. The hubbub that would characterize the Democratic convention three weeks later was nowhere to be found—which was exactly what Marcus Alonzo Hanna had wanted. For three years, Hanna had been working diligently to lock up the Republican nomination for his friend Ohio governor William McKinley, and he certainly didn't want any disturbances unlocking it.

After his election, McKinley (shown here with Hanna in an 1899 cartoon) named Ohio senator John Sherman as his secretary of state to create a Senate vacancy for Hanna, whose lifelong ambition it had been to serve there.

A WEALTHY INDUSTRIALIST with interests in transportation and finance, Mark Hanna exemplified the growing influence of big business in American politics. Born into money and marrying into even more, he built up a stake in coal and iron before expanding into shipping, street railways, banking, and even an opera house. Hanna's enormous financial success demonstrated his mastery of the new industrial system and also confirmed his faith in that system's durability. "There isn't going to be any revolution," he told jittery members of Cleveland's Union League Club during the 1893 panic. "You're all a lot of damned fools."

Hanna became involved in Republican politics around 1880, devoting most of his efforts to raising funds from fellow industrialists for the support of probusiness candidates. He became a particular supporter of Rep. William McKinley after the Ways and Means Committee chairman successfully boosted tariff rates in 1890. Thereafter, Hanna used his money, influence, and political expertise to build McKinley's career. First, he helped McKinley become governor of Ohio in 1892; then, even before the 1896 Republican convention began, Hanna spent a hundred thousand dollars of his own money promoting McKinley for president. As a result, the candidate and the kingmaker arrived in St. Louis with enough delegates for a first-ballot nomination.

A McKinley "goldbug" pin from the 1896 campaign.

Only the silver question proved dicey. A fair number of southern and western Republicans were leaning toward free coinage, and McKinley's own record on the issue was confused. As Bryan later demonstrated, McKinley had been a silverite from 1877 until as late as 1891. He had even written a letter in 1890 to the Stark County (Ohio) Farmers' Alliance stating, "I am in favor of the use of all the silver product of the United States for money as circulating medium. I would have silver and gold alike." Speaker of the House Thomas B. Reed, who had been McKinley's only real competition for the nomination, derided his rival's waffling: "McKinley isn't a gold-bug, McKinley isn't a silver-bug. McKinley is a straddle-bug." Yet Hanna kept the issue in check, writing into the party platform a plank endorsing bimetallism through international agreement—that is, only if England and America's other trading partners went along, a highly unlikely prospect. This plank satisfied most delegates, though a few dozen Silver Republicans walked out. The nominee wasn't concerned. As he told a friend, "Thirty days from now, you won't hear anything about silver." The friend disagreed. "Thirty days from now," he told McKinley, "you won't hear about anything else."

The Populist Convention

EVEN AFTER THE DEMOCRATS MET in Chicago, there was still one more important party convention to be held in this extraordinary election year. The Populists, who convened in St. Louis beginning July 22, faced a quandary: Should they, or should they not, endorse William Jennings Bryan for president? There were many different analyses: If the Populists joined with the Democrats, silver might sweep the nation. However, if the Populists endorsed a competing ticket, the silver vote would surely split, and Hanna's Republicans would have an easy victory. Yet most Populist leaders realized that, if they supported Bryan, they risked losing their party identity.

A Bryan lapel badge from the 1896 campaign.

The Populist delegates who marched into St. Louis bore little resemblance to the Republicans who had preceded them there. They were a ragtag group drawn from the margins of American political activity: suffering farmers, former Grangers and Greenbackers, Socialists, and even a few urban radicals and labor organizers. Not the usual free-spending convention crowd, many were simply poor. Some had walked to St. Louis, or skipped meals to get there, or both. Even their faces, which featured a wide array of beards and whiskers, seemed strange in an era when it was the fashion to be clean shaven.

The support for Bryan was largely sectional. Midwestern and western delegates, accustomed to cooperating with Democrats in local races, favored "fusion." Southern Populists, however, resisted any alliance. They remembered all too well the violence and fraud committed by southern Democrats in response to Populist efforts to organize blacks, and so the convention struggled. Because there was no "smoke-filled room" in St. Louis to help build consensus, it took time for a compromise to emerge. In the end, it was decided that the delegates would support Bryan for president; but for vice president, instead of Maine Democrat Arthur Sewall, Tom Watson would be nominated. (Unusually, the vice-presidential ballot was held first so that the southerners might be assured that the fusionists planned no betrayal.) The 1896 general election campaign was now formally under way.

WILLIAM JENNINGS BRYAN
1860–1925

BORN TO MIDDLE-CLASS PARENTS in Salem, Illinois, William Jennings Bryan attended both college and law school in his home state. In 1887, however, seeing little future for himself there, he moved his family to Lincoln, Nebraska, where a law school classmate had offered him a partnership. Although Nebraska was at the time a solidly Republican state, its demographics were changing fast; three years later, the voters of Lincoln elected Bryan, a life-long Democrat, to Congress. The transplant served two terms in the House before giving up his seat in 1894 to run for the Senate.

After his defeat in that race, Bryan had to make an important decision. His wife, Mary, wanted him to resume his legal career so that he might spend more time at home and she wouldn't have to raise the children on her own. "Mary, I admit that all you say is true," he replied, "but you have asked me the impossible. It would seem to me as if I was born for this life, and I must continue to fight the battles of the people for what I think is right and just if I have to do so single-handed and alone."

Without his congressional salary, Bryan now had to find other ways to support his family. In addition to writing editorials for the *Omaha World-Herald*, he enrolled with a number of lecture bureaus, delivering speeches for fifty- or hundred-dollar fees. Always skillful at discoursing in public, Bryan performed well, and his notoriety spread. When an ailing Rep. Richard P. Bland, cosponsor of the Bland-Allison Act, withdrew from a series of lectures on silver, Bryan was recruited as a replacement. The Brockway Lecture Bureau promised him no fewer than four bookings a week at two hundred dollars an appearance. Bryan appreciated the money, of course, but his primary interest lay in spreading the gospel of silver (along with the fame of Bryan). Often he spoke for small fees or no compensation at all, and once he even paid for the hall himself when the sponsoring group ran short of funds. By the time he took the stage at the Chicago convention in July 1896, his year of relentless touring had made him one of the most recognizable free-silver advocates in the country.

IN BRYAN, THE DEMOCRATS and the Populists had a candidate whose man-of-the-people style perfectly matched their grassroots issues. While McKinley ran a leisurely front-porch campaign from his home in Canton, Bryan embarked on an unprecedented tour of the country to promote his own candidacy. Most previous presidential candidates had spoken publicly only to express how pleased and flattered they were by all the attention. The hard stumping was left to party surrogates, because—so the parties claimed—the candidates were themselves far too modest to campaign on their own behalf. Yet during the four months between his July nomination and the November 3 election, Bryan traveled eighteen thousand miles and made six hundred speeches to some five million people. Never before had a presidential candidate toured systematically the entire country, nor had any taken the time to appear in small towns and villages. But Bryan did, and the response he received usually matched his own enthusiasm, even in the supposedly hostile East. After a triumphant tour of New England, Bryan was told by a friend that he had never seen such a reception. "You ought to come with me to Ohio, Indiana, and Kansas," the confident Nebraskan replied. "These people have given us a great reception in the East, but the West is on fire."

A McKinley banner overhangs Broadway in New York City during the 1896 campaign. In November, the Republicans carried New York State, the most populous in the nation, by nearly twenty percentage points.

Hanna didn't panic. Nor was he taking any chances. He used the momentum Bryan had generated to raise millions of dollars from industrialists for an equally unprecedented electioneering effort on McKinley's behalf. Joined by Great Northern Railway owner James J. Hill, Hanna began visiting corporate offices in New York City and elsewhere to remind wealthy Americans of the danger that Bryan and his followers posed to their interests. Rockefeller and Morgan each contributed $250,000, four Chicago meatpackers gave $100,000 apiece, and Hanna pressured banks and insurance companies into tithing one-quarter of 1 percent of their total assets. The books of the Republican National Committee showed a total of $3.5 million collected by Hanna, but estimates of what he really took in range from $7 million to $16 million. Using this money, he recruited hundreds of speakers, including many turncoat Democrats, whom he sent out to precede and follow Bryan around the country. (Hanna himself caused a brief public stir when he complained that some of his Democratic converts weren't worth the money it had taken to convert them.) Meanwhile, fourteen hundred Hanna-funded Republican workers spent the summer and fall mailing millions of political leaflets to voters all over the country—many of them in German, Swedish, Polish, Italian, Yiddish, and other immigrant languages. As managed by Hanna, the 1896 Republican campaign was by far the most costly and, depending on one's viewpoint, the best conducted yet. "He has advertised McKinley as if he were a patent medicine!" exclaimed a young Theodore Roosevelt.

In comparison, the Democrats raised only five hundred thousand dollars (most of it from silver mine owners), and Bryan had other difficulties with his party. Following Whitney's lead, most of the major Democratic newspapers in the East refused to support him, and the party's gold faction held a separate convention in September to nominate Sen. John M. Palmer of Illinois for president and former Kentucky governor Simon Bolivar Buckner for vice president. Backed by Cleveland, the two Civil War veterans (one a former Union general, the other a former Confederate general) campaigned actively but less for themselves than to shake Democratic voters loose from Bryan. Near the end of the race, Palmer announced to his "fellow Democrats" that he would "not consider it any great fault if you decide to cast your vote for William McKinley." In the meantime, when Secretary of the Interior Hoke Smith came out for Bryan, Cleveland demanded his resignation.

The Labor Vote

IT WAS HANNA WHO FINALLY grasped Bryan's weakness: "He's talking silver all the time, and that's where we've got him." The Democrats' prounion platform had won Bryan either the outright endorsement or the tentative support of influential labor leaders such as Samuel L. Gompers and Eugene V. Debs. But the Nebraskan never reached out to the segment of the electorate that these men represented. Even when he did speak to workers, Bryan talked about currency much more often than jobs or wages or working conditions. Compared to heavily indebted farmers, steelworkers putting in twelve-hour days couldn't have cared less about the silver issue, and Bryan apparently saw no need to broaden his appeal. As one observer put it, he was leading a political revolution without ever understanding it.

Yet even had Bryan courted urban voters more assiduously, he would still have had problems with them because many were recent immigrants—and their troubles were outside his personal experience. A fervent Protestant who nearly always cloaked himself in rural, prudish evangelism, Bryan neither smoked, nor drank, nor gambled. These aspects of his personality, accentuated by his rich midwestern twang and revivalist speaking style, created a cultural divide that made many urban workers, especially Catholics, feel uneasy. On the other hand, both McKinley and Hanna had excellent relationships with many labor groups. As governor of Ohio, McKinley had signed several prolabor bills, and his recent refusal to use state militiamen to break up a strike had led the *Chicago Herald* to

Bryan's speeches during the 1896 campaign, especially those he gave in the West, seemed more appropriate to revival meetings than political rallies. Sometimes the crowds were so thick that he had difficulty reaching the speaker's platform. At other times, out in the sparsely populated countryside, his platform might literally be a tree stump. Yet Bryan never failed to work hard for these small gatherings as well.

compare him favorably to Altgeld. Meanwhile, Hanna had fastidiously avoided labor trouble in his own far-flung enterprises and was famous for having bellowed once during a major strike, "Any [businessman] who won't meet his men halfway is a goddamn fool!"

Even so, many industrialists sought to ensure that the labor vote would go their way with threats of tangible repercussions. "You may vote any way you wish," some of them were alleged to have informed their workers, "but if Bryan is elected on Tuesday, the whistle will not blow on Wednesday." Workers also reported receiving similar warnings from shop foremen and in their pay envelopes.

For all of these reasons and a few others of lesser significance, Bryan came up half a million votes short. He carried on Election Day all the states of the former Confederacy, the Plains (except for North Dakota), and the mountain West; but his inability to reach urban voters in the former Granger states of the upper Midwest cost him the election, 271 electoral votes to 176. In Altgeld's home state of Illinois, for example, where the downstate farm vote was strong, Bryan received just 42.7 percent of the popular total, compared to 55.7 percent for McKinley. The Democrats complained that the Republicans bought the election, but the true deciding factor was Bryan's inability to transcend labor's fear that free coinage of silver would produce an even more calamitous financial meltdown.

"I might just as well put up a trapeze on my front lawn and compete with some professional athlete as go out speaking against Bryan," observed McKinley, who spent most of the 1896 campaign at home. Nevertheless, while Bryan went out to meet America, 750,000 Americans came to see McKinley and hear him speak from his front porch in Canton. Reduced fares offered by Republican-friendly railroads encouraged these junkets— prompting one Democratic newspaper to comment that it was cheaper to visit McKinley than to stay home.

AFTER MCKINLEY'S ELECTION, most of the radicalism quieted down as an economic recovery, begun during the campaign, finally took hold. Farm prices rose significantly, more gold was discovered in Colorado, and there seemed to be less immediate need for an increase in the money supply. Mark Hanna had advertised McKinley as "the advance agent of prosperity," and he appeared to have been correct.

Appreciative of the benefits of governing during a period of peace and prosperity, McKinley did little to rock the boat. The only exception he made was to continue his career-long pursuit of higher tariff rates. These he advocated not merely as an economic benefit but for profoundly nationalistic reasons as well. Protective tariffs, McKinley insisted, would deliver prosperity for workers, high prices for farmers, *and* stable markets for domestic manufacturers and retailers.

Nationalism was a new theme for the Republicans, who had spent the previous three decades beating on the Democrats for starting the Civil War—and, in retrospect, it was the most lasting feature of the 1896 election, enabling the party to put together a majority coalition that cut across many class lines. McKinley won not only the votes of factory owners and the urban middle class but also those of a majority of the industrial workforce. Many of those workers concluded, evidently, that a probusiness Republican could advance their interests more effectively than a rural Democrat obsessed with farming. The ensuing realignment transformed American politics—though not in the way that the spent Populists had expected.

Four years after their first encounter, McKinley faced Bryan again in the presidential election of 1900. Although a reluctant convert to the cause of the 1898 Spanish-American War, McKinley benefited from its wide popularity, and Bryan made little headway attacking the president as an imperialist and demanding independence for the Philippines. Nor did Bryan's repeated condemnations of McKinley's close ties to the trusts influence voters as strongly as the Republican slogan, "Four more years of a full dinner pail." Peace and prosperity won out, and McKinley was reelected by an even wider margin.

The McKinley Assassination

YET THERE WERE TROUBLING undercurrents in American society that proved impossible to ignore. These surfaced most shockingly in September 1901, when the president was shot while visiting the Pan-American Exposition in Buffalo. On the afternoon of September 6, McKinley attended a reception at the exposition's Temple of Music, where admirers had been waiting in line for several hours to shake the president's hand. At seven past four, as McKinley reached for another set of fingers, the three Secret Service agents on duty heard two shots fired. Twenty-eight-year-old Leon Czolgosz, an unemployed mill worker with very large hands, had concealed a short-barreled revolver in his palm, which he had covered with a handkerchief. (Because the day was so hot, the Secret Service had relaxed the rule that every person in line must have his hands exposed and empty before reaching the president.) One shot missed McKinley, but the other entered his abdomen. Although he survived the initial impact, two separate operations failed to remove the bullet, and McKinley died a week later. His successor, ironically, was Theodore Roosevelt, a man put on the 1900 ticket specifically to sidetrack his political career.

The Detroit-born son of Polish immigrant parents, Czolgosz had barely survived the economic dislocations of the 1890s. Although he hadn't joined any particular political group or party, he had begun reading anarchist newspapers and often espoused their ideas. Drifting from one city to another in the upper Midwest, he had allowed his class hatred to grow until he finally decided to do something about it. "I killed the president because he was the enemy of the people—the good working people," Czolgosz explained after the shooting. McKinley was indeed a potent symbol. According to historian Morton Keller, he was "a transitional man, straddling the Americas of the late nineteenth and early twentieth centuries" who was "felled by a product of the social anomie that came with mass, industrialized, urban society." In other words, Czolgosz was a troubled product of the America being born, in which Bryan and the Populists had failed to find a lasting place.

This special September 9, 1901, edition of Frank Leslie's Weekly *featured on its cover the first photograph taken of McKinley assassin Leon F. Czolgosz after his imprisonment.*

16

BECOMING A WORLD POWER

The Filipino Revolt

O N APRIL 24, 1898, THE DAY that Spain declared war on the United States, the U.S. consul in Singapore, E. Spencer Pratt, summoned twenty-nine-year-old Emilio Aguinaldo to the elegant Raffles Hotel, a legendary center of Southeast Asian intrigue. At the time, Aguinaldo was living in exile, having been forced out of the Philippines as a result of his involvement with the Katipunan, a Filipino independence movement that had challenged Spanish colonial rule during 1896 and 1897. Pratt's agenda was unmistakable: Seeing no reason to limit the new Spanish-American War to the Caribbean theater, elements within the U.S. government wanted to go after the Spanish colonies in the Pacific as well. Pratt obviously sought to enlist Aguinaldo's help.

Yet the accounts offered later by Pratt and Aguinaldo of their conversation at the Raffles disagree in nearly every respect—even as to whether they had one or two subsequent meetings. Only this much seems clear: Pratt asked Aguinaldo to accompany the U.S. Asiatic Squadron to the Philippines and, once there, to revive his insurgent campaign. Aguinaldo responded positively but requested that Pratt give him some written assurance that the United States backed Filipino independence. At this

AT LEFT: *Members of the **Thirtieth** U.S. Infantry Regiment inspect an abandoned Philippine village. American soldiers in the field routinely burned such villages (and towns with populations in the thousands) as part of their three-year-long pacification campaign.*

point, according to Aguinaldo's account, Pratt became evasive. He told the Filipino that an agreement in writing was unnecessary because the word of the U.S. government was "sacred." He also continued to offer Aguinaldo effusive verbal assurances.

When the meeting ended, Pratt cabled Asiatic Squadron commander George Dewey, then in Hong Kong outfitting his ships for battle, to let the commodore know that Aguinaldo had agreed to join the expedition and would provide "insurgent cooperation." Dewey replied tersely, "TELL AGUINALDO COME AS SOON AS POSSIBLE." Two days later, Aguinaldo left Singapore for Hong Kong, but by the time he arrived in the British colony, Dewey had already left for Manila.

As became apparent later, Pratt had been freelancing. Even if he did, as Aguinaldo insisted, tell the Filipino leader that the United States "would at least recognize the independence of the Philippines under a naval protectorate," the American consul had no authority to make any such promises. In subsequent self-congratulatory dispatches that he sent to his superiors in Washington, Pratt boasted of having "assisted the cause of the United States by securing Aguinaldo's cooperation." Yet after reading Pratt's full report, a concerned Secretary of State William R. Day instructed the consul sternly "to avoid unauthorized negotiations with Philippine insurgents" lest Aguinaldo and his colleagues "form hopes which it might not be practicable to gratify."

EMILIO AGUINALDO
1869–1964

BORN TO PROSPEROUS CHINESE and native Tagalog parents on the main Philippine island of Luzon, Emilio Aguinaldo studied at the University of Santo Tomás in Manila before becoming mayor of Cavite in 1896. About the same time, he joined the movement for Filipino independence from Spain, which had ruled the islands since the late sixteenth century. The Katipunan, as it was called, arose in response to Spanish unwillingness to consider even the most minor political reforms.

Fighting between the Katipunan and the Spanish broke out in August 1896 and continued for more than a year until rebel losses and the government's need to divert military resources to Cuba made both sides willing to talk peace. On December 14, 1897, at Biak-na-bato, Aguinaldo (who had become acting president of the Katipunan's provisional government) and Spanish governor-general Miguel Primo de Rivera signed an armistice. In addition to offering vague promises of reform, Primo de Rivera agreed to pay Aguinaldo eight hundred thousand dollars, while Aguinaldo and some thirty other Katipunan leaders voluntarily entered exile.

When no reforms emerged, many disgruntled Filipinos came to suspect (as Primo de Rivera had intended) that the Katipunan leaders had sold out the insurgent rank and file. As a result, when Aguinaldo returned to the Philippines in May 1898, he had some initial difficulty restoring the trust he had previously enjoyed. Fortunately, he had kept intact the money that Primo de Rivera had paid him (only a portion of the total promised) and used it to purchase arms for the renewal of the fighting.

The question of whether Pratt (and other representatives of the U.S. government) promised independence to Aguinaldo as a means of securing his support would take on paramount importance later. But for now, Spain still controlled the Philippines, and it was in Aguinaldo's interest to ally himself with the Americans, even if he did so on the basis of a wink and a nod.

THE FACT THAT DEWEY had sailed even before Aguinaldo's arrival would seem to suggest that the commodore had little regard for the Filipino rebels. While this was true—Dewey once called Aguinaldo an "unimpressive little man" and often referred to the Katipunan leaders as "little brown men"—the neutral British had, in fact, ordered Dewey's seven-ship squadron out of Hong Kong on April 25. After putting in briefly at Mirs Bay on the Chinese coast to take on coal and an American diplomat lately stationed in Manila, Dewey sailed for the Philippines on April 27, arriving off the main Philippine island of Luzon on the morning of April 30 and passing through the lightly defended entrance to Manila Bay between 11 P.M. and 2 A.M. that evening.

Dewey's immediate target wasn't Manila City, but the Spanish naval base six miles away at Cavite. Spanish admiral Patricio Montojo had prepared for Dewey's arrival as best he could, but his fleet—if it could be called that—was small and decrepit, with more than a few of the Spanish ships either rotting dockside or out of the water with their engines removed. Montojo's most modern vessels were more than a decade old, and his largest warship was wooden hulled, making it no match for the Americans' impressive modern steel navy.

Just after 5 A.M. on May 1, the Cavite shore batteries opened up on the approaching U.S. ships. At 5:41, Dewey delivered to Charles V. Gridley, captain of the flagship *Olympia*, his famous order to "fire when you are ready." The Asiatic Squadron made five passes along the Spanish line, gradually decreasing its range from five thousand to two thousand yards.

The battle of Manila Bay, as floridly depicted by Kurz & Allison in an 1898 lithograph.

At 7:35, however, Dewey was informed that the *Olympia* had only fifteen rounds of rapid-fire ammunition left. At that point, the commodore broke off the attack and ordered his ships to withdraw into the middle of the bay for a review and redistribution of ammunition. Subsequently, Dewey learned that he had been misinformed; there was actually no shortage of ammunition aboard the *Olympia*. He also learned, as the smoke cleared, that his squadron had sunk the Spanish flagship, destroyed two other vessels, and mastered the bay. Instead of reengaging, he sent a message to the Spanish governor-general at Manila demanding that the shore batteries immediately cease firing or Manila would be shelled. At the same time, he signaled his squadron captains to "let the people go to breakfast."

After giving his men a little extra time to digest their food, Dewey resumed the attack at 11:16 A.M. The Spanish had only four ships left, and these put up little resistance. At 12:30 P.M., all firing stopped as a white flag was raised above the Cavite arsenal. Thus ended the battle of Manila Bay. Every ship in the Spanish Pacific fleet had been destroyed without the loss of a single American life and without serious damage to any U.S. ship. Dewey had accomplished his mission, yet the war in the Philippines was far from over.

O
N MAY 2, COMMODORE DEWEY proposed joint use of the submarine Manila–Hong Kong telegraph cable. When the Spanish refused his offer, Dewey ordered the cable cut. But news of his victory had already been sent to Madrid, whence it trickled across the Atlantic to Washington. Pres. William McKinley, it was reported, immediately rushed to a map, saying that he couldn't locate the Philippines within two thousand miles. Most Americans, in fact, didn't know that Spain even had colonies in the Pacific. (Newspaper columnist Finley Peter Dunne, in the persona of his humorous creation Mr. Dooley, observed that Americans weren't sure whether the Philippines were an archipelago or something to eat.) But information was scarce, and it wasn't until May 5 that Dewey sent his dispatch boat, the *McCulloch*, to Hong Kong with a full account of the battle. His cabled report finally reached the U.S. mainland on May 7, at which point Dewey became a national hero. Later that day, an elated McKinley promoted him to rear admiral.

Commo. George Dewey in 1899.

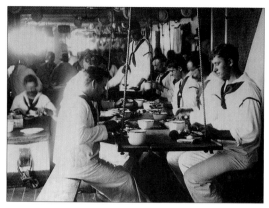

The crew's mess aboard the Olympia. *This 1899 photograph by Francis Benjamin Johnston shows sailors eating on a table suspended by ropes.*

In Manila Bay, Dewey waited for orders, but none were immediately forthcoming. Until the opportunity presented itself, neither the president nor his most senior advisers had seriously considered ordering the conquest of the Philippines. In a speech delivered in October 1899, McKinley recalled that "when Dewey sank the ships at Manila, as he was ordered to do, it was not to capture the Philippines—it was to destroy the Spanish fleet, the fleet of the nation against which we were waging war, and we thought that the soonest way to end that war was to destroy the power of Spain to make war, and so we sent Dewey." Corroborating McKinley's version of events is the account of a foreign diplomat in Washington who observed that senior U.S. officials "seemed to be surprised…by the demand for reinforcements from Dewey. No troops were ready to be sent to him, and there was even discussion for several days in the Department of War before the number of reinforcements was decided upon."

Within the Navy Department, however, acquisition of the Philippines had been a long-term, if discreet, goal. The U.S. Navy of 1898 was an expanding, ambitious service with quiet plans for the Pacific that required a major base of

SEA POWER

DURING THE 1890s, the chief spokesman for American expansionism was Alfred Thayer Mahan, a career naval officer and president of the Naval War College. Mahan presented his views in a number of important works, including *The Influence of Sea Power upon History, 1660–1783* (1890), the single most influential foreign policy document of its time. Mahan believed that history's greatest empires had all been shaped by their control of the sea. Therefore, he advocated that the United States construct a large and powerful navy capable of protecting American commerce overseas and winning great military victories. He also pushed for territorial expansion so that the new navy could have local bases at which to refuel and to which it could retire.

In 1897, Mahan told his close friend Theodore Roosevelt, McKinley's new assistant secretary of the navy, that the country needed to station its "best admiral" in the Pacific. Through Roosevelt's machinations, George Dewey was given this job in October 1897. Then on February 25, 1898, just ten days after the explosion of the *Maine*

Alfred Thayer Mahan

in Havana Harbor, Roosevelt's boss, Navy Secretary John D. Long, took the afternoon off.

Although Roosevelt's appointment to the Navy Department had been strongly urged by Massachusetts senator Henry Cabot Lodge, McKinley had resisted at first because of TR's seeming recklessness. Even after Roosevelt became assistant secretary, Long kept a watchful eye on him to make sure he didn't act to set (rather than follow) administration policy. Yet on that particular afternoon in February 1898, an exhausted Long let his guard down, and in a few hours Roosevelt refashioned a great deal of navy policy—probably with the help of Lodge, who spent at least part of the afternoon in Roosevelt's office. When Long returned to the Navy Department the next morning, he found that Roosevelt had issued a number of important unauthorized directives, including one requisitioning a large new order of armaments and another ordering the U.S. Asiatic Squadron from Japan to Hong King. Roosevelt's message to Dewey included instructions that, should war with Spain come, Dewey was to attack the Philippines.

the sort that Manila Bay provided for Spain. McKinley's cabinet soon came to see the logic of this, and when Dewey cabled on May 13 that he could "take Manila any time" but needed five thousand troops to hold it, the army made the necessary arrangements. The first troop convoy, however, wouldn't leave San Francisco until May 25 and wouldn't arrive at Manila (after a short stopover in Honolulu) until June 30, or nearly two months later.

Dewey and Aguinaldo

HERE AGUINALDO REENTERS the story. Dewey had completely destroyed the Spanish fleet, but his naval victory had done little to cripple the Spanish army, whose commander saw no reason to surrender. The guns of the U.S. warships allowed the Americans to occupy and hold the Spanish naval base at Cavite, but the marine battalion assigned to Dewey's squadron was far too small to permit further land operations. With army reinforcements still an ocean away, Dewey had to look elsewhere, at least temporarily, for friendly manpower. He had assumed that the natives would naturally ally themselves with him, but this turned out not to be the case. In fact, the Spanish authorities were persuading many Tagalogs to give up their rebellion and support the familiar colonial government in repulsing the American attack. So Dewey sent for Aguinaldo, who returned to the Philippines aboard the *McCulloch* on May 19.

That afternoon, Aguinaldo was brought aboard the *Olympia* for an interview with Dewey. Like those of the Pratt-Aguinaldo conversations, the accounts of this meeting with Dewey differ markedly on most key points. According to Aguinaldo, the American admiral repeated Pratt's assurances that he "must have no doubt concerning the recognition of Philippine independence on the part of the United States" because "America was rich in lands and money and did not need colonies." Later, Dewey explicitly denied making any such statements—and if he did, it was certainly without any direction from Washington. In response to a May 20 cable from Dewey reporting the arrival of Aguinaldo, Navy Secretary John D. Long replied on May 26, "It is desirable…not to have political alliances with the insurgents or any faction in the islands that would incur liability to maintain their cause in the future." On June 3, Dewey assured Long that he had "acted according to the spirit of Department's instructions therein from the beginning, and I have entered into no alliance with the insurgents or with any faction."

At the same time, rumors were reaching Washington (and presumably Dewey as well) of a Spanish relief mission to Manila, including armored cruisers and perhaps a battleship as well. Given this possibility, Dewey had to be allowed some flexibility, and the Navy Department was much more concerned with the safety of his ships than with the Filipino political situation. Under these circumstances, Dewey may well have told Aguinaldo whatever was necessary to win the Filipino's allegiance.

The USS Olympia, *commissioned in February 1895, was part of the United States' new Steel Navy, begun in 1883 at the insistence of Pres. Chester A. Arthur, who saw the need to modernize the nation's aging, wooden, Civil War–era fleet.*

WHATEVER DEWEY DID SAY, it was enough to set Aguinaldo to organizing a rebel army as quickly as possible. The exiled insurgent leaders who had returned with Aguinaldo aboard the *McCulloch* immediately established a headquarters outside the naval base in the town of Cavite and spread the word that they had allied themselves with the Americans to win Philippine independence. This claim of American support proved most helpful in reviving the opposition to the Spanish, and even after Aguinaldo became personally aware that the United States likely intended to retain possession of the Philippines, he continued for several months to promote the impression that he was acting with the full backing of Dewey and the other U.S. commanders.

Meanwhile, Aguinaldo tried to position the independence movement as best he could. In a letter written May 20, the day after his return to Cavite, Aguinaldo informed the "Revolutionary Chiefs of the Philippines" that he had "promised, not only the American admiral, but also the representatives of other nations with whom I have conferred, that the war they will see here shall be of the sort that is called war among the most civilized nations, to that end that we may be the admiration of the civilized powers and they may concede us independence." Aguinaldo considered it imperative that the rebels avoid conducting themselves in a manner that would allow the United States, or any other nation, to justify continued colonization.

Cavite's Calle Real in 1899. Although the Filipinos had become quite Westernized during three centuries of Spanish rule, the Americans still perceived them as savages. "These people do not know what independence means," Brig. Gen. Robert P. Hughes declared bluntly. "They probably think it is something to eat. They have no more idea what it means than a shepherd dog."

During the last week of May, Aguinaldo armed his troops with Spanish rifles provided by Dewey, and quickly the great central valley of Luzon fell to the insurgents. Next, Manila was besieged, and beginning June 1, rifle fire could be heard in the suburbs every day. Even so, the rebel forces weren't nearly strong enough to dislodge the thirteen thousand Spanish troops holding the walled and well-defended city.

Although Aguinaldo's first priority was military organization, he never neglected the political situation. On May 24, he issued a proclamation establishing a "Dictatorial Government" under his personal leadership. This government would rule the islands, he said, until they were "completely conquered and able to form a constitutional convention, and to elect a President and a Cabinet, in whose favor I will duly resign the authority." Aguinaldo then staged a ceremony in Cavite on June 12 proclaiming the "flag of the Philippines." This event wasn't a formal declaration of independence, but many Filipinos considered it such, which was certainly Aguinaldo's intention. (Dewey was invited to attend, but he declined, excusing himself because it was "mail-day.") On June 23, Aguinaldo issued another proclamation, this one creating the Revolutionary Government of the Philippines, which was to become the islands' new representative central government. Thereafter, he referred to himself as "president" rather than "dictator."

The Conquest of the Philippines

BY THE TIME AGUINALDO formally declared Philippine independence on August 1, the American army troops had already landed. The first contingent under Brig. Gen. Thomas M. Anderson arrived at Manila on June 30 after a short detour to capture the small Spanish garrison at Guam. (Guam was considered such a backwater that one of its military governors was said to have boarded a merchant steamer, spent a year living secretly in Europe, and then returned to the island just in time to be relieved. Upon his return, his secretary greeted him with the report, "Nothing new.") Anderson arrived with twenty-five hundred men, expecting that he would simply take over the occupation of Cavite. Instead, Anderson said later, he found "matters were seriously complicated because he [Dewey] had set Aguinaldo up in business."

Aguinaldo (seated, center) and members of his Revolutionary Government of the Philippines.

What Anderson soon learned—and became the first to communicate unambiguously to Washington—was that the Filipino rebels expected independence and that any U.S. colonial government set up in the archipelago would almost certainly come into conflict with them. At the same time, the transformation of the American presence from sea-based to land-based forces dismayed the insurgents, who resisted making room on shore for any new U.S. arrivals. For the most part, this resistance was passive, but it reflected a growing sense of resentment and hostility.

More troops were indeed on their way. During late July, additional deployments under Brig. Gen. Francis V. Greene, Brig. Gen. Arthur MacArthur, and Maj. Gen. Wesley E. Merritt brought the total number of U.S. soldiers in the Philippines to eleven thousand. Merritt had been appointed commander of the new Department of the Pacific, and following his arrival, planning for the reduction of Manila began in earnest. After Aguinaldo's cooperation was first requested and then demanded, U.S. troops began replacing Filipinos in the trenches the insurgents had dug around the city's defenses. The Spanish troops then made a brief show of defiance before capitulating rather easily on August 13. Earlier, the Americans had assured the Spanish that they would not allow any insurgents to enter and sack the city. Aguinaldo's appeals for a joint occupation of Manila were also denied.

LEFT: This magazine cover from November 1896 shows the queen of Spain having difficulty holding two boys— one labeled "Cuba" and the other, "Philippine Islands"—who are struggling to free themselves.

THE SPANISH-AMERICAN WAR actually ended six hours before the surrender of Manila. Halfway around the world in Washington, Secretary of State Day and French ambassador Jules M. Cambon, acting on behalf of the Spanish, signed an armistice on August 12, after which President McKinley ordered an immediate halt to all hostilities. With the telegraph cable to Manila inoperative, however, McKinley's order didn't reach Dewey until the afternoon of August 16. By this time, Manila was already in American hands.

What lay in store for the Philippines beyond this military occupation was anyone's guess. In Washington, senior government officials still had to reconcile the fact of conquest with the many arguments for and against U.S. territorial expansion. McKinley himself was the source of most of the hand-wringing. On the one hand, he wanted to show the imperialist nations of Europe that "a lofty spirit" guided American actions; on the other, he supported the "general principle of holding on to what we get." Later, the president tried to create the impression that public opinion and the course of events had directed the outcome in the Philippines, but he was a shrewd enough politician to have realized early on that one does not give away what one might ultimately wish to keep.

During the negotiations that preceded the signing of the December 1898 Treaty of Paris, McKinley held numerous discussions with his closest advisers concerning the fate of the Philippines. On a cruise that he took with his cabinet in early August to discuss the terms of the proposed armistice, he had voiced doubts about the wisdom of acquiring islands so far away, yet he also acknowledged that the American people "would never be satisfied if they were given back to Spain." During the weeks that followed, religious newspapers emerged as some of the strongest advocates of annexation. "The conquest by force of arms must be followed up by conquest for Christ," the *Baptist Union* demanded on August 27 (choosing to overlook the fact that Spanish friars had already converted most Filipinos to Roman Catholicism). The nation's business community also favored annexation because of the access it would provide into new Asian markets, especially in China. Sen. Henry Cabot Lodge specifically called Manila "the great prize, and the thing which will give us the Eastern trade."

In his September 16 instructions to the peace commissioners he was sending to Paris, McKinley pointed out that the United States had engaged Spain in the Philippines without "any original thought of...even partial occupation," yet the country's military success had brought with it certain obligations that now required the United States to annex at least the island of Luzon. By the time the Treaty of Paris was finalized, McKinley had extended that demand to include the entire chain.

The signing of the armistice with Spain on August 12, 1898. President McKinley stands at the head of the table, with George B. Cortelyou to his left. During the Spanish-American War, Cortelyou, who was the president's private secretary, became unofficially the first presidential press secretary as well.

The Prelude to Revolt

WHILE THE NEGOTIATIONS BETWEEN Spain and the United States were under way, Aguinaldo tried desperately to gain international recognition for his revolutionary government. On August 6, he sent a memorandum to several foreign powers, requesting that they grant belligerent status to the Filipino insurgents as a prelude to full diplomatic recognition. He noted his government's control of fifteen provinces and asserted that the nine thousand Spaniards his men had taken prisoner were all being treated with the "same consideration observed by cultured nations." He concluded his appeal with the declaration that the Philippines had "arrived at that state in which it can and ought to govern itself." Yet no recognition came, and the United States seemed no more willing than it had been to grant Philippine independence unilaterally.

By steps, the tension between the Americans and the Filipinos mounted. After the signing of the Treaty of Paris, McKinley sent a message to Maj. Gen. Elwell S. Otis, the new military commander in Manila, ordering him to extend U.S. control over the Philippines to the entire archipelago. Otis was instructed to demonstrate to the natives that "that the mission of the United States is one of benevolent assimilation." However, McKinley also wrote that Otis should not hesitate to use the "strong arm of authority to repress disturbances and to overcome all obstacles to the bestowal of the blessings of good and stable government upon the people of the Philippine Islands under the free flag of the United States."

Up to this point, most influential Filipinos had withheld their judgment of the Americans, pending some formal statement of U.S. intentions. Aware of how badly the Filipinos would take McKinley's unequivocal statements concerning U.S. sovereignty, Otis chose to edit severely the president's proclamation before publishing it in Manila. Unfortunately, a copy of McKinley's statement was also transmitted to the U.S. base at Iloilo, where Brig. Gen. Marcus P. Miller published it as received. The Filipino nationalists, already disturbed by the redacted version, became irate when they realized what Otis had done, and their suspicion and distrust deepened rapidly.

AGUINALDO RESPONDED in early January with a proclamation of his own, rejecting the U.S. claim to sovereignty and accusing the Americans of acting in bad faith. He pointed out sharply that, in using military power to impose their will on the weaker Filipinos, the people of the United States were violating their own professed ideals regarding personal liberty and government by the consent of the governed. His memorandum concluded with a warning that, given the present explosive circumstances, a single accidental or impetuous act might trigger war.

On February 4, 1899, just such an incident occurred in a Manila suburb. An American soldier on guard duty challenged a Filipino to halt. When the man ignored the order, the sentry shot and killed him. The Filipino might not have heard or understood the American, or he might have been acting on instructions from a local insurgent commander eager to test the American sentries. Whatever the case, fighting between the Americans and the Filipinos broke out in general all over the islands. The Filipino Revolt had begun.

HIT HIM HARD!

This February 1899 issue of the political humor magazine Judge *appeared just as the Filipino Revolt began. Its cover illustration depicts Aguinaldo and other Filipino insurgents as mosquitoes annoying President McKinley. "Mosquitoes seem to be worse here in the Philippines than they were in Cuba," its caption read. Another work first published in the United States in February 1899 was "The White Man's Burden" by Rudyard Kipling. This popular, influential poem intermixed exhortations to empire with sober warnings concerning the difficulties of imperialism.*

The Roots of American Imperialism

ONCE IT BECAME APPARENT that the United States would be keeping at least a portion of the Philippine Islands, members of the newly created Anti-Imperialist League began pressing the question: Just whose interests were being served by the deployment of tens of thousands of troops to the other side of the world? The answer, of course, lay in both the recent and not-so-recent past.

Thus far, Americans had been largely content to exploit the natural resources of their own continent, and few had looked elsewhere for wealth. Overseas trade remained an important sector of the U.S. economy, as it had been during colonial times, but the federal government generally heeded its first president's parting advice to avoid foreign entanglements. Only once in its history had the nation allied itself with a foreign power and that had been more than a century earlier, when the Continental Congress accepted—and needed—French assistance during the Revolutionary War.

Two major factors combined to change this attitude: One was the rapid growth of U.S. industry during the late nineteenth century, which created enough excess manufacturing capacity that additional markets were needed. By 1900, the United States had become the world's leading economic power; no longer could it expect to grow primarily within its own borders.

The second factor promoting U.S. interest in overseas colonies was European imperialism, then at its height. America's primary economic rivals—Britain, France, and Germany—were all busily engaged in creating captive markets in Asia and Africa. Unless the United States became involved fairly soon, some Americans argued, the nation would lose out on many potentially lucrative economic opportunities. With domestic markets apparently reaching their saturation point, few questioned the premise that future American prosperity depended on the acquisition of new foreign outlets for excess U.S. production.

YET AMERICANS REMAINED troubled by the prospect of acquiring colonies in Asia or anywhere else. Some believed that it was simply wrong to impose U.S. sovereignty on independent peoples, but these were a small minority; many more opposed colonization either because they feared the burden of having to civilize "heathen" populations or because they distrusted globalism and wanted the United States to remain politically as well as geographically isolated from Europe and its intrigues. Most weren't sure what they thought.

Nearly all Americans felt conflicted to one degree or another, and, as noted earlier, even President McKinley struggled. Yet in the end, the expansionist impulse prevailed, predictably enough. It turned out that once Americans got used to the idea, they saw within imperialism enough of the ideology of manifest destiny to make them feel comfortable with the prospect of becoming colonizers. Their sense of Anglo-Saxon racial and cultural superiority was strong, and it prompted them to conclude, for both selfish and humanitarian reasons, that the country had a moral obligation to uplift and enlighten less civilized peoples. This transition was made even easier by events taking place just ninety miles offshore in Cuba.

American politicians had been eyeing Cuba for generations. Andrew Jackson nearly took it from Spain in 1818, and the Ostend Manifesto of 1854 contemplated much the same thing. By 1898, with Spain even more

> "The truth is I didn't want the Philippines, and when they came to us, as a gift from the gods, I did not know what to do with them."
>
> — *William McKinley, speech to the General Missionary Committee of the Methodist Episcopal Church, November 21, 1899*

deeply in decline, Cuba entered American politics once again as part of the nation's growing commercial interest in Latin America as a whole. In 1889, the Harrison administration had hosted the first International Conference of American States, or Pan-American Conference, intended to improve trade relations and expand U.S. involvement in Latin American affairs. Although congressional Republicans later blocked meaningful tariff reform (they wanted to keep rates high), the federal government did become much more active in the region, and during the 1890s a significant number of American businesses began investing large sums of money there.

Cuba

THE CUBANS THEMSELVES resented Spanish rule because it was repressive and corrupt. Already between 1868 and 1878, they had fought a ten-year war, which ended when Spain promised to reform Cuba's political and economic systems. But the minor reforms introduced didn't come close to satisfying the nationalists. The Cuba Libre movement became militant again during the 1890s and, in February 1895, resumed fighting the two hundred thousand Spanish soldiers deployed on the island. Both sides killed civilians, destroyed private property, and burned towns and plantations, bringing the sugar trade with America—the foundation of the Cuban economy—to a halt.

*This **Puck** cartoon from September 1900 shows anti-imperialists offering a bloated Uncle Sam "a dose of this anti-fat." Uncle Sam declines. Meanwhile, McKinley, depicted as a tailor, measures him for new clothing to be made from imperialist cloth. The cartoon appeared near the end of the 1900 presidential campaign, during which Democratic candidate William Jennings Bryan attacked McKinley for annexing the Philippines.*

Yet, like the Filipinos, the Cubans lacked the military strength to oust the Spanish entirely. So they fought as guerrillas, hounding the Spanish, who responded by imprisoning the rebels (and anyone suspected of helping them) in *reconcentrados*, or concentration camps. Thousands died in those camps—some from malnutrition, some from diseases brought on by inadequate sanitation, some from the lack of proper medical care—but whatever the cause of these deaths, their sheer number caught the attention of circulation-hungry newspapers in the United States.

This June 1898 cartoon shows Pulitzer (left) and Hearst both dressed as the Yellow Kid, a cartoon character created by Richard F. Outcault. When Pulitzer's World *first began publishing Outcault's strip in February 1896, the Yellow Kid caused such a sensation that Hearst moved quickly to hire Outcault away from Pulitzer. A bidding war ensued, and Hearst won. At the same time, Hearst and Pulitzer's shenanigans resulted in the origination of the phrase* yellow journalism *to describe sensational and unscrupulous publishing.*

Reporting in an overtly sensationalist manner on Spanish oppression in Cuba, two rival newspapers, William Randolph Hearst's *New York Journal* and Joseph Pulitzer's *New York World*, helped create an atmosphere of interventionist frenzy. Each paper vied to outdo the other with gaudier and gaudier stories (some of them known to be lies) describing the brutality of the Spanish and praising the sincerity of the rebels. Their stories spread to newspapers in other markets, and jingoism took hold of the country. (The word, a new coinage, came from a popular 1878 song and was used in 1898, as today, to describe fervent nationalism backed by a belligerent foreign policy.) President McKinley, who strongly objected to what he called this "jingo nonsense," resisted the appeals of expansionists—notably Alfred Mahan, Henry Cabot Lodge, and Theodore Roosevelt—to intervene in Cuba. But events took the matter out of his hands.

USING DIPLOMATIC PRESSURE, McKinley had persuaded the Spanish to recall Valeriano Weyler, the notorious military governor of Cuba who had established the *reconcentrados*. McKinley also obtained Spanish assurances that the camps would be closed and more reforms would be forthcoming—which the president thought would be enough to hold off the interventionists in his party. On February 9, 1898, however, Hearst's *Journal* published a letter stolen from the Havana post office. Written by Spanish minister to the United States Enrique Dupuy de Lôme, it characterized McKinley as "weak and a bidder for the admiration of the crowd, besides being a would-be politician who tries to leave a door open behind himself while keeping on good terms with the jingoes of his party." Because there was a good deal of truth to what Dupuy de Lôme had to say, McKinley found himself cornered. When the USS *Maine* exploded in Havana Harbor six nights later, he soon followed the rest of the country down the road to war.

The immediate Spanish inquiry into the February 15 explosion that killed 266 U.S. sailors and sank their battleship found the cause to be an internal explosion. Although never able to identify a particular external cause, the American investigators disagreed. For its part, the American public didn't much care what either report said. Most Americans had already decided that a Spanish mine had sunk the U.S. warship, and they wanted retaliation. "Remember the *Maine!*" became the warmongers' favorite cry. McKinley didn't want to fight, yet he felt compelled on March 27 to demand concessions from Spain, including an armistice between the colonial forces and the rebels on Cuba.

Under pressure from conservative elements at home and not wanting to lose too much face, the Spanish government agreed on March 31 to everything McKinley was asking for except the armistice; and after several visits from the U.S. minister in Madrid, it even agreed to that on April 9. But by then, the president was already at work on his war message, which he delivered to Congress on April 11. (McKinley was so intimidated by the jingoes in his party that he went through with the request for a declaration of war even though Spain had already conceded every point.) On April 25, Congress adopted a formal declaration; and, to demonstrate the purity of its motives, it also passed the Teller Amendment, which guaranteed independence for Cuba. (Pratt and Dewey probably cited the Teller Amendment in their attempts to persuade Aguinaldo that the United States had no territorial ambitions regarding the Philippines.)

The Spanish-American War

JOHN HAY, THEN THE U.S. AMBASSADOR to Great Britain, called the conflict that followed "a splendid little war." It lasted only a few months yet demonstrated the fearsome superiority of the American military—at least relative to that of Spain, the weakling of Europe. U.S. combat casualties were light, though tropical diseases did kill several thousand Americans.

Because the Spanish forces on Cuba greatly outnumbered the peacetime U.S. Army (which had only twenty-eight thousand regulars in April 1898), the decision was made to establish a naval blockade while a larger army was raised. In early June, McKinley sent the Fifth Army Corps under Maj. Gen. William R. Shafter to Santiago de Cuba, where Adm. William T. Sampson had trapped the squadron of Spanish admiral Pascual Cervera. Following landings at Daiquiri and Siboney on June 20, Shafter marched his men west along an interior route to the outskirts of Santiago. In response, the Spanish commander there arranged his ten-thousand-man garrison into three defensive lines. Because he intended to make his principal stand closer to the city, the first Spanish line, established atop San Juan Heights, contained just five hundred soldiers. On July 1, Shafter overran this line, took control of the heights, and commenced a siege.

The wreck of the USS Maine, *which McKinley had sent to Havana as a sop to the jingoes. More recent inquiries into the cause of the February 1898 explosion have suggested that the Spanish were right: An internal explosion most likely sank the* Maine.

YELLOW FEVER

DURING THE SPANISH-AMERICAN WAR, 5,462 Americans died in Cuba, but only 379 of those deaths were the result of enemy fire. The rest were caused by other maladies, principally yellow fever. Doctors and nurses worked with relentless dedication to save infected soldiers, yet they were ineffective because so little was known of the disease and its cause. Most medical experts still thought it was spread through contact with the bedding and clothing of infected people. When a yellow-fever epidemic broke out among Americans stationed in Havana in early 1900, the army sent physicians Walter Reed, James Carroll, Aristides Agramonte, and Jesse W. Lazear to investigate, with Reed acting as the commission's chairman. Following up on work done by a Cuban epidemiologist that suggested yellow fever was transmitted by insect bite, Major Reed and his colleagues decided to devote their efforts to proving or disproving this theory.

Maj. Walter Reed

On August 27, 1900, Carroll exposed himself to a suspect mosquito and subsequently developed a severe case of yellow fever. Shortly afterward, Lazear was bitten, developed an even worse case, and died. In November, Reed ordered a more extensive series of controlled experiments. In one building, volunteers slept on bedding that had earlier been used by yellow-fever patients; in another, volunteers slept on uncontaminated bedding but were exposed to the suspected mosquitoes. Only those volunteers bitten by mosquitoes developed yellow fever. Thus Reed demonstrated that the disease was transmitted by the bite of the species *Stegomyia fasciata* (later renamed *Aëdes aegypti*).

Acting on these findings, Maj. William C. Gorgas, the U.S. Army's chief sanitary officer in Cuba, began a program in February 1901 to eradicate the disease by destroying its carriers. Within ninety days, Gorgas had freed Havana of yellow fever, and in 1904 he was sent to Panama, where his work exterminating mosquitoes made construction of the Panama Canal possible.

General Shafter's force included the First Volunteer Cavalry Regiment, known as the Rough Riders. Teddy Roosevelt (standing, center) was its commanding officer.

The Americans' position on San Juan Heights unsettled the new Spanish governor-general of Cuba, Ramón Blanco. Fearing that Shafter was somehow about to capture Cervera's squadron, he ordered the admiral to leave Santiago immediately. This was a mistake: Inside Santiago Harbor, Cervera's wooden ships were relatively safe from U.S. attack; outside, they were sitting ducks. On July 3, as Cervera attempted an escape to Cienfuegos, four of his five ships were sunk near the harbor entrance. (The fifth ship did manage to stay afloat for a short time but later had to be beached.) Although fighting continued elsewhere on Cuba until August 12, the destruction of Cervera's squadron had, for all practical purposes, decided the war.

AT FIRST, IN ADDITION TO independence for Cuba and the cession of Puerto Rico and Guam, the United States government demanded only Manila; then, after September 16, it wanted the rest of Luzon as well. By late October, the entire archipelago was being demanded. Spain had no choice but to submit. In its final form, signed on December 10, the Treaty of Paris liberated Cuba and ceded Puerto Rico, Guam, and the Philippines to the United States in exchange for a payment of twenty million dollars and some commercial concessions. "There was nothing left for us to do," McKinley told a group of Methodist ministers in November 1899, "but to take them all, and to educate the Filipinos, and to uplift and civilize and Christianize them, and by God's grace do the very best we could by them as our fellow men for whom Christ also died."

Most Americans had supported the war with Spain, but the acquisitive, imperialistic nature of the Paris accord aroused opposition. The annexation of the Philippines became the principal focus of contention. The anti-imperialists feared that annexation would tarnish American democracy—some for moral reasons, some for racist reasons, and some for both. The moral argument was that nations such as the United States shouldn't subjugate weaker societies simply because they were powerless to resist. The racist argument was that governing the nonwhite Filipinos would become a burdensome responsibility. Both views were influential.

Joined by a few Republican defectors, the Democratic senators who opposed the Treaty of Paris seemed strong enough to block it. The final vote came on February 6, 1899. It was close, 57–27, or just one vote more than the two-thirds majority necessary for ratification. Afterward, opponents suggested that, had fighting between the Filipinos and the U.S. occupation forces not broken out two days earlier, the vote would have gone the other way.

HAWAII

ONE WAY TO MEASURE THE EFFECT of the Spanish-American War on America's sense of itself as a world power is to consider the history of Hawaii, which Congress annexed by joint resolution in July 1898. Until January 1893, the island chain had been an independent kingdom. On January 16, however, with the help of marines ordered ashore by U.S. minister John L. Stevens, a cabal of American sugar planters led by lawyer Sanford B. Dole overthrew the native government of Queen Liliuokalani and immediately applied for annexation. (Although Hawaii had enjoyed privileged trade status since 1875, annexation would have made the planters eligible for bounties being offered domestic sugar producers under the 1890 McKinley Tariff.) On February 15, the Harrison administration submitted a hastily negotiation treaty of annexation to the Senate.

Before the Senate voted, however, Harrison left office, and new president Grover Cleveland withdrew the treaty because he suspected improprieties. When Cleveland learned later from a diplomat he sent to Hawaii of Stevens's inappropriate involvement, the president attempted to restore the deposed queen; failing at that, he did manage to block annexation throughout his second term.

McKinley felt no such moral misgivings, and just three months after taking office, his secretary of state, John Sherman, negotiated a new treaty of annexation with the Americans running Hawaii. Even so, that treaty lingered in the Senate for more than a year before events in Cuba and the Philippines made the construction of a U.S. colonial empire, including Hawaii, palatable.

Queen Liliuokalani

The Pacification of the Philippines

AT THE OUTSET OF THE FILIPINO REVOLT, Major General Otis boasted that his nearly thirty thousand troops could suppress the rebellion within a few weeks—and he repeated this prediction, with depressing regularity, several times over the next fifteen months. The gap that existed between Otis's optimistic fantasies and the reality of the situation can easily be seen in the general's ongoing refusal to accept the additional troops being offered by the Secretary of War Elihu Root. And when Otis's subordinate Maj. Gen. Henry Lawton told the press that one hundred thousand soldiers would be needed to pacify the Philippines, Otis forced Lawton to deny he had ever made such a statement. In fact, one hundred thousand troops were exactly the number that Arthur MacArthur requested when he relieved Otis as military governor of the Philippines in May 1900.

Macabebe scouts employed by the U.S. Army on the march in 1900. Members of other Filipino tribes who continued to resist the Americans were often subjected to harsh treatment. The U.S. Army even set up "security camps" similar to the Spanish reconcentrados that had so enraged the American public only months earlier.

The U.S. Army had so much difficulty suppressing the Filipino insurgency because the insurgents weren't fighting a conventional war. During early 1899, Otis had successfully driven Aguinaldo's men from the larger provincial towns, but he halted U.S. offensive operations in the late spring because the rainy season was beginning. While it passed, Aguinaldo made an important adjustment. With his military staff, he decided that henceforth the rebels would blend in with the civilian population and fight the Americans as guerrillas. When the American offensive resumed in October 1899, the U.S. troops had a great deal more trouble distinguishing the minority combatants from the majority noncombatants. According to Brig. Gen. Robert P. Hughes, "As to actual engagements, they were very few. It was very hard to get an engagement of any kind. You could get what we would call a little skirmish, and probably there would be ten or twelve killed." These skirmishes did little to safeguard U.S. Army patrols, many of which were ambushed by rebel bands hoping to wear down the occupation forces.

In the meantime, McKinley appointed in January 1899 a five-man Philippine Commission to confer with prominent Filipinos, study conditions in the islands, and make recommendations for the establishment of a civilian government there. The chairman of this commission was Cornell University president Jacob G. Schurman; its members, in addition to Dewey and Otis, were diplomat Charles Denby and Dean C. Worcester, an assistant professor of zoology at the University of Michigan who had made two field trips to the archipelago as a student. Although Schurman generously praised Aguinaldo's honesty and sincerity, his report (issued in January 1900) whitewashed the situation in the Philippines—understandably so in that 1900 was a presidential election year. The commission's conclusions emphasized the impossibility of immediate self-government for the Filipinos and confirmed the necessity of maintaining a U.S. presence there to ensure peace and order. "Whatever the future of the Philippines may be," the commissioners declared, "there is no course open to us now except the prosecution of the war until the insurgents are reduced to submission." McKinley was delighted.

S OON AFTER THE REPORT WAS ISSUED, acting on one of its recommendations, the president appointed a Second Philippine Commission with the authority to implement limited self-government in the colony. To chair this group, McKinley named federal judge William Howard Taft, who would become the first U.S. civilian governor of the Philippines on July 4, 1901. Taft's attitude was typically paternal. "Our little brown brothers," he wrote to the president shortly after his arrival, would need "fifty or one hundred years to develop anything resembling Anglo-Saxon political principles and skills."

As Taft began the process of setting up a civilian government, MacArthur harried the guerrillas while carefully plotting the capture of Aguinaldo himself. The rebel leader's whereabouts were a mystery, and Otis had declared that he was "probably dead." But MacArthur got a break: In February 1901, U.S. troops intercepted a messenger carrying a request for additional troops from Aguinaldo to his brother. Presumably using the "water cure," a form of torture favored by Americans to extract information from reluctant rebels, Col. Frederick Funston learned that Aguinaldo was operating out of the village of Palanan, high up in the northern mountains of Luzon. (The "water cure" involved forcing prisoners to swallow large quantities of salted water "until their bodies became distended to the point of bursting," according to one report in the *New York World*. Although military officials routinely denied such accounts, Taft later admitted that the "so-called water cure" was used "on some occasions.")

Taft during his three-year tenure as governor of the Philippines.

Shrewdly, Funston recruited a group of eighty-one Tagalog-speaking Macabebe scouts to pose as the reinforcements that Aguinaldo had requested. He provided them with rebel uniforms and transported them by ship (the USS *Vicksburg*) to Casiguran Bay on Luzon's northeastern coast. Accompanying the Macabebes were the captured courier; a rebel defector and a former Spanish secret service officer, masquerading as the group's leaders; and five American officers, Funston among them, posing as captives. The party followed difficult jungle trails for more than fifty miles before reaching Palanan on March 23 in the middle of Aguinaldo's thirty-second birth-day celebration. Having learned of the "captured" Americans, the few insurgents who were in Aguinaldo's camp at the time saluted the disguised Macabebes with rifle shots. Giving the appearance of returning the salute, the scouts opened fire on the insurgents. Aguinaldo was taken prisoner and rushed to the coast before his guerrillas could organize a pursuit. By March 28, the raiding party was back in Manila, and Aguinaldo was imprisoned in the governor's mansion.

A Filipino insurgent leader (center) surrenders his force to the Americans in 1901.

Because the U.S. military had recently been publicizing its claim that the Filipino rebels were committing atrocities against American prisoners, many newspapers called for Aguinaldo's trial and execution. But MacArthur and Taft were careful not to transform Aguinaldo into a martyr. Instead, they persuaded him to swear allegiance to the United States and request that other rebel leaders

The captured Aguinaldo on his way to Manila aboard the Vicksburg in March 1901. Throughout the Filipino Revolt, U.S. military officials had tried to demean Aguinaldo, portraying him as a bandit who lived in luxury by looting his own people.

do so as well. Aguinaldo's April 19 proclamation—the purpose of which, he said, was to avoid further bloodshed—dealt a heavy blow to rebel morale. The fighting continued but gradually diminished until April 1902, when the last element of armed resistance to American colonial rule surrendered in Luzon's Batangas Province. In all, the Filipino Revolt lasted more than three years and cost the United States about $160 million, or eight times what it had paid Spain for the islands in the first place. But now the country had an empire.

Big Stick Diplomacy

THE USEFULNESS OF HAVING a colony in the Far East became immediately apparent during the summer of 1900, when the Boxer Rebellion threatened the lives of Americans and other Westerners living in China. For decades, the leading commercial nations of the world had been carving up China into carefully delineated spheres of economic and political influence. Finally acknowledging that access to China would not be possible without political involvement in Asia, the United States proposed in September 1899 that all countries be allowed to trade with China on an equal basis. McKinley's new secretary of state, John Hay, floated this initiative in a set of diplomatic notes he sent to Great Britain, France, Germany, Italy, Russia, and Japan. In March 1900, Hay optimistically announced that his "open door" policy had been accepted.

Three months later, a group of Chinese nationalists, responsible for recent attacks against Christian missionaries in the countryside, began an all-out effort to expel all foreigners from China. The nationalists called themselves the Righteous and Harmonious Fists, but Westerners referred to them as the Boxers because their calisthenic rituals resembled boxing. (Like the Ghost Dancers, the oppressed Boxers believed that performing these rituals would make them impervious to bullets.) On June 18, the empress dowager gave the Boxers her unequivocal support and ordered that all foreigners in China be killed. On June 20, the Boxers reached Peking, where they murdered the German minister and trapped hundreds of

Western diplomats and Chinese Christians in the barricaded, well-armed British legation. An international army subsequently fought its way through to Peking from the port of Tientsin, arriving on August 14 to restore imperialist rule. The force included British, French, Russian, and Japanese troops, along with twenty-five hundred Americans hurriedly transferred from the Philippines.

Another important factor contributing to America's new sense of itself as a world power was the passionate expansionism of forty-two-year-old Theodore Roosevelt, who became the nation's youngest chief executive ever upon McKinley's assassination in September 1901. As president, Roosevelt initiated an aggressive foreign policy known as Big Stick Diplomacy. (One of TR's favorite adages was, "Speak softly and carry a big stick; you will go far.") Unlike McKinley, Roosevelt felt no reluctance when it came to projecting U.S. power overseas, and he pursued every opportunity he could to expand the nation's influence. One such opportunity presented itself in Panama.

F OR HALF A CENTURY, ever since the California gold rush, the U.S. government had been wondering how it might shorten voyages from the East Coast to the West Coast. Because Great Britain, the world's most formidable naval power, shared this same goal, the two nations agreed in the 1850 Clayton-Bulwer Treaty to guarantee the neutrality of any canal built across Central America. The most likely spots for such a canal were Nicaragua and the Isthmus of Panama (then a part of Colombia).

This lithograph from 1900 shows the Allied armies occupying the Peking palace of Empress Dowager T'zu-hsi during the Boxer Rebellion.

By 1901, however, America's new taste of empire had made the country increasingly eager to build a canal that it could control exclusively. In November 1901, Secretary of State Hay negotiated a new arrangement with British diplomat Julian Pauncefote that abrogated the Clayton-Bulwer Treaty and granted the United States "the exclusive management and policing" of a Central American canal, so long as ships of all nations could use the canal on an equal basis.

The next step was to decide where this canal would be built. A commission recommended Nicaragua, but the New Panama Canal Company began lobbying Roosevelt hard to site the canal in Panama. A French company led by Ferdinand de Lesseps, the man who built the Suez Canal, had begun work on a sea-level waterway in Panama in 1881, but political and financial trouble forced an end to that venture in 1888. Subsequently, the New Panama Canal Company had optioned the French rights, which were now being offered to the U.S. government for $109 million. Roosevelt waited until the price dropped to $40 million before buying them. Once the canal commission had revised its recommendation accordingly, Congress passed the June 1902 Spooner Act, which authorized the president to proceed with the construction of a canal across the Isthmus of Panama, provided that the government of Colombia could be induced to cede the United States an appropriate amount of land (the French lease being about to expire).

In January 1903, Secretary of State Hay and Colombian foreign minister Tomás Herrán signed a treaty that turned over to the United States a ten-mile-wide strip of land in Panama. In exchange for a hundred-year lease, the U.S. government agreed to pay $10 million plus annuities of $250,000 beginning after nine years. The U.S. Senate ratified the deal immediately, but the Colombian senate held out for more money. When Roosevelt refused to give any more, the Colombians rejected the treaty in August 1903 amid a burst of patriotic pride and complaints of "Yankee imperialism."

An angry Roosevelt decided to cut the Colombians out of the deal entirely and began supporting opposition politicians in Panama who favored the construction of a canal. In October, he ordered three navy warships to the region, and on November 3, when the anticipated uprising came, he used those ships to prevent Colombian troops from landing in the province. With indecent haste, the United States recognized the new independent government of Panama on November 6, and Hay nearly as quickly negotiated a deal with French engineer Philippe Bunau-Varilla, an agent of the New Panama Canal Company lately named Panamanian minister to the United States, whose financial terms matched exactly those of the recently rejected Hay-Herrán Treaty. Some members of Congress griped about the heavy-handed role Roosevelt had played in securing the canal zone, but the president simply ignored their objections. "I took the canal zone and let Congress debate," TR declared in a 1911 speech, "and while the debate goes on, the canal does also."

Roosevelt salutes the Great White Fleet that he sent on a two-year, around-the-world "goodwill tour" in December 1907 to project American force internationally.

THE ROOSEVELT COROLLARY

THEODORE ROOSEVELT'S PARTICULAR CONCERN with Latin America became obvious to the world even before the trouble in Panama began. In late 1902, when the Venezuelan government defaulted on some debts it owed to European bankers, Great Britain, Germany, and Italy sent warships to blockade the Venezuelan coast. The German ships even bombarded a Venezuelan port. At first, Roosevelt showed little interest. Then, when rumors reached Washington of German intentions to seize Venezuelan territory for the purpose of establishing a permanent naval base there, the president warned the Germans that he would send Admiral Dewey and the U.S. Navy to defend Venezuela should any such land grab be attempted.

The Germans withdrew; more importantly, Roosevelt established a policy of interventionism that long survived his presidency. This new policy, which came to be called the Roosevelt Corollary to the Monroe Doctrine, was articulated by the president in a December 1904 congressional address. The original 1823 Monroe Doctrine had warned European nations not to act aggressively in colonizing the Western Hemisphere; the Roosevelt Corollary extended this warning to include instances in which "chronic wrongdoing" by Latin American nations (rather than European aggression) had put those countries at risk. According to Roosevelt, it was the duty and obligation of the United States—and not the aggrieved Europeans—to act as an "international police power" and set matters right.

Under this policy, which laid the groundwork for Taft's Dollar Diplomacy, Roosevelt took control of Dominican finances early in 1905 so that the Dominican Republic's debts to France and Italy could be repaid. Numerous additional U.S. interventions followed during the next two decades, placing a great strain not only on U.S. government resources but also on the country's relations with other nations in the hemisphere. The State Department finally repudiated the Roosevelt Corollary in 1930.

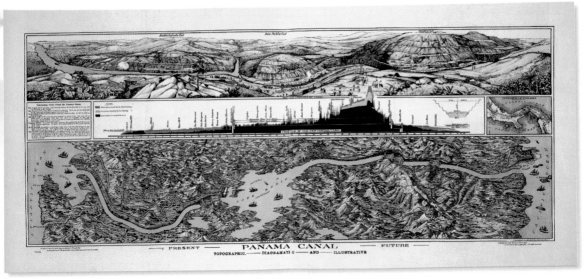

Dollar Diplomacy

ROOSEVELT'S HANDPICKED SUCCESSOR in the White House was William Howard Taft, whom TR had appointed secretary of war following Taft's return from the Philippines in 1904. Taft shared Roosevelt's desire to expand American influence in both Latin America and the Far East, but he favored as president an economic rather than military approach. Taft's policy, known as Dollar Diplomacy, advocated the economic penetration of foreign nations—backed up, only if necessary, by U.S. military force. At the new president's urging, U.S. capitalists began investing hundreds of millions of dollars in overseas ventures, especially in the Caribbean. These investments, Taft was sure, would enrich Wall Street and also promote American stewardship of the Western Hemisphere, which would in turn benefit the people of Latin America by ensuring political stability and economic growth.

The first important challenge to Dollar Diplomacy came in Nicaragua, where Pres. José Zelaya had lately been attempting to unify the nations of Central America against the United States. In 1909, Zelaya canceled some special economic privileges that had previously been granted to an American mining company. Later, he executed two Americans for taking part in a coup attempt allegedly instigated by that mining company. Taft responded by sending U.S. Marines to overthrow the Zelaya government and install a regime much friendlier to the United States. Meanwhile, Secretary of State Philander C. Knox, a former corporate lawyer, prevailed upon his friends in the U.S. banking community to provide large loans to Nicaragua so that Washington might have a stronger financial hold on the new government. Elsewhere, Knox used American economic resources to purchase the Haitian national debt and finance new railroad construction in China, lest the Russians and the Japanese create a transportation monopoly there.

During the 1912 presidential campaign, Democrat Woodrow Wilson made an issue of Dollar Diplomacy, attacking Republican imperialism and promising that under his administration the United States would "never again seek one additional foot of territory by conquest." Following his victory in a three-way race over Taft

This 1903 map illustrated the Panama Canal project for curious Americans. The top panel showed the excavations already conducted by Ferdinand de Lesseps; the middle panel showed the project in profile; and the bottom panel showed a bird's-eye view of the canal as it was expected to look upon completion.

and Roosevelt, Wilson named staunch anti-imperialist William Jennings Bryan as his secretary of state and declared that his goal in Latin America was to support "the orderly processes of just government based upon law, and not upon arbitrary or irregular force." Nevertheless, when the economies of Nicaragua, Haiti, and the Dominican Republic became unstable, and those countries suspended their debt payments to U.S. banks, Wilson sent in troops so that debt service might resume. By the end of his second term in office, the supremely idealistic Wilson had become, in the words of historian Walter LaFeber, "the greatest military interventionist in U.S. history."

Yet the most significant intervention of Wilson's first term had nothing at all to do with debt (although it did have something to do with money). It came in Mexico, where U.S. investment had so expanded during recent decades that Americans now owned more than 40 percent of all Mexican real estate. In 1910, an armed uprising began that a year later overthrew dictator Porfirio Díaz; in November 1911, Francisco Madero was elected president. Madero promised comprehensive democratic reforms, but his government was immobilized by militant attacks from both the left and the right, the latter supported by U.S. business interests that considered Madero's program a threat to their billion-dollar investment. On February 19, 1913, with the approval of the U.S. ambassador, Gen. Victoriano Huerta, commander of the government's forces, arrested Madero and assumed the presidency. Three days later, as the lame duck Taft prepared to recognize the Huerta government, Madero was shot while allegedly trying to escape.

This Clifford Berryman cartoon appeared on March 10, 1916, the day after Pancho Villa attacked Columbus, New Mexico. U.S. military involvement in Mexico (and, later, Europe) came as a complete surprise to President Wilson, who remarked as he left New Jersey on the way to his first inauguration, "It would be an irony of fate if my administration had to deal chiefly with foreign affairs."

An outraged Wilson vowed that he would never recognize a "government of butchers," even one receptive to U.S. investment. After taking office two weeks later, he demanded that Huerta resign and free elections be held. Huerta, of course, refused to do any such thing, yet Wilson remained determined to "teach the South [sic] American republics to elect good men." He persuaded the British to end their support for Huerta and began selling guns to Mexico's Constitutionalist opposition, led by Venustiano Carranza. Matters escalated in April 1914, when an officer in Huerta's army arrested a group of U.S. sailors who had gone ashore in Tampico. A superior officer quickly freed the sailors from the USS *Dolphin* and apologized personally to their captain, but the *Dolphin*'s commander pressed for a public apology in the form of a twenty-one-gun salute to the American flag. When the Mexicans refused, Wilson used the incident as an excuse to increase the U.S. naval presence in Mexican waters.

A few days later, on April 21, Wilson ordered some of these ships to seize the port of Veracruz to prevent a German ship from delivering munitions to Huerta's forces. Although intended by Wilson to be a bloodless operation, the occupation of Veracruz provoked fighting in the streets, during which 126 Mexicans were killed. The entire country—even the Constitutionalist opposition—was outraged by Wilson's heavy-handedness, and the unexpected intensity of its reaction gave the American president pause. Withdrawal of the U.S. troops was subsequently arranged through the international mediation of "the ABC powers"—Argentina, Brazil, and Chile.

W HEN CARRANZA'S ARMY CAPTURED Mexico City in August 1914, forcing Huerta into exile, it seemed as though Wilson's problems in Mexico were over. But Carranza's rejection of American guidelines regarding the establishment of a new Mexican government angered the U.S. president. Carranza didn't care much; he had more pressing problems. As the coalition that ousted Huerta broke apart, two dissatisfied factions began to threaten Carranza's rule. One, operating around Cuernavaca, was led by Emiliano Zapata; the other, active in the North, was commanded by Francisco "Pancho" Villa. For a time, Wilson considered supporting Villa in the Mexican civil war, but Latin American diplomats eventually led the American president back to Carranza, whose government received preliminary recognition from the United States in October 1915.

Feeling betrayed, Villa decided to strike back at the United States in the hope that escalating tensions between the two countries would undermine U.S. support for Carranza. In January 1916, he took seventeen American mining engineers off a train in northern Mexico and had them shot (one feigned death and escaped). Two months later, he led nearly five hundred Villistas in a cross-border raid, attacking the Thirteenth U.S. Cavalry Regiment at Camp Furlong before setting fire to nearby Columbus, New Mexico. Fourteen U.S. soldiers and ten Columbus residents died in the spree. Wilson told Carranza that he would be sending U.S. troops into northern Mexico to search for Villa, and the Mexican leader had little choice but to agree.

Commanded by Brig. Gen. John J. "Black Jack" Pershing, the hastily organized "punitive expedition" included forty-eight hundred soldiers, mostly cavalry, supported by motorized vehicles and aircraft. (It was the first time either of these new technologies was used by the U.S. Army in combat.) The Villistas couldn't be found, but Pershing's troops did fight a bloody skirmish with Carranzistas (whom they mistook for Villistas) on June 21, 1916, at Carrizal. The misguided American attack could have led to war with Mexico, had it not been for the European situation and Wilson's fear that deteriorating U.S. relations with Germany might require American troops to be sent overseas. Therefore, Wilson agreed to submit the Mexican grievance to an international commission, which eventually ruled that "the Carrizal affair" had been Pershing's fault.

The son of a field laborer, Pancho Villa (foreground) was orphaned at an early age. As a teenager, he killed one of the owners of the estate on which he worked in retaliation for an assault upon his sister. Afterward, Villa fled into the mountains, where he spent the rest of his adolescence before joining Francisco Madero's 1910 uprising against Porfirio Díaz.

Meanwhile, Villa continued to elude the Americans, whose presence up to three hundred miles inside Mexican territory seemed increasingly ridiculous and dangerous. Finally, in late January 1917, Wilson withdrew all U.S. forces from Mexico and ended the ten-month campaign. By this time, like the rest of the world, he was focusing his attention entirely on Europe.

The Great War

DURING THE CENTURY that followed the defeat of Napoléon in 1815, continental Europe had enjoyed a remarkable era of peace. To be sure, there had been some armed conflicts, such as the Franco-Prussian War of 1870, but these were few and relatively contained. In June 1914, however, the assassination of Archduke Francis Ferdinand, heir presumptive to the Austro-Hungarian throne, by a Serbian nationalist in Sarajevo triggered a chain reaction of diplomatic ultimatums that by early August had produced a general war. In many respects, the Great War was a conflict waiting to happen, born of imperialist rivalries among the world's leading military powers. On one side were the Central Powers, including Germany, Austria-Hungary, and Turkey. Opposing them were the Allied Powers, among them France, Great Britain, and Russia (a traditional ally of the Serbs).

Wilson tried to keep the United States out of the fighting. Isolationist sentiment among Americans was strong, and there were enough German immigrants living in the country to make U.S. entry into the war on the Allied side a contentious issue, at least in 1914. In any case, Wilson preferred to present himself as an impartial arbiter of peace: On August 5, the day after Great Britain declared war on

By the time the United States joined the fighting in late 1917, the Great War was already three years old. Tens of millions of Europeans were dead, wounded, or facing starvation; and the front lines, where soldiers huddled in miles and miles of wretched trenches, hadn't moved significantly in years.

Germany, he announced U.S. neutrality and called on all Americans to remain nonpartisan "in thought as well as in action." This proved easier said than done.

The most significant cause of friction between Germany and the United States involved Germany's use of submarine warfare. At the time the First World War began, the German army was the mightiest on the planet, but the German navy left much to be desired. The unsurpassed British Royal Navy immediately imposed a stifling blockade on all German ports. Aware that they couldn't compete with the British on the water's surface, the Germans began investing in a relatively new naval technology: the submarine. The idea of warships that could operate underwater had been around since the sixteenth century, but only since the turn of the twentieth century had submarines become practical weapons. In 1900, American inventor John Holland sold the first sub with a practical propulsion system to the U.S. Navy. (It employed an internal-combustion engine for surface operation and a battery-driven electric motor for propulsion while submerged.) Germany began the war with just thirty-eight submarines; during the next four years, it built nearly four hundred more.

AT FIRST, IT WAS GERMAN POLICY to torpedo enemy vessels on sight. Exactly what type of ship qualified as an enemy vessel, however, was sometimes unclear. In May 1915, for example, a German *Unterseeboot*, or U-boat, sank the British passenger liner *Lusitania* off the coast of Ireland—killing 1,198 people, of whom 128 were Americans. As the Germans later pointed out, the *Lusitania* was also carrying a substantial quantity of munitions, but this detail was lost in the public outcry over German "barbarism." An irate Wilson exchanged a series of diplomatic notes with Germany, in which he demanded an end to U-boat attacks on civilian vessels and respect for the rights of neutral nations. Seeking to avoid U.S. intervention on the side of the Allies, the Germans backed down and agreed to restrict their submarine operations.

This German poster from 1914 shows Great Britain surrounded by predatory U-boats. To protect their shipping from submarine attack, the British and Americans eventually developed the convoy system.

Tensions continued, however, in large part because American neutrality was not all that neutral. When the war began and Britain imposed its blockade on Germany, the United States could have not merely denounced the blockade as illegal but actually cut off trade with Britain until the illegal blockade was lifted. Instead, Wilson tolerated the embargo and gave up America's right as a neutral nation to trade freely with Germany. His policy made a great deal of economic sense, because trade with Germany was slight compared to U.S. commerce with Great Britain. Even before the war, Britain had been America's most important trading partner, and British wartime munitions orders proved to be a fantastic boon to the U.S. economy. Overall, between 1914 and 1916, Allied purchases of American goods quadrupled. Meanwhile, Wilson berated the Germans for threatening U.S. commerce—a rather insincere position, given the British interdiction. In the aftermath of the sinking of the *Lusitania*, however, Secretary of State Bryan argued that fairness demanded that the president make equally strong demands of Great Britain regarding its blockade. When Wilson refused, Bryan resigned.

Early in 1916, the Allies began arming merchant ships to attack the submarines, which (because of their limited battery capacity) had to spend most of their time on the surface. The German government's response was to announce that, once again, all enemy ships would be attacked without warning. A few weeks later, a U-boat sank the unarmed cross-channel steamer *Sussex*, injuring several American passengers and provoking another round of demands from Wilson that the Germans abandon their "unlawful" tactics. Again, Germany backed down.

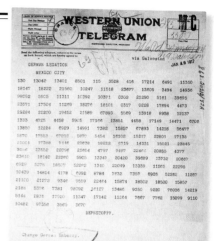

By early 1917, however, with its soldiers stuck in the same trenches they had occupied for three years, the Germans became impatient. Deciding to risk everything for victory, they massed their ground forces for a major offensive in France while simultaneously deploying their entire U-boat fleet to cut off shipments of supplies to the Allies. When all was ready, the German ambassador to the United States informed Wilson that, beginning February 1, German U-boats would again sink all ships—enemy or neutral, military or merchant—that came within a wide zone around Great Britain. It was made quite clear that U.S. ships entering this area would be subject to attack. The Germans knew that such a declaration would likely mean war with the United States, but they gambled that the German army would conquer France before large numbers of U.S. troops could be mobilized and sent overseas.

The United States Enters the War

WILSON PREPARED TO ASK CONGRESS for a declaration of war, but he waited for the right moment in order to maximize his public support—wisely, it turned out, because subsequent developments in February and March greatly enhanced his position. On February 24, the British ambassador provided to Wilson a copy of a telegram that the British had recently intercepted and decoded. Sent by German foreign minister Arthur Zimmermann to his embassy in Mexico City, it proposed that, in the event of hostilities between the United States and Germany, the Mexicans enter the war on the side of the Central Powers and proceed to reclaim their "lost provinces" in Texas and the Southwest. A transcript was released to the American press several days later. Two weeks after that, U-boats torpedoed five American merchant ships without warning.

On April 2, 1917, Wilson requested from Congress a declaration of war against Germany. In his message, he made clear his ambitions for a universalistic peace rooted in American moral values—especially in the principle of self-governance, which he considered a panacea for nearly all political ills. "We shall fight," Wilson declared, "for the things we have always carried nearest our hearts—for democracy, for the right of those who submit to authority to have a voice in their own governments, for the rights and liberties of small nations, for a universal dominion of right by such a concert of free peoples as shall bring peace and safety to all nations and make the world itself at last free…. The world must be made safe for democracy." The specifics of Wilson's approach, the so-called Fourteen Points, were later enunciated in a speech he delivered to Congress on January 8, 1918.

Two decades after the Spanish-American War, Americans had become accustomed to their status as citizens of a world power and so responded eagerly to Wilson's crusade. Because the U.S. Army had returned after the "liberation" of Cuba to its traditionally small peacetime force status, the government initiated a hugely successful recruiting drive, which enlisted hundreds of thousands of volunteers. It also enacted a draft, which met with little objection. By war's end, more than four million Americans had been sent overseas.

Pershing at his headquarters in Chaumont, France, in October 1918.

CHOSEN TO COMMAND the American Expeditionary Force (AEF), which began shipping out in late 1917, was Black Jack Pershing, recently recalled from Mexico, where he had not fared well but had somehow managed to escape with his good reputation intact. Allied supreme commander Ferdinand Foch wanted to integrate the new American troops into existing French command structure, but Pershing insisted that the AEF operate as an independent army under his command. Consequently, the Americans were given their own sector of the front and assigned a distinct role in the counteroffensive that began in early August 1918 following the only partially successful German offensives of March and July. On August 8—which German general Erich Ludendorff later called "the black day of the German army"—British troops struck with 450 tanks along the

Somme, overwhelming the forward German positions. On September 14, Pershing's army captured the Saint-Mihiel salient, which the Germans had held since late 1914. On October 3, a new German parliamentary government replaced Kaiser Wilhelm II's autocratic regime and that night sent a message to Wilson, requesting an armistice and peace negotiations based on his Fourteen Points.

After a formal armistice was signed on November 11, Wilson

The Big Four *at the Hotel Crillon in Paris on May 27, 1919. From left to right: Lloyd George, Orlando, Clemenceau, and Wilson.*

turned all his energies to the task of brokering a fair and lasting peace. A treaty conference was convened at Versailles in mid-January 1919. It featured the Big Three powers—the United States, Great Britain, and France—which were represented personally by their heads of state: Wilson, British prime minister David Lloyd George, and French premier Georges Clemenceau. As part of his plan for a new world order, Wilson sought to substitute international cooperation for the dangerous brinkmanship that had characterized the prewar era. The last of his Fourteen Points had proposed the creation of a "general association of nations" to resolve international disputes—a suggestion readily accepted by Clemenceau and Lloyd George—but it also had endorsed national self-determination for ethnic groups, which did not at all please the British and the French. The United States, which had only belatedly joined the fighting, might be willing to forgo the spoils of victory, but not so Great Britain and France. After enduring four years of horrific warfare, these imperial powers felt justified in taking everything they could get.

Clemenceau's obsession with French security and Lloyd George's hunger to bolster the sagging British Empire gave Wilson the most trouble. Despite the American president's call for "open covenants of peace, openly arrived at," most of the negotiations took place in secret conferences from which even Prime Minister Vittorio Orlando of Italy, a junior member of the Allied coalition, was typically excluded. Capitulating on national self-determination, Wilson allowed Lloyd George and Clemenceau to redraw Europe's political map and divide up Germany's overseas possessions with little regard to the wishes of their inhabitants. He also permitted Great Britain and France to load down Germany with staggering reparations payments that would cause no end of trouble later. Nonetheless, some of his Fourteen Points were incorporated into the final agreement, which Wilson still considered compatible with his overall goals. Most importantly, the treaty included a covenant establishing the League of Nations.

The Ratification Fight

IN JULY 1919, WILSON BROUGHT the Treaty of Versailles home. A small group of fourteen Senate "irreconcilables" refused to support it—or any other form of U.S. participation in the League of Nations—because they considered the league a violation of their isolationist principles. There were still plenty of other senators, however, who could be induced to support the treaty if only Wilson would assuage some of their doubts concerning its alleged infringements on U.S. sovereignty. These doubts were distilled into a list of forty-nine "reservations" prepared by Senate Foreign Relations Committee chairman Henry Cabot Lodge, who offered them up as amendments to the treaty after keeping it bottled up in his committee for two long months. Wilson's advisers warned him that he would have to accept at least some of the reservations in order to win ratification, but Wilson, who had been acting haughtily throughout, refused. "I shall consent to nothing," he said. "The Senate must take its medicine."

THE LAMB FROM THE SLAUGHTER.

This September 1919 Clifford Berryman cartoon of Henry Cabot Lodge escorting the Versailles Treaty was entitled, "The Lamb from the Slaughter."

To mobilize public support for the treaty, Wilson undertook an arduous cross-country tour. On September 25, 1919, he delivered a particularly impassioned speech at Pueblo, Colorado; the next day, he awoke with uncontrollable facial twitching. A stroke soon followed that paralyzed his entire left side. Wilson returned immediately to Washington, where he remained in bed for six weeks, seeing almost no one except for his doctor and his second wife, Edith, who managed his political affairs while he recuperated.

Just about the time in mid-November that Wilson resumed a partial public schedule, the Senate voted to accept fourteen of Lodge's reservations. A still-defiant Wilson instructed Democratic senators loyal to the administration to vote down the amended treaty, which they did on November 19. Later, when the Senate voted on the original treaty without reservations, it was also defeated. The United States, therefore, never ratified the Treaty of Versailles and never joined the League of Nations. Wilson began looking ahead to the 1920 presidential election, which he hoped would become a "solemn referendum" on U.S. membership in the league. But that campaign became instead a referendum on Wilsonian universalism, and by then Americans had had enough of global involvement. In overwhelming numbers, they abandoned the Democratic party and voted for Republican Warren G. Harding, who promised a return to "normalcy" and took advantage of the new women's vote to win a record landslide victory. Imperialism survived, but internationalism was dead.

Lodge (third from the right) and his Senate Foreign Relations Committee colleagues.

Henry Cabot Lodge
1850–1924

by Thomas Fleming

HENRY CABOT LODGE has suffered an unfortunate historical fate. He has been demonized as the prototypical isolationist because he led the fight in the Senate against Woodrow Wilson's plan to make the United States a founding member of the League of Nations. In fact, Lodge strongly supported U.S. involvement in world affairs. As early as 1893, when he first took his seat as a senator from Massachusetts, Lodge saw an active foreign policy as crucial to the development of America's national character.

Like many members of his generation, Lodge (born in 1850) was profoundly influenced by the Civil War, which he interpreted as a conflict between good and evil. This assessment later brought him to the conclusion that America's role in the world should be to fight similar battles beyond its shores. To do so, the United States would have to be strong, so Lodge pushed for military expansion and supported the Spanish-American War, which he called "a great broad question" in which "right and wrong are involved." He even welcomed the controversial annexation of the Philippine Islands and Puerto Rico because, he said, "we have risen to become one of the world's great powers." He hoped that new, idealistic American leadership would provide the world with "fresh sources of energy" more ennobling than the often "sordid" imperialism of Britain, France, Germany, and Russia, which then dominated two-thirds of the globe.

When fellow Republican Theodore Roosevelt became president in 1901, Lodge enthusiastically backed TR's internationalism, supporting the Panama Canal and Roosevelt's mediation of the Russo-Japanese War. Lodge was equally enthusiastic about Secretary of State John Hay's Open Door policy for China, and he exulted when Roosevelt sent America's Great White Fleet on its around-the-world, flag-waving junket. The worst possible foreign policy, Lodge thought, was inaction—which is why he simply couldn't abide the pale neutrality that President Wilson seemed to embody during the first three years of the Great War. Certain that Great Britain and France were fighting for "the right"—and that Germany was not merely wrong but evil—Lodge wanted the United States to side with the Allies right away. He even supported the idea of a postwar League to Enforce Peace, modeled on the 1815 Congress of Vienna, which had created a new European order in the aftermath of Napoléon's defeat.

While Wilson called repeatedly for "peace without victory," Lodge condemned the president for being weak and indecisive—an opinion he refused to moderate even after Wilson asked Congress in April 1917 for a declaration of war. Later, Lodge particularly objected to the clause in Wilson's beloved Versailles peace treaty that required the United States, as a member of the new League of Nations, to participate in all future wars conducted by the league. This provision, he was certain, violated the Constitution, which reserved to Congress the power to declare war; it also violated Lodge's conviction that American military force should only be used when backed by the united will of the American people.

For his part, Wilson saw Lodge as a narrow, mean-spirited man who would "break the heart of the world" for partisan political gain. In fact, their policy battle became so entangled with personal hatred that any hope of compromise soon vanished. In the end, Lodge won the political battle: The United States never joined the League of Nations, and Wilson's Democrats

Lodge as he appeared *during the first decade of the twentieth century.*

were routed in the 1920 election. Yet Wilson and his adherents have so far won the historiographical war, having demonized Lodge so thoroughly that his once bright vision of America as a source of idealism in international affairs has largely been forgotten.

17

THE PROGRESSIVE ERA

The Triangle Fire

O^{N MONDAY}, September 27, 1909, owners Isaac Harris and Max Blanck locked two hundred young Jewish and Italian women out of their jobs at the Triangle Shirtwaist Company in New York City. The reason was that all but seven members of Triangle's mostly immigrant, overwhelmingly female workforce had attended a meeting the previous Thursday night at which officials of the International Ladies' Garment Workers' Union (ILGWU) discussed the possibility of unionizing Triangle. On Friday, September 24, Harris and Blanck, known as "the shirtwaist kings," had "called the girls together and expostulated with them more in sorrow than in anger," *The Survey* magazine reported. "Terms were once more arranged between a delegation of operators and the firm and the next day everyone went back to work as usual. On Monday, however, when the girls reported for work the shop was found closed. The next day it was once more open. But no union girls were taken back so...the lockout began."

Shirtwaists, essentially fitted blouses, were the most popular garments worn by young women at the turn of the twentieth century. Glamorized by commercial artist Charles Dana Gibson, they became the standard attire of the millions of women then entering the workforce. Available in many fabrics and designs, they were generally worn with tailored skirts. The shirtwaists made by the Triangle Company, the largest firm in the

AT LEFT: **Two women unionists** *take a break from their picketing to pose for this news photograph in February 1910. Their strike against the New York City garment industry became known as the Uprising of the Twenty Thousand.*

business, were of medium quality and intended for mass sales.

Aware of the growing sentiment for unionization, Harris and Blanck had established a year earlier the Triangle Employees Benevolent Association, a so-called company union; but this club for favored employees did little to blunt nascent demands of other workers for better pay, shorter hours, and improved working conditions. During 1908 and 1909, groups of Triangle workers began appearing at the nearby headquarters of ILGWU Local 25 asking for help. Unfortunately, there was little the struggling union could do for them; it had only four hundred members and was nearly penniless itself.

In this respect, the garment trade resembled most other American industries at the time. Despite the persistent efforts of union organizers over the past quarter century, no strong industry-wide unions had emerged in the United States. At the turn of the twentieth century, ten million Americans, or a third of the total labor force, worked in factories; of these, fewer than 4 percent belonged to unions. Large-scale efforts to organize them—such as Eugene Debs's American Railway Union—had consistently been defeated by the joint action of employers. The ILGWU was merely labor's latest attempt to organize the garment industry, all earlier ones having failed to accomplish the task.

Rank-and-file organizers kept at it, however, because factory workers desperately needed the help. The Triangle workers, for example, like most other garment workers in New York City, toiled in crowded, unkempt lofts where windows and doors were often nailed shut (to prevent pilferage) and the humidity could rise to oppressive levels (perhaps contributing to the coinage in 1892 of the word *sweatshop*). Most garment workers put in fifty-six-hour, six-day workweeks for as little as three dollars a week, and when factory owners needed a rush order filled, they often "sweated" their powerless employees at night and on Sundays for no additional pay. Some employers even deducted from worker pay penalties assessed for mistakes made while sewing, and others levied fines for violations of work rules regarding talking, smoking, and singing while on the job.

O NCE THE TRIANGLE lockout began, ILGWU Local 25 immediately declared a strike and organized picket lines that became the talk of the town. One reason for their notoriety was the unusual solidarity among Jewish and Italian women at a time when ethnic groups generally kept their distance from one another. In fact, it was the first time that immigrant workers from different backgrounds had so publicly set aside their fears and suspicions in favor of a common economic interest. Previously, when Jews went on strike, employers hired Italians, and vice versa. (More often than not in 1909, the supply of immigrant labor greatly exceeded the demand, and employers had little difficulty

THE NEW LOFT FACTORIES

THE BRINGING TOGETHER of garment workers under a single roof was a relatively recent development in New York City, which dominated the nation's garment industry at the turn of the twentieth century. Before 1900, manufacturers typically farmed out their sewing to immigrants working in their tene-ment homes. (Families often labored together at this work, for which they were paid by the piece.) With the advent of electrified loft buildings, however, it became much more efficient to bring immigrants into the workplace. Even so, families still worked together, as mothers, daughters, aunts, and cousins helped one another land jobs at the same factory.

New York City law required that factories allow 250 cubic feet of air space per worker. This requirement kept down the number of workers an employer could pack into Manhat-tan's old, low-ceilinged buildings. But the new lofts, with their high ceilings, permitted factory floors to become much more crowded and, therefore, efficient—at least from the owners' point of view. New electric equipment also enabled workers to sew much faster and pro-duce more goods for the same cost in wages.

Under this new system, skilled machine operators, usually men, supervised teams of young women, who performed the simpler tasks that preceded the final construction of the garment. At large companies such as Triangle, the factory owners paid these team leaders, known as contractors, according to the number and style of the garments they produced. Each con-tractor, in turn, paid his female assistants whatever he thought their work was worth. Following the prevailing social mores, the young women showed their appreciation for whatever they received by accepting it meekly and without complaint.

Jacob A. Riis took this photograph of Jewish immigrants working in a Ludlow Street tenement on New York City's Lower East Side in 1889.

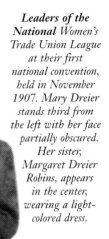

Leaders of the National Women's Trade Union League at their first national convention, held in November 1907. Mary Dreier stands third from the left with her face partially obscured. Her sister, Margaret Dreier Robins, appears in the center, wearing a light-colored dress.

filling unskilled or semiskilled positions.) But the Triangle action—and the wider, industrywide strike that it sparked—set a pattern for future cooperation in the labor movement that spurred its growth. Jewish union organizers learned some Italian, Italian organizers learned some Yiddish, and they all pitched in on behalf of the strikers. Notably active among local politicians were Meyer London, who became in 1914 one of the first Socialist congressmen, and Fiorello La Guardia, who won election himself to the House in 1916 before becoming a three-term mayor of the city.

Another reason for all the talk about the Triangle Shirtwaist Company strike was the involvement of wealthy ladies who wanted to demonstrate the solidarity they felt for less fortunate workingwomen. In 1903, some of these "uptown" ladies had helped to found the National Women's Trade Union League (NWTUL), which emerged in response to the American Federation of Labor's reluctance to organize women. Many members of the NWTUL's New York branch, known simply as the Women's Trade Union League (WTUL), joined the Triangle picket lines and were arrested along with the strikers. Their involvement generated an enormous amount of publicity—especially after November 4, when the police arrested WTUL president Mary Dreier, sister of NWTUL president Margaret Dreier Robins.

On another occasion in mid-December, wearing a hat so large that it required six jeweled pins to keep it in place, Mrs. Alva Belmont appeared at night court on behalf of four arrested strikers. After waiting nearly six hours for their case to be heard, Mrs. Belmont put up her Madison Avenue mansion as collateral for their bail. The presiding magistrate, a man named Butts, asked her, jokingly, whether the house was worth enough to cover the eight-hundred-dollar bail. She replied, "I think it is. It is valued at four hundred thousand dollars. There is a mortgage of one hundred thousand dollars on it which I raised to help the cause of the shirtwaist makers and the women's suffrage movement." The time noted on the bail bond that Butts then approved was 2:45 A.M.

> "One man whom I advised to install a fire drill replied to me: 'Let 'em burn. They're a lot of cattle, anyway.'"
>
> —
>
> *H. F. J. Porter, fire prevention expert quoted in the* New York Times *after the Triangle fire*

WOMEN'S SUFFRAGE

SUFFRAGE FOR WOMEN had been at the center of the women's rights movement ever since 1848, when Elizabeth Cady Stanton's controversial Resolution Nine was adopted at the Seneca Falls convention. Yet not much seemed to have been achieved since then. Several western states had granted women the right to vote, beginning with Wyoming in 1869, but these did so only as part of a larger power struggle between settlers and itinerants. (Allowing women to vote gave farm families a clear majority over the cowboys, miners, and railroad workers who were only passing through.) By 1900, when Carrie Chapman Catt became president of the two-million-member National American Woman Suffrage Association (NAWSA), women had organized themselves thoroughly, yet Congress still refused to grant them the vote.

As NAWSA president, Catt pursued a state-by-state campaign. Between 1910 and 1914, her slow, methodical work brought women the vote in eight more states. But in 1915, women's suffrage referenda failed in Massachusetts, New Jersey, New York, and Pennsylvania. Men who drank feared that women would enact temperance laws; men who owned factories thought women might ban child labor; men who ran political machines didn't want their franchises upset; and many others thought the reality of women voting would unpleasantly disrupt the traditional social order.

Alice Paul had a different view than Catt did of how best to obtain the vote for women. She wanted to force Congress to pass a constitutional amendment enfranchising all American women at once, and her primary target

***Carrie Chapman Catt** was Susan B. Anthony's personal choice to succeed Anthony as president of NAWSA in 1900.*

Before becoming a full-time suffrage activist, Alice Paul spent three years in England as a caseworker at a London settlement house.

was the Democratic party then in power. On January 10, 1917, she unleashed her organization, the hundred-thousand-member National Woman's Party (NWP), on Pres. Woodrow Wilson, picketing the White House on a daily basis. "MR. PRESIDENT," one of the NWP's many banners read, "HOW LONG MUST WE WAIT FOR LIBERTY?"

Catt considered Paul's approach unwisely combative—and, after the United States entered the Great War in April 1917, positively appalling. Paul thought Catt's strategy was getting women nowhere. In fact, according to historian Nancy Cott, "neither the shocking militancy of the National Woman's Party nor the ladylike moderation of NAWSA was so solely responsible for victory as each group publicly claimed of itself—and neither was as counterproductive as each group privately complained of the other. In retrospect, it's clear that the two organizations complemented each other, although they believed they worked at cross purposes."

Both claimed credit when the House approved the Nineteenth Amendment on January 10, 1918; both worked hard to prod the Senate to follow suit, which it did rather belatedly on June 4, 1919; and both celebrated on August 18, 1920, when Tennessee's narrow approval of the Nineteenth Amendment completed the ratification process. As a result, on November 2, 1920, Catt, Paul, and millions of other American women voted for the first time in a U.S. presidential election.

The Triangle strikers needed all the help they could get because Harris and Blanck had the police on their side. According to Joseph Flecher, an assistant cashier at Triangle, "You could get a man on the beat to look away by giving him a box of cigars with a hundred-dollar bill in it. Then the hoodlums hired by the company could do their work without interference. They couldn't hit women, even on the picket line. So they brought their lady friends—prostitutes. They knew how to start fights." And when the fights started, the pickets were arrested. "The girls have been entirely orderly but police interference has made them appear otherwise," *The Survey* reported on November 13. "The officers break in upon any who are talking together…and the least refusal to answer the officers is made excuse for prompt arrest. Unfair treatment has not stopped there for in court the judges railroaded through a whole batch of girls at a time without as much as a hearing."

The Uprising of the Twenty Thousand

AS WORKERS AT OTHER shirtwaist companies in the city watched the events unfold at Triangle, they, too, began approaching the ILGWU for help. On the evening of November 22, unionization meetings were held at assembly halls all over town. The principal gathering took place in the Great Hall of the Cooper Union. AFL president Samuel L. Gompers (who had come around to supporting the ILGWU) and Mary Dreier were among those who spoke, but the climax of the evening came when young Clara Lemlich, a shirtwaist worker and member of the Local 25 executive committee, rose to say that there had been enough talk. She called for a general strike, which formally began when the crowd at Cooper Union approved her passionate motion by acclamation.

New York City policemen arrest picketers during the Uprising of the Twenty Thousand. The Women's Trade Union League was especially helpful in raising money to post bail and pay fines, but some women did have to spend time in the workhouse on Blackwells Island.

At the time, New York City's six hundred garment-industry factories employed more than thirty thousand people, of whom 80 percent were women. The strike that began on November 22, which the ILGWU billed as "the Uprising of the Twenty Thousand," affected five hundred of those companies and lasted most of the winter. It was the first industrywide strike undertaken in New York City by immigrant workers and the nation's largest female job action yet. Three-quarters of the pickets were young women between the ages of sixteen and twenty-five. Almost all were foreign born or the children of recent immigrants; most were either Jewish or Italian.

Many employers responded by showering higher pay (up to twenty dollars a week) and other perks (such as free lunches) on employees willing to cross the picket lines and remain at work. Harris and Blanck installed a phonograph on the factory floor and permitted dancing at lunchtime. "Mr. Blanck even used to give out prizes to those who were the best dancers," one of the faithful recalled. "But once the

strike was over—no more dancing, no more prizes, no more phonograph."

Outside in the cold winter weather, the poorly clad women pickets did their best to keep up their morale despite accelerating arrests, which totaled 723 by Christmas Day. With the benefit of bail money provided by the Women's Trade Union League, however, most of those arrested were out of jail the next day and back on the picket lines.

Members of ILGWU Local 25 carry a special edition of the New York Call *explaining their strike in English, Yiddish, and Italian.*

Mulberry Street in New York City at the turn of the twentieth century. The activity shown here was typical of life on the Lower East Side.

IN ADDITION, a host of journalists, social workers, academics, and other professionals contributed their time, money, and efforts to make the strike a success. Many were middle- and upper-class German Jews, whose forebears had arrived in America several generations earlier. Participating in the strike gave them a chance to aid poorer Jews from eastern Europe, most of whom had only recently arrived. Other ILGWU benefactors included New Yorkers who had initially opposed unionization but had been persuaded by the tumult of the 1890s of the need to remedy the deepening class conflict.

Within the immigrant community itself, officials from other labor unions, Socialist party leaders, priests, rabbis, local newspaper editors, and ordinary workers aided the ILGWU pickets as best they could. An open meeting on December 5 drew more than eight thousand people and helped turn public opinion sharply against the factory owners, who began to feel mounting pressure from City Hall to resolve the dispute.

The process of settlement began with arbitration. Several compromise proposals were made, all of which were rejected by the workers. Then, a number of smaller manufacturers, eager to resume production, started settling privately with the ILGWU. By February 15, 1910, enough companies had come to terms with the union that it declared the strike officially over. By the ILGWU's own count, however, thirteen of the largest shirtwaist firms, employing more than a thousand workers, still refused to settle with the union. Chief among these was Triangle.

The garment workers had made several important gains in the new union shops: Workweeks were reduced to fifty-two hours, with a two-hour limit on evening overtime; wages were increased 12 to 15 percent; and employers promised to end the contractor system and pay all workers directly. As a result, in the months following the "uprising," ILGWU membership surged from several hundred to sixty thousand. "But," as Leon Stein, the former editor of *Justice* (the ILGWU's official magazine), has pointed out, "the strike that began at Triangle was not won at Triangle." The union remained unrecognized there, and no concessions were made.

A little over a year later, a fire broke out at the Triangle factory. "On the twenty-fifth of March [1911]," one survivor recalled, "it was the same policemen who had clubbed [the pickets] back into submission who kept the thousands in Washington Square from trampling upon their dead bodies, sent for ambulances to carry them away, and lifted them one by one into the receiving coffins."

Reform Movements of the Late Nineteenth Century

THE FATE OF THE TRIANGLE WORKERS shocked New Yorkers—and Americans in other cities as well. Few outside the neighborhoods of the Lower East Side had paid much attention to the goings-on there, and little was known in general about the new industrial conditions. Yet, as noted earlier, there were several reform writers during the late nineteenth century who thought seriously about the problems of the new American industrial society— even as the rest of the country remained, for the most part, blissfully unaware of the dislocations to come.

Most prominent among these writers was a group of socialist writers who agreed that communal control of factories, land, and other resources was necessary (although they disagreed on how best to achieve this end). They expressed their ideas in landmark books that advocated the complete overhauling of American economic and political institutions. In *Progress and Poverty* (1877–1879), Single Taxer Henry George attacked the inequities of private landownership and the evils of urban-industrial life. A decade later, the best-selling novel *Looking Backward* (1888) expressed Edward Bellamy's vision of a socialist utopia based on the guarantee of material equality. In 1894, journalist Henry Demarest Lloyd published *Wealth Against Commonwealth*, in which he called for the abolition of monopolistic and other corrupt business practices, particularly those developed by John D. Rockefeller's Standard Oil Company.

Uppermost in the minds of these and other late-nineteenth-century reformers was the sense that the United States would soon be consumed by class warfare unless something drastic was done to ameliorate the terrible conditions in the nation's slums and factories. At the same time, however, another group was

This cartoon from a September 1904 issue of Puck depicts Standard Oil as an octopus with its tentacles wrapped around the steel, copper, and shipping industries, as well as a statehouse and the U.S. Capitol. Another tentacle extends toward the White House.

emerging whose viewpoint was considerably less apocalyptic. Beginning in the late 1880s, young college-educated women formed organizations and institutions dedicated to gradually improving the lives of the immigrant poor. Among the most effective of these efforts were the settlement houses that provided a variety of social services to foreign-born working people who were having difficulty acclimating themselves to life in America. By 1910, there were more than four hundred settlement houses operating in the major cities of the East and Midwest, where immigrants tended to congregate. The most famous of these were Lillian Wald's Henry Street Settlement on Manhattan's Lower East Side and Jane Addams's Hull House in Chicago, both founded in 1889.

JANE ADDAMS
1860–1935

DURING THE LATE 1880s, Jane Addams was touring Europe with a friend when she visited Toynbee Hall in London's industrial East End. Founded in 1884 by Samuel Augustus Barnett, Toynbee Hall was the first social settlement, or settlement house. Its original purpose was to provide a residence for well-to-do Oxford- and Cambridge-educated students who wanted to learn more about working-class life. In addition to collecting social data, however, these "settlers" soon began offering adult education courses to neighborhood residents and otherwise sought to improve local conditions. Addams and her companion, Ellen Gates Starr, were so impressed with the work being done at Toynbee Hall that they decided to found their own settlement house in Chicago upon their return. (Two disciples

of Barnett, Charles B. Stover and Stanton Coit, had already started the Neighborhood Guild, later the University Settlement, on New York City's Lower East Side in 1886.)

The most suitable building that Addams and Starr could find was the decaying Hull mansion, located in the heart of one of Chicago's poorest immigrant neighborhoods. The two women moved in on September 18, 1889, and other young men and women soon joined them. They immediately invited their neighbors to visit, and before long many neighborhood residents did begin attending the lectures being held at Hull House and joining the clubs that met there. During the next four years, Hull House expanded to include a day-care center, a gymnasium, a dispensary, a playground, and a cooperative boardinghouse for single working-women. It also offered cooking and sewing classes; lessons in art, music, and language; and even theatrical productions. Each week, two thousand people passed through its doors.

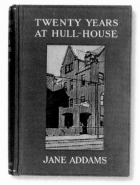

Furthermore, under Addams's leadership, Hull House became an important center for Progressive reform. She and her fellow residents pressured state and federal legislators to act on such critical issues as child labor, factory inspection, and union recognition. In fact, Addams was among those in 1903 who founded the National Women's Trade Union League.

YET ANOTHER REFORM element focused its energies on cleaning up municipal politics. Members of organizations such as the National Civic Federation abhorred the waste and corruption generated by urban political machines and thought that city governments should be run much more efficiently. In New York City, for example, a number of wealthy Protestant businessmen went after the Catholic Tammany Hall machine, though without much success.

Quite often, fundamental cultural differences made it difficult, if not impossible, for reformers and immigrants to work together. For example, most immigrants tolerated gambling and drinking, while the bulk of the Protestant upper class held to a more puritanical moralistic code. Economic factors also kept the two groups apart: Recent immigrants depended for jobs on the very political patronage that municipal reformers sought to eliminate.

One thing that helped break down these barriers was information. Following the example set by Henry Demarest Lloyd, more and more journalists began examining and exposing social ills in the belief that the first step toward solving problems was to publicize them. These early investigative journalists were called "muckrakers" because, as Theodore Roosevelt liked to say, their task was to "rake through the muck" of dishonesty and misconduct. Ida Tarbell's articles for *McClure's Magazine* on John D. Rockefeller's business dealings encouraged Roosevelt to pursue as president an antitrust suit against Standard Oil; Lincoln Steffens, also writing for *McClure's*, penned a series on municipal corruption later published in book form as *The Shame of the Cities* (1904); and David Graham Phillips eventually tried Roosevelt's patience with a series on federal corruption entitled *The Treason of the Senate*. As a result, by 1910, numerous Americans had come to understand the dangers of unrestrained industrial capitalism, and this made it much easier for different reform constituencies to come together. Historians have since labeled the movement that they formed Progressivism.

An issue of McClure's Magazine *from May 1903.* McClure's *was the leading organ of the muckrakers during the early twentieth century.*

The Progressive Movement

UNLIKE THE LATE-NINETEENTH-CENTURY reformers, the Progressives of the early twentieth century feared no imminent social cataclysm. Instead, they were motivated by strong nationalistic feelings and a supremely optimistic sense of America's future. Nationalism and reform went hand in hand for these people because both impulses emerged from the same idealistic appreciation of American potential. Most Progressives simply wanted a decent society and believed that one could be had through steady effort and gradual improvement. The sort of revolutionary change envisioned by Henry George and Edward Bellamy seemed altogether unnecessary and a great deal of trouble.

By and large, Progressives were also deeply committed to Christian morality, and much of their political agenda took shape within a strongly ethical framework. Frances Perkins, who later became secretary of labor under Franklin Roosevelt, described the Progressive philosophy as dominated by "the idea that poverty is preventable, that poverty is destructive, wasteful, demoralizing, and that poverty in the midst of potential plenty is morally unacceptable in a Christian and

In this October 1903 Puck *cartoon, New York City reformer Seth Low uses ammunition labeled "clean record," "capable administration," and "just return for taxes" to subdue Tammany Hall.*

democratic society." For similar reasons relating to Christian stewardship, Progressives also sought to regulate dangerous concentrations of economic power, preserve the nation's natural resources, and return honesty to government.

Yet an equally important quality of Progressive ideology was its rationalism. For example, Progressives had unshakable confidence in the ability of "experts" to manage public affairs with propriety and efficiency. Trained professionals, such as social workers and social scientists, were presumed able in nearly all instances to develop rational, scientific solutions to the country's problems—given enough time and money, of course. This rather elitist approach was sometimes used to cloak efforts to keep power out of the hands of immigrant political organizations; nevertheless, most Progressives believed sincerely in expertise and remained oblivious to its antidemocratic implications.

On the local level, Progressives often echoed the calls of earlier municipal reformers for the creation of nonpartisan investigating agencies to root out government corruption. They also wanted regulatory agencies established to oversee business practices and panels of experts appointed to devise programs of reform. Beginning in the late 1890s, electoral successes enabled them to gain

MULLER V. OREGON

DURING THE FIRST DECADE of the twentieth century, a number of states enacted broad programs of legislation designed to regulate the wages and hours of factory workers, especially those of women and children. Maryland, for example, passed the first workmen's compensation law in 1902, and in February 1903 Oregon passed a measure prohibiting employers from working female employees more than ten hours a day. A year and a half later, steam laundry owner Curt Muller was charged with violating this law because he had forced Emma Gotcher to work overtime until she met her quota for the day.

Because a New York State law limiting the number of hours bakers could work had been overturned by the Supreme Court in *Lochner v. New York* (1905), Muller thought he had a pretty good case. Even after two Oregon courts found against him, he still appealed to the Supreme Court, which agreed to hear the case. To help the overmatched Oregon attorney general,

Florence Kelley

Florence Kelley, executive secretary of the National Consumers' League (NCL), recruited Harvard law professor Louis Brandeis. Aided by his sister-in-law, NCL legislative director Josephine Goldmark, Brandeis put together a document, known as the Brandeis Brief, which contained 113 pages of social science data proving that women's maternal capabilities were irreparably harmed by long hours of work.

The Court had found in *Lochner* that state governments could not restrict the hours worked by employees on the grounds that such restrictions negated the constitutional right of employees to contract freely with their employers. It was the contention of Kelley, Goldmark, and Brandeis, however, that the state of Oregon had a right to limit the freedom of women in this regard because society had a special interest in protecting the ability of women to reproduce and mother their offspring. Brandeis won the case, but his argument later ended up hurting the cause of women's rights when others began using it to justify a host of new legal restrictions.

control of large municipal governments and put some of these ideas into practice. In 1901 in New York City, for example, Columbia University president Seth Low won the mayoralty and drove Tammany Hall temporarily from power. During the next two years, Low worked diligently to rein in patronage, tighten the city's housing laws, improve parks and playgrounds, and expand health services for the poor. Yet despite these efforts, much remained to be done in New York City, as conditions there at the time of the Triangle fire later demonstrated.

AROUND THE COUNTRY, other mayors—such as Hazen Pingree, who urged public ownership of municipal utilities in Detroit, and Samuel M. "Golden Rule" Jones, who provided free day care for working mothers in Toledo—joined Low in proposing and enacting helpful reforms. On the state level, too, important progress was made by governors Robert M. La Follette in Wisconsin, Charles Evans Hughes in New York, Hoke Smith in Georgia, Hiram Johnson in California, and Woodrow Wilson in New Jersey. Yet none of these reformers could match the impact of the country's new, young, and quite Progressive president, Theodore Roosevelt.

As all good Progressives did, TR wanted to transform the federal government into an efficient, modern manager of American society. He began with the trusts, ordering Attorney General Philander C. Knox in March 1902 to bring suit under the Sherman Anti-Trust Act against the Northern Securities Company, a new four-hundred-million-dollar railroad combination in the Northwest. Put together by J. P. Morgan, James J. Hill, and Edward H. Harriman, it merged three major railroad systems: the Great Northern, the Northern Pacific, and the Chicago, Burlington & Quincy. Upon learning of the suit, Morgan immediately rushed to the White House. "If we have done any-thing wrong," he told the president, "send your man to my man and they can fix it." Roosevelt declined to do as Morgan suggested and afterward informed Knox, "Mr. Morgan could not help regarding me as a big rival operator, who either intended to ruin all his interests, or else could be induced to come to an agreement to ruin none."

In fact, Roosevelt adhered to a middle path. Born into wealth, he had nothing against profit and had no desire to eliminate all industrial combinations, or even blunt the trend toward business consolidation. He merely wanted to discipline those companies that "have done something we regard as wrong" so that the economy—and the economic elite—could prosper. After March 1904, when the Supreme Court declared the Northern Securities Company an illegal combination and ordered it dissolved, the Roosevelt Justice Department brought more than forty additional suits against trusts it considered to be misbehaving. Yet many more monopolies, he declined to challenge—such as U.S. Steel, another Morgan project, whose reorganization he personally approved in a private arrangement with Morgan. "Our objection to a given corporation," Roosevelt wrote, "must be not that it is big, but that it behaves badly."

Outdoorsman
Teddy Roosevelt also became famous for his efforts to conserve the nation's natural resources. Using the 1891 Forest Reserve Act, for example, he set aside more than two hundred million acres of land—an amount greater than the land set aside under the act by his three predecessors combined.

WASHINGTON AND DU BOIS

Born into slavery in 1856, Booker T. Washington was educated at the Hampton Institute, a Freedmen's Bureau school in southeastern Virginia.

A LESSER BUT STILL IMPORTANT aspect of the Progressive agenda was civil rights for African Americans. Unlike his recent predecessors in the White House, Theodore Roosevelt was sensitive to the issue, even inviting Booker T. Washington to dine with him at the White House in October 1901. But like many whites of his era, Roosevelt avoided deeper involvement with the issue.

Known as the Great Accommodator, Booker Washington believed that blacks should forgo political equality until they had accumulated more economic power through patient industry. At the Tuskegee Institute he founded in 1881 in Alabama with the help of wealthy northern whites, Washington emphasized vocational education and personal self-improvement. He wasn't terribly concerned in 1896 when the Supreme Court upheld the constitutionality of "separate but equal" segregation in *Plessy v. Ferguson* because he believed that the social and psychological consequences of racial segregation were much less important than the education and economic advancement of his people.

On the other hand, there were a number of well-educated northern blacks who vehemently opposed Washington's philosophy, which they believed encouraged black subordination. Some met at Niagara Falls in November 1905 to compose a list of alternative demands, including

immediate political equality for African Americans and an end to segregation. (Ironically, they had to meet on the Canadian side of the border because no hotel on the American side would allow them to register.) Atlanta University professor W. E. B. Du Bois, the leader of what came to be called the Niagara Movement, asserted that Booker Washington's much-desired economic power would come only once political power had been achieved.

In May 1909, a group of mostly white social activists sponsored the first biracial National Negro Conference at the Charity Organization hall in Lower Manhattan, just a short walk from the Triangle Shirtwaist Company. Among those in attendance were many whites who would figure prominently in the garment workers' strike still four months away. Significantly, Booker Washington was not among those invited to speak, but W. E. B. Du Bois was.

For the first time since the abolitionist heyday of the 1850s and the early suffrage movement, black and white men and women came together to promote the cause of African-American civil rights. Out of this meeting emerged the National Committee for the Advancement of the Negro, which became in 1910 the National Association for the Advancement of Colored People (NAACP), the first activist civil rights organization.

William Edward Burghardt Du Bois became in 1895 the first African American to receive a doctorate from Harvard. His dissertation concerned the African slave trade.

The Square Deal

THE ANTHRACITE COAL STRIKE of 1902 provided the president with another opportunity to serve the public good through the assertion of federal authority over private economic interests. The goals of the strike, organized by the United Mine Workers, were an eight-hour workday, a 20 percent pay increase, and recognition of the union; but the mine owners were determined to concede nothing, so the often violent strike dragged on for months. However, when it began to threaten winter coal supplies, Roosevelt intervened. He invited both sides to the White House and proposed federal arbitration. The miners agreed, but the owners refused. An angry TR next threatened to use federal troops to seize the mines and resume production. This possibility, along with pressure from J. P. Morgan (who believed that Roosevelt was serious), finally persuaded the mine operators to relent and agree to arbitration. The settlement was a 10 percent wage increase, a nine-hour workday, and no recognition of the union.

Coal miners in southern Illinois eat their dinner by the light of safety lamps. According to the caption that accompanied this 1903 photograph, this scene took place more than two and a half miles underground.

During President Roosevelt's second term in particular, he did as much as any Progressive to educate his fellow Americans about the need for political and social change. Calling the presidency "a bully pulpit," he often mounted its steps to criticize "malefactors of great wealth"—not merely the trusts, but also political bosses, railroads, lumber companies, and anyone else threatening either to rend the nation's social fabric or plunder its natural resources. During his 1904 reelection campaign, TR promised to ensure a "square deal" for all Americans, regardless of their social or economic standing. Later, he sought to redeem this pledge with legislation such as the Hepburn Act of June 1906, which strengthened the power of the Interstate Commerce Commission to *regulate* railroad rates. (Even so, the final version of this act had considerably fewer teeth than the bill originally proposed, and "Fighting Bob" La Follette never forgave Roosevelt for his concessions.)

Another crop of reform legislation followed publication of muckraker Upton Sinclair's 1906 novel *The Jungle*, which exposed the nauseating conditions then prevalent in most Chicago slaughterhouses and meatpacking factories. President Roosevelt used public outrage to push Congress into passing the Meat Inspection Act and the Pure Food and Drug Act, both of which mandated government regulation of the national food supply. Yet for some reason, most readers—Roosevelt included—ignored Sinclair's equally horrific depiction of life among Chicago's immigrant poor—and conditions in New York City were just as bad.

THE JUNGLE
BY
UPTON SINCLAIR

DOUBLEDAY, PAGE & CO
NEW YORK

LEFT:
A poster advertising the 1906 publication of The Jungle. *In terms of its popularity and political influence, Upton Sinclair's novel was the* Uncle Tom's Cabin *of its generation.*

THE ELECTION OF 1912

ALTHOUGH PRESIDENT TAFT's Justice Department actually initiated many more antitrust lawsuits than President Roosevelt's had, most Americans considered Taft much more conservative and probusiness than his bullish, outspoken predecessor. One reason was the Ballinger-Pinchot affair. In 1910, U.S. Forest Service chief Gifford Pinchot, a TR intimate, accused his superior, Interior Secretary Richard Ballinger, of improperly disposing of some government-owned coal fields in Alaska. Taft's response—to fire Pinchot for insubordination—deeply upset Roosevelt, who became further enraged a year later when Taft's attorney general, George W. Wickersham, filed an antitrust suit against U.S. Steel, even though TR had personally approved the company's 1907 reorganization. It wasn't long before Roosevelt announced that he would challenge his erstwhile friend for the Republican presidential nomination in 1912.

Because Taft had spent four years as president attending to the needs of the party while Roosevelt was off on safari, he won renomination handily. Roosevelt, however, vowed to stay in the race, backed by the hastily formed Progressive party. Among those prominently supporting TR's quixotic run were Robert La Follette, then a U.S. senator from Wisconsin; Jane Addams; and George W. Perkins, a member of the Committee on Safety set up by the Women's Trade Union League in the aftermath of the Triangle fire.

The Socialists, who had won nearly five hundred thousand votes in 1908 with Eugene V. Debs as their candidate, nominated Debs again. (Including the 1900 and 1904 campaigns, the 1912 effort was Debs's fourth presidential race.) The Democrats nominated Gov. Woodrow Wilson of New Jersey. This time, Debs tallied nearly a million votes; but the bigger story was the Republican split that allowed Wilson to capture the presidency with just 41.8 percent of the popular total. Wilson won forty states and 435 electoral votes, yet in only ten of those states did he win an actual majority. It's likely that, had either Taft or Roosevelt dropped out of the race, the other would have won convincingly. Instead, Roosevelt finished a distant second, with Taft close behind in third.

THE TRIANGLE SHIRTWAIST COMPANY occupied the top three floors of the Asch Building, located on the northwest corner of Washington Place and Greene Street. In addition to its ten-foot-high ceilings, the ten-story loft structure had enormous open floors measuring just under one hundred feet on a side. Put up by Joseph J. Asch between July 1900 and January 1901, the building was part of a $150 million construction boom in Lower Manhattan. Like other factories erected at the same time, it had a brick shell that was supposed to make it fireproof. However, buildings under 150 feet tall weren't required by law to use metal trim, metal window frames, or concrete flooring, so the 135-foot-tall Asch Building was built with wooden trim and wooden flooring to save money.

In 1909, when Isaac Harris and Max Blanck applied for additional fire insurance, their carrier sent P. J. McKeon, a Columbia University expert on fire prevention, to inspect the factory. McKeon immediately noticed the large number of workers crammed into the workshops on the eighth and ninth floors (the tenth was used largely for shipping and administration). He asked whether Triangle staged regular fire drills and was told that none had ever been held—to which McKeon replied that, unless they were given some training, the workers would surely panic during an emergency. He recommended fire-drill expert H. F. J. Porter and even persuaded Porter to write a letter to the Triangle owners offering his services, but Harris and Blanck never responded. Meanwhile, McKeon reported to the insurance company that the doors to the stairway on the Washington Place side of the Asch Building were "usually kept locked" because, he was told, "it was difficult to keep track of so many girls." Even though Triangle had experienced several small fires during 1909, none of McKeon's safety recommendations were ever implemented.

As the workday at Triangle drew to a close on Saturday, March 25, 1911, the 225 employees who worked on the eighth floor finished their chores and prepared to leave through the open door on the Greene Street side of the building. The time was about 4:30 P.M., and the weather outside was brisk and sunny, making for a perfectly delightful early-spring afternoon. A company watchman stationed at the Greene Street door prepared to check the handbags of the workers as they left to make sure that they weren't stealing any clothing fragments. As usual, huge piles of cloth, paper patterns, and cuttings covered the factory tables, shelves, and floor. The wooden flooring was also soaked with oil from the sewing machines, which often leaked; barrels filled with more oil lined the walls.

The Asch Building stood just around the corner from New York University and only a block east of Washington Square Park.

The Fire

THE CLOSING BELL had just sounded when a young woman on the eighth floor ran up to Samuel Bernstein, Triangle's production manager, shouting, "There is a fire, Mr. Bernstein." Aided by several other men who had successfully put out a small blaze in the factory two weeks earlier, Bernstein poured pails of water into a long under-table bin of burning cuttings near the Greene Street windows. But fed by so much flimsy cotton fabric and the many paper patterns clipped to lines running above the cutting tables, the fire spread more rapidly than it could be doused. After a few minutes, Bernstein realized that he couldn't control it, and he began hustling workers out through the Greene Street door. At the same time, he sent machinist Louis Brown to unlock the Washington Place door, in front of which more and more frightened workers were gathering.

Section 80 of the New York State Labor Law required that all factory doors open outward "where practicable," but the landings in the Asch Building were so small that building inspectors exempted its stairway doors from this provision. As a result, the crowd of workers struggling to get out made the Washington Place door nearly impossible to open. "I had to push the girls away from the door," Brown recalled. "I couldn't open it otherwise. They were packed there by the door, you couldn't get them any tighter. I pulled with all my strength. The door was open a little while I was pulling. But they were all against the door and while I was pulling to open it they were pushing against it as they tried to get out." Finally, Brown wrenched the door open, and young women began passing through the twenty-inch-wide doorframe one at a time because no more could fit.

Panic and confusion spread with the flames. As workers ran to escape the heat and smoke, many called out the names of relatives who also worked for Triangle.

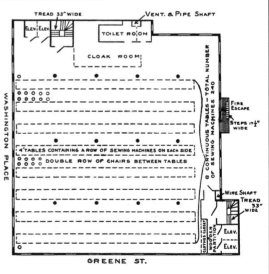

A plan of the Triangle shop on the Asch Building's ninth floor.

A young eighth-floor employee, Dinah Lifschitz, sent an urgent message by interoffice teletype to the executive offices on the tenth floor, but the pen on the receiving machine jammed, which happened fairly often. Lifschitz then used the interoffice telephone to alert switchboard operator Mary Alter, a cousin of Isaac Harris, to the fire on the eighth floor. "All right, all right," Alter responded, then left the tenth-floor switchboard unattended. Without her help, Lifschitz couldn't reach the ninth floor to warn employees there of the danger.

The remains of the Triangle workplace on the eighth floor of the Asch Building, photographed on the day after the fire.

Joseph Zito operated one of the fifteen-passenger elevator cars that succeeded in rescuing some of the Triangle workers. He made seven or perhaps eight trips before his car became too weighted down with bodies on its roof.

BECAUSE THE SUPERSTRUCTURE of the Asch Building was fireproof, the flames couldn't spread through its walls and floors. But they did pour up and out of the eighth-floor windows, igniting first the window frames and then the interiors of the ninth and tenth floors. The seventy employees on the tenth floor, alerted by Lifschitz, were given just enough time to escape, most of them taking the Greene Street stairs up to the roof and then passing over it to the roofs of adjacent buildings. However, by the time the 260 workers on the ninth floor learned of the fire, it was already an inferno, and most found themselves trapped.

Some workers, paralyzed by their fear, remained at their machines, staring blankly across the burning shop floor. Most, however, pressed against one another in a frantic rush to escape the intense heat that was already beginning to sear their bodies. As on the eighth floor, the ninth-floor Washington Place stairway door was locked, so most of the workers tried to reach the stairway on the Greene Street side. A number made it safely down this narrow, thirty-three-inch-wide spiraling staircase, but quickly the burning eighth-floor landing blocked the passageway for others. A few more managed to break through some rusted metal shutters and scamper onto the fire escape at the back of the building, but most of the unprepared employees didn't even know there was a fire escape behind those always-closed shutters. For them, the two passenger elevators on the Washington Place side of the building seemed the only means of escape.

"When I first opened the elevator door on the ninth floor all I could see was a crowd of girls and men with great flames and smoke right behind them," elevator operator Joseph Zito said. "When I came to the floor the third time, the girls were standing on the window sills with the fire all around them." Soon, the bodies of ninth-floor workers, flinging themselves down the elevator shaft to escape the flames, began to accumulate on the roof of Zito's car, preventing further ascents. (Firemen later found nineteen bodies stacked there, one on top of another.) Meanwhile, the heat emanating from the eighth floor blaze bent the other elevator car's tracks, disabling it as well. By 4:45 P.M. there was no longer any way to escape the ninth floor.

EGINNING WITH THE FIRST sound of glass breaking, a crowd had gathered on the streets below to see what was happening. Suddenly, an object that looked to be a bale of dress material was dropped from an eighth-floor window. Some on the ground assumed that workers were simply trying to save the best fabric. A *New York World* reporter who happened to be passing by described what happened next:

> From the crowd of 500 persons there came a cry of horror. The breeze had disclosed the form of a girl shooting down to instant death on the stone pavement beneath. Before the crowd could realize the full meaning of the horror, another girl sprang upon the window ledge. It seemed that she had broken open the window with her fists. Her hair, streaming down her back, was all ablaze, and her clothing was on fire. She stood poised for a moment, her arms extended, and then down she came. Three other girls at the same moment threw themselves from various windows, and other girls could be seen clinging to the window frames, struggling for breath and trying to decide between the death within the factory room and the death on the stone pavement and sidewalk below.

Arriving firemen stretched out life nets to catch those who jumped, but the bodies, falling from such great heights, landed with much more force than the firemen or the nets could handle. Nothing the firemen did could prevent the jumpers from crashing into the stone pavement or smashing through the glass blocks that had been set into the sidewalk to allow some light to reach the Asch Building's basement. Often, several girls jumped at once, holding hands to soothe themselves as they fell.

The front page of the New York World *on March 26, 1911.*

Eighteen minutes after the firemen arrived, the flames were brought under control, but there was no one left to save. Forty-six people had already jumped to their deaths, and the charred remains of one hundred more were found inside the factory. Seven bodies were so badly burned that relatives couldn't identify them, and they were buried in coffins marked with numbers rather than names. All but twenty-one of the victims were women.

The Morgue

THE FOUR HUNDRED INJURED, stunned, and weeping workers who did survive the Triangle fire soon returned to their Lower East Side apartments, some via local hospitals, to share their grief with their neighborhoods. Meanwhile, the Triangle dead lay in piles on the sidewalk as firemen continued to hose down the Asch Building and police officials searched for enough coffins to accommodate 146 bodies. The coroner's office set up a temporary morgue in a huge enclosed pier on East Twenty-sixth Street, to which corpses were shuttled throughout the evening. Some of the victims had stuffed their skimpy pay envelopes into their clothing for safekeeping; others still had their wages clutched in their hands. The police placed all such valuables in envelopes marked with the corpse's tag number and waited for relatives to arrive so that a positive identification could be made.

So many Jews on the Lower East Side had friends or family working at Triangle that tens of thousands showed up at the East Twenty-sixth Street morgue that night looking for the missing. Joining them were numerous Italian families. The police allowed a few dozen in at a time to look for loved ones among the

dozens of coffins laid out in neatly ordered rows. Throughout the night, mothers, discovering the lifeless bodies of their daughters, would begin wailing. Some in their sorrow tried to kill themselves by jumping off the pier. The police stopped no fewer than a dozen such attempts.

On April 5, more than a hundred thousand people, most of them residents of the Lower East Side, took part in a solemn funeral parade, marching silently in the rain for five hours. As the parade approached the Asch Building, many in

Until the sun rose on Sunday morning, policemen at the East Twenty-sixth Street morgue stood with lanterns over the victims' bodies as their friends and families filed past. Once a corpse was identified, its coffin was closed and moved aside.

its vanguard yielded to their emotions and, according to one newspaper account, uttered a "long-drawn-out, heart-piercing cry, the mingling of thousands of voices, a sort of human thunder in the elemental storm—a cry that was perhaps the most impressive expression of human grief ever heard in this city."

WHO WAS TO BLAME? The question dogged New Yorkers in the weeks after the tragedy. "That a terrible mistake was made by somebody," the *New York Times* observed, "is easier to say now than to point out just where the blame for this destruction of human life may be placed." The city's fire department was later assigned a portion of the responsibility, mostly because its equipment was inadequate to fight blazes higher than six stories, even though more than three hundred thousand New Yorkers worked in loft factories located above the sixth floor. (The department's tallest ladders were too short, and most of its hydrants lacked the pressure necessary to send water that high.) Fault was also found with the city's buildings department, whose inspectors had found violations in the Asch Building but never followed up to make sure that they were remediated. In its defense, the department pointed out that it had only forty-seven inspectors to examine more than fifty thousand buildings.

The largest measure of blame, however, fell on Harris and Blanck, who were indicted for manslaughter on April 11. (A day earlier, Samuel Bernstein and Louis Brown had been thrown out of the criminal courts building for allegedly tampering with grand jury witnesses.) The trial of the Triangle owners opened on December 4, 1911. Each day over the next three weeks, crowds of women gathered outside the courtroom to chant, "Murderers! Murderers!" The police eventually thought it necessary to post a guard to protect the defendants.

To simplify the presentation of its case, the district attorney's office decided to try Harris and Blanck merely for the death of Margaret Schwartz, one of those who might have escaped the ninth floor of the Asch Building had the Washington Place stairway door not been locked. The testimony of the prosecution's 103 witnesses focused on three key points: (1) Was the ninth-floor Washington Place stairway door kept locked on a regular basis? (2) Was it locked at the time of the fire? (3) Did Harris and Blanck know that it was locked? The defense called mostly supervisory personnel related to the owners either by blood or by marriage. It maintained that the ninth-floor Washington Place door *was* open at the time of the fire, that the heat of the eighth-floor blaze prevented workers from descending this way, and that Margaret Schwartz would have survived had she only suppressed her panic and thought quickly enough to use the Greene Street stairway instead.

The narrow spiral staircase on the Greene Street side of the Asch Building.

It took the jurors less than two hours to reach a verdict. They found the shirtwaist kings not guilty of manslaughter. Apparently, they accepted the argument offered by defense counsel Max D. Steuer that, although the deaths had been a terrible tragedy, they had not been Harris's and Blanck's fault. As one jury member later told a newsman, "I believed that the [door] was locked at the time of the fire. But I could not make myself feel certain that Harris and Blanck knew that it was locked." A year later, the district attorney's office brought seven new indictments against Harris and Blanck, but Steuer complained that his clients would be facing essentially the same evidence, which was a violation of their double-jeopardy rights. The judge agreed and ordered the case dismissed.

After the Triangle Fire

MANY NEW YORKERS HAD HOPED that a guilty verdict would provide some sort of emotional resolution to the Triangle tragedy; instead, the December 27 acquittal of Harris and Blanck made the deaths seem once again horribly pointless. Because this was an untenable situation for a city still consumed by uncertainty and grief, other outlets had to be found. Indeed, as historian Richard B. Morris has suggested, "It is doubtful whether the social consequences of the Triangle fire would have been as far-reaching had Steuer lost his case."

The mechanism through which these consequences were realized turned out to be the New York Factory Investigating Commission, created in June 1911 by the state legislature in response to pressure from the Women's Trade Union League, the National Consumers' League, trade unions, and the public. Its leaders were two politically powerful New York City Democrats: senate majority leader Robert F. Wagner Sr. and assembly minority leader Alfred E. Smith. The commission's nine members also included Mary Dreier and Samuel L. Gompers. Its initial mandate was to study and report back

Triangle Shirtwaist Company owners Max Blanck (left) and Isaac Harris during their December 1911 trial.

on fire hazards—for which the legislature in Albany appropriated the rather paltry sum of ten thousand dollars, or just barely enough to pay a competent attorney to perform the basic legal tasks. Realizing that they needed help, Wagner and Smith went to see real estate mogul Henry Morgenthau Sr., who was then chairing the Committee on Safety, a civic group established by WTUL members soon after the Triangle fire to create the broadest possible movement for change in factory working conditions.

Alfred E. Smith in 1913, shortly after he became speaker of the New York State Assembly. This photograph was preserved in a Smith family album and later distributed to the press during the Happy Warrior's 1928 presidential campaign.

Within a few hours of this meeting, Morgenthau made arrangements for not one but *two* excellent lawyers to manage the commission's investigation free of charge. Wagner and Smith also enlisted the services of such dogged and capable investigators as H. F. J. Porter, the man who had offered to set up fire drills for Triangle in 1909; social worker Henry Moskowitz, who had recently helped found the NAACP; Moskowitz's wife, Belle, a politically active Progressive who became an important adviser to Smith during his later gubernatorial and presidential campaigns; and Frances Perkins, who had been visiting friends on Washington Square when the Triangle fire broke out and had witnessed dozens of workers jumping to their deaths.

THUS FORTIFIED, the Factory Investigating Commission took its work far beyond the study of fire hazards to conduct, according to its preliminary report, "a thorough and extensive investigation into the general conditions of factory life." It researched almost every category of labor problem in New York State, sending staff members to inspect 1,836 factories in its first year alone. At public hearings held throughout the state, it heard testimony relating to unsafe machinery, lack of proper sanitation, child labor, and the spread of disease. The commission's investigators got up at five in the morning to talk with exhausted women leaving their factory workplaces after putting in ten-hour shifts, and they observed children as young as five years old working full-time jobs in canneries across the state. In fact, the conditions in many industries were so bad that an entirely new set of labor laws seemed the only possible remedy.

Between 1911 and 1914, the commission issued more than sixty recommendations, fifty-six of which became the basis of new legislation, thanks to the political muscle of Tammany Hall. Taken together, these new laws overhauled the operation of the state department of labor, doubling its inspection staff and creating an industrial board whose regulatory decisions had the force of law. The use of dangerous machinery was restricted, stronger sanitation and lighting standards were set, and the department's authority to supervise tenement labor was significantly expanded. In addition, the commission established the Bureau of Fire Prevention and wrote new fire safety codes that included compulsory fire drills and the installation of automatic sprinkler systems in factory buildings more than six stories tall.

The result of all this effort was the most enlightened set of labor laws in the country. They served as a model for many other states and foreshadowed much that would be enacted on the federal level—with the help of Senator Wagner and

Labor Secretary Perkins—under the New Deal. "We got there just as they started to jump. I shall never forget the frozen horror which came over us as we stood with our hands on our throats watching that horrible sight, knowing that there was no help," Perkins recalled many years after the Triangle blaze. "Out of that terrible episode came a self-examination of stricken conscience in which the people of this state saw for the first time the individual worth and value of each of those 146 people who fell or were burned in that great fire."

Among those with a "stricken conscience" was a young Democratic state senator who rose one day in 1912 in Albany to speak on behalf of a bill that Smith and Wagner had devised, legislating a fifty-four-hour workweek for women. Earlier, the measure had been defeated by a single vote. Now Wagner had found the additional vote he needed, but one of the bill's previous supporters, Lower East Side Democratic boss Big Tim Sullivan, happened to be out of town at the time. It was the young senator's job to stall while Sullivan raced back to the capital to cast his tie-breaking vote. Mainly, the thirty-year-old spoke about birds, and when Republican leaders complained that birds had nothing to do with the bill being considered, he replied that he was "trying to prove that nature demands shorter hours." As soon as Sullivan appeared in the chamber, Franklin Delano Roosevelt sat down, and the voting proceeded.

Frances Perkins in 1918.

THE NEW FREEDOM

DURING THE 1912 presidential campaign, Woodrow Wilson sought to compete with Theodore Roosevelt's New Nationalism by promoting his own New Freedom plan. Not surprisingly, this same label was later applied to the array of antitrust, proregulation legislation that Wilson guided through Congress during his remarkably successful first term in office.

Although he could be stubbornly moralistic in foreign relations, Wilson usually acted with skillful realism in domestic affairs. He quickly disregarded his campaign pledge to break up the trusts, trading it in for congressional approval of more extensive regulation of the giant corporations. The Federal Trade Commission Act of 1914 created a new, quasi-judicial body to investigate and remedy unfair methods of competition. The Clayton Anti-Trust Act, passed the same year, was less successful in its attempt to strengthen the Sherman Anti-Trust Act, but it did exempt trade unions from the antitrust laws—at least until the Supreme Court struck down this provision during the 1920s.

Meanwhile, the new Democratic Congress had already passed both the Underwood Tariff and the Federal Reserve Act. The Underwood Tariff, enacted in October 1913, lowered import duties substantially (to an average of 27 percent) and also included the nation's first constitutional income tax—courtesy of the Sixteenth Amendment, ratified in February 1913. The Federal Reserve Act of December 1913, also known as the Glass-Owen Act, replaced the uncoordinated subtreasury system with the present banking system, under which twelve regional Federal Reserve banks supervise the nationally chartered banks within their respective geographic areas. The Glass-Owen Act also empowered Federal Reserve banks to lend money to other banks at a price known as the discount rate. It is through adjusting the discount rate that the Federal Reserve controls most consumer interest rates.

Pres. Woodrow Wilson during his first term in office.

AMERICAN PROFILE

Theodore Roosevelt
1858–1919

by Michael Barone

THEODORE ROOSEVELT WAS the first president to take office during the twentieth century and the man who shaped the presidency as we know it today. Born in 1858 in New York City to the scion of an old New York Dutch family and the daughter a Georgia plantation owner, he led a privileged and colorful life from the start. After his graduation from Harvard College in 1880, he returned to New York City, where he won election to the state assembly in 1881. Three years later, however, his wife and mother died in the same house on the same day—his wife from complications related to the birth of their first child, Alice. Leaving his infant daughter in the care of relatives, Roosevelt fled to the Dakota Territory, where he raised cattle, hunted the few buffalo that were left, and allowed his spirit to heal. He returned home in 1886, a year in which he also married Edith Kermit and ran for mayor of New York, finishing third. Undaunted, Roosevelt continued to pursue a career in politics, winning appointment to the U.S. Civil Service Commission in 1889 and becoming president of the New York City Police Board in 1895.

TR received yet another political appointment in 1897, when President McKinley named him assistant secretary of the navy. During the next year, Roosevelt played an important role in bringing about the Spanish-American War; then, once war came, he resigned his office to organize a volunteer regiment to fight in Cuba. He filled its ranks with Ivy League graduates, western ranch hands, and other rowdies of his acquaintance. The press ate it up; by the time the First Volunteer Cavalry, nicknamed the Rough Riders, shipped out for Santiago in June 1898, it was obvious to everyone that Lieutenant Colonel Roosevelt had mastered the art of manipulating the media and bending its coverage to his will.

During his time in Cuba, as throughout his public career, Roosevelt nurtured favorable press coverage with a great deal of success. Always important to a politician, good relationships with the media were particularly important at the turn of the twentieth century, when the powerful barons of the "yellow press" could be remarkably supportive if pleased and quite dangerous if crossed.

There seemed to be little danger of the latter for Roosevelt, who understood instinctively how to provide good, colorful copy. In Cuba, he made sure that Richard Harding Davis, the nation's most famous war correspondent, had plenty of access to the Rough Riders; and Davis returned the favor by making heroes of Roosevelt and the regiment. (In fact, Davis was so close to the Rough Riders that he took up arms with them during their well-publicized charge up San Juan Heights.) After the war, Roosevelt's new celebrity made him a natural gubernatorial candidate for New York State's scandal-tarred Republican party, and he was elected narrowly in November 1898.

Demonstrating a media savvy much more familiar to the late rather than the early twentieth century, TR used his well-covered war exploits and colorful personal history to build up name recognition until he became the obvious choice to replace the late Garret Hobart as McKinley's running mate in 1900. Mark Hanna distrusted Roosevelt and objected to his nomination, but the draft-Teddy movement was too strong to be stepped. The Republican leadership went along because the vice presidency promised to sidetrack TR's reform efforts in Albany. However, when McKinley died just six months into his second term, Roosevelt suddenly became president.

"Now, look!" Hanna raged after learning of McKinley's assassination. "That damned cowboy is president of the United States."

Although Roosevelt initially pledged to continue McKinley's policies, he soon became a very different kind of chief executive—all the time showing the same flair for attracting favorable press coverage that he had demonstrated in Cuba. He cleverly took friendly reporters into his confidence, leaking them stories and granting them exclusive interviews that put his views into their words. Even when Roosevelt refused to be quoted directly, he made sure that each story had the proper spin. Reporters who violated his rules were made members of the Ananias Club, named after the biblical liar, and denied access to the White House.

TR's life ended in frustration with his inability to alter Woodrow Wilson's neutrality policies and the death of his son Quentin, an Army Air Service pilot, in combat over France. Yet his energy, activism, acknowledgment of the new realities of industrial life, and appreciation of America's emergence as a world power came to define what it meant to be a chief executive in the modern era, and these qualities made him, in fact as well as in name, the first twentieth-century U.S. president.

Roosevelt in 1904.

18

THE NEW ERA

Lindbergh's Flight

ROUGH WEATHER OUT OVER the Atlantic kept Charles Augustus Lindbergh grounded on Long Island throughout the third week of May 1927. Each day, he shuttled back and forth between his room at the Garden City Hotel and his plane at Curtiss Field, but there was little he could do at either place, other than wait until the weather cleared. While he waited, the pressure intensified, as did the media attention. Already, six prominent, well-financed aviators had died in recent attempts to become the first to fly nonstop from New York City to Paris. Other rivals remained, yet it was Lindbergh who now held the spotlight. In just a few weeks, swarming reporters had transformed him from an obscure twenty-five-year-old airmail pilot into a national sensation. Most of the time, he was simply "Lindy"; however, because he intended to fly the thirty-six hundred miles to Paris alone (to save the weight of a copilot), he was also nicknamed "the Flying Fool."

Numerous promoters pursued the tall, slim pilot from St. Louis, offering him lucrative contracts contingent on the success of his flight: $250,000 for a movie, $50,000 for appearances on the stage, equally profitable book deals. But Lindbergh paid little attention, turning them all down except one: He did agree to a license arranged by his backers giving the *New York Times* the exclusive rights to the story of his flight. Even so, Lindbergh continued to meet with reporters from other newspapers, and nobody much seemed to mind.

AT LEFT: **Charles Lindbergh,** *photographed shortly after his arrival at Curtiss Field on Thursday, May 12, 1927. Lindbergh was ready to take off for Paris at daybreak on Monday, May 16, but poor weather kept him grounded until Friday, May 20.*

The light rain that fell on Thursday, May 19, made the prospect of a takeoff anytime soon seem quite remote, so Charles Lindbergh spent the day visiting the Wright Aeronautical factory in Paterson, New Jersey. Among his companions were Ken Lane, Wright's chief engineer, and Dick Blythe, a public relations man hired by the Wright company to help Lindbergh (whose plane carried a Wright engine) with whatever he needed. Early that evening, the group drove back into New York City, where Blythe had arranged for Lindbergh to take in a Broadway musical, *Rio Rita*, one of the season's biggest hits. However, as the group drove across Forty-second Street, Lane suggested that they stop to call Dr. James H. Kimball, Lindbergh's contact at the local weather bureau, whose office sat atop the Whitehall Building on lower Broadway. The Manhattan skyline was still enshrouded in fog, but Kimball told Blythe that a new high-pressure system was moving in quickly and clearing patches of sky over the ocean. Forgetting about the play, Lindbergh and the others headed straight for Long Island, stopping along the way only for a quick bite to eat in Queens. While Lindbergh finished his meal, Lane went on ahead to Curtiss Field to begin the plane's final inspection, while Blythe ran around the corner to a drugstore to buy some sandwiches for Lindbergh to take with him on the flight.

When Lindbergh himself arrived at the Curtiss Field hangar sometime after nine o'clock, he noted with surprise and apprehension that neither of his two primary rivals, Richard E. Byrd and Clarence Chamberlin, were preparing their respective aircraft for dawn departures. Apparently, he was the only one heeding Kimball's preliminary estimate.

After working with his mechanics for several hours, Lindbergh returned to the Garden City Hotel "to get whatever sleep the night still holds for me," he wrote later. Unfortunately, a crowd of reporters, having learned of the activity at his hangar, delayed him in the lobby. By the time he reached his room, it was nearly midnight. He left instructions to be awakened at 2:15 A.M., then posted a friend outside his door to stand guard and went to bed.

> *Now I must sleep. I ought to have been in bed three hours ago—that was a serious slip in plans; a pilot should be fresh for the start of a record-breaking transoceanic flight. Your mind doesn't work as well when it's short of sleep.*

Just as Lindbergh began to drop off, however, he was awakened by a loud knock. His friend wanted to know, "Slim, what am I going to do when you're gone?" Lindbergh tried to get back to sleep but couldn't.

> *Why did that fellow have to ask such a fool question, just as I was dozing off? Maybe I won't sleep at all. That's a bad start for flying over the ocean—a full day without sleep before the take-off.*
>
> *But would I have slept anyway, even if my friend hadn't come in?… The days in New York have been tiring—there's no question about that—but tiring in an unhealthy sort of way. If I had been working on the plane, pouring fuel in the tanks, and walking over the field to watch its surface, I'd now be asleep. That's what I would have been doing except for the newspapers, and the crowds they've brought. But I wanted publicity on this flight. That was part of my program. Newspapers are important. I wanted their help. I wanted headlines. And I knew that headlines bring crowds. Then why should I complain?…*
>
> *Well, I'll be away from it all in the morning—this same morning, if the weather breaks. It will all be gone once I'm in the air, left behind.*

A S HE HAD INTENDED, the newspapers and public relations firms made a hero of the boy from the nation's heartland even before his heroic act had been accomplished. The way they told his story, Lindbergh was Ragged Dick (the Horatio Alger character) with a pilot's license, David against the ocean Goliath, Icarus spreading his wings. His celebrity was manufactured for the moment to sell newspapers, yet it was also merited: Lindbergh had come out of nowhere with an inexpensive single-engine aircraft to challenge not only the formidable Atlantic Ocean but also a collection of better-financed pilots flying the most expensive, modern aircraft in the world.

The public image that Lindbergh presented during his eight days in New York was that of a shy, small-town youth who had mastered modern technology yet retained the premodern American virtues of modesty, dignity, and courage. Through the eyes of the New York City press corps, the rest of the country came to see Lindy this way as well. The image was attractive and, for the most part, accurate—but not completely so. At the time of his Paris flight, Lindbergh was believed to have descended from typically robust, uncomplicated, hardworking immigrant stock. Yet biographers later discovered some checkering in the Lindbergh family past; for example, they weren't actually Lindberghs.

Lindbergh's paternal grandfather, a man named Ola Månsson, had come to America in 1859 from Sweden, where he had been a banker and a powerful member of Parliament. However, Månsson had been convicted in June 1859 of embezzlement, and following his trial, he had fled Sweden with his mistress and their infant son, Karl August. Sometime during the ten-week journey from Stockholm, Månsson decided to change his name. Thus, it was as the Lindbergh family—August, Louisa, and Charles August—that the three Swedes appeared in a Minnesota courtroom in August 1859 to declare their intention to become citizens of the United States.

Soon after his arrival, August Lindbergh began the modest life of a mid-nineteenth-century homesteader. He built his family a log cabin near Sauk Centre in central Minnesota and traded the gold medal his erstwhile constituents had given him for a plow that he used to break the sod of the 160 acres he had claimed under the Homestead Act. Two years later, he was milling wood for a frame addition to his house when some of his clothing became caught in the spinning saw blade. Pulling him in, the blade mangled his left arm and cut such a deep gash in his back that his heart and part of a lung were exposed. Somehow, August Lindbergh survived, even though the nearest doctor lived sixty miles away and didn't arrive until the third day after the accident. By that time, all the doctor could do was bind Lindbergh's wounds, amputate his arm, and marvel at his physical endurance. August Lindbergh's stoicism in the face of adversity, in particular, set an example that all his descendants would thereafter try to emulate.

THE SON WHOM AUGUST LINDBERGH brought to America—the first of seven he would have with Louisa—grew up to become a lawyer in Little Falls, Minnesota, about fifty miles northwest of Sauk Centre. Known simply as C. A., Charles August Lindbergh represented both prosperous local businesses and eastern investors who speculated in the region's farmland. He married in 1887 and had two daughters before his first wife died of an abdominal tumor in 1898. Three years later, he married Evangeline Lodge Land, the college-educated daughter of an eccentric Detroit dentist, who had come to Little Falls to teach science at the local high school. On February 4, 1902, she gave birth to the couple's only child, named Charles Augustus after his father and grandfather. The marriage, though, had never been a happy one, and after Charles's birth, it became even more troubled.

A carte-de-visite portrait of August Lindbergh (the former Ola Månsson), taken in 1873.

August Lindbergh's home in Melrose, Minnesota, as it appeared in 1880.

C. A. Lindbergh and his son, photographed in Washington, D.C., in 1910.

In 1906, after C. A. ran for Congress as a Progressive Republican and won, he moved to Washington while sending the rest of his family to live with his wife's parents in Detroit. It was a scandal-free way of separating from his wife. "I seldom spent more than a few months in the same place," Charles Lindbergh explained later. "Our winters were passed in Washington, and our summers in Minnesota, with intermediate visits to Detroit." Though young Charles lived primarily with his mother, he did spend significant amounts of time with his father, especially once he was old enough to accompany his father on campaign trips. In 1916, when he was fourteen—and already nearly six feet tall—Charles spent a few weeks driving his father around Minnesota in a Saxon Light Six automobile. (He was the only member of the family who could drive, having learned on a Model T Ford that C. A. had bought in 1912.) After five terms in the House, C. A. had decided to run in 1916 for the Republican Senate nomination, but he finished an embarrassing fourth. The reason was his outspoken opposition to U.S. involvement in World War I. Like many midwestern reformers, Congressman Lindbergh wanted no part of a conflict that he blamed on bankers, munitions makers, and other war profiteers in Europe and the United States. Yet his isolationism was so radical that it unsettled Minnesota's deeply patriotic Republicans at a time when American entry in the Great War seemed increasingly inevitable.

In 1918, C. A. ran for governor backed by the Nonpartisan League, a group of agrarian socialists whose goal was to replace agricultural trusts with state owner-ship. By now a pariah, he was arrested, shot at, hanged in effigy, and threatened with lynching. After one rally, C. A. confronted a mob that had already beaten his

driver. Standing down the crowd, he walked back to his car, assisted his injured aide into the driver's seat, and began to leave. Even though he could hear gunshots being fired as the car drove off, he told his driver not to speed away. "They will think we are afraid of them if we do," C. A. said. He lost the nomination by fifteen percentage points and afterward, embittered, pursued various business ventures until his death from a brain tumor in May 1924. In the meantime, he began deeding over his farmland in Little Falls to his son.

Lindbergh loved internal combustion engines. He learned how to drive a car at age eleven and poses here in 1921 (while a student at the University of Wisconsin) with a motorcycle he bought at age sixteen.

Charles Lindbergh worked his father's land from the time he moved back to Little Falls in 1917 (to complete his final year of high school) until the fall of 1920, when he became a mechanical engineering student at the University of Wisconsin at Madison. His mind, however, wasn't on his studies, and in his third semester he flunked out. In April 1922, rather than go back to the farm, he enrolled in a flight school being run at Lincoln Standard Aircraft, a company in Lincoln, Nebraska, that specialized in refurbishing old airplanes. For his five-hundred-dollar tuition, Lindbergh received four weeks of training in the company's factory, a week of lessons on its airfield, and several more weeks' instruction in the air.

Aviation

AVIATION ITSELF WASN'T ANY OLDER than Charles Lindbergh, who was not yet two when Orville and Wilbur Wright engineered the first engine-powered, heavier-than-air flights in December 1903 at Kitty Hawk, North Carolina. Orville made the first Kitty Hawk flight, remaining aloft for twelve seconds. Later that day, Wilbur managed a fifty-nine-second flight, during which the brothers' Flyer I traveled 859 feet. The next year, the Wrights' Flyer II model hung the air for five minutes. In 1905, the Flyer III performed half-hour flights that covered nearly twenty-five miles. (That model could also bank, turn, and circle.) Further advances were made by the Wrights and others during the next decade, but as World War I began, airplanes were still flimsy machines made by trussing up wooden frames with wire and then covering the entire contraption with linen.

When the Great War began, there were only a few hundred planes in the world, and neither side's generals knew what to do with them. At first, they were used exclusively for reconnaissance; then someone got the idea of arming a few to attack enemy reconnaissance missions. These were the first fighter aircraft. As with any defense-related technology during wartime, research and development was accelerated and substantial government funds invested. In Great Britain alone, more than fifty thousand technologically superior aircraft were built between 1914 and 1918, as the number of people employed in British aviation work rose from several hundred to 350,000.

Even so, commercial aviation didn't take off after the war. Despite the headline-grabbing dogfights that promoted a remarkable awareness of heavier-than-air flight, the large number of equally well reported accidents kept most people out of the air. In 1922, for example, there were fewer than twelve hundred civilian airplanes in the United States—and most of those were war-surplus models, barely fit to fly. The work of Lincoln Standard Aircraft was to recondition those planes, and Lindbergh spent his first week there replacing engines and converting cockpits to hold two passengers. Later, he learned to fly in one of Army Air Service trainers he had refitted.

LINDBERGH'S QUICK REFLEXES and excellent hand-eye coordination made him a natural pilot, but flight time he found hard to come by. So after his lessons ended, he approached barnstormer Erold G. Bahl and pleaded for a job as an unpaid assistant. The word *barnstormer*, which dated back to the early 1880s, was originally used to describe the actors who traveled the back roads of the country, staging single-night performances in local barns. During the early twentieth century, however, the fledgling aviation industry adopted the term to describe the pilots who traveled from town to town, staging aerial shows and offering sight-seeing rides. In southeastern Nebraska in 1922, the going rate for

Piloting the Flyer I on December 17, 1903, Orville Wright makes the first sustained, powered flight in history as his brother, Wilbur, looks on. The two Dayton, Ohio, bicycle shop owners transported their equipment all the way to Kitty Hawk, North Carolina, because of the favorable winds on the Outer Banks.

a five-minute flight was five dollars; in comparison, entry-level jobs at Lincoln Standard Aircraft paid about fifteen dollars a week.

Soon Lindbergh began performing the stunts that the barnstormers used to attract a paying clientele when they arrived in a new town. These stunts included "wing walking" and parachuting into the pasture where the show would take place. According to Lindbergh's own description of a typical performance,

> *We started with wing-walking. The performer would climb out of the cockpit and walk along the entering edge of the wing to the outer bay strut, where he climbed up onto the top wing and stood on his head as we passed the grandstand. After finishing his stunts on the wing, he would go to the landing gear and from there to the center section, where he sat while the plane looped....*
>
> *After wing-walking came the breakaway. This was accomplished by fastening a cable to the landing gear. The performer went out to the wing-tip, fastened his harness to the loose end of the cable and to all appearances fell off the wing. No one on the ground could see the cable, and a breakaway always produced quite a sensation.*

In this way, Lindbergh became accustomed to risk. At least twice during his barnstorming career (and twice more as an airmail pilot), he had to parachute for his life from planes about to crash.

I N APRIL 1923, a year after he began taking flying lessons, Lindbergh persuaded his father to underwrite the purchase of an airplane. For five hundred dollars, he bought a war-surplus Curtiss JN4-D, known as a Jenny. The biplane had been a popular army trainer, and it suited Lindbergh's purposes well. He used it to barnstorm the upper Midwest and even put it to work in C. A.'s last political campaign: a special election being held in 1923 to replace Minnesota's senior senator, who had recently died. One time Charles carried his father aloft with hundreds of handbills that they planned to release over a town. Recalled Lindbergh, "It did not occur to me that he might throw them out all at once; but he did, and the thick stack of sheets

Lindbergh adjusts *a parachute strap before taking off in an experimental plane in 1925. As a barnstorming daredevil around this time, he specialized in "the plane change"—a stunt that involved two biplanes. As the planes flew together past the grandstand, Lindbergh would stand on the top wing of one plane and reach up to grab a rope ladder hanging down from the lower wing of the other (so that he could climb aboard it). "We usually made two fake attempts to effect the change and actually counted on the third for success," Lindbergh wrote. "In this way, the feat looked more difficult."*

struck the stabilizer with a thud." As a result, Lindbergh noted, "the distribution of literature in the town wasn't very broad."

He billed himself as "Daredevil Lindbergh" and made a pretty good living barnstorming during 1923. But he soon became eager to fly the more advanced planes available only to military pilots, so he wrote to the head of the Army Air Service in Washington, asking for an appointment. After passing mental and physical examinations in January 1924, he was accepted as a cadet; two months later, he began a yearlong training course at Brooks Field in San Antonio, Texas. Except for a brief leave of absence in May 1924 occasioned by the death of his father, Lindbergh applied himself to his studies and was graduated in March 1925 at the top of his class, which the rigors of training had meanwhile reduced from 104 cadets initially to just 19 at graduation.

Lindbergh had assumed that, after completing his studies, he would be put on active duty, but there weren't many openings for army pilots in 1925, so he became a second lieutenant in the Air Service Reserves. To support himself, he began barnstorming again (billing himself now as "the Flying Fool") and found work as a test pilot at Lambert Field outside St. Louis. One of the planes he tested for the Robertson Aircraft Corporation was a De Havilland DH-4, another army-surplus observation plane. At the time, Robertson was bidding for a government airmail contract, and it wanted to use DH-4s to transport the mail sacks. In October 1925, the postal service awarded Robertson the route between St. Louis and Chicago. Right away, the company hired Charles Lindbergh as its chief airmail pilot.

Airmail

IN GENERAL, THE FEDERAL GOVERNMENT was slow to recognize the potential of aviation. Three separate times in 1905, the War Department refused the Wright brothers' offer to share their new technology, and even after the Wrights brought their latest Flyer to France and wowed Europeans in August 1908, the U.S. government still saw no reason to own more than one rather dilapidated plane. Its attitude began to change in 1911, however, when the postal service authorized the first experimental mail flights. These took place on Long Island between Garden City and Mineola. Pilot Earle Ovington made daily runs from Garden City; when he reached Mineola, he simply dropped the mail bags out of his plane so that the Mineola postmaster could pick them up. Thus persuaded of the feasibility of airmail, the postal service began requesting funds in 1912 to roll out the service, but four years passed before Congress appropriated fifty thousand dollars for more extensive tests. Even then, the postal service had difficulty spending the money: Because suitable planes were in short supply, not a single company responded to its requests for bids to set up pilot programs in Massachusetts and Alaska.

In 1918, however, Congress appropriated another hundred thousand dollars, and the War Department agreed to provide on short-term loan both planes (Curtiss Jennies) and pilots (cadets who needed more flight experience). The first regular airmail runs began on May 15, 1918, between New York City and Washington, D.C. In August 1918, the postal service replaced the army pilots and aircraft with new civilian employees and six custom-built mail planes.

Charles Lindbergh in his U.S. Army Air Service uniform, about 1925. After receiving his commission, Lindbergh was offered a year's worth of work dusting crops in Georgia, but he turned down the job because the pay seemed too low. Instead, he headed for Lambert Field, the busiest airfield in the Midwest, where he had spent some enjoyable time during his barnstorming days.

The next major step was the creation of an attention-grabbing transcontinental route between New York City and San Francisco. The first legs—from New York City to Cleveland and Cleveland to Chicago—were launched in 1919; a year later, the postal service added Chicago–Omaha and Omaha–San Francisco segments. Of course, no ordinary plane in 1920 could fly from Omaha to San Francisco (or even from Cleveland to Chicago) without making stops, so the postal service built airfields along the way. Flying from Omaha to San Francisco, for instance, airmail pilots stopped in North Platte, Cheyenne, Rawlins, Rock Springs, Salt Lake City, Elko, and Reno—and maybe in a pasture somewhere else if they hit bad weather or had engine trouble. Forced landings were common, yet fatal accidents remained rare because the early biplanes were small and highly maneuverable and landed at relatively slow speeds.

IMPRESSED WITH WHAT HAD BEEN accomplished thus far, Congress passed in February 1925 its first major act to "encourage commercial aviation." The new law directed the postmaster general to contract out additional airmail routes as a prelude to privatizing the entire system. The first two Contract Air Mail routes, known as CAM-1 and CAM-2, fed into the postal service's already established network. CAM-1 linked New York City and Boston, while CAM-2, the contract won by Robertson, joined St. Louis and Chicago.

Lindbergh helps load mail sacks on April 15, 1926, before making the first CAM-2 airmail flight. The DH-4 that he flew had fabric-covered wings (painted silver) and a plywood fuselage, (painted maroon). The pilot sat in the rear cockpit so that he could keep an eye on the mailbags in the front seat.

Before CAM-2 service could begin, however, Lindbergh had to survey the route, arrange for landing fields along the way, and note locations where he and the two other Robertson pilots could put their planes down in an emergency. Lindbergh pursued this work diligently—eventually choosing nine way stations along the 285-mile route, most of them cow pastures with telephones nearby— but he wasn't especially looking forward to the drudgery of flying the same route day after day after day. That's why, when he heard in late 1925 of navy commander Richard E. Byrd's plans to overfly the North Pole, he applied for the job of copilot. Lindbergh noted in his letter of application that he had logged eleven hundred hours in thirty different types of planes and also had "lived in northern Minnesota most of my life"; unfortunately, the position had already been filled.

Lindbergh made his first airmail flight for Robertson on April 15, 1926— quickly becoming, as biographer A. Scott Berg has noted, St. Louis's "poster boy for the Air Mail." Lindbergh appeared in print advertisements, attended chamber of commerce luncheons, and gave presentations to businessmen, encouraging them to use the new service. There was resistance, however, because of the additional fifteen cents' worth of postage the service required and also because of the risk that mail might be lost in a crash.

Despite all of Lindbergh's promotion, after six weeks Robertson was still carrying just half of the twenty-five hundred pieces of mail it needed to haul each day to break even. The experiment might have ended right then had it not been for several civic-minded St. Louis banks, which offered to cover some of Robertson's losses as an investment in their city's future prosperity.

The Orteig Prize

WHILE FLYING HIS MAIL ROUTE, Lindbergh often daydreamed. In September 1926, he began daydreaming about owning a Wright Bellanca, a new monoplane with remarkable fuel efficiency. "If only I had the Bellanca, I'd show St. Louis businessmen what modern aircraft could do," he later recalled thinking to himself. The Bellanca could whisk Missourians away to New York City in just eight or nine hours. Alternatively, throttled down and carrying nothing but fuel, "it could break the world's endurance record, and the transcontinental, and set a dozen marks for range and speed and weight. Possibly...I could fly nonstop between New York and Paris."

The New York City–Paris flight held a special significance because in May 1919, Raymond Orteig had offered twenty-five thousand dollars to "the first aviator of any Allied country crossing the Atlantic in one flight from Paris to New York or New York to Paris." A wealthy New York City hotelier of French origin, Orteig made the offer in a burst of postwar jubilation, later revising it (in 1924) to include pilots from any country. By 1926, when Lindbergh first began seriously considering the journey, there had been numerous transatlantic flights—most by dirigibles, some by airplanes traveling in stages—but none had challenged for the prize. The two British pilots who made the Newfoundland–Ireland hop in 1919, for example, covered only 1,936 miles, or just about half the distance of the 3,636-mile Orteig Prize route.

Lindbergh knew that no existing plane, not even the Wright Bellanca, could make the Paris flight without some special, costly modifications. So it was with great interest that he followed the work of engineer Igor Sikorsky, who was building a customized plane for French World War I ace René Fonck. A Russian-born American, Sikorsky had built the world's first practical multiengine aircraft in 1913, and the plane he was building for Fonck, paid for by an American syndicate determined to win the Orteig Prize, had three engines. The S-35 also had a copilot, a navigator, a radio operator, two radio sets, flotation bags (in case of a forced water landing), a bed, leather upholstery, and hot meals. Once construction was completed in September 1926, Sikorsky wanted to run extensive tests, but Fonck and his backers were eager to make their attempt before the onset of wintry weather postponed the flight until spring. On the morning of September 15, 1926, the S-35, heavily laden with fuel and all the elegant appurtenances of a Pullman car, rolled down the runway at Roosevelt Field on Long Island, straining to take off. It couldn't. Instead, Fonck drove the plane into an embankment at the end of the runway, where the S-35 exploded. Only the pilot and copilot survived.

The Sikorsky S-35 was a sesquiplane— that is, a biplane whose bottom wing was much shorter than its top wing. The giant aircraft, shown here in September 1926, weighed thirty-two thousand pounds.

DURING THE FALL OF 1926, Lindbergh spent hours pondering the lessons of Fonck's failure, concluding that the French pilot's mistake had been trying to carry far too much weight. Success, Lindbergh reasoned, would require keeping the plane itself as light as possible so that it could hold the large amount of fuel necessary to cross the Atlantic and still get off the ground. Later, Lindbergh would become obsessed with weight. The less a plane weighed, the more fuel it could carry; in addition, reducing a plane's weight made it that much more fuel efficient. As Lindbergh made his mail runs back and forth between St. Louis and Chicago, he visualized the Paris flight often and decided that, if he ever did make an attempt,

Harold Bixby

Harry F. Knight

Harry H. Knight

A. B. Lambert

Wooster Lambert

E. Lansing Ray

William B. Robertson

Earl Thompson

***These eight men
financed** Charles
Lindbergh's venture.
Bixby was a vice
president of the
State National Bank.
Harry F. Knight,
father of Harry H.,
was the eponymous
Knight in the
brokerage firm
Knight, Dysart &
Gamble. Maj. Albert
Bond Lambert,
proprietor of Lambert
Field, was the first to
pledge money to
Lindbergh; Wooster,
his brother, was the
second. Ray edited the
St. Louis Globe
Democrat. Robertson
was Lindbergh's boss.
Thompson was an
insurance executive to
whom Lindbergh had
given flying lessons.*

his plane would contain only the most vital equipment. There would be no radio, no heater, no parachute, and none of the special navigation gear that Sikorsky had crammed onto the S-35. Instead, his craft would have just one engine and just one pilot. Sometime during October, he made up his mind: He *would* try for Paris. On October 30, he wrote his mother, "I am working on a new proposition in St. Louis and have been very busy lately."

Lindbergh's immediate problem was financing. His competitors had already committed upward of a hundred thousand dollars apiece on special aircraft, and Lindbergh didn't see how a serious attempt could be made for much less than fifteen thousand dollars. Because he had neither the money to finance the flight by himself nor the fame to win the backing of a major aircraft manufacturer, he decided to ask the St. Louis business community for funding. He had recently given flying lessons to a number of leading chamber of commerce members and had met others promoting the airmail. He would appeal not only to their interest in aviation but also to their desire to advertise St. Louis.

In late November, having raised several thousand dollars, he bought a new suit and took a train to New York City. The day after his arrival at Pennsylvania Station, he visited the Wright offices in New Jersey to talk about the purchase of a Bellanca. Disappointingly, he learned that Wright had no plans to manufacture Bellancas beyond the one that already existed, which had been built merely to show off the company's new Whirlwind engine. The executive who talked with Lindbergh, however, did put him in touch with the plane's designer, Giuseppe Bellanca.

The next evening, Lindbergh met with Bellanca at the Waldorf-Astoria Hotel. Bellanca explained that his plane was still tied up in talks that Wright was having with several possible manufacturers, all interested in obtaining the rights. But Bellanca did promise to stay in touch, which made Lindbergh hopeful enough to redouble his efforts to obtain sufficient financing. A few weeks later, he called on Harry Knight, the insouciant scion of St. Louis's leading brokerage firm. Knight also happened to be president of the St. Louis Flying Club and one of Lindbergh's students. He asked Slim (Lindbergh's Lambert Field nickname) how much money he needed, then he made a call to banker Harold Bixby, the president of the St. Louis Chamber of Commerce; Bixby came to Knight's office to join the meeting. After a few minutes of discussion, he and Knight told Lindbergh to concentrate henceforth solely on the technical aspects of the flight. They would raise the fifteen thousand dollars.

The Plane

IN THE LATE FALL OF 1926, Lindbergh identified three main rivals for the Orteig Prize. The first was Richard Byrd, who had announced in late October that he was preparing his hundred-thousand-dollar trimotored Fokker for an attempt the following summer. The second was the American team of Noel Davis and Stanton Wooster, who had the backing of the American Legion and were planning a spring flight. The third rival was the French team of Charles Nungesser and François Coli, two World War I aces who were rumored to be planning a flight from Paris.

Time was clearly of the essence, so when weeks passed and Lindbergh still hadn't heard from Bellanca, he began contacting other aircraft manufacturers, without much success. Finally, he tried Ryan Aeronautical, a San Diego firm that he knew because it made high-wing monoplanes for some western airmail routes. "CAN YOU CONSTRUCT WHIRLWIND ENGINE PLANE CAPABLE FLYING NONSTOP BETWEEN NEW YORK AND PARIS STOP IF SO PLEASE STATE COST AND DELIVERY DATE," he cabled Ryan on February 3, 1927. The next day, Lindbergh's twenty-fifth birthday, Ryan replied, "CAN BUILD PLANE SIMILAR [MODEL] M ONE BUT LARGER WINGS CAPABLE OF MAKING FLIGHT COST ABOUT SIX THOUSAND WITHOUT MOTOR AND INSTRUMENTS DELIVERY ABOUT THREE MONTHS." Lindbergh asked for the plane's specifications and whether it could be built any faster; Ryan wired back that it could hold 380 gallons of fuel, cruise at a hundred miles an hour, and be ready in two months following the receipt of a 50 percent down payment.

Lindbergh was about to move ahead with Ryan when Bellanca telegraphed him on February 6, "WILLING TO MAKE ATTRACTIVE PROPOSITION ON THE BELLANCA AIRPLANE FOR PARIS FLIGHT STOP SUGGEST YOU COME NEW YORK SOON POSSIBLE SO WE CAN GET TOGETHER IN QUICKEST MANNER." It turned out that Bellanca had recently gone into business with twenty-eight-year-old war-surplus millionaire Charles Levine, the fast-talking new owner of Columbia Aircraft, whose offices were on the fifty-first floor of the sixty-story Woolworth Building. There, Levine and Bellanca offered to sell Lindbergh the only existing Bellanca for fifteen thousand dollars. After returning to St. Louis to consult with his backers, Lindbergh accepted. Later, as the cashier's check was being cut, Bixby suggested that Lindbergh name the plane the *Spirit of St. Louis.*

On February 19, Lindbergh was back at the Woolworth Building to present Levine with his check. But before Levine accepted the money, he insisted on a new condition: He wanted to choose the pilot who would fly the plane to Paris. A flabbergasted Lindbergh refused to go along with this and returned with the check to St. Louis. Only later did he realize that Levine had been planning his own attempt all along and was merely interested in selling the naming rights to the St. Louis group. Now Slim was right back where he was on February 5, except that two more precious weeks had passed. After a quick meeting with his backers, Lindbergh got on the next train to California. His fare to San Diego was $75, on top of which he spent $22.50 for a sleeping berth in one of the train's Pullman cars.

Richard E. Byrd, shown here in 1925, points to the spot on the globe where he hopes to find an arctic continent. On May 8, 1926, he and Floyd Bennett made the first flight over the North Pole.

LINDBERGH ARRIVED IN SAN DIEGO at noon on February 25 and took a taxi to the Ryan factory down by the harbor. There was no airfield nearby, and the building was a bit seedy, but the company's youthful, energetic staff talked the lingo of experimental aviation that Lindbergh recognized immediately. After a brief tour of the plant, he met with owner Benjamin Franklin Mahoney and chief engineer Donald Hall. They discussed some basic specifications, after which Hall asked Lindbergh what the mileage was between New York City to Paris. Because Lindbergh didn't know exactly, they drove to a library to find out. By the time they returned, Mahoney had run some financials on the plane. Complete with a Wright Whirlwind J-5 engine and instrumentation, which Ryan would install at cost, the price of the custom-built plane would be $10,580. From Mahoney's office, Lindbergh wired the details to Knight; the next day, Knight wired back that Lindbergh should close the deal.

Charles Levine (left) and Clarence Chamberlin (right) pose in early 1927 with Lloyd Bertaud, who would have been Chamberlin's copilot on the Paris flight had Levine given them permission to take off that Friday morning.

Remaining in San Diego and working directly with Hall, Lindbergh monitored every aspect of the plane's design and construction. "Every part of it can be designed for a single purpose," he wrote. "I can inspect each detail before it's covered with fabric and fairings. And by knowing intimately both the strengths and weaknesses of my plane, I'll be able to tax the one and relieve the other according to conditions which arise." Knowing that others might take off at any time come April, the Ryan staff worked nights and weekends to put the plane together as quickly as possible. "During this time," Lindbergh recalled, "it was not unusual for the men to work twenty-four hours without rest, and on one occasion Donald Hall, the Chief Engineer, was over his drafting table for thirty-six hours." According to mechanic Douglas Corrigan, "everyone was glad to do that as they all seemed to be inspired by the fellow the plane was being built for."

Lindbergh told Hall that his design priorities should be fuel efficiency first, pilot safety second, and pilot comfort last. The cockpit seat that Ryan installed, for example, resembled a cramped wicker lawn chair, but its light construction saved a few pounds of weight, which was all that mattered to Lindbergh.

The factory work was completed on April 25. That afternoon, the aircraft's fuselage was towed out to the Ryan hangar at the Dutch Flats airfield on the outskirts of town. Moving the aircraft's separately constructed wing assembly proved much more difficult, however. The problem was its size. At forty-six feet across, the wing assembly was ten feet longer than any previously built at Ryan, and no one had measured the doors to the loft in which it was built to see whether it could ever be taken out. "For a time it looked as though we'd have to tear out a section of the wall; but careful measurement showed that we could get by if we tipped the wing over at an angle and removed the loft's double doors," Lindbergh recalled. The plane's final assembly took place over the next three days at Dutch Flats.

San Diego to New York

MEANWHILE, ON THE EAST COAST, Lindbergh's competition waited impatiently for acceptable flying weather over the Atlantic. To most aviation experts, Lindbergh seemed hopelessly outclassed. Byrd's North Pole adventure had made him world famous. Nungesser and Coli were also considered among the finest—and bravest—aviators in the world, performing at the peak of their abilities. Even Columbia Aircraft test pilot Clarence Chamberlin had grabbed headlines on April 14, when he broke the world endurance record during a test flight in the Bellanca. He and his copilot, Bert Acosta, remained aloft for more than fifty-one hours, smashing the old record by nearly six hours. Of all the serious contenders for the Orteig Prize, in fact, only Charles Lindbergh stood out as unfamiliar, untested, unknown.

Yet the onset of better weather brought with it a series of accidents that tragically narrowed the field. On April 16, Byrd's huge trimotored Fokker crashed during a test flight in New Jersey, overturning on landing. Two crew members were badly injured, Byrd's wrist was broken, and the monoplane was badly damaged: One of its engines, its propeller, and its cockpit were all ruined. "The accident may force Commander Byrd to abandon his plans for a trans-oceanic flight this spring," Lindbergh read in the next day's newspaper.

On April 26, there was another crash. Testing their enormous Keystone Pathfinder at Langley Field in Virginia before setting out for Paris, Noel Davis and Stanton Wooster took off with the equivalent of a full transatlantic fuel load. The weight proved to be too much, however, and their trimotored airplane wasn't able to clear the tree line at the end of the runway. Davis turned the plane sharply to the right to avoid some branches, lost altitude, and crashed into a nearby marsh. Both men were killed.

Two days later, Lindbergh flew in the *Spirit of St. Louis* for the first time. By then, the national press had caught such a bad case of "Atlantic fever" that even the airmail pilot was getting some coverage. During the next ten days, he flew the plane two dozen times, increasing the duration and the load with each flight. On May 4, he took off with 300 gallons of gasoline, or just about three-quarters of the expected 425-gallon New York–Paris load. The plane held up well, needing only minor adjustments, but the landing was sufficiently hard on the tires that Lindbergh decided not to strain them again. "I had intended to take off with loads up to 400 gallons; but if I keep on, and a tire blows, it may wreck our whole project," Lindbergh wrote. "After all, one can carry tests so far that instead of adding to safety they increase the over-all danger." On Thursday, May 6, he made ready to leave for St. Louis, but bad weather over the Rockies held him up.

Workers carefully extricate the Spirit of St. Louis's *wing assembly from the Ryan Aeronautical factory, using a freight car for support.*

LEFT: *Charles Nungesser in March 1921. During World War I, Nungesser was France's third leading ace, with forty-five dogfight victories.*

ON SUNDAY, MAY 8, he was still in San Diego when Nungesser and Coli took off from Paris's Le Bourget Aerodrome. If all went well, the Frenchmen were expected to land in New York City on Monday. Lindbergh began making alternate plans to fly westward across the Pacific. But all didn't go well. Late on Monday, Nungesser and Coli still hadn't arrived, which meant that they must have gone down somewhere because they didn't have enough fuel with them to be still in the air. Lindbergh put away his Pacific charts and on May 10 left San Diego for St. Louis, taking off in the late afternoon so that he could get some practice navigating unfamiliar territory in the dark. Fourteen and a half hours later (a new record for a nonstop flight of that distance), Lindbergh landed in St. Louis, where he had breakfast and got status reports on Nungesser and Coli (still lost) and on the Bellanca (still on the ground). He spent the rest of the day with his old cronies at Lambert Field, went to sleep early, and took off the next morning—Thursday, May 12—for Long Island. On landing at Curtiss Field, Lindbergh learned that he, too, had become a celebrity.

Although the young aviator certainly had the rough good looks and boyish charm of a matinee idol, his physical appearance was responsible for only a small part of his appeal. Lindbergh captured the imagination of his era because he personified and transcended so many of the contradictions that had, by then, come to characterize life in the United States during the "roaring" 1920s. To an America increasingly surfeited with technological change, Lindbergh brought a recognition that individuals could still master new technologies and set the course of their own lives. Furthermore, in a culture publicly dominated by affluent, self-absorbed, middle- and upper-class pleasure seekers, Lindbergh's apparent commitment to traditional American values—devotion to family, loyalty to friends, modesty, self-discipline—made him all the more compelling to reporters and their audiences.

As the son of a former congressman, Lindbergh couldn't be entirely mistaken for a country bumpkin, yet the mass media blurred this aspect of his past as best it could in order to present him as an Everyman hero. Playing on the cynicism and moral laxity of the Jazz Age, print and radio journalists created about the boy wonder a cult of virtue and innocence. "Romance, chivalry, self-dedication—here they were, embodied in a modern Galahad for a generation which had forsworn Galahads," wrote Frederick Lewis Allen, the decade's most perceptive chronicler. To his fellow Americans, Lindbergh represented not only the freedom and prosperity of what was then being called the New Era but also the persistence of deeper American values in a time of rapid change.

Lindbergh with Ryan Aeronautical owner B. F. Mahoney, sometime in 1927. While working in San Diego, Lindbergh ordered a waterproof cloth flying suit from A. G. Spalding & Bros., the sporting goods manufacturers. The custom-made garment had a thick wool lining (because there would be no heater on the plane) and one long zipper. However, what Lindbergh liked best about it was its weight: only nine pounds.

PROHIBITION

ALTHOUGH WELL-TO-DO AMERICANS of the 1920s liked to complain about the "licentiousness" of the country's youth—a licentiousness made possible, incidentally, by the new automobility—the great public sin of the New Era was the illegal consumption of alcohol. In December 1917, aided by the growth of religious fundamentalism, the temperance movement had finally persuaded Congress to send to the states a constitutional amendment banning "the manufacture, sale, or transportation of intoxicating liquors." Thirteen months later, the Eighteenth Amendment was ratified, and in October 1919, Congress passed the Volstead Act enforcing the ban. (Of course, by this time, many states had already been "dry" for years.)

Detroit police raid an illegal underground brewery during the Prohibition era.

During the era of Prohibition, however, millions of Americas refused to take part in "the noble experiment," and they created a thriving market for "bootleg" liquor that urban crime syndicates rushed to exploit. These gangs, including Al Capone's notorious mob in Chicago, smuggled in spirits from abroad and serviced the many, not-so-discreet "speakeasies" that opened to satisfy the urban public's thirst for sophisticated adult recreation. New York City alone had thirty-two thousand speakeasies, or twice the number of legal saloons it had before Prohibition, according to the city's police commissioner. Enforcement of the Volstead Act reduced the country's alcohol consumption considerably (mostly by quintupling the price of beer and liquor), and there were concurrent drops in the prison population and in medical statistics that tracked diseases associated with alcoholism. But the social and economic costs of the lawlessness eventually proved too high, leading to repeal of the Eighteenth Amendment in December 1933.

Automobiles

THE GREATEST OF THE CHANGES taking place in American life during the 1920s resulted from the many new machine technologies that had recently been developed. When the decade began, electricity provided only a third of the energy used to power U.S. industry; by the time of Lindbergh's flight, widespread electrification had raised that figure to almost two-thirds. At the same time, mass-production techniques revolutionized U.S. manufacturing, making consumer goods much more plentiful and affordable. The automobile industry, in particular, led the way.

In 1900, the first year that the Department of Commerce began keeping track, there were 8,000 automobiles in the United States—nearly all of them playthings for the rich. In 1903, when Henry Ford established the Ford Motor Company in Detroit, there were 23,000 cars on the nation's few suitable roads. Five years later, when Ford introduced the inexpensive Model T, Americans owned 194,000 cars. However, by 1918, that number had exploded to 5,554,000. The difference was the assembly line, introduced by Ford in 1913. It divided manufacturing tasks according to function, speeded up the work, and reduced Ford's labor costs considerably.

The first Model Ts had cost $850, quite a reasonable price in 1908, and Ford sold 10,607 of them that year. With the efficiencies of its new assembly line, however, the company was able to drop the Model T's price steadily and thereby increase sales. In 1916, three years after introducing the assembly line at its manufacturing plants, the Ford Motor Company sold 730,041 Model Ts for just $360 apiece. Ford also made motor cars affordable by offering them on the installment plan. Instead of having to come up with $360 on delivery, average Americans could make weekly or monthly payments while enjoying full use of the car.

Workers assemble a Model T in 1913, the first year in which Henry Ford used assembly lines to manufacture his cars. With the inexpensive Tin Lizzie, Ford was able to create the first true mass market for automobiles and make good on his promise to "build a motorcar for the multitudes."

Meanwhile, the explosion in automobile ownership changed American social practices both immediately and profoundly. The construction of numerous new roads crisscrossing the country produced a sense of easy mobility nearly unimaginable before 1900. Railroads began to decline as a result, along with other forms of public transportation. (Quietly, the automobile companies accelerated this trend by purchasing trolley car lines and closing them down so that passengers would have to use motor buses or passenger cars to get around.)

THE SUCCESS OF THE AUTOMOBILE industry during the early decades of the twentieth century also fed expansion in a number of collateral industries—such as rubber, glass, petroleum, and road construction, even restaurants and the new "motor inns." Soon, with wartime purchases from Europe also contributing, the U.S. economy was booming again after several years of lean times. Big business even regained the respectability it had lost during the Progressive era—and then some. Soon, business values hijacked the culture. "The man who builds a factory builds a temple; the man who works there worships there," Republican vice-presidential candidate Calvin Coolidge observed in 1920. The new advertising industry played perhaps the most interesting role in this image makeover. During the 1920s, as corporate expenditures on advertising tripled, the Madison Avenue agencies came into their own. They developed new ways to sell perfumes, sewing machines, and door locks— and, more importantly, they helped Americans feel comfortable replacing the nation's traditional thrift ethic with a ravenous new desire to consume. The unshackling of this demand, in fact, produced a release of economic energy so powerful that making money began to seem easy and those in positions of privilege became arrogant.

THE NEW FORD CABRIOLET

A convenient, convertible car. In summer, the airy freedom of the roadster. In winter, the comfort and protection of a coupe. The side windows, as well as the windshield, are made of Triplex shatter-proof glass. Rumble seat is included as standard equipment.

RIGHT: An ad for a Ford Cabriolet from the period of Lindbergh's flight. In 1920s America, automobiles and advertising grew up together.

Urban Americans, in particular, saw in the New Era the triumph of entrepreneurial capitalism and believed that all levels of society benefited. They admired leading businessmen, abhorred political radicalism, and demanded

THE LOST GENERATION

THE PARIS IN WHICH CHARLES LINDBERGH landed in May 1927 was a world quite far removed from the business-oriented United States—and thus a place quite attractive to the many Americans who lived there during all or part of the 1920s. These expatriates included many prominent writers and artists who belonged to what Gertrude Stein called the "lost generation" because they had been disillusioned not only by the carnage of World War I but also by the failure of Wilsonian universalism at Versailles. Young men such as Ernest Hemingway, who had originally crossed the ocean to take part in the Great War, remained behind rather than reenter America's aggressively bourgeois New Era society.

"I was always embarrassed by the words *sacred, glorious,* and *sacrifice,* and the expression *in vain,*" Hemingway wrote. "We had heard them…and read them on proclamations… and I had seen nothing sacred, and the things that were glorious had no glory and the sacrifices were like the stockyards at Chicago, if nothing was done with the meat except to bury it." The Great War had been fought, complained the poet Ezra

In 1918, Ernest Hemingway volunteered to drive a Red Cross ambulance on the Italian front, where he was severely wounded after just a few weeks of service.

Pound, for a "botched civilization." The rancor was everywhere, and these writers gradually transformed their bitterness—toward war, toward the ruling classes, toward their own country, toward themselves—into searing literary masterworks, such as John Dos Passos's *Three Soldiers* (1921), T. S. Eliot's *The Waste Land* (1922), Hemingway's *The Sun Also Rises* (1926) and *A Farewell to Arms* (1929), and many others.

Meanwhile, in the United States, equally young authors expressed a related sense of alienation and disillusionment. Gone was the exuberance and optimism of pre-1914 American literature, replaced by an aimlessness of the sort found most notably in the work of F. Scott Fitzgerald, who populated his 1920 novel *This Side of Paradise* with wealthy and flamboyant youth "grown up to find all Gods dead, all wars fought, all faiths in man shaken." Like their counterparts in expatriate fiction, Fitzgerald's pleasure seekers were morally conflicted and often found themselves torn between old duties and new desires. "So we beat on," Fitzgerald wrote, "boats against the current, borne back ceaselessly into the past."

"stability" from the government (by which they meant that the government shouldn't limit business decision making, either by regulation or by oversight). More so than the Democrats, the Republicans championed this viewpoint and enjoyed much greater electoral success as a result. "Brains are wealth," Coolidge said on another occasion, "and wealth is the chief end of man."

The degree to which this business gospel pervaded even traditional religion became apparent in 1925, when advertising executive Bruce Barton topped the best-seller lists with *The Man Nobody Knows.* In Barton's book, a modern retelling of the Jesus story, the Nazarene became a model corporate executive who "picked up twelve men from the bottom ranks of business and forged them into an organization that conquered the world." Jesus' parables, according to Barton, were "the most powerful advertisements of all time."

Business and Politics

ONE REASON THAT BARTON'S vulgarization of Christianity succeeded so well was that its message echoed the worshipful attitude that the federal government showed private enterprise throughout the 1920s. Progressive concerns about the dangers posed by large corporations died with the Wilson presidency, and beginning in 1921, the Republican party enjoyed a dozen years of preeminence, controlling both the White House and Congress until well after the October 1929 stock market crash. Pres. Calvin Coolidge, in particular, believed wholeheartedly in the benevolence of American capitalism. He admired men of wealth and accepted absolutely the social Darwinist principle that economic prosperity depended on the ability of these men to guide their companies as they saw fit. Therefore, during the 1920s, the regulatory agencies of the federal government, populated by Republican appointees dedicated to noninterference, did virtually nothing to restrain mergers, price fixing, or any other noncompetitive business practice. Coolidge's appointee to chair the Federal Trade Commission, William T. Humphrey, even denounced the work of his own agency as oppressive and socialistic.

Coolidge was disturbed by the enormous amount of stock speculation but did nothing to curb it; in fact, his treasury secretary—Andrew Mellon, the third richest man in the country—*promoted* investment in stocks. A holdover from the Harding administration, Mellon believed that the government could best help the economy by leaving it alone; on the other hand, he didn't see how a large tax cut could hurt. In 1924 and again in 1926, he proposed tax reduction bills that Congress duly enacted, halving the top income-tax rate and similarly slashing the estate tax. The Wilson administration's Progressive tax legacy was wiped out, and wealthy Americans suddenly had a great deal more money to spend. Most invested their windfalls in the quickly rising stock market.

The market kept going up during the 1920s, not only because of all the new investment but also because corporate dividends were soaring. By the late 1920s, stocks seemed such sure bets that people borrowed from brokers merely to buy more. This practice, called buying "on margin," drove stock prices even higher, beyond all rationality. Price-to-earnings ratios skyrocketed, and there were other danger signs as well, such as the fact that corporate profits were increasing at more than twice the rate of productivity gains. But all that most middle- and upper-class Americans could see was the impressive value (on paper) of their market portfolios. The fever got so bad that some corporations began investing their own cash in the stock market, rather than in new research or plant expansion, because they anticipated greater returns from speculation than from production.

Supporting all this reckless economic behavior was the unfortunate political assumption that the public interest and the interests of the business community were identical. ("The chief business of the American people is business," Coolidge declared in 1925.) What such thinking produced was a warped and unsound financial structure that only *seemed* prosperous. Under such conditions, however, it did seem reasonable for firms to use real productivity gains to fund higher stock dividends rather than better equipment or higher wages. Yet this practice only

Calvin Coolidge (shown here at the White House) succeeded to the presidency upon Warren Harding's death in August 1923. In contrast to his slick, gregarious predecessor—whom Teddy's daughter, Alice Roosevelt Longworth, called "not a bad man... just a slob"— Coolidge presented himself as a crisp, ascetic business executive.

enhanced the disastrous maldistribution of income, promoted by Mellon's tax cuts, that eroded the very consumer purchasing power that had begun the New Era boom in the first place. Because the federal government supported any and all business policies during the 1920s, and because labor unions were weak, there was no countervailing force in the New Era economy to lobby for reason and balance.

O N FRIDAY, MAY 20, 1927, after being awakened by his friend at 12:30 A.M., Lindbergh lay in his bed until 2 A.M., then got dressed and drove to Curtiss Field. He still wasn't sure whether he would take off that morning, and neither Chamberlin nor Byrd (whose plane had been sufficiently repaired) were making any preparations. Lindbergh got an updated weather report—clearing along the North American coast, clearing over the Atlantic, only local storms in Europe—then ordered the *Spirit of St. Louis* towed from Curtiss to neighboring Roosevelt Field, where Byrd had offered Lindbergh use of its longer, better runway. Light rain continued to fall as a small band of newsmen, mechanics, and police accompanied the plane on its slow transit between the two fields. "It's more like a funeral procession than the beginning of a flight to Paris," Lindbergh later wrote.

It wasn't until after daybreak, when he sat in the cockpit of the fully loaded *Spirit of St. Louis*, its motor on and idling, that Lindbergh decided to go for Paris. "It's less a decision of logic than of feeling," he explained later, "the kind of feeling that comes when you gauge the distance to be jumped between two stones across a brook." Fonck and Davis had both crashed because their planes couldn't generate enough lift to offset full loads of fuel; on the other hand, the Bellanca (during its record endurance flight) and the French Levasseur had both managed to take off fully laden. Would Lindbergh's plane manage the feat? Even he wasn't sure, but he decided to try. He motioned the mechanics to remove the chocks restraining his wheels and opened his engine wide. With his crew pushing on the wing struts to help the heavy plane overcome its inertia, the *Spirit of St. Louis* began to creep forward. After about a hundred yards, the men fell away as the plane picked up speed. Halfway down the runway, though, Lindbergh still wasn't sure he would make it into the air.

"Civilization and profits go hand in hand."
—
*Calvin Coolidge,
speech,
November 27,
1920*

*A truck begins
to tow the* Spirit
of St. Louis *from
Curtiss Field to
Roosevelt Field
during the predawn
hours of May 20.*

Seconds now to decide—close the throttle, or will I get off? The wrong decision means a crash—probably in flames—I pull the stick back firmly, and—the wheels leave the ground. Then I'll get off! The wheels touch again. I ease the stick forward— almost flying speed, and nearly 2000 feet of field ahead—A shallow pool on the runway—water spews up from the tires—A wing drops—lifts as I shove aileron against it—the entire plane trembles from the shock—Off again—right wing low— pull it up—Ease back onto the runway—left rudder—hold to center—must keep straight—Another pool—water drumming on the fabric—The next hop's longer—

*The **Spirit of St. Louis** overflies Long Island on its way to Paris. "What freedom lies in flying!" Lindbergh once wrote. "What godlike power it gives to man! I'm independent of the seaman's coast lines, of the landsman's roads…. I'm like a magician concocting magic formulas."*

I could probably stay in air; but I let the wheels touch once more—lightly, a little bow to earth, a gesture of humility before it—Best to have plenty of control with such a load, and control requires speed. The Spirit of St. Louis *takes herself off the next time.*

The time was 7:54 A.M. when Lindbergh cleared the line of telephone poles at the end of the Roosevelt Field runway by about twenty feet. Newspaper reporters rushed off to file the story: The Flying Fool was off to Paris.

New York City to Paris

LINDBERGH'S FLIGHT PATH followed the North American coastline up into Canada before turning east over the Atlantic. Because of the low cloud cover, he had to fly close to the ground in order to monitor his course by sighting visual landmarks. For a time, several newspapermen in hired planes escorted the *Spirit of St. Louis* so that they could track and photograph Lindbergh. Then, as he headed out over Long Island Sound, the last of the escort planes dipped its wing in farewell and left him alone. As long as the daylight lasted, there were occasional sightings of the plane by fishing boats and people on shore, and these were instantly relayed to a fascinated nation and world over the radio. But once darkness fell, there was little anyone could do but handicap Lindbergh's chances and pray for his safety. "No attempt at jokes today," began Will Rogers's newspaper column on Saturday, May 21. "A slim, tall, bashful, smiling American boy is somewhere over the middle of the Atlantic Ocean, where no lone human being has ever ventured before."

As Lindbergh passed over Cape Cod Bay on his way to Nova Scotia, he flew low over the water, sometimes just ten feet above the waves. He perused fishing boats, dodged cloudbursts, and fought the slow onset of drowsiness, wishing he'd gotten at least some sleep the night before. About 7:15 P.M. New York time, he reached St. John's, Newfoundland, where he turned east over the North Atlantic. From this point on, a number of new dangers presented themselves: There would be no place to land in the event of trouble, of course, and there would also be a much greater potential for ice to build up on his wings at night in the moist ocean air. If this happened, he could easily lose control of the *Spirit of St. Louis* and spiral down into the water. It took an extraordinary effort for Lindbergh to keep his mind alert at all times—yet he managed to do so, not only staying awake but also remaining on course despite the obvious lack of landmarks.

Darkness set in about 8:15 New York time and a thin, low fog formed through which the white [ice]bergs showed up with surprising clearness. This fog became thicker and increased in height until within two hours I was just skimming the top of storm clouds at about ten thousand feet. Even at this altitude there was a thick haze through which only the stars directly overhead could be seen.

There was no moon and it was very dark. The tops of some of the storm clouds were several thousand feet above me and at one time, when I attempted to fly through one of the larger clouds, sleet started to collect on the plane and I was forced to turn around and get back into clear air immediately and then fly around any clouds which I could not get over.

The moon appeared on the horizon after about two hours of darkness; then the flying was much less complicated.

Dawn came at about 1 A.M. New York time and the temperature had risen until there was practically no remaining danger of sleet....

After a few miles of fairly clear weather the ceiling lowered to zero and for nearly two hours I flew entirely blind through the fog at an altitude of about 1500 feet. Then the fog raised and the water was visible again.

On several more occasions it was necessary to fly by instrument for short periods; then the fog broke up into patches. These patches took on forms of every description. Numerous shorelines appeared, with trees perfectly outlined against the horizon. In fact, the mirages were so natural that, had I not been in the mid-Atlantic and known that no land existed along my route, I would have taken them to be actual islands.

MASS COMMUNICATIONS

CHARLES LINDBERGH WAS ONE OF THE FIRST American heroes spawned with the complete connivance of the new mass media, radio included. After Alexander Graham Bell's invention of the telephone in 1876, the next great communications advance was the "wireless telegraphy" developed by Italian physicist Guglielmo Marconi and others at the turn of the twentieth century. By the 1920s, radio sets had joined telephones as standard equipment in middle-class American homes. Lindbergh's ability to project himself with eloquence and self-confidence over the airwaves enhanced his celebrity and caused radio stations to air frequent bulletins reporting the progress of his flight to Paris as he overflew the North American coast.

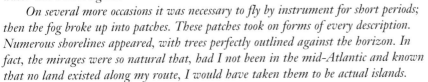

A clothing manufacturer in St. Paul, Minnesota, created these Lucky Lindy hats and coats to cash in on the country's "Atlantic fever."

T HE FIRST SIGN OF LINDBERGH'S APPROACH to the European mainland was a small fishing boat. Gliding his plan down within fifty feet of the vessel, the American closed his throttle and yelled at a man sticking his head out of a cabin porthole, "Which way is Ireland?" Lindbergh circled a few times, waiting for a response that never came, then continued on his previous course. Less than an hour later, not long after 3 P.M. local time (11 A.M. New York time), he spotted a rugged coastline—more than two hours ahead of schedule, thanks to strong tailwinds. Circling with his chart spread out on his knees, he checked and rechecked his position before concluding that he had made land at the entrance to Dingle Bay on Ireland's southwestern coast. To his amazement, he was fewer than three miles from the point he had projected as his landfall three months earlier in San Diego. Paris was now just six hundred miles away.

The cockpit of the **Spirit of St. Louis,** *photographed from the perspective of a person sitting in the pilot's seat. Note that the plane had no forward window; the engine would have blocked Lindbergh's view in any case. There was, however, a skylight.*

From Ireland, his course took him across first the St. George's Channel, then southern England, and finally the English Channel. Except for a few brief interludes, he was never out of sight of a ship or land the rest of the way. He struck France over Deauville, about which time the sun set and Lindbergh picked up the beacons of the Paris–London airway. Realizing that he hadn't eaten since taking off thirty-three hours earlier, he pulled out the bag of sandwiches that Dick Blythe had bought for him and forced one of them down.

I first saw the lights of Paris a little before 10 P.M., or 5 P.M. New York time, and a few minutes later I was circling the Eiffel Tower at an altitude of about four thousand feet.

The lights of Le Bourget were plainly visible, but appeared to be very close to Paris. I had understood that the field was farther from the city, so continued out to the northeast into the country for four or five miles to make sure that there was not another field farther out which might be Le Bourget. Then I returned and spiraled down closer to the lights. Presently I could make out long lines of hangars, and the roads appeared to be jammed with cars.

I flew low over the field once, then circled around into the wind and landed. After the plane stopped rolling I turned it around and started to taxi back to the lights. The entire field ahead, however, was covered with thousands of people all running toward my ship.

Arrival

LEARNING OF LINDBERGH'S APPROACH, more than a hundred thousand people had rushed out to Le Bourget, and even though French military and police units had also been deployed there, the crowds were simply too large and excited to be controlled. When Lindbergh landed at 10:24 P.M., thousands of celebrants broke free of the barricades and, chanting the American's name, rushed his plane. The U.S. ambassador to France, Myron T. Herrick, had come out to Le Bourget with a number of French officials to greet Lindbergh formally, yet the eruption of humanity prevented the dignitaries from getting anywhere near the by-now disoriented pilot.

After so many hours without sleep, alone with his thoughts in the small plane, Lindbergh wasn't prepared for the frenzied reception that greeted him in Paris. To say that it rattled him initially would be an understatement. He could hear the sounds of snapping wood and tearing fabric, which he knew meant that souvenir hunters were already at work on his plane. He cut his engine and disengaged the propeller so that no one would be injured, then moved to get out of the plane in order to draw the crowds away from it. "I started to climb out of the cockpit," he recalled, "but as soon as one foot appeared through the door I was dragged the rest of the way without assistance on my part. For nearly half an hour I was unable to touch the ground, during which time I was ardently carried around in what seemed to be a very small area, and in every position it was possible to be in."

Lindbergh was finally rescued by a pair of French aviators who diverted the crowd by jerking Lindbergh's helmet from his head and tossing it to a nearby American reporter, Harry Wheeler, who caught it instinctively. "There is Lindbergh! There is Lindbergh!" the French pilots shouted, setting the crowd upon Wheeler, who was carried on innumerable shoulders to the edge of the airfield, where Ambassador Herrick and the French dignitaries were waiting. "I am not Lindbergh," Wheeler insisted, as Herrick presented him with a bouquet of red roses. "Of course you are," the diplomat replied before Wheeler managed to explain the situation.

Meanwhile, pilots Michel Détroyat and George Delage pushed Lindbergh into Delage's Renault and hustled him into a nearby hangar. There, the American managed to catch his breath and compose himself. He asked first about his plane and was assured that everything possible was being done to protect it. Then, because he had never obtained a visa, he asked whether there would be any problems with customs or immigration. The only response he got was laughter. France, Détroyat and Delage told him, was his.

AFTER ABOUT AN HOUR, a major in the French air force arrived to escort Lindbergh to an office on the military side of the aerodrome, where—after another hour's wait—Lindbergh was finally presented to Herrick. Until word came from Ireland that the *Spirit of St. Louis* had been sighted, Herrick hadn't thought the plane would make it, so he'd been forced to make arrangements for Lindbergh's arrival in a hurry. "Young man," Herrick said after taking a few moments to look the pilot over, "I am going to take you home with me and look after you." A relieved Lindbergh accepted the ambassador's offer but insisted on examining his aircraft first. "It was a great shock to me to see my plane," he wrote later. "The sides of the fuselage were full of gaping holes, and some souvenir hunter had pulled a lubrication fitting right off one of the rocker-arm housings on my engine. But in spite of surface appearances, careful inspection showed that no serious damage had been done. A few hours of work would make my plane airworthy again."

It was almost 2 A.M. by the time Lindbergh reached the American embassy, and it took Herrick, who traveled separately, even longer to negotiate the traffic jams around Le Bourget. While Lindbergh waited, he ate a sandwich and drank a glass of milk. When Herrick finally arrived, he asked whether Lindbergh might consent to a brief meeting with American reporters waiting elsewhere in the building. With the permission of the *New York Times* bureau chief still awaiting the paper's exclusive, Lindbergh agreed to hold an impromptu press conference in the ambassador's bedroom. By then, the exhausted Flying Fool had changed into Herrick's generously cut pajamas. Sitting on the edge of the bed, he answered a flurry of questions with poise and candor. Could the *Spirit of St. Louis* have flown farther? "A thousand, or at least five hundred miles," Lindbergh said. "What about you? Could you have flown on? Weren't you too tired?" another newsman asked. "I could have flown half the distance again. You know, flying a good airplane doesn't require nearly as much attention as driving a motor car." After about ten minutes of this, Herrick ended the session, and at 4:15 A.M. local time, Lindbergh finally went to sleep.

In Paris the next day, and later in the United States, the response to Lindbergh was overwhelming. The delight taken in his achievement was universal, even among the notoriously cynical sophisticates of the Jazz Age, and celebrations greeted the pilot everywhere he went. At his public appearances, Lindbergh usually spoke as little as possible, adhering to a few carefully chosen themes: his high hopes for the future of aviation, the pleasure he took in his accomplishment, and the need for greater international amity.

LINDBERGH HAD UNDERSTANDABLY never given much thought to his return to the United States, except to assume that one way or another he would fly the *Spirit of St. Louis* back to America himself. Instead, President Coolidge sent a navy cruiser to carry both plane and pilot home as safely as possible. Not long after dawn on June 11, the USS *Memphis* docked at the Washington navy yard, where Captain Lindbergh of the (recently renamed) Army Air Corps Reserves was met by members of the cabinet and the heads of the nation's military services. During the months ahead, Lindbergh flew the *Spirit of St. Louis* to every state in the Union and received similarly glorious welcomes in each.

During the second week of December 1927, Congress voted Lindbergh the Congressional Medal of Honor, which had previously been reserved for war heroes. It was later presented to him by President Coolidge at a White House ceremony.

He continued to turn down nearly all of the promotional offers he received—including proposals to make movies, join daredevil barnstorming tours, and otherwise exploit his national celebrity. But he did pen a series of exclusive articles for the *New York Times* and seclude himself for a few weeks that summer to write the terse memoir *We*, which became a best-seller and guaranteed his financial security. (The title of the book referred to the union of plane and pilot.)

Beginning in 1928, Lindbergh devoted an increasing amount of his time and energy to the promotion of commercial aviation. He worked with several groups of entrepreneurs, including two that created the nation's first great transcontinental airlines: Pan American and Trans World. Although in later life Lindbergh tried to avoid publicity as best he could, he remained in the public eye for decades, and his heroism never diminished, even as others replicated his flight and the press moved on to other, more current excitements.

The Election of 1928

AMONG THOSE EXCITEMENTS was the presidential election of 1928, one of the hottest in American history. After Calvin Coolidge announced his retirement in August 1927, the Republicans nominated Commerce Secretary Herbert C. Hoover. A member of Stanford University's first graduating class, Hoover had majored in geology and afterward become a mining engineer, working all over the world. (In China in 1900, he and his wife, Lou, had helped defend the foreign community in Tientsin during the Boxer Rebellion.) By 1914, the forty-year-old Hoover was a multimillionaire, and he spent the Great War leading American efforts to help starving Europeans. As head of the Commission for the Relief of Belgium (1914–1919) and later as director of the American Relief Administration (1919–1920), he distributed thirty-four million tons of food, clothing, and other supplies to needy refugees. His remarkably efficiency—a product, he said, of his engineering and entrepreneurial backgrounds—made him famous, and the verb *hooverize* came into popular usage, meaning "to conserve." The Great Engineer seemed the perfect successor to President Coolidge—a technocrat who promised to keep the prosperity going (through "scientific" management of the economy) and a humanitarian to boot.

Hoover's Democratic opponent was Alfred E. Smith, late of the New York Factory Investigating Commission and more recently governor of New York State, an office to which he was elected four times. There couldn't have been a more conspicuous contrast between the two major party candidates. Hoover, like Lindbergh, was a man who embodied old-stock, rural values; Al Smith was unmistakably a city slicker, and a Catholic one at that. Never before had a Catholic run for president on the ticket of a major party, nor a nominee so closely identified with immigrant politics and urban machines. Smith's campaign demonstrated why. Members of the newly resurgent Ku Klux Klan, who hated Catholics and Jews

Four sailors pose with Lindbergh's plane aboard the Memphis. *This photograph was taken on June 12, 1927, the day after the* Memphis *docked in the Washington navy yard.*

THE RESURRECTION OF THE KLAN

AMONG AL SMITH'S MANY PROBLEMS during the 1928 campaign were the attacks directed at him by the newly resurgent Ku Klux Klan. Yet as much as Klan members hated Catholics and Jews, they despised blacks more. During the final years of Reconstruction, under substantial pressure from the federal government, the Klan had become dormant; around the turn of the twentieth century, however, a revival of Confederate "lost cause" sentimentalism led to its resurrection in the South and elsewhere.

During the late 1910s and early 1920s, gross distortions of the history of both the antebellum South and the Reconstruction period proliferated throughout the culture. For example, D. W. Griffith based his 1915 epic *Birth of a Nation* on *The Clansman*, an absurdly racist 1905 novel by

Thomas Dixon Jr. Yet, at a private White House screening, Woodrow Wilson praised the veracity of Griffith's film highly. ("It is like writing history in lightning," the president said.) This sort of racist attitude, along with the superpatriotism that swept the country during World War I, encouraged the Klan to become increasingly bold. The group staged numerous public marches during the 1920s, fed on nativist fears, and by the time Congress passed the National Origins Act in May 1924 had recruited about three million members nationwide. Most of these people were disturbed by America's apparent drift away from the small-town Protestant values on which they had been raised. "The Klan…has now come to speak for the great mass of Americans of the old pioneer stock," Imperial Wizard Hiram W. Evans wrote in 1926.

Meanwhile, African Americans continued to suffer at the hands of these and other whites. In the South—and also in the North, where hundreds of thousands of southern blacks had recently migrated—there was continued segregation and violence. While the American Expeditionary Force (including many black soldiers) fought in France, deadly race riots broke out in East St. Louis, Houston, Philadelphia, Chicago, and elsewhere—most inflamed by economic tensions arising from the competition for wartime jobs. After the war, when African-American veterans returned home from unsegregated France, many felt compelled by their wartime experiences to press much more militantly for fair and equitable treatment. The white response to these demands was often violent, and between 1918 and 1927, 416 blacks were lynched.

During the 1920s, the Klan campaigned openly for like-minded politicians and enjoyed widespread support among "respectable" white Americans in every region of the country. In fact, wearing Klan regalia became so popular during the mid-1920s that several leaders of the organization made personal fortunes selling the gear. In this photograph, several members of the KKK attend Klan Day at Denver's Overlook Park race track.

nearly as much as they despised blacks, burned crosses outside Democratic rallies and hanged Smith in effigy. Smith's New York accent proclaimed his ghetto origins and made voters outside the Northeast think of ward politics, saloons, and the sort of urban anomie that had gotten McKinley killed.

Hostility toward immigrants, especially those from southern and eastern Europe, had rebounded strongly during the 1920s. In 1921 and again in 1924, Congress had passed immigration laws that used national origin as the basis for restricting entry into the country. The Emergency Quota Act of May 1921 had limited annual immigration from each country to 3 percent of the number of that country's nationals living in the United States in 1910, with no more than 357,000 allowed from all sources. The National Origins Act of May 1924 lowered the cap from 3 percent to 2 percent and moved the basis date back from 1910 to 1890. Beyond reducing the overall number of immigrants to 150,000, the 1924 law also discriminated blatantly against Italians and Jews, who didn't begin arriving in the United States in large numbers until after 1890. "America must be kept American," Coolidge explained as he signed the new law.

*LEFT: **New York governor** Alfred E. Smith in 1928. Smith was raised in a slum but rose to prominence and some wealth through machine politics. He was, nevertheless, a reformer.*

S OME OF THE VOTERS who scorned Al Smith were nativists who couldn't abide his Catholicism; others were Prohibitionists who objected to his support for repeal of the Eighteenth Amendment; still others were appalled by his links to Tammany Hall. Yet, as political columnist Walter Lippmann pointed out, there was still another source of antagonism,

which is as authentic and, it seems to me, as poignant as his support. It is inspired by the feeling that the clamorous life of the city should not be acknowledged as the American ideal…. That, at bottom, is the opposition to Al Smith, and not the nonsense about setting up the Pope in the East Wing of the White House…. Here is no trivial conflict. Here are the new people, clamoring to be admitted to America, and there are the older people defending their household gods.

As a result, the election of 1928 became easily the most symbolic contest for the presidency since the McKinley-Bryan battle of 1896. Small-town and urban America met head-on in 1928, and for the last time, the cities lost. Hoover carried forty states, including New York, and even won the vote of the industrial working class, which believed his claim that Republican rule had brought the country near a "final triumph over poverty." At the news that the Republicans had won again, the stock market commenced another dizzying spurt upward. The Dow Jones Industrial Average rose from 257.58 on Election Day to a record close of 381.17 on September 3, 1929. Although margin debt also spiked during this period, there seemed to be no end to the prosperity.

*As **commerce secretary** to both Harding and Coolidge, Herbert Hoover (shown here during his presidency) had spent eight years helping shape the economic policies that he hoped to inherit.*

AMERICAN PROFILE

Robert A. Millikan

1868–1953

by Daniel J. Kevles

In 1923, Robert A. Millikan—a minister's son from Maquoketa, Iowa—won the Nobel Prize in physics for his study of the electron, a building block of atoms. Later in the decade, he appeared on the cover of *Time* magazine for a story on his scientific accomplishments and views about religion. (He had the "face of a witty and successful banker," the editors said.) In short, he was the most famous American scientist during an era marked not only by the increasing strength of the discipline but also by the blossoming interrelationship among science, industry, the defense establishment, and cultural authorities that would come to characterize the twentieth century.

Born in 1868, Millikan entered physics at a time when the field crackled with the excitement of recent experimental discoveries—X rays in 1895, electrons in 1897, radioactivity in 1898—and faced the paradoxes posed by the new quantum theory enunciated by Max Planck in 1900. Millikan was a young faculty member at the University of Chicago when he performed his Nobel work in 1910, using his famous "oil drop" experiment to measure the charge of a single electron and prove that all electrons are distinct, identical subatomic particles. Because Millikan's work involved matters of high interest to the burgeoning telephone and radio industries, he consulted regularly for AT&T and produced students for its laboratories.

During World War I, he headed the mobilization of academic scientists for the war effort and coordinated their work in areas related to national defense. Under the auspices of the National Research Council of the National Academy of Sciences, he facilitated efforts in submarine detection, airplane instrumentation, and defense of the American Expeditionary Force against enemy artillery. In 1921, he was appointed head of the new California Institute of Technology, where he insisted on taking enough time off from his administrative and fund-raising duties to continue his program of basic research into quantized radiation and cosmic rays. Through this scientific leadership, and also because of his wide connections among philanthropists and businessmen, Millikan was able to achieve world-class standing for Cal Tech within just a few years.

It also helped that Millikan's cultural persona matched perfectly the conservative tenor of the times. He became during the 1920s one of the chief defenders of scientific rationalism and responded to the attacks of Christian fundamentalists by touting the recent "reconciliation" of science and religion. Declaring that even more important than science was "a belief in moral and spiritual values," he recruited forty-five prominent Americans—including Herbert Hoover, sixteen Protestant theologians, and some leading members of the National Academy of Sciences— to sign a statement testifying not only to the harmony of science and religion but also to the value of both. A dozen of the nation's leading scientists, he confidently asserted, had already attested to their faith in a higher being.

At the same time, Millikan rebutted charges being made by humanists that science and technology dehumanized human labor and threatened civilization by escalating the destructiveness of war. To the contrary, Millikan contended, the greatest threat to civilization was not science but the "emotional, destructive, over-sexed" content of modern literature and art. In his view, "no efforts toward social readjustment or toward the redistribution of wealth have one thousandth as large a chance of contributing to human well-being as have the efforts of the physicist, the chemist, and the biologist toward the better understanding and the better control of nature."

Millikan's conservative syllogism—that business was good for America, that science was good for business, and that, therefore, science was good for America, both economically and spiritually—fell out of fashion during the Great Depression, when business became good for virtually no one. However, like his friend President Hoover, Millikan remained conservative to the end, even opposing the federal funding of scientific research on the grounds that it would harmfully politicize the discipline.

When Millikan died in 1953, he was buried in Los Angeles at Forest Lawn Memorial Park. The cemetery's directors had promised him that they would donate several thousand dollars to Cal Tech if Millikan allowed them to lay his final remains to rest in their establishment. The deal was good business all around.

Robert A. Millikan during his years at the University of Chicago.

19

THE NEW DEAL

The Hundred Days

"THE ONLY THING WE HAVE TO FEAR is fear itself," Franklin Delano Roosevelt declared in his first inaugural address. In the rest of that speech, the new president offered remarkably little to justify such a bold statement, considering the country's terrifying economic situation; yet, for the time being at least, his confidence alone proved enough to calm fears and ease panic. For reasons perhaps having to do with Roosevelt's remarkable political appeal, Americans were comforted by his words as they never had been by Herbert Hoover's. FDR's gift for inspiring confidence, in fact, became a defining attribute of his presidency—as important as any bill he proposed or executive order he issued.

On the day that Roosevelt took office—March 4, 1933—the country was in the depths of its worst financial crisis ever. Specifically, the U.S. banking system was collapsing. Four years of depression had put such pressure on American financial institutions that the weaker ones had already failed, and a chain reaction was now threatening to bring down even the strongest. Quite naturally, as Americans watched neighbor after neighbor lose a lifetime's worth of savings to bank failures, they, too, became concerned about the stability of the financial system and began withdrawing their own funds, just to be safe. Once such bank runs get started, however, they can be very difficult to stop, and in late 1932 the pace of withdrawals accelerated. By February 1933, there was widespread panic. The governor of Michigan closed all the banks in his

AT LEFT: *A worker inspects the interior of a scroll case at the Norris Dam, one of five dams built (and twenty improved) by the Tennessee Valley Authority.*

state to prevent their immediate collapse, and other states soon joined Michigan in declaring bank holidays. By March 4, banks in thirty-eight states had been closed; the New York Stock Exchange and the Chicago Board of Trade had also been shut down. "We are at the end of our string," President Hoover said despairingly just before leaving office.

Roosevelt's mandate was to act, so he did just that. The day after his inauguration, he proclaimed (with questionable legality) a four-day national bank holiday, beginning March 6. He also ordered teams of examiners into the nation's banks to evaluate their soundness. Those institutions whose books passed muster would receive infusions of federal capital to help them stay solvent; those that didn't measure up would be closed, with as much money as possible returned to depositors. At the same time, the president summoned the Seventy-third Congress into special session.

The banking bill that he sent up to Capitol Hill on March 9, the first day of the special session, was a rather mild measure given the circumstances, yet its provisions didn't really matter. The country was in crisis, and the voters wanted the government to do *something*. "The house is burning down," one leading Republican congressman declared, "and the President of the United States says this is the way to put out the fire."

The Emergency Banking Act ratified the actions Roosevelt had taken on March 5, provided a mechanism for reopening the sound banks, and gave the president additional broad powers to get the system back on its feet. On March 10, some banks reopened, and on March 12, the president delivered the first of many informal radio speeches that came to be called "fireside chats." In a calm and confident voice, he assured the nation that its remaining banks were sound and that there was no need to panic. "In one week," columnist Walter Lippmann marveled, "the nation, which had lost confidence in everything and everybody, has regained confidence in the government and in itself." Within two months, in fact, more than twelve thousand banks—holding 90 percent of the nation's deposits—reopened, and bankers were astounded to find that deposits topped withdrawals.

A New York City policeman informs *depositors on March 4, 1933, that their bank has been closed. On June 16, the last of the Hundred Days, Congress passed the Glass-Steagall Act, which established the Federal Deposit Insurance Corporation to guarantee bank deposits up to five thousand dollars. The Glass-Steagall Act also required commercial banks within the Federal Reserve system to divest their investment banking affiliates.*

THE SUCCESSFUL resolution of the banking crisis set a number of important precedents for the New Deal, as Franklin Roosevelt's program to end the Great Depression was called. Importantly, it established, from the very outset, public confidence in the new administration's effectiveness. It also demonstrated to many conservatives that Roosevelt preferred to rehabilitate the existing American economic system rather than impose an entirely new one. Had FDR wanted to nationalize the banks, for example, a Congress made pliant by four years of crisis probably would have gone along.

Instead, the president opted for a moderate solution that bought him some time to grapple with the country's other pressing problems. Many of these he addressed in bills sent up to Congress during its March 9–June 16 special session. During this period of exactly one hundred days, Congress approved and the president signed most of the legislation—experimentation, really—that formed the basis of the "first" New Deal.

Franklin Roosevelt was a forty-seven-year-old governor of New York State when the stock market collapsed in 1929 and fifty-one years old when he became president. Thus, his ideas about the world were already quite well formed, and there is no reason to believe that either event changed his thinking substantially, other than perhaps to make him more flexible. At his core, Roosevelt remained a traditionalist, and why not? He was born into wealth and privilege, educated at Groton and Harvard, and enamored of his family's Hudson Valley estate, Hyde Park, at which he liked to play the gentleman farmer. A suave, smiling, confident aristocrat, Roosevelt generally got what he wanted—with the notable exception of the poliomyelitis he contracted in 1921, when he was thirty-nine. It was easy for Roosevelt to take the nation's social and economic institutions for granted—so he did. As Walter Lippmann pointed out during the 1932 campaign, "Franklin D. Roosevelt is no crusader. He is no tribune of the people. He is no enemy of entrenched privilege. He is a pleasant man who, without any important qualifications for the office, would very much like to be president."

Yet Roosevelt's confidence in himself, born of class and personal privilege, made him comfortable with innovation because he always believed that things would work out. Furthermore, his confidence in the fundamental strength of the country's values and institutions made him willing to consider almost any proposal for reform as long as it didn't involve junking the system entirely. Although FDR fully appreciated the seriousness of the depression, he was nevertheless certain that, sooner or later, the economy would recover. He focused, therefore, in the short term on using federal funds to generate more economic activity and in the long term on passing laws and devising regulations that would prevent the worst mistakes of the 1920s from ever being repeated.

The Origins of the Great Depression

DESPITE THE WELL-PUBLICIZED prosperity of the 1920s, there were many signs—appearing long before the stock market crash—that the economy was in trouble. For one thing, the nation's wealth remained concentrated in the hands of very few people; even with installment buying, most consumers had reached the limit of their purchasing power early in the decade. For another, the savings rate was abysmally low. The families of workers who lost their jobs or farmers who lost their crops could plunge instantly from the middle class to poverty—with no money left to pay for automobiles, radio sets, or anything else, even on the installment plan.

The situation on the farms was the worst. Encouraged by wartime subsidies and patriotic pleadings, U.S. farmers had increased their production during the late 1910s far beyond all market demand in order to feed a starving Europe. As a result, when the Great War ended and Europeans began growing their own food again, agricultural prices nose-dived. Rather than cut production, the farmers asked for additional subsidies under the McNary-Haugen farm bill. First proposed in 1924, this legislation would have supported farm income by establishing a government corporation to buy surplus grain, cotton, livestock, and tobacco at a fixed high price. The corporation would then either store its holdings until the world market price rose or "dump" them abroad at a loss. Because McNary-Haugen contained no production limits, it was extremely popular among

FRANKLIN DELANO ROOSEVELT
1882–1945

FRANKLIN ROOSEVELT HAD BEEN preparing himself for the presidency for many years. Although a fifth cousin of Theodore Roosevelt, he came from the Democratic side of the family and so didn't join the federal government until Woodrow Wilson's election in 1912. He served as assistant secretary of the navy (the same job held by TR) from 1913 until 1920, when he resigned to accept his party's vice-presidential nomination. After contracting polio in 1921, he spent three years convalescing before beginning one of the most remarkable comebacks in American political history with his speech nominating Al Smith at the 1924 Democratic national convention. Four years later, he succeeded Smith as governor of New York. During FDR's two terms in Albany, he assembled a remarkable group of academics and social policy experts that reporters nicknamed the "brain trust." Its members, including Frances Perkins and Harry Hopkins, distrusted New Era economics and believed strongly in the efficacy of social welfare programs.

Roosevelt, propped up against a car door, poses during his first presidential campaign in 1932.

agricultural constituencies, whose representatives won passage of the bill in 1927 and again in 1928. Both times, however, Pres. Calvin Coolidge vetoed the measure, which he considered price fixing at its worst and also too "socialistic." Like most prosperous easterners, Coolidge was generally indifferent to the plight of midwestern and western farmers.

Of course, there was a great deal of reckless stock speculation as well during the 1920s, as millions of ordinary Americans joined the nation's wealthiest citizens in playing the market. Between 1923 and 1929, volume on the New York Stock Exchange quadrupled, while prices rose nearly as sharply to keep pace with the expanding investor demand. Further encouraging stock speculation were the low-tax, easy-credit policies of the Treasury Department, the Federal Reserve, and other government agencies. Borrowing money to finance additional stock purchases became standard practice—much of it funded by brokerage houses that wanted to stimulate more trading and thus generate more commission income.

Pres. Calvin Coolidge poses with Treasury Secretary Andrew Mellon (center) and Commerce Secretary Herbert Hoover (right) outside the Executive Office Building in Washington, D.C., in 1928.

These "call loans" were backed by the market value of a client's portfolio. Therefore, the higher the market went, the more an investor could borrow. In the early 1920s, the total value of all call loans hovered around $1.5 billion; by 1926, however, this figure had doubled to $3 billion, and from there, it kept rising—to $6 billion in 1928 and a staggering $8.5 billion at the time of the October 1929 crash. Normal interest on call loans ran about 5 percent, but the intense demand for nearly any company's shares and the growing concern (among brokers) as to the reliability of some of the new issues pushed rates up to 12 percent in December 1928 and over 20 percent by March 1929. In early 1929, many brokerages also began raising their margin requirements to 50 percent. In other words, investors now had to fund half the cost of new stock purchases with cash. Even so, the market kept going up.

OPTIMISM REGARDING THE FUTURE of the economy remained nearly universal as late as the fall of 1929. "The economic condition of the world seems on the verge of a great upward movement," financial wizard Bernard Baruch opined in June. Irving Fisher, one of the country's leading academic economists, agreed: "Stock prices have reached what looks like a permanently high plateau." President Hoover, Treasury Secretary Andrew Mellon (serving his third consecutive Republican administration), and other senior federal officials shared this assessment. During the summer of 1929, shares in American Telephone & Telegraph (AT&T) rose from 209 to 304, while General Motors went up an equivalent percentage from 268 to 391. The market's high point was reached on September 3; then the slide began, at first slowly but picking up speed in late October. "The stock market crash," literary critic Edmund Wilson explained, "was to count for us almost like a rending of the earth in preparation for the Day of Judgment."

The deep plunge began on Thursday, October 24, 1929. Thirteen million shares were sold that day, and prices plummeted across the board, even those of such blue-chip issues as General Electric, U.S. Steel, and Westinghouse. The news stunned the country, especially the 1.5 million Americans who owned stock. Leaders in Washington and on Wall Street responded with public statements designed to reassure. "The fundamental business of the country—that is, production and distribution—is on a sound and prosperous basis," the president declared. "There has been a little distress selling on the Stock Exchange," J. P. Morgan Jr. explained, adding that "I see nothing in the present situation that is either menacing or warrants pessimism." Then came Black Tuesday, October 29, the most calamitous day in the history of the New York Stock Exchange. The volume that day was sixteen million shares, and when the session finally ended, the market value of the exchange's listed companies had fallen by more than a third, from eighty-seven billion dollars down to fifty-five billion dollars. Even worse, brokers began calling in billions of dollars' worth of call loans that investors could repay only by selling more shares from their portfolios—and driving down prices still farther.

Against this tide, efforts by wealthy investors, such as the Rockefellers and the Morgans, to prop up stock prices with their own buying had little effect. Over the next several months, personal bankruptcies mounted, dramatically reducing consumer spending; without customers, businesses began to fail. Business failure, of course, meant higher unemployment and even less consumer spending, which meant even more business failures. The cycle kept going for years, as the situation grew ever more desperate. The stock market, in fact, didn't hit bottom until July 8, 1932, when the Dow Jones Industrial Average closed at 41.22, down 89 percent from its September 3, 1929, high of 381.17. During this same period, AT&T dropped from 304 to 72, U.S. Steel from 262 to 22, Montgomery Ward from 138 to 4.

> "October. This is one of the peculiarly dangerous months to speculate in stocks in. The others are July, January, September, April, November, May, March, June, December, August, and February."
>
> — *Mark Twain,*
> *Pudd'nhead*
> *Wilson (1894)*

There was so much selling at the height of the panic that tickers ran two hours behind the current prices.

The Great Depression

THE DOWNWARD ECONOMIC SPIRAL seemed irreversible, and not a single sector of the economy escaped its deleterious effects. Five thousand banks failed during the first three years of the Great Depression, wiping out the savings of millions of people. Overall, personal income dropped from $85.9 billion in 1929 to just $47.0 billion in 1933, with an even steeper decline in foreign trade from $7.0 billion in 1929 to $2.4 billion in 1933. Meanwhile, during this same period, industrial production fell by 46 percent to a point somewhat less than its 1913 level. A factory closed somewhere almost every day, and on average a hundred thousand workers lost their jobs each week.

The greatest human cost was the unemployment. In April 1929, there were 1.6 million Americans out of work, representing just 3.2 percent of the workforce. In April 1930, however, 4.3 million Americans were unemployed (8.9 percent of the workforce), and that was only the beginning. A year later, there were 8.0 million people out of work (16.3 percent of the workforce); and by April 1932, that figure had jumped to 12.1 million (24.1 percent of the workforce). Entire cities seemed to be jobless: 50 percent of the workforce in Cleveland, 60 percent in Akron, 80 percent in Toledo. In New York City alone, there were a million people who wanted work but couldn't find any.

It was in 1931 that hospitals first began reporting deaths from starvation; about the same time, jobless workers began raiding stores, warehouses, and even delivery trucks, desperate for food. In many working-class neighborhoods, residents organized rent strikes (and sometimes used other, more forceful means) to prevent landlords from evicting indigent tenants. By the time Roosevelt took office in March 1933, more than one in four Americans was out of work.

For a remarkably long time, Americans clung to their New Era optimism, believing the exhortations of businessmen, politicians, and economists that the crisis would soon pass. "Prosperity is just around the corner," Hoover said again and again. After several years of moving from bad to worse, however, the country's "cheerful desperation" became simply despair, as most jobless Americans blamed themselves for the shame of poverty. Novelist Sherwood Anderson later recalled "picking up hitchhikers on the highway who apologized for being down and out. They accepted the whole responsibility themselves." Initially, private charities offered some aid, but after several years of hard times, they ran out of money themselves, with donations falling while demand exploded. State and local governments provided aid as well, but declining tax revenues limited these efforts, too. In Boston, for example, only one in four jobless families received any aid.

To those who could afford to buy one, each day's newspaper brought further tales of woe, such as the story of a Pennsylvania man who was arrested in 1930 for stealing a loaf of bread to feed his starving children. He hanged himself in jail while awaiting trial. Sometimes, desperation of this sort found an outlet in radical politics. Many previously apolitical men and women took part in "hunger marches" organized by the Socialist and Communist parties to demand more help from local and state governments, and they showed their interest in political change in other ways as well. During 1932, for instance, more than a hundred thousand Americans applied for jobs in the Soviet Union.

An unemployed man visiting a Volunteers of America soup kitchen in Washington, D.C., in June 1936. During the Great Depression, malnutrition was pervasive in every section of the country. In 1931, for example, an average of thirty-one breadlines operated each day in New York City alone.

ALTHOUGH HOOVER CAME TO THE PRESIDENCY with a much greater fondness for activism than either of his two predecessors, Harding and Coolidge, he was still invested in their laissez-faire, probusiness policies, having developed many of them himself as secretary of commerce from 1921 until 1928. Proceeding from the flawed premise that the U.S. economy was generally sound, Hoover refused to pursue structural change and instead focused his energies on promoting optimism. (At least at first, he considered the Great Depression far more psychological than economic.) Beginning shortly after the crash, he convened a series of White House conferences that brought together businessmen, labor leaders, and politicians to discuss the crisis. Such cooperation between the private sector and government, Hoover believed, could restore New Era prosperity in a relatively short period of time; sadly, this proved not to be the case.

Henry Ford arrives at a November 1929 conference called by President Hoover to discuss the nation's industrial situation.

The president had underestimated grotesquely the seriousness of the nation's economic problems. The December 1929 tax cut he supported was trifling compared to what the country really needed: more jobs and higher personal income. Yet it was a far sight better than Congress's next fix, the Smoot-Hawley Tariff, which actually did a great deal of harm. This attempt to protect American businesses by raising tariff rates to an average of 42 percent was a profoundly bad idea. A thousand U.S. economists signed a petition begging the president not to sign the bill, but Hoover rejected their nearly unanimous advice, and Smoot-Hawley became law on June 17, 1930. The problem was that, by this point, the depression had become a worldwide calamity, and the Europeans (America's best trading partners) were not much better off. The result was a trade war that hurt everyone, but none more so than the still-overproducing American farmer. The tariff fiasco merely shut off foreign markets for grain, causing the domestic price for wheat to tumble from $1.05 a bushel in 1929 to just 39¢ a bushel in 1932.

It wasn't until late 1931 that Hoover finally abandoned his wishful thinking and came to a belated understanding of the severity of the situation. He continued to oppose direct federal assistance to the poor, believing that cash payments would undermine traditional American individualism and make the population unacceptably dependent on the government. Instead, he decided to provide federal funds to state and local governments so that they could expand their own public works projects and provide at least some temporary employment while the private sector sorted itself out. Hoover also proposed a bill creating the Reconstruction Finance Corporation (RFC), which Congress approved in January 1932. Capitalized with $500 million and authorized to raise (through the sale of tax-exempt bonds) another $1.5 billion, the RFC was directed to provide massive new loans to the country's struggling financial institutions—including insurance companies, farm mortgage associations, agricultural credit bureaus, and building-and-loan societies, as well as commercial banks. It was Hoover's hope that, by strengthening private sources of capital, he could stimulate investment and growth. The RFC opened offices in fifty cities and in its first six months loaned more than $1.2 billion to five thousand borrowers. The flaw in Hoover's plan, however, was that RFC loans did little to increase the purchasing power of individuals, without whose participation there could be no recovery.

THE BONUS MARCH

PERHAPS THE MOST POLITICALLY damaging episode of Hoover's presidency was the Bonus March staged by World War I veterans during the spring and summer of 1932. Eight years earlier, Congress had passed the Soldiers' Bonus Act, granting these veterans Adjusted Compensation Certificates payable in 1945. In May 1932, however, the first elements of the Bonus Expeditionary Force, or Bonus Army, began arriving in the nation's capital to lobby Congress for early redemption of the certificates. As starving demonstrators told anyone who would listen, they might not live until 1945 the way things were going. Eventually, more than seventeen thousand desperate veterans converged on Washington to force passage of a new bonus bill.

Army chief of staff Douglas MacArthur defended his actions by calling the Bonus Army (shown here on July 13, 1928) "a mob animated by the essence of revolution."

Although the "invading" Bonus Army behaved remarkably peacefully, it nevertheless terrified Washington residents. According to Gore Vidal, who was six years old at the time, "The grownups were fearful that, at last, in those bad days, revolution had begun. Only fifteen years earlier the Russian Revolution had taken place. The same thing could happen here, everyone agreed." Yet the only violence that occurred was at the government's instigation. After the Senate rejected a $2.4 billion House-approved bonus bill on June 17, the government offered to pay the fare home for each "Boner" willing to leave Washington. Thousands accepted the offer, yet thousands more remained encamped on the Anacostia Flats, across the Potomac from central Washington, in a ramshackle Hooverville (as depression-era shantytowns were called).

Finally, on July 28, when the D.C. police moved to evict the veterans, a riot broke out, and two Boners were killed. Hoover sent in federal troops with orders to secure the shantytown and contain the veterans. But commanding general Douglas MacArthur (son of Arthur MacArthur) exceeded those orders, dispersing the Boners with tear gas and setting fire to their shacks. "The spectacle of the United States Army routing unarmed citizens with tanks and firebrands outraged many Americans," historian David M. Kennedy has written, and it "came to symbolize Hoover's supposed insensitivity to the plight of the unemployed."

The Election of 1932

YET ON THE ISSUE OF DIRECT RELIEF, Hoover held firm. In July 1932, congressional Democrats passed a bill sponsored by Speaker of the House John Nance Garner (recently named Roosevelt's running mate) and New York senator Robert F. Wagner that would have established federal jobs programs in states that had none of their own. Calling it "the most gigantic pork-barrel raid ever proposed to an American Congress," Hoover vetoed the bill and instead signed a law authorizing the RFC to loan state and local governments another $1.5 billion for public works programs. The same compromise law also provided $300 million to fund the direct relief programs of states facing bankruptcy.

To be fair, Hoover had traveled a remarkable distance during his presidency from New Era boosterism to depression-era crisis management. Many of his programs were truly innovative and remarkable for a man who had once believed so piously that business alone knew best. A number of Hoover's initiatives clearly anticipated more ambitious programs developed later under the New Deal. Yet Hoover was never able to shake his basic caution and scorn for intrusive governmental intervention. To most Americans, he always seemed too interested in saving businesses and not sufficiently concerned with helping individual people and families survive.

Almost any candidate could have beaten Hoover in 1932, but the Democrats chose New York governor Franklin Roosevelt. In an unprecedented gesture, Roosevelt flew to Chicago to accept the nomination personally. "I pledge you, I pledge myself, to a new deal for the American people," he told the convention delegates on July 2. The phrase, reminiscent of his fifth cousin's Square Deal, quickly caught on, underscoring FDR's professed willingness to help the country make a fresh start. Yet few details were offered to back up the pledge. The Democratic party platform was nearly identical to the Republican agenda: Both campaigns said they wanted less government spending, a balanced federal budget, and a strong currency. The only real difference involved Prohibition, which the Democrats wanted to end and the Republicans merely wanted to modify so that individual states could opt out. Because neither party platform offered anything in the way of new ideas, the campaign devolved into the usual game of rhetorical thrust and parry. No one thought Hoover had much of a chance, yet even his harshest critics remained unpersuaded that Roosevelt offered much of an improvement.

In the meantime, the election campaign presented many Americans with the opportunity to release some of their economic and political anger. The "farmers' holiday" movement, which encouraged farmers (sometimes through coercion) to withhold low-priced crops from market, began forcibly blocking foreclosure sales and threatening rebellion in the heartland. "Unless something is done for the American farmer," the president of the Farm Bureau Federation told a Senate committee, "we will have revolution in the countryside in less than twelve months." In the cities, labor protests also increased in both number and ferocity. In March 1932, the Communist-led Auto Workers' Union organized a

"Ford Hunger March" in which three thousand protesters descended on the Ford Motor Company's River Rouge plant in Dearborn, Michigan. They demanded jobs for laid-off workers and a halt to evictions of the unemployed. When local police and armed company guards tried to stop the march, fighting broke out, with the police and the Ford "detectives" firing into the crowd. Some policemen even used machine guns on the demonstrators. Somehow, only four marchers were killed, though more than sixty were injured. "When I saw the blood flowing on Miller Road," one of the protesters recalled, "that was the point I became a radical." Charles M. Schwab, the head of Bethlehem Steel, spoke for many in 1932 when he said, "I'm afraid, every man is afraid."

"Meeting Roosevelt was like uncorking your first bottle of champagne."

—

Winston Churchill, remark during a visit to Hyde Park, 1946

A campaign cap from 1932. Before Roosevelt flew to Chicago that year to accept his nomination in person, it had been considered immodest for a nominee to deliver an acceptance speech at the convention.

Election Day, as expected, brought a Democratic sweep. Roosevelt won twenty-three million votes (57.4 percent of the popular total) to sixteen million votes for Hoover (39.6 percent), with Socialist Norman Thomas not even reaching the million-vote mark and Communist William Z. Foster barely topping one hundred thousand. Meanwhile, Democratic candidates for the House won 310 of 432 seats, and the party also took back the Senate with Democrats controlling 60 of that chamber's 96 seats. The mandate for change could hardly have been more clear, and it prompted one of Roosevelt's friends to remark shortly after his inauguration that should FDR's programs succeed, he would probably be considered the greatest U.S. president ever. If they failed, however, he would likely be reviled as the worst. "If I fail," Roosevelt said, "I shall be the last."

Peter Arno created this cover for The New Yorker's *1933 inauguration-week issue well in advance of the actual event. On February 15, however, would-be assassin Giuseppe Zangara shot at the president-elect's motorcade in Miami. FDR was unhurt, but Chicago mayor Anton Cermak was fatally wounded. Afterward,* The New Yorker *editors decided to use a more subdued image.*

AFTER MARCH 9, when the Emergency Banking Act was passed, Congress and the nation waited expectantly for an announcement of the administration's next legislative initiative. The problem was that FDR and his advisers hadn't really worked any out. During the 1932 campaign, Roosevelt had gone along with his party's calls for spending cuts and a balanced budget. Now, he could see that these would hardly be adequate, so he began to improvise. Although the New Deal may appear today a comprehensive legislative program emanating from a single philosophical base, it actually developed experimentally, by trial and error, as a pastiche. First one policy was tried and then another until the administration found some variation that worked. Still, when the New Dealers were done, their zigzagging had indeed altered the nature of American government and profoundly reshaped the structure of American life.

Eight days after his first fireside chat, the president signed the Economy Act, which fulfilled a campaign promise to reduce federal salaries and otherwise cut the cost of government overhead. Two days after that, Congress amended the Volstead Act to legalize beer and wine while the various state legislatures considered repealing Prohibition entirely. The next big move, however, didn't come until March 31, when Congress passed the Reforestation Relief Act establishing the Civilian Conservation Corps (CCC). This highly popular program—which carried out reforestation, irrigation, and flood control projects—immediately created 250,000 jobs for young men between the ages of eighteen and twenty-five. The workers lived in army-style camps, and the government sent a portion of their paychecks home to help their struggling families.

In April, the president decided to take the country off the gold standard. No longer backed by U.S. gold reserves, the dollar fell sharply in international trading. This disadvantaged trade but also stimulated the domestic economy by making money cheaper and more plentiful. Meanwhile, Congress considered a number of bills sent up by the administration. On May 12, a rather momentous day, members approved the Federal Emergency Relief Act, while President Roosevelt signed the already-passed Agricultural Adjustment Act. The former created the Federal Emergency Relief Administration (FERA), which provided $500 million for direct aid to individuals. Later, more funds were approved.

The First Relief

THE 250,000 JOBS THAT THE CCC CREATED were a help, but Secretary of Labor Frances Perkins, the first female cabinet member, and Harry Hopkins, the social worker who had headed New York State emergency relief under Governor Roosevelt, knew that much more assistance would be needed. With the help of three powerful Democratic senators—Wagner, Robert M. La Follette of Wisconsin, and Edward Costigan of Colorado—they twisted the president's arm until he repressed his fantasy of a balanced budget and agreed to their program. During the last seven months of 1933, the FERA distributed (through state agencies) $1.5 billion in "relief," as government aid was then called, to seventeen million impoverished Americans so that they could feed and clothe themselves. Aghast at such colossal giveaways, conservatives accused the administration of rash decision making and made particular trouble for Hopkins. They insisted that, in the long run, the economy would right itself without such expensive government programs. "People don't eat in the long run," Hopkins responded tartly. "They eat every day."

The Agricultural Adjustment Act was an even more provocative departure from the Republican policies of the New Era. Its purpose was to control the farmers' wrongheaded tendency to combat falling prices with greater production. Under Roosevelt's plan, the new Agricultural Adjustment Administration (AAA) would pay farmers to stop growing underpriced crops and to hold back certain types of livestock from market. Because spring planting had already taken place by the time the law was enacted, the AAA actually paid farmers about $200 million during 1933 to plow under ten million acres of grain crops and kill six million pigs. This extensive destruction of food produced a great deal of controversy at a time when millions of Americans had less than they needed to eat, yet it did succeed in boosting farm income, which rose from $1.9 billion in 1932 to $4.6 billion in 1935. (In comparison, though, farm income at its peak during World War I had been $9.8 billion a year.)

Of course, nearly everywhere people were suffering, yet nowhere was the depression felt more severely than in the Tennessee River Valley. One reason was that this seven-state area had been remarkably poor to begin with. Nearly every year, swelled by fifty inches of average annual rainfall, the Tennessee River flooded, making agriculture in its forty-one-thousand-square-mile valley enormously difficult. Nor was there much industry in the area, so incomes were low—less than half the national average, in fact. On May 18, however, Congress created the Tennessee Valley Authority (TVA) to vitalize the region. It was easily the most creative and far-reaching experiment in regional planning ever undertaken in the United States. An independent public corporation, the TVA was authorized by Congress to construct dams along the course of the

A CCC employee photographed during the late 1930s. Americans given jobs by the federal government were said to be on "work relief." Those receiving direct cash payments were on "straight relief."

Tennessee River and its major tributaries that would control floods and power new hydroelectric plants. Generating cheap electricity, it was believed, would promote industrial development, job growth, and a higher standard of living in the region; it did. TVA programs built schools, improved health facilities, increased recreational opportunities, expanded reforestation, and provided other social benefits as well.

At Stiner's Store in Lead Mind Bend, Tennessee, a TVA agent interviews applicants in November 1933 for work on the Norris Dam. The men in the background are seeing who can pull up the most weight on the scale.

Construction of the Wilson Dam, the first on the Tennessee River, began in 1918. The TVA added thirteen generators to make it the most productive hydroelectric dam in the region.

O N JUNE 16, the last of the Hundred Days, Congress passed the cornerstone of the early New Deal: the National Industrial Recovery Act. This law represented Roosevelt's best effort to bring together government, management, and labor in the service of economic recovery. It established a federal agency, the National Recovery Administration (NRA), which had the power to suspend antitrust laws in order to facilitate improved economic planning. Taking such a step meant ending price competition, but the administration was prepared at this low point in economic activity to sacrifice competition for market stability, higher profits, and more take-home pay. Under the NRA's "codes of fair competition," one of which was drawn up for each major U.S. industry, price fixing became legal; in exchange, employers agreed to increase wages, end child labor, and recognize the collective bargaining rights of workers. Eventually, the NRA created 750 different codes, covering twenty million workers. Most were developed with input from labor and management—but when an industry refused to cooperate, the NRA simply imposed a code of its own devising.

The NRA launched the code program with a great deal of fanfare. Any company that embraced the codes was awarded a flag emblazoned with a blue eagle, the NRA symbol, that it could fly above its premises to show its patriotism. However, there was also opposition. Many of the nation's largest corporations (notably the Ford Motor Company) refused to participate, and soon small producers began complaining that big companies were using price fixing to squeeze them out of business. Consumer prices rose sharply because of the NRA codes, and a 1934 commission headed by Clarence Darrow concluded that the NRA was promoting dangerous monopoly control. A year later, the Supreme Court joined the controversy as well.

Meanwhile, the National Industrial Recovery Act also created the Public Works Administration (PWA) under Interior Secretary Harold Ickes. Like most New Deal "work relief" programs, this one provided construction jobs within the public sector. Its many high-profile projects included the Triborough Bridge and the Queens-Midtown Tunnel in New York City and the Bonneville and Grand Coulee Dams on the Columbia River in Washington. In all, the PWA spent more than five billion dollars constructing sewage and waterworks, public housing, power stations, and airports in addition to its many bridges, tunnels, and dams.

One of the placards used by businesses to advertise their compliance with the NRA code for their industry.

Opposition to the New Deal

LONG BEFORE THE EFFECTIVENESS of the president's Hundred Days programs could be gauged, it had become clear that Roosevelt had captured the American imagination. FDR's smiling, confident face appeared on the walls of homes across the country, and journalists estimated the president's approval rating at about 90 percent. "Mr. Roosevelt is the only man we ever had in the White House who would understand that my boss is a son of a bitch," one of his many admirers explained. Yet the president did have enemies, and when the spring of 1934 arrived with only a slight easing of the crisis—a reduction in unemployed to 11.3 million (22.0 percent of the workforce), a small uptick in consumer spending—critics attacked the administration from both the left and the right.

Although both the Socialist and Communist candidates had fared poorly in the 1932 presidential election, by 1934 the left was experiencing a definite revival. During the latter Hoover years, labor unions (many of them led by Communists) had been reluctant to strike because, with so many Americans unemployed, the risk of losing one's job was too great. Beginning in 1934, however, daring unions staged job actions all over the country, including a general strike in San Francisco. Even so, the most serious threat to Roosevelt from the left came not from any Marxist but from a Louisiana senator, Huey P. Long, who insisted that the New Deal hadn't gone nearly far enough.

Members of the Civilian Conservation Corps stationed at Camp Fechner cheer President Roosevelt, seated at the head of their mess table. This photograph was taken on August 12, 1933, a day that FDR toured five CCC camps in Virginia.

Conservatives, of course, argued that Roosevelt had gone much too far, and in August 1934 they organized the American Liberty League to rally the right. Initially financed by the Du Pont family, the league soon gained enthusiastic support from senior management at General Motors, General Foods, and Montgomery Ward. Its membership was largely Republican yet included two noteworthy Democrats: 1924 presidential candidate John W. Davis and 1928 nominee Alfred E. Smith. Believing that he had been robbed by Roosevelt of the 1932 nomination, an embittered Smith actively promoted the Liberty League even though doing so often forced him to disavow both his personal background and his political principles. "There can be only one capital," Smith warned the nation, "Washington or Moscow."

With this sort of strident criticism increasing on all sides, the New Dealers waited with some trepidation for the 1934 midterm elections. Privately, they expected to lose about forty seats in the House. When the results came in, however, the administration was both stunned and delighted: The Democrats had actually *gained* nine seats in the House and another nine in the Senate, giving them veto-proof majorities in both chambers. Because no seat had yet opened on the Supreme Court, however, the justices were still overwhelmingly Republican.

OF THE COURT'S NINE JUSTICES, seven had been appointed by Republican presidents. William Howard Taft had elevated the most senior justice, ultraconservative Willis Van Devanter, in 1911. Warren Harding had two of his nominees still on the bench—George Sutherland and Pierce Butler, both of whom believed that most legislation designed to regulate the economy was unconstitutional. Coolidge's sole appointment, Harlan Fiske Stone, tended toward the liberal end of the spectrum, while Hoover's three choices—Benjamin Cardozo, Owen J. Roberts, and Chief Justice Charles Evans Hughes—were all less predictable. Of the two Democrats appointed by Woodrow Wilson, Louis D. Brandeis was the most consistently liberal justice on the Court, while James C. McReynolds turned out to be one of its most dogged conservatives. Handicappers in the press typically grouped the justices this way: four (Van Devanter, Sutherland, Butler, and McReynolds) solidly against the New Deal, three (Stone, Cardozo, and Brandeis) tending to sustain it, and two (Roberts and Hughes) liable to go either way.

It took nearly two years for the first major New Deal litigation to reach the Court. The case in question, *Schechter Poultry v. U.S.*, involved a small Brooklyn firm charged with violating the NRA's poultry code. In its May 27, 1935, decision, the Court not only found for Schechter but also struck down most of the National Industrial Recovery Act. Writing for the unanimous majority, Chief Justice Hughes held that the law was unconstitutional for two reasons: It sought to regulate intrastate commerce, and it unacceptably transferred legislative power from Congress to the executive branch by granting the president "virtually unfettered" authority to impose NRA codes on reluctant industries. "Extraordinary conditions do not create or enlarge constitutional power," Hughes wrote.

In a way, the Court did Roosevelt a favor. However successful the NRA might have been in avoiding destruction competition during 1933 and 1934, it had, by 1935, outlived its usefulness. The complaints the system was generating had already softened the administration's popularity and would likely have led to a repeal of the NRA codes in the not-too-distant future; the *Schechter Poultry* decision, therefore, saved the president from having to admit a failure. But Roosevelt didn't see it that way. He denounced the Court for adhering to a "horse and buggy" definition of interstate commerce. Nevertheless, the administration would henceforth propose new legislation with the knowledge that the justices would sooner or later have their say.

> "Franklin Roosevelt has done his part, now you do something. Buy something— buy anything, anywhere. Paint your kitchen, send a telegram, give a party, get a car, pay a bill, rent a flat, fix your roof, get a haircut, see a show, build a house, get married."
>
> —
>
> *Sign posted in a factory, 1933*

HUEY P. LONG
1893–1935

BECAUSE OF AN ASSASSIN'S bullet, Americans will never know just how serious a threat Huey P. Long posed to their political institutions. The most potent demagogue of the Great Depression, Long attracted support well beyond his native Louisiana with a program of wealth redistribution that extended little beyond its admittedly seductive slogan, "Every Man Is a King." Attacking the New Deal as excessively timid, he called his own program Share Our Wealth, and by 1935 Long had attracted enough interest that the president's political advisers were predicting he might poll several million votes as a third-party presidential candidate. Roosevelt retaliated by cutting off federal patronage to Long's machine in Louisiana, and he sent a small army of Treasury agents into the state to examine the former governor's income tax returns. ("Long and his gang are stealing everything in the state," one agent reported.)

On September 10, 1935, however, Long's political career— and life—came to an end, two days after he was shot in a corridor of the Louisiana State Capitol at Baton Rouge. "I wonder why he shot me?" Long asked before falling into a coma. The question was never really answered because Long's bodyguards had immediately shot and killed the gunman, a doctor named Carl Weiss whose father-in-law the Kingfish had ruined. It's highly unlikely that Long could have ousted Roosevelt in 1936 (or even contributed to a Republican victory), but there's no telling how much other trouble he might have caused had he lived.

The Second New Deal

THE BILLS PASSED by the Seventy-fourth Congress (1935–1937) differed greatly from the legislation of the Hundred Days in that they were both less hodgepodge and more consistently liberal. Recoiling from his Supreme Court defeats and the American Liberty League's attacks, Roosevelt began listening more and more attentively to his most liberal advisers—including Perkins; Hopkins; and especially his wife, Eleanor, who played a critical role in persuading his husband during this period to fund more relief. Downplaying his earlier goals of stabilization and cooperation, the president now began devoting many more resources to improving the lives of the poor and the powerless, whether or not big business was keen to go along.

PACKING THE COURT

THE SUPREME COURT DIDN'T STOP with *Schechter*. In January 1936, in *U.S. v. Butler*, it struck down the Agricultural Adjustment Act on the grounds that the AAA usurped state and local authority. As a result, all through the 1936 campaign, Roosevelt nursed a grudge against the Court. Afterward, he decided to use his record mandate to get even. On February 5, 1937, he announced to his flabbergasted cabinet that he would ask Congress to reorganize the federal judiciary. Under the guise of improving its efficiency, FDR wanted to add justices to each level of the federal system (including the Supreme Court) for each judge or justice over seventy years old. Because six of the current justices were older than seventy, that meant Roosevelt would be able to make six new

The Supreme Court in 1937 (clockwise from bottom left): Brandeis, Roberts, Butler, Stone, Cardozo, Sutherland, McReynolds, Hughes, and Van Devanter.

appointments immediately, expanding the Court to fifteen members and presumably creating a majority in support of the Wagner Act, Social Security, and other New Deal legislation that would soon be coming up for judicial review.

Roosevelt's barely disguised power grab stunned the nation—including many of the most dedicated New Dealers in Congress, who lined up with Republicans in opposition to the bill. "Boys," the chairman of the House Judiciary Committee told his colleagues, "here's where I cash in my chips." Even worse for Roosevelt, many voters began to wonder whether the Liberty League had been right: Perhaps the president did dream of becoming a dictator akin to Benito Mussolini in Italy or Adolf Hitler in Germany. The rise of fascism in Europe was causing Americans to cling ever more tightly to their free institutions, and few of those ranked as high as the Supreme Court.

Roosevelt pushed hard for his plan, but the justices fought back. Eighty-year-old Louis Brandeis, the oldest and most liberal member of the Court, lobbied personally against the bill. The infighting continued for three months before it ended with a vote to recommit. Roosevelt thus failed in his attempt to "pack" the Court, yet his efforts did apparently produce some movement on the part of the centrist judges. In April 1937, in deciding *Associated Press v. National Labor Relations Board*, the Court upheld the Wagner Act; a month later, it ruled that the Social Security Act was constitutional as well.

In April 1935, with unemployment still unacceptably high at 10.6 million people (20.3 percent of the workforce), Roosevelt finally gave up all pretense of balancing the budget and made use of the political capital he had gained in the 1934 elections to win approval of the Emergency Relief Appropriations Act. At $4.8 billion, it was the largest peacetime appropriation yet in U.S. history. Funds from this act were used to set up various work relief programs, the most important of which was the Works Progress Administration (WPA). Run by Hopkins, the WPA created jobs for 3.5 million Americans, or about a third of those out of work. Because most of its projects involved constructing public facilities—from hospitals and schools to ball fields and municipal swimming pools— it soon became the most visible and popular New Deal agency.

The summer following *Schechter* also saw passage of the two bills that would become the New Deal's most significant legislative legacy: the National Labor Relations Act, passed in July, and the Social Security Act, which Roosevelt signed in August. Had the president still believed that the NRA's cooperative model could work, he might not have pushed ahead with these controversial measures. But he was angry— because of the *Schechter* decision and also because of all the business attacks on his administration. He didn't see how cooperation could be revived, so he declared the National Labor Relations and Social Security Acts "must" legislative items and demanded their immediate passage.

O F ALL THE NEW DEAL LEGISLATION, the measure that most affected the American power structure was the National Labor Relations Act—more commonly known as the Wagner Act after its chief sponsor, Robert Wagner. Coming at a time when organized labor had almost given up on Roosevelt, the Wagner Act required employers to recognize labor unions favored by a majority of their employees. To enforce this new right to collective bargaining, the act created the National Labor Relations Board (NLRB), to which it gave two primary responsibilities: the supervision of union elections and the policing of unfair employment practices. The NLRB had both investigative powers and the authority to hold proceedings whose decisions were enforceable by federal courts. Although it could theoretically curb union activities as well, the NLRB generally acted—at least during the 1930s—to aid workers in their efforts to organize and empower unions in their negotiations with management.

During the next six years, union membership in the United States more than doubled, from 3.8 million in 1935 to 8.7 million in 1941. This period of astounding growth, however, was marked by divisions within the labor movement that ran deeper than usual. During labor's lean years at the turn of the twentieth century, the AFL under Samuel Gompers had limited its efforts to the organization of skilled workers into craft unions. Even in 1934, 70 percent of those voting at the

Harry Hopkins eventually became the second most powerful figure in the Roosevelt administration (after the president himself). Thin and pale, apparently existing on little more than cigarettes and black coffee, he seemed perpetually on the point of death from consumption, yet his appetite for social work never diminished.

ELEANOR ROOSEVELT
1884–1962

THE COAL MINERS WERE evidently far below the surface of the earth. Only the lamps in their helmets illuminated the darkness and revealed the surprise on their faces. "For Gosh Sakes!" one of them exclaimed. "It's Mrs. Roosevelt!"

Eleanor Roosevelt may never have actually descended a mine shaft, but one of the most famous cartoons of the 1930s made its point nonetheless. During the most fearful years of the Great Depression, Mrs. Roosevelt went to places that no first lady had ever been and did things that none had ever considered doing. She went to Appalachia, to the rural Deep South, and to Puerto Rico to see the worst U.S. poverty for herself. She explored the slums and back alleys of the District of Columbia, places in which few politicians ever set foot despite lifetimes spent in the capital. She met people who had never imagined they would ever speak to a first lady and, through her membership in the Women's Trade Union League, kept in touch with workingwomen and their concerns. She gave civil rights leaders access to the White House and lobbied her husband on their behalf. Walter White, head of the National Association for the Advancement of Colored People (NAACP), remarked once that only the thought of Mrs. Roosevelt kept him from hating all white people.

Although her husband's extramarital affairs made their personal life difficult, Eleanor found consolation in acting to keep the president aware of the plights of numerous oppressed groups. From her large correspondence, she selected particularly evocative letters and placed them on his desk with the scribbled injunction, "F—read."

Among first ladies, *Eleanor Roosevelt (shown here on a plane in 1936) was the first to create a public role for herself beyond being simply the president's wife. She wrote a daily newspaper column, spoke frequently on the radio, and held her own press conferences, to which only female reporters were invited. With the exception of her husband, she was probably the best-known person in the country.*

AFL national convention refused to support a proposal for organizing unskilled workers. In 1935, therefore, John L. Lewis of the United Mine Workers, Sidney Hillman of the Amalgamated Clothing Workers, and David Dubinsky of the ILGWU formed within the AFL the Committee for Industrial Organization. After this group was expelled from the AFL in 1936, its members founded the Congress of Industrial Organizations (CIO) in 1938.

As the CIO's first president, Lewis moved aggressively to build membership in the sort of industrial unions that Eugene V. Debs had promoted four decades earlier. He was opposed, however, by some of the most antiunion corporations in the country, primarily in the steel and automobile industries. In fighting these entrenched interests, Lewis employed as his weapon of choice the "sit-down strike," the most famous of which began on December 30, 1936, in Flint, Michigan.

The Flint Sit-Down Strike

THE HOME OF GENERAL MOTORS (then the world's largest corporation), Flint was essentially a company town: Four out of five workers in Flint toiled in one of the numerous GM plants there, and most of the municipal officials, from the mayor and police chief on down to the members of the school board, had been on the GM payroll at one time or another. On December 30, managers at the Fisher Body No. 2 plant attempted to discipline some union members, but the move backfired when fifty workers occupied the building. The next day, nearly a thousand more workers gathered at the United Auto Workers (UAW) hall before marching on the Fisher Body No. 1 plant and shutting it down as well. When their job action spread to the Chevrolet and Buick plants in town and to GM factories elsewhere around the country, the Flint sit-down strike developed into the pivotal labor battle of the decade.

The primary worker complaints related to frequent layoffs (GM tended to run its factories on a seasonal schedule rather than spreading out the work over the entire year); management's arbitrary hiring and firing practices (foremen played favorites and discriminated against union "troublemakers"); and, most of all, the

"speed-up" (the debilitating acceleration of the assembly line used to increase production during busy periods). At first, GM officials responded to the plant occupations with unsuccessful attempts to obtain court orders evicting the strikers; then GM turned off the heat inside the occupied buildings (during sixteen-degree weather). When the workers still wouldn't budge, the Flint police stormed the plants. Three times on January 11, sheriff's deputies charged, and three times they were repulsed by strikers armed with wrenches and other makeshift weapons.

Sit-down strikers occupying the Fisher Body No. 3 plant in early January 1937. Other General Motors divisions with factories in Flint included Chevrolet, Buick, and AC Spark Plugs.

The stalemate lasted until February 3, when GM finally agreed to negotiate. A week later, it recognized the UAW (a CIO affiliate), granted amnesty to the striking workers, and promised to consider the strikers' specific demands at a national labor–management conference to be held sometime in the near future. This resolution was an enormous victory for both the UAW and the CIO (whose membership by 1939 exceeded two million). Although President Roosevelt refused Lewis's call for federal intervention during the strike (because he disapproved of the sit-downers' tactics), it was FDR's support for the Wagner Act, the most significant prolabor law ever signed by an American president, that made the CIO's gains possible. Exceeding even Roosevelt's expectations (and perhaps his wishes as well), the Wagner Act transformed "big labor" into a political juggernaut whose support in money and manpower produced in 1936 even more impressive Democratic victories at all levels. That

SOCIAL SECURITY

IN SEPTEMBER 1933, a sixty-six-year-old Long Beach, California, physician named Francis Everett Townsend wrote a letter to his local newspaper calling for the government to provide pensions to the nation's elderly. At the time, thousands of ordinary Americans were proclaiming their own plans to cure the depression, yet Townsend's was a good deal more rational than most. Specifically, he wanted the government to pay two hundred dollars a month to each American over the age of sixty with two conditions attached: The recipients had to be retired, and they had to spend the money within the same month it was paid (it couldn't be hoarded).

The idea had strong grassroots appeal. By 1935, there were nearly five thousand Townsend Clubs nationwide with more than two million members, and twenty-five million Americans had signed a petition demanding enactment of Townsend's plan.

At the start of the Seventy-fourth Congress in January 1935, several California congressmen (elected with strong Townsendite support) introduced a bill promoting Townsend's goals.

A monthly check to you—

FOR THE REST OF YOUR LIFE .. BEGINNING WHEN YOU ARE 65

GET YOUR SOCIAL SECURITY ACCOUNT NUMBER promptly

APPLICATIONS ARE BEING DISTRIBUTED AT ALL WORK PLACES

WHO IS ELIGIBLE...

HOW TO RETURN APPLICATION

Social Security Board

INFORMATION MAY BE OBTAINED AT ANY POST OFFICE

But that's where the movement ended because the bill conflicted with another pension scheme about to be introduced by the Roosevelt administration. The Social Security Act, which became law in August 1935, required both workers and employers to contribute small portions of their earnings to a common fund that would finance old-age and other pensions beginning in 1942. In addition to retirees, disabled workers and the families of deceased workers would also receive benefits. The monthly amounts were much less than the two hundred dollars suggested by Townsend, and many of those who needed pensions most, such as farm workers and domestics, were excluded; yet the program did involve the federal government for the first time in the long-term financial well-being of its citizens.

Most European countries had already set up public pension programs funded entirely by the state. Yet Roosevelt insisted that American workers contribute to Social Security to guarantee the longevity of the program. "With those taxes in there," he explained, "no damn politician can ever scrap my Social Security program."

year, the largest single contributor to the Democratic party was Lewis's United Mine Workers union, which provided $469,000 in addition to thousands of campaign workers. Although a September 1935 U.S. Chamber of Commerce poll revealed that the chamber's member organizations opposed the New Deal by a margin of thirty-five to one, labor's new political strength more than made up for management antagonism.

EAGER TO SAVE THE COUNTRY from bureaucracy and Bolshevism, the Republicans nominated in 1936 mild-mannered Kansas governor Alfred M. "Alf" Landon. Although Landon had been the only Republican governor to win reelection in 1934, he was overall a rather weak choice to represent the fervent anti–New Dealers. For one thing, he actually favored portions of the New Deal. He was also a dull speaker, and Democrats derided his single great accomplishment, the balancing of his state's budget, by mirthfully pointing out that the budget of Kansas was not much larger than the budget of the New York City Department of Sanitation.

While Landon promised a cheaper, more efficient federal government, the Liberty Leaguers waged a whispering campaign against Roosevelt, whose policies they considered both socialistic and un-American. FDR's polio had destroyed his brain, they said, and late at night Secret Service agents could hear maniacal laughter coming from the Oval Office. The anti-Semites among them often referred to the president as Franklin Rosenfeld, and others called him "a traitor to his class."

Backed by some hopeful economic signs, the president welcomed the opportunity that the 1936 campaign provided for him to confront his most determined political enemies. In general, he ignored Landon and focused instead on the plutocrats of the American Liberty League. In his annual message to Congress, delivered in January 1936, Roosevelt boasted of having "earned the hatred of entrenched greed." On another occasion, he compared his business critics to the elderly gentleman who, having been rescued from drowning, turns angrily on his rescuers for failing to save his top hat. The president's campaign staff established an extraparty organization so that sympathetic Republicans could support the New Deal without ostensibly supporting the Democrats, and, of course, labor unions worked hard to get out the vote.

The Roosevelt Coalition

ROOSEVELT'S CHIEF POLITICAL operative, Democratic National Committee chairman (and postmaster general) James A. Farley, predicted that his boss would win every state except Maine and Vermont. Not even the candidate believed him, yet Farley was right. In addition to carrying forty-six of the forty-eight states, FDR took 60.8 percent of the popular vote, eclipsing Harding's record performance of 60.3 percent in 1920. The president also swept more Democrats into office with him, reducing the Republican caucus in the Senate to just sixteen votes and the House caucus to just eighty-nine.

However, Franklin Roosevelt accomplished much more in 1936 than simply winning the election. As became clear later, his victory completed the recent restructuring of American politics. Al Smith's 1928 campaign had shown those who knew where to look that a major shift in voting patterns was under way. For instance, working-class women began voting in significant numbers in 1928, and most of them favored Smith. Catholics as well began lining up behind Democratic candidates in that election, and so did other urban immigrants. To these constituencies and the Solid South (the name given to the Democrats' post-Reconstruction stranglehold on that region), Roosevelt added even more immigrants (especially Jews), union members, and African Americans.

In 1932, most black voters had remained loyal to the party of Lincoln, but the difficulties of the depression, which struck African Americans hardest of all, eventually turned this group around politically. President Roosevelt hadn't signed a single piece of civil rights legislation, nor had he made any significant black appointments (although he did provide new opportunities for previously excluded Catholics and Jews); what made the difference for blacks was New Deal relief.

Catholics and Jews *had voted Democratic before, but Roosevelt (shown here in July 1937) gave them, for the first time, substantial representation in the upper echelons of government.*

These funds—especially monies distributed in the South, where state governments were notoriously penurious as well as discriminatory—helped millions of African Americans rise out of the poverty that had oppressed them even before the Great Depression began. When Harry Hopkins set up a jobs program under the FERA, for instance, he established a national minimum wage of thirty cents an hour, the least that administrators in Washington believed a worker could live on. Only later did FERA officials discover that southern blacks had been routinely earning as little as five cents an hour for years. Jobs with the FERA and the WPA, therefore, provided genuine economic advancement for blacks, who responded gratefully with their votes.

At first, few of the groups in the new Roosevelt coalition felt particularly strong ties to the Democratic party; their political loyalties were to the president personally (and, in some cases, to his wife). Yet, at FDR's urging, they voted for Democratic congressmen, Democratic governors, and Democratic state legislators. After a while, all this voting for Democrats became habit forming. Since 1896, thanks to William McKinley and Mark Hanna, the Republicans had been the nation's majority party; now and for the next half century, the Democrats would be.

ALTHOUGH ROOSEVELT had come close during his first four years in office to accepting the theories of John Maynard Keynes, he began his second term still unpersuaded that government needed to have a permanent role in the economy. In Keynes's latest work *The General Theory of Employment, Interest, and Money* (1936), the British economist had argued that national governments could lessen troughs in the business cycle by providing public jobs to spur consumption and also by increasing the money supply to stimulate investment. Yet Roosevelt remained reluctant to adopt Keynesian remedies because they entailed substantial deficit spending. It was generally believed that a government, just as a private household, should spend no more than what it had. FDR tolerated deficits during his first term because the nation was in crisis; in March 1937, however, with many economic indicators approaching predepression levels, he decided to pull back. There were still 7.7 million Americans unemployed, yet the president began sharply reducing relief expenditures and bringing government "pump priming" virtually to an end.

With startling suddenness, the bottom dropped out of the recovery. The Dow Jones Industrial Average fell from 191.63 on the day of FDR's second inauguration to just 120.85 by year's end; during this same period, another three million people (almost 5 percent of the workforce) lost their jobs. The press began calling the downturn "the Roosevelt recession." In November 1937, the president recalled the Seventy-fifth Congress, but little came of the brief special

The black community's particularly strong attachment to Roosevelt is displayed in this image of mourners lining the route of the late president's funeral procession through the streets of Washington, D.C., on April 14, 1945.

session because of Roosevelt's reluctance to resume the heavy spending of 1933–1936. "Everything will work out all right if we just sit tight and keep quiet," he explained, using language that sounded remarkably like Hoover's.

Meanwhile, the New Dealers fought an internal battle for influence with the president. Treasury Secretary Henry Morgenthau Jr. led the faction that argued against continued government support of the economy—which, Morgenthau believed, simply had to right itself eventually. On the other side, Perkins and Hopkins pushed for more Keynesian deficit spending. The debate raged for months. In April 1938, however, with the Roosevelt recession worsening and the midterm elections approaching, the president gave in to the liberals. He asked Congress for another Emergency Relief Appropriations Act and used the four billion dollars it provided in June to revitalize both the WPA and the PWA. Slowly, the economy began to turn around again.

The End of the New Deal

NEVERTHELESS, in the November 1938 midterm elections, President Roosevelt felt the depth of middle-class alarm over the recession, the sit-down strikes, and his court-packing bill. Although the Democrats still held sixable majorities on Capitol Hill, the Republicans picked up seventy-five seats in the House and seven in the Senate. This forced the administration to pay much more attention to the wishes of conservative southern Democrats, who threatened defection at times if changes in certain bills weren't made.

Meanwhile, the rise of fascism in Europe, the Spanish Civil War, and Japanese aggression in the Far East all compelled Roosevelt to spend a great deal more time and energy on foreign policy than he had previously. Early on, the president recognized the trend of events and sought to prepare the United States for war. Yet southern congressmen refused to support his preparedness program unless FDR agreed to soft-pedal domestic reforms. It wasn't a difficult choice. Having moved already about as far to the left as he ever wanted to go, Roosevelt subordinated his domestic agenda to pressing national security concerns and never looked back.

A Civilian Conservation Corps poster from 1941, the year in which the outfit that Roosevelt called his "tree army" was finally disbanded. By that time, it had employed nearly three million young men, most of them for periods of six months to a year.

Jim Braddock & Joe Louis
1905–1974   1914–1981

by Geoffrey C. Ward

IN THE SPRING OF 1937, twenty-three-year-old Joe Louis seemed entitled to a shot at the world heavyweight boxing championship—at least on paper. He had beaten thirty-four of thirty-five opponents, knocking out thirty (including three former champions). Louis had excellent trainers, a stable of top sparring partners, and a canny manager with good connections. Only one potential obstacle remained: He was black, and American sports were still overwhelmingly segregated. No black ballplayer played in the big leagues; no black jockey rode at the major racetracks; and no black heavyweight had been allowed to fight for the title since 1915, the year after Louis's birth, when the flamboyant Jack Johnson had lost the crown to the Great White Hope, Jess Willard. Every heavyweight champion since then had been careful to draw the "color line" against African-American challengers, and there seemed no reason why Jim Braddock, the current title-holder, would make an exception for Louis.

Few men had worked harder to win the title than Braddock, and none had more reason to want to keep it. Born in Manhattan's Hell's Kitchen in 1906 and raised on the tough streets of North Bergen, New Jersey, he had been expelled from parochial school at age thirteen for fighting and had worked as an errand boy and a printer's devil before turning to the ring. By 1929, he seemed well on his way to a title when everything began to go wrong. He lost a fight for the light-heavyweight championship, saw the taxi company in which he'd carefully invested his earnings go under, and dropped twenty-three of his next thirty-three bouts. After breaking his hand, Braddock was forced to look for work on the docks, and finally, like millions of others during the Great Depression,

he had to swallow his pride and go on relief to support his wife and three children. By this time, most promoters considered Braddock just another "opponent," a battered veteran they could hire to make up-and-coming young boxers look good—when somehow he turned things around, beating three top heavyweights to win a shot at the champion, Max Baer. Braddock was a ten-to-one underdog when he entered the ring on June 13, 1935, but Baer had underestimated him and failed to train properly. Braddock outpointed Baer to win the title. It was the greatest upset yet in a heavyweight championship fight and earned Braddock the nickname Cinderella Man, a gift from newspaper columnist Damon Runyon.

As fair-minded as he was tenacious, Braddock seems never to have even considered denying Louis a shot at the title. If the deal could be made, he told his manager, make it.

The two men met in Chicago's Comiskey Park on June 22, 1937. "Sentiment," reported one Detroit sportswriter, "is all on the side of the Irishman, because he is a Cinderella man with a wife and a brood of kids and short of dough as a family man always is." But sentiment didn't matter much. Braddock knocked down the challenger in the first round, after which the fight was all Louis. Braddock lasted into the eighth before Louis knocked him out. Afterward, the Cinderella Man required twenty-three stitches.

Joe Louis would remain champion for twelve years, still the longest reign in heavyweight history—during which he became a hero to African Americans and millions of white Americans as well. Jim Braddock made no excuses; Louis had just been too much for him, he told the press. He signed for one more fight, won it, then retired for

good. He was proud that his brief period in the spotlight had earned him enough money to start a little restaurant and to pay back the state of New Jersey every penny of the relief he'd been forced to accept when times were bad.

Jim Braddock (left) shakes hands with Joe Louis in February 1937 after the two heavyweights signed to fight their title bout in Chicago.

20

WORLD WAR II

The Attack on Pearl Harbor

A T 7:02 A.M. ON DECEMBER 7, 1941, Pvt. George Elliot noted the appearance of a huge "echo" on his oscilloscope, indicating the presence of a radar contact some 137 miles to the north of his position. At the time, Elliot was being trained by another private, Joseph Lockard, in the use of the new radar equipment then being tested on Hawaii. Their station was one of six mobile SCR-270B detectors operating on the island of Oahu, where the Pearl Harbor naval base was located. The equipment required four trucks to transport and had recently been set up at Opana, a knoll near Kahuku Point at the northern tip of the island. Although the idea of using radio signals to detect and track distant objects was nearly as old as radio itself, the technology needed to accomplish this feat was still being developed. In fact, the U.S. Navy didn't begin using the acronym RADAR (which stands for "radio detection and ranging") until 1942.

Concerned because their plottings showed that the target was moving rapidly toward their position on Oahu, Elliot and Lockard reported what they had found to the information center at Fort Shafter, near the main Pearl Harbor naval facilities on the southern shore of Oahu. A shift change was under way, however, so the soldier at the switchboard turned Lockard's call over to the only officer he could find, a fighter pilot named Kermit Tyler. (Ironically, Elliot and Lockard were themselves still on duty only because the truck scheduled to pick

AT LEFT: *The Office of War Information published this poster by Bernard Perlin in early 1942. Throughout World War II, the slogan that most readily aroused Americans was, "Remember Pearl Harbor!"*

them up at 7 A.M. was late.) The information center assignment was new to Lieutenant Tyler; December 7 was only his second day on the job there. He listened to Lockard's report, quickly reaching the conclusion that the radar contact was a flight of thirteen B-17 bombers expected to arrive from California later that morning. Tyler told Lockard and Elliot to forget about the signal, and the privates were too inexperienced to point out that the echo was much too large to be merely a single squadron of planes, even airplanes as massive as the B-17 Flying Fortresses.

Lockard and Elliot continued tracking the incoming planes until 7:39 A.M., when background interference obscured the signal. (Because of the effects of mountainous terrain to the south of Opana, the equipment there couldn't track anything within twenty miles of Oahu.) About the same time, the transport truck finally arrived to take the two men to breakfast. They secured their equipment and headed back down to their quarters at Kawailoa. "About halfway to camp," Lockard recalled, "we passed our other truck with the rest of our operating crew speeding back toward Opana. They excitedly waved and shouted at us as they passed, but we couldn't understand what they were saying. As we proceeded toward Kawailoa, we saw huge black billows of smoke rising high into the sky in the direction of Pearl Harbor. We knew something had happened but we didn't know what it was. When we arrived at camp, we were told that the Japanese had attacked. We knew immediately that what we had tracked were the Japanese attack planes."

AT WHEELER FIELD IN CENTRAL OAHU, most of the U.S. Army Air Force pilots were still asleep, but Lts. George Welch and Ken Taylor had risen early on this Sunday morning and were breakfasting at the officers' club when they saw Japanese dive-bombers plunging down from the sky. Rushing to a car, they drove at a hundred miles an hour to an auxiliary airstrip, unknown to the Japanese, where they took off in waiting fighters. Heading for the first wave of attack planes, they shot down three Japanese aircraft before landing to refuel. During the dogfighting, Taylor was wounded twice.

The commanding officer of the Kaneohe Naval Air Station on Oahu's eastern shore was drinking his morning coffee when he heard the sound of aircraft engines. Looking up, he saw—much to his consternation—several formations of planes, all flying lower than regulations allowed. He watched them turn to the right into Kaneohe Bay, where most of his thirty-three new flying boats were moored. He leaped to his feet, shouting, "Those fools know there is a strict rule against making a right turn!" His young son added, "Look, red circles on the wings!" Realizing that his son was right and the planes were Japanese, the commander rushed to his headquarters to direct the base's antiaircraft fire.

Adm. Husband E. Kimmel, commander in chief of the U.S. Pacific Fleet, and Maj. Gen. Walter C. Short, the army commander in charge of all the land-based aircraft in Hawaii, were neither friendly nor close. In fact, they rarely interacted, although this particular morning they were scheduled to play golf together. At about 7:30, Kimmel received a phone call from an officer on his staff who told him that the destroyer *Ward* had just attacked a Japanese two-man submarine trying to sneak into Pearl Harbor. Kimmel didn't think the incident worthy of a general alert, but he did decide to head in to his office. Before he left, however, the phone rang again, and Kimmel took the call. He was listening to some additional details about the midget submarine when the officer making the report paused and then shouted into the telephone that the Japanese were attacking Pearl Harbor. Kimmel immediately ran outside, and what he saw froze him. From his house overlooking the harbor, he could see the sky alive with attack planes, and he understood immediately that his ships were doomed.

The Neutrality Acts

UNTIL JAPAN'S AUDACIOUS surprise attack, America had been sharply divided between isolationists and interventionists. The profound disillusionment brought on by the botching of the Versailles peace had persisted throughout the 1920s and 1930s. Woodrow Wilson may have declared the Great War a crusade to "make the world safe for democracy," but many Americans had come to see it merely as a war fought to safeguard loans made by American banks and enrich the country's arms manufacturers. Sen. Gerald P. Nye, a North Dakota Republican, promoted this perspective during the mid-1930s with a series of public hearings investigating World War I munitions sales.

Nye's special Senate committee exposed exorbitant profiteering and emphasized that the arms manufacturers—or "merchants of death," as Nye and others liked to call them—had sold their wares to all belligerents. The Nye Committee also investigated allegations that the Morgan banking empire, acting as financial

Adm. Husband E. Kimmel during his brief eleven-month tenure as commander of the U.S. Pacific fleet. Kimmel reached his headquarters at 8:10 A.M. on December 7 during the peak of the attack. All he could do was stand by a window and watch. At one point, a spent bullet broke through the window and bounced off his chest. "It would have been merciful had it killed me," Kimmel wrote later. He was stripped of his command on December 17 and soon retired.

agent for Great Britain and France, had somehow pressured President Wilson into asking Congress for a declaration of war. In this regard, at least, the committee's work was less successful; yet, overall, the hearings helped shape public opinion and persuade Congress to pass the first of four Neutrality Acts.

The act of August 1935 sought to preserve U.S. neutrality by restricting both the conduct of the government and the behavior of private citizens. It required the president to embargo arms shipments to all belligerents once he had established that a state of war existed among them. (With the sinking of the *Lusitania* in mind, it also required the president to warn U.S. citizens who planned to travel on the ships of belligerent nations that they did so at their own risk.) However, because the 1935 Neutrality Act made no distinction between victims and aggressors, its rules sharply limited the president's ability to respond to foreign expansionism, especially the expansionism then being undertaken by Japan in East Asia.

When the Neutrality Act was renewed in February 1936, a further provision was added banning loans to belligerents. In May 1937, the law was again tightened, this time in response to the outbreak of a civil war in Spain between the republican government and fascists led by Gen. Francisco Franco. The Neutrality Act of 1937 appended civil wars to the list of applicable conflicts, added strategic materials (such as steel and oil) to the embargoed commodities, and made travel by Americans on the ships of belligerents illegal. It also required belligerent nations buying nonmilitary goods in the United States to pay cash and transport their purchases using their own ships (the so-called cash-and-carry policy). The requirements of the neutrality law became so rigid and burdensome, in fact, that when Japanese and Chinese troops began fighting in July 1937, President Roosevelt chose not to acknowledge the war formally because doing so would automatically trigger an embargo much more harmful to the victim, China, than to the aggressor, Japan.

Sen. Gerald P. Nye meets with reporters on September 12, 1939, less than two weeks after the German invasion of Poland. He called the press conference to announce his determination to preserve the embargo provisions of the Neutrality Act.

LEFT: **Charles Lindbergh** *(second from left) appears at a 1941 Madison Square Garden rally with other members of the Committee to Defend America First, a leading isolationist organization. The group, also known as the America First Committee, asserted that World War II was none of their country's business.*

MILITARISM HAD BEEN ON the rise in Japan since the Japanese victory over Russia in the Russo-Japanese War of 1904–1905. During the Great Depression, in particular, Japanese army and navy officers became convinced that their country's persistent economic problems could be solved only by territorial expansion. In 1930, Japan controlled about 146,000 square miles of territory (an area about the size of the Dakotas), into which some sixty-five million people were crowded. Because there wasn't enough arable land on Japan's home islands to feed all its people, the country had to import an increasingly large percentage of its food supply. Even worse, the home islands had few mineral resources, which concerned the militarists deeply. Unless Japan could establish reliable access to the raw materials necessary for the health of its highly industrialized economy, the nation would continue to struggle and eventually become a third- or fourth-rate power.

THE WASHINGTON CONFERENCE

ALTHOUGH THE UNITED STATES never joined the League of Nations, it did—under the leadership of future chief justice Charles Evans Hughes, who served as secretary of state from 1921 until 1925—pursue alternative means of promoting world peace and stability. During the winter of 1921–1922, for example, the United States hosted the Washington Conference, which sought to defuse an expanding naval arms race among America, Great Britain, and Japan. Although Hughes proposed extensive disarmament, the delegates eventually settled on a plan that set limits on naval tonnage and established ratios of weaponry among the signatories. For every 5 tons of American and British warship, Japan was allowed 3 tons and France and Italy 1.75 tons each. Because Great Britain and the United States had to spread their fleets over the entire globe, this agreement nearly guaranteed Japanese dominance in the Pacific; yet it also codified the militarists' sense that the rest of the world considered Japan an inferior power and led to even harsher attacks by the military establishment on the Japanese civilian government.

The militarists considered this prospect intolerable, so they took action. In September 1931, the Kwangtung Army—stationed on southern Manchuria's Kwangtung (Liaotung) Peninsula, which had been taken from Russia in 1905—accused Chinese troops of attempting to bomb a South Manchurian Railway train. This unlikely charge gave the army the excuse it needed to seize the rest of Manchuria from a helpless China—a development that the weak Japanese civilian government was also powerless to prevent. Later, the army forced the government to reconstitute Manchuria as the "independent" state of Manchukuo under the Kwangtung Army's control. The United States and the nations of Western Europe all condemned the action strongly but ineffectually. When the League of Nations called on member nations to withhold recognition of the new Manchukuo puppet state, Japan simply withdrew from the league in March 1933.

For the next several years, political violence in Japan (including the assassinations of a prime minister and other top government officials) diverted the army's attention and put its expansionism on hold. On July 7, 1937, however, Japanese troops engaged Chinese units in the demilitarized zone that had been established between the Great Wall and Peking. A full-scale invasion followed, during which Japan conquered China's major ports and much of the Chinese interior. The slaughter was particularly brutal in Nanking, where as many as three hundred thousand civilians were killed in what came to be known as the "rape of Nanking." Once again, Western protests were strongly worded but empty.

> "The political situation in the world, which of late has been growing progressively worse, is such as to cause grave concern and anxiety."
>
> —
> *Franklin D. Roosevelt, Quarantine Speech, October 5, 1937*

The Quarantine Speech

IN OCTOBER 1937, President Roosevelt delivered an important foreign policy address in Chicago that took on America's isolationists directly. "There is a solidarity and interdependence about the modern world, both technically and morally," he said, "which makes it impossible for any nation completely to isolate itself from economic and political upheavals in the rest of the world, especially when such upheavals appear to be spreading." He pointed out how fortunate the United States was that it could put its money into "bridges and boulevards, dams and reforestation, …rather than into huge standing armies and vast supplies of implements of war.

"Nevertheless, my friends," the president continued, "I am compelled, as you are compelled, to look ahead. The peace, the freedom, and the security of 90 percent of the population of the world is being jeopardized by the remaining 10 percent who are threatening a breakdown of all international order and law." In conclusion, FDR compared the lawlessness in the world to an epidemic disease and proposed a commonsense solution: "a quarantine of the patients in order to protect the health of the community against the spread of the disease." Specifically, the president wanted Congress to revise the neutrality law to give him greater flexibility in aiding victim nations and thwarting aggression. "Let no one imagine that America will escape, that America may expect mercy, that this Western Hemisphere will not be attacked," Roosevelt warned.

Yet even his deliberately vague request for a "quarantine" was rejected. Hostile public reaction to the speech fortified the isolationist bloc in Congress and caused Roosevelt to pull back. Most isolationists were not pacifists, however; they favored rearmament, especially the construction of a large two-ocean navy. They called their strategy Fortress America and believed that a well-armed United States could always repel military threats from Europe or Asia because of the great difficulties involved in transporting troops and war matériel across the vast expanses of the Atlantic and Pacific Oceans.

A SMALL BUT EXPANDING GROUP of interventionists in Congress did argue that the Berlin-Rome Axis (formed by Germany and Italy in October 1936) would, if left unchecked, threaten America. But their warnings went unheeded by the vast majority of Americans, even as the prevailing European policy of appeasement brought the world closer to war. In 1936, German dictator Adolf Hitler remilitarized the Rhineland in violation of the Locarno treaties of 1925; in March 1938, he annexed Austria in the Anschluss; and then he wanted Czechoslovakia—or at least the Sudetenland, an area of western Czechoslovakia in which many ethnic Germans lived. The Czechoslovakians were prepared to fight, but not so their European allies, which left little the diplomatically marginalized Czechoslovakian government could do.

Japanese soldiers *leading a group of* *Chinese prisoners in* *1937.*

At the Munich Conference held in September 1938, Hitler met with British prime minister Neville Chamberlain and French premier Edouard Daladier to resolve the crisis. So eager were Chamberlain and Daladier to avoid another European war that they simply agreed to let Germany take the disputed territory, accepting Hitler's promise that "this is the last territorial claim I have to make in Europe." Such concessions, of course, only brought new demands. Just six months after Munich, Hitler disregarded his September pledge and brazenly occupied the rest of Czechoslovakia; six months after that, Germany invaded Poland.

In the meantime, Foreign Ministers Joachim von Ribbentrop and Vyacheslav M. Molotov had negotiated the Nazi-Soviet Nonaggression Pact, which they signed on August 23, 1939. This agreement, which stunned the world, allowed the Nazis to begin their invasion of Poland on September 1 without fear of Soviet intervention. (Only later did it become known that the Nazi-Soviet pact included secret protocols dividing the rest of Eastern Europe between the two governments.) Meanwhile, Britain and France, honoring mutual defense treaties with Poland, declared war on Germany, and World War II began.

THE HOME FRONT

NEARLY FOUR MILLION AMERICANS were out of work when the Japanese attacked Pearl Harbor. Millions more still labored at government-sponsored jobs for such agencies as the WPA.

Some 40 percent of American families earned less than fifteen hundred dollars a year, which was then considered the minimum necessary for a family of four. In other words, the Great Depression wasn't over.

During four years of war, however, the federal government spent $306 billion, two-thirds of it borrowed from the public through programs such as war bonds. As a result, annual personal income in the United States rose from $78 billion in 1940 to $171 billion in 1945, and unemployment fell to 1.2 percent, the lowest rate ever recorded.

The home front became one gigantic factory. Initially, few Americans believed that the country could meet President Roosevelt's call for an annual defense output of sixty thousand planes, forty-five thousand tanks, and eight million tons of shipping. By 1944, however, with its factories open twenty-four hours a day on continuous shifts, the United States produced ninety-six thousand planes, and similar levels were also reached in other areas of production.

With wartime unemployment so low and factories desperate for workers, the federal government urged women to take full-time jobs in heavy industry. Previously, such jobs had been exclusively given to men.

The Anglo-American Relationship

As late as the Munich Conference, Franklin Roosevelt had supported Prime Minister Chamberlain's policy of appeasement; yet by early 1939, the American president had come to reject this view. He began pressing harder for repeal—or at least liberalization—of the neutrality law but made little headway. Only after the outbreak of war in September did Congress agree (in November 1939) to modify the Neutrality Act so that Britain and France could buy arms and munitions in the United States. Yet the British and the French still had to pay cash and carry the goods away in their own ships; otherwise, it was feared, U-boat attacks might once again draw the United States into war.

Many Americans hoped that arms sales to the Allies would be enough to defeat the Axis powers. Then, in June 1940, the impossible happened: Germany conquered France. The sight of Hitler in Paris particularly tested American neutrality. With the Low Countries and Scandinavia already occupied, only Britain remained as a bulwark against Nazi domination of Western Europe. How long the British might hold out, and what the Nazis might do with the Royal Navy should they win the battle of Britain, remained open questions that few Americans cared to contemplate—so most ignored them as best they could. Meanwhile, President Roosevelt and his interventionist allies in Congress concentrated all their efforts on aiding Britain so that when the United States did eventually enter the war (as Roosevelt knew it must), there would still be a democratic Great Britain left to help.

Adolf Hitler visits the Eiffel Tower in July 1940. Images such as this of Hitler inspecting his new toy, the city of Paris, unsettled many Americans and substantially shifted the interventionist-isolationist balance.

Anglo-American cooperation was particularly enhanced during this period by the close relationship that devilloped between Roosevelt and Winston Churchill, who became Britain's prime minister following Chamberlain's resignation in May 1940. Because 1940 was also a presidential election year, and because FDR was running for an unprecedented third term, he moved cautiously at first in assisting Great Britain, paying attention both to what was politically possible and to what was legally permissible. On September 3, he arranged the transfer of fifty aging U.S. destroyers to the Royal Navy (for use in Atlantic convoy duty) in exchange for rights to naval and air bases in several British possession in the Western Hemisphere, including Newfoundland, Bermuda, and the British West Indies.

After trouncing Wendell Willkie in the 1940 election, however, Roosevelt became much bolder in his requests for aid to the British, whose financial reserves were beginning to run out. On December 17, 1940, he held a press conference at which he announced that he would soon be asking Congress to liberalize the terms under which Great Britain purchased arms from the United States. Specifically, he wanted Congress to permit the British to defer all payments until after the war. The president explained his reasoning to the American people

An aircraft spotter stands on a rooftop near St. Paul's Cathedral, scanning the sky above London for German planes. With the enactment of Lend-Lease, however, the battle of Britain gave way to the battle of the Atlantic, during which Hitler's goal was to choke off Anglo-American merchant shipping.

in this way: If your neighbor's house is on fire and he asks you for your garden hose to put it out, you don't haggle over price. You simply loan him the hose until the fire is out, at which point he will surely return it to you. "I think you all get it," Roosevelt said.

Twelve days later, the president delivered one of his most memorable fireside chats, in which he instructed Americans at length in the fundamentals of U.S. national security policy. "If Great Britain goes down, the Axis powers will control the continents of Europe, Asia, Africa, Australasia, and the high seas—and they will be in a position to bring enormous military and naval resources against this hemisphere," he explained. "It is no exaggeration to say that all of us, in all the Americas, would be living at the point of a gun…. All our present efforts are not enough. We must have more ships, more guns, more planes—more of everything. And this can be accomplished only if we discard the notion of 'business as usual.' …We must be the great arsenal of democracy." The country must also move quickly, Roosevelt added, "so that we and our children will be saved the agony and suffering of war which others have had to endure."

This last point shows that—even as the president detailed Nazi intentions to "enslave the whole of Europe, and then to use the resources of Europe to dominate the rest of the world"—he refused to relinquish the public fiction that the United States could remain a nonbelligerent. He even called rumors that he had plans to send soldiers overseas "deliberate untruth." Yet Roosevelt's actions, including his current Lend-Lease proposal, contradicted such denials.

Passed despite fierce isolationist opposition, the Lend-Lease Act of March 1941 authorized the president, using funds appropriated by Congress, to transfer arms and other military supplies to "the government of any country whose defense the President deems vital to the defense of the United States." The program, which quickly became the main conduit of U.S. military aid to Britain, was soon extended to include the Soviet Union (after the German invasion of that country in June 1941), China, and other Allied nations as well. Ultimately, more than fifty billion dollars' worth of aid would be provided through the mechanism of Lend-Lease.

The Battle of the Atlantic

AS USUAL, FRANKLIN ROOSEVELT remained sensitive to his electorate. Most Americans were frightened by events in Europe, and newsreel coverage of the heroic resistance of the British to the German air assault known as the Blitz gave American an additional emotional reason to tolerate aid for the Allies. Further support for the British came in mid-April 1941, when President Roosevelt announced that the United States would extend its antisubmarine patrols to twenty-five degrees west longitude, thus covering most of the North Atlantic and freeing the Royal Navy for operations closer to home.

Roosevelt acted because the problems being caused by the German subs had recently become extraordinarily serious. In April 1941 alone, U-boats sank 650,000 tons of Allied shipping, and there seemed little point in spending billions of dollars on Lend-Lease if none of the aid was making it to Europe. The Germans were turning out four new submarines each month, providing U-boat service chief Karl Dönitz with more than enough vessels to institute an offensive strategy known as the "wolf pack." Once a single patrolling submarine discovered an Allied convoy, Dönitz's headquarters in Brittany would use coded radio messages to direct other U-boats to join in the attack. The first submarine would fire a torpedo into the convoy and run. When the escorting Allied destroyers gave chase, the rest of the German wolf pack would attack the now-defenseless convoy.

The strategy was so successful that the Germans began sinking British merchant ships at three times the rate new ones could be built. "The decision for 1941 lies upon the seas," Churchill warned Roosevelt pointedly; and although politically vulnerable because of his assertions that Lend-Lease would be sufficient, Roosevelt responded (as noted above) by extending the American patrols to Iceland—and thus overlapping, not coincidentally, the western third of the German-declared combat zone. This policy change inevitably led to confrontations with U-boats, and several U.S. destroyers and merchant ships were sunk. Making political use of these incidents, Roosevelt persuaded Congress in early November to grant two more concessions: Merchant ships would be armed, and they would be allowed to transport supplies into combat zones (thus repealing the neutrality law's remaining "carry" provision). As a result, the United States clearly became a participant in the Atlantic war, if only on a limited basis.

Another important milestone in Allied solidarity was the Atlantic Charter. Following a secret three-day August 1941 meeting aboard the USS *Augusta* in

U.S. Coast Guard officers on the deck of the cutter Spencer *watch depth charges explode in April 1943. The charges sank the German sub U-175, which had been attempting to sneak into the center of the convoy being escorted by the* Spencer.

Placentia Bay, Newfoundland, Roosevelt and Churchill issued on August 14 a document that became in 1945 the blueprint for the United Nations. The Atlantic Charter, which the Soviet Union and a dozen other nations soon endorsed, declared that the Allies renounced territorial aggrandizement, recognized the right of self-determination as belonging to all peoples, and stated that they sought only to ensure that "all the men in all the lands may live out their lives in freedom from fear and want." Of course, this could happen only after "the final destruction of the Nazi tyranny."

Winston Churchill aboard the HMS Prince of Wales *in Placentia Bay during the August 1941 conference with Roosevelt that produced the Atlantic Charter. The two heads of state met almost a dozen times during the war, developing the close partnership that made Joseph Stalin suspicious of their motives.*

Throughout the late summer and fall of 1941, the "all-outers" in Roosevelt's cabinet—especially Secretary of War Henry L. Stimson, Treasury Secretary Henry Morgenthau Jr., and Interior Secretary Harold Ickes—pushed for an immediate declaration of war against Germany. But Roosevelt told them (and Churchill) that he was "not willing to fire the first shot"—not when his political instincts told him that the American people would not support an all-out war. The president would continue to arm Britain; he would continue the undeclared war in the Atlantic; but he would not ask Congress for a formal declaration of war against Germany. As it turned out, he wouldn't have to.

By 1940, THE MILITARISTS had largely taken over Japanese civil society, and they yearned for more. Seeking to capitalize on the recent Nazi conquests of France and the Netherlands, the Japanese government began forcing concessions from weak French and Dutch colonial governments in Southeast Asia. Authorities in the Dutch East Indies (now Indonesia) were pressured into granting Japanese companies access to the colony's rich oil fields. Similarly, the Vichy French were leaned upon until they agreed to close off Chinese supply routes through French Indochina (present-day Vietnam, Laos, and Cambodia). Even Churchill felt compelled to suspend the aid to Chiang Kai-shek's Nationalist Chinese army that was currently passing through British Burma. In July 1940, alarmed by these developments, Roosevelt halted all sales of aviation fuel and high-grade scrap metal to Japan. Two months later, after the Japanese extracted from the Vichy regime its reluctant consent to the stationing of Japanese troops in northern Indochina, the president extended the U.S. embargo to include all grades of scrap iron and steel. Also in September 1940, Japan signed the Tripartite Pact, initiating a ten-year mutual-defense and economic alliance with Germany and Italy.

The next major deterioration in U.S.-Japanese relations came in late July 1941, when Japanese troops invaded southern Indochina. Responding to this development just prior to their meeting in Newfoundland, Roosevelt and Churchill froze all Japanese assets in their respective countries and extended the existing trade embargo to include all shipments of oil as well. (Japanese access to Dutch

East Indian oil was also cut off.) This put Japan, which imported 88 percent of its oil, in an untenable position. In Tokyo, Emperor Hirohito and his military leadership saw three options: Japan could abandon its plans to establish a Greater East Asia Co-Prosperity Sphere and live within the limits of its domestic resources, becoming a minor regional power; it could make concessions to the Americans in order to win a resumption of trade; or its could attack its enemies and take what it wanted. After the first option was eliminated, it was decided to proceed with the other two simultaneously.

Prime Minister Konoe Fumimaro was given until mid-October 1941 to reach a diplomatic settlement. On October 2, Konoe presented to Washington a comprehensive plan under which Japan agreed to remove its troops from Indochina following the conclusion of its war with China. When Secretary of State Cordell Hull responded unenthusiastically that the United States would also need to know when the Japanese planned to withdraw from China, Konoe resigned under pressure from the army. He was succeeded a day later (October 16) by hard-line war minister Tojo Hideki, who had risen to power during the late 1930s as chief of staff of the Kwangtung Army. Although nicknamed the Razor for his sharpness of mind, Tojo tended to view global issues narrowly and rarely considered any perspective other than that of the Japanese military.

Operation Z

JAPAN COVETED THE OIL, rubber, and tin resources of the Dutch East Indies and British Malaya. In order to conquer those colonies, however, the Japanese would have to establish long supply lines through the South China Sea—which would be vulnerable to interdiction by American B-17s stationed on Luzon. Therefore, any offensive war plan targeting the East Indies or Malaya would also have to include significant operations against the American bases in the Philippines.

The Japanese officer most responsible for initiating and planning the attack on Pearl Harbor was Adm. Yamamoto Isoroku—commander in chief of the imperial navy and, ironically, an opponent of war with the United States. Having spent several years in Massachusetts (where he studied at Harvard University) and a few more in the U.S. capital (where he served in the Japanese embassy as a naval attaché), Yamamoto returned to Japan in 1928 sobered by America's industrial might and harboring no illusions about Japan's ability to defeat such a country. Yet he was also deeply patriotic and believed that, given the realities of the Japanese political situation, war was inevitable. Therefore, he would do his best to win—or, in this case, not lose.

Of course, an invasion of the continental United States never figured seriously in any Japanese war plan because the Japanese lacked the resources to mount such an enormous long-range effort. Even an attack on Pearl Harbor would be a stretch. Yet Yamamoto knew that Japan's only chance to survive a war with the United States was to punish America so severely at the outset that the Japanese gained enough time to establish an impenetrable ring of defenses in the western

Tojo Hideki served as Japan's prime minister until July 1941, when the success of the American island-hopping campaign (especially Japan's loss of the Mariana Islands) resulted in his ouster. He is shown here in November 1948, being sentenced to death at the conclusion of his war crimes trial.

Pacific. Conquest of the Philippines would not be sufficient. The only target important enough to meet the need for a staggering blow to American power was the U.S. naval base at Pearl Harbor, headquarters of the Pacific Fleet. Moreover, the only way to succeed at Pearl Harbor was with a surprise attack.

Yamamoto's plan called for a strike force built up around six heavy aircraft carriers with a complement of 360 dive-bombers, torpedo bombers, high-level bombers, and escort fighters. (The Japanese had ten heavy carriers in all, compared to three for the U.S. Pacific Fleet.) The carriers would leave Japanese waters and sail in a wide arc, avoiding all shipping lanes, through the nearly deserted waters of the North Pacific. Then, at a point 500 miles north of Hawaii, the fleet would turn sharply south, closing to within 220 miles of Oahu before launching its first wave of planes. In all, the strike force *Kido Butai* would have to travel 3,500 miles, adhere to a rigidly precise timetable, maintain absolute radio silence, and hope that it wasn't discovered before it could savage Pearl.

This captured Japanese photo shows Mitsubishi dive-bombers warming up on the deck of one of Nagumo's carriers prior to taking off for Pearl Harbor. Yamamoto had code-named the attack Operation Z after a signal flag that his hero, Adm. Togo Heihachiro, had hoisted during Japan's annihilation of the Russian fleet at Tsushima in May 1905.

UNDER THE OPERATIONAL COMMAND of Adm. Nagumo Chuichi, the *Kido Butai* sailed on November 26, the day before Thanksgiving. Sunday morning, December 7, had been chosen for the attack because most U.S. military personnel were still being given the weekends off despite the dangerous international situation, and many servicemen would still be sleeping off a late Saturday night out. The Pacific Fleet's ships, therefore, would also be in port—sitting ducks for Nagumo's planes. Because of the ongoing negotiations in Washington, the admiral was instructed to wait for a final radioed command before preparing his attack. If the talks with the Americans succeeded (this was considered unlikely), his orders were to hold his fleet in the North Pacific and await further instructions. Instead, on December 2, his flagship received the message "Climb Mount Niitakayama" (the highest peak on Taiwan). This was the "go" code, irrevocably ordering the attack.

Although the Japanese had sent veteran diplomat Kurusu Saburo to Washington to revive bilateral talks with the Americans, little flexibility was expected from the U.S. government. Now that the European war had thoroughly discredited appeasement as a response to aggression, the Roosevelt administration was holding firm to its insistence that all Japanese troops be withdrawn from Indochina *and* China. U.S. resolve was further stiffened by intelligence produced by Magic, the code name given to the naval intelligence operation that had broken Japan's diplomatic code. From decoded intercepts, Roosevelt, Hull, and Stimson had already learned that the Japanese were prepared to go to war should negotiations with the United States fail.

On November 20, Kurusu presented to Hull his government's final offer: Japan would withdraw from southern Indochina if the United States would agree to end its embargo and suspend aid to Chiang's Nationalists. Hull dismissed these terms, and in his reply of November 26 (the day that the *Kido Butai* left port), he forcefully reiterated the U.S. position that the embargo would continue until Japan withdrew from all of China and Indochina. Hull's note infuriated Tojo, who considered it proof of his contention that America was seeking the complete humiliation of Japan. The prime minister requested an audience with the emperor, at which he persuaded Hirohito to allow Operation Z to proceed. In the meantime, the Magic cryptographers decoded and sent up the chain of command an ominous November 22 cable to Kurusu that read: "THIS TIME WE MEAN IT, THAT THE DEADLINE CANNOT BE CHANGED! AFTER THAT THINGS ARE AUTOMATICALLY GOING TO HAPPEN."

The Situation at Pearl

NONE OF THE TOP MILITARY or civilian personnel who had access to Magic knew for certain what those "things" were, yet they had to assume that war was likely among them. On November 27, the Navy Department alerted all U.S. commanders in the Pacific to the possibility of an imminent hostile move by Japan. A December 2 message to Pearl Harbor began, "This is a war warning." Yet the service chiefs in Washington never gave Magic clearance to either Kimmel or Short, so the warnings remained vague and were generally disregarded. Few of the planners at Pearl believed that the Japanese could actually strike Hawaii, so they focused their attention instead on the defense of the Philippines, a much more obvious target.

Earlier, Admiral Kimmel had considered the suggestion that he ship out his eight battleships; but he eventually concluded that they would be more vulnerable on the open sea, especially without carrier air support. (In early December, not a single one of Kimmel's three aircraft carriers was in port: The *Enterprise* was delivering planes to Wake Island, the *Lexington* was out on patrol, and the *Saratoga* was in San Diego, having just come out of dry dock in Bremerton, Washington.) On Oahu, however, General Short had hundreds of Army Air Force planes ready to protect the ships, should that prove necessary.

Short's own response to the war alerts was to increase his antisabotage measures. Then, as now, the Japanese-American community on Oahu was large, and there was a great deal of concern that hidden among these people were numerous spies and saboteurs. Unfortunately, one of Short's tactics was to line up his planes wingtip to wingtip. This way, they occupied a smaller area and required fewer soldiers to guard. Because he didn't anticipate an air attack, Short wasn't at all concerned that such a tactic made his planes much more vulnerable to Japanese bombers.

IN ORDER TO DIVERT THE AMERICANS' ATTENTION from the strike force then crossing the North Pacific, the Japanese government had Kurusu keep talking to Hull. But on the morning of December 7, the Japanese embassy in Washington received a lengthy, top-secret cable that the ambassador, Adm. Nomura Kochisaburo, was directed to handle personally and present to Secretary of State Hull at precisely 1 P.M. Washington time (8 A.M. Hawaii time). Because the message was so highly classified, Nomura and Kurusu had to decode and type it themselves. As a result, they were sixty-five minutes late for their appointment with Hull.

Before joining the Roosevelt administration as secretary of state in 1933, Cordell Hull had been a congressmen from Tennessee and a favorite of southern Democrats. He resigned from the State Department following the 1944 election because of poor health.

INTERNMENT

WHITES ON THE WEST COAST had distrusted and persecuted Asian immigrants since the first "coolies" arrived in the mid–nineteenth century to build the transcontinental railroads. Not surprisingly, therefore, the attack on Pearl Harbor produced an outpouring of public fear concerning the "threat" posed by Japanese Americans, whose loyalty could presumably not be trusted. The pressure on President Roosevelt became so great so quickly that he felt compelled to order the internment of 112,000 Americans of Japanese ancestry, more than half of whom had been born in the United States. The American Civil Liberties Union later called this order "the worst single invasion of citizens' liberties" during the war.

Although no evidence was ever presented to support the charge that Japanese Americans were more likely than anyone else to be saboteurs, officials such as California attorney general Earl Warren (later a

The owner of this Oakland grocery was a University of California graduate of Japanese descent. He was forced to abandon his store in March following President Roosevelt's evacuation order.

great libertarian chief justice) insisted that Japanese Americans had to be removed from the West Coast in order to protect the region's military and civil defense installations. In February 1942, President Roosevelt issued an executive order authorizing the imprisonment of Japanese Americans in nine inland "relocation centers." Forced from their homes into what were essentially prisoner-of-war camps, loyal Japanese Americans lost their land, their businesses, and their dignity, while many well-placed whites profited substantially from purchases made at bargain prices.

Even so, more than thirty-three thousand young Japanese Americans volunteered for military service during the war and fought bravely in Europe to demonstrate not only their own loyalty but also the patriotism of their families and their community. During the late 1980s, Congress finally voted compensation to redress partially the wrong of internment.

The Magic code breakers worked much faster. Shortly before noon Washington time, as Admiral Nagumo ordered his carriers into the wind, U.S. Army Chief of Staff George C. Marshall read the text of the decrypted message. It was a point-by-point refutation of Hull's November 26 note that concluded with instructions to Nomura that he must break off negotiations "AT 1:00 P.M. ON THE 7TH, YOUR TIME."

Marshall immediately ordered a warning sent by radio to army commanders in the Philippines, Hawaii, Panama, and San Francisco. "Japanese are presenting at 1:00 P.M. Eastern Standard Time what amounts to an ultimatum…. Just what significance the hour set may have we do not know but be on the alert accordingly. Inform naval authorities of this communication." Unfortunately, atmospheric static temporarily blocked the channel to Honolulu, so the signal officer on duty used the next fastest method of communication: the Western Union cable. His telegram left Washington at 12:17 P.M. and reached Honolulu sixteen minutes later, at 7:33 A.M. local time. A motorcycle messenger was immediately dispatched from the Western Union office to carry the urgent telegram to General Short at Fort Shafter, several miles away. He was en route when the attack began.

Japanese envoys Nomura (left) and Kurusu smile for photographers as they leave the State Department following their December 7 meeting with Hull.

FLIGHT COMMANDER FUCHIDA MITSUO, a veteran pilot of the China war, led the first wave of 183 planes, personally flying one of the high-level bombers. As he approached Pearl Harbor, he could see the battleships moored off Ford Island in the same position described by intelligence reports provided by the Japanese consulate in Honolulu. Seeing also that the surprise was complete, he broke radio silence at 7:53 to shout into his mouthpiece, *Tora! Tora! Tora!* The Japanese word for "tiger" was code to let Admiral Nagumo know that Yamamoto's gamble had paid off. The high-level bombers attacked first—at Wheeler and Hickam Fields, where the Army Air Force planes sat clustered together like sheep in a pen. A third were destroyed, and nearly all the rest damaged. The Barber's Point marine base and NAS Kaneohe were also targeted by the first wave of attacking Japanese planes.

Fuchida's torpedo and dive-bombers concentrated their firepower on Battleship Row. Because Pearl Harbor wasn't very deep, the Japanese torpedo bombers had been outfitted with special shallow-running "fish" that used wooden fins to generate extra buoyancy. (Normal torpedoes would likely have hit obstructions on the harbor bottom and exploded before reaching the battleships.) The dive-bombers also had special munitions: naval shells outfitted with metal fins so that they would fall like bombs yet still pierce the battleship's thick armor plating.

Although the Japanese were disappointed that none of the American carriers was in port, they were happy to find the eight U.S. battleships nearly defenseless. As the attack began, only one-quarter of the battleships' antiaircraft guns were manned, and land-based artillery was of no use at all because its ammunition had been stored to prevent deterioration. The USS *Oklahoma* took four torpedo hits within the first minute and began to capsize. So it went on down the line, with the *California*, the *West Virginia*, the *Maryland*, and the *Tennessee* all suffering serious damage. The USS *Pennsylvania*, moored across the channel in dry dock, was mostly overlooked, and the USS *Nevada* was able to steam nearly out of port before it was beached. The *Arizona*, however, escaped nothing. One of the dive-bombers' shells exploded in its forward magazine, triggering such a powerful explosion that Fuchida felt the shock wave in his bomber thousands of feet above the harbor. Of the 2,403 American military personnel who lost their lives in the Pearl Harbor attack, 1,103 died in the *Arizona* when she sank.

At 8:55, shortly after the first wave of Japanese planes had pulled out, a second wave of 167 planes arrived. These encountered much more antiaircraft fire, as well as towering columns of smoke that obscured the pilots' visibility. Given such conditions, the second wave still performed effectively, knocking out some destroyers that the first wave had missed; however, when it pulled out just before 10 A.M., Nagumo decided not to risk all that he had accomplished by sending in another wave.

The scene on the morning of December 7 at Ford Island, where the squadron of B-17s arriving from California expected to land. Weary after fourteen hours in the air, the B-17 pilots thought at first that they had flown into a nightmare. Incredibly, none of the planes was shot down, although some were destroyed on the ground after landing at various other fields.

The battleships West Virginia *and* Tennessee *burn in Pearl Harbor.*

Infamy

IN WASHINGTON, Cordell Hull was waiting at his desk when his phone rang at 2:05 P.M., just as Nomura and Kurusu were arriving. It was President Roosevelt calling to tell him that Pearl Harbor had been attacked. Roosevelt made the call exactly eighteen minutes after learning himself of the attack from Navy Secretary Frank Knox. Once the president finished his call, the secretary of state had Nomura and Kurusu brought into his office, where they handed him the document that he, Stimson, and Marshall had already read two hours earlier. Nevertheless, Hull read it again so that the Japanese wouldn't suspect their code had been broken. Then he told the Japanese diplomats, "In all my fifty years of public service, I have never seen a document that was more crowded with infamous falsehoods and distortions—infamous falsehoods and distortions on a scale so huge that I never imagined that any government on this planet was capable of uttering them."

RIGHT: *The first official word of the Pearl Harbor attack came in a hurried dispatch from CINCPAC (Commander in Chief Pacific) headquarters. This copy was received by the USS* Ranger, *an aircraft carrier returning to Norfolk, Virginia, after an Atlantic Ocean patrol.*

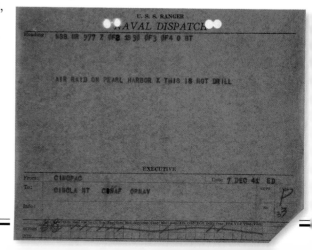

The fact that poor typing skills caused Nomura and Kurusu to miss their 1 P.M. deadline later allowed American officials to emphasize that Japan had attacked Pearl Harbor while still disingenuously discussing peace. Yet even had the diplomats met with Hull minutes before the first bombs fell on Hickam Field, it's difficult to imagine how that might have made a difference in the outcome. The isolationist–interventionist debate was over. The United States, with twenty times the industrial capacity of Japan and a hundred times its natural resources, was going to fight. Moreover, as Stephen E. Ambrose has pointed out, the Japanese started the war "with a brilliant victory so humiliating to the vanquished that the Americans vowed to fight on until retribution was total." Even Michigan Republican Arthur H. Vandenberg, a leading Senate isolationist, conceded that December 7 "ended isolationism for any realist."

On December 8, grim-faced and resolved, President Roosevelt went before Congress to ask for a declaration of war against Japan:

Yesterday, December 7, 1941—a date which will live in infamy—the United States of America was suddenly and deliberately attacked by naval and air forces of the Empire of Japan.

The United States was at peace with that nation and, at the solicitation of Japan, was still in conversation with its Government and its Emperor, looking toward the maintenance of peace in the Pacific. Indeed, one hour after Japanese air squadrons had commenced bombing in Oahu, the Japanese Ambassador to the United States and his colleague delivered to the Secretary of State a formal reply to a recent American message. While this reply stated that it seemed useless to continue the existing diplomatic negotiations, it contained no threat or hint of war or armed attack.

It will be recorded that the distance of Hawaii from Japan makes it obvious that the attack was deliberately planned many days or even weeks ago. During the intervening time, the Japanese Government has deliberately sought to deceive the United States by false statements and expressions of hope for continued peace.

The attack yesterday on the Hawaiian Islands has caused severe damage to American naval and military forces. Very many American lives have been lost. In addition American ships have been reported torpedoed on the high seas between San Francisco and Honolulu.

Yesterday, the Japanese Government also launched an attack against Malaya. Last night, Japanese forces attacked Hong Kong. Last night, Japanese forces attacked Guam. Last night, Japanese forces attacked the Philippine Islands. Last night, the Japanese attacked Wake Island. This morning, the Japanese attacked Midway Island.

Japan has, therefore, undertaken a surprise offensive extending throughout the Pacific area. The facts of yesterday speak for themselves. The people of the United States have already formed their opinions and well understand the implications to the very life and safety of our nation.

President Roosevelt *delivers his "day of infamy" speech, asking Congress for a declaration of war against Japan. The vote in the Senate was unanimous; in the House, there was only one dissenter: pacifist Jeannette Rankin of Montana.*

JAPAN'S AGGRESSOR: ADMIRAL YAMAMOTO
His was the daring execution of a brilliant treachery.

NEARLY ALL JAPANESE greeted the news of victories at Pearl Harbor and elsewhere with jubilation. Extra editions of newspapers appeared on the streets, radio stations broadcast martial music, and patriotic slogans were on everyone's lips. Although Admiral Yamamoto remained cautious, even he thought that the Greater East Asia Co-Prosperity Sphere might now be achieved. The infantry campaign in the Philippines was going particularly well, and in early January 1942, Lt. Gen. Douglas MacArthur was forced to retreat with the bulk of his army to the thickly forested Bataan Peninsula. Other American troops withdrew to fortifications on Corregidor Island at the entrance to Manila Bay. Vowing "I shall return," MacArthur left for Australia in mid-March pursuant to FDR's orders that he avoid capture. Three weeks later, on April 9, the seventy thousand American and Filipino soldiers whom MacArthur had left behind on Bataan surrendered; Corregidor fell on May 6. British Malaya and the Dutch East Indies put up much less resistance.

DID FDR KNOW?

EVER SINCE THE ATTACK on Pearl Harbor, some conspiracy theorists have insisted that FDR knew it was coming. They allege that he learned about Operation Z from Magic intercepts and that he ordered Kimmel and Short kept in the dark so that the attack would succeed and America would enter World War II united. They also charge—without any evidence—that Roosevelt sacrificed the U.S. battleships at Pearl Harbor because he (and, apparently, he alone) knew that carrier air power would determine the outcome of the war. Such a scenario, however, lacks credibility. While it may be true that FDR's hard-line policy during the summer and fall of 1941 gave the Japanese no option other than war (at least from the Japanese point of view), the undeclared naval war that he was fighting in the Atlantic would sooner or later have led to war with Germany, regardless of anything the Japanese did, as Hitler's December 11 declaration of war demonstrated.

Yet Operation Z did have its shortcomings—over and above the flawed premise that the Japanese could sufficiently cripple American military power. One blunder was that the port facilities at Pearl Harbor weren't badly damaged; an even more significant mistake was that the base's oil storage tanks weren't targeted. Had the navy's fuel supply been destroyed (as it easily could have been), Japan might have forced those elements of the U.S. Pacific Fleet that survived the attack, including the carriers, back to California for refueling. This would have made Pearl Harbor useless to the Americans for months, perhaps even an entire year. Instead, Pearl was able to serve immediately as a staging area for the greatest buildup of American military power in history. With its surprise attack, Japan did gain, as Yamamoto had predicted, six months in which to loot Southeast Asia as it wished. Beginning with the battle of the Coral Sea in early May 1942, however, the United States began to strike back.

The Grand Alliance

ON THE DIPLOMATIC FRONT, the Japanese asked Hitler immediately after the attack on Pearl Harbor to honor his pledge to declare war on the United States should Japan initiate hostilities. The Nazi leader had made this offer to encourage Japanese aggression so that the Americans would have to fight a two-front war, thus diverting U.S. resources from the Atlantic theater. Now that war in the Pacific was irrevocable, Hitler could have reneged—nothing new for him—yet he decided instead to declare war on the United States on December 11, and Mussolini followed suit.

What Roosevelt might have done had Hitler not declared war is anyone's guess. Certainly, the German declaration simplified matters enormously, because American military planners had always considered Germany the greater threat. Having already taken their best shot, the Japanese could be dealt with later. Yet the "infamous" nature of the Japanese attack on Pearl Harbor did mean that the Pacific war couldn't be ignored entirely.

The group of nations that joined together to fight the Axis powers called itself the Grand Alliance. By 1945, it had forty-seven members; yet, for all practical purposes, it was directed by three men: Roosevelt, Churchill, and Soviet premier Joseph Stalin. The Big Three met for the first time at Tehran in late November 1943. During the four-day summit, Stalin pressed his demand for the British and Americans to open immediately a second front in western Europe. Although American troops had been fighting in the greater European theater since November 1942, the first landings had come in North Africa in support of the British Eighth Army, then fighting Erwin Rommel's vaunted Afrika Korps in Egypt. These operations, however, had done little to relieve the pressure on the Soviet troops dying in large numbers on the eastern front, especially at Stalingrad. Stalin became even angrier in mid-January 1943, when he learned that Roosevelt and Churchill, meeting in Casablanca, had decided to invade Sicily and Italy next, rather than France. At Tehran, however, the British and American leaders committed themselves to a cross-channel invasion in 1944. Its code name was Operation Overlord.

The invasion of Normandy that took place on D day (June 6, 1944) remains the largest amphibious military operation in history. It employed 6,200 ships, 10,000 aircraft, and landed 156,000 soldiers and thousands of vehicles on just the first day. Within two months, Paris was liberated, and Lt. Gen. George S. Patton's Third Army, having broken through the German lines at Avranches, was hustling its tanks toward the Rhine. The German army was too strong to be defeated in 1944, however, and Hitler still nurtured fantasies of revival. He refused to let his generals retreat behind the Rhine and instead, against all advice, ordered a risky counteroffensive in mid-December 1944. Hitler hoped to exploit a weakness in the Allied lines passing through the Ardennes Forest, and with the help of several Panzer tank divisions transferred from the eastern front, the German army did achieve a limited success. The Germans were able to push back Allied troops far

U.S. Coast Guard photographer Robert F. Sargent took this D day photograph of American soldiers wading ashore through waist-high water. At first, expecting the major allied assault to come at Calais, Hitler dismissed the Normandy invasion as a diversion and refused to concentrate his forces there.

enough to create a "bulge" in the lines. By late January 1945, however, Patton had erased the bulge, and the Germans, their position now compromised, were forced to withdraw. With the end of the Third Reich now coming into view, elements within the German bureaucracy hastened the conclusion of the Nazi murder of millions in concentration camps.

The Big Three sit for a photo opportunity on February 9, 1945, on the grounds of the Livadio Palace outside Yalta. Standing directly behind Churchill, Roosevelt, and Stalin are British war transport minister Lord Leathers, British secretary of state for foreign affairs Anthony Eden, U.S. secretary of state Edward Stettinius, British Foreign Office secretary Alexander Cadogan, Soviet foreign minister V. M. Molotov, and U.S. ambassador to the Soviet Union W. Averell Harriman.

IN EARLY FEBRUARY 1945, the Big Three met again in the Crimean resort town of Yalta to discuss the rapidly approaching postwar world. Certain territorial questions could no longer be avoided, despite Roosevelt's predilection to win the war first and settle differences later. The fate of eastern Europe—of Poland, in particular—was the source of the greatest antagonism. Stalin acted assertively, as one might expect of a man whose army held Bulgaria, Romania, Hungary, Poland, and East Prussia—all of which had been taken from the Germans at great cost. The Red Army was even then nearing Berlin, whereas the British and the Americans had only just won the Battle of the Bulge. According to historian David M. Kennedy, "Stalin now moved to translate his hard-won military advantage into permanent political gains."

Calling the final disposition of Poland "a question of honor and security... [even] one of life and death," the Soviet premier insisted that Churchill and Roosevelt recognize as the legitimate government of Poland the Communist regime he had set up in Lublin, rather than the government in exile that had operated in London since September 1939. ("It was to extinguish elements aligned with the London Poles," David M. Kennedy has noted, "that Stalin in 1940 had ordered the massacre of thousands of captured Polish army officers in the Soviet-occupied Katyn Forest near Smolensk.") Because the Red Army already controlled the territory in question, there was little either Roosevelt or Churchill could do to resist Stalin, short of declaring war on the Soviets.

Similarly, there was little Stalin could do to win his demand for ten billion dollars in war reparations, because the British and Americans controlled the German industrial heartland in the Saar and Ruhr basins. For domestic political reasons, a hollow, vague Declaration on Liberated Europe was issued, pledging all parties "to arrange and conduct free elections." At the same time, Roosevelt sent a private note to Stalin assuring him that the United States would "never lend its support in any way to any provisional government in Poland that would be inimical to your interests."

At the same time, Roosevelt was dying. "To a doctor's eye," Churchill's physician, Lord Moran, observed, "the President appears a very sick man.... I give him only a few months to live." For this reason, some historians have since blamed the territorial and economic concessions FDR made at Yalta on his poor health. They argue that he "sold out" Poland and compromised China out of weakness, in exchange merely for Stalin's promise to enter the Pacific war against Japan. Yet, as David M. Kennedy persuasively concludes, Roosevelt did little at Yalta "that he had not signaled his willingness to do at Tehran, where he was in full possession of his faculties, and did little differently than any American leader could have done at this juncture." As the president himself acknowledged, "I didn't say the result was good. I said it was the best I could do." On April 12, 1945, Franklin Roosevelt died at his Warm Springs, Georgia, retreat; on April 30, Adolf Hitler killed himself in his bunker beneath the Chancellery; on May 7, Admiral Dönitz (whom Hitler had named as his successor) surrendered to Allied supreme commander Dwight D. Eisenhower at Reims.

The War in the Pacific

MEANWHILE, THE JAPANESE OFFENSIVE that had begun at Pearl Harbor received its first setback in early May 1942 in the Coral Sea, where American carriers turned back a Japanese invasion force headed for Port Moresby, New Guinea. The battle turned out to be the first engagement in naval history in which the opposing fleets never came within sight of one another. Carrier-based torpedo and dive-bombers inflicted approximately equal damage—each side losing one aircraft carrier and sustaining serious damage to another—yet the Americans won a strategic victory when the Japanese called off their Port Moresby invasion.

The next important encounter in the Pacific came a month later at Midway Island, where a truly decisive battle was fought in early June. The American base at Midway in the central Pacific was so important to the U.S. war effort that any serious threat to it, Yamamoto knew, would draw out all the remaining elements of the U.S. Pacific Fleet. Therefore, Yamamoto targeted Midway in order to gather together and destroy those warships, especially the carriers, that had escaped the Japanese at Pearl Harbor. Admiral Nagumo once again commanded the strike force, but this time with much

A U.S. naval officer in the South Pacific took this June 1942 photograph of a torpedoed Japanese destroyer through the periscope of his submarine.

Navy fighters taking part in the June 1942 battle of Midway. Below them, a burning Japanese destroyer is visible. Even though the Americans had the intelligence advantage, having broken the Japanese naval code, the Japanese still had considerably more firepower at Midway. Their fleet included four heavy and two light carriers, along with seven battleships, fifteen cruisers, and forty-four destroyers. The Americans had only three carriers, eight cruisers, and fifteen destroyers.

less success. Although Nagumo had more than twice as many ships as the Americans, he was still a novice with regard to naval aviation and wasn't comfortable fighting an enemy that he couldn't see.

Yamamoto had premised his plan on his belief that Adm. Chester Nimitz, who had replaced Kimmel as commander in chief of the U.S. Pacific Fleet, knew nothing of his intentions. But the Americans, by that point, had broken the Japanese naval code, too, and Nimitz knew everything. By the time Nagumo's reconnaissance planes discovered the presence of the American fleet, it was too late to stop U.S. dive-bombers from sinking all four of the Japanese heavy carriers. With the Americans losing but a single flattop, the battle of Midway restored a measure of naval balance in the Pacific and marked the end of all Japanese offensive operations.

Potsdam

THE VICTORIES IN THE CORAL SEA and at Midway set the stage for America's own offensive operations in the South Pacific, which began in August 1942 with landings at Guadalcanal in the Solomon Islands. The ferocious fighting there, which lasted six months, provided a warning of what lay ahead for the U.S. military in its "island-hopping" campaign. By April 1945, when U.S. Marines invaded Okinawa, the cost of such fighting had become quite clear. The toll on Okinawa alone was twelve thousand American dead, in addition to the hundred thousand Japanese fatalities. Furthermore, the Japanese were stepping up their suicidal "kamikaze" raids, and no one doubted that they would fight to the last man. A plan for the defense of the home islands distributed to Japanese field commanders on April 8, 1945, called for suicide attacks on the U.S. fleet, followed by more suicide attacks on the beaches, followed by perpetual guerrilla resistance inland. This was the situation that Harry Truman faced when he became president on April 12. According to Truman's military advisers, the loss of American life would likely be in the hundreds of thousands before Japan was pacified.

As vice president, Truman had never been informed of the Manhattan Project, the code name given the American effort to develop an atomic bomb. In fact, Truman wasn't fully briefed on the bomb until April 25, when Secretary of War Stimson told the new president that "within four months we shall in all probability have completed the most terrible weapon ever known in human history." The British knew about the bomb, having provided some assistance, but Roosevelt had chosen to keep Stalin in the dark, even at Yalta, despite FDR's numerous other efforts to win the Soviet leader's trust. In late July, at a summit meeting with Churchill and Stalin in the Berlin suburb of Potsdam, Truman did, according to his memoirs, "casually [mention] to Stalin that we had a new weapon of unusually destructive force. The Russian premier showed no special interest." (The American president never suspected, of course, that Stalin knew all about the bomb already from his spies within the Manhattan Project.) It was about this time at Potsdam, while considering the political repercussions of Soviet entry into the Pacific war, that Truman decided to use atomic bombs on Hiroshima and Nagasaki in early August.

His reasoning has been the subject of contentious argument ever since. Truman's public explanation was quite simple: "My object is to save as many American lives as possible." Therefore, he would do nearly anything to avoid the necessity of invading the Japanese home islands, even if that meant sacrificing the lives of 210,000 Japanese civilians—which it did. The Hiroshima bomb, dropped on August 6, is believed to have killed about 140,000 people, with perhaps another 70,000 dying in the August 9 bombing of Nagasaki. (Of course, nonatomic fire bombing of other cities throughout the war, from London to Dresden, to Berlin to Tokyo, had killed even greater numbers of civilians.) On August 10, the Japanese government announced its intention to surrender.

Yet, as the diary that Truman kept at Potsdam makes clear, the new president had a great deal more on his mind than simply ending the war with Japan. The Soviet Union, in particular, was prominent in his thoughts as he made the decision to use the bombs. To what extent he was influenced by his desire to keep Stalin out of postwar China and Japan—and to intimidate the Soviet military with America's new superweapon—no one can say. In any event, the bombing of Hiroshima and Nagasaki certainly had a profound effect on U.S.-Soviet relations. Hitler's June 1941 invasion of the Soviet Union had forced Stalin into an alliance with Roosevelt and Churchill—what other choice did he have?—yet the Soviet leader had never relinquished his suspicions concerning the intentions of his allies. Such distrust did not augur well for the postwar world.

The safety plug from the plutonium bomb dropped on Nagasaki on August 9, 1945.

This unusual view of the Hiroshima cloud was taken at ground level by a photographer in nearby Kure.

AMERICAN PROFILE

Wendell L. Willkie

1892–1944

by Robert Dallek

THE FACT THAT THE REPUBLICAN party nominated utility executive Wendell Willkie to run for president in 1940 is itself reason enough to assure his permanent place in history books. Yet Willkie is one of those twentieth-century Americans whose lives provide a vehicle for something more: the understanding of a national transformation.

The most important issue separating the two major parties in 1940 was the role the United States should play in the current world crisis. How far should America extend itself to help Great Britain? Should the country risk war with Nazi Germany to prevent the triumph of authoritarianism in Europe? Although Willkie was personally as much of an internationalist as his opponent, incumbent president Franklin Roosevelt, he was persuaded by the strength of isolationist sentiment in the country to make opposition to U.S. involvement in the war the principal theme of his campaign. Repeatedly, Willkie warned voters that reelecting Roosevelt would mean, sooner or later, sending hundreds of thousands of American boys overseas. The positive response generated by Willkie's antiwar message led directly to Roosevelt's own promise that he would not take the United States into war unless the country was attacked by a foreign power. Later, as the campaign neared its close and Willkie seemed to be gaining even more, Roosevelt dropped the qualification and promised not to join the fighting under any circumstances.

Pearl Harbor, of course, changed the political landscape entirely, and Willkie finally showed his true colors. After completing an around-the-world inspection tour and visiting all of the fighting fronts on FDR's behalf, he wrote a book about the experience called *One World*, published in March 1943. Overnight, it became the greatest nonfiction best-seller in U.S. history to that point, and though a slender volume, it still provides marvelous insights into the thinking of the time.

Reflecting the desire of most Americans for a postwar triumph of Wilsonian universalism, Willkie's book described a world intent on becoming more and more American. Russian grain fields running to the horizon reminded Willkie of Texas; an irrigated valley near Tashkent looked just like southern California; stately mansions along the Volga recalled for him the great houses lining the Hudson River. Willkie even described the thirty-seven-year-old leader of the Siberian republic of Yakutsk as a go-getter who "talked like a California real estate salesman." Similarly, the sturdy, handsome farmers Willkie met in China reminded him of his own forebears on the Indiana and Iowa frontiers. Overall, the message Willkie brought back from his globe-trotting was that inside people of all nationalities was an American waiting to be born.

One World thus combined Woodrow Wilson's vision of a peaceful world committed to American values—that is, a world "made safe for democracy"—with Henry Luce's prediction of an American century. The book remains worthy of reading today because it so clearly evokes the optimism regarding international affairs that Americans felt before Yalta. Producer Darryl F. Zanuck even bought the film rights. He wanted Spencer Tracy to star as Willkie.

Willkie poses just before (or during) *his 1940 campaign for president.*

21

THE COLD WAR AT HOME

The Hiss-Chambers Case

THERE WERE JUST A HANDFUL of reporters in the hearing room when six of the nine members of the House Un-American Activities Committee (HUAC) took their seats on August 3, 1948. The half-dozen congressmen included Acting Chairman Karl E. Mundt of South Dakota, John McDowell of New Jersey, John E. Rankin of Mississippi, J. Hardin Peterson of Florida, F. Edward Hébert of Louisiana, and Richard M. Nixon of California. The committee's chief investigator, Robert E. Stripling, called the only witness he had scheduled for that day: Whittaker Chambers.

Physically, Chambers was an unprepossessing figure, but his intellectual credentials were impressive. In addition to being a gifted journalist, he was a talented linguist and had translated numerous works from German into English, including the children's classic *Bambi*. Currently, he was a senior editor at *Time* magazine.

The initial questioning was desultory. Chambers had received the committee's subpoena only the day before, but it had not come as a surprise to the witness. Chambers had already told State Department officials and FBI agents on several occasions beginning in 1939 of his past involvement with secret Communist cells in the U.S. government. In answer to one of Stripling's preliminary questions, Chambers described in general terms his activities as "a paid functionary of the party" during the

AT LEFT: **Whittaker Chambers** (left) glances at newspaper coverage of his August 25, 1948, confrontation with Alger Hiss before the House Un-American Activities Committee.

1920s and 1930s. He explained that he had been part of an eight-member Washington, D.C., "underground group" that had included Alger Hiss. "The purpose of this group at that time was not primarily espionage," Chambers said. "Its original purpose was the Communist infiltration of the American government. But espionage was one of its eventual objectives." Chambers also made sure to point out that he had "repudiated Marx's doctrines and Lenin's tactics" when he left the party a decade earlier.

The committee members then questioned Chambers at length about Hiss, with whom he claimed to have been particularly close:

MR. STRIPLING: *When you left the Communist party in 1937, did you approach any of [the other seven underground group members] to break with you?*

MR. CHAMBERS: *No. The only one of those people whom I approached was Alger Hiss. I went to the Hiss home one evening at what I considered considerable risk to myself and found Mrs. Hiss at home. Mrs. Hiss is also a member of the Communist party. Mr. Hiss came in shortly afterward, and we talked and I tried to break him away from the party. As a matter of fact, he cried when we separated; but when I left him, he absolutely refused to break. I was very fond of Mr. Hiss.*

As the questioning continued, Chambers stood by his story. He described in further detail his close relationship with Hiss while still pointedly denying that he, Hiss, or any other member of their Communist cell had ever committed espionage. "These people were specifically not wanted to act as sources of information," Chambers told the committee. "These people were an elite group, which it was believed would rise to positions—as, indeed, some of them did—notably Mr. Hiss—in the government. Their position in the government would be of much more service to the Communist party." When the hearing ended, the few newsmen in the room filed their stories. The lead was obvious: A *Time* magazine editor had accused the respected president of the Carnegie Endowment for International Peace, a former high State Department official, of having been a secret Soviet agent.

Two DAYS AFTER Chambers gave his initial testimony, it was Alger Hiss's turn to appear before the committee. Hiss's tall, lean frame and poised bearing offered a striking contrast to the image presented by his stout, untidy accuser. He clothed himself elegantly, and his handsome face shone with self-confidence. Under questioning, Chambers had seemed extremely nervous; by contrast, Hiss was cool and relaxed. He began his testimony with a prepared statement:

I am not and never have been a member of the Communist party. I do not and never have adhered to the tenets of the Communist party. I am not and never have been a member of any Communist-front organization. I have never followed the Communist party line, directly or indirectly. To the best of my knowledge, none of my friends is a Communist. To the best of my knowledge, I never heard of Whittaker Chambers until 1947, when two representatives of the Federal Bureau of Investigation asked me if I knew him and various other people. I said that I did not know Chambers. So far as I know, I have never laid eyes on him, and the statements made about me by Mr. Chambers are complete fabrications. I think my record in the government service speaks for itself.

When this official portrait *was taken in April 1946, forty-one-year-old Alger Hiss was nearing the end of his tenure as director of the State Department Office of Special Political Affairs. He left in December of that year to head the Carnegie Endowment for International Peace.*

Hiss, a lawyer, was then given an opportunity to describe his impressive government career, which included a clerkship with Supreme Court justice Oliver Wendell Holmes, service as assistant counsel to the Nye Committee, and a decade with the State Department. He had traveled to Yalta with President Roosevelt and spent the rest of 1945 overseeing, as temporary secretary general, the creation of the United Nations. In December 1946, Hiss had resigned his post at State to head the Carnegie Endowment.

When Hiss had finished his opening statement, committee members questioned him about Chambers's accusations. "I wonder what possible motive a man who edits *Time* magazine would have for mentioning Alger Hiss in connection with [the Communist party]," Congressman Mundt began. "So do I, Mr. Chairman," Hiss replied. "I have no possible understanding of what could have motivated him."

By this time, the committee members had recognized that there was, in Stripling's words, a "very sharp contradiction" between the two men's accounts. One had to be lying. Yet, according to Mundt, both men were "witnesses whom normally one would assume to be perfectly reliable. They have high positions in American business or organizational work. They both appear to be honest. They both testify under oath [yet their] stories fail to jibe." Therein lay the problem for the committee: Which witness would it choose to believe?

Richard Nixon made the reasonable suggestion that Hiss and Chambers "be allowed to confront each other so that any possibility of a mistake in identity may be cleared up." But the other HUAC members ignored their freshman colleague. After concluding his testimony, Hiss was surrounded by a large crowd of reporters, who seemed to accept his frankness and honesty. After that day's hearing, Nixon agreed that a terrible mistake had been made. The committee, he said, should not have allowed Chambers to testify publicly without first checking into the truth of his story. "How is the committee going to dig itself out of this hole?" one journalist asked Hiss.

THE HOUSE UN-AMERICAN ACTIVITIES COMMITTEE

ALTHOUGH THE House Un-American Activities Committee (HUAC) was formed in May 1938 to investigate fascists as well as Communists, in practice, especially during and after World War II, it concentrated almost exclusively on the latter. Under Texas congressman Martin Dies, who chaired the committee while the Democrats controlled the House, HUAC became famous for making reckless and seemingly arbitrary accusations of disloyalty. Broad popular support for its anti-Communist goals, however, gave the committee enviable political power—despite its often-deplored methods.

Under Republican chairman J. Parnell Thomas (who was bed-ridden with a bleeding ulcer at the outset of the Hiss-Chambers case), HUAC held a series of well-publicized hearings in late 1947 to investigate Communist infiltration of the motion-picture industry. The Hollywood studio heads, fearful of bad publicity, testified as friendly witnesses. However, a group of left-wing screenwriters and directors chose to defy the committee and refused to testify. Known as the Hollywood Ten, they were later cited for contempt of Congress and blacklisted.

The film-industry hearings, packed with celebrity witnesses, made good copy and helped heighten HUAC's profile, but the real drama remained in Washington. According to Thomas, it was HUAC's mission "to expose the New Deal as a Communist project and New Dealers as subversive per se." The Hiss-Chambers hearings allowed Thomas and his colleagues to pursue this goal.

Members of HUAC visit committee chairman J. Parnell Thomas at his home in March 1948. From left to right, they are Rep. Richard B. Vail, Thomas, Rep. John McDowell, chief HUAC counsel Robert E. Stripling, and Rep. Richard M. Nixon.

EVEN BEFORE THE HISS-CHAMBERS controversy developed, the House Un-American Activities Committee had come under attack from both the Truman administration and the press for its careless handling of hearings. Partisan political concerns also played a part. In the 1946 midterm elections, sixteen years of Democratic domination had ended when the Republican party won control of the House. With the 1948 congressional and presidential elections now only three months away, the Democrats sought issues that could help them take back the House. It was rumored that President Truman, if reelected, would ask Congress to disband HUAC. On the same morning that Hiss gave his initial testimony, the president denounced the committee's current spy investigations. He called them a "red herring," organized by the Republicans to divert public attention from their failure to enact needed domestic economic programs. The Eightieth Congress should be passing legislation, Truman said, not "slandering a lot of people that don't deserve it."

"This case is going to kill the committee unless you can prove Chambers's story," one reporter warned Nixon after the August 5 session with Hiss. But the young and ambitious California congressman already recognized this. As he recalled later, the committee "was in a virtual state of shock." Nevertheless, It devised an approach to proceeding: "While it would be virtually impossible to prove that Hiss was or was not a Communist—for that would simply be his word against Chambers's—we should be able to establish whether or not the two men knew each other," Nixon later explained. "If Hiss were lying about not knowing Chambers, then he might also be lying about whether or not he was a Communist."

To determine this, Nixon led a small delegation of committee members and staff to New York City to question Chambers again. This time, the session would be held in private so that HUAC might avoid further embarrassment from conflicting witnesses.

On August 7, 1948, Nixon's subcommittee questioned Chambers secretly in a windowless room in the federal courthouse on Foley Square. During what time period, Nixon asked, had Chambers known Hiss as a Communist? "Roughly between the years 1935 and 1937," the witness answered, adding that Hiss had known

RICHARD M. NIXON
1913–1994

RICHARD MILHOUS NIXON was sixteen years old when the stock market crashed. During the Great Depression, his already struggling family suffered along with millions of other Americans (though not the Roosevelts or the Kennedys). A hard worker and studious, he managed to put himself through both college and law school. After his admission to the California bar in 1937, he practiced for a few years in his hometown of Whittier until World War II broke out.

Although raised a Quaker, Nixon yearned for some role in the war effort. Beginning in January 1942, he worked in the tire-rationing section of the Office of Price Administration, a new government agency set up to regulate wartime price levels. In June, however, he resigned, disillusioned with the bureaucracy, and joined the navy. His service as a supply officer—efficient, if not particularly distinguished—ended with his discharge in March 1946. That year, like a number of other young veterans (including John Kennedy), Nixon ran for Congress and won.

him not by his real name but "by the party name of Carl." Nixon then plunged into a rapid-fire series of detailed questions designed to test whether Chambers had indeed known Hiss as well as he now claimed to have. Apparently, Chambers remembered a great deal about the Hisses. According to Nixon, "All of this information might have been obtained by studying Hiss's life without actually knowing him. But some of the answers had a personal ring of truth about them beyond the bare facts themselves." Chambers claimed to have visited the Hiss home several times and described their furniture, their eating and drinking habits, their pets, their personal mannerisms, and even their nicknames for one another.

Nixon, Hébert, and McDowell were most interested in two of Chambers's recollected anecdotes. One involved the transfer of a car owned by Hiss to another Communist—in which Chambers had acted as an intermediary. The other concerned bird-watching, a hobby that the Hisses and Chambers shared. According to Chambers, "I recall once they saw, to their great excitement, a prothonotary warbler." At this point, Congressman McDowell, also an amateur ornithologist but one less experienced than Chambers, interrupted to ask, "A very rare specimen?" "I never saw one," Chambers replied. By the end of the session, the breadth and depth of Chambers's answers had restored the subcommittee's faith in his honesty.

Hiss shakes hands with President Truman in June 1945 at the San Francisco conference at which the United Nations was founded. At Truman's left is Secretary of State Edward R. Stettinius Jr. After the conference, the highlight of his governmental career, Hiss accompanied the UN Charter back to Washington aboard a special plane. "That was the day," Hiss said later, "when I realized exactly how important I really was—the charter had a parachute, and I didn't."

THE FULL COMMITTEE held another closed session on August 16, at which it pressed Hiss with questions based on Chambers's August 7 testimony (the details of which it kept from Hiss, despite his repeated protests that he be allowed to review a copy). In stark contrast to his earlier appearance, Hiss now seemed under severe strain. His composure, in particular, yielded to a blend of anxiety and anger. Nixon began by showing Hiss two photographs of Chambers and asking him whether he knew the man "either as Whittaker Chambers or as Carl or as any other individual." Hiss wavered, admitting that "the face has a certain familiarity."

As the questioning continued, Hiss became increasingly hostile. He asked resentfully how the committee members could take the word of "a confessed former Communist" and "self-confessed traitor" over the testimony of a highly respected public servant such as himself. Stripling snapped back that Chambers had "sat there and testified for hours. He said he spent a week in your house, and he just rattled off details like that. He has either made a study of your life in great detail or he knows you." Moments later, a subdued Hiss announced that he had "written a name on this pad in front of me of a person whom I knew in 1933 and 1934 who not only spent some time in my house but sublet my apartment." Hiss said that he didn't know for certain whether this person, a freelance journalist named George Crosley, was Chambers, and he insisted that he hadn't seen Crosley since 1935. At the committee's request, he gave a more detailed account of his relationship with Crosley, whom he said he had met while attached to the Nye Committee.

Crosley, Hiss recalled, had been interested in writing magazine articles about the Nye Committee's work investigating the munitions industry, and Hiss had become friendly with him. In fact, after moving his own family into a new apartment, Hiss had sublet his old residence to Crosley and even "threw in" an old Ford roadster that he no longer wanted. However, according to Hiss, Crosley never paid the rent, and in the end, "I finally decided it wasn't any use expecting to collect from him, that I had been a sucker and he was a sort of deadbeat; not a bad character, but I think he was just using me as a soft touch." Hiss also said that after ending his relationship with Crosley in 1935 (a date he later changed to mid-1936), he gave no more thought to the man until he realized that morning on the train to Washington to testify that "Crosley is the only person I know who has been in my house, who knows the layout of any house or apartment I lived in." At one point Nixon asked Hiss about his hobbies. When the witness mentioned bird-watching, McDowell asked, "Did you ever see a prothonotary warbler?" Yes, Hiss replied, "right here on the Potomac."

The scene in the HUAC hearing room on August 25, 1948. Chambers can be seen testifying at the lower right. Hiss is seated at the table two rows behind.

THE EXECUTIVE SESSION that followed Hiss's August 16 testimony was tense. HUAC's Democratic members wanted to let the Justice Department take over the investigation (and presumably protect Hiss, at least until after the election); the Republicans, however, wanted more, and they were in the majority. At first, the committee voted to have Chambers and Hiss confront one another in public on August 25. But this was switched to a private session on Tuesday, August 17, in New York City—changed, in Nixon's words so that Hiss wouldn't gain "nine more days to make his story fit the facts." At the August 17 hearing, Hiss was again defensive and irritable. After the Carnegie Endowment chief was sworn in, Chambers entered the hearing room from an adjoining room, where he had been asked to wait.

MR. NIXON: *Sit over here, Mr. Chambers. Mr. Chambers, will you please stand? And will you please stand, Mr. Hiss? Mr. Hiss, the man standing here is Mr. Whittaker Chambers. I ask you now if you have ever known this man before.*

MR. HISS: *May I ask him to speak? Will you ask him to say something?*

MR. NIXON: *Yes. Mr. Chambers, will you tell us your name and your business?*

MR. CHAMBERS: *My name is Whittaker Chambers. [Hiss walks over to Chambers.] I am senior editor of* Time *magazine.*

MR. HISS: *Are you George Crosley?*

MR. CHAMBERS: *Not to my knowledge. You are Alger Hiss, I believe.*

MR. HISS: *I certainly am.*

MR. CHAMBERS: *That was my recollection.*

After Chambers read from a magazine so that Hiss could listen to his speech pattern, Hiss announced that Chambers was probably the man he had known a s Crosley. Nixon and Stripling then pursued a lengthy series of questions that compared Hiss's version of the Crosley relationship to the information previously supplied by Chambers. Denying that Crosley had been more than a casual acquaintance, Hiss said, "He meant nothing to me." Chambers maintained that the two men had shared a secret bond: "I was a Communist, and you were a Communist." Although Hiss pointed out that "it was a quite different atmosphere in Washington then than today," he continued to claim that he had known Crosley only as a journalist.

THE NATION'S INTEREST had been piqued. The committee's next session, held on August 25, was jammed with reporters and televised live (a first for a congressional hearing). In the meantime, the other six people (in addition to Hiss) whom Chambers had named as members of the underground cell had all been called before the committee. All had invoked their Fifth Amendment rights, except Hiss's brother, Donald, who denied everything.

Accompanied by his lawyer, Alger Hiss treated the August 25 hearing as a legal proceeding. By then, he was certain that the HUAC members believed Chambers and were looking to develop evidence that the Justice Department could use to obtain a perjury indictment. Therefore, he was extremely cautious

At the August 25 hearing, Hiss counterattacked—reviewing his impressive fifteen-year record of public service, denouncing HUAC's investigation as a partisan political attack on liberal Democrats, and naming thirty-four prominent public figures as guarantors of his loyalty. Nixon later derided this effort by Hiss to prove his "innocence by association," an ironic phrase given HUAC's own reputation for determining guilt by association.

in his answers, qualifying nearly all of his responses with phrases such as "to the best of my recollection," which he used more than two hundred times. On several occasions, he accused the committee of pursuing Chambers's allegations for partisan political reasons—because his government career had been so closely associated with Democratic accomplishments, such as the New Deal, the Yalta agreements, and the United Nations.

The August 25 session lasted nine hours and did not go well for Hiss. The animosity that had been building between Hiss and Nixon finally came out into the open, and Nixon got the better of the exchange. Some of the most damaging testimony involved Hiss's old Ford car:

MR. NIXON: *Did you give Crosley a car?*
MR. HISS: *I gave Crosley, according to my best recollection—*
MR. NIXON: *You certainly can testify yes or no as to whether you gave Crosley a car. How many cars have you given away in your life, Mr. Hiss?*
MR. HISS: *I have had only one old car of a financial value of twenty-five dollars in my life. That is the car I let Crosley use.*
MR. NIXON: *My point now is, is your present testimony that you did or did not give Crosley a car?*
MR. HISS: *Whether I transferred title to him in a legal, formal sense; whether I gave him the car outright; whether the car came back—I don't know.*

According to Chambers biographer Sam Tanenhaus, as much as the Time *editor "abhorred the HUAC spectacle, he secretly welcomed the opportunity to give witness, to speak out directly as an 'I,' explaining what he had done and seen, after so many years of concealment.... Chambers leaned toward the microphone, sometimes clutching its base. In staccato sentences he reiterated, a touch hoarsely, the story he had been telling since August 3."*

UNFORTUNATELY FOR HISS, a title search revealed that he had transferred ownership of the car on July 23, 1936, to a Washington dealership, which had immediately resold the car (without issuing an invoice) to a man named William Rosen. This supported Chambers's description of the transaction as an inside deal. It also called into question Hiss's original testimony that he had ended his relationship with Crosley/Chambers in 1935. (The next day, Rosen, testifying in secret session, pleaded the Fifth.)

With the August 25 hearing now turning quite dramatically against him, Hiss went on the offensive, attacking Chambers's credibility. He claimed that, with access to *Time* magazine's excellent research department, Chambers could easily have discovered in such publications as *Who's Who* most of the personal information he had passed on to the committee. "Nobody could have read in *Who's Who* that you found a rare bird," Congressman Hébert retorted. Hiss then tried to explain that he had "told many, many people" of the warbler sighting, but his excuses failed to persuade the committee. Instead, Chambers appeared the more sympathetic figure, denying that he wanted to ruin Hiss and fighting back tears as he said softly, "The story has spread that in testifying against Mr. Hiss I am working out some old grudge, or motives of revenge or hatred. I do not hate Mr. Hiss. We were close friends, but we are caught in a tragedy of history. Mr. Hiss represents the concealed enemy against which we are all fighting and I am fighting."

By the time the committee adjourned its hearing at 8 P.M., Alger Hiss was in deep trouble. Three days later, HUAC issued an interim report describing Hiss's testimony as "vague and evasive" while characterizing Chambers's as "forthright and emphatic." In the committee's opinion, "the verifiable portions of Chambers's testimony have stood up strongly; the verifiable portions of Hiss's testimony have been badly shaken." As a result, many Americans, including a number of Democrats, no longer viewed *this* HUAC investigation as either a red herring or a witch hunt.

The First Red Scare

THROUGHOUT AMERICAN HISTORY, perceived threats to governmental institutions have periodically generated waves of hysteria, leaving social and political turmoil in their wake. The Salem witch trials were an early instance; another egregious example involved the persecution of Americans who opposed U.S. involvement in World War I. These victims included pacifists, Socialists, members of radical labor unions such as the Industrial Workers of the World (IWW), and German Americans.

To encourage zealous public support of the nation's war effort, Congress had created in April 1917 a massive propaganda agency, the Committee on Public Information (COPI), run by a former Progressive journalist, George Creel. Under Creel's enthusiastic leadership, the COPI distributed seventy-five million pieces of literature explaining the Wilson administration's idealistic war aims and denouncing alleged German battlefield atrocities. The COPI also paid for tens of thousands of speakers ("four-minute men") to tour the country, delivering brief speeches designed to rally prowar emotions. Creel was so successful that, within a few months, the war became enormously popular with most Americans. Yet Creel's work helped to unleash irrational hatreds and suspicions that menaced not only America's enemies in Europe but also anyone at home who might be considered "subversive" of the war effort. "Americanization" movements pressured recent immigrants to change their names, and many German-sounding words were also Anglicized. *Sauerkraut*, for example, became "Liberty cabbage."

Encouraged by the Wilson administration, Congress buttressed these popular efforts with legal sanctions designed to silence internal dissent. The most notorious of the new laws was the Espionage Act of June 1917, which mandated stiff jail sentences for Americans who revealed national defense information or interfered with the recruiting of troops. The act also punished all those who encouraged disloyalty or refused to perform military duty. In September 1918, Eugene V.

The Hun ~ his Mark
Blot it Out
with
LIBERTY
BONDS

This poster, designed by Allen St. John, was published in 1917.

Eugene V. Debs delivers a speech in Canton, Ohio, in 1918, not long before his imprisonment for violation of the Espionage Act.

Debs was sentenced to ten years in jail under the Espionage Act for delivering a speech in which he defended the Bolshevik Revolution, pacifism, and the Wobblies (as members of the IWW were called). Socialist congressman Victor Berger was sentenced to twenty years in jail for similar remarks, and nearly five hundred conscientious objectors were also imprisoned.

Libertarians challenged the Espionage Act, but in *Schenck v. U.S.* (1919), the Supreme Court upheld the statute's constitutionality. Writing for the majority, Oliver Wendell Holmes asserted that the principal question involved was whether the offensive words were of such a nature and used in such circumstances "as to create a clear and present danger that they will bring about the substantive evils that Congress has a right to prevent." Yet even Charles Schenck's alleged crime—the distribution of antidraft leaflets—did not appear to meet this standard. Others convicted under the Espionage Act similarly posed no immediate threat to the war effort. Neither traitors nor seditious, most were simply Americans who peacefully opposed their country's involvement in the war.

A FTER THE WAR'S END, the harassment of left-wing groups continued—with even less justification under Holmes's "clear and present danger" standard. The roots of repression could be traced to the high level of tension that still existed in the country. Millions of U.S. soldiers left Europe and returned home, where they found high unemployment, labor unrest, and widespread racial tensions. Meanwhile, the Bolsheviks consolidated their control in Russia, causing the focus of xenophobic hostility in the United States to shift from the so-called Huns of a defeated Germany to the alleged new Soviet threat. Wilson opposed Bolshevik participation at Versailles, and U.S. troops intervened several times between 1918 and 1920 in the Russian Civil War on the side of anti-Communist armies. The fear of revolutionary unrest at home was strong, which accounted for America's first Red Scare in 1919–1920.

Once Wilson's stroke paralyzed him in September 1919, leadership in the fight against "subversion" fell to Attorney General A. Mitchell Palmer. Old-stock Americans such as Palmer generally had difficulty distinguishing between supporters of Bolshevism (who favored armed revolution) and Socialists (who advocated gradual, peaceful change).

RIGHT: *Alexander Mitchell Palmer in 1913, while he was still a member of the U.S. House of Representatives from Pennsylvania.*

Palmer even had trouble telling Bolshevism and unionism apart. He also counted among his country's enemies Negroes, Jews, and women's rights advocates.

After mobilizing an army of government agents (foremost among them, J. Edgar Hoover), Palmer conducted in late 1919 and early 1920 a series of nation-wide raids, invading the homes, offices, and meeting places of tens of thousand of Americans. His favorite targets were immigrants, thousands of whom were illegally deported. Palmer hoped that such exploits would gain him the Democratic presidential nomination in 1920. In April, he warned that American Bolsheviks were planning a May Day revolt. State militias were called out and extra guards placed at key government buildings and the homes of important public officials. When nothing happened, an embarrassed Congress turned its attention away from radicalism and began investigating Palmer's own behavior instead. Yet the country's fear of political radicalism lingered and reasserted itself in the late 1940s as the Cold War with the Soviet Union intensified.

The Pumpkin Papers

THE NEXT ACT in the Hiss-Chambers "tragedy of history" took place on Friday evening, August 27. Chambers had agreed to appear on the radio news program *Meet the Press*, and an estimated twelve million listeners tuned in. Hiss had previously dared Chambers to repeat his charges outside the protective immunity of the congressional hearing room, and that night Chambers did so, stating again that "Alger Hiss was a Communist and may be now." Several weeks passed without a response from Hiss. His supporters grew impatient. "Mr. Hiss has created a situation," the liberal *Washington Post* complained, "in which he is obliged to put up or shut up." Finally, on September 27, Hiss filed suit for slander. By then, however, Harry Truman's remarkable surge in the 1948 presidential campaign had knocked the Hiss-Chambers case off the front pages, and with November's Democratic victories, a continuation of the HUAC investigation—even of HUAC itself—seemed unlikely.

Deeply depressed by Truman's November 2 reelection, Chambers grew anxious over the possibility that the Justice Department might now indict him (and not Hiss) for perjury. He even contemplated suicide. At this low point, when pressed by Hiss's attorneys for written proof of his charges and under severe emotional strain, Chambers decided finally to produce some incriminating documents that he had been withholding. He traveled to Brooklyn in mid-November 1948 to visit his wife's nephew, from whom he retrieved a sealed envelope that he had left for safekeeping with the nephew at the time of his break with the party. (Chambers, fearful at that time of assassination by Soviet agents, called the envelope's contents his "life preservers.") The envelope, hidden in a disused dumbwaiter shaft for ten years, contained some papers and five rolls of microfilm.

Chambers hid the microfilm and a few of the papers on his farm in Westminster, Maryland; the rest he presented to Hiss's lawyers at a deposition session on November 17. Dated between December 1937 and February 1938, the documents

John Edgar Hoover joined the Justice Department as a file reviewer in 1917. Two year later, he became a special assistant to Attorney General Palmer. At the time this photograph was taken in December 1924, Hoover had just been confirmed as director of the Justice Department's Bureau of Investigation (later the FBI).

included a large number of typed copies of State Department reports and memoranda, as well as transcriptions of diplomatic cables in Alger Hiss's handwriting. (Investigators later showed that the copied State Department documents had been produced on the Hisses' Woodstock-brand typewriter because they matched personal letters typed by Priscilla Hiss during the same period.) If genuine, as they appeared to be, the handwritten notes and typed papers were a bombshell. Not only did they demonstrate that Hiss had lied about ending his relationship with Crosley/Chambers in 1936, but they also suggested strongly that Hiss had been deeply involved in espionage.

CHAMBERS TOLD Hiss's lawyers that he had kept the papers hidden because "I was particularly anxious, for reasons of friendship, …not to do injury more than necessary to Mr. Hiss." The papers, he continued, "indicate a kind of activity, the revelation of which is somewhat different from anything I have testified about before."

Now Chambers confessed that he had been a Soviet spy from 1935 until 1938 and had acted as a courier for Hiss, who had been passing along secret State Department documents. (The three-year statute of limitations on espionage had already expired, but this new information left Chambers open to a perjury charge because he had told the committee that he had left the party in 1937 and not in April 1938, as the new evidence showed.) Hiss vigorously denied the espionage charge, and his lawyers grilled Chambers about contradictions between his previous story and the new testimony.

Meanwhile, attorneys for both sides agreed that the new evidence had to be turned over to the Justice Department. Criminal Division head Alexander Campbell warned all parties involved in the slander suit not to discuss the contents of the envelope until the material had been investigated. (At this time, neither Campbell nor Hiss nor anyone other than Chambers knew of the microfilm.) Nevertheless, one of Chambers's lawyers leaked what had happened to Stripling and Nixon. The next day, December 1, Stripling served Chambers with a subpoena demanding that he relinquish any other evidence in his possession. On December 2, Chambers drove with two HUAC investigators to his Maryland farm, where he led them to a pumpkin patch and removed from a hollowed-out gourd the withheld microfilm. The filmstrips contained even more stolen State Department documents. "What is this, Dick Tracy?" one of the astounded HUAC men exclaimed.

Beginning December 6, the Justice Department called both Hiss and Chambers several times before a federal grand jury sitting in New York City. HUAC also began a new round of hearings. At one of the sessions, Assistant Secretary of State John Peurifoy (in charge of security for the State Department) testified that any foreign country possessing the documents shown on the microfilm would have been able to break every U.S. diplomatic code then in use.

Stripling and Nixon inspect on December 6 the microfilm recovered from Chambers's farm. Two days earlier, Nixon had been aboard a Panama-bound cruise ship with his wife when the Pumpkin Papers story broke and a Coast Guard seaplane was sent to fetch him. The urgent summons was something of a charade, however. Nixon had ordered the Chambers subpoena himself and had told the House doorkeeper as he left on December 2, "I'm going out to sea, and they're going to send for me."

The Trials of Alger Hiss

CLEARLY, THE HOUSE UN-AMERICAN Activities Committee—which the lame-duck Republicans would control for only a few more weeks—had no legal authority to indict Hiss. Only the Justice Department could do that. Yet the publicity generated by the Pumpkin Papers ensured that the investigation (and the committee) would continue after the change in House leadership the following month. Nixon made doubly sure by asserting in the press that the committee "did not trust the Justice Department to prosecute the case with the vigor it deserved." On December 10, *Time* accepted Chambers's resignation. On December 13, Hiss took a three-month paid leave of absence from the Carnegie Endowment (he never returned). On December 15, the federal grand jury in New York indicted Hiss on two counts of perjury: for denying he had transmitted stolen State Department records to Chambers and for stating that he had not seen Chambers since January 1, 1937.

Hiss's first perjury trial began on June 1, 1949. Federal prosecutor Thomas Murphy introduced evidence to show that Hiss had been a Communist, that he and Chambers had known one another after 1936, and that he had stolen the State Department documents in question. Chambers testified at length, describing Hiss's recruitment during the fall of 1936 and his activities as a Communist agent through April 1938, when Chambers broke with the party and ended his relationship with Hiss. The documents, however, were the heart of the case against Hiss—"immutable witnesses," Murphy called them. An FBI expert testified that they had unquestionably been typed on the Hisses' Woodstock machine. The defense never challenged his testimony because several of their own experts had reached the same conclusion. Instead, Hiss claimed vaguely that he and his wife had given away the Woodstock sometime earlier.

The first trial ended on July 8 with a hung jury, deadlocked at eight to four in favor of conviction. The government retried the case in November, with Murphy again serving as prosecutor. As at the first trial, Hiss's lawyers paraded a distinguished group of public officials before the jury, all of whom testified to Hiss's outstanding personal character and service to his country. The defense also tried to undermine Chambers's credibility by calling two psychiatrists, one of whom described him as "a psychopathic personality" with irrational tendencies. Murphy ridiculed these defense efforts, pointing repeatedly to the evidence that Hiss's lawyers could never adequately explain: the stolen government documents. Overlooking some minor inconsistencies in Chambers's testimony, the jury at the second trial voted unanimously to convict Hiss on January 21, 1950.

Chambers arrives by subway on June 3, 1949, at the New York City federal courthouse. He had been called to Foley Square that day to testify at Hiss's first perjury trial.

TO U.S. COURT HOUSE

"Such pipsqueaks as Nixon and McCarthy are trying to get us so frightened of Communism that we'll be afraid to turn out the lights at night."

—

Helen Gahagan Douglas, 1950

AT HIS SENTENCING on January 25, Hiss received the maximum: five years in federal prison for each count, the sentences to run concurrently. He eventually served forty-four months, emerging from prison in November 1954. Now a convicted perjurer (and de facto spy), he couldn't return to public service. Instead, he held an assortment of obscure business jobs, wrote a book presenting his side of the story, and worked continuously to revive public interest in his case. Because it was the Hiss case that first made Richard Nixon famous, the matter received some renewed attention during the Watergate crisis, but this was short lived. In November 1996, Hiss died, still protesting his innocence. Meanwhile, Chambers retired to his farm in Maryland and completed a best-selling 1952 memoir, *Witness*, which became a central text for American conservatives in the half century that followed. He died of a heart attack in July 1961.

Richard Nixon used his new fame to obtain his party's nomination in 1950 for a Senate seat from California. His opponent in that race was Democratic congresswoman Helen Gahagan Douglas, whom Nixon dubbed the Pink Lady in order to call attention to her alleged "softness" on Communism. One of Nixon's most effective tactics was to distribute "pink sheets" that compared Douglas's liberal voting record to the stated goals of the Communist party. (It was during this campaign that Democrats first began calling Nixon Tricky Dick.) Once elected, he served on the Senate's Permanent Investigations Subcommittee, then chaired by Sen. Joseph R. McCarthy of Wisconsin. A year later, Nixon's outspoken criticism of the Truman administration and his continued warnings against unwarranted Communist influence in government won him a spot on the Republicans' 1952 national ticket with World War II hero Dwight D. Eisenhower.

Until February 9, 1950, Joseph McCarthy had been an obscure Republican senator, elected largely on the basis of a self-inflated war record. That evening, however, less than three weeks after Hiss's conviction, McCarthy gave a speech in Wheeling, West Virginia, that ended his obscurity. "I have here in my hand," McCarthy announced, "a list of 205 people known to be members of the Communist party and who, nevertheless, are still working and shaping the policy of the State Department." Although even the junior senator from Wisconsin had no idea at the time, this speech formally inaugurated a new period of anti-Communist hysteria in the United States—a second Red Scare.

Who Lost China?

IN ADDITION TO THE HISS CASE, other recent developments in international affairs contributed to the media and public attention given McCarthy's charges. The most important of these was the victory in the Chinese civil war of Mao Tse-tung's Communist army over the Nationalist forces of Chiang Kai-shek. Beginning in August 1945, both the Communists and the Nationalists had raced to fill the power vacuum left by the surrender of Japan. At first, each side had consolidated its own strength, avoiding armed conflict as much as possible; in late 1946, however, the fighting became generalized throughout China. During 1947 and early 1948, the Nationalists held the advantage; but major Communist victories in late 1948 and throughout 1949 forced Chiang and his allies into exile on the island of Formosa (later Taiwan). Meanwhile, on the mainland, Mao established the People's Republic of China on October 1.

Chiang Kai-shek addresses his troops in 1942 or 1943. The war against the Japanese temporarily united the Nationalists and the Communists. With the defeat of Japan, however, the Chinese civil war resumed.

In Washington, the question became, Who Lost China? Republicans blamed the Truman administration, repeating their now-familiar charge that Democrats were "soft" on Communism. Truman reacted angrily, insisting that the Nationalists had lost not because of a lack of American support but because of Chiang's military and political inadequacies. Yet the president's denials did little to silence Republican critics, who continued to blame Truman and Secretary of State Dean Acheson publicly and personally for the "loss" of China.

In fact, Truman was far from soft. Despite assurances from the FBI that the security situation was well under control, the president had issued in March 1947 an executive order setting up review boards in every government department and agency to investigate the "loyalty" of federal employees. During the next five years, these loyalty boards investigated 6.5 million people. No cases of espionage were uncovered, although 490 government workers were dismissed and thousands more had their careers ruined because of reckless allegations.

DIPLOMATICALLY, the United States refused to recognize China's new Communist government. Soon enough, however, Americans would confront the Chinese army in combat. The battleground would be the Korean Peninsula. General Order No. 1—drafted on August 11, 1945—had outlined the Japanese surrender terms for Korea: Japanese troops north of the thirty-eighth parallel would surrender to the Soviets; Japanese troops south of that line would give themselves up to the Americans. Thus Korea was partitioned, and separate governments were established in the North and South. During 1949, South Korea began to form its own hundred-thousand-man army, and by late June the last of the U.S. occupation forces were gone. Meanwhile, North Korea established a much larger military, and on June 25, 1950, its forces invaded the South.

This 1949 poster celebrates the founding of the People's Republic of China on October 1 of that year. It says, "The central people's government constitutes the only legitimate government of all the people of the People's Republic of China."

LSTs (the military acronym for "landing ship, tank") unload men and equipment during MacArthur's September 15, 1950, amphibious landing at Inchon, South Korea.

The next day (though still June 25 in New York City), the UN Security Council approved a resolution condemning the North Korean invasion as "an action of aggression" and urging all UN member nations to help restore the peace. (The Soviet Union failed to veto this resolution aimed at its client state, because it was absent from the Security Council; its delegation was boycotting UN proceedings to protest the fact that Mao's government hadn't been granted China's seat in the General Assembly.) On June 27, President Truman authorized U.S. air and sea forces to resist Communist aggression in South Korea; that same day, the Security Council approved UN military aid as well. The first of 1.8 million U.S. ground troops reached the battlefield on July 4. Three days later, Gen. Douglas MacArthur, who had been supervising the occupation of Japan, was named supreme commander of all U.S. and UN forces.

The North Koreans kept advancing throughout July until they had overrun all of South Korea except for a small beachhead around the southeastern city of Pusan—the "Pusan perimeter." On September 15, MacArthur counterattacked at Inchon, a port on the west coast of South Korea, just outside Seoul. His masterful amphibious landing behind enemy lines trapped thousands of North Korean soldiers and caused the rest to flee north in panic. On September 27, the Joint Chiefs of Staff ordered MacArthur to eliminate the North Korean army; two days later, the president authorized him to pursue the enemy across the thirty-eighth parallel into North Korea itself. On October 20, UN forces reached the North Korean capital at Pyongyang, and a week later, they neared the Yalu River, which separated North Korea from China. Unwilling to tolerate hostile forces so close to its border, the Chinese government intervened massively in early November, using such overwhelming force that its army pushed the UN troops all the way back to the thirty-eighth parallel. In fact, the Chinese offensive wasn't stopped until mid-January, when MacArthur launched a counteroffensive with limited success.

Frustrated by the limitations placed on him by political necessity, MacArthur publicly recommended extending the war into China (and privately demanded that he be permitted to use nuclear weapons). Quite reasonably, Truman interpreted the general's statements as a challenge to his own authority. Therefore, he dismissed MacArthur on April 11, 1951; yet he and his party paid a political price. The 1952 Republican platform attacked the Democrats for not resisting Communism in Korea and elsewhere as strongly as they should have, while praising Eisenhower and Nixon for their determination to resist the Red menace. Not content to contain Communism, the Republicans seemed prepared in 1952 to advocate active efforts to reclaim the countries of Eastern Europe now under Soviet control.

McCarthyism

THE FACT THAT SECRETARY OF STATE Acheson had been a strong defender of Alger Hiss created political problems for the Truman administration and political opportunities for Joe McCarthy. It didn't matter that McCarthy had never produced any genuine list of State Department subversives; it didn't even matter that he kept changing the number of names on this imaginary list from one speech to the next. With China gone and U.S. soldiers dying in Korea, most Americans had little doubt that the Communists hoped to injure the United States by any means available, including treachery. Much regrettable behavior was justified in the name of this perceived yet largely overblown threat.

There were, of course, Soviet spies working in the United States during the 1940s and 1950s, many quite successfully. The most famous of these were Julius Rosenberg, a machine shop owner in his early thirties, and his wife, Ethel. Through British scientist Klaus Fuchs, an admitted atomic spy, the FBI tracked down David Greenglass, an army sergeant who had been stationed during the war at the secret Manhattan Project laboratory in Los Alamos, New Mexico. Greenglass had provided information about the bomb to Soviet agents, having been recruited for the task by his wife and by the Rosenbergs (his sister and brother-in-law). FBI agents arrested the couple in July 1950; at their spring 1951 trial, Greenglass appeared as the chief government witness, receiving a reduced prison sentence and immunity for his wife. Julius and Ethel Rosenberg were both convicted and sentenced to death. They were executed on June 19, 1953.

In Washington, Sens. Margaret Chase Smith of Maine and Ralph Flanders of Vermont objected to McCarthy's exponentially expanding charges and denounced their Republican colleague publicly on the floor of the Senate. Yet McCarthy was proving himself so useful to the party that most other Republicans, whether they found his tactics distasteful or not, chose to let him continue savaging the Democrats. Most polls showed that a majority of Americans tolerated McCarthy's braggadocio and applauded his relentless search for subversives in government.

LIKE MANY successful demagogues, McCarthy made use of what journalist Richard H. Rovere called "the multiple untruth"; that is, his allegations grew so complex that refuting them became extremely difficult. In other ways as well, his methods were tried and true. Nixon and others gave McCarthy access to HUAC files and even tutored him in the aggressive tactics for which the committee had become famous.

The Truman administration also spent much of its last two years in office conducting a hunt for subversives. In addition to the ongoing executive branch loyalty reviews (which spilled over into the private sector, especially at universities and within the entertainment industry), the Justice Department successfully prosecuted eleven leaders of the American Communist party under the 1940 Smith Act,

Ethel and Julius Rosenberg leave federal court in New York City on August 23, 1950, after being indicted on charges of espionage. Prosecutors later asserted that their atomic spy ring had sped up by years the development of Soviet nuclear weapons.

which prohibited Americans from advocating the desirability of overthrowing the government by force. After their October 1949 conviction was upheld by the Supreme Court in June 1951, more Communists were arrested. Meanwhile, such episodes persuaded Congress to enact stronger laws intended to protect the nation against domestic Communism. The September 1950 McCarran Internal Security Act compelled all Communist organizations (and their members) to register with the attorney general. It also barred Communists from working in defense-related industries; from becoming naturalized citizens, if aliens; and from using their U.S. passports, if citizens.

By the time Dwight D. Eisenhower made it known in January 1952 that he would accept the Republican nomination for president, perhaps any Republican could have been elected. But Eisenhower, the orchestrator of Operation Overlord and the most popular man in America, was as close as a candidate could come to a sure thing. After his election in November 1952, however, Eisenhower found that the activities of his party's extreme right wing were seriously interfering with his ability to govern.

Sen. Joseph R. McCarthy consults with aides David Schine (left) and Roy Cohn (right) during the Army-McCarthy hearings in mid-1954. When critics attacked the methods McCarthy used to "expose" alleged Communists, the Wisconsin senator often responded by accusing the critics of being Communists, too.

McCarthy was a particular irritant. For example, the marauding Wisconsin senator had challenged Eisenhower's nomination of career diplomat Charles E. Bohlen to be U.S. ambassador to the Soviet Union because Bohlen had been Roosevelt's interpreter at Yalta. (Bohlen was nevertheless confirmed by the Senate.)

DURING ITS FIRST YEAR in office, the Eisenhower administration tried to accommodate the senator. In early 1954, however, a dispute developed over McCarthy's investigation into subversion at Fort Monmouth, New Jersey (where an army dentist accused of being a Communist had nevertheless been promoted). The army's reluctance to cooperate with McCarthy had prompted the senator to accuse Army Secretary Robert Stevens of "coddling" Communists within his service. On April 22, the Senate began public hearings into the matter. McCarthy plied his usual trade in half-truths and innuendo, while the army counterattacked with its own charge that McCarthy had sought favors for a recently drafted aide, David Schine.

The lengthy televised hearings eventually exposed the senator as a reckless bully. The denouement came on June 9, when army lawyer Joseph N. Welch took on McCarthy personally. The proximate cause was a menacing aspersion McCarthy had just cast on a young Welch assistant. "Until this moment, Senator," Welch responded with dignified fury, "I think I never really gauged your cruelty or your recklessness.... Have you no decency, sir, at long last? Have you left no sense of decency?"

As a direct result of these televised hearings, McCarthy's influence in the Senate and the country quickly declined, encouraged by Eisenhower's offstage maneuverings. In December 1954, McCarthy's fellow senators voted to censure him for "conduct unbecoming a member." He died in May 1957 of complications related to his cirrhosis of the liver. Yet McCarthyist blacklisting continued well into the 1960s, with many Americans suffering because twenty years earlier they had innocently (and legally) attended meetings or joined groups that, often without their knowledge, had some hidden Communist connection.

The Election of 1960

MOST AMERICANS, however, entered the 1960s with a remarkably positive, confident outlook, sure of their purpose as well as their power. Both presidential candidates in 1960 held similar views regarding America's place in the world—yet Massachusetts senator John F. Kennedy, more than Vice President Richard Nixon, recognized and responded to the country's desire for vigorous young leadership. Because Eisenhower had been a remarkably popular president, the election was close. In fact, had Ike been a little less tentative in his endorsement of Nixon, the vice president would probably have won. Instead, Kennedy captured one of the closest presidential elections ever, defeating Nixon by 118,000 votes, or just 0.2 percent of the popular tally.

During the campaign, Kennedy had labeled his program the New Frontier, and in his inaugural address, he trumpeted the theme of rejuvenation:

Nixon's running mate in 1960 was Henry Cabot Lodge, grandson of the Massachusetts senator who defeated the Versailles Treaty.

> *Let the word go forth from this time and place, to friend and foe alike, that the torch has been passed to a new generation of Americans—born in this century, tempered by war, disciplined by a hard and bitter peace, proud of our ancient heritage—and unwilling to witness or permit the slow undoing of those human rights to which this nation has always been committed, and to which we are committed today at home and around the world.*
>
> *Let every nation know, whether it wishes us well or ill, that we shall pay any price, bear any burden, meet any hardship, support any friend, oppose any foe, in order to assure the survival and the success of liberty.*
>
> *This much we pledge— and more.*

Pres. John F. Kennedy delivers his January 20, 1961, inaugural address from the steps of the Capitol's West Portico.

A sense of promise and hope was felt strongly that day, as the new forty-three-year-old chief executive—the first U.S. president born in the twentieth century—called on his fellow Americans to "bear the burden of a long twilight struggle, year in and year out, …against the common enemies of man: tyranny, poverty, disease, and war itself." Few Americans doubted on January 20, 1961, that their country was up to the task.

AMERICAN PROFILE

Lillian Hellman

1905–1984

by Alice Kessler-Harris

L ILLIAN HELLMAN IMAGINED herself as someone passionately committed to the simple human values of honor, loyalty, and social justice. When pushed, she could sum these up in a single word: *decency*.

Until the early 1950s, Hellman, arguably one of the midcentury's great playwrights, explored these values in half a dozen beautifully crafted dramas and screenplays. *The Children's Hour* (1934), *The Little Foxes* (1939), and *Autumn Garden* (1951) became, each in its turn, icons of the American theater and films as well. Rewarded with a place among the literati of her day, Hellman reaped the material comforts that enabled her to dress well, divide her time between city and country houses, and entertain with legendary warmth and generosity. Like many members of her generation, she acted on her impulse for social justice by participating in left-wing and Communist-inspired causes of various sorts. In the late 1940s, however, when Hollywood moguls began blacklisting writers, actors, and others suspected of Communist sympathies, Hellman found herself struggling with the meaning of honor and justice in her own life.

Called before the House Committee on Un-American Activities on May 21, 1952, Hellman wrote a famously controversial letter to the committee chair in which she volunteered to testify freely about her own past if the committee would agree not to ask her to identify others with whom she had been involved. "I was raised in an old-fashioned American tradition," she wrote, "and there were certain homely things that were taught to me: to try to tell the truth, not to bear false witness, not to harm my neighbor, to be loyal to my country, and so on." She asked the committee to respect these "simple rules of human decency" and allow her to testify only about herself. The attention drawn to this letter (which became public when the committee chair introduced it into the congressional record) got Hellman off the hook. She was treated lightly when she invoked the Fifth Amendment to deflect repeated prodding about her past associations. Yet her stance, and her subsequent defense of it, did produce a vitriolic debate about whether she had herself acted with decency.

Hellman claimed that others could have done what she did: that there was no excuse for the "friendly witness" who gave the committee the names of others. Eloquently, she attacked those, especially liberals with a shared commitment to social justice, who had gone before the committee with "a little breast-beating, a little apology." She would never understand, she said later, why members of the intellectual community did not resist these incursions on their integrity.

In turn, Hellman was attacked for refusing to acknowledge the human cost of Stalinism and for her failure to denounce the inhumanity of an economic system that deprived individuals of intellectual freedom. While she offered herself up as a model of integrity, her critics charged, she had obscured her own commitment to the left. She accused others of lacking an honesty that she herself had betrayed. By the mid- and late 1970s, many of Hellman's former friends and admirers charged her with outright fabrication: with aggrandizing her own actions in ways that diminished the roles of her friends and allies—and even with making up stories about her own life out of whole cloth. The champion of honesty countered these accusations with social snubs and libel suits.

Hellman always insisted that she reserved her most fervent admiration for those willing to live by their beliefs: for those who refused to do "the indecent thing" in order to save their own skins.

Yet the McCarthy period in American history posed a tragic dilemma for those who sought both to act decently and to acknowledge at long last that they had worshiped a dishonorable idol. Acting decently in the face of an indecent interlocutor required that witnesses hide, even from themselves, certain complicated truths about their pasts; yet without the confession of these truths, repentance could not proceed.

Hellman in December 1935.

22

PAX AMERICANA

The Cuban Missile Crisis

FOR THIRTEEN DAYS in October 1962, the United States and the Soviet Union confronted one another in nuclear combat readiness. Given the state of nuclear weaponry at the time, there were probably half a billion people in danger. A year earlier, the Department of Defense had estimated that an all-out war with the Soviets would produce 120 million American casualties. A like number of Soviets would also die, along with the bulk of the populations of Europe and Canada. If the war spread to China, of course, the final death toll would run incalculably higher.

The crisis began on Sunday, October 14, when cloud cover over Cuba broke long enough for an American U-2 high-altitude spy plane, making a regular reconnaissance flight, to photograph some new construction in Cuba's remote western highlands. That day, Pres. John F. Kennedy had traveled to Indiana to campaign against Republican senator Homer Capehart, who was up for reelection in three weeks. Capehart's repeated assertions that the Soviets planned to install offensive weapons on Cuba had been particularly annoying to the president, who ridiculed the possibility and considered Capehart's grandstanding a political obstacle to enactment of the administration's domestic agenda. When the president returned to the White House around 2 A.M. Monday, analysts inside the National Photographic Information Center were still developing and assessing the film the U-2 had shot. Their work proceeded slowly. Finally,

at eight o'clock the next evening, they concluded that the pictures showed eight ballistic missile launch pads being built on the edge of the Sierra del Rosario in west-central Cuba.

The head of the Defense Intelligence Agency dispatched two officers to notify his superior, Deputy Secretary of Defense Roswell Gilpatric, who relayed the information immediately to the president's special assistant for national security affairs, McGeorge Bundy. At eight forty-five the next morning—Tuesday, October 16—Bundy took the photographs to the president. "Mr. President," he said, "there is now hard photographic evidence, which you will see, that the Russians have offensive missiles in Cuba." All Kennedy saw at first was a construction site; after being briefed, however, he understood that the images showed launch sites for medium-range ballistic missiles, capable of carrying nuclear warheads more than six hundred miles.

IN HIS TWENTY-ONE months as president, Kennedy had become intimately familiar with "the Cuban question." Campaigning in 1960 as a dynamic alternative to the bland Eisenhower years, he had blamed the Republicans for the creation of a Communist state in Cuba, just as the Republicans had blamed Harry Truman for "losing" China. In office, however, Kennedy had learned that plans were already in place for the retaking of Cuba. With President Eisenhower's approval, the Central Intelligence Agency had been training and supplying an army of fifteen hundred anti-Castro exiles; now Kennedy could either endorse the plan or kill it. Heeding the counsel of his military advisers (and because he had advocated this sort of scheme as

AT LEFT: *Members of Women Strike for Peace* *demonstrate near UN headquarters in New York City* *during the Cuban Missile Crisis.*

*The original
U-2A high-altitude
reconnaissance plane,
first deployed in
August 1955, had
a wing span of 80
feet and a ceiling of
eighty-five thousand
feet. This U-2R
model, introduced
in 1967, had a
wingspan of 103 feet.*

*One of the
photographs taken
by the U-2 that
overflew Cuba on
October 14, 1962.
On a follow-up
mission two weeks
later, the plane's
pilot, Maj. Rudolf
Anderson Jr., was
shot down and killed.*

a candidate), Kennedy told the CIA to proceed. Just as John Brown had expected a mass slave uprising to follow his Harpers Ferry raid, the American planners of the invasion and their counterparts among the Cuban exiles believed that, once the exiles landed at the Bay of Pigs on Cuba's southwestern coast, a third of Fidel Castro's army would desert the Communists and join them. Another third, it was estimated, would simply desert, and the remaining third would be unable to withstand the exiles' attack.

The April 1961 invasion, however, proved to be a military and political disaster. CIA officials had promised the exiles U.S. naval and air support should they encounter strong opposition; but Kennedy, eager to limit U.S. involvement, refused to authorize either. Cuban troops remained loyal, fought well, and easily routed the exiles, capturing the last of them within seventy-two hours. A year later, eleven hundred survivors were ransomed with fifty-three million dollars in U.S. food and medical supplies.

Because the exile army had traveled to Cuba from Puerto Cabeza, Nicaragua—where it had been mobilized with the permission of Nicaraguan dictator Anastasio Somoza Debayle—the State Department at first tried to deny U.S. involvement. Within a few days, however, the truth came out: The United States had been caught trying to remove the government of another country—and, worse still, doing so clumsily and ineffectually. Although most of the invasion planning had been carried out under Eisenhower, President Kennedy was left with little choice but to assume full responsibility for the fiasco.

The failure at the Bay of Pigs severely undermined the president's faith in the wisdom of his military, yet it hardly diminished his resolve to "take Cuba away from Castro." In late 1961—under the direction of his brother, the attorney general—Kennedy had established Operation Mongoose, whose goal was the overthrow of the Castro regime. Later, the Kennedy administration developed three full-scale invasion plans. Beginning on October 6, 1962, more than one hundred thousand U.S. troops, prepositioned at bases from North Carolina to Key West, were ready on eight days' notice to overrun Cuba. An October 8 memorandum written by Defense Secretary Robert McNamara outlined several scenarios under which the president might conceivably give the order to proceed. The first was "the positioning of [Soviet] offensive weapons on Cuban soil," though Kennedy himself still discounted this possibility. In fact, Soviet premier Nikita S. Khrushchev had recently assured Kennedy personally that no offensive weapons would be placed on Cuba in the foreseeable future.

The Executive Committee

ONCE BUNDY HAD FINISHED briefing Kennedy on the missile sites, the president told him to set up a meeting for later that Tuesday morning in the Cabinet Room. He rattled off the names of fourteen top officials whose

MRBM FIELD LAUNCH SITE
SAN CRISTOBAL NO 1
14 OCTOBER 1962

ERECTOR LAUNCHER EQUIPMENT

TENT AREAS

EQUIPMENT

ERECTOR LAUNCHER EQUIPMENT

8 MISSILE TRAILERS

CONSTRUCTION

CUBA

AFTER THE U.S. OCCUPATION ended in 1902, Cuba was governed by a series of increasingly corrupt administrations, each supported in turn by the lucrative U.S. sugar trade. Tourism, essentially hotels and casinos, also enriched Cuba's economic elite, as well as many American mobsters. In the Cuban countryside, however, the poverty was appalling, and the extreme governmental neglect helped Fidel Castro build during the mid-1950s a guerrilla movement strong enough to overthrow Cuban dictator Fulgencio Batista.

When the Fidelistas took control of the Cuban government on January 1, 1959, the State Department wasn't quite sure what to make of Castro. Yet the company he kept—including Argentine revolutionary Ernesto "Che" Guevara—made the Eisenhower administration suspicious. As the Cuban government

became increasingly dominated by Communists, and Castro moved to nationalize hundreds of millions of dollars' worth of property belonging to American citizens, the CIA began making plans for an invasion. Meanwhile, Castro steadily strengthened his relationship with the Soviet Union.

Fidelistas wave their rifles in front of the presidential palace in Havana after Batista's ouster.

participation he wanted, starting with his brother. Although the size and composition of this new Executive Committee of the National Security Council (known as Ex Comm, for short) would fluctuate over the next two weeks, its key members included Robert F. Kennedy, McNamara, Gilpatric, Bundy, Vice Pres. Lyndon B. Johnson, Secretary of State Dean Rusk, Treasury Secretary Douglas Dillon, CIA director John McCone, Joint Chiefs of Staff chairman Maxwell Taylor, Assistant Secretary of Defense Paul Nitze, UN ambassador Adlai Stevenson, and former secretary of state Dean Acheson.

McNamara, Rusk, and Taylor had already been up most of the night, working with their staffs to develop diplomatic and military options. Everyone in the room agreed that the missiles had to go, one way or another. Cuba's proximity to the United States (as well as to Central and South America) meant that U.S. forces would have virtually no warning should nuclear missiles ever be launched from there. Furthermore, because Pentagon planners had never anticipated a nuclear threat to the south, all of America's radar and antiaircraft resources faced north to detect and intercept Soviet planes and missiles flying over the North Pole. The presence of nuclear weapons in Cuba was simply not a situation that any U.S. government could tolerate under any circumstances.

Khrushchev understood this well, yet had he chosen to build secret missile bases in Cuba—taking an extraordinary risk—because he also knew how far behind the United States the Soviets had fallen in the accelerating nuclear arms race. Although Kennedy had denounced the Eisenhower administration during the 1960 campaign for allowing the Soviets to move ahead in intercontinental ballistic missile (ICBM) technology, his "missile gap" charge had no credence.

> "I guess this is the week I earn my salary."
>
> —
> *John F. Kennedy, remark to Dean Acheson, October 19, 1962*

The Soviets might have astounded the world (and frightened Americans) with their successful launch of Sputnik, the earth's first artificial satellite, in October 1957. And cosmonaut Yuri Gagarin's orbital flight less than four years later was another impressive scientific accomplishment. Yet in nuclear weapons, the

Members of the Ex Comm convene on October 29. Clockwise from President Kennedy: McNamara, Gilpatric, Taylor, Nitze, United States Information Agency deputy director Don Wilson, speechwriter Theodore Sorensen, Bundy (obscured), Dillon, Johnson (obscured), Robert Kennedy, former ambassador to the Soviet Union Llewellyn Thompson, U.S. Arms Control and Disarmament Agency director William C. Foster, McCone (obscured), Undersecretary of State George Ball, and Rusk.

Soviets were far, far behind the Americans. During the first Ex Comm meeting, Kennedy had asked, "What is the reason for the Russians to set this up...? It must be that they're not satisfied with their ICBMs." To which Rusk responded, "Khrushchev knows that we have a substantial nuclear superiority.... We don't really live under the fear of his nuclear weapons to the extent that he has to live under fear of ours."

In October 1962, the United States had approximately five thousand deliverable nuclear weapons. These included 156 land-based ICBMs and 144 Polaris missiles, capable of being fired from submerged nuclear submarines. The rest were in the form of nuclear bombs that would be delivered to their targets by the 1,300 aircraft of the Strategic Air Command (SAC). (One-third of SAC's bomber force was armed and in the air at all times.) In comparison, U.S. intelligence estimated that the Soviet Union had only three hundred deliverable weapons, and even these were of inferior quality. The 75 ICBMs in the Soviet arsenal had guidance systems so primitive that no one on either side expected them to hit anywhere near their intended targets. The Soviets also had 97 short-range submarine-launched missiles, but their subs had to surface first (and become vulnerable) before they could fire. A Soviet missile base in Cuba, therefore, would substantially remediate the balance of nuclear power. In fact, on the basis of such new strength, Khrushchev might even demand U.S. concessions in other parts of the world, such as the withdrawal of American forces from Europe.

E X COMM DELIBERATED all that day and every day throughout the crisis. Usually, the president was elsewhere. He was determined to keep U.S. knowledge of the missile bases secret until an appropriate response could be formulated, so he kept to his regular public schedule, meeting with foreign dignitaries and campaigning for Democratic candidates in the upcoming 1962 midterm elections. His brother generally kept him informed with regard to each day's deliberations. On this first morning, however, the president had his own questions. "How long have we got...how long before it can be fired?" There was a pause before CIA deputy director Marshall Carter answered, "Two weeks. Maybe one." Next, he asked for Rusk's recommendation. "I don't think we can sit still," the secretary of state replied. "I think that, by and large, there are these two broad alternatives: one, the quick strike; the other, to alert our allies and Mr. Khrushchev that there is an utterly serious crisis in the making here, and that, facing a situation that could well lead to general war; that we have an obligation to do what has to be done but do it in a way that gives everybody a chance to…back down."

Next, McNamara gave his assessment:

There are two propositions I would suggest. My first is that, if we are to conduct an air strike, we must agree now that we will schedule that prior to the time these missile sites become operational. Because, if they become operational before the air strike, I do not believe we can knock them out before they can be launched. Secondly, I would submit the proposition that any air strike must be directed not solely against the missile sites, but against the missile sites plus the airfields plus the aircraft which may not be on the airfields but hidden by that time, plus all potential nuclear storage sites. A fairly extensive air strike.

After an hour of discussion, the president left the meeting inclined to remove the missiles and the bases with an air strike, but he wanted to hear more. For the rest of Tuesday afternoon and all of Wednesday, October 17, Ex Comm met at the State Department, where such a gathering would attract less attention than at the White House. The group considered diplomatic options first, but these were deemed inadequate and likely to delay matters long enough for the missile bases to become operational. Maxwell Taylor and the rest of the Pentagon brass wanted to send in bombers, but they acknowledged that even the eight hundred sorties they were recommending would likely destroy only 90 percent of the missiles. Furthermore, Llewellyn Thompson, former ambassador to the Soviet Union and the group's Kremlinologist, warned that Soviet technicians would likely be killed in such a raid and that Khrushchev's response could not be safely predicted. An invasion was also discussed, both as a stand-alone operation and as a follow-up to air raids. The toll in both Cuban and American lives, it was believed, would be high.

The Blockade

THE MOST IMPASSIONED OPPOSITION to the bombing and invasion options came from the president's closest adviser, his brother Robert. Although the attorney general was still in his late thirties and inexperienced in global affairs, his intimate relationship with his brother added great weight to his comments. A "sneak attack," Robert Kennedy argued persistently, failed to honor the nation's military traditions and would also hurt its standing overseas. As British ambassador David Ormsby-Gore told the president at one point during the crisis, other countries had little sympathy for the sense of entitlement that Americans felt toward their complete, ocean-guarded security. Other governments wouldn't perceive the Soviet missiles in Cuba as a significant threat to the United States and would consider any military response an egregious overreaction. "My brother is not going to be the Tojo of the 1960s," Robert Kennedy said. Instead, the attorney general argued for an intermediate measure: a blockade of Cuba to keep out further deliveries of missiles while the situation was resolved.

The Strategic Air Command tests one of its Atlas ICBMs in 1963.

A decisive moment came on Friday, October 19, when Treasury Secretary Dillon, a Republican who had been undersecretary of state for economic affairs in the Eisenhower administration, changed his mind. At first, Dillon had joined the older members of Ex Comm in favoring bombing. As historian Richard Reeves has pointed out, "He had a bit of contempt for Kennedy's new boys, calculating that the men around the table, talking about the possibility of nuclear war for the first time, were more frightened than men like himself, Acheson, McCone, and Nitze. The older hands had thought the unthinkable before. The new boys, he thought, did not comprehend the true extent of U.S. military superiority, nor did they understand that the Soviets were more afraid than they were, for good and simple reasons."

By Friday, however, Dillon found himself swayed by Robert Kennedy's emotional arguments for the blockade, especially by his repeated references to sneak attacks and Pearl Harbor. "Waves of bombers appearing over the horizon at dawn began to register with him, too, as somehow wrong," Reeves continued. "...So, Dillon switched sides. He was willing to try blockade first; then if it did not work, we could still bomb, there would be nothing sneaky about it by then." That evening, Robert Kennedy told his brother that a consensus to blockade was forming.

AT AN EX COMM MEETING held at the White House on Saturday afternoon, the president agreed to the blockade. He knew that he had to take some action; to do nothing would be political suicide and might even lead to his impeachment. Kennedy also wanted, if at all possible, to avoid forcing Khrushchev so far into a corner that the Soviet leader had no room to back down. The blockade seemed the most reasonable course. Nevertheless, he ordered McNamara to ready the U.S. military for war.

On the morning of Monday, October 22, U.S. Navy ships and planes began evacuating 2,810 women, children, and other noncombatants from the American naval base at Guantánamo Bay, while moving in additional marines. (The base at Cuba's eastern end had been granted to the United States by treaty in 1903 and kept by the Americans after the 1959 revolution despite Cuban protests.) Meanwhile, the president's favorite speechwriter, Theodore Sorensen, completed work on the address that the president was to deliver on national television at seven o'clock that evening. At the request of State Department counsel Abram Chayes, Sorensen used the word *quarantine* rather than *blockade*, because international law considered a blockade an act of war.

"Good evening, my fellow citizens," the seventeen-minute speech began. "This Government, as promised, has maintained the closest surveillance of the Soviet military buildup on island of Cuba. Within the past week, unmistakable evidence has established the fact that a series of offensive missile sites is now in preparation on that imprisoned island. The purpose of these bases can be none other than to provide a nuclear strike capability against the Western Hemisphere."

Kennedy went on to outline a number of actions that would be undertaken immediately. The first was the imposition of the quarantine: "All ships of any kind bound for Cuba from whatever nation or port will, if found to contain cargoes of offensive weapons, be turned back." The second was that close surveillance would

Douglas Dillon in May 1962. Having served in the Eisenhower administration, Dillon consulted the general before accepting Kennedy's offer to become treasury secretary. Ike tried to discourage Dillon, telling him that he was being used by liberals who didn't share his commitment to sound money.

be continued and increased. The third was ominous: "It shall be the policy of this Nation," Kennedy declared, "to regard any nuclear missile launched from Cuba against any nation in the Western Hemisphere as an attack by the Soviet Union on the United States, requiring a full retaliatory response." Finally, after making references to the reinforcement of Guantánamo and calling for meetings of the Organization of American States (OAS) and the United Nations, the president appealed directly to his Soviet counterpart: "I call upon Chairman Khrushchev to halt and eliminate this clandestine, reckless, and provocative threat to world peace and to stable relations between our two nations. I call upon him further to abandon this course of world domination, and to join in an historic effort to end the perilous arms race and to transform the history of man."

President Kennedy addresses the nation from the Oval Office on October 22. Fifty-one hours earlier, speechwriter Ted Sorensen had retired to his office with copies of two speeches that he wanted to use for reference: one made by Woodrow Wilson on April 2, 1917; the other by Franklin Roosevelt on December 8, 1941. Both were requests for declarations of war.

The Truman Doctrine

THE CONFRONTATION BETWEEN the two nuclear titans over the missiles in Cuba was nearly two decades in the making. Following Yalta and Potsdam, cooperation between the Soviets and the Americans broke down completely. Along with Poland, the rest of eastern Europe swiftly came under Soviet control. The Baltic republics of Latvia, Lithuania, and Estonia—granted to the USSR by one of the secret protocols of the 1939 Nazi-Soviet Nonaggression Pact—lost their independence and became "Soviet socialist republics" (of which the USSR was the "union"). Finland avoided such a fate only by forswearing an independent foreign policy. To the south, the countries between the Soviet border and Western-occupied Germany (plus the Balkan nations) also became Soviet satellites—including Hungary, Romania, Bulgaria, Albania, and Yugoslavia (although Yugoslavia later broke away in June 1948). As the new Soviet empire emerged, the nonaligned countries on its borders—particularly Greece, Turkey, and Iran—felt an increasing pressure to genuflect.

There was little the other Allies could do to prevent what Churchill memorably called an "iron curtain" from descending across Europe. Few Americans expected the U.S. government to pull back from international engagement as it had after World War I. But theSecond World War had left Britain and France completely

exhausted, and, at first, the United States was slow to oppose Soviet-sponsored insurgencies in Europe and Asia on its own. In Greece, for example, where Communist and anti-Communist partisans had fought together against the Germans, a civil war broke out in 1944. With the help of the British army, the anti-Communists prevailed in hard fighting during that winter. When the civil war resumed in 1946, however, the British could no longer offer much aid, and the anti-Communists turned to the United States for help. Turkey, another Mediterranean nation threatened by Soviet expansionism, also needed U.S. support.

Given the weakness of America's European allies in early 1947, it seemed that only substantial U.S. intervention could keep Greece and Turkey out of the Soviet sphere. Therefore, on March 12, 1947, President Truman asked a joint session of Congress to approve four hundred million dollars in aid to Greece and Turkey. He also enunciated what came to be known as the Truman Doctrine: Henceforth, it would be the policy of the United States to aid any foreign nation threatened by Communist aggression—economically, politically, and militarily, if necessary. "At the present moment in world history, nearly every nation must choose between alternative ways of life," Truman explained.

President Truman delivers his Truman Doctrine speech on March 12, 1947. By then, the Cold War was already well under way. The phrase Cold War, *originated in 1945, was used to describe the postwar ideological conflict between the United States and the Soviet Union conducted by means other than sustained military action.*

> *The choice is too often not a free one. One way of life is based upon the will of the majority and is distinguished by free institutions, representative government, free elections, guarantees of individual liberty, freedom of speech and religion, and freedom from political oppression. The second way of life is based upon terror and oppression, a controlled press and radio, fixed elections, and the suppression of personal freedom. I believe that it must be the policy of the United States to support free peoples who are resisting attempted subjugation by armed minorities or by outside pressures.*

Even with American aid, however, the Greek anti-Communists didn't gain the upper hand until Yugoslavia's defection from the Soviet bloc closed supply lines that the Soviets had been using to arm the Greek Communists. Furthermore, the democratic nations of Western Europe were themselves becoming unstable. Their war-ravaged economies were sliding even deeper into stagnation, and the resulting financial chaos seemed merely a prelude to the political and social maelstrom to come. It was becoming clear that, for the United States to contain the Soviet empire within its 1947 borders, more would have to be done.

CENTER: *As George Marshall understood, Europe had a great deal of damage to recover from. This April 1945 aerial view of Cologne, Germany, shows the sort of devastation caused by massive Allied air attacks.*

WITHIN THREE MONTHS of the Truman Doctrine speech, Secretary of State (and former army chief of staff) George C. Marshall signaled in a Harvard commencement address arguably the most important and creative initiative of America's emerging Cold War strategy. As presented to Congress in December 1947, Marshall's European Recovery Program (ERP) called for seventeen billion dollars in U.S. aid to Europe over the next four years. Its purpose was not merely to feed the Europeans (some were indeed starving) but also to rebuild their homes, apartment buildings, factories, shops, and economic infrastructure. The most controversial aspect of the plan was that Marshall envisioned offering aid to all Europeans, including the Germans and the Soviets. After attending a preliminary conference, however, the Soviets declined Marshall's offer for themselves and also on behalf of their client states (including Soviet-occupied eastern Germany, soon to become the German Democratic Republic).

Meanwhile, the French expressed concern that a rebuilt western Germany might once again threaten world peace, and there was even some opposition at home to the ERP's massive cost. But Marshall argued persuasively that a weak western Germany would be highly vulnerable to Communist destabilization, and he eventually won his case. Although Congress moved cautiously at first, the Communist takeover of Czechoslovakia in February 1948 spurred funding of the Marshall Plan, and billions of dollars quickly flowed into Western Europe. By mid-1948, with bipartisan support, the U.S. policy of "containment" was firmly in place.

Around the same time, a crisis was developing in Berlin. As part of their postwar planning, the Big Three had agreed in 1944 to divide occupied Germany into four zones controlled, respectively, by the United States, Great Britain, France, and the USSR. Although Berlin fell within the Soviet zone of occupation, it was considered a special case and was also divided among the four powers. Once it became clear that the Soviets were not going to permit free elections within any territory they occupied, the three Western nations decided in March 1948 to merge their zones, creating the Federal Republic of Germany and unifying West Berlin. In response, the Soviets cut off all road access to the city. To sustain West Berlin, the United States and Great Britain began a massive airlift of food, coal, and other necessary supplies. It began on June 20, 1948, and continued even after the Soviets abandoned their blockade on May 12, 1949, so that a year's supply of essential goods could be stockpiled.

A C-54 transport plane prepares to land at Templehof air base in West Berlin during the 1948–1949 blockade. At the height of the Berlin Airlift, American and British aircraft flew around the clock, taking off or landing every ninety seconds in Berlin.

Massive Retaliation

IN APRIL 1949, the Western allies took the added step of creating a formal military alliance: the North Atlantic Treaty Organization (NATO). Its original members included the United States, Canada, and ten Western European nations. Pursuant to the mutual defense clauses in the NATO treaty, large numbers of American troops were stationed permanently in West Germany, and the U.S. Navy supplanted the waning British Royal Navy in the Mediterranean. Although the Soviet military threat increased substantially when the USSR exploded its first nuclear weapon in September 1949, even the toughest hard-liners in the Kremlin knew that, because of NATO and the Marshall Plan, further expansion in Europe would not be possible without another world war.

In December 1950, NATO's governing body, the North Atlantic Council, chose Dwight D. Eisenhower to become its first supreme military commander—a post that he held until May 1952, when he resigned to run for president. Once in the White House, Eisenhower chose as his secretary of state a man whom he believed was ideally suited to help him move beyond Truman's policy of containment. At the time of his appointment, John Foster Dulles was a sixty-four-year-old Wall Street lawyer who had long been one of the Republican party's leading foreign policy experts. Dulles's paired convictions in the righteousness of the American republic and the iniquity of the Soviet system made him eager to liberate the "captive nations" of Eastern Europe from the yoke of Communist "oppression." Guided by this highly moralistic view of the world, he managed U.S. foreign policy from 1953 until 1959, when failing health forced him to resign. (He died a month later.) During his six years in office, Dulles held Eisenhower's special trust and became the most influential secretary of state of the postwar era, with the possible exception of Henry Kissinger.

Dulles's diplomatic strategy came to be known as brinkmanship, because he repeatedly asserted that the United States was "not scared to go to the brink" of war into order to frustrate the Soviet goal of world domination. As the Truman administration had, and the Kennedy administration would, Dulles assumed a bipolar world manipulated by the United States and the Soviet Union in that order. Because much of American diplomacy rested on the power of the U.S. nuclear arsenal, Dulles set forth a policy in January 1954 that he called "massive retaliation." In other words, the United States would maintain a stockpile of nuclear weapons so large that it could survive any preemptive attack and still obliterate Soviet society.

Massive retaliation had an economic benefit as well. The high cost of the Korean War had nearly quadrupled the defense budget in recent years, from twelve billion dollars in 1950 to forty-four billion in 1953. The fiscal conservatives in Eisenhower's cabinet were pressuring the president to cut defense spending sharply so that the federal budget could be brought more nearly into balance. One way to accomplish this was to reduce the outlay for conventional forces (soldiers, tanks, airplanes, ships, etc.) and instead rely more heavily on much less expensive

Secretary of State John Foster Dulles, photographed on his arrival in London in August 1956 for talks with the British on the Suez Crisis. Dulles made diplomacy a much more personal affair than had previous American secretaries of state. He visited forty-seven countries during his tenure at State, flying nearly half a million miles.

nuclear weapons. Pentagon public relations officers termed this "more bang for the buck" approach the New Look, after Christian Dior's acclaimed 1947 fashion line.

B RINKMANSHIP WAS PUT to the test right away in Korea. During the 1952 election campaign, Eisenhower had promised, "I will go to Korea," and on November 29, the president-elect did fly there for a three-day inspection tour. Later, Dulles met with regional intermediaries and let it be known that the United States was seriously considering "intensifying" the war. (He didn't need to use the word *nuclear* to make his point.) Shortly after Dulles's May 1953 meeting with Indian prime minister Jawaharlal Nehru, the Chinese agreed to a settlement. At Panmunjom on July 27, 1953, North Korean and UN representatives signed an armistice that ended the Korean War and reestablished the thirty-eighth parallel as the dividing line between North and South. Brinkmanship appeared to be working.

Along with the death of Stalin in March 1953, the peace in Korea made Dulles much more assertive. "This is the time to crowd the enemy—and maybe finish him, once and for all," the secretary of state declared, and he seemed to be right. The period between 1953 and 1956, during which Khrushchev emerged as the new Soviet leader and consolidated his power, was marked on the Soviet side by an easing of tensions with the West. In May 1955, the USSR agreed to withdraw its occupation troops from Austria so that the country could reunify. Overtures were even made regarding a similar arrangement for Germany, but Dulles remained suspicious. Soviet concessions, he said, indicated Soviet weakness, which the United States should actively exploit.

In early 1954, for example, Dulles set out to cleanse Communism from Southeast Asia. Using NATO as a model, he organized the Southeast Asia Treaty Organization (SEATO), and he also became much more deeply involved in French Indochina. Following the surrender of Japan, France had reestablished its colonial government in Indochina—but not without opposition. The Vietnamese nationalist Ho Chi Minh, who had led his people's resistance against Japan, now contested the French for control of the country. His Communist Vietminh organization was so militarily successful that France appealed for U.S. aid. President Truman approved the first support in May 1950, and soon the U.S. government was paying 80 percent of the French war cost. Yet even this much support wasn't enough. On March 13, 1954, forty thousand Vietminh troops under Gen. Vo Nguyen Giap besieged the fifteen-thousand-man French garrison at Dien Bien Phu. On May 7, the French surrendered, marking the end of their rule in Indochina.

Ho Chi Minh in early September 1954, shortly after he became premier of the new North Vietnamese government. Ho posed for this photograph while in the village of Thai Nguyen for meetings with an international truce commission.

A cease-fire agreement signed in Geneva on July 20 established a temporary demilitarized zone along the seventeenth parallel and partitioned the country into North and South, pending an internationally supervised reunification election to be held within two years. The Vietminh occupied the North, making Hanoi their capital. In the South, however, following questionable elections, Ngo Dinh Diem declared himself president of a new, independent, anti-Communist South Vietnam.

Once U.S. military and intelligence (CIA) aid began flowing to his government, Diem refused to hold a reunification election, citing the lack of freedom in the North. This prompted Ho Chi Minh to begin making plans for a guerrilla war in the South.

The Spirit of Geneva

MEANWHILE, THE PROSPECTS for détente with the Soviet Union seemed particularly good during the summer of 1955—when, shortly after the agreement on Austrian reunification, Eisenhower met with Khrushchev and Nikolai Bulganin (Khrushchev's partner in power at the time) at a super-power summit in Geneva. Neither the Soviet nor the American negotiators expected much to result from the conference, and little did, but the media was nevertheless impressed by the friendly "spirit of Geneva" that pervaded the talks. Only Dulles was unhappy. He worried that the amity merely indicated American acceptance of the status quo, including the Soviet domination of Eastern Europe. Accordingly, he made several public statements following the Geneva summit about what a high priority "liberation" of the "captive nations" remained for U.S. foreign policy.

Eisenhower and Diem take part in a motorcade following Diem's arrival at Washington's National Airport in May 1957. The South Vietnamese leader was already quite familiar with America. He had spent much of the past decade at a Roman Catholic seminary in New Jersey, accepting voluntary exile to protest French colonial rule in his country.

But how much (or little) would the United States be willing to risk to achieve such liberation? This wouldn't become clear until late 1956. Emboldened by Khrushchev's February 1956 speech to the Twentieth Party Congress denouncing Stalinism, and by a brief Polish challenge to Soviet rule that spring, students in Hungary staged an October 23 protest march to air long-standing grievances against their pro-Soviet government. When police fired into the crowd, however, the demonstration became a revolution. The Hungarian army joined, and former prime minister Imre Nagy, ousted in early 1955 because of his reformist policies, was returned to power.

Nagy's new regime lasted less than two weeks. After announcing Hungary's withdrawal from the Warsaw Pact (the Soviet-bloc equivalent of NATO), Nagy asked the United States to recognize and protect Hungarian neutrality; but while Eisenhower and Dulles temporized, Soviet tanks massed on the Hungarian border. At four in the morning on November 4, Soviet troops entered Budapest, deposing Nagy's government and installing a new administration consisting entirely of Soviet-oriented Communists. The United States did nothing. Given the realities of the nuclear stalemate and America's reduced conventional forces, there was little it could do.

TWO AND A HALF YEARS LATER, after an ailing Dulles resigned in April 1959, Eisenhower resumed East–West summitry. Determined to leave office as a peacemaker, he sent Vice Pres. Richard Nixon to Moscow in July and conducted Khrushchev on a tour of the United States two months later. Another summit was set for Paris the following May. On May 1, 1960, however, two weeks before the scheduled start of the Paris summit, the Soviets shot down an American U-2 spy plane over Sverdlovsk, deep within Soviet territory. Informed by Pentagon officials that no evidence would have survived the crash, the State Department initially claimed that the downed aircraft was a weather plane that had strayed off course. However, when the Soviets produced the plane's living pilot, former air force captain Francis Gary Powers, who confessed fully to his mission, the United States had to admit that it had been engaged in espionage. Nevertheless, Eisenhower refused to apologize, insisting that U.S. national security required him to keep a close watch on the Soviet Union (and pointing out that the Soviets

THE SUEZ CRISIS

AT THE TIME OF THE HUNGARIAN uprising in October 1956, the Suez Canal was already the scene of an international crisis involving two of America's closest allies. In part, the situation developed as the result of Dulles's own clumsiness. Earlier, the secretary of state had attempted to improve Egyptian-American relations by offering U.S. financing for the construction of a dam at Aswan on the upper Nile River—one of Egyptian leader Gen. Gamal Abdel Nasser's most cherished projects. When Nasser began flirting with the Soviet Union, however, Dulles withdrew the offer of aid, and the British also withdrew a similar offer. Seven days later—on July 26, 1956—feeling humiliated and angry, Nasser retaliated. He seized the Suez Canal from the British and French stockholders who owned and operated it, boldly predicting that the tolls from the newly nationalized canal would pay for the Aswan Dam within five years.

Fearing that Nasser might soon move to block oil shipments from the Persian Gulf, which passed through the canal daily on their way to western Europe, Great Britain and France began plotting

A British troopship delivers reinforcements in November 1956 to Port Said at the Mediterranean end of the Suez Canal.

to take the canal back. Without consulting the Americans, they arranged with Israel (the victim of Nasser-sponsored commando raids since 1955) to conduct a secret joint offensive. On October 29, ten Israeli brigades invaded Egypt's Sinai Peninsula and headed for the canal. As previously arranged, the British and French announced that they would deploy their own troops to enforce a recent UN cease-fire order unless all combatants left the canal zone immediately. When Egypt refused, British and French troops landed on November 5–6 and began occupying the canal zone.

Not only the Soviet Union but also the United States reacted angrily. President Eisenhower demanded the immediate withdrawal of the European troops, while Khrushchev, bidding for greater Soviet influence in the Arab world, issued a much more strongly worded threat outlining possible Soviet reprisals. Under this sort of pressure, the British and French had no choice but to withdraw, which they did under UN supervision on December 22. Israel pulled back its forces from the Sinai three months later.

had known about the U-2 flights for years without protesting). Predictably, Khrushchev was outraged, and he canceled the Paris summit amid substantial acrimony.

By the time that Kennedy took office eight months later, the spirit of Geneva was completely dead. Believing that Eisenhower's New Look defense policy unacceptably limited his options in responding to Communist aggression, the new president swiftly replaced Dulles's concept of massive retaliation with a new, much more expensive policy that his own national security team called "flexible response." Its centerpiece was a massive buildup of conventional forces, especially the creation of new counterinsurgency units (such as the Green Berets) that could respond quickly and effectively to emergencies.

In June 1961, two months after the Bay of Pigs invasion, President Kennedy met with Khrushchev in Vienna. Skeptical of the new president's strength and contemptuous of his youth, Khrushchev tried to bully Kennedy into "adjusting" the situations on Taiwan and in West Berlin. Neither polity could retain its independence indefinitely, Khrushchev said; in reply, Kennedy warned that the

THE MILITARY-INDUSTRIAL COMPLEX

PERHAPS DWIGHT D. EISENHOWER'S most important presidential legacy was the farewell address that he gave on the evening of January 17, 1961, three days before leaving office. Televised live, the speech expressed Eisenhower's concern that the nation's military leadership, acting in concert with its industrial titans, might lead the country down the road to war.

As the outgoing president explained, the megalithic U.S. military establishment, created during the Cold War to protect some American freedoms, was now, ironically, threatening others:

Until the latest of our world conflicts, the United States had no armaments industry. American makers of plowshares could, with time and as requested, make swords as well. But now we can no longer risk emergency improvisation of national defense; we have been compelled to create a permanent armaments industry of vast proportions. Added to this, three and a half million men and women are directly engaged in the defense establishment….

This conjunction of an immense military establishment and a large arms industry is new in the American experience. The total influence—economic, political, even spiritual—is felt in every city, every statehouse, every office of the federal government. We recognize the imperative need for this development. Yet we must not fail to comprehend its grave implications. Our toil, resources, and livelihood are all involved; so is the very structure of our society.

In the councils of government, we must guard against the acquisition of unwarranted influence, whether sought or unsought, by the military-industrial complex. The potential for the disastrous rise of misplaced power exists and will persist. We must never let the weight of this combination endanger our liberties or democratic processes.

United States would never countenance Communist expansion in either area without taking action. Khrushchev answered that Communism was sweeping the world and that history required the Soviet Union to assist the process as it could. Kennedy left the meeting shaken. "The Vienna summit," Richard Reeves has written, "came as a particular shock to Kennedy, a man convinced that he could always prevail one-on-one with men and with women. This time, he'd been outmaneuvered and out-thought by the Soviet leader—a fact cleaned up for American consumption by a protective staff misleading a patriotic press. But Kennedy was no fool, and he came away from Vienna with a valuable seed of experience."

The Berlin Wall

AT VIENNA, KHRUSHCHEV had seemed most perturbed by the status of Berlin. "This is unbearable for Khrushchev," Kennedy told an aide not long after the summit. "East Germany is hemorrhaging to death. The entire East bloc is in danger. He has to do something to stop this. Perhaps a wall…." In fact, the enormous flow of educated young East Germans to the West through West Berlin was a colossal problem for the Soviets. Worse than embarrassing, it threatened the future of the East German state. Since the end of the war, three million East Germans had escaped to the West, and by early 1961 they were leaving the German Democratic Republic at the rate of three thousand a day.

In late June 1963, President Kennedy toured West Berlin. More than two million Berliners turned out for his visit, and nearly two hundred thousand jammed the Rathausplatz for his speech. "Today," the president said, "in the world of freedom, the proudest boast is, 'Ich bin ein Berliner.'" Kennedy is shown here inspecting an American checkpoint.

Khrushchev continued to demand changes; Kennedy continued to resist. As tensions related to the situation in Berlin increased, the United States began preparing for a possible confrontation. The president tripled the draft call, mobilized 150,000 reservists, and sent another 40,000 troops to Europe. When the president of East Germany threatened to reinstitute a blockade, Kennedy went on national television to deliver a defiant speech. "I hear it said that West Berlin is militarily untenable," he told Americans on July 25. "And so was Bastogne. And so, in fact, was Stalingrad. Any dangerous spot is tenable if men—brave men—will make it so." Privately, however, Kennedy made it clear to the Soviets that, so long as the autobahn to West Berlin remained open, the Communists could do as they pleased on their own side of the border.

During the early-morning hours of August 13, 1961, Communist troops rolled out a long barbed-wire fence just inside the East German border with West Berlin. The fence, later replaced by a steel-reinforced concrete wall, ended the emigration problem overnight—and though it violated existing international agreements with regard to Berlin, the United States, as Kennedy had indicated, took no action.

It was within this context of frayed U.S.-Soviet relations that President Kennedy—and the rest of the world—awaited the Soviet response to his October 22 speech. All over the globe, people were genuinely and reasonably concerned that they might not live out the week.

UNDERSECRETARY OF STATE George Ball spent the night of October 22 sleeping on a couch in Dean Rusk's office. He was awakened early the next morning by the secretary of state. "We have won a considerable victory," Rusk told Ball. "You and I are still alive." That morning, Rusk presented the American case to the OAS, the group of twenty South and Central American countries that the United States had organized into a regional political alliance after World War II. The State Department was not sanguine about the response Rusk would get from the often-recalcitrant Latin American nations. According to the assistant secretary of state for inter-American affairs, there was only one chance in four that the necessary two-thirds of member nations would vote to approve the U.S.-sponsored resolution condemning the missiles in Cuba. After eight hours of debate, however, the delegates, one after another, voted to endorse the U.S. position. The final tally was 19–0, with only Uruguay abstaining. (Later, the Uruguayans made the vote unanimous.) The president waited until after the OAS vote to sign the proclamation that put the quarantine into effect beginning at 10 A.M. on Wednesday, October 24. He authorized the navy to cripple, by firing at propellers or rudders, any vessel bound for Cuba that refused to stop and be inspected.

Wednesday's Ex Comm meeting also began at 10 A.M. As had become the usual practice, the session began with CIA director John McCone's summary of the overnight intelligence. At the missile sites in Cuba, workers were rapidly assembling structures considered suitable for the storage of nuclear weapons. In the Caribbean, three ships with hatches big enough to handle missiles had been joined by Soviet submarine escorts. The president was holding his hand over his mouth, opening and closing his fist, but his eyes showed the strain. "We must expect that they will close down Berlin," he interjected. "We must make the final preparations for that." Then McCone resumed his briefing until, at ten twenty-five, he was interrupted by a messenger. "Mr. President," McCone said after reading the note, "we have a preliminary report that seems to indicate that some of the Russian ships have stopped dead in the water." After a brief pause, Rusk was the next to speak. "We're eyeball to eyeball," he said, "and the other fellow just blinked." The president wasn't quite so sure, but he wanted to avoid a confrontation if that's what the Soviets had in mind. "If the ships have orders to turn around," he told Taylor, "we want to give them every opportunity to do so."

This promotional photograph from 1955 shows a Kidde Kokoon underground bomb shelter, manufactured by Walter Kidde Nuclear Laboratories of Garden City, Long Island. The shelter fad of the 1950s and early 1960s was encouraged by the government's position that nuclear warfare was manageable.

The Soviet decision not to run the blockade gave both governments some additional time, but time was mainly on the side of the USSR. As new reconnaissance photos showed, work on the missile sites was continuing around the clock, and there were already enough warheads on Cuba to devastate large portions of the United States. While pressure mounted for the president to order an invasion, the members of Ex Comm looked for additional ways to impress upon Khrushchev the urgency of the situation. Officials talked openly of American readiness, and Robert Kennedy visited Soviet ambassador Anatoli Dobrynin to warn him that there were at most two days left before the United States would feel compelled to take further military action.

Khrushchev's Responses

THE FIRST INTIMATION of Khrushchev's response came in a roundabout way. Early Friday afternoon while eating at his desk in the State Department press room, John Scali, a diplomatic correspondent for ABC News, received a phone call from Alexander Fomin, an official at the Soviet embassy whom Scali knew slightly. More important, Fomin was known to the intelligence community as the Washington station chief for the KGB (the Soviet CIA). At Fomin's urgent request, Scali met him for a second lunch. "The situation is very serious," Fomin began. Then he asked Scali to find out whether the State Department would be interested in a reciprocal settlement: The Soviet Union would remove its missiles from Cuba in exchange for a U.S. pledge not to invade Cuba.

John Scali holds up a copy of the message from Dean Rusk that he passed on to Alexander Fomin. Two decades earlier, Fomin (whose real name was Col. Alexander Feklisov) had served as KGB case officer for both Julius Rosenberg and Klaus Fuchs.

Returning to the State Department, Scali went to see intelligence chief Roger Hilsman, who took him to see Rusk. The secretary left a meeting with Robert Kennedy and McGeorge Bundy to listen to Scali's story, then he went back into the meeting. A few minutes later, he returned with a handwritten response for the television correspondent to memorize: "I have reason to believe that the United States Government sees real possibilities in this and supposes that representatives of the two governments could work this matter out with [UN Secretary General] U Thant and each other. My impression is, however, that time is very urgent."

Meanwhile, at six o'clock that evening, the teletypes at the State Department begin clacking out the first section of a long letter from Khrushchev to Kennedy that had been delivered earlier that day to the U.S. embassy in Moscow. U.S. ambassador Foy Kohler had received the letter at 7:43 A.M. Washington time (4:43 P.M. Moscow time), but translation difficulties and problems with the Soviet telegraph lines had delayed transmission. The letter was rambling, personal, and quite strange, Kohler reported. "This reads as if he wrote it himself without anyone around, without consultation," Llewellyn Thompson, Kohler's predecessor in Moscow, opined. "He's worried. He seems to be under a lot of strain."

KHRUSHCHEV WROTE that he had seen war firsthand and detailed his experiences during two German invasions of his country. There were Soviet missiles in Cuba, he admitted, but only because the United States had already sponsored one invasion of the island and Fidel Castro legitimately feared another. "Mr. President," the Soviet leader wrote,

I appeal to you to weigh well what the aggressive, piratical actions, which you have declared the U.S.A. intends to carry out in international waters, would lead to…. If you did this as a first step towards the unleashing of war, well then, it is evident that nothing else is left to us but to accept this challenge of yours. If, however, you have not lost your self-control and sensibly conceive what this might lead to, then, you have tied the knot of war, because the more the two of us pull, the tighter that knot will be tied. And a moment may come when that knot will be tied so tight that even he who tied it will not have the strength to untie it, and then it will be necessary to cut that knot, and what that would mean is not for me to explain to you, because you yourself understand perfectly of what terrible forces our countries dispose.

Amid all the verbiage was the outline of a deal nearly identical to the one that Fomin had floated by Scali: If the United States agreed to lift its blockade and pledged not to invade Cuba, the Soviet Union would no longer perceive the need to maintain nuclear weapons in Cuba. The members of Ex Comm met at 10 A.M. on Saturday, October 27, to consider Khrushchev's letter. Less than fifteen minutes into the discussion, Press Secretary Pierre Salinger burst into the room with news that Khrushchev had just released a public letter, transmitted from Moscow over the Associated Press wire, in which he demanded removal of U.S. Jupiter missiles in Turkey in exchange for any missile withdrawal from Cuba. Apparently, the Politburo had not appreciated Khrushchev's freelancing of the night before.

Thirty-four-year-old Fidel Castro and sixty-six-year-old Nikita Khrushchev meet for the first time at a session of the UN General Assembly in late September 1960. In the end, Khrushchev's failure in Cuba would lead to his removal as premier in October 1964.

No one in the Cabinet Room was particularly surprised by the new demand. In fact, Kennedy had wondered aloud several times when the fifteen U.S. nuclear missiles in Turkey would come into play. The Jupiters were obsolete: They were wildly inaccurate, took hours to fuel, and could be disabled by a single shot from a sniper parked on a nearby public road. The president himself had ordered their removal months earlier, but the Turks had balked. The removal of nuclear missiles from their territory would be seen domestically as a loss of prestige, and Turkish governments had fallen over less. Furthermore, now that Khrushchev was demanding their removal, Kennedy certainly couldn't acquiesce without appearing faithless. French president Charles de Gaulle had been causing a great deal of trouble lately with his repeated assertions that the United States couldn't be trusted to risk its own security in defense of Western Europe. If the United States now "sold out" the Turks to remove the missile threat from Cuba, de Gaulle's point would be made, and NATO would suffer. The alliance might even be dissolved.

Resolution

THE PRESIDENT FELT boxed in. He didn't want to remove the Jupiters, nor did he wish to invade Cuba. "They've got a very good case," he said of the Soviets during the Saturday-morning Ex Comm meeting. "This one is going to be very tough, I think, for us…. We're going to be forced to take action that might seem, in my opinion, not a blank check but a pretty good check to take action in Berlin on the grounds we were totally unreasonable…. The only thing we've got on him [Khrushchev] is the fact that now they've put forth varying proposals in short periods of time, all of which are complicated, and under this shield this work [on the missile sites] goes on."

Sometime that afternoon, the president made up his mind: He would not go to war over the obsolete Jupiters in Turkey. "We can't very well invade Cuba… when we could have gotten them out by making a deal on the same missiles in Turkey," he told the members of Ex Comm after meeting privately with the commander of all U.S. forces in Europe. "If that's part of the record, I don't s ee how we'll have a good war." Later, it was decided that Kennedy would follow a strategy suggested earlier in the day by Bundy: He would agree to the terms offered by Khrushchev in his first letter, ignoring the second.

Robert Kennedy left the White House at 7:30 P.M. that Saturday, carrying the final version of the president's response to Anatoli Dobrynin at the Soviet embassy. Moments earlier, Rusk had suggested telling Dobrynin that, although the president could make no public deal concerning the Jupiters, they would be removed once the crisis had passed. "Right, do it," the president said. At the Soviet embassy, the attorney general told Dobrynin that he didn't know how long his brother could hold off the military's demand for war. He emphasized that the president's letter offered the last chance for peace. "This letter does not mention the missiles in Turkey," Dobrynin replied. That could be worked out, Robert Kennedy said—but not now, not in public. "I am not optimistic," Dobrynin told Kennedy as the conversation concluded. "The Politburo is too committed to back down now."

At 8:05 P.M., the president released his answer to Khrushchev and ordered it broadcast over the Voice of America so that it could be picked up in Moscow right away. At 9 P.M., the third Ex Comm meeting of the day began. McNamara advised that twenty-four squadrons of U.S. Air Force reserves be called to active duty. The president agreed. "Now," Kennedy said, "it can go either way."

Just before nine o'clock the next morning—Sunday, October 28—President Kennedy was lounging in bed, reading the *New York Times*, when a news bulletin interrupted the flow of music from his bedside radio. The Associated Press was reporting that Radio Moscow was about to broadcast an important announcement at the top of the hour. At nine o'clock precisely, the Soviets went on the air with a public letter from Khrushchev to Kennedy. "In order to complete with greater speed the liquidation of the conflict…and to calm the American people, who, I am certain, want peace as much as the people of the Soviet Union," the Radio Moscow announcer read in English, "the Soviet government…has issued a new order on the dismantling of the weapons, which you describe as 'offensive,' and their crating and return to the Soviet Union." The letter ended: "I regard with respect and trust your statement in your message of October 27, 1962, that no attack will be made on Cuba."

During the Cuban Missile Crisis, the U.S. Army deployed Hawk antiaircraft missiles on public beaches in Key West (this is Smathers Beach) and elsewhere in Florida.

M ANY HISTORIANS have since found in the Cuban Missile Crisis a convenient dividing line, marking the end of one period of U.S.-Soviet relations and the inauguration of another. Before October 1962, Soviet and American Cold War diplomacy had consisted largely of threat and counterthreat. Afterward, having peered into the nuclear abyss and been frightened by what they saw, the leaders of both superpowers behaved much more soberly and with greater circumspection.

Of course, the United States and the Soviet Union did not resolve their differences in the aftermath of the Cuban crisis. They still pursued widely divergent objectives in the world, and conflicts continued to develop. Yet steps were also taken to prevent a repetition of the terrifying events of mid-October 1962. These included communication improvements, such as the installation of a direct "hot line" between the White House and the Kremlin, and the deescalation of nuclear diplomacy.

In August 1963, the same month that the new hot line became operational, the two superpowers, along with Great Britain, signed the Limited Nuclear Test Ban Treaty, prohibiting all aboveground nuclear testing. Environmentalists applauded the agreement, and Kennedy called it the most important achievement of his presidency, even though the People's Republic of China and France later declined to ratify the document.

Vietnam

YET KENNEDY'S growing empathy toward the Soviet Union apparently didn't extend to the Communist insurgency in South Vietnam. As early as April 1954, President Eisenhower had likened the nations of Southeast Asia to a row of dominoes. "You knock over the first one," he had said, "and what will happen to the last one is the certainty that it will go over very quickly." In practical terms, this widely held "domino theory" meant that if one nation in a region fell to the Communists, its neighbors would soon follow in a chain reaction. Therefore, during the late 1950s, the United States had kept up the flow of aid to South Vietnam and even sent over several hundred military advisers. During 1961, Kennedy's first year in office, more equipment and more advisers were sent, and in January 1962, the United States launched Operation Ranch Hand, the spraying of chemical defoliants (including Agent Orange) on the jungle trails used by the Vietcong, the Communist guerrillas in South Vietnam. During 1962 and 1963, still more advisers were sent until there were more then eleven thousand "in country."

Yet Ngo Dinh Diem's government in Saigon continued to decline because it lacked popular support. Although Diem was a Catholic in a predominantly Buddhist country, his chief problem wasn't his religion; rather, it was his brutality and corruption. During 1963, the demands for his ouster intensified, and the size and number of popular demonstrations against his rule increased accordingly. Several Buddhist monks immolated themselves in the middle of busy Saigon intersections to call attention to Diem's murderous anti-Buddhist policies.

An antipersonnel mine of the sort used by the Vietcong.

Kennedy's goal was to establish a strong, pro-Western government in South Vietnam to show that U.S. aid could defeat Communist insurrection. Obviously, this was not going to happen under Diem. Therefore, on November 1–2, with the knowledge and consent of the U.S. government, Gen. Duong Van Minh led a group of South Vietnamese army officers in a coup against Diem and his brother, Ngo Dinh Nhu. Both were murdered. Three weeks later, Kennedy himself was killed in Dallas. Shortly after that, Ho Chi Minh's government began sending the first North Vietnamese regulars to fight in the South.

W HAT JOHN F. KENNEDY might or might not have done in Vietnam, had he lived, has been the subject of much speculation. During Lyndon Johnson's first year in office, the new president generally followed his predecessor's lead in gradually increasing U.S. aid and military support to South Vietnam. The substantial escalation of the Vietnam War that followed Johnson's landslide reelection in November 1964, however, cannot be attributed to anyone other than Johnson himself. Given the chance, Kennedy might have done the same thing—or perhaps he wouldn't have. Certainly, Lyndon Johnson *did* escalate the war in Vietnam.

Having accepted the domino theory, Johnson feared greatly the loss of American prestige in the world should the Communists overrun South Vietnam. Although he moved cautiously before the 1964 election, he did take advantage of two incidents in early August 1964 to gain all the legitimacy he would ever need for the war. According to naval reports, three North Vietnamese patrol boats attacked the U.S. destroyer *Maddox* in the Gulf of Tonkin on August 2. (A second attack on a U.S. destroyer in international waters was reported but never actually took place.) Congress responded with the Gulf of Tonkin Resolution, approved unanimously in the House and 88–2 in the Senate. It authorized the president to "take all necessary measures to repel any armed attack against the forces of the United States and to repel any further aggression." During the next four years, the Johnson administration referred repeatedly to the Tonkin Gulf Resolution as its authority for all subsequent escalation.

President Johnson shakes hands in July 1966 with Vietnam-bound soldiers at Fort Campbell in Kentucky.

Because Republican nominee Barry Goldwater criticized severely the Democrats' "no-win" approach to Vietnam and talked vaguely of using nuclear weapons to win the war, LBJ ran in 1964 as the "peace" candidate. "We don't want our American boys to do the fighting for Asian boys," he declared, adding often that he sought "no wider war." In March 1965, however, Johnson launched Operation Rolling Thunder, the sustained bombing of North Vietnam, and ordered the first U.S. combat troops into South Vietnam. These were two battalions of marines sent to Da Nang to guard the American air base there.

By now, about 75,000 American soldiers were serving in Vietnam, up from 23,000 at the start of the year. On July 28, 1965, however, the president held a press conference in the East Room of the White House at which he announced a substantial troop increase: "I have asked the commanding general, General [William C.] Westmoreland, what more he needs to meet this mounting aggression. He has told me. And we will meet his needs. We cannot be defeated by force of arms. We will stand in Vietnam." Immediately, Johnson announced, U.S. troop strength there would be increased to 125,000 men, with additional soldiers to be "sent as requested." What the president didn't say was that Westmoreland had already requested a total of 175,000 troops, and Johnson had already secretly approved the request.

The president concealed the extent of his plans for increased U.S. military involvement in Vietnam—which exceeded half a million troops by 1968—because he didn't want to alarm the nation and thus put at risk his enormously ambitious domestic agenda, especially his Great Society programs. Defense Secretary Robert McNamara, one of the many holdovers from the Kennedy foreign policy team (and Ex Comm), estimated that the cost of the war would rise to ten billion dollars in fiscal year 1966. National Security Adviser McGeorge Bundy urged Johnson to build support for this commitment by explaining his decision fully to the public. The president declined, believing that Congress and the American people wouldn't go along. "Nevertheless," historian David Kaiser has written, "the decision to go to war had been made, and within three years it destroyed not only Johnson's presidency but also the national consensus that had hitherto seemed likely to carry him to the loftiest heights of national leadership."

Johnson Steps Down

LIKE WESTMORELAND, Johnson believed that North Vietnamese and Vietcong troops couldn't stand up to superior American firepower. However, he underestimated tragically two other factors: The Communists were prepared to sustain heavy losses nearly indefinitely in order to reunify their country, and the leadership of South Vietnam was inadequate to the task of counterinsurgency. After the fall of Diem, governments came and went in Saigon with distressing frequency until September 1967, when Gen. Nguyen Van Thieu came to power. Thieu's regime was more stable but hardly less oppressive or dishonest than its predecessors. Unable to unite the anti-Communist elements in South Vietnamese society, control the corruption in the South Vietnamese army, or win the loyalty of the peasantry, Thieu's administration remained a government kept alive by U.S. aid and military might. (American planes ultimately dropped more munitions during the Vietnam War than during all of World War II.) Meanwhile, in engagements such as the November 1965 battle fought in the Ia Drang Valley, the North Vietnamese army proved that it was prepared to absorb many casualties in order to injure and kill many fewer Americans. "Ironically," according to David Kaiser, "this engagement persuaded *both* sides that the war could be won through a series of such engagements. The North Vietnamese, of course, were the ones who proved to be right on this count."

At home, opposition to the war was growing, especially among college students subject to the draft. In October 1967, antiwar activists staged a march on the Pentagon that Norman Mailer chronicled in his influential 1968 book *The Armies of the Night*. After the march, President Johnson watched his approval rating fall to just 28 percent.

Three months later, North Vietnamese and Vietcong soldiers launched the Tet Offensive. Beginning on January 30, 1968, during a cease-fire called to celebrate the Vietnamese New Year (known as *Tet* in Vietnamese), eighty-four thousand Communist troops attacked urban centers throughout the South. Hue, South Vietnam's second largest city, was temporarily overrun, and the fighting in Saigon

McNamara and Westmoreland talk with a South Vietnamese corps commander during the defense secretary's mid-July 1965 fact-finding trip to Vietnam. Upon his return, McNamara recommended to President Johnson that Westmoreland's request for additional troops be approved.

American soldiers belonging to the Twenty-fifth Division enter a Vietnamese village in May 1967. During 1967, U.S. troop levels in Vietnam rose from 385,000 to 485,000.

reached the gates of the U.S. embassy before the assault was turned back on January 31. In the end, the Tet Offensive proved to be a military defeat for the Communists but a sensational public relations victory. General Westmoreland had been claiming for years that the United States was winning the war and that victory was nearly at hand; television news footage of Vietcong soldiers outside the American embassy, however, put the lie to those statements.

Inside the White House, too, members of the Johnson administration were reconsidering the wisdom of continued U.S. involvement in Vietnam. On March 1, Clark Clifford replaced Robert McNamara as secretary of defense. After facilitating the war's escalation for three years, McNamara had finally become disillusioned with its conduct and resigned. Now Clifford, a Johnson confidant, undertook his own policy review and came away with the same conclusion: The United States needed to get out of Vietnam.

THE FIRST PRESIDENTIAL PRIMARY of 1968 was held on March 12 in New Hampshire. Running on an antiwar platform, Minnesota senator Eugene McCarthy nearly upset the president, taking 41.9 percent of the Democratic vote to the president's 49.6 percent. The results immediately shifted America's political landscape. Seeing Johnson's weakness and believing that he could take the peace vote away from McCarthy, Robert F. Kennedy (now a senator from New York) also entered the race.

On March 31, President Johnson announced on national television a partial halt to the bombing of North Vietnam. He was offering this unilateral move, he said, to induce the North Vietnamese to resume peace talks. He emphasized his sincerity and, near the end of the speech, reiterated how important it was that his action not be interpreted as an election-year ploy. "Accordingly," he said, "I shall not seek, and I will not accept, the nomination of my part for another term as your president." Lyndon Johnson thus became yet another casualty of the Vietnam War.

AMERICAN PROFILE

George F. Kennan

1904–

by Robert Dallek

GEORGE F. KENNAN WAS the architect of America's victory in the Cold War. In Kennan's view, the essence of the Soviet Union was a combination of Marxist-Leninist evangelism and traditional Russian imperialism. As the only great power in Europe after 1945 (with Germany's defeat and Franco-British decline), the Soviets had two fundamental postwar aims: first, to assure their national security; and second, to spread their Communist ideology around the globe. Kennan understood that the USSR's determination to dominate Eastern Europe rested on the former of these principles, while its messianic activities in Asia, Africa, and elsewhere could be attributed to the latter. He concluded, therefore, that while efforts to recover Eastern Europe were unlikely to succeed, Western firmness with regard to the expansion of Communism into other spheres could contain Soviet ambitions. Having just lost twenty million people in World War II, Kennan believed, Moscow was unlikely to risk another devastating war against a superior U.S. military.

Kennan joined the foreign service shortly after his 1925 graduation from Princeton and was immediately posted overseas to State Department "listening posts" in Tallinn, Riga, and elsewhere. (For a decade and a half after the Russian Revolution—a period when the United States and the Soviet Union had no formal diplomatic relations—these embassies were used to monitor events within Soviet Russia.) From 1929 until 1931, Kennan immersed himself in Russian studies at the University of Berlin, which prepared him for later duties accompanying Amb. William C. Bullitt to Moscow after U.S. recognition of the Soviet government in 1933. Kennan spent World War II in Berlin (where he was briefly interned

after America's entry into the war), Lisbon, and Moscow; and it was from Moscow in February 1946 that he sent his first cablegram proposing the policy of "containment." Kennan's formulation provided the Truman administration with a useful framework for understanding and responding to Soviet aggression around the world, and it soon became the core of America's Cold War strategy.

A year later—following announcement of the Truman Doctrine in March 1947 and release of the Marshall Plan three months after that—Kennan outlined the reasoning behind containment in a *Foreign Affairs* article that he signed only "X." In that July 1947 article, Kennan pointed to four regions of the globe vital to U.S. national security: the Western Hemisphere, Western Europe, Japan, and the oil-rich Middle East. He doubted that the Soviet Union would invade any of those regions but did predict that it would attempt to topple pro-Western governments through subversion and the exploitation of economic and political instability. Therefore, by propping up those governments—as the United States was already doing with aid to Greece and Turkey—Washington could keep Moscow from making significant international gains. Moreover, Kennan saw the Soviet system as a perilous marriage of command economics and political oppression that would either have to liberalize or eventually self-destruct. If this was true, as long as America kept applying sufficient counterpressure to Soviet expansionism, there would be no need to militarize the Cold War further. Following this logic, Kennan saw no need for NATO or SEATO and opposed the creation of any global military alliances on the grounds that they would only provoke Soviet countermeasures, such as creation of the Warsaw Pact.

Kennan in November 1951, while he was on leave from the State Department to run a Ford Foundation fund set up to help anti-Communist Soviet exiles in the United States.

Kennan also doubted the wisdom of building large arsenals of nuclear weapons because the Soviets would have to keep pace, thus creating a potentially destabilizing arms race. He warned that stockpiling weapons of mass destruction, just a few of which would suffice to deter Soviet attack, was a prescription for human extinction. As he pointed out vigorously, the twentieth century's two world wars had already demonstrated that advanced industrial powers could not fight one another without producing ruinous devastation.

Because America's political leaders had the wisdom to follow most of Kennan's advice, they managed between 1947 and 1991 to avoid a nuclear holocaust while simultaneously fostering the demise of the Soviet Union. Yet whatever plaudits other U.S. policy makers deserve for their restraint, none is more deserving of credit than George Kennan, one of the twentieth century's great peacemakers.

23

THE SIXTIES

The March on Washington

ON JUNE 21, 1963, A. Philip Randolph and Martin Luther King Jr. announced that a coalition of national civil rights groups would be staging a March on Washington for Freedom and Jobs later that summer. King joined Randolph in making the announcement because he was then the most famous black leader in the country. The march, however, had been Randolph's idea, and he would be leading the effort, which sought to consolidate and extend the recent gains the civil rights movement had made.

At seventy-four, Randolph was the movement's elder statesman. In 1925, he had founded the Brotherhood of Sleeping Car Porters to organize the predominantly black workers who tended the nation's Pullman cars. Because all existing railroad unions excluded blacks (even Eugene Debs's short-lived American Railway Union had barred them), Randolph had come to see labor organizing as a means of advancing the civil rights cause. W. E. B. Du Bois had promoted the concept of the Talented Tenth—a cadre of committed, college-educated, urban blacks who would lead the civil rights crusade from the top down—but not Randolph. He thought the key to equality lay in mobilizing the black proletariat and encouraging grassroots leaders.

The 1963 March on Washington wasn't the first mass rally that Randolph had planned for the nation's capital. In early 1941, with the help of the NAACP and the Urban League, he had made plans for a huge demonstration to protest

racial segregation in the armed forces. Franklin Roosevelt wanted no part of such a march. He feared its divisiveness, especially if it turned violent, and also resented the pressure that it put upon him to move ahead more quickly with desegregation on the eve of war. He sent his wife, Eleanor, and New York mayor Fiorello La Guardia—two eminent emissaries whom Randolph knew well and respected—to talk with the union leader and persuade him to cancel the march. Randolph was warned that the July 1 demonstration would incite bigoted whites and do more harm than good. Still, Randolph refused to call it off. Finally, one week before the march, President Roosevelt issued Executive Order 8802, prohibiting racial discrimination in the country's defense industries and establishing a Fair Employment Practice Committee to enforce the order. In exchange, Randolph called off the march.

Like FDR, Pres. John F. Kennedy recognized the pervasive unfairness encountered by African Americans in their daily lives; yet he also, like Roosevelt, gave primacy of place to his own political agenda and didn't appreciate being challenged or upstaged. At a White House meeting on June 22 with Randolph, King, NAACP executive secretary Roy Wilkins, and other prominent civil rights leaders, the president attempted to talk them out of the Washington march. When this effort failed, he tried to manage the inevitable as best he could, assigning his brother Robert to work with Randolph and Randolph's deputy, Bayard Rustin. Ultimately, Robert Kennedy provided hundreds of thousands of dollars in Justice Department funds to ensure that the demonstration remained

AT LEFT: **In addition to the participants,** *three thousand reporters attended the March on Washington, and all three U.S. networks chose to televise the proceedings live.*

peaceful, orderly, and pro-Kennedy. The government, for example, paid for the best sound system available because Justice Department officials feared that protesters on the fringe of the crowd might lose interest and turn to mischief instead if they couldn't hear the proceedings. The Kennedy administration's involvement became so extensive, in fact, that the Nation of Islam refused to take part, and its spokesman, Malcolm X, denounced the march as "government controlled."

AUGUST 28, 1963, was a Wednesday. The Justice Department had pressured the march organizers to choose a day in the middle of the week so that the marchers, most of whom couldn't afford to miss more than one day of work, would have to arrive in the capital and leave on the same day. For similar reasons, the three-hour rally was scheduled to end at 4 P.M., so that the Mall could be cleared before sunset.

For most of the marchers, the day began in the middle of the night, when they boarded "freedom buses" and "freedom trains" bound for the capital. So many chartered buses were scheduled to leave New York City at midnight that they caused a 1:30 A.M. traffic jam in the Lincoln Tunnel. According to Rustin's carefully choreographed plan, most reached Washington by 9 A.M. Military police stationed at key intersections throughout the city guided the buses—more than fifteen hundred of them—to their predesignated unloading points.

MARTIN LUTHER KING JR.
1929–1968

MARTIN LUTHER KING JR.'S maternal grandfather became pastor of Atlanta's Ebenezer Baptist Church in 1894. In 1913, after his grandfather's death, his father took over the prosperous church. Yet in 1944, when fifteen-year-old Martin Jr. began attending all-black Morehouse College, he still wasn't sure that *he* wanted to take up the family calling. The emotional evangelism practiced by most black ministers at the time seemed to him overly crude, and he found it difficult to accept his father's literal interpretation of the Bible. At Morehouse, however, college president Benjamin Mays explained to King how a minister could fight poverty and injustice without sacrificing his intellect. Gradually, King changed his mind, and he was ordained a Baptist minister in 1948. Later that year, he entered Crozer Theological Seminary, a small private school outside the city of Philadelphia.

It was during a lecture at Crozer that King first became acquainted with the nonviolent strategies devised by Mohandas K. Gandhi to win India's recent independence from Great Britain. As King learned, Gandhi had taken Henry David Thoreau's principle of civil disobedience—that each person has a moral responsibility to disobey unjust laws—and applied it to a mass political movement. By filling the Indian jails with peaceful demonstrators and calling the world's attention to their plight, Gandhi forced the British government into ending its colonial rule—or, from a theological point of view, he used love to transform the British and redeem their sins. After Crozer, King attended Boston University, where he earned a Ph.D. in theology in 1955. He was at work on his dissertation when Montgomery's Dexter Avenue Baptist Church offered him a job in March 1954.

The staging area for the march itself was the plaza around the Washington Monument, from which point the crowd would walk less than a mile down Independence and Constitution Avenues to the Lincoln Memorial. The march portion of the program was supposed to begin at 11:30 A.M., but King and other movement leaders were delayed in meetings on Capitol Hill. When word reached them shortly after noon that the crowd was getting restless in the August heat and would begin marching soon with or without them, the leaders dashed out of the House and began frantically hailing taxicabs, forgetting that they already had limousines waiting for them. When President Kennedy head about his later in the day, he laughed.

Along with the rest of America, Kennedy watched the march and rally on television. The organizers had been hoping for 100,000 marchers; instead, they got 250,000, about a quarter of whom were white. Each speaker at the Lincoln Memorial was allotted seven minutes; Randolph gave the first address. "Fellow Americans," he began, "we are gathered here in the largest demonstration in the history of this nation. Let the nation and the world know the meaning of our numbers. We are not a pressure group; we are not an organization or a group of organizations; we are not a mob. We are the advance guard of a massive moral revolution for jobs and freedom."

The Bus Boycott

FRANKLIN ROOSEVELT'S EXECUTIVE ORDER 8802 had been a milestone in the African-American struggle for equal rights. Seven years later, in July 1948, Harry Truman followed it up with another executive order desegregating the armed forces. Yet in the Congress, southern Democrats blocked all civil rights legislation, and in the South, state laws mandating racial segregation remained as pervasive as ever.

More than 450 buses brought marchers to Washington from New York City alone. Given the close working relationship between the Justice Department and the march organizers, the event inevitably became identified with the administration's proposed civil rights bill. This meant that President Kennedy had a great deal riding on the march, and he was nervous. A recent Gallup poll had shown that 63 percent of Americans opposed the march and 38 percent thought that Kennedy was moving too quickly on integration. "We're all in this up to our necks," he told King at one point.

One such Jim Crow law required blacks in Montgomery, Alabama, to sit apart from whites on public buses. However, the specific segregation practiced by the Montgomery City Lines hardly met the "separate but equal" standard established by the Supreme Court in *Plessy v. Ferguson* (1896). Officially, Montgomery bus drivers were instructed to divide their buses into two sections—whites in the front and blacks in the rear—according to an imaginary line that moved in relation to the number of whites and blacks on the bus at any given time. As additional whites got on the bus, the white section was supposed to expand toward the back. The bus company's official policy was that it couldn't expand beyond the middle of the bus if all the seats farther back were taken. However, this wasn't the practice. During the early 1950s, no white person on a Montgomery city bus ever stood while a black person sat. Nor was it unusual for a crowd of blacks to stand while seats remained open in the white section.

Segregation in the South extended well beyond schools and public transportation to nearly every aspect of daily life.

On the night of Thursday, December 1, 1955, after an exhausting day of work at a downtown department store, forty-two-year-old seamstress Rosa Parks boarded a City Lines bus at Court Square for her trip home. She sat in the middle section, open to blacks as long as no white people were standing. At the next stop, more white riders boarded. After all the available seats in the front section were taken, one white man remained standing. Bus driver James F. Blake told the four blacks sitting in the fifth row to stand up. Three complied, but Rosa Parks refused. So Blake called the police. "A policeman approached me and asked me if the driver had asked me to stand," Parks recalled. "I said yes. He said, 'Why don't you stand up?' I said, 'I don't think I should have to stand up.' And I asked him, I said, 'Why do you push us around?' He said, 'I do not know, but the law is the law and you are under arrest.'"

Rosa Parks was often warned by her mother that one day her civil rights activities would get her lynched.

ROSA PARKS WAS NOT THE FIRST African American to refuse to give up her seat on a Montgomery bus. In fact, just a few months earlier, fifteen-year-old Claudette Colvin had been pulled off a bus in handcuffs for refusing to give up her seat. ("I done paid my dime. I ain't got no reason to move," Colvin had told the bus driver repeatedly.) E. D. Nixon, a former head of the local NAACP, began to raise money for Colvin's defense, and Parks, herself a former NAACP official and currently an adviser to the group's Youth Council, also became involved. When Nixon and Parks learned that the teenaged Colvin was pregnant, however, they decided to abandon their efforts because the defendant in any segregation test case, they believed, had to be above moral reproach.

When Nixon heard of Parks's arrest on the evening of December 1, he raised the money for her bond. Then he asked her whether she would consider using her case to challenge bus segregation in Montgomery. After discussing the matter with her husband and her mother, Parks agreed.

The first thing that Nixon did was make a list of Montgomery's black ministers. (Nixon, a sleeping car porter, wanted to avoid working through the Montgomery NAACP because he lacked influence with the group's current leaders, some of whom had snubbed Nixon because of his sixth-grade education.) At the top of Nixon's list was twenty-nine-year-old Ralph Abernathy, who was asleep when Nixon called at 5 A.M. on December 2. After discussing the situation with Abernathy, then pastor of Montgomery's First Baptist Church, Nixon called eighteen other ministers and scheduled a meeting for that Friday evening. By the time of the meeting, however, a boycott of the buses set for Monday, December 5—the day of Parks's trial—had already been organized. Late Thursday evening, Parks's lawyer, Fred Gray, had called Jo Ann Robinson, an Alabama State College English professor who was active in the black Women's Political Council, to tell her what had happened to Parks. Robinson knew Parks from the Colvin case and told Gray that Parks's arrest would make an ideal test case. After consulting with other Women's Political Council members, Robinson drove out to the college and worked all night, mimeographing thirty-five thousand handbills that she and her students distributed the next morning throughout Montgomery.

"This is for Monday, December 5, 1955," Robinson's text began. "Another Negro woman has been arrested and thrown into jail because she refused to get up out of her seat on the bus for a white person to sit down…. This has to be stopped. Negroes have rights, too, for if Negroes did not ride the buses, they could not operate. Three-fourths of the riders are Negroes, yet we are arrested, or have to stand over empty seats…. This woman's case will come up on Monday. We are, therefore, asking every Negro to stay off the buses Monday in protest of the arrest and trial. Don't ride the bus to work, to town, to school, or anywhere on Monday." A story on the impending boycott appeared in Sunday's *Montgomery Advertiser*; also that morning, the city's black ministers—including twenty-six-year-old Martin Luther King Jr., a newcomer to the community—reinforced Robinson's call from their pulpits.

The Montgomery Improvement Association

NO ONE KNEW WHAT WOULD HAPPEN on Monday. A few years earlier, King's predecessor at the Dexter Avenue Baptist Church, the Rev. Vernon Johns, had been told to give up his seat on a bus. Johns stood up but then urged the other black riders to leave the bus with him in protest. No one did.

"I was in the kitchen drinking my coffee, when I heard [my wife] Coretta cry, 'Martin, Martin, come quickly,'" King later recalled. "As I approached the front window, Coretta pointed joyfully to a slowly moving bus: 'Darling, it's empty!' I could hardly believe what I saw." That Monday, the forty thousand blacks who normally rode Montgomery's buses walked, taxied, bicycled, and even hitchhiked their way around town. None rode the buses. The protest was a complete success, and at a community meeting that night it was decided to continue the boycott.

Before December 1956, all buses in the South were segregated. Black riders paid their fares up front, then got off the bus and reentered it through the rear. Also, in black neighborhoods, the stops were farther apart than in white neighborhoods.

The mass meeting that night proved a turning point—not only in the struggle to desegregate Montgomery's buses, but in the national civil rights movement as a whole. Abernathy had been eager to get King involved in civil rights work, but King had thus far demurred, explaining that he was still too busy getting his new church in order. On the afternoon of December 5, however, before the public meeting began, the city's black ministers met with other black leaders to prepare an agenda. Abernathy persuaded the group to form an organization called the Montgomery Improvement Association (MIA) to coordinate the boycott. King was elected its president. According to E. D. Nixon, Reverend King was "a very intelligent young man [who] had not been here long enough for the city fathers to put their hand on him."

The December 5 meeting at the cavernous Holt Street Baptist Church was packed. "I parked many blocks from the church just to get a place for my car," *Advertiser* reporter Joe Azbell remembered.

I went on up to the church, and they made way for me because I was the first white person there.... The audience was so on fire that the preacher would get up and say, "Do you want your freedom?" And they'd say, "Yeah, I want my freedom!"... They were on fire for freedom. There was a spirit there that no one

SCHOOL INTEGRATION

THE CULMINATION OF THE NAACP'S effort to defeat segregation through legal means came on May 17, 1954, when the Supreme Court decided in *Brown v. Board of Education of Topeka, Kansas* that segregation in public education was unconstitutional. In overturning *Plessy v. Ferguson* (1896), the Court concluded unanimously that "in the field of public education the doctrine of 'separate but equal' has no place. Separate educational facilities are inherently unequal."

For more than a decade, the interracial staff of the NAACP Legal Defense Fund, headed by Thurgood Marshall, had carefully plotted the reversal of *Plessy.* One of the many steps along the way was the 1950 Texas Law School case, in which the Court ruled that an all-black law school hastily created by the

In one Virginia county, *the local board of education closed all the public schools rather than integrate them.*

state of Texas to meet the *Plessy* standard wasn't sufficient because it didn't measure up to the University of Texas's own all-white law school. Following this success, Marshall took up the *Brown* case to challenge segregation in public primary and secondary education.

The plaintiff in the case was the Rev. Oliver Brown, whose daughter Linda had to cross dangerous railroad tracks to reach her all-black school because she was barred from attending an all-white school in her own neighborhood. To buttress his argument, Marshall introduced into evidence research produced by psychologist Kenneth B. Clark that demonstrated the effect of segregation on black self-esteem. Clark had shown African-American children a black doll and a white doll, then asked them standardized questions. More than half answered that the white doll was the "nice" one and the black doll the "bad" one. Persuaded by Clark's work, Chief Justice Earl Warren wrote for the Court that separating schoolchildren "solely because of their race generates a feeling of inferiority as to their *could capture again…it was so powerful. And then King stood up, and most of them didn't even know who he was. And yet he was a master speaker…. I went back, and I wrote a special column. I wrote that this was the beginning of a flame that would go across America.*

THE HOLT STREET MEETING was the beginning of a new era in the struggle for African-American civil rights. For the past several decades, Philip Randolph (and E. D. Nixon) had worked through the labor movement while NAACP lawyers challenged racial segregation in the federal courts. The Montgomery boycott, however, launched a new phase of mass protest, and Martin Luther King Jr. became that movement's new voice and leader. He also gave it a new philosophy—based on the teachings of Gandhi and Thoreau, in addition to Jesus—that emphasized the redemption of racism through nonviolent civil disobedience. The civil rights struggle, King declared, was not against whites but against injustice; its most important weapons, he said, were not anger and hate but love and forgiveness. During the next year, he and his family were arrested and threatened—their house was bombed—yet King refused to go into hiding or accept the armed guards offered him. He would not succumb to hatred, he said.

status in the community that may affect their hearts and minds in a way unlikely ever to be undone."

Although the nation's public school systems were ordered to integrate "with all deliberate speed," those in the Deep South and Virginia resisted. In Little Rock, Arkansas, for example, a well-publicized integration battle took place in the fall of 1957. Defying a federal court order, Arkansas governor Orval Faubus called out the Arkansas National Guard to prevent nine black students from attending all-white Central High. State NAACP president Daisy Bates personally escorted the students to school on September 4 but was turned away.

The standoff continued for sixteen days until federal district court judge Ronald Davies ordered Faubus on September 20 to remove the National Guard. The following Monday, as several black journalists (mistaken for parents) were being beaten by a mob

Thurgood Marshall *during the early 1950s.*

U.S. Army soldiers escort *the Little Rock Nine from Central High in September 1957.*

outside the school, the Little Rock police slipped the students into Central High through a side door. By noon, however, the mob had swelled to more than a thousand people, persuading Police Chief Gene Smith to remove the Little Rock Nine from the school for their own safety. When the mob returned the next day, President Eisenhower reluctantly dispatched a thousand soldiers of the 101st Airborne Division to Little Rock to enforce Judge Davies's order. The federal troops remained in Little Rock until September 30, when federalized Arkansas national guardsmen replaced them.

A strategy of civil disobedience fit the African-American situation in Montgomery well, King believed, because Alabama's segregation code contradicted not only moral law but also federal law. Therefore, the MIA had a legal basis for its protests, and after the city commissioners refused to compromise, Fred Gray filed suit in federal court, challenging the constitutionality of bus segregation. Meanwhile, as the weeks and months passed, the boycott continued with close to 100 percent participation. A private taxi system was organized to help the boycotters travel around town, and many white women, reluctant to lose their maids and baby-sitters, picked up and dropped off their servants each day. A number of black churches used funds provided by members of Montgomery's Jewish community to buy station wagons, and three whites from nearby Maxwell Air Force Base volunteered their cars and their services as drivers.

In June 1956, a special three-judge federal panel ruled in favor of the boycotters. The city commissioners appealed, and the case eventually reached the Supreme Court, which on November 13 affirmed the lower court's opinion that bus segregation violated the Fourteenth Amendment. On December 20, the Court's written mandate arrived in Montgomery; the next day, the city's blacks ended their 382-day boycott, riding the buses again and sitting where they pleased. Yet the confrontation with Montgomery's whites wasn't over: Snipers fired rounds into passing buses, and a pregnant black woman was shot in the leg. In mid-January 1957, Ralph Abernathy's home was bombed.

Also in January 1957, ministers from eleven southern states met at Martin Luther King Sr.'s Ebenezer Baptist Church in Atlanta to discuss the success of the Montgomery boycott and how its lessons might be applied elsewhere. Before leaving, they created the Southern Christian Leadership Conference (SCLC), electing Martin Luther King Jr. as its president.

Ralph Abernathy (front row, left) and Martin Luther King Jr. (second row, left) ride in the front section of a Montgomery City Lines bus on December 21, 1956, the day that the boycott ended.

Sit-Ins and Freedom Rides

THE DIRECT-ACTION STRATEGY promoted by King and the SCLC quickly displaced the NAACP's gradualist legal approach as the movement's main focus. Inspired by the Montgomery boycotters, other southern blacks began organizing mass protests of their own, many focusing on the desegregation of public schools. After the 1957 school integration fight in Little Rock, the next major showdown came in Greensboro, North Carolina.

The downtown Woolworth's in Greensboro resembled most other American five-and-dimes. It sold cosmetics, school supplies, toys, and other inexpensive goods; it also had a lunch counter that refused to serve blacks. No chain store in the South did at the time. Nevertheless, on the afternoon of February 1, 1960, four polite, well-dressed freshmen from the all-black North Carolina Agricultural and Technical College sat down at the Woolworth's lunch counter in Greensboro and waited all day for service that never came.

Unsure of what to do next, Ezell Blair Jr., David Richmond, Franklin McCain, and Joseph McNeil approached a prominent black dentist in Greensboro, who wrote to the Congress of Racial Equality (CORE) in New York City on their behalf. A week later, CORE sent Gordon Carey to Greensboro to help the four students organize sustained sit-ins at all the downtown lunch counters. One by one, the chain stores agreed to integrate.

When SCLC executive director Ella Baker learned what was going on, she began telephoning her numerous contacts on college campuses throughout the South, urging them to become involved. "It's time to move," she said. In Little Rock, Daisy Bates recruited students to organize sit-ins there, while students from Alabama State College met at Ralph Abernathy's house to plan similar lunch-counter

Angry whites pour mustard and *ketchup on sit-in demonstrators at a Jackson, Mississippi, lunch counter in 1960. Anne Moody, author of the influential 1968 autobiography* Coming of Age in Mississippi, *can be seen seated at the far right.*

protests in Montgomery. Attracted by all the media attention, more students joined the sit-ins each day—including some whites. By April 1960, the campaign had spread to seventy-eight cities, bringing into the civil rights movement some seventy-five thousand college students.

Ella Baker was particularly excited by the emergence of committed young black leaders, among them John Lewis and Robert Moses. As one of the SCLC's more militant staff members, the fifty-six-year-old Baker knew that "there was a great deal of dissatisfaction among the young with the older leadership." To give the student leaders some direction, Baker persuaded King and the other SCLC ministers to sponsor a conference for them. The event took place over Easter weekend at Shaw University in Raleigh, North Carolina. John Lewis attended, as did white University of Michigan undergraduate Tom Hayden, who would soon become a key figure in Students for a Democratic Society (SDS). Baker spoke at the 1960 conference and, much to the chagrin of the more moderate SCLC leadership, encouraged the three hundred students gathered at Shaw to go their own way, rather than become a youth arm of the SCLC organization. The students took her advice and, before concluding their meeting, formed the Student Nonviolent Coordinating Committee (generally referred to by its acronym, SNCC, pronounced "snick").

BY EARLY 1961, the student sit-in movement, now being led by SNCC, had largely ended restaurant segregation in the South. The next battleground, it was decided, would be interstate transportation. Although most segregation was still legal in the South, travel between states presented a special case because it was subject to federal rather than state regulation. In fact, citing the Constitution's interstate commerce clause, the Supreme Court had recently ruled in *Boynton v. Virginia* (1960) that segregation on interstate buses was illegal. To pressure the new Kennedy administration into enforcing *Boynton*, James Farmer, CORE's national director, recruited an interracial group of Freedom Riders to travel on interstate buses through the South. Farmer's plan called for the white Freedom Riders to sit in the back of each bus and the blacks to sit up front. According to Farmer, "We felt we could count on the racists of the South to create a crisis so that the federal government would be compelled to enforce the law." He continued:

We wrote letters in advance, following the Gandhian program of advising your adversaries or the people in power of just what you were going to do.... I sent letters to President Kennedy, Robert Kennedy, J. Edgar Hoover, the chairman of the Interstate Commerce Commission, the president of Greyhound.... We got replies from none of those letters.

Just as the Freedom Rides were beginning, however, Robert Kennedy telephoned Martin Luther King Jr. and asked the SCLC leader to use his influence to arrange a postponement of the rides and a cooling-off period. King called Farmer, and Farmer consulted with Diane Nash of SNCC before calling King back: "I asked Dr. King to tell Bobby Kennedy that we'd been cooling off for 350 years, and that if we cooled off any more, we'd be in a deep freeze."

On May 4, 1961, thirteen Freedom Riders (including Farmer and SNCC's John Lewis) boarded buses in Washington, D.C., bound ultimately for New Orleans. Among the six whites in the group were forty-six-year-old James Peck, a CORE staff member who had been jailed during World War II for his pacifism, and Walter and Frances Bergman, both of whom were over sixty. Each of the Freedom Riders was committed to nonviolence; unfortunately, many southern whites were not. At first, there were a few scuffles. Then, on May 14, as a Greyhound bus carrying half of the Freedom Riders pulled into the station at Anniston, Alabama, a mob of two hundred whites attacked it. The bus sped away, but when slashed tires forced it to stop six miles outside of town, the mob caught up with it. A firebomb sailed in through a window, and the passengers barely escaped before the coach exploded.

Meanwhile, an equally enraged mob beat the other Freedom Riders as they got off their Trailways bus in Birmingham. (One Freedom Rider was paralyzed for life.) Birmingham commissioner of public safety Eugene "Bull" Connor later explained that none of his officers was on duty at the bus station that afternoon because it was Mother's Day. However, declassified FBI documents have shown that an informant warned the bureau in advance that the Birmingham police knew of the planned violence and intentionally stayed away.

The President Intervenes

INCREDIBLY, PRESIDENT KENNEDY didn't know about the Freedom Rides until he read about the beatings in the *New York Times* on Monday, May 15. His first reaction was anger: at the propaganda value the story would have for Soviets trying to make America look bad around the world; at the distraction the rides were causing just three weeks before his Vienna summit with Khrushchev; at the trouble he would ultimately have calming southern Democrats in Congress. He and his brother decided quickly, however, that the federal government would have

James Farmer (shown here in July 1966) later worked for a short time as an assistant secretary of health, education, and welfare in the Nixon administration.

to take the side of the Freedom Riders because that was the law and also the right thing to do. Attorney General Robert Kennedy sent the only southerner on his personal staff, John Seigenthaler, to Birmingham to help the trapped riders get out of town. Because neither Greyhound nor Trailways would carry them to New Orleans, they had to take a plane out of Birmingham. But the Freedom Rides didn't end there.

"If the Freedom Riders had been stopped because of violence," SNCC's Diane Nash recalled, "I strongly felt that the future of the movement was going to be cut short. The impression would have been that whenever a movement starts, all [you have to do] is attack it with massive violence and the blacks [will] stop." So a group of students from Nashville went down to Birmingham to continue the rides. Seigenthaler, who knew Nash, tried to persuade her to call off the protest, but she refused.

An irony of the situation was that it had been the president's own rhetoric that had inspired Nash and many other young black activists to become involved with the civil rights movement in the first place. They had all wanted to do something for their country—although Freedom Rides weren't exactly the sort of thing that Kennedy had had in mind. "We're going to show those people in Alabama who think they can ignore the president of the United States," Nash said. Meanwhile, in Washington, President Kennedy told his brother that he just wanted "this Goddamned civil rights mess" to go away.

On Friday, May 19, Seigenthaler met with Alabama governor John Patterson, who told him, "There's nobody in the whole country that's got the spine to stand up to the goddamned niggers except me." Patterson also warned Seigenthaler that

Some Freedom Riders watch their *bus burn outside Anniston, Alabama, on Mother's Day, 1961. Pictures of the flaming Greyhound were sent all over the country and appeared on most front pages the next morning— including President Kennedy's copy of the* New York Times.

KENNEDY AND CIVIL RIGHTS

JOHN F. KENNEDY's political relationship with Martin Luther King Jr. began during the 1960 campaign, when King was arrested during a lunch-counter sit-in and Senator Kennedy intervened to arrange his release. (By contrast, Vice President Nixon refused even to comment on King's situation.) During this episode, although Kennedy called King's wife to express his personal concern, the civil rights leader understood that the gesture was motivated by political expediency rather than any genuine commitment to the civil rights cause.

Once in the White House, however, Kennedy did more for that cause than any president since Lincoln— though he did so only when pushed. After the Freedom Rides, the next large shove came in the fall of 1962, when James Meredith attempted to integrate the University of Mississippi. A quiet air force veteran who said that he had been inspired by Kennedy's inaugural address, Meredith first filed suit for admission to Ole Miss during the summer of 1961. His case was handled by the NAACP Legal Defense Fund.

At first, Meredith lost when the federal district court judge in Jackson accepted the state's absurd contention that no policy of segregation existed at the all-white school. That ruling was reversed on appeal, but the circuit court withheld its final order until it met with Assistant Attorney General for Civil Rights Burke Marshall and asked him directly whether the president would enforce a desegregation order. Marshall told the judges that Kennedy (already planning for a second term) preferred a negotiated settlement but would use force, if necessary.

Mississippi governor Ross Barnett had a much simpler position: "No school in our state will be integrated while I am your governor," he had promised Mississippi's voters, nearly all of whom were white. On September 20, 1962,

Reporters approach James Meredith as he walks to class *on his first day as a student at the University of Mississippi.*

Barnett appeared at the Ole Miss campus in Oxford to turn Meredith away; then, five days later, he repeated the performance when Meredith tried to register at the university's Jackson office. At this point, Kennedy ordered five hundred federal marshals to Oxford under the command of Deputy Attorney General Nicholas Katzenbach. The marshals arrived on Sunday, September 30, planning to secure the campus and bring Meredith in that night, registering him the following morning.

At first, the operation went smoothly. The campus was quiet because many students had traveled to Jackson for the weekend to attend the Saturday football game against Kentucky. When they began to return on Sunday night, however, the presence of federal marshals caused tempers to flare. By 7 P.M., there was a riot under way. Students and others threw firebombs made from Coca-Cola bottles into the campus building where Katzenbach had established his headquarters, and sporadic gunfire could be heard throughout Oxford. At 10 P.M., after a dozen marshals had been shot and one reporter killed, Katzenbach called the White House to ask for the army troops that the president had already authorized.

Army Secretary Cyrus Vance gave the necessary order, but for some reason that has never been explained—perhaps reluctance, perhaps incompetence—the troops needed five hours to make the one-hour trip from Memphis. "They always give you their bullshit about their instant reaction and their split-second timing," the president complained as the siege at Oxford continued, "but it never works out. No wonder it's so hard to win a war." Finally, by dawn, sixteen thousand soldiers had secured Ole Miss, and at 9 A.M., James Meredith attended his first class there: Colonial American History.

there would be "warfare" if the federal government tried to enforce desegregation in Alabama. However, when Seigenthaler informed Patterson that the president was prepared to send in federal marshals, the governor agreed to have state police protect the Freedom Riders.

THE NEXT DAY, the twenty-one Freedom Riders waiting in Birmingham boarded a Greyhound bus for Montgomery. A plane monitored its progress, and highway patrol cars lined its route. But at the Montgomery city limits, the state police peeled off, and the bus entered the Montgomery terminal unescorted. Another mob attacked the riders, and even John Seigenthaler was knocked unconscious by a man swinging a pipe. When Robert Kennedy reached Seigenthaler that afternoon at a Montgomery hospital, he told his aide that the president would immediately be sending six hundred federal marshals to Montgomery.

By May 1961, Martin Luther King Jr. had shifted his base of operations to his father's church in Atlanta, but now he flew to Montgomery to take part in a Sunday-night rally at Ralph Abernathy's First Baptist Church. Later, several thousand angry whites surrounded the church, trapping King and fifteen hundred others inside. At 3 A.M., fearing that the federal marshals ringing the church might not be able to withstand the mob much longer, King called Robert Kennedy and angrily demanded whether or not there was law and order in the United States. According to Kennedy, "I said that I didn't think that he'd be alive if it hadn't been for us, that we were going to keep him alive, and that the marshals would keep the church from burning down." Soon thereafter, Deputy Attorney General Byron R. White called the White House from his command post at Maxwell Air Force Base and recommended that the president send in army troops. Learning of the call (and everything else going on at Maxwell) from the base's switchboard operator, Governor Patterson preempted the federal move by sending in Alabama national guardsmen to disperse the crowd and escort King to safety.

On May 24, two days after the church siege, twenty-seven Freedom Riders left Montgomery for Jackson. At the Mississippi state line, they found a phalanx of national guardsmen flanking the highway, scanning the forest on either side for snipers. In Jackson, instead of a mob, policemen escorted them through the terminal and straight to jail for violating the state's segregation laws. The Kennedys had made a deal with Mississippi's powerful, ardently segregationist senator, James O. Eastland: no violence, but also no federal enforcement of *Boynton*. Over the rest of that summer, while Robert Kennedy formally petitioned the Interstate Commerce Commission to issue a specific ruling against interstate bus segregation, more than three hundred additional Freedom Riders were arrested in Mississippi. To the president's relief, however, the story left the front pages.

Project "C"

ALTHOUGH KING HAD belatedly associated himself with the Freedom Rides, he was beginning to fall behind his own movement. John Lewis and the other SNCC leaders who had kept the CORE initiative going resented King's calls for moderation and disdained the SCLC leader's refusal to board a bus himself. (They felt that to share in the publicity, he should also share in the danger.) At the same time, King's primary constituencies, black ministers and churchgoers, pressured him to abjure actions that might encourage white violence. For two years, King

"I will never be concerned about [what people in other parts of the world are thinking]. In the first place, the average man in Africa or Asia doesn't even know where he is, much less where Alabama is."

—

George C. Wallace, May 1963

tried to find a middle path; in early 1963, however, he decided to make a stand in Birmingham—where white violence, he knew, would be unavoidable.

Known throughout the country as one of the South's most intransigently racist cities, Birmingham had been nicknamed "Bombingham" because of the fifty bombings directed at local blacks that had taken place there since the end of World War II. The victim of two of those attacks, the Rev. Fred L. Shuttlesworth of the Sixteenth Street Baptist Church, was King's chief local contact. With Shuttlesworth's help, King and other SCLC leaders developed a detailed plan for challenging segregation in Birmingham. The campaign, called Project "C" (for "Confrontation"), began on April 3, 1963, with a series of marches and boycotts directed against segregation in the downtown stores.

On April 10, an Alabama Circuit Court judge enjoined 133 specified civil rights leaders—including King, Abernathy, and Shuttlesworth—from taking part in the demonstrations. But King chose to defy the order and was arrested with Abernathy and fifty others on Good Friday, April 12. While imprisoned, King wrote his famous "Letter from Birmingham Jail," in which he declared:

> *For years now I have heard the word "Wait!" It rings in the ear of every Negro with piercing familiarity. This "Wait" has almost always meant "Never." We must come to see, with one of our distinguished jurists, that "justice too long delayed is justice denied."*

Birmingham firemen turn *their hoses on black demonstrators in May 1963. On May 2, Robert Kennedy called King to challenge his use of children, arguing that Bull Connor's tactics might permanently injure them. King apparently believed that the images Connor's brutality would produce were more important. Indeed, they were pivotal. Blacks should thank Connor, President Kennedy observed ironically at his June 1963 meeting with King: "After all, he's done more for civil rights than any of the rest of us."*

ON APRIL 20—realizing that, in their absence, the Birmingham demonstrations were losing momentum—King and Abernathy accepted release on bond so that they could launch the next phase of Project "C." Because many adults had been reluctant to participate in marches, fearing that they would lose their jobs if arrested, King aide James Bevel had suggested using children as demonstrators. "A boy from high school has the same effect in terms of being in jail, in terms of putting pressure on the city," Bevel pointed out, "…yet there's no economic threat to the family, because the father is still on the job." On Thursday, May 2, 6,000 children between the ages of six and eighteen marched; by the end of the day, 959 had been arrested and hauled off to jail in school buses. The next day, another thousand children stayed out of school to march. An angry and frustrated Bull Connor deployed the city's police dogs and ordered its firemen to use their hoses against the young marchers. The resulting images of black children being bitten by large dogs and knocked off their feet by powerful jets of water horrified countless Americans watching the news that night on television.

On Monday, May 6, the marching resumed. In one black elementary school, 1,339 of the 1,426 students were absent. By Monday night, more than twenty-five hundred marchers were in jail, two thousand of them children. On Tuesday, Jefferson County sheriff Melvin Bailey met with members of the city's business community and told them that Connor's police force was losing control of the situation. The store owners knew, of course, that rioting was bad for business, so they decided to make a deal with King and Shuttlesworth. On May 10, a settlement was announced: All downtown lunch counters and rest rooms would be integrated within ninety days. Also, black workers would henceforth be hired as clerks and salesmen on an equal basis with whites.

Both parties to the agreement hoped that Birmingham would now cool down, but on the night of May 11, the Ku Klux Klan held a rally outside the city at which Grand Dragon Robert Shelton declared, "Martin Luther King's epitaph…can be written in Birmingham." Several bombs were later exploded, including one at the Gaston Motel, where King had been staying. When a large crowd of blacks gathered there, Gov. George C. Wallace (who had replaced Patterson in January 1963) ordered state troops into Birmingham over the objection of Sheriff Bailey. Now the rioting began in earnest, with the state troopers and Connor's police beating black residents with clubs and rifle butts. Fearing that the violence in Birmingham might trigger outbreaks elsewhere, Robert Kennedy persuaded his brother to send in federal troops. The agreement between the businessmen and the SCLC was too important, the president said, to be "sabotaged by a few extremists."

When George Wallace (shown here in July 1963) first ran for governor of Alabama in 1958, he was considered a racial moderate and was endorsed by the NAACP. But he lost to a little-known racist and vowed never to forget. "John Patterson out-niggered me," Wallace said after that election. "And boys, I'm not going to be out-niggered again."

THE FEDERAL TROOPS quieted the city, but Alabama remained a trouble spot. Governor Wallace had promised during his 1962 campaign to "stand in the schoolhouse door" to prevent the integration of the University of Alabama, and on June 11 he did just that, physically blocking the enrollment of two black students until President Kennedy federalized the Alabama National Guard, and the general in charge ordered the governor to step aside. That night, Kennedy spoke to the nation about civil rights:

If an American, because his skin is dark, cannot eat lunch in a restaurant open to the public; if he cannot send his children to the best public school available; if he cannot vote for the public officials who represent him; if, in short, he cannot enjoy the full and free life which all of us want, then who among us would be content to have the color of his skin changed and stand in his place? Who among us would be content with the counsels of patience and delay?...

We face, therefore, a moral crisis as a country and as a people. It cannot be met by repressive police action. It cannot be left to increased demonstrations in the streets. It cannot be quieted by token moves or talk. It is a time to act in the Congress, in your state and local legislative bodies and, above all, in all of our daily lives.

I am, therefore, asking the Congress to enact legislation giving all Americans the right to be served in facilities which are open to the public—hotels, restaurants, theaters, retail stores, and similar establishments. This seems to me to be an elementary right. Its denial is an arbitrary indignity that no American in 1963 should have to endure.

During the week before the march, some Washington notables predicted violence and bloodshed, yet these fears turned out to be groundless. As New York Times reporter Russell Baker observed, "The sweetness and patience of the crowd may have set some sort of national high-water mark in mass decency."

The civil rights bill that Kennedy sent up to Capitol Hill on June 19 outlawed segregation in all interstate public accommodations, empowered the attorney general to halt the funding of federal programs in which discrimination was practiced, and declared that any person with a sixth-grade education was to be presumed literate for the purpose of voting (to prevent southern states from using rigged literacy tests to disqualify black voters). Two days later, King and Randolph announced their plans for the Washington march.

The Fragile Coalition

ALL THE MAJOR CIVIL RIGHTS organizations lined up behind the administration's bill—except for SNCC, which found Kennedy's proposals inadequate. In the speech that John Lewis originally intended to deliver at the Lincoln Memorial, he had declared that SNCC could not support the Kennedy bill because more definitive action was necessary.

"We will march through the South, through the heart of Dixie, the way Sherman did," Lewis was going to say. "We shall pursue our own scorched-earth policy and burn Jim Crow to the ground nonviolently." However, when copies of the speeches were circulated the day before the march and Washington archbishop Patrick Cardinal O'Boyle read Lewis's words, he told Rustin that he would refuse to give the rally's invocation unless Lewis changed his speech.

The civil rights movement in August 1963 was supported by a large yet fragile interracial coalition, of which O'Boyle represented an important constituency—the white clergy. The march couldn't afford to lose him, so King, Rustin, and even Robert Kennedy went to work on Lewis, pressuring him to accommodate the cardinal. It wasn't until an aging Philip Randolph took the young man aside and spoke to him, however, that Lewis agreed to alter his speech in deference to Randolph's many past sacrifices.

Lewis's edited speech remained one of the highlights of a program that also included numerous musical performances and celebrity cameos. By midafternoon, however, the day had grown long and hot, and the marchers restive. Near the end of the rally, Mahalia Jackson sang the weary crowd back to life with a memorable rendition of "I've Been 'Buked and I've Been Scorned." Then Martin Luther King Jr. approached the podium and began to speak. Ignoring the seven-minute time limit, he addressed the crowd and the nation for nineteen minutes. No one complained or moved to cut him off. His speech was perhaps the greatest ever given by an American:

I have a dream today! I have a dream that one day down in Alabama—with its vicious racists, with its governor having his lips dripping with the words of interposition and nullification—one day right there in Alabama, little black boys and black girls will be able to join hands with little white boys and white girls as sisters and brothers….

This is our hope. This is the faith that I go back to the South with. With this faith, we will be able to transform the jangling discords of our nation into a beautiful symphony of brotherhood. With this faith, we will be able to work together, to pray together, to struggle together, to go to jail together, to stand up for freedom together, knowing that we will be free one day…. And if America is to be a great nation, this must become true.

So let freedom ring from the prodigious hilltops of New Hampshire! Let freedom ring from the mountains of New York! Let freedom ring from the heightening Alleghenies of Pennsylvania! Let freedom ring from the snow-capped Rockies of Colorado! Let freedom ring from the curvaceous slopes of California! But not only that. Let freedom ring from Stone Mountain of Georgia! Let freedom ring from Lookout Mountain of Tennessee! Let freedom ring from every hill and mole hill of Mississippi. From every mountainside, let freedom ring.

The response, then as now, was overwhelming. Some people wept; others cheered. All appreciated that King had put into words the emotional legacy of three hundred years of discrimination and oppression. King's delivery impressed even the president, a fair elocutionist himself. "He's damned good," Kennedy remarked as he watched the minister speak on a television in the White House living quarters. "Damned good!"

Martin Luther King Jr. delivers his "I Have a Dream" speech at the Lincoln Memorial. The Justice Department had chosen this site for the rally because it was open, surrounded by water on three sides (making it easier to police), and far from commercial and residential districts (in case any violence did break out). As an added precaution, one of the president's advance men was stationed behind Lincoln's statue with a switch that controlled the power to the sound system. He was told to shut it down if any speaker became too incendiary.

"THE MARCH ON WASHINGTON took place because the Negro needed allies," Rustin later explained. "…The march was not a Negro action. It was an action by Negroes and whites together. Not just the leaders of the Negro organizations, but leading Catholic, Protestant, and Jewish spokesmen called the people into the street. And Catholics, Protestants, and Jews, white and black, responded." As Rustin suggests, the interracial quality of the civil rights movement of the late 1950s and early 1960s was important and undeniable, yet there was also a growing militancy among young blacks that couldn't be suppressed, no matter what John Lewis said or didn't say. In Birmingham and elsewhere, as white violence escalated, many African Americans began to doubt the wisdom of King's nonviolent approach and reconsidered whether the proper response to white violence was not, in fact, self-defensive violence of their own. Less than two weeks after the March on Washington— on Sunday, September 15—a bomb ripped through the Sixteenth Street Baptist Church in Birmingham, killing four young girls who had been participating in a Bible class. Two months after that, the president was killed in Dallas.

Some of the organizers of the March on Washington gather for a group photograph prior to the start of the rally. Randolph is seated in the middle, with King to his left and Lewis standing behind him.

There is no adequate way to describe the enormity of the effect that John Kennedy's November 22 assassination had on American politics, society, and culture. An entire generation had come to idolize the man, and his death deeply affected their beliefs and attitudes moving forward. Lincoln had had many enemies, even among northerners, and Kennedy, too, was reviled by numerous Americans, especially in the South. Yet among those of college age, such as Diane Nash and James Meredith, his call to "pay any price, bear any burden…to assure the survival and the success of liberty" had rerouted their lives.

"Whether you liked him politically or not," folksinger Phil Ochs explained in a 1968 interview, "Kennedy represented a whole force, a whole positive force, as a person, as a personality, as an image, as a man, as an American. He represented something great, and he was destroyed." Blacks in the civil rights movement began to suspect the motives of whites marching alongside them, and young whites, for their part, found themselves confronted with unquiet fears about America's goodness that would not be quelled through civil rights marches alone.

Among young white activists, the president's death was seen as proof that change couldn't come from within the political system. Furthermore, it caused many to wonder whether their work with the civil rights movement hadn't been merely vicarious protest. Many young blacks couldn't help wondering the same thing, and soon a faction within SNCC, attracted by Malcolm X's black nationalism, began to challenge the group's interracial leadership. In 1966, the black members of SNCC voted to expel all whites from the organization. The move was largely symbolic, however, because nearly all of the whites had already left.

BLACK POWER

THE TERM *BLACK POWER* first gained popularity during 1966, when Stokely Carmichael of SNCC promoted it in a series of speeches. Later, it came to describe a diverse array of militant civil rights politics, especially the aggressive alternatives being offered by those who had rejected King's nonviolence.

One primary source for Black Power ideology was the black nationalist movement of the early twentieth century, whose avatars (men such as Marcus Garvey and Elijah Muhammad) counseled African Americans to separate rather than integrate. An even more proximate source was Malcolm X, the chief spokesman for Muhammad's Nation of Islam, who preached self-determination and the right to retaliate with force against white violence.

After traveling to Mecca in early 1964 and learning that Islam (as opposed to the Nation of Islam) taught the equality of all races, Malcolm X stopped preaching that whites were devils and repudiated Elijah Muhammad, changing his name to El-Hajj Malik El-Shabazz. A year later—on February 21, 1965—he was murdered by Nation of Islam gunmen as he gave a speech at Harlem's Audubon Ballroom.

The Great Society

IN WASHINGTON, meanwhile, Lyndon Johnson masterfully used John Kennedy's martyrdom to achieve much more than a living Kennedy ever could have. A former Senate majority leader, Johnson was probably the most effective legislator this country has ever produced, and he understood the direction in which its history was moving—at least in domestic affairs. Although a Texan, LBJ recognized, as the Kennedys had, that integration was both inevitable and right. Yet his vision of what could be accomplished extended far beyond anything that John Kennedy, at heart a pragmatist, had ever imagined. Johnson didn't merely want to end segregation in interstate travel; he wanted to end it everywhere, while also improving education, ending poverty, and providing health care to all underprivileged Americans—black, white, and otherwise.

During early 1964, Johnson cannily made use of the nation's grief to force through Congress a civil rights bill significantly stronger than the one Kennedy had proposed. The Civil Rights Act of July 1964 outlawed racial discrimination in all public places, ending Jim Crow forever; it also banned discrimination in employment, union membership, and programs financed by the federal government. In the meantime, the president sent a special message to Congress on March 16, 1964, calling for a "war on poverty." His $962 million program, expanded to $3 billion by 1966, brought New Deal–style relief to the most intractable pockets of rural and urban poverty in America. It funded Head Start (preschool education for disadvantaged children), the Job Corps (vocational training for older youth), food stamps, VISTA (the domestic equivalent of Kennedy's much-lauded Peace Corps), and many more social welfare programs.

Nevertheless, as broad as it was, the War on Poverty represented but a single aspect of the president's Great Society program, which he announced to Congress in his January 1965 State of the Union address. During the first six months of that year—as LBJ also sent the first combat troops to Vietnam—he signed into law, courtesy of a a receptive Democratic Congress, the Appalachian Regional Development Act, a TVA for Appalachia; the Elementary and Secondary Education Act, which provided billions of dollars for school construction and teacher salaries; and Medicare, health care for the elderly that three previous Democratic presidents (including his idol, FDR) had wanted but failed to obtain. Other Great Society initiatives protected consumers, safeguarded the environment, and created the Department of Housing and Urban Development, along with public radio and television.

President Johnson delivers the January 1965 State of the Union address in which he outlined his goals for the Great Society. Johnson's personal goal was also greatness—even beyond that achieved by his political idol, Franklin Roosevelt.

IN THE MINDS of many black leaders, however, there remained an important issue that Lyndon Johnson had overlooked: voter registration. Beginning in 1961 with SNCC's early efforts in Mississippi, the civil rights movement had been devoting more and more resources to this task, especially after the 1964 Civil Rights Act settled the matter of segregation. Voter registration required a great deal of grassroots organizing, SNCC's specialty, yet in late 1964, even the SCLC got involved, targeting Selma, Alabama, for its own highly publicized registration campaign. At the time, blacks in Selma made up more than half of the city's population, yet fewer than 1 percent of them were registered to vote.

SNCC was already well established in Selma when King arrived on January 2, 1965. Its field-workers had been helping organize local residents for more than two years; lately, however, SNCC's effort had flagged because of persistent funding problems and staff exhaustion. For this reason (and because of their general preference for the SCLC over SNCC), Selma's black ministers welcomed King's involvement gratefully; among the SNCC staff, however, there was resentment. A strong rivalry already existed between the two organizations—one whose eager young members lived in the communities in which they worked; the other whose older professional staff came and went as they believed they were needed. To the SNCC volunteers in Selma, Reverend King seemed a mixed blessing at best: They appreciated the money and attention he brought with him, yet they disliked what they considered his flashiness and his habit of jetting off to yet another trouble spot before truly settling anything in the place where he had been. As many of them knew from personal experience, the letdown following King's departure could be crushing; local conditions often got worse in the short run, not better.

THE MISSISSIPPI SUMMER PROJECT

ROBERT MOSES was one of many northern blacks drawn to the South in 1960 by the sit-in movement. Early on, however, he realized that desegregating lunch counters, though symbolically important, mattered little as long as southern blacks were denied the right to vote. During the summer of 1961, he led a SNCC initiative to register voters in Mississippi, where only sixty thousand of the state's approximately one million blacks were then able to exercise their franchise. Moses set up field offices around the state and staffed them with workers, who went door to door persuading blacks to register and helping them with the forms. Of course, white Mississippians resisted as they always had, with stonewalling and with physical intimidation to keep as many blacks as possible off the voter rolls.

In 1962, SNCC and CORE formed the Council of Federated Organizations (COFO) to coordinate their activities in Mississippi. The SCLC and the NAACP were also nominally involved, but SNCC and CORE set COFO's agenda, emphasizing grassroots organizing. COFO's goal for the summer of 1964 was to create a black political structure within the state. To accomplish this, Moses worked closely with New York City lawyer Allard Lowenstein. (Moses had once taught mathematics at Lowenstein's alma mater, the private Horace Mann School.) Together, they created the Mississippi Summer Project, which set out to mobilize an interracial army of northern volunteers, most of them college students on summer break.

Although some black COFO staffers wanted to restrict the role of white volunteers, Moses defended their participation—and even those reluctant to include whites acknowledged that their involvement would bring national media attention

to Mississippi and help expose the appalling conditions there. The whites would also be paying their own way, guaranteeing COFO $150 for traveling expenses and $500 in bail money. Moses knew that sending student volunteers into rural Mississippi to register blacks was dangerous, but he also knew that little in Mississippi in 1964 was safe for civil rights workers.

The volunteers' primary task was to register voters for the new Mississippi Freedom Democratic party (MFDP) so that it could challenge the legitimacy of Mississippi's all-white Democratic regulars. By the time the interracial MFDP held its state convention on August 6, Summer Project volunteers had signed up sixty thousand members. Two weeks later, MFDP delegates traveled to Atlantic City to press their case at the Democratic national convention.

Furious because of the embarrassment he expected the MFDP to cause him, President Johnson twisted numerous arms to prevent the credentials fight from reaching the convention floor. In the end, the MFDP was offered two at-large seats and a promise that no segregated delegations would be seated at the 1968 convention. But MFDP vice chair Fannie Lou Hamer thought this wasn't enough, and she persuaded her group to decline Johnson's offer. "We didn't come all this way for no two seats when all of us is tired," Hamer said.

After the convention, feeling betrayed by the Democratic party, Robert Moses left Mississippi. He spent several years resisting the draft before leaving the United States altogether in 1969 to teach mathematics in Tanzania.

Queens College student Andrew Goodman left COFO's Ohio training center for Mississippi on Saturday, June 20, 1964. He was assigned to the CORE office in Meridian, and on Sunday, June 21, he traveled with CORE workers Michael Schwerner and James Chaney to Neshoba County to investigate a church burning. Just after 3 P.M., all three were arrested for speeding by Deputy Sheriff Cecil Price, who jailed them until the sun had set without allowing them any phone calls. After their 10:30 P.M. release, Goodman, Schwerner, and Chaney disappeared. A reward eventually led the FBI on August 4 to their badly beaten bodies. Price and five others were convicted on civil rights charges after Mississippi governor Paul Johnson refused to prosecute them for murder.

At first, for the sake of the Selma community, the two groups worked together. Their joint effort began on January 18, 1965, with a series of marches to the Selma courthouse. The purpose of these marches was to show the nation watching on television the sort of violence to which southern blacks were routinely subjected whenever they tried to register to vote. On February 1, King was arrested and jailed, joining three thousand other demonstrators already in prison. On February 4, at SNCC's invitation, Malcolm X came to Selma, where he told a capacity crowd at Brown's Chapel that "the white people should thank Dr. King for holding people in check, for there are other [black leaders] who do not believe in these [nonviolent] measures."

On February 6, Lyndon Johnson became involved, announcing that he would soon send to Congress a new voting rights bill. To keep the pressure on, a nighttime march was held on February 18 in the town of Marion, a few miles west of Selma. Suddenly, all the streetlights went out—at which point, auxiliary policemen, state troopers, and angry white civilians rushed the peaceful demonstrators with clubs and sticks raised. One of those beaten was Jimmie Lee Jackson's eighty-two-year-old grandmother. Jackson helped her into a local café to escape further injury. However, when several policemen followed him in, and one began beating his mother, the twenty-six-year-old Jackson struck back. One officer smashed his face with a billy club, while another pulled a gun and shot Jackson fatally in the stomach. Jimmie Lee Jackson died seven days later.

The Selma-to-Montgomery March

TWO DAYS AFTER JACKSON'S DEATH—on Sunday, February 28—James Bevel proposed in a sermon that a protest march be staged from Marion to the state capitol at Montgomery, sixty-five miles away. (As the plan developed, it was decided instead that the march would begin in Selma.) Governor Wallace announced that he would not allow the march because it would tie up traffic on one of the state's major highways. Nevertheless, on March 7, six hundred people lined up behind King aide Hosea Williams (the SCLC leader was off in Atlanta for the day) to cross the Edmund Pettus Bridge leading out of Selma.

On the far side of the bridge, the demonstrators encountered several hundred Alabama state troopers, most of them slapping billy clubs across their palms in an intimidating fashion. Maj. John Cloud ordered the marchers to disperse, then he told his men to advance. The officers knocked the first row of marchers off their feet. "The police were riding along on horseback, beating people," future UN ambassador Andrew Young recalled. "The tear gas was so thick you couldn't get to where the people were who needed help." All three networks interrupted their regular programming to show footage of the police assault. "When that beating happened at the foot of the bridge, it looked like war," Selma mayor Joseph Smitherman remembered. "That went all over the county. And…the wrath of the nation came down on us."

From Atlanta, King immediately sent telegrams all over the nation, asking prominent clergymen to join him in Selma for "a ministers' march" on March 9. On Monday, March 8, he petitioned federal district court judge Frank M. Johnson to issue an injunction barring Governor Wallace from interfering with the march. Instead, Johnson enjoined King, pending a hearing later that week. On Tuesday morning, King began the march in Selma as scheduled. However, when he encountered Cloud's state troopers, once again stationed on the far side of the Pettus Bridge, he knelt in prayer and then turned the dismayed marchers around. SNCC staffers accused King of selling them out, but he later explained that he had promised only to proceed until violence became imminent.

Marchers led by King cross the *Edmund Pettus Bridge in Selma on March 9, 1965, before encountering the Alabama state police and turning around.*

Later on March 9, King asked those who had traveled to Selma to stay on a few days longer until the injunction could be lifted. One of those who stayed, white Unitarian minister James Reeb, was beaten to death that night as he left a soul food restaurant in Selma. Ironically, white America's outraged reaction to Reeb's death left many blacks embittered. According to SNCC executive committee member Stokely Carmichael, who had spoken at Jimmie Lee Jackson's funeral, "It seemed to me that the movement itself was playing into the hands of racism. What you want is the nation to be upset when anybody is killed…but it almost [seems that] for this to be recognized, a white person must be killed."

ON SATURDAY, MARCH 13, while Judge Johnson deliberated, Governor Wallace flew to Washington to meet with the president. Assistant Attorney General for Civil Rights Burke Marshall was at the meeting. "Governor Wallace didn't quite grovel, but he was [very] pliant by the end of two hours, with President Johnson putting his arm around him and squeezing him and telling him it's a moment of history, and how do we want to be remembered in history? Do we want to be remembered as petty little men, or do we want to be remembered as great figures that faced up to our moments of crisis?" Two nights later, President Johnson himself appeared before a joint session of Congress to present his new voting rights bill, which would become five months later the Voting Rights Act of 1965. In his speech, Johnson caused quite a stir when he invoked the civil rights movement's most powerful slogan:

Alabama state troopers on the steps of the capitol in Montgomery, awaiting the arrival of the marchers from Selma who traveled only by daylight. At night, they slept in tents along the roadside.

> *Even if we pass this bill, the battle will not be over. What happened in Selma is part of a far larger movement which reaches into every section and state of America. It is the effort of American Negroes to secure for themselves the full blessings of American life. Their cause must be our cause, too, because it is not just Negroes but really it is all of us who must overcome the crippling legacy of bigotry and injustice. And we shall overcome.*

"We were all sitting around together…and when LBJ said, 'And we shall overcome,' we all cheered," SCLC organizer C. T. Vivian recalled. "And I looked over…and Martin was very quietly sitting in the chair, and a tear ran down his cheek. It was a victory like none other. It was an affirmation of the movement." The next day, Judge Johnson lifted the injunction.

Calling King and his colleagues "Communist-trained anarchists," Governor Wallace still refused to provide police protection for the marchers, claiming that his state couldn't afford the expense. So President Johnson federalized the Alabama National Guard and ordered eighteen hundred guardsmen (along with two thousand army troops, a hundred FBI agents, and a hundred federal marshals) to defend the marchers along the entire length of their route. On Sunday, March 21, the fifty-four-mile Selma-to-Montgomery march began once more, with King leading the way across the Edmund Pettus Bridge. Their column reached Montgomery four days later, by which time it had swelled to more than twenty-five thousand people. Tens of millions more watched on national television, as King walked up the steps of the Alabama state capitol with Rosa Parks, Philip Randolph, Roy Wilkins, and John Lewis at his side. Then King spoke:

> *Last Sunday, more than eight thousand of us started on a mighty walk from Selma, Alabama. We have walked through desolate valleys and across the trying hills…. But today, as I stand before you and think back over that great march, I can say, as Sister Pollard said—*
>
> *A seventy-year-old Negro woman who lived in this community during the bus boycott, one day she was asked while walking if she didn't want to ride. And when she answered, "No," the person said, "Well, aren't you tired?" And with her ungrammatical profundity, she said, "My feets is tired, but my soul is rested." And in a real sense this afternoon, we can all say that our feet are tired, but our souls are rested.*

The New Left and the Counterculture

THE SELMA MARCH WAS, as King asserted, a great victory for the movement. It helped win passage of the 1965 Voting Rights Act, which eliminated literacy tests and other obstacles to black registration and also created a corps of federal examiners to ensure that the process of registration would be fair and open. Yet the Selma march nevertheless marked the end of the coalition that had brought blacks and white, moderates and radicals, together. There would be no more mass interracial demonstrations. Instead, King pursued broader and more national causes, such as halting the escalating war in Vietnam and alleviating poverty, while more radical African Americans embraced Black Power and young whites created their own political organizations.

Development of a separate white radical political consciousness had lagged behind white involvement in the civil rights movement because whites, at first, lacked a radicalizing spur equivalent to racial prejudice in the black community. However, all that changed during the mid-1960s, as white northerners gained political experience in the South and President Johnson decided to send hundreds of thousands of young draftees to Vietnam. Among the earliest and most active groups in the New Left (as the white youth movement was called) was Students for a Democratic Society, which began campaigning for political change in 1960 as a renamed version of the Student League for Industrial Democracy.

With roots reaching all the way back to the Progressive era, the venerable League for Industrial Democracy had been a staple of the Old Left of the 1930s. The creation of SDS, however, marked the supersedure of the Old Left and its class-based ideology by a new generation of social activists promoting "participatory democracy." Meeting in June 1962 at a United Auto Workers vacation camp in southeastern Michigan, the leaders of SDS produced the landmark Port Huron Statement. Primarily the work of Tom Hayden, the manifesto set as the goal of the organization the creation of a political system in which power was vested not in representative institutions but in communities and individuals. Before 1965, of course, most SDS members focused their efforts on supporting the civil rights

Tom Hayden tries to stand after being assaulted by a segregationist in McComb, Mississippi, in October 1961. Hayden was in Mississippi working as a freelance reporter to spread news of the civil rights activities taking place there.

movement as SNCC and CORE volunteers. Yet, by the time of the Selma march, their attention had shifted to raising the political consciousness of the nearly six million students then attending U.S. colleges and universities.

In 1963, University of California president Clark Kerr had boasted in *The Uses of the University* that his Berkeley campus was the first "multiversity," a huge new public investment in the training of cogs for the machinery of American industrial democracy. Many Berkeley students, however, failed to share Kerr's vision. One was Mario Savio, a New Yorker studying philosophy at one of Berkeley's graduate schools. Savio had spent the summer of 1964 in Mississippi, registering blacks and learning the methodology of civil disobedience. After returning to Berkeley in the fall, he realized that some of the same rights for which he had been crusading on behalf of Mississippi's blacks were currently being denied to him at his own university.

WHAT CAME TO BE CALLED the Free Speech Movement (FSM) began on September 15, 1964, when Dean of Students Katherine Towle notified all student organizations on the Berkeley campus that, beginning the following week, tables for distributing political literature would no longer be allowed on Bancroft Avenue, the most heavily traveled strip on campus. On September 30, after two weeks of minimally successful negotiations, five students still manning tables there were summoned to Towle's office in Sproul Hall for disciplinary action. Five hundred students showed up, staging a sit-in that lasted all night. Later, under Savio's leadership, a strike was called, rallies were held, and in December Bob Dylan played on the steps of Sproul before a thousand students and faculty members began another sit-in. In January 1965, the Berkeley administration recanted, lifting the restrictions governing on-campus political activity.

Although the Free Speech Movement ostensibly involved a First Amendment dispute, it actually represented much, much more. It expressed, most importantly, the widespread disaffection that many white students felt toward the society to which Clark Kerr had pledged them and also helped participants recognize the strong bonds of age, ideology, and lifestyle that joined them together. These bonds provided the basis for what soon became known as "the counterculture"—the attempt of the under-thirty generation to establish its own cultural norms and mores within, yet apart from, the society of their parents. There was more to the counterculture, however, than simply New Left politics.

Another crucial element was the "hippie" subculture then developing in the Haight Ashbury, a low-rent neighborhood across the bay in San Francisco. During the mid-1960s, San Francisco and Berkeley represented two distinct states of mind,

> "We must have a try at bringing society under human control."
>
> —
> *Tom Hayden, SDS memo, early 1962*

Mario Savio addresses a November 1966 rally outside Sproul Hall on the campus of the University of California at Berkeley.

often existing in varying measures within the same person. Both the hippies and the student radicals generally agreed on the goal—happiness in the here-and-now—yet they disagreed substantially on the proper means of attaining it. In the Haight, where utopianism (or romantic escapism) prevailed, direct political action was distrusted. "Instead of protesting about the war with twenty people," Paul Kantner of the Jefferson Airplane complained, "I'd rather take those same twenty people out into the woods and get 'em high and swimming in a stream. And just doing that shows them a much better way to live and will convert them a lot faster than yelling in their faces at a rally. That's the difference between Berkeley and San Francisco." In Berkeley, meanwhile, the radicals had a great deal of difficulty reconciling such attitudes with Karl Marx's famous dictum that "a revolution involves a change in structure. A change in style is not a revolution."

A San Francisco concert poster from December 1967. Before accepting the "hippie" moniker (a gift of the media) in early 1967, the bohemians in the Haight referred to themselves as "freaks." The distinction is philologically instructive: A freak is an isolated social anomaly, whereas a hippie can only exist as part of a group bound by a common hipness. The San Francisco freaks met each other and became hippies on the dance floors of the Fillmore and Winterland ballrooms.

By early 1967, however, these distinction had blurred. Many Berkeley students had begun spending time in the Haight, still espousing political action but looking and acting rather differently. They were sharing the hippies' drugs, following their fashions, and believing, as the hippies did, that all revolutions must start with the self. The radicals even came to accept the hippie quest for a new community, and this acceptance gave them access to powerful cultural weapons they had previously disdained.

NINETEEN-SIXTY-SEVEN, the year of the Summer of Love, was also the year in which opposition to the war in Vietnam, previously confined to college campuses, emerged as a national issue. Even the most cloistered hippies couldn't ignore it, because the males all had draft cards. With Martin Luther King Jr. leading peace marches in March and April 1967, the antiwar "mobilization" quickly came to overshadow the civil rights movement as the focus of most political protest in the United States. Since the Selma march, King had been struggling to redefine himself and his crusade. In June 1966, he had moved his family to Chicago, where he began organizing black tenants to force improvements in slum housing. He found, however, that opposition in the North was much subtler and more sophisticated than the confrontational violence he had encountered in the South. Chicago mayor Richard Daley commanded one of the most effective political machines in the history of American politics, and he enjoyed the loyalty of several key black leaders in the community. Unable to mold the rest into an effective opposition, King stumbled badly. His interjection of southern strategies into a northern environment produced mostly frustration and, unfortunately, some rioting.

After Chicago, King continued to pursue economic equality for African Americans, yet he also became much more involved in the antiwar movement as he became convinced that blacks were paying disproportionately the social cost of U.S. involvement in Vietnam. In December 1967, he began planning a Poor People's March on Washington to take place the following April; in addition to the usual mass rally, the march would include boycotts, strikes, and sit-ins at federal office buildings designed to shut down the city. King called the nonviolent protest "disruptive without being destructive" and summarized its goal as "Jobs or

Income," to be provided by WPA-style government relief. "We have got to confront the power structure massively. We can't live with another summer like the last," the SCLC leader told a reporter in January 1968. He was referring to the ghetto violence in Detroit, Newark, and elsewhere during the summer of 1967, which had left nearly a hundred people dead.

While King was planning the Poor People's March, sanitation workers in Memphis, nearly all of them black, staged a strike against the city over their demand for union recognition. SCLC's Memphis office became deeply involved, eliciting the support of such national luminaries as Bayard Rustin, Roy Wilkins, and United Auto Workers president Walter Reuther, whose integrated union had long supported the cause of civil rights. As usual, King was expected to hold the diverse coalition together, yet the task proved difficult, primarily because of the militancy of many young blacks. They shouted, "Black Power!" at the mass meetings King held in Memphis and threw rocks and bottles at the police, who responded with much more effective and systematic violence.

Beginning in July 1964 with a riot in Harlem, the United States experienced five consecutive summers of racial violence. The worst occurred in the Watts neighborhood of Los Angeles in August 1965, in Newark in July 1967, and in Detroit later that month. This photograph shows New Jersey national guardsmen patrolling Newark, where twenty-three people died in four days of chaos.

Assassination

ON APRIL 3, 1968, a depressed King gave a melancholy speech in which he said, "Like anybody, I would like to live a long life. Longevity has its place. But I'm not concerned with that now. I just want to do God's will. And He's allowed me to go up to the mountain. And I've looked over, and I've seen the promised land. I may not be there with you, but I want you to know that we as a people will get to the promised land." The next day, as King stood on the balcony of the Lorraine Motel in Memphis, sniper James Earl Ray shot and killed him. Captured a month later at London's Heathrow Airport, Ray confessed to the crime but later recanted. Because he had no apparent motive for the killing, a congressional committee investigating the assassination in 1976 concluded that Ray had likely been hired by others, though all such conspiracy theories remain unproven.

The congressional investigation also confirmed that FBI director J. Edgar Hoover had been using his agency to conduct a "war" to "destroy" King, whom Hoover considered a threat because he could "unify and electrify" the African-American community. Furthermore, the campaign against the civil rights leader, which included electronic surveillance and anonymous notes to his wife revealing infidelities exposed by the bugs, was part of a much larger FBI program, Cointelpro, that Hoover used to attack the New Left. The offices of the Socialist Workers party, for example, were burglarized by FBI agents ninety-two times between 1960 and 1966, and the names gathered used to single out more than ten thousand people for special tax audits.

After learning of the April 4 assassination, Robert F. Kennedy sent a Kennedy family plane to transport King's body back to Atlanta. On April 9, he marched personally in the slain leader's funeral cortege. More so than anyone else, the former attorney general had been profoundly shaken by his brother's assassination. Having identified himself completely with Jack Kennedy's political career, Bobby had to reassemble himself from the ground up after Jack's death. At first, he thought about running for vice president in 1964, but Lyndon Johnson (no friend) refused to choose him. Instead, he ran for a Senate seat from New York and won.

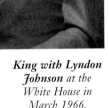

ALTHOUGH RFK DISLIKED the routine of the Senate and the details of state party leadership, he persevered with these tasks as he built a national constituency for a future run at the White House. His allies within the antiwar movement pushed him to challenge President Johnson in 1968, but Kennedy refused, believing that it would be impolitic to take on a sitting president from his own party (especially one as wily as Johnson). Instead, Minnesota senator Eugene McCarthy picked up the antiwar standard—and nearly beat Johnson in the March 1968 New Hampshire primary. Recognizing the president's vulnerability, Robert Kennedy changed his mind and entered the race; once Johnson bowed out at the end of March, Vice Pres. Hubert Humphrey also became a candidate.

King with Lyndon Johnson at the White House in March 1966.

April 1968 was a particularly difficult month in which to campaign for president. In addition to King's assassination, which produced a great deal of spontaneous ghetto rioting, there was also the disappointment of the Poor People's March (which Ralph Abernathy led in King's absence) and the occupation of administration buildings on the Columbia University campus by SDS leaders who objected to the school's involvement in defense research and its condescending treatment of the largely black Morningside Heights and Harlem communities. On April 30, Columbia president Grayson Kirk signed a formal police complaint charging the

A mule-drawn wagon carries King's casket through the streets of Atlanta on April 9, 1968.

students with trespassing. The New York City police then moved in to "bust" the students both figuratively and literally.

That same day, Eugene McCarthy won the Massachusetts Democratic primary. A week later, however, Kennedy won the Indiana primary, and on May 14, he also won in Nebraska. Thus, the two leading antiwar candidates approached the June 4 primary in California running neck and neck. The winner would face off against Humphrey,

The scene inside the convention hall on the second night of the Republican convention in early August 1968. Curiously, because of Wallace's presence in the presidential race, Nixon received two million fewer votes winning in 1968 than he did losing in 1960.

who had the support of most party regulars, at the Democratic convention in Chicago. Just before midnight on the night of the California primary, Kennedy appeared before a capacity crowd in the ballroom of the Ambassador Hotel to claim a hard-fought victory. As he left through the hotel kitchen, however, he was shot by Palestinian immigrant Sirhan B. Sirhan, dying two days later.

The Silent Majority

FOR REPUBLICAN CANDIDATE Richard Nixon, the sense of disarray in the country was an important political asset. He spoke often of the "silent majority" of Americans, who rejected political protest and sought stability above all. Many voters had indeed heard enough about their country's shortcomings, and they responded well to such gestures as John Wayne's "inspirational reading" of "Why I Am Proud to Be an American" at the Republican National Convention in Miami. Casting aside his previous political persona, Nixon presented himself now as a harmonizer, even promising that he had a secret plan to end the Vietnam War "with honor."

Nixon's eventual Democratic opponent, Hubert Humphrey, didn't have the same opportunity to express his own misgivings about the war. Instead, he carried the burden of the president's Vietnam policy as best he could. A proud and accomplished liberal, Humphrey would probably have beaten Nixon in another year—but not in 1968, not after the Chicago convention. Inside the convention hall, the bitter fight between the McCarthy delegates, who had won their seats in primary elections, and the Humphrey delegates, who controlled the party machinery, alienated most of the party's liberal activists. Meanwhile, outside the hall, the damage was much worse. During the months preceding the convention, Jerry Rubin, Abbie Hoffman, and several other antiwar radicals with a taste for political theater had made plans for thousands of other young men and women to demonstrate in Chicago under the auspices of their Youth International party, created specifically for the occasion. (Intending to nominate a pig for president, the Yippies even brought a swine with them to Chicago to parade before the media.)

Chicago's Mayor Daley simply could not abide such shenanigans. He angrily ordered the removal of the demonstrators, whom he considered a personal embarrassment, and the Chicago police complied with excessive (at times brutal) force. Along with the Yippies, many journalists were also beaten in what newspaper and television reporters called a "police riot." The outcome for Humphrey couldn't have been much worse, and the vice president never recovered. Nevertheless, Nixon's margin of victory was less than 1 percent of the popular vote, and even with all his troubles, Humphrey might still have won had it not been for both an electoral boycott by many Democrats and the independent candidacy of George Wallace, whose calls for victory in Vietnam and "law and order" at home appealed to many northern blue-collar Democrats. Wallace won nearly ten million votes, or 13.5 percent of the popular total, including decisive margins in several key battleground states.

ONCE IN OFFICE, Nixon indeed attempted to promote retrenchment and tranquility, but his ambivalence on U.S involvement in Vietnam quickly got him into trouble. Nixon's secret plan to end the war in Southeast Asia turned out to be "Vietnamization," or the transfer of all combat responsibilities to South Vietnamese troops, which Lyndon Johnson had already begun. It was Nixon, however, who announced on June 8, 1969, the first withdrawal of American combat troops from Vietnam—twenty-five thousand soldiers, or about 5 percent of the U.S. military presence. The problem Nixon encountered, however, was that, even with increased aid, the withdrawal of American troops meant more battlefield losses for the South Vietnamese. To compensate for this, Nixon announced on April 30, 1970, that the United States would temporarily invade Cambodia, where the North Vietnamese had established supply bases for the Vietcong. His explanation, delivered in a nationally televised speech, was that he had to intensify the war in order to end it.

Many college students and other opponents of the war dismissed this reasoning as pure sophistry and participated in angry demonstrations that weekend on campuses all over the country. At Kent State University in Ohio, a follow-up rally was planned for Monday, May 4, beginning at noon. Unwisely, Gen. Robert H. Canterbury of the Ohio National Guard had authorized his soldiers, ordered to the campus over the weekend, to use live ammunition. One unit of 113 guardsmen became separated from the rest and began marching up Blanket Hill. A group of students followed the guardsmen, taunting them from about a hundred yards away. "At 12:24," James Michener wrote in *Kent State*, his comprehensive 1971 investigation of the tragedy, "with the escape route back to ROTC completely unimpeded…, some guardsmen on the trailing right flank stopped, wheeled 135 degrees to the right—that is, they turned almost completely around—faced the students who had collected on the south side of Taylor Hall, and dropped their rifles to ready position." According to tape recordings made by several journalism students, the shooting that followed lasted about ten seconds. Four people were killed, two of them bystanders. "Have we come to such a state in this country that a young girl has to be shot because she disagrees deeply with the actions of the government?" the father of one of the slain students asked.

A Kent State student picks up one of the many tear-gas canisters used on May 4 and throws it back at the National Guard. Later, it was suggested that the gas masks worn by the guardsmen contributed to the tragedy because they made the soldiers feel disassociated from their environment.

AMERICAN PROFILE

Coya Knutson
1912–1996

by Richard Reeves

BEFORE THE advent of "women's liberation," a woman's place was clearly "in the home." Betty Friedan dismantled this notion in her landmark 1963 study *The Feminine Mystique*. Later, New Yorker Bella Abzug won a noisy congressional race with her combative slogan, "This Woman's Place Is in the House"—as in the House of Representatives. But it mustn't be forgotten that the shift in thinking from "house" to "House" was relatively abrupt and rather grudgingly accomplished. As late as 1958, the phrase "A woman's place is in the home"—and the ideas behind it—were so well ingrained in the American psyche that they cost Rep. Coya Knutson her job.

Before entering politics, Cornelia Gjesdal Knutson was a high school music teacher, a farmer's wife, and a boardinghouse operator in Oklee, Minnesota, population 495. Like many women, she left the kitchen again for full-time work when her country went to war. The man who had been the local Agricultural Adjustment Administration agent was drafted, and Mrs. Knutson took over his job serving the farmers who tilled the hard, windy land along the Minnesota–North Dakota border. She already knew most of them by sight because she often performed at local weddings, playing the accordion and singing along in both English and Norwegian, her first language.

Knutson campaigning in Minnesota's Ninth Congressional District in 1955.

In those days, northwestern Minnesota was Republican country, so the Democratic-Farmer-Labor (DFL) party wasn't risking much when it decided to run Coya for state assembly in 1950. "What a campaigner [she was]," recalled former vice president Walter Mondale of his days as a young Minnesota political wannabe. "Coya could go into a room and get the dead to wake up." After winning that 1950 race and an easy reelection campaign in 1952, Mrs. Knutson decided to run for Congress in 1954, even though it meant challenging the candidate already endorsed by her party.

Knutson won the primary and then narrowly upset a six-term incumbent in the general election. But her independence angered a number of DFL leaders, and she made even more enemies when she decided to back Estes Kefauver for the Democratic presidential nomination in 1956, despite DFL boss Hubert H. Humphrey's strong endorsement of Adlai Stevenson. With Knutson chairing his Minnesota campaign, Kefauver swept nearly all the state's delegates and embarrassed Humphrey—after which the DFL leadership decided to get even.

When Coya came up for reelection in 1958, some DFL insiders got her husband, Andy, to write a devastating open letter—or, more likely, to sign a letter they had already composed—demanding that she not run again. They knew that Andy Knutson, a failed and alcoholic farmer, wanted his wife to stay home, cook for him, and presumably do the plowing, too. (Apparently, when Coya left for Washington the first time, she had been forced to run through the snow to the Oklee train station because Andy was right behind her with a shotgun, shouting that he'd kill her before letting any wife of his leave hearth and home.) The letter was distributed to the press in late April 1958 on the eve of the Ninth Congressional District nominating convention.

Washington had been a lonely place for Coya Knutson because the mores of the day precluded her socializing with any man not her husband—including male members of her staff. Even so, she had performed well, playing a key role in the establishment of a federal loan program for college students and introducing the first bill to create a tax-form checkoff for funding presidential campaigns. Yet her husband's letter demanded that she quit Congress and return home: "My dear wife, Coya, I want you to tell the people of the 9th District this Sunday that you are through in politics. That you want to go

home and make a home for your husband and son. As your husband I compel you to do this.... I'm sick and tired of having you run around with other men all the time and not your husband. I love you, honey." The headline in the next day's *Fargo Forum* read "COYA COME HOME," and the story made national news.

Local voters were persuaded: A woman's place was indeed in the home, most of them thought. Coya still won the DFL nomination, but she lost the general election (to a man) by 1,390 votes after winning the district handily in 1956. Two years later, even after Andy admitted that the letter had been a setup, she lost again. That year, 1960, was both too late and too early for Coya Knutson.

Coya in Oklee with *her husband, Andy, in November 1954.*

24

THE SEVENTIES

The Watergate Crisis

FORMER WHITE HOUSE COUNSEL John W. Dean III was in trouble. He had obstructed justice, and federal prosecutors already possessed enough evidence against him to put him in jail for many years. Now the four-month-old Senate Watergate Committee (formally the Senate Select Committee on Presidential Campaign Activities) wanted him to appear under a grant of limited immunity (which the prosecutors had not yet seen fit to offer him).

Dean began testifying before the committee on Monday, June 25, 1973, in the old Senate Caucus Room. He started by reading a 245-page opening statement, which took him all day to get through. Dean droned on for hours, yet the three commercial television networks (and the new Public Broadcasting System) aired the entire hearing live, gavel to gavel. Afterward, four more days of questioning followed.

The mundane manner in which Dean made his presentation belied the sensational nature of his charges. He said that his first conversation with Pres. Richard M. Nixon regarding the burglary of the Democratic National Committee (DNC) offices in the Watergate office building occurred three months after the break-in. The date Dean gave was September 15, 1972—the same day that a federal grand jury handed down seven indictments in the case, two of them naming former White House employees. According to Dean, the president had congratulated him on the effectiveness of his efforts to limit the

AT LEFT: ***Richard Nixon*** *and his chief of staff, H. R. Haldeman, walk past the Rose Garden in this photograph taken through the French doors in the Oval Office.*

scope of the Justice Department investigation. "I left the meeting with the impression that the president was well aware of what had been going on regarding the success of keeping the White House out of the Watergate scandal, and I also had expressed to him my concern that I was not confident that the cover-up could be maintained indefinitely," Dean read.

Dean's next meeting with the president took place on February 27, 1973. (Even though Dean was the president's lawyer, he had relatively little contact with Nixon, access to whom was carefully controlled by Chief of Staff H. R. Haldeman.) At the February 27 meeting, Dean testified, he told the president that he feared the cover-up would collapse, and the next day he expressed to Nixon his fears concerning his own criminal liability. "[The president] reassured me not to worry, that I had no legal problems," Dean said. As a lawyer, however, Dean knew better.

On March 13, he told the president that the seven Watergate defendants were demanding hush money—as much as a million dollars. "That's no problem," Nixon replied. (This was Dean's most sensational charge: that Nixon had personally approved paying off the burglars.) Eight days later, Dean again met with the president in the Oval Office and briefed him on all the details of the cover-up. Dean told Nixon that there was "a cancer growing on the presidency," which might force Nixon from office if it wasn't removed. According to Dean, Nixon took the news calmly, without shock or outrage, indicating prior knowledge. "I guess you are fully aware, Mr. Dean, of the gravity of the charges you have made under oath against the highest official of our land, the president of the United States?"

John Dean reads his lengthy opening statement before the Senate Watergate Committee. Later, Nixon described Dean's voice on June 25 as a

"The American people are tired of disorder, disruption, and disrespect for law. America wants to come back to the law as a way of life."

—

Richard M. Nixon, speaking at the funeral of FBI director J. Edgar Hoover, May 4, 1972

the committee's majority counsel, Sam Dash, asked once Dean had finished his opening testimony. "Yes, I am," Dean replied. "And, being so aware, do you still stand on your statement?" Dash continued. "Yes, I do," Dean said.

There was a good deal of reason at the time to be skeptical of Dean's allegations. By his own admission, he had illegally impeded a federal investigation; he also admitted to having had advance knowledge of the plan to bug the DNC offices. One way to soften his punishment would undoubtedly be to implicate others more important than himself, such as Haldeman or domestic policy chief John D. Ehrlichman (both of whom had already resigned). There was no target larger, however, than President Nixon. For hours, the millions of Americans watching Dean on television scanned his face for clues to his reliability. At the end of Dean's testimony, however, the committee and the public knew only that he—or Nixon—was lying.

The First Term

NIXON HAD RECEIVED ENOUGH of the core Republican vote in 1968 to defeat the divided Democrats with a scant 43.4 percent plurality, but his support was soft and most of the opposition despised him. The American left, in particular, had hated Nixon ever since his days as a Red-hunter, and its members made use of every opportunity to embarrass the president that they could. Describing Nixon as "the Republican that Democrats and liberals most loved to hate," former *New York Times* columnist Tom Wicker has written that "Nixon bore the scars, real or imagined, of a single-minded thirty-year ambition to win the presidency." He also had a warlike view of life that required others to choose sides: Either you were with him, or you were against him. "What starts the process really are laughs and slights and snubs when you are a kid," Nixon once told deputy White House communications director Kenneth Clawson. "…But if you are reasonably intelligent and if your anger is deep enough and strong enough, you learn that you can change those attitudes by excellence [and] personal gut performance, while those who have everything are sitting on their fat butts."

In January 1969, as Nixon took the oath of office, he believed sincerely, as did many Americans, that dissent and disorder were tearing the country apart. To control at least the latter, he encouraged his staff to develop a comprehensive plan to use FBI and CIA assets to investigate and undermine civil rights workers, antiwar protesters, and other left-wingers. Mail would be opened, telephones tapped, and secret searches conducted. (Internal Revenue Service files were considered especially valuable, and during his Senate testimony John Dean made specific reference to IRS audits conducted at the administration's request.) The president personally approved the plan in July 1970, but it never went into effect because FBI director J. Edgar Hoover wouldn't go along, believing that the accompanying reorganization of intelligence assets would undermine his bureaucratic authority.

At the same time, Nixon had to grapple with an economy nearing recession. After two decades of unprecedented, triumphal growth, the U.S. economy had finally been drained by the cost of funding both the Vietnam War and the Great Society. During Nixon's first two years in office, unemployment surged from 3.5 percent to 5.9 percent. Inflation also rose during this period, creating (with stagnant consumer demand) an unusual combination that economists termed *stagflation*. At first, the president tried to cut the budget while raising taxes; when those two policies proved politically untenable, however, he demonstrated remarkable ideological flexibility in proposing wage and price controls, which took effect in August 1971. While in place, the controls kept inflation in check; however, their removal following Nixon's 1972 reelection produced the first double-digit rise in the cost of living since World War II.

Haldeman (left) and Ehrlichman outside the White House in April 1969 at the height of their power.

THE UNITED STATES THUS FACED a number of difficult domestic challenges as the 1970s began, but the president never became fully engaged because, as he liked to say, when it came to domestic affairs, the country could nearly run itself. Foreign affairs was Nixon's preferred bailiwick, and the most pressing issue on his agenda during his first years in office was the war in Vietnam. Realizing that the conflict had ruined Lyndon Johnson's presidency, Nixon wanted to get the 536,000 U.S. troops out of Southeast Asia as expeditiously as possible. But he also wanted to avoid a humiliating defeat, so he sent his trusted national security adviser, Henry Kissinger, to Paris in February 1970 to conduct secret peace talks with North Vietnamese diplomat Le Duc Tho. Unfortunately, those talks dragged on for more than two years without any substantial progress.

Meanwhile, Kissinger pursued another secret diplomatic initiative. Richard Nixon had been one of the country's leading anti-Communists for the past two decades, yet he sent Kissinger to the People's Republic of China (PRC) in early July 1971 to arrange a presidential visit. The United States had never formally accepted the legitimacy of the Communist government in mainland China, and it still opposed the PRC's admission to the UN, where the Taiwanese government-in-exile represented China. Yet Nixon decided to seek a normalization of relations with "Red" China because doing so promoted a larger ambition that he and Kissinger shared: the creation of a new international order. The world, Nixon realized, was no longer bipolar: Japan and Western Europe had become economic powers once again; disunity within the Communist bloc, particular between China and the USSR, had increased; and the developing nations of the Third World were becoming more and more nationalistic. New alliances would have to be formed to perpetuate the world's political equilibrium—and American preeminence.

In Nixon's view, no U.S. relationship was more obsolete than its lack of contact with Communist China. China was the second largest nation on earth and a nuclear power, yet the United States still acted as though the remnants of the Nationalists on Taiwan ruled the mainland. Determined to reverse U.S. policy on this issue and persuade China to emerge from its decades-long isolation, Nixon announced shortly after Kissinger's return that he would be visiting Peking within the next several months. His disclosure startled the nation and the world; it also generated a great deal of controversy. Nixon's impeccable anti-Communist credentials meant that no one could accuse him of being soft on Communism, yet there was nevertheless a fear that his China initiative would destabilize the already touchy U.S.-Soviet relationship. This proved not to be the case, for just three months after Nixon's historic February 1972 visit to Peking, the president traveled to Moscow to sign the first Strategic Arms Limitation Treaty (SALT I).

The Election of 1972

ALTHOUGH SALT I REQUIRED little from both sides, it did promote détente, and Nixon returned home in triumph. His stunning diplomatic successes in China and the Soviet Union, along with the slackening of inflation produced by the wage and price controls, put him in the strongest political position of his presidency. Furthermore, the Democrats were floundering. After the 1968 convention debacle in Chicago, the party's liberal activists had forced through a number of rule changes concerning delegate selection. These allowed candidates—primarily ultraliberal South Dakota senator George S. McGovern, who had chaired the rules commission—to acquire delegates without the backing of state party organizations. These delegates—mostly young, many of them women and minorities—gave McGovern the 1972 nomination, yet they also alienated most party regulars, without whose support McGovern had no chance of winning.

WOMEN'S LIBERATION

BY THE EARLY 1970s, the counterculture was well into decline—but not so women's liberation. The modern women's rights movement had gotten under way during the early 1960s, when several female authors and scholars began reevaluating sexual stereotypes and reconsidering gender roles. Betty Friedan's pioneering work, *The Feminine Mystique* (1963), challenged the view that all American women should be able to find satisfaction exclusively in housewifery. After her book became a best-seller, Friedan turned from research to activism, helping to found the National Organization for Women (NOW) in June 1966.

Avoiding aggressive attacks on men in favor of a more humanistic ideology, Friedan's brand of feminism emphasized practical reform. During the late 1960s, however, a new generation of feminists, alienated by male domination of the civil rights and antiwar movements, pursued a more radical critique. In her 1970 book *Sexual Politics*, thirty-five-year-old Kate Millett wrote, "Our society, like all other historical societies, is a patriarchy. The fact is evident at once if one recalls that… every avenue of power within the society…is entirely in male hands." Rather than seek greater personal fulfillment as individuals (the Friedan approach), the new feminists urged women to band together for a united assault on "male chauvinism" and the male power structure.

Most women, however, pursued less extreme means. NOW members continued to use traditional political techniques to seek an end to sexism in employment, win stronger penalties for rape, and legalize abortion. Other women joined consciousness-raising groups and concentrated on the reform of social institutions, such as marriage and motherhood.

During the campaign, Nixon tried to appear above politics by confining himself to the White House and ignoring nearly all of the reelection activities carried out in his name. The details of the campaign he left to Attorney General John N. Mitchell, who resigned from the cabinet to become director of the Committee for the Re-Election of the President (CRP). Even though a Nixon landslide seemed likely, the president neglected the needs of Republican congressional candidates so that his campaign staff could focus its efforts entirely on the enfeebling of McGovern. Nixon surrogates had little trouble presenting the president as the moderate choice for 1972 and the Democrat McGovern, with his plan to guarantee all Americans a minimum income, as an extremist. Kissinger even announced on October 26, just two weeks before the election, that peace was "at hand" in Vietnam. (This, of course, was not so. Negotiations broke down shortly after the election, and on December 18, American B-52s began the twelve-day "Christmas bombing" of North Vietnam.) McGovern had no chance. On Election Day, he carried just one state (Massachusetts) and only 37.5 percent of the popular vote, compared to Nixon's 60.7 percent. Nixon thus achieved the broad mandate he had craved, but in other ways his campaign strategy limited his ability to govern. Because he had done so little for his party's other candidates, the Republicans remained in the minority in both the House, where they picked up only a dozen seats, and the Senate, where they lost two. Nixon's campaign staff had also, it turned out, been overeager in finding new ways to humble the Democrats.

A poster from the 1972 campaign. In addition to CRP, the Committee for the Re-Election of the President was also known by the acronym CREEP.

GIVEN HIS INSULAR, somewhat paranoid personality, Richard Nixon simply couldn't tolerate the leaks to reporters that sometimes become epidemic in official Washington. By July 1971, in fact, the president had become so frustrated with repeated foreign policy leaks that John Ehrlichman set up a special unit in the White House to investigate and stop them. Nicknamed the Plumbers, the task force included Ehrlichman deputy Egil "Bud" Krogh Jr., Kissinger aide David R. Young, former CIA agent E. Howard Hunt Jr., and former FBI man G. Gordon Liddy. "On July 23, the morning before we were scheduled to present our formal position at the SALT I talks in Helsinki," Nixon recalled, "the *New York Times* carried a front-page leak of our fallback negotiating position. I tried to motivate Krogh in the strongest terms, and I told him, 'We're not going to allow it. We just aren't going to allow it.'"

A month later, over the Labor Day weekend, the Plumbers burglarized the office of Daniel Ellsberg's psychiatrist, hoping to find in the psychiatrist's files information about Ellsberg's motivation for leaking the Pentagon Papers, his future plans, his possible co-conspirators, and anything else that might be used to discredit him. "I do not believe I was told about the break-in at the time, but it is clear that it was at least in part an outgrowth of my sense of urgency," Nixon admitted in his 1978 memoir. "…Given the temper of those tense and bitter times and the peril I perceived, I cannot say that had I been informed of it beforehand,

THE PENTAGON PAPERS

IN JUNE 1967, INCREASINGLY TROUBLED by the war he had helped Lyndon Johnson to orchestrate, Defense Secretary Robert McNamara commissioned a top-secret study of U.S. involvement in Southeast Asia dating back to World War II. The forty-seven-volume report wasn't completed until January 1969, just as the Johnson administration was leaving office. Two years later, Daniel Ellsberg, who had worked on the study as a consultant to the Pentagon, leaked it to the *New York Times*, which began publishing a series of articles based on its contents on June 13, 1971.

The information in the Pentagon Papers, as the study came to be called, was extremely embarrassing to the government because it revealed the extent to which policy makers had misled the public about the reasons for and extent of U.S. involvement in the war. Citing the need to protect national security, the Nixon Justice Department obtained a temporary restraining order halting further publication of the study. On June 30, however, the Supreme Court ruled in *New York Times v. U.S.* that the government had failed to offer sufficient cause for the newspaper to be restrained. After publication resumed, the Justice Department went after Ellsberg personally, but the charges against him were dropped in May 1973 when it was revealed that the government had engaged in improper conduct—specifically, the burglary of Ellsberg's psychiatrist's office.

I would have automatically considered it unprecedented, unwarranted, or unthinkable.... Today the break-in at Ellsberg's psychiatrist's office seems wrong and excessive."

The Plumbers unit was disbanded in late September 1971, but Liddy soon became the CRP's general counsel (later its finance counsel) and, discreetly, the chief of its political intelligence operation. A self-dramatizer who enjoyed reveling in his own cloak-and-dagger expertise, Liddy once showed John Dean a burn mark on his palm that he said he had obtained while deliberately holding his hand over a flame to demonstrate his tolerance for pain.

In January 1972, before Mitchell resigned to run the CRP, Liddy proposed to the attorney general a comprehensive million-dollar plan for covert operations against the Democrats. Its components included bugging potential candidates, procuring prostitutes to compromise convention delegates, and even forming kidnap squads to detain radical leaders until after the 1972 Republican convention had ended. Mitchell told Liddy to downsize his plans, which Liddy did—twice. Finally, Mitchell approved $250,000 for Operation Gemstone. Liddy then recruited James W. McCord Jr., who had once been chief of physical security for the CIA and was now working as a security consultant for the CRP. Howard Hunt helped by recruiting three anti-Castro Cubans whom he had known while in the CIA—Bernard L. Barker, Virgilio R. Gonzalez, and Eugenio R. Martinez— along with their anti-Communist friend Frank A. Sturgis, also a Miami resident. (Barker and Martinez had already taken part in the Ellsberg break-in.)

CENTER: *The Watergate complex (shown here in April 1973) encompassed two office buildings, a hotel, and three blocks of luxury apartments. Among its more notable residents was Kansas senator Bob Dole.*

The Break-In

On Sunday, May 28, 1972, McCord and the four Miamians broke into the Watergate offices of the Democratic National Committee to bug two telephone lines: one belonging to the secretary of DNC chairman Lawrence F. O'Brien and another belonging to an O'Brien deputy. Transcripts of the calls made on those lines, monitored from a motel room across the street, were passed on to Deputy Campaign Manager Jeb Stuart Magruder—and, according to Magruder, Mitchell as well. The information proved useless, however, so Liddy's unit went in again, this time to bug O'Brien's personal telephone line. It was during this second break-in early on the morning of Saturday, June 17, that Watergate security guard Frank Wills found tape covering a door lock and called the police. The officers who responded found McCord, Sturgis, and the three Cubans in the DNC offices and arrested them.

The five burglars were arraigned that afternoon. Along with sophisticated electronic equipment and pen-sized tear-gas guns, they were carrying approximately twenty-three hundred dollars in cash, most of it in consecutively numbered hundred-dollar bills. When the presiding judge asked the men to state their occupations, one answered for all of them, "Anti-Communists." Judge James A. Belsen then had McCord step forward and asked him again to state his occupation. "Security consultant," McCord said. The judge wanted to know where. Twenty-nine-year-old *Washington Post* reporter Bob Woodward leaned closer to hear. "CIA," McCord replied softly.

Woodward had been assigned to help write the *Post*'s story on the break-in. The next day, the front-page article to which he contributed ran under the byline of Alfred E. Lewis, the newspaper's police reporter. It began, "Five men, one of whom said he is a former employee of the Central Intelligence Agency, were arrested at 2:30 A.M. yesterday in what authorities described as an elaborate plot to bug the offices of the Democratic National Committee here." The story seemed promising, yet as Woodward and colleague Carl Bernstein recalled later, "The thought that the break-in might somehow be the work of the Republicans seemed implausible," because the president was already so far ahead in the polls.

Because the *Post*'s national staff rarely covered police stories, Woodward and Bernstein, both metro reporters, were assigned to follow up. Late Sunday night, Woodward got a call from another of the *Post*'s police reporters, Eugene Bachinski, who had been given a tip: Two of the burglars had been carrying address books in which the name Howard Hunt had been listed next to the notations "W.H." and "W. House." On Monday, Woodward called the White House and asked for Howard Hunt. He was transferred to a

Police discovered the address book of Watergate burglar Bernard Barker on June 18 in a room at the Watergate Hotel. Under the listing "HH" (for Howard Hunt), FBI investigators found Hunt's White House phone number, one of the first links between the burglars and the president's staff.

Bob Woodward (left) and Carl Bernstein in the newsroom of the Washington Post *in April 1973. This pair of young reporters became important players in the developing national scandal when they reported on October 10, 1972, that the Watergate burglary was merely one facet of a much larger "dirty tricks" campaign being waged by the Republicans.*

secretary in the office of presidential aide Charles W. Colson, who told him that Hunt, then merely a consultant to Colson, spent most of his week working as a writer at a Washington public relations firm. Later that day, Woodward telephoned Hunt at the PR firm and explained why he was calling. "Good God!" Hunt blurted out before refusing further comment and slamming down the receiver. Meanwhile, other reporters uncovered the relationship between McCord's security company and the CRP.

O N TUESDAY, JUNE 20, presidential press secretary Ron Ziegler responded briefly to a question about the break-in, describing it as "a third-rate burglary attempt" and not worthy of official White House comment. During the summer of 1972, however, more evidence was developed, mostly by newspaper reporters, tying Liddy and Hunt to the break-in. (Suspiciously, the FBI was doing very little to advance the case, the *Post* reported.)

On September 15, 1972, Liddy, Hunt, and the five burglars were indicted before federal district court judge John J. Sirica. The charges included conspiracy, burglary, and violation of federal laws pertaining to electronic surveillance. During a pretrial hearing, however, as the government outlined its case, Sirica realized that prosecutor Earl J. Silbert was avoiding the issue of motive and focusing instead on the minimum facts necessary to support the relatively narrow indictment. The judge wanted to know more: Why had the DNC offices been burglarized? Who had paid the defendants, and for what purpose? "There were simply too many unanswered questions," Sirica explained later. "…I'd have had to be some kind of moron to believe that no other people were involved. No political campaign committee would turn over so much money to a man like Gordon Liddy without someone higher up in the organization approving the transaction. How could I not see that?"

Meanwhile, President Nixon prepared for the start of his second term by isolating himself within the White House to an even greater degree than he had previously. A shy man, he had never liked the social aspects of being president and always preferred to spend his time by himself, thinking, or planning strategy with

Kissinger and other close aides. After the 1972 election, the Berlin Wall—as Washington insiders called Haldeman, Ehrlichman, and Kissinger—rose even higher around Nixon, and even cabinet members had difficulty getting in to see him.

The Cover-Up

THE TRIAL OF THE WATERGATE defendants began on January 10, 1973. All seven had previously entered not-guilty pleas, but Hunt changed his plea that day to guilty. The next day, the four Miamians changed their pleas as well. Sirica asked them why—whether they had been paid off. They all said no; but, as Dean later revealed, they were lying. The White House had already made arrangements to pay them from a secret slush fund. "Where did you get this money, these hundred-dollar bills that were floating around like coupons?" Sirica demanded of Barker before he would accept the defendant's guilty plea. He had received them in the mail in a blank envelope, Barker said. "I'm sorry, I don't believe you," Sirica snapped back.

The trial of the two remaining defendants, Liddy and McCord, ended on January 30 with guilty verdicts for both on all counts. Because the prosecution's theory of the case was that Liddy had misused CRP funds intended for legitimate security purposes, the defendants' stonewalling might have worked—except that Sirica still wasn't satisfied. At one point, upset with the limpness of the prosecution, the judge had interrupted Silbert's examination of CRP treasurer (and former Haldeman aide) Hugh W. Sloan to ask forty-one questions of his own regarding the campaign's money-laundering practices, run by Liddy. Now, after the verdict, Sirica declared in open court that he still didn't believe all the pertinent facts had been disclosed. Therefore, he was going to withhold final sentencing to give the defendants some time to contemplate the long sentences they were likely to receive. Sirica hoped that the pressure might persuade one or more of them to cooperate with the Senate and Justice Department investigators.

Lenient judges were abetting the breakdown of law and order, President Nixon liked to complain. Yet even by Nixon's standards, John J. Sirica (shown here in September 1973) was a tough judge. The son of an Italian immigrant, he worked his way through law school as a boxing coach before developing a stern sentencing reputation as a judge. His nickname was Maximum John.

Just before the sentencing hearing, which Sirica had scheduled for March 23, McCord decided that he wasn't going to risk a long sentence to protect his CRP superiors. On March 20, he hand-delivered to Sirica's chambers a letter in which he wrote, "Several members of my family have expressed fear for my life if I disclose knowledge of the facts in this matter either publicly or to any government representatives." Nevertheless, he wrote, he wanted to talk to Sirica "in the interest of justice and in the interest of restoring faith in the criminal justice system." He went on to inform the judge that pressure had been applied to the defendants to remain silent, that perjury had been committed in his courtroom, and that others had been involved in planning and approving the burglary. The letter was exactly the break for which Sirica had been hoping.

WITHIN DAYS, McCORD BEGAN briefing investigators working for the Senate Watergate Committee (formed February 7), naming John Mitchell as "the overall boss" of the operation and asserting that both Magruder and Dean had prior knowledge of the break-in. Meanwhile, President Nixon, monitoring the cover-up, met with Dean on March 21—the "cancer on the presidency" meeting—at which point he approved (or at least seemed to approve) more hush money for the burglars. That night, an agent of the White House paid seventy-five thousand dollars to Hunt through his lawyer. It wasn't very long, however, before Magruder and Dean, realizing the implications of McCord's letter, began negotiating with federal prosecutors to trade their testimony for leniency.

Because he met regularly with Haldeman and Ehrlichman (and even the president on occasion), Dean was the key. In early April, Haldeman had warned him not to talk, but Dean, according to a statement he released on April 19, had no intention of becoming the "scapegoat in the Watergate case." Dean's statement had come in response to a front-page

Testifying before the Senate Watergate Committee in May 1973, James McCord demonstrates how he bugged the Democratic National Committee's telephones.

Woodward and Bernstein article in that morning's *Washington Post*, reporting that on April 14 Magruder had told prosecutors that Mitchell and Dean had approved the bugging operation in advance and later helped buy the silence of the burglars. At this point, according to Woodward and Bernstein, "Those who had once served Richard Nixon as one and had forged the superstructure of rigid White House discipline and self-control were [now] in open warfare with one another." Soon, other top administration officials who had known nothing about the break-in yet had participated in the cover-up began volunteering testimony to prosecutors in order to escape obstruction-of-justice charges. The cover-up had, as Dean predicted, begun to unravel.

On April 30, Ziegler announced the resignations of Haldeman, Ehrlichman, and Dean. Because he had known of perjured testimony by administration officials, Attorney General Richard G. Kleindienst was also out, replaced by Defense Secretary Elliot L. Richardson. That night, President Nixon gave a nationally televised address, his first specifically on the Watergate scandal. The question on everyone's mind was, Had the president been involved in the cover-up? In his memoir, Nixon acknowledged that "if I had given the true answer, I would have had to say that without fully realizing the implications of my actions I had become deeply entangled in...the Watergate cover-up." However, he continued, given his belief that "any admissions I made would be used to keep the Watergate issue—and the issue of my behavior in office—festering during the rest of my term," he decided to say that he had not been involved and "had known nothing at all."

These Chap Stick tubes wired for sound were discovered inside Howard Hunt's White House safe after the break-in.

GOVERNMENT
EXHIBIT
133

The Tapes

DURING THE FOUR DAYS of questioning that followed the reading of John Dean's opening statement on June 25, senators from both parties tried to shake his story. So did the White House, which prepared a list of questions for its allies on the committee to use to discredit Dean. Yet the former White House counsel stuck to his story. At the time and later, Nixon complained that much of Dean's testimony was self-serving and that some of it was false. Yet he also understood how damaging it was:

> It no longer made any difference that not all of Dean's testimony was accurate. It only mattered if any of his testimony was accurate. And Dean's account of the crucial March 21 meeting was more accurate than my own had been. I did not see it then, but in the end it would make less difference that I was not as involved as Dean had alleged than that I was not as uninvolved as I had claimed.

For the next three weeks, the issue of the president's role remained essentially a question of whose account one believed. Haldeman and Ehrlichman both testified before the Senate committee—chaired by seventy-six-year-old Sam Ervin, a North Carolina Democrat— that Dean had masterminded the cover-up and misled them—and for a time, it seemed that their version, supporting the president, might prevail. On Friday, July 13, however, at Woodward's suggestion, investigators for the Ervin Committee interviewed former White House deputy chief of staff Alexander P. Butterfield— whose responsibilities, Woodward had learned, had included "internal security." The next day, a member of the committee's staff called the reporter at home to congratulate him. "We interviewed Butterfield," the man said. "He told the whole story." What story? Woodward wanted to know. "Nixon bugged himself," the source replied. On Monday, July 16, testifying before the Senate committee on national television, Butterfield repeated his story, explaining that President Nixon had been secretly taping Oval Office (and other) conversations since February 1971. Apparently, not even Kissinger had known. More important, it would no longer be simply Dean's word against Nixon's.

Majority counsel Sam Dash (right) confers with Watergate Committee chairman Sam Ervin, while Tennessee senator Howard Baker uses his hand to cover a live microphone. Although a Republican, Baker became famous for repeatedly asking witnesses, "What did the president know, and when did he know it?"

Once the existence of the taping system became public knowledge, both the Ervin Committee and Archibald Cox (whom Richardson had named special prosecutor for Watergate on May 18) wrote polite letters to the president, requesting access to the tapes. On July 23, the president announced that he would not comply with either request, citing executive privilege. Cox then asked Sirica to approve a subpoena for nine specific tapes, which Sirica did. Meanwhile, the Senate committee voted to issue its own subpoena. Three days later, Nixon rejected both.

AGNEW RESIGNS

ON OCTOBER 10, 1973, Vice Pres. Spiro T. Agnew accepted a plea bargain and resigned his office; otherwise, he likely would have been jailed. Over the summer, federal prosecutors in Maryland had built a strong case indicating that, while serving as governor of Maryland and later as vice president, Agnew had accepted illegal cash kickbacks. Citing constitutional grounds, the vice president tried to argue that a sitting vice president couldn't be indicted, but his compli-cated legal maneuverings fell short, and he finally took the deal offered by Attorney General Elliot Richardson: his resigna-tion, and a no-contest plea on a single count of tax evasion, in exchange for a ten-thousand-dollar fine and three years' probation (but no jail time).

Agnew got off lightly, but the deal served Nixon well because it stopped the political bleeding and prevented Agnew's case (a loser) from testing whether or not a vice president

(or a president) could be prosecuted while in office. Moreover, a long bribery trial would have left the matter of presidential succession in doubt should Nixon have been impeached. Instead, Agnew was shown the door, and a new vice president, Michigan congressman Gerald R. Ford, was chosen. Meeting with the two top congressional Democrats, Speaker of the House Carl Albert and Senate majority leader Mike Mansfield, immediately after the announcement of Agnew's resignation, Nixon began the conversation by asking the two men if they had any suggestions regarding Agnew's replacement. "We gave Nixon no choice but Ford," Albert said later. "Congress made Jerry Ford president."

During Nixon's first term in office, his political staff used the abrasive Agnew to attack political dissenters, the news media (whom Agnew called "nattering nabobs of negativism"), and intellectuals in general ("an effete corps of impudent snobs").

Refusing to accept the president's claim that he had "absolute power" over the tapes because they belonged to the executive branch, Sirica backed Cox's efforts to force the president to comply with the court's subpoena. On August 29, the judge issued an opinion ordering the president to turn over the tapes so that Sirica could review them in his chambers and determine for himself whether there was any merit to Nixon's privacy claim—or whether it was simply a ruse to avoid political embarrassment. The president appealed Sirica's order but lost when the circuit court ruled, 5–2, on October 12 that he would have to turn over the nine tapes sought by Cox.

A WEEK OF NEGOTIATIONS followed during which the White House tried to persuade Cox to accept a compromise: The tapes would be given to a third-party "verifier" (Nixon later chose Sen. John Stennis, a pro-Nixon Mississippi Democrat), who would compare the original tapes to summaries prepared by the White House. Cox ultimately refused the deal, but Nixon imposed it anyway on Friday, October 19. At the same time, he ordered Cox "as an employee of the executive branch to make no further attempts by judicial process to obtain tapes, notes, or memoranda of presidential conversations." That night, the special prosecutor announced that he would refuse Nixon's order because it violated the conditions under which he had agreed to serve. The next day, he held a press conference during which he explained reasonably and with great patience specifically why he was refusing. Afterward, public opinion turned noticeably against the president. But Nixon could no longer consider retreat; he was committed to his course, and later that afternoon, he had Haldeman's replacement, Alexander Haig, order Attorney General Richardson to fire Cox for refusing the Stennis compromise.

Richardson, however, had promised the Senate during his confirmation hearings in May that he would not fire Cox, except for gross improprieties. Rather than betray this promise, Richardson resigned. Next, Haig called Richardson's deputy, William Ruckelshaus, who also resigned rather than fire Cox. Finally, Solicitor General Robert H. Bork agreed to become acting attorney general and carry out the president's wishes, which also included the abolition of the office of the special prosecutor. The events of that evening became known almost immediately as the Saturday Night Massacre. "As I watched the story unfold on television," Sirica recalled, "I couldn't get away from the feeling that the president had lost his grip on reality."

The public reaction was overwhelmingly negative. Beginning with that evening's White House announcement of Cox's dismissal, callers jammed the Western Union switchboards, wanting to send irate telegrams to Washington. During the next ten days, nearly half a million such telegrams arrived. Almost unanimously, they denounced the president's action. Meanwhile, major national periodicals—including *Time* magazine, in its first editorial ever—began calling for Nixon's resignation. For three days, the president held firm; then he capitulated. On October 23, appearing before Sirica, Nixon lawyer Charles Alan Wright surprised the courtroom with his announcement that the president would comply with the appeals court ruling and turn over the nine tapes after they had been properly itemized and indexed.

However, a week later, during a meeting in his chambers, the judge learned from White House counsel J. Fred Buzhardt that, in fact, two of the nine tapes didn't exist. An incredulous Sirica scheduled a public hearing for the next day to hear testimony on the taping system, the tapes, and how they were being handled; it dragged on for months. In Sirica's words, "The whole episode was a sad one. It seemed that every explanation they offered had to be revised a few days later." On November 21, for example, the day before Thanksgiving, Buzhardt had to inform the judge that while reviewing the June 20, 1972, tape of a conversation among the president, Haldeman, and Ehrlichman—recorded just three days after the break-in—his staff

From the start, Nixon detested the choice of Archibald Cox as special prosecutor because Cox (shown here in early June 1973) had been U.S. solicitor general under the Kennedys.

The White House tape recorder on which the recordings of Nixon's Oval Office conversations were made.

had discovered an eighteen-minute "obliteration." Buzhardt later claimed that Nixon secretary Rose Mary Woods had erased that portion of the tape accidentally while transcribing it.

U.S. v. Nixon

MEANWHILE, EAGER TO REPAIR SOME of the political damage caused by the Saturday Night Massacre—and to appease the House Judiciary Committee, which had recently announced its own investigation into the president's alleged abuse of power—Nixon instructed Bork to appoint a new special prosecutor. On November 1, the acting attorney general named to the post Texan Leon Jaworski, a former American Bar Association president who had been a close friend of Lyndon Johnson.

On April 29, 1974, facing a Judiciary Committee ultimatum to turn over more tapes or risk impeachment, Nixon made one last, dramatic attempt to suppress the scandal. He announced in a televised address that he would be releasing to the

Seated at her desk in the White House, Nixon secretary Rose Mary Wood demonstrates how she may have inadvertently erased eighteen minutes from the June 20, 1972, tape. Nevertheless, many disbelievers dismissed her account and contended that she would have had to have been a contortionist to have erased the tape in the manner she described.

Congress and the public transcripts made from the subpoenaed White House tapes. Twelve hundred pages in all, they revealed a surprisingly indecisive president consumed by plotting and political expediency. The transcripts also revealed how foulmouthed Nixon was, using the phrase *expletive deleted* repeatedly to indicate where profanities had been edited out. As Sirica wrote, "He was apparently willing to humiliate himself to save himself."

Even so, the Democrats on the Judiciary Committee weren't satisfied. When committee staff members compared the White House transcripts to the few actual tapes in their possession, they found numerous discrepancies and omissions. On May 1, the committee voted 20–18 to reject the transcripts and continue demanding the tapes; the White House responded that it would release no more Watergate-related material. On May 30, the committee sent a letter to the president telling him that his refusal was a "grave matter" and could be grounds for impeachment. The vote approving the letter was 28–10, reflecting a substantial erosion of the president's support among Republicans.

CENTER: *The twelve hundred pages of tape transcripts released by Nixon on April 29, 1974, as they appeared stacked on his desk just prior to his nationally televised address that evening. Instead of cauterizing his wounds, as he had intended, the release of the transcripts merely set off another round of demands for his resignation.*

Meanwhile, on April 18, Jaworski had subpoenaed sixty-four more tapes, including a particularly sensitive one from June 23, 1972. On May 20, Sirica upheld the subpoena and ordered all sixty-four tapes turned over to his court. When Nixon again moved to appeal Sirica's decision to the circuit court, Jaworski insisted that the Supreme Court hear the case immediately because of its "imperative public importance." On May 31, the Court granted certiorari. Two months later, on July 24, Chief Justice Warren Burger, a Nixon appointee, announced the unanimous decision in *U.S. v. Nixon:* The president would have to turn over the subpoenaed tapes "forthwith." That evening, Special Counsel to the President James D. St. Clair announced live on the network news programs that the president would comply.

NEVERTHELESS, ST. CLAIR REFUSED to set a delivery date for the tapes, and the House Judiciary Committee decided not to wait. On July 27, its members voted 27–11 to approve the first of three articles of impeachment, charging that the president had "impeded the administration of justice." With six Republicans joining the Democratic majority, it appeared certain that the House would impeach Nixon, and he would have to stand trial in the Senate. Meanwhile, Sirica insisted that St. Clair listen personally to the subpoenaed tapes— including the June 23 tape, which was the surviving tape closest to the break-in now that the June 20 tape had been erased.

New York congresswoman Elizabeth Holtzman (foreground) makes some notes as Peter Rodino (background, seated) converses with other members of the House Judiciary Committee during its impeachment deliberations on July 27, 1974.

For more than a year, Nixon's lawyers, aides, and the president himself had insisted that he knew nothing of the cover-up until Dean briefed him on March 21, 1973. However, once St. Clair and others (including Haig) listened to the June 23 tape, they knew this was a lie and insisted that a transcript of the tape be released immediately so that they wouldn't be implicated themselves in the conspiracy. The transcript of the president's June 23 conversation with Haldeman was, in fact, released on Monday, August 5. It was the "smoking gun" for which all the investigators had been looking, definitively contradicting the president's defense that he had known "nothing at all." On the tape, Haldeman tells the president, "The FBI is not under control," because it had begun tracing the money found on the burglars. Haldeman then tells Nixon that Mitchell has suggested the president ask the CIA to order the FBI to "stay the hell out of this." After some additional discussion, Nixon tersely approves the cover-up. "All right, fine," he says. The transcript was direct evidence that the president had helped plan and carry out the cover-up from the very beginning.

Immediately, seven Republican members of the House Judiciary Committee who had voted against Nixon's removal from office only the week before announced that they would vote for impeachment when the issue reached the House floor. Now that Nixon's eventual removal from office was all but certain, the Republican

A crowd gathers by the White House gates on August 9, 1974, the day of Richard Nixon's resignation. After releasing the June 23, 1972, tape four days earlier, the president had admitted that its contents were "at variance with certain of my previous statements." Even so, he insisted, the new evidence did not justify impeachment.

leaders on Capitol Hill sought a quick resolution and got it. During a nationally televised speech on Thursday night, August 8, the president announced that he would resign his office effective at noon the next day, thus becoming the first U.S. chief executive to leave office voluntarily before the expiration of his term. Following Nixon's August 9 departure from the White House, new president Gerald R. Ford delivered a brief acceptance speech. "My fellow Americans," Ford said, "our long national nightmare is over."

After Watergate

INITIALLY, FORD RECEIVED a great deal of public support. His openness and integrity came as a welcome change from the secretiveness of the grim, hunched figure who had inhabited the White House previously. The media gushed about his ordinary lifestyle—how he opened his own front door to pick up each morning's newspaper, how he toasted his own English muffins for breakfast. As the president himself once admitted, he had seemed "disgustingly sane" during the madness of Watergate. Yet Ford's isolation from the scandal ended on September 8, when he pardoned Richard Nixon for any crimes Nixon may have committed while in office. The widespread condemnation that followed Ford's pardon was understandable; even Ford realized that many Americans might think he had made a deal for the presidency. Yet, as later became clear, Ford genuinely believed that the pardon was the right thing to do to spare the country the further trauma and division of putting a former president on trial. Even so, the negative reaction was much more severe than Ford had anticipated. "I began to wonder," he later wrote, "whether, instead of healing the wounds, my decision had only rubbed salt into them."

At the same time, President Ford inherited other problems as well, the most pressing ones being those related to energy and the economy. By early 1975, the country was entering the second year of its most severe recession since the 1930s, with inflation spiking and unemployment nearing double digits. The job losses were particularly troubling in the manufacturing sector—especially in the automobile, construction, and aerospace industries. A large part of the problem was the skyrocketing cost of energy. The United States was still suffering from the effects of a petroleum embargo imposed in October 1973 by Arab oil exporters in retaliation for U.S. support of Israel during the recent Yom Kippur War.

On October 6, 1973, during the most sacred Jewish religious holiday, Egyptian and Syrian troops launched a joint surprise attack on Israel. Although the Nixon administration was in turmoil over the impending Agnew resignation and the standoff with Cox, the president still managed to act decisively on behalf of an important U.S. ally. He ordered a huge airlift of supplies to the Israelis, who had been struggling for ten days to recover from the initial shock of the attack. (Fearful of jeopardizing their own oil imports, America's NATO allies offered no similar aid.) In November, after Israel had captured the Sinai Peninsula from Egypt and the Golan Heights from Syria, Nixon and Kissinger pressured the Jewish state to accept a cease-fire. In the meantime, however, the Arab members of the Organization of Petroleum-Exporting Countries (OPEC) voted to cut off all shipments of oil to the United States.

At the time, the United States was importing more than 10 percent of its petroleum—about two million barrels a day—from the Middle East and North Africa. Conservation and a mild winter helped the country through the embargo, yet the experience heightened awareness of the nation's growing energy problems. For years, consumption had been increasing far more rapidly than domestic production, and now production was suffering under new environmental laws that restricted the use of polluting fuels, especially coal. Furthermore, both the Arab and non-Arab members of OPEC agreed to a series of steep price increases between October 1973 and January 1974, so that even when the embargo was lifted in mid-March 1974, the cost of imported oil had quadrupled.

A gas station owner in Detroit posted this sign in November 1973 to announce (with some humor) that he would be complying with President Nixon's directive that filling stations conserve their stock by halting sales on Sunday.

F OR TWO YEARS, GERALD FORD did his best to manage the difficult economic situation, but the effective leadership ability that had helped him move the country beyond Watergate failed him in domestic policy. Rather than resort to the wage and price controls employed by Nixon, Ford began what amounted to a mere publicity campaign, declaring inflation "public enemy number one" and exhorting Americans to "whip inflation now." He even promised to hand out "WIN" buttons to each American who enlisted in his campaign. Unfortunately, the economy continued to decline, leading the president to reverse himself and accept a Democratic tax cut intended to "jump-start" the economy.

President Ford stumbles down the steps of Air Force One on his arrival in Salzburg in June 1975. His unfortunate, widely publicized misstep reinforced the observation (attributed to Lyndon Johnson) that Ford, an All-America center at Michigan, had "played too much football with his helmet off." As a healer, President Ford was magnificent; as a head of state, however, he often appeared slow-witted, if beneficent.

Ford also suffered from his public image as a bumbler. After the former University of Michigan football star fell down a flight of stairs while deplaning in Austria in June 1975, reporters began to focus on his every misstep, and Chevy Chase became famous impersonating the president on NBC's *Saturday Night Live*, enacting a pratfall each week. During this period, the editor of the president's daily news summary monitored his boss's transformation from "good-hearted, not-very-bright jock" to "klutz."

When Ford announced that he would seek the Republican nomination in 1976, the declaration made him seem more presidential and less the political accident, yet there was still some chuckling and strong opposition from within the Republican party's conservative wing. Former California governor Ronald Reagan pressed Ford hard during the primaries and nearly beat him at the convention, losing by only 117 votes out of 2,257 cast. As a result, Ford left the convention so far behind Democratic nominee Jimmy Carter that, still burdened by the pardon issue, few gave him much chance of catching up. He didn't.

The Carter Administration

AT LEAST A DOZEN prominent Democrats expressed interest in running for president in 1976, but the candidate who emerged from the pack wasn't one of them. He was a former Georgia governor, little known outside his state. James Earl Carter Jr., who preferred to be called Jimmy, possessed a permanent smile and a disarming informality. He ran as a Washington outsider, and the strategy worked. Once in office, however, Carter faced many of the same problems that had plagued Ford, especially disturbingly high inflation coupled with slow growth. In 1977, President Carter set 4 percent as his target for containing inflation; by 1980, however, inflation had risen to three times that level, and it was still going up.

Carter's energy policies were a little more successful. In addition to persuading Congress to create a cabinet-level Department of Energy, he emphasized conservation measures (rather than production increases) to lower prices and stabilize demand. Among other proposals, President Carter suggested a surcharge on cars with poor fuel mileage, higher taxes on gasoline and domestic oil production, and tax incentives for public utilities and other businesses to switch from petroleum to alternative sources of energy, such as "clean" (low-sulfur) coal. The president also asked Congress to approve tax incentives for homeowners who insulated their houses and made other energy-efficient improvements. "Energy will be the immediate test of our ability to unite this nation," Carter asserted in a major July 1979 address, having already described the effort to reduce American dependence on foreign oil as the "moral equivalent of war."

Americans did conserve—driving slower and less often, buying more fuel-efficient cars and appliances, turning down their thermostats—but they resisted the president's more costly proposals, such as the punitive gas tax—as did their representatives in Congress. In the meantime, demand for energy and American reliance on foreign sources continued to grow, as did oil company profits.

THE END IN VIETNAM

In January 1973, following the Christmas bombing of North Vietnam, the United States, North Vietnam, the Vietcong, and South Vietnam (under strong pressure from the American government) signed a cease-fire agreement in Paris. Soon afterward, the draft was ended, and the first American POWs began coming home. By the end of March 1973, the last U.S. combat troops had left Vietnam. In January 1974, however, South Vietnamese president Nguyen Van Thieu announced, "The war has restarted." (In fact, nearly sixty thousand Vietnamese soldiers had been killed since the signing of the cease-fire agreement.)

On April 4, 1974, the House rejected President Nixon's request for more aid to South Vietnam, and it also refused several subsequent appeals made by President Ford. In March 1975, after the Communists launched a major ground offensive, the South Vietnamese retreat quickly turned into a rout. On April 8, the final battle of the Vietnam War began at Xuan Loc, the last defensive line before Saigon. Ten days later, Secretary of State Henry Kissinger ordered the evacuation of all Americans from the South Vietnamese capital. As the North Vietnamese army began closing in on April 29–30, Operation Frequent Wind, the largest helicopter evacuation in history, carried the remaining Americans to U.S. Navy ships waiting in the South China Sea. On April 30, Gen. Duong Van Minh, who had led the November 1963 coup against Diem, announced the surrender of his country.

During the evacuation, *U.S. Marines had to fight off the thousands of terrified Vietnamese who came to the American embassy in Saigon, begging for protection. (Many had earlier been promised safe conduct by the Americans.) One marine guard devised a simple, hard rule for himself: "Don't look in their eyes."*

In foreign affairs as well, Carter proved to be better intentioned than successful. From the moment he took office, he seemed determined (inordinately, according to some critics) to champion "human rights" as the basis of U.S. foreign policy. He wrote to Soviet dissident Andrei Sakharov, expressing his solidarity with those in the Soviet Union (and throughout the world) who were striving to expand their political freedoms. Yet this sort of moralistic pronouncement, while heartening to those oppressed, severely irritated the leaders of nondemocratic regimes, many of them long-standing U.S. allies, who resented Carter's effort to link diplomatic relations to improvements in their treatment of "prisoners of conscience."

Conversely, Carter believed that the United States should no longer automatically oppose revolutionary movements in the Third World, even those led by Marxists. This policy was put to the test in Central America, where growing unrest in Nicaragua and El Salvador threatened pro-American right-wing dictatorships during the late 1970s. In July 1979, in fact, the Nicaraguan opposition, led by the Marxist Sandinistas, deposed Anastasio Somoza Debayle, whose family had

THE CAMP DAVID ACCORDS

THE GREAT, ENDURING TRIUMPH of the Carter presidency was the settlement he helped to negotiate between Egyptian president Anwar el-Sadat and Israeli prime minister Menachem Begin at Camp David in September 1978. The peace talks that had begun following Sadat's historic visit to Jerusalem in November 1977—easily the most stunning diplomatic development since Nixon's 1972 trip to China—had stalled by the time President Carter invited both sides to resume their discussions at the presidential retreat in Maryland. After twelve days of intense, highly personal, trilateral bargaining, the three heads of state emerged on September 17 to present to the world the framework they had devised for peace in the region. Difficulties arose later concerning autonomy for the Palestinians (a question ultimately left unsettled); nevertheless, Sadat and Begin did transform the Camp David accords into a formal peace treaty, which they signed in March 1979, ending a thirty-one-year state of war between their two nations.

Begin (left), Carter, and Sadat converse in the president's Camp David study during the September 1978 Middle East summit.

"The most emotional time of all was after the agreement. I read in the news that Israeli teachers who were out on strike, having heard about the Camp David agreement, voted unanimously to go back to work."

—

Jimmy Carter, diary, September 18, 1978

ruled Nicaragua since 1937. An earlier U.S. government would likely have intervened to assure the creation of a reliably pro-American regime, but Carter's State Department offered aid to the new alliance government in Nicaragua while monitoring its associations, especially its increasingly close ties to Cuba and the Soviet Union—much to the displeasure of American conservatives, who feared that the Sandinistas would take Nicaragua into the Communist bloc.

On November 4, 1979, however, concern over Central America was overshadowed when Iranian militants overran the U.S. embassy in Tehran and took its occupants hostage. For twenty-five years, Iran had been ruled by Mohammed Reza Shah Pahlavi, who had used oil revenues to attempt a modernization of his country. The shah had ordered land redistribution, developed heavy industries, encouraged Iranians to attend colleges and universities in the West, and introduced social reforms, such as liberalization of the Islamic divorce laws and other restrictions on women. Yet the opposition his policies generated among fundamentalist Muslims and his ruthless repression of dissent led to his ouster in January 1979.

On April 1 of that year, after a landslide victory in a national referendum, the Ayatollah Ruhollah Khomeini, an aging extremist cleric who had been living in exile in Paris, declared an Islamic republic in Iran. He reinstituted all Islamic laws concerning the comportment of women and suppressed other Western influences with increasing rigor. During the summer of 1979, most of the country's wealthy, Western-educated elite left to join the shah in exile; that fall, using the shah's recent entry into the United States for cancer treatment as an excuse, Iranian "students" seized the Tehran embassy. Although fourteen of the sixty-six hostages—the women, the African Americans, and one white male who was seriously ill—were soon released, the remaining fifty-two were held for 444 days (a figure familiar to many Americans because television news broadcasts typically began or ended with a running count). After months of diplomacy failed to resolve the crisis, Carter approved a military rescue mission for late April 1980 that turned back, well before reaching Tehran, when several of its helicopters malfunctioned in the desert. Even the shah's death in Egypt in July 1980 did little to alleviate the situation.

This photograph—taken on November 4, the day that Iranian militants occupied the U.S. embassy in Tehran—shows blindfolded American hostages being paraded about by their captors.

The Election of 1980

BECAUSE OF THE HOSTAGE CRISIS—and because of other frustrations, such the decline of the U.S. automobile industry in relation to European and especially Japanese manufacturers—hostility toward the Carter administration mounted. On the eve of the 1980 election, the president's approval rating sank to 29 percent, the lowest ever measured by the Gallup poll. Meanwhile, the nation was becoming increasingly conservative—a shift particularly visible among blue-collar Democrats, who bolted from the Roosevelt coalition in 1980 to support Republican nominee Ronald Reagan. (Truly, the Roosevelt coalition had begun dissolving in 1964.) Reagan's most effective issue was the economy. Uniquely comfortable in front of any camera, the former movie and television actor ended his October 28 debate with Carter by looking directly into the lens of the television camera focused on him and telling viewers, "I think when you make that decision [on Election Day], it might be well if you could ask yourself, Are you better off than you were four years ago?" The answer was a resounding No! and the president conceded on Election Night even before the polls had closed on the West Coast.

Furthermore, Reagan had long coattails. The Republicans picked up thirty-two seats in the House, cutting significantly into the Democratic majority, and a dozen more seats in the Senate, giving them control of that body for the first time in twenty-six years. On the state level, Republican candidates also performed well. Richard Nixon had once hoped that the 1972 election would transform the GOP into a majority party capable of controlling the national agenda for the next fifty years as the Democrats had for the past half century. Now, with conservative southern Democrats prepared to give Reagan a working majority in the House, the 1980 election seemed to have done just that.

LEFT: *Ronald Reagan was known* as the Great Communicator *because his acting experience made him seem at ease before the television cameras and because his likable, engaging personality made Americans want to believe him.*

Jimmy Carter

1924–

by William E. Leuchtenburg

AMERICA HAS NEVER HAD A MORE morally earnest public figure than James Earl Carter Jr., known to all the world as Jimmy. A single-term governor of Georgia, Carter was so obscure when he began his campaign for president in 1976 that the media called him "Jimmy Who?" He seemed highly unlikely to win, but Americans were reeling then from the seamy Watergate scandal, and Carter's message of integrity resonated with disaffected voters. He further distanced himself from Richard Nixon by telling a television interviewer, "If I'm elected, at the end of four years or eight years I hope people will say, 'You know, Jimmy Carter made a lot of mistakes, but he never told a lie.'"

On his very first day in office, Carter showed how determined he was to discard the trappings of Nixon's imperial presidency. Following his inauguration, he made his way up Pennsylvania Avenue from Capitol Hill to the White House not in the usual bulletproof black limousine but walking hand-in-hand with his wife, Rosalynn, and their nine-year-old daughter, Amy. Later, he gave his first televised address wearing a simple cardigan, and when he traveled, he usually carried his own luggage.

As president, Carter did a number of good things—he named women and African Americans to high federal posts, created cabinet-level departments devoted to education and energy, safeguarded the environment, and brought Egypt and Israel together. But he also found that goodwill alone does not make an effective leader. A technocrat by nature, he was politically insensitive and didn't know how to interact with the power brokers in Washington. After watching his boss scold congressional leaders instead of massaging their egos, Vice Pres.

Walter "Fritz" Mondale remarked, "Carter's got the coldest political nose of any politician I ever met." Nor did the president's uninspired speeches arouse much enthusiasm. "Carterism does not march and it does not sing," wrote historian Eric Goldman, a former White House aide. "It is cautious, muted, grayish, at times even crabbed."

Carter also learned painfully that personal values sometimes clash with public ones and that worthwhile aims can occasionally conflict. When Republicans accused budget director Bert Lance of corruption, Carter stood by his closest friend—an act of loyalty that did him credit as a man but seriously impaired his reputation for rectitude. Similarly, when he pursued fiscal responsibility by proposing cuts in social programs, including funds for school lunch programs, he was accused of balancing the budget on the backs of the poor.

Carter's commitment to doing good also produced mixed results in foreign affairs. When he said, "A strong nation, like a strong person, can afford to be gentle," he voiced a welcome departure from America's previous Yankee arrogance. He insisted that all governments respect human rights and took up the cause of the Soviet dissidents—an admirable stance but one that damaged his efforts to reach understandings with the Kremlin on critical issues such as arms control.

Despite warnings of the perilous consequences that might follow, Carter permitted the exiled shah of Iran to enter the United States for cancer treatment. This compassionate but unwise act infuriated the Islamic fundamentalists who had recently deposed the shah and provoked them into overrunning the U.S. embassy in Tehran. Fifty-two members of the embassy staff were held hostage for more than a year. The president responded with patient diplomacy, but as his initiatives failed again and again to free the hostages, the country became increasingly exasperated. During his final summer in office, Carter's approval rating fell to just 21 percent, lower even than Nixon's had been in the abyss of Watergate.

After his resounding loss to Ronald Reagan in 1980, Carter left the presidency, but not public life. Freed from the constraints of the White House, he has since engaged in a multitude of activities that have earned him worldwide plaudits as a remarkable humanitarian and the greatest ex-president in U.S. history. Even these accomplishments, however, have not greatly altered the negative assessment of his presidency. More than one historian has likened Carter to the Wizard of Oz. When Dorothy discovers that the Wizard is a humbug, she cries, "You are a very bad man!" "No, I am a very good man," he replies. "I'm just a very bad Wizard." Jimmy Carter was, and is, a very good man. But, sadly, like the Wizard, he wasn't very good at his craft.

Carter leans against a pillar outside the Oval Office.

25

THE END OF
THE COLD WAR

The Last Days of the Soviet Union

LATE IN THE EVENING ON SUNDAY, August 18, 1991, Pres. George Bush was relaxing at his summer home in Kennebunkport, Maine. At a nearby hotel, his national security adviser, Brent Scowcroft, was reading through some diplomatic cables while watching CNN on his bedroom television set. At 11:30 P.M., the network interrupted its regular broadcast with some breaking news from Moscow: Soviet president Mikhail Gorbachev had just resigned for "reasons of health." Initially disbelieving the report, Scowcroft telephoned his deputy, Robert Gates, and asked him to "check it out." At 11:45 P.M., Scowcroft called the president, who had just fallen asleep. The two men discussed the situation and decided that Scowcroft should continue seeking confirmation of the report while Bush got some rest.

At five-thirty the next morning, according to Bush's diary, he "called the [White House] Situation Room…and they gave me the update that Gorbachev has been put out." By then, Scowcroft had confirmed that a junta of eight hard-line Soviet officials had indeed overthrown Gorbachev and established a Committee for the State of Emergency. Bush began telephoning friendly heads of state in Europe and elsewhere, while his staff prepared a public statement for him to deliver on this dangerous yet still obscure development.

AT LEFT: **Bush and Gorbachev** *walk through Red Square on July 30, 1991. Bush flew to Moscow just three weeks before the attempted coup to sign the Strategic Arms Reduction Treaty (START).*

In Washington, meanwhile, at 4 A.M. that same Monday, Allen Weinstein, president of the Center for Democracy (and a coauthor of this book), also awoke to a ringing telephone. Hearing only garbled Russian speech on the other end before the line went dead, he decided, despite the hour, to dress and visit his downtown Washington office. In late June, Weinstein's small, nongovernmental democratic assistance organization had joined Senate majority leader George Mitchell and Senate minority leader Bob Dole in hosting a visit to the United States by Boris Yeltsin, the recently elected president of the Russian Republic (the most influential of the fifteen republics that made up the Soviet Union). Furthermore, only a week before, he and his Center for Democracy colleagues had helped Yeltsin's government stage a successful conference in Moscow at which issues related to Soviet political reform were discussed.

At one of his meetings with Weinstein in Moscow, Yeltsin, who was then Gorbachev's main rival for leadership of the Soviet reform movement, had ridiculed speculation that reactionary Communists might soon stage a coup. Although Gorbachev's policies had taken a number of unnecessary twists and turns, the Russian president said, the processes of democratization, marketization, and decentralization of power that he had initiated could not now be reversed. A coup would be pointless and, therefore, was unlikely. The top CIA analysts agreed.

Yet, arriving at his office just before dawn, Weinstein found waiting for him a fax from Moscow, sent only a few hours earlier by one of Yeltsin's closest associates. It confirmed Weinstein's worst fear: "It is Military Coup. Tanks are everywhere." Another fax, sent moments later, read: "Tanks are around the Council. BY [Boris Yeltsin] denounces the coup. Ukraine and other republic are against. Everybody go on strike. BY tried to contact Gorbi. and failed."

T HE PROXIMATE CAUSE for the rather hastily and incompetently plotted coup was the new Union treaty that Gorbachev, Yeltsin, and the leaders of other Soviet republics expected to sign on Tuesday, August 20. This agreement, announced to the public on August 2, would have significantly reduced the political and economic power of the Soviet central government—a prospect deeply troubling to the top apparatchiks. Unwilling to permit their authority to be decentralized, the conspirators, led by KGB chief Vladimir Kryuchkov, moved to topple Gorbachev.

On Sunday afternoon, August 18, Gorbachev was nearing the end of a vacation at Foros, his lavish estate on the Black Sea, when his chief of security entered his study to tell him that a delegation had arrived from Moscow without an appointment, wanting to see him immediately. Sensing trouble, the Soviet president picked up his telephone to call for help, but all five of his lines were dead. Several of the conspirators soon came upstairs to inform him that he had been deposed. They demanded that he sign a document transferring all his power to Vice Pres. Gennadi Yanayev, the Emergency Committee's front man. When Gorbachev refused, he was placed under house arrest. Because his personal bodyguards remained loyal to him, the ousted leader wasn't in any immediate physical danger, but he was isolated from the outside world. His only information came from a shortwave radio receiver, found in a servant's room, over which he monitored reports of the coup's progress broadcast by the BBC and other Western media.

*A **Red Army** soldier loyal to Defense Minister Dmitri Yazov stands atop his tank in Red Square on August 21, 1991. Later that day, Yazov was arrested along with other members of the Emergency Committee.*

At the same time, the managers of the coup were largely ignoring Boris Yeltsin, who took refuge with his staff inside the Russian parliament building, known as the White House. For some inconceivable reason, the conspirators allowed Yeltsin's phone and fax lines to remain in operation, and the Russian president used them effectively to communicate with his allies in the Soviet military and rally popular opposition to the coup. Responding to his calls, a hundred thousand Muscovites formed a human shield around the Russian White House to prevent military units loyal to the Emergency Committee from entering the compound and arresting Yeltsin. The Russian president also contacted political leaders throughout the Soviet Union and the world, urging them to denounce the coup and support the imprisoned Gorbachev.

Several of the military leaders who came over to Yeltsin's side advised him to declare himself commander in chief of the army in Gorbachev's absence. Agreeing to this, Yeltsin read a declaration to that effect while standing on a tank (and risking assassination by sniper fire) in the courtyard of the Russian White House. Because the Emergency Committee had not yet secured every broadcast outlet, many Russians witnessed Yeltsin's courageous defiance on television. The powerful image of Yeltsin standing atop that tank fueled debate within the Soviet military as to whom it should support: Defense Minister Dmitri Yazov and his apparently inept Emergency Committee or Yeltsin and the brave reformers.

The Bush Response

In Washington, Weinstein received additional faxes from the Russian White House with queries and instructions. This one arrived on the evening of August 19 (which means it was sent during the middle of the night in Moscow):

> *Did Mr. Bush make any comments upon the situation in this country? If he did, make it known by all means of communication. Make it known to the people of this country.*
>
> *The Russian Government has No ways to address the people. All radio stations are under control.*
>
> *The following is BY's address to the Army. Submit it to USIA [the United States Information Agency, proprietor of the Voice of America]. Broadcast it over the country.... Do it! Urgent!*

In fact, President Bush's initial response to the coup was extraordinarily cautious. "Our dilemma," Scowcroft wrote in his joint memoir with Bush, "was that we didn't know the current status of the coup. The president's inclination was to condemn it outright, but if it turned out to be successful, we would be forced to live with the new leaders, however repulsive their behavior. We decided he should be condemnatory without irrevocably burning his bridges."

Jack Matlock, who had served as Bush's ambassador to the Soviet Union until his retirement a few weeks before the coup, found the president's morning statement disappointing. According to Matlock, Bush "sounded as if he thought the coup had been successful and he intended to deal with the emergency committee." Rather than *illegal* or even *unconstitutional*, the president described the coup as "extraconstitutional" and emphasized that he expected the Emergency Committee to "live up fully to its international obligations."

Media criticism of this statement led Bush to make a stronger one later that day. Appearing before the press at the White House (to which he had returned), the president used the words *unconstitutional* and *illegal* and endorsed Yeltsin's demand for Gorbachev's release and restoration. However, as Matlock has pointed out, "the initial statement was damaging, particularly within the Soviet Union," where the leaders of the Emergency Committee "used it repeatedly in the controlled media on August 19 and 20, ignoring Bush's subsequent correction." Moreover, throughout that first dramatic day, the U.S. president declined to call Boris Yeltsin, who could have used the president's moral support to strengthen his own legitimacy.

Gennadi Yanayev blows his nose at a press conference held by the Emergency Committee at 6 P.M. on August 19. According to one reporter who was present, the Soviet vice president was "plainly drunk," as were several other nervous members of the cabal. Although Yanayev was the group's titular leader, KGB chief Vladimir Kryuchkov and Interior Minister Boris Pugo were the masterminds of the coup.

EVERTHELESS, EARLY ON THE SECOND DAY of the crisis, after trying unsuccessfully to reach Gorbachev several times, President Bush did place a call to Yeltsin at the Russian White House—"and much to my surprise," Bush wrote later, "I got him." Yeltsin described his perilous situation and said that he expected an armed attack to begin at any moment. "We're anxious to do anything we can to be helpful. Do you have any suggestions?" Bush asked. "The main thing is moral support," Yeltsin replied. "We need to hear statements that will call the attention of the world to our plight." He also asked Bush to continue insisting that Gorbachev be released and warned the president not to communicate with the conspirators, lest such contact legitimize them.

Encouraged by growing internal resistance to the coup and Yeltsin's firm leadership, Bush did as the Russian president requested. He denounced the putsch in even stronger terms and called again for Gorbachev's return to power. During the Persian Gulf War, British prime minister Margaret Thatcher had told Bush, "This is no time to go wobbly." The president went much less "wobbly" now.

By Wednesday, August 21, it had become clear that the coup was failing. That morning, Kryuchkov and Yazov commandeered an Aeroflot jet and flew to the Crimea. Whether they expected to negotiate with Gorbachev or plead for his mercy, no one knew. Not far behind was a second jet carrying a delegation led by Yeltsin's vice president, Alexander Rutskoi. Catching up to Kryuchkov and Yazov at Foros, the Rutskoi party arrested them and freed Gorbachev. In Moscow, meanwhile, several conspirators killed themselves rather than face arrest and imprisonment.

Elsewhere in the Soviet capital, the devoted faxer on Yeltsin's staff dispatched two final messages to Weinstein in Washington. The first was sent on the evening of August 21 (Moscow time) before news of the coup's collapse had spread: "Sunset over Moscow is beautiful…. One can feel 'Victory!' in the air…[but] it is going to be a night of crucial importance for us." The next, sent on the morning of August 22, read simply: "It's all over. We won! There is sunrise of freedom. [Signed] Mikhail Galyatin. The White House of Russia."

Yeltsin waves to a cheering crowd in front of the Russian White House on Thursday, August 22, 1991, after his steadfastness helped defeat the coup. American diplomats in Moscow had an excellent view of the proceedings, because the U.S. embassy was just across the street.

Why had the coup failed? Yeltsin himself later stated the principal reason: "The putschists had underestimated the changes that had occurred in the country. Under Gorbachev's rule, aside from the official government, there had emerged leaders of public opinion, political forces, independent authorities in culture, the democratic press, and others. Their mouths could be stopped only with the most brutal bloody persecution, with a wave of arrests and executions...but [the putschists] were not even capable of that." The policies initiated by Gorbachev to which Yeltsin refers were *glasnost* ("openness"), which encouraged political debate within the Soviet Union by relaxing state censorship, and *perestroika* ("restructuring"), which began the transformation of Soviet state socialism into a market economy. By August 1991, these reforms had moved the Russian people (if not their central government) far from the repressive, totalitarian polity that Pres. Ronald Reagan had once called "an evil empire."

Détente

IN THE FORTY-SIX YEARS SINCE the end of World War II, an uneasy "balance of terror" had persisted between the United States and the Soviet Union. At the same time, there had been modulation within the superpower relationship: Some periods had been marked by negotiation, others by confrontation. After 1964, when stolid Leonid Brezhnev replaced the mercurial Nikita Khrushchev as Soviet premier, a period of slow improvement in relations ensued. During the early 1970s, Nixon and Kissinger built on this détente to negotiate not only the SALT I accord but also significant trade deals, including the Soviet purchase of nearly 25 percent of the 1972 American wheat crop. (Later, this deal was called "the Great Grain Robbery," because the Soviets were charged far less than the world market price for the wheat—the difference being made up by U.S. government subsidies to American farmers.)

After Nixon resigned from office, détente continued under Kissinger, whom Ford retained as secretary of state. The SALT talks continued, and in August 1975 the United States and the Soviet Union, meeting with thirty-three other nations at the Helsinki Conference on Security and Cooperation in Europe (CSCE), signed an agreement recognizing the boundaries established in Eastern Europe after World War II but also pledging the signatories to "respect human rights and fundamental freedoms." Therefore, by the time President Carter took office in 1977, it had become difficult to characterize U.S. foreign policy as an anti-Communist crusade.

Yet the superpower relationship shifted again during the late 1970s, when massive Soviet military aid to the Marxist faction in the Angolan civil war focused international attention on Soviet expansionism in the Third World. Simultaneously, the persecution of Jewish and other dissidents within the USSR—a flagrant violation of the Helsinki Accords—also became a cause célèbre. Thereafter, détente limped along until late December 1979, when a hundred thousand Soviet troops invaded Afghanistan to prop up a tottering Communist regime there. The Soviet incursion reportedly made Jimmy Carter angrier than at any other time during his presidency. Although many Kremlinologists interpreted the move as a Soviet attempt to defend the status quo, Carter called it "a stepping-stone to their possible control over much

Nixon and Kissinger at the latter's swearing-in as secretary of state in September 1973. A Jewish refugee from Nazi Germany, Kissinger rose to prominence during the 1960s as a professor of government at Harvard, where he specialized in the balance of power that defined European politics during the nineteenth century. During his years in the Nixon and Ford administrations, Kissinger looked to re-create this period of stability in international affairs, first as Nixon's national security adviser and later as his (and Ford's) secretary of state.

of the world's oil supplies" (because of Afghanistan's proximity to Iran and the Persian Gulf). He suspended the sale of advanced technologies to the Soviet Union, instituted a grain embargo, and led a sixty-four-nation boycott of the 1980 Summer Olympics in Moscow. Carter also withdrew from Senate consideration the SALT II treaty that he and Brezhnev had signed in June 1979.

COMING WITHIN TWO MONTHS of one another, the seizure of American hostages in Iran and the Soviet invasion of Afghanistan dramatically altered public opinion within the United States, resurrecting Cold War animosities and intensifying them to levels not seen since 1962. An overwhelming majority of Americans came to support large increases in the U.S. defense budget and a stronger national military posture. Ronald Reagan took advantage of these attitudes during the 1980 campaign, when he lambasted Carter for being too dovish and promised to support actively anti-Communist movements around the world. Later, after Reagan's overwhelming election victory, his policy of intervening to oppose Communism in the Third World became known as the Reagan Doctrine.

Mobilizing support among influential Cold War Democrats (notably Washington senator Henry M. Jackson), President Reagan won congressional funding for a massive buildup of the nation's nuclear and conventional forces.

CENTRAL AMERICA

WITHIN DAYS OF TAKING OFFICE, the new Reagan administration reversed former president Jimmy Carter's policy of patience with regard to Nicaragua and suspended all aid to the new revolutionary government there. The reason, it charged, was that the Sandinistas were covertly supporting leftist rebels in neighboring El Salvador. Soon, Reagan began his own program of covert aid to the guerrilla opposition in Nicaragua, a consortium of democrats and backers of the former Somoza regime collectively known as the "contras." At the same time, in El Salvador, Reagan placed the military and economic resources of the United States squarely behind the fragile government of José Napoléon Duarte, a centrist beset by Cuban-armed Marxists on the political left and reactionary "death squads" on the right. Military aid to El Salvador increased fivefold during Reagan's first term, yet even so, the future of the Duarte government remained uncertain.

In the meantime, Democrats and others on Capitol Hill became concerned that President Reagan's attitude might lead the United States into a Central American war. As the overthrow of the Sandinista government in Nicaragua became the all-but-stated policy of the U.S. government, Congress passed the Boland Amendment. This December 1982 law banned further military aid to the contras. Even so, Reagan was reluctant to relinquish his support. praising the contras in March 1985 as "freedom fighters" and "the moral equal of our Founding Fathers."

The government of Sandinista leader Daniel Ortega Saavedra remained in power in Nicaragua until an indigenous regional peace process, orchestrated largely by Costa Rican president Oscar Arias Sanchez, led to free elections there in February 1990 and a peaceful transfer of power to victorious opposition leader Violeta Barrios de Chamorro.

(During his first term in office, Pentagon spending rose nearly 50 percent.) At the same time, Reagan decided to postpone serious arms control negotiations until the new U.S. force status had been achieved. Critics charged that his policies undermined the détente sought by every American president since John Kennedy, but Reagan responded confidently that the end of détente was no great loss. At his first press conference, in fact, he dismissed détente as "a one-way street the Soviet Union has used to pursue its own aims."

Because of the steep tax cuts that the Reagan administration also pushed through Congress during its first year in office, the fattening of the defense budget soon produced shocking federal deficits. In 1983, for example, the U.S. government took in $601 billion but spent $808 billion (including $205 billion on defense)—yielding a deficit of $207 billion, or nearly triple the shortfall in Carter's final budget. Reagan was gambling that the Soviet Union couldn't keep up in such an all-out arms race, and he proved to be right.

Pressing America's technological advantage, the president proposed in a nationally televised March 1983 speech that the nation build a new, hugely expensive missile shield to protect the country from nuclear attack. According to the president, the Strategic Defense Initiative (SDI) would use laser beams and other advanced technologies to destroy incoming ICBMs before they could reach their targets. Although SDI's many opponents called the science unrealistic (dismissively referring to it as "Star Wars"), Soviet officials reacted with outrage and alarm. In every respect, SDI threatened the existing strategic balance between the two nations, which had centered since the New Look of the 1950s around the concept of "mutually assured destruction." As the cornerstone of nuclear deterrence, MAD (as it was known) had maintained the peace for nearly two generations, albeit by means of a tense standoff. Now that it was being challenged, many on both sides felt the deepest unease.

Following Reagan's speech, the Soviets began to insist on U.S. abandonment of SDI as a precondition for any new arms control agreement. This was fine with Reagan, who wasn't yet prepared to conclude an agreement in any case. Nor, in truth, were the Soviets, who were experiencing a leadership crisis. Beginning with Brezhnev's death in November 1982, the USSR quickly went through two more aging premiers, Yuri Andropov (who died in February 1984) and Konstantin Chernenko, before fifty-four-year-old Mikhail Gorbachev rose to power following Chernenko's death in March 1985.

Poland

AT THE SAME TIME, the Soviet Union was also beginning to have difficulty maintaining its control over Eastern Europe. The initial trouble spot was Poland, where the visit of Pope John Paul II (né Karol Cardinal Wojtyla, archbishop of Kraków) in June 1979 had rekindled national pride among the country's numerous Roman Catholics. A year later, dissatisfaction with Poland's Communist government (because of food shortages, insufficient housing, and the rationing of electricity) produced an enormously disruptive strike at the Lenin Shipyard in Gdansk, where seventeen thousand workers walked off their jobs on August 14,

Mikhail Gorbachev grew up as the son of peasants in the northern Caucasus. After four years at a machine-tractor station in his native Stavropol, he joined the Communist party in 1952, when he was twenty-one. Three years later, he earned a law degree from Moscow State University, rising to become first secretary of the Stavropol party in 1970. He was elevated to the Central Committee in 1971 and became a full member of the Politburo in 1980, specializing in agricultural issues.

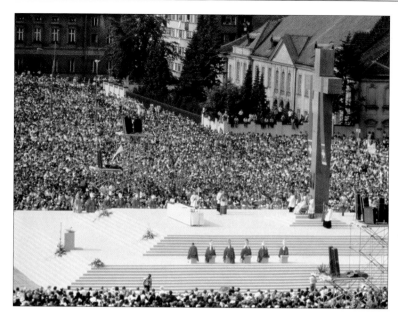

Pope John Paul II celebrates an afternoon mass in Warsaw's Victory Square in June 1979. The podium and enormous cross were specially erected for the occasion. When the former Cardinal Wojtyla was elected pope in October 1978, he became the first non-Italian to lead the Roman Catholic Church in 456 years.

1980. Quickly, the strike, led by electrician Lech Walesa, spread to other industrial centers on the Baltic coast and to coal mines in Silesia as well.

The uprising toppled Polish premier Edward Babiuch, who was dismissed by Communist party first secretary Edward Gierek on August 24. After further consultation with the Soviets, Gierek appointed deputy premier Mieczyslaw Jagielski to negotiate with Walesa's new independent trade union Solidarnosc (Solidarity). A week later, Walesa and Jagielski signed an agreement acknowledging the central role of the Polish Communist party but also recognizing the independence of Solidarity, whose ranks would soon number about ten million workers. In addition, all of Solidarity's major labor-related demands were met.

Although the Soviets had encouraged Gierek to compromise with the workers, the deal that was eventually struck displeased Moscow because it encouraged Walesa to push for more. Gierek was soon ousted, and after a few false starts and some reshuffling, Defense Minister Wojciech Jaruzelski became the new Polish head of state. Walesa and Archbishop Jozef Glemp met with General Jaruzelski on November 4, 1981, to discuss the creation of a Council of National Understanding, but their talks went nowhere. Finally, on December 12, the leaders of Solidarity proposed nationwide referenda on the questions of establishing a non-Communist government in Poland and redefining the country's military relationship with the Soviet Union. The next day, Jaruzelski imposed martial law, which remained in effect until July 1983.

DETERMINED TO SUPPORT oppositional movements such as Solidarity within the Communist bloc, President Reagan placed American foreign policy on a much more aggressive footing. Some of America's new anti-Communist allies were democrats; other not. In Afghanistan, for example, President Reagan greatly expanded covert American aid to the Mujahideen, a loose coalition of Islamic forces that was carrying on a guerrilla war against the Soviet army of occupation. Handheld Stinger antiaircraft missiles, supplied by the CIA, offset the Soviet advantage in airpower, and other arms smuggled into Afghanistan through refugee camps in Pakistan eventually forced the Soviet army to begin pulling out of the country in early 1988.

RIGHT: Lech Walesa became radicalized in 1970 after watching several demonstrators being gunned down in the street.

Supporting Reagan strongly in these anti-Communist policies were three staunch European allies—Margaret Thatcher, French president François Mitterand, and West German chancellor Helmut Kohl. All backed the president's confrontational stance and applauded his decision to deploy new Cruise and Pershing missiles in Europe beginning in December 1983—despite the vehement objections of peace groups and, of course, the Soviets.

After winning a landslide reelection in 1984, however, President Reagan began to soften his rhetoric and segue back from confrontation to negotiation. By then, his defense modernization program had created a much more robust American military, and this gave him a much stronger position at the bargaining table. Even the highly conservative Thatcher, known as the Iron Lady, agreed that the time had come for engagement. After meeting the rising Soviet leader in December 1984, she declared, "I'm cautiously optimistic. I like Mr. Gorbachev. We can do business together."

Reagan and Gorbachev

EXCEPT FOR A BRIEF COURTESY CALL made by Foreign Minister Andrei Gromyko in 1984, Reagan hadn't met with a single high-ranking Soviet official during his entire first term. In mid-November 1985, however, he flew to Geneva for a summit with Gorbachev. During their meetings, the two men began to develop something of a friendship, but because of the summit's focus on arms control, there was also a great deal of blame to be exchanged for the lack of progress made during the early 1980s. Gorbachev was

particularly eager to reach an accommodation with the West so that he could divert funds from defense to domestic production, yet Reagan remained reticent. (Although Gorbachev had little to show for it as yet, he had already begun to install within the Kremlin the cadre of sympathetic younger officials that would help him implement *glasnost* and *perestroika*.)

The next meeting between Reagan and Gorbachev took place in Reykjavík, Iceland, in October 1986. The Reykjavík summit also ended without a formal agreement; however, there was a brief flurry of activity when it was revealed that Reagan had agreed preliminarily to accept Gorbachev's dramatic proposal that both sides reduce their nuclear arsenals immediately by 50 percent or more as a prelude to complete nuclear disarmament within the next decade. Reagan later pulled back because of Gorbachev's continuing insistence that SDI be abandoned, because the Soviets were unwilling to permit on-site verification, and because of the shock expressed by America's European allies when they learned of his apparent willingness to abandon casually the West's long-standing and effective nuclear deterrent.

President Reagan reminded the world that he was still a Cold Warrior in June 1987, when he delivered a speech at the Brandenburg Gate in West Berlin challenging Gorbachev to make good on glasnost and perestroika. "If you seek peace," Reagan declared, "...come here to this gate! Mr. Gorbachev, open this gate! Mr. Gorbachev, tear down this wall!"

THE IRAN-CONTRA SCANDAL

ONCE IRAN RELEASED THE AMERICAN HOSTAGES on the first day of his presidency, Ronald Reagan generally avoided public contact with that nation and other Islamic states known to be unfriendly to U.S. interests. He did provide American troops for an international peacekeeping mission in Lebanon, but that undertaking failed tragically in October 1983, when terrorists exploded a truck bomb inside the marine compound at the Beirut airport, killing 241 servicemen.

When the civil war between the Lebanese Christians and Muslims restarted in February 1984, Reagan ended the military mission but felt that he still needed to remain engaged in Lebanon because of the seven American hostages being held by Islamic militants there. He referred often at this time to his commitment never to negotiate with terrorists. Yet in late 1986, rumors began to circulate that his administration had been trading arms for hostages. As it turned out, National Security Adviser Robert C. McFarlane and NSC staff member Oliver L. North had arranged a secret shipment of arms to Iran in July 1985, after which one of the seven hostages was released. A second covert shipment took place in May 1986. In the meantime—on April 4, 1986— North sent a memo to McFarlane's replacement, John M. Poindexter, suggesting that twelve million dollars of the proceeds from the second arms sale be diverted to fund weapons for the contras. This was indeed what happened, according to Attorney General Edwin Meese, who revealed the illegal

Oliver North was a lieutenant colonel in the marines before being assigned to the National Security Council. He is shown here in December 1986 being sworn in to testify before a House committee conducting one of the early investigations into the Iran-Contra affair.

diversion to the nation on November 26, 1986. Later that day, President Reagan personally announced both Poindexter's resignation and North's dismissal.

As part of the congressional hearings and court trials that followed, North testified (often fervently) that the late CIA director William J. Casey—who died conveniently in May 1987, two months before North's congressional appearance—had approved the entire operation. Although special prosecutor Lawrence E. Walsh dropped more serious conspiracy charges once the White House refused to release relevant documents (for reasons of national security), North and Poindexter were convicted of obstructing Congress and making false statements under oath. But their convictions were overturned on appeal when a federal circuit court ruled that their testimony to Congress, compelled under grants of limited immunity, had prejudiced their subsequent trials. Walsh also charged McFarlane, Defense Secretary Caspar W. Weinberger, and four other top Reagan administration officials with lying to Congress and withholding information, but Pres. George Bush pardoned them on Christmas Eve 1992. The extent of President Reagan's involvement in the scandal was never made clear; however, his popularity fell precipitously once the investigating congressional committees concluded that he bore "ultimate responsibility" for the illegal actions of his staff.

The first practical result of the Gorbachev-Reagan entente emerged only in December 1987, when the two men signed the Intermediate-range Nuclear Forces (INF) Treaty at their next meeting in Washington, D.C. The INF Treaty eliminated an entire class of nuclear missiles—those with ranges between three hundred and thirty-four hundred miles—and resulted in the dismantling of more than twenty-five hundred weapons, two-thirds of them American. Equally significant were the provisions of the treaty that permitted rigorous on-site inspection: Each side was allowed to conduct short-notice searches and even assign resident inspectors to monitor compliance at major military facilities.

Gorbachev and Reagan were joined by President-elect Bush for their final meeting on Governors Island in New York Harbor in December 1988. The discussion followed Gorbachev's stunning December 7 speech before the United Nations General Assembly, in which he announced his unilateral decision to reduce the Soviet military by half a million men and withdraw from East Germany, Czechoslovakia, and Hungary six armored divisions, all of which would be disbanded within two years. "However," Gorbachev recounted in his memoir, "my main intent was to show the international community that mankind was on the threshold of a fundamentally new era—the traditional principles governing international relations, which were based on the balance of power and rivalry, to be superseded by relations founded on creative cooperation and joint development."

Soviet weapons inspectors stand with their American escorts among the remains of Pershing II missiles dismantled in accordance with the INF Treaty. This photograph was taken in January 1989 at the Pueblo Army Deport in southeastern Colorado.

The speech confirmed Gorbachev's position as the most visionary figure in international politics since World War II. "Not since Woodrow Wilson presented his Fourteen Points in 1918 or since Franklin Roosevelt and Winston Churchill promulgated the Atlantic Charter in 1941 has a world figure demonstrated the vision of Mikhail Gorbachev," the *New York Times* editorialized on December 8. "…Breathtaking. Risky. Bold. Naive. Diversionary. Heroic. All fit. So sweeping is his agenda that it will require weeks to sort out. But whatever Mr. Gorbachev's motives, his ideas merit—indeed compel—the most serious response from President-elect Bush and other leaders."

THE POLITICAL AND PERSONAL CONTRAST between Ronald Reagan and George Bush could hardly have been more stark: Reagan was a "conviction" politician, governed by deeply ingrained principles that guided him in his daily actions. Although ideologically conservative as well, Bush was a pragmatist, temperamentally cautious and reluctant to engage in unnecessary confrontation, even regarding some matters of principle. Although it was Reagan's hard line that had fatally weakened the USSR's imperialist superstructure, it was Bush who would preside over the empire's collapse.

This disintegration occurred in two phases: First, in 1989, the Soviet satellites began to break away. In his General Assembly speech, Gorbachev had promised political "freedom of choice" to the people of Eastern Europe, and they took him at his word, moving rapidly to unseat unpopular Communist governments. Again, Poland led the way. In June 1989, a new Polish legislature was chosen in the first truly free elections in Eastern Europe since 1939. (Walesa's Solidarity movement was the overwhelming victor.) On September 10, 1989, Hungary opened its border with Austria, allowing thousands of East German "vacationers" to cross over into the West. On November 9—following massive demonstrations in East Berlin, Leipzig, and other East German cities—the Berlin Wall came down, followed shortly thereafter by the Communist government that had erected it. In December 1989, Czech playwright and recent political prisoner Vaclav Havel led the so-called Velvet Revolution, peacefully ending Communist rule in Czechoslovakia.

The Bush administration initially responded to these developments with skepticism. National Security Council officials still weren't sure that Gorbachev meant what he said—and even if he did, they weren't sanguine that conservatives in the Kremlin would let him continue. An American policy review, conducted at Bush's request, concluded that the United States should remain agnostic with regard to Soviet liberalization—at least until Gorbachev had demonstrated consolidation of his domestic support. Yet, as Bush watched televised images of Germans breaking off pieces of the Berlin Wall on November 9, he told an aide, "If the Soviets are going to let the Communists fall in East Germany, they've got to be really serious—more serious than I realized."

One of the many souvenir hunters who chipped away at the Berlin Wall after November 9, 1989, when East Germany made the wall obsolete by allowing free access to the West.

A MONTH LATER, Bush and Gorbachev met aboard U.S. and Soviet naval vessels anchored off the island of Malta. By then, Bush had surrendered the bulk of his doubts about Gorbachev's intentions; however, the reward he offered the Soviet leader was slight: proposals for arms reduction and some modest economic initiatives to help the failing Soviet economy. Gorbachev countered with more talk of demilitarization, which Bush resisted. Nevertheless, it did seem as though, by the last day of the summit, the two men had begun to warm to one another. "The world will be a better place if *perestroika* succeeds," the American president said at one point. "We don't consider you as an enemy anymore. Things have changed," Gorbachev told Bush at another.

The Malta summit thus ended on a positive note, yet the period between December 1989 and August 1991 proved difficult and disquieting for Gorbachev and his allies, who were caught between popular demands for more rapid change in the Soviet economy and hard-line insistence that the central government reassert its authority—with force, if necessary—over the rebellious Soviet republics now wanting "freedom of choice" for themselves.

RIGHT: *A button advertising the Civic Forum, an umbrella organization of Czechoslovakian opposition groups that Vaclav Havel helped to form in November 1989.*

Of course, this second phase of Soviet disintegration—the breaking away of the republics—was already well under way. On March 11, 1990, the Lithuanian parliament publicly declared its independence from the USSR. (Lithuania was one of three Baltic republics granted to the Soviet Union by the secret protocols of the 1939 Nazi-Soviet Nonaggression Pact.) Gorbachev immediately declared the move "illegitimate and invalid" but for nearly a year did little else. Meanwhile, on February 7, 1990, the Central Committee of the Communist Party of the Soviet Union (CPSU) reluctantly accepted Gorbachev's proposal that it end its seven-decade monopoly on political power.

Boris Yeltsin was overjoyed by this development. Having risen through the party ranks as a civil engineer specializing in construction, he had been made a member of the Central Committee of the CPSU in March 1981 and a nonvoting member of the Politburo in February 1986. On October 21, 1987, however, he had delivered a Central Committee speech highly critical of the slow pace of *perestroika* and also of the "cult of personality" surrounding CPSU general secretary Gorbachev. Three weeks later, the party dismissed Yeltsin from his post as first secretary of the Moscow Gorkom (city committee), demoting him to deputy chairman of the USSR State Construction Committee. Yeltsin remained highly popular in Moscow, however, where (at Gorbachev's direction) he had been rooting out corruption in the Moscow party hierarchy.

When Gorbachev introduced multicandidate elections in March 1989, Yeltsin ran for a seat in the new Congress of People's Deputies of the USSR and won with 92 percent of the vote in his Moscow district. Fourteen months later, he was elected chairman of the Supreme Soviet of the Russian Soviet Federated Socialist Republic (RSFSR)—despite Gorbachev's objections—and in that capacity presided over the June 12 adoption of the RSFSR's Declaration of Sovereignty, a document that described Russia as a "democratic" state within a "renewed" Soviet Union. A month after that—on July 12, 1990—Yeltsin announced his resignation from the CPSU.

Demonstrators at an independence rally held in Vilnius, Lithuania, in February 1989. Their signs read "OCCUPYING POWER, GET OUT" and "WE WANT TO RETURN TO EUROPE."

The Persian Gulf War

THIS WAS THE SITUATION ON AUGUST 2, 1990, when Iraqi leader Saddam Hussein invaded the tiny oil-rich emirate of Kuwait on the northwestern coast of the Persian Gulf. Acting to protect U.S. political and economic interests in the Gulf region, President Bush sent the first of 541,000 American troops to Saudi Arabia beginning on August 8. Meanwhile, he worked to put together a global coalition in support of economic (and ultimately military) sanctions designed to free Kuwait from Iraqi control.

Despite Baghdad's strong ties to Moscow, Gorbachev became a crucial member of that coalition, suspending Soviet arms sales to Iraq and using other diplomatic means to pressure Saddam into leaving Kuwait. When these proved insufficient, the United States and its allies attacked. Operation Desert Storm began on January 17, 1991, with five weeks of bombing; then, on February 24,

Coalition soldiers in Kuwait remove a dead Iraqi from a tank along the Highway of Death, the name given to a stretch of road leading north out of Kuwait City that was clogged with retreating Iraqis when the ground war began. Nearly everyone on it was killed. This photograph was taken on March 1, 1991, the day after President Bush proclaimed Kuwait's liberation.

the ground assault began. Four days later, President Bush proclaimed the liberation of Kuwait. He also announced his decision to suspend hostilities rather than conquer Iraq. Bush was fearful that U.S. casualties might be high and also that Arab members of the coalition might defect if he continued the fighting. Debate over the merits of Bush's decision to leave Saddam in place continues unabated today.

Although Gorbachev succeeded in bending the Politburo to his will on Iraq, the experience of backing the United States against one of the Soviet Union's erstwhile allies offended many conservatives within the government (and even some of Gorbachev's close associates). But when it came time to deal with the increasingly assertive independence movements in the Baltic republics, the CPSU leadership found itself in a far less generous mood. In January 1991—only weeks after Foreign Minister Eduard Shevardnadze had resigned, warning of an impending "dictatorship"—Soviet paratroopers began cracking down in Lithuania. Estimating that the world would be too distracted by the onset of Desert Storm, the Soviet military took over the main printing plant in Vilnius on January 11 and two days later moved to seize a television transmitter that had been broadcasting regular reports of the Soviet repression. By the time the confrontation between two Soviet tanks and several hundred Lithuanians guarding the tower ended, fifteen Lithuanians were dead, including a teenage girl crushed to death by a tank.

The crackdown in Lithuania and elsewhere in the Baltics backfired, however, when six republics announced (on February 6) that they would be boycotting the upcoming referendum on Gorbachev's latest plan for reorganizing the Soviet Union and Yeltsin gave a televised speech (on February 19) in which he "dissociated" himself from Gorbachev's policies and called for the general secretary's "immediate resignation." Finally, on April 23, Gorbachev moved to reclaim his leadership of the reform movement, inviting the leaders of nine republics (including Yeltsin) to his dacha at Novo-Ogarevo to begin the talks that would eventually produce the new Union treaty.

The Bush administration reacted to all this warily and at times clumsily. The president criticized the Soviets for using force in Lithuania—but not as strongly as did Boris Yeltsin, who flew to Estonia and signed on behalf of the RSFSR a "mutual support pact" with the Baltic republics. In late July, Bush flew to Moscow to sign the Strategic Arms Reduction Treaty (START), which mandated deep cuts in nuclear weapons. Afterward, he flew on to Ukraine where he planned to give a speech before the Ukrainian parliament in Kiev. Two weeks earlier, however, Bush had received a secret message from the Soviets imploring him not to visit Ukraine, where surging nationalism was rapidly destabilizing the political situation. Although Bush went anyway, he tried to offset the symbolism of his presence by counseling the Ukrainians against secession, even making reference to "suicidal nationalism" in his August 1 speech (which *New York Times* columnist William Safire memorably named the "Chicken Kiev speech"). Bush's performance pleased no one and probably weakened Gorbachev's already tenuous position. The coup began seventeen days later.

ALTHOUGH GORBACHEV DIDN'T YET REALIZE IT, by the time he returned from Foros at 2 A.M. on August 22, nearly all of his authority had, as a practical matter, passed on to Boris Yeltsin. Initially, Gorbachev acted as though he could merely pick up where he had left off, but the empire that he had governed for six years had changed dramatically during its last three days of turmoil. From the time that Yeltsin frustrated the coup, events moved ahead rapidly. On August 24, Gorbachev, finally recognizing some of the inevitability of the situation, resigned as general secretary of the Communist party. On September 5, the Congress of People's Deputies dissolved itself. On December 8, meeting outside Minsk, Yeltsin joined the leaders of Ukraine and Belarus in dissolving the Soviet Union and replacing it with a loose confederation, the Commonwealth of Independent States (CIS), that most of the other now-independent republics subsequently joined.

In the meantime, Gorbachev clung stubbornly to the vestiges of his power. When Secretary of State James A. Baker III visited Moscow in mid-December 1991, Gorbachev was still occupying his office in the Kremlin, while Yeltsin ran a competing government from the Russian White House. At Baker's December 16 meeting with Yeltsin, the two men were joined by Soviet military commander Yevgeni Shaposhnikov, demonstrating to Baker that the armed forces had cast their lot with the CIS. At the secretary of state's afternoon meeting with Gorbachev, the Soviet leader argued that he still had an important part to play. "There have been many miscalculations and even serious mistakes on my part, but that's not the point," Gorbachev said. "I see a role for myself…to prevent even greater disintegration in the process of creating the commonwealth." That turned out not to be the case. Instead, Gorbachev and Yeltsin announced the next morning that as of January 1, 1992, the Soviet Union and its governmental structures would cease to exist. As for the Cold War, in February 1992, Presidents Bush and Yeltsin issued a joint statement officially ending the almost half-century-old conflict.

"The thing about Yeltsin I really like…is that he's not a Russian bureaucrat. He's an Irish poet. He sees politics as a novel he's writing."

—

Bill Clinton, quoted by Deputy Secretary of State Strobe Talbott

26

A NEW MILLENNIUM

September 11, 2001

MOST DAYS FOR MOST PEOPLE pass privately and unmemorably. Only a very few become fixed in the imagination, as personal experience fuses with societal memory. For Americans of the Great Depression era, December 7, 1941, was such a pivotal day, evoking strong feelings of horror, sorrow, and determination that never fully subsided. Members of the Sixties generation recall November 22, 1963, and April 4, 1968, in similar terms. These were days that never quite ended, despite the setting of the sun. Now, September 11, 2001, has joined them in the first rank of historical touchstones—both for Americans, all of whom were indirect targets of the attacks, and for billions of other people around the world, who watched the grisly events unfold on television. "Shock is, of course, one goal of terrorism: The greater the number of people in shock, the better," the editors of the German newsweekly *Der Spiegel* wrote in the aftermath of the raids on the World Trade Center and the Pentagon. "That is why the attacks of September 11 are to date the most perfect act of terror in history."

The shocks in question were especially stunning to Americans because they ended what had been arguably the most secure, self-confident, even smug period in their country's history. Propelled by a band of young Internet tycoons and their dazzling dot-com ventures, the so-called New Economy of the 1990s had

just produced the longest economic expansion in U.S. history. At the same time, the collapse of the Soviet Union and the end of the Cold War had created a sense of global invulnerability that matched America's unprecedented financial good fortune. Then, hijacked American Airlines Flight 11 crashed into the North Tower of New York City's World Trade Center, and some of the American psyche came crashing down along with the 110-story building.

It was in March 1991, a decade earlier, that eight months of recession ended and the United States began a record 120 consecutive months of economic growth. Yet prospects for recovery hardly seemed bright at the time. The 1990–1991 recession had been deeply troubling to most Americans, and Democrats began emphasizing the issue in their attacks on Pres. George Bush, who had served Ronald Reagan as vice president for eight years and then succeeded him as president in 1989. During the 1988 campaign, in fact, Bush had pledged himself to continue the policies of the Reagan administration—memorably asserting in his acceptance speech at the Republican national convention, "Read my lips: No new taxes!" In office, however, Bush had watched the federal deficit climb from $153 billion in 1989 to $220 billion in 1990 to $269 billion in 1991. Under pressure from the Democratic majority in Congress, he finally reversed himself in June 1990, agreeing to a budget compromise that included both spending cuts and new taxes. Although President Bush later backed away from the tax hikes, calling them "a mistake," he had already signed them into law, and the political damage was done.

AT LEFT: *A fire truck covered with debris from the collapsed World Trade Center. During the days following the tragedy, some of the tens of thousands of mourners who visited The Site (as rescue workers called the area of devastation) decorated the demolished vehicle with flowers.*

REAGANOMICS

DURING HIS YEARS in the White House, Jimmy Carter often lectured Americans for leading profligate lives and told them that national resources were limited. Ronald Reagan, however, ran a campaign in 1980 based on encouraging optimism. According to the Republican candidate, there was more than enough opportunity for everyone in America—if only federal spending could be restrained. "Government is not the solution to our problem," Reagan liked to say. "Government is our problem." Americans who wanted desperately to regain the sense of unlimited opportunity that many considered their birthright voted for him overwhelmingly.

The solution that Reagan offered was based on "supply-side economics"—or "voodoo economics," as his Republican rival, George Bush, called the plan before joining the Reagan ticket. The essence of supply-side economics was the belief that a sharp cut in taxes would, by putting more money in people's pockets, stimulate additional investment and consumer spending. These would, in turn, yield greater

Reagan's first term in office *was marked by the worst recession since World War II. Lower oil prices kept inflation down, but unemployment reached 10.8 percent in December 1982, its highest since 1940.*

prosperity. The tax cuts needed to be concentrated in the highest income brackets, the supply-siders argued, because it was the wealthiest Americans who would most likely invest the extra cash; yet, Reagan was quick to point out, the middle and working classes would benefit also because the prosperity would "trickle down." Furthermore, government tax revenue would rise, because the increase in economic activity would more than offset the reduction in rates.

To begin this beneficial chain of events, conservative southern Democrats joined Republicans in enacting a 25 percent reduction in individual income-tax rates, to be phased in over three years. This August 1981 tax cut was slightly less than the 30 percent the new president had asked for but still the largest in American history. Unfortunately, supply-side economics didn't work out the way the theorists had anticipated: It failed to generate much additional investment, and the increases in consumer spending it did produce were generally unproductive because the money tended to be spent on aerobics classes and Japanese-made videocassette recorders (two popular trends of the early 1980s) rather than on durable goods manufactured in America. Thus, from a macroscopic point of view, the tax cuts merely underscored America's shift from a manufacturing to a service economy and from a creditor to a debtor nation.

Meanwhile, despite the deep spending cuts made by the Reagan administration (especially in social welfare programs), the federal budget deficit kept rising as revenues fell. As a result, during President Reagan's two terms in office, the U.S. national debt nearly tripled, and interest payments of more than $150 billion a year became the third largest budget item. During much of Reagan's second term, Congress tried—with little success—to muster the political will to bring these deficits under control. In December 1985, for example, the president signed the Gramm-Rudman-Hollings Act, which included a timetable for reaching a balanced budget and mandated automatic, across-the-board cuts in federal spending should Congress fail to meet any of the Gramm-Rudman-Hollings targets. In June 1986, however, the Supreme Court ruled that such automatic cuts were unconstitutional.

Because both the Cold War and the Persian Gulf War were over, the presidential election of 1992 became the first since 1936 in which foreign policy failed to become a major issue. This hurt Bush, whose impressive Gulf War approval ratings had disappeared as quickly as they had materialized, and benefited Arkansas governor Bill Clinton, the Democratic nominee, whose campaign advisers kept reminding him and themselves, "It's the economy, stupid."

Although economic statistics have since shown that Bush was technically correct—the recession was over—the $290 billion federal budget deficit for 1992 and the general uneasiness that most Americans felt concerning the economy gave Clinton a victory in the close three-way race among himself, Bush, and Texas billionaire H. Ross Perot—who ran as an independent, spent much of his time attacking the Republicans, and won 18.9 percent of the popular vote. Widespread concern about the future of the economy also helped President Clinton win passage in August 1993 of a controversial five-year deficit-reduction plan totaling $496 billion, half in spending cuts and half in tax increases. The extremely close vote was 218–216 in the House and 51–50 in the Senate, where Vice Pres. Al Gore had to cast a dramatic tiebreaking vote. "Unless we did something about [the budget deficits]," Clinton said later, "we would not have the capacity to deal with a whole range of other issues."

The result of that legislation was a steady decrease in the budget deficit from $255 billion in 1993 to $22 billion in 1997. The next year, the federal government reported its first budget surplus since 1969. Nevertheless, the budget battles of the mid-1990s were some of the most raucous and contentious ever. During the 1994 midterm elections, House Minority Whip Newt Gingrich of Georgia led an enormously successful campaign that put Republicans in control of both houses of Congress for the first time since 1955. The centerpiece of his effort was the Contract with America, which promised an end to unfunded federal mandates and enactment of a balanced-budget amendment, a line-item veto, and tort reform, among other proposals. ("Republicans did a good job of defining us as the party of government," Clinton explained, "and that [wasn't] a good place to be.") Yet the combative Gingrich proved much less effective as a Speaker than he had been as a campaigner. Most Contract with America legislation failed to survive the Senate, where Republicans were more moderate than in the House, and President Clinton outmaneuvered the highly ideological Gingrich more often than not.

The Government Shutdowns

THE BATTLE OVER THE FISCAL YEAR 1996 budget continued well into the fall of 1995 before the House and Senate finally agreed in late October on a spending plan that cut taxes and balanced the budget by 2002. President Clinton vetoed the bill, however, asserting that its deep cuts into health, education, and environmental spending were unacceptable. After the Republicans rejected his compromise offer, the two sides stopped talking, and with no budget law in place, the government began to run out of money. Choosing not to move forward with

Clinton with Gingrich in June 1995. In addition to their battles over the budget, Clinton's tenure was marked by an acceleration of the trend toward economic "globalization." Two milestones were the House's narrow approval in November 1993 of the North American Free Trade Agreement and the December 1994 ratification of the General Agreement on Tariffs and Trade (GATT).

CLINTON'S FOREIGN POLICY

WITH THE DOMESTIC ECONOMY booming (and scandals undermining his authority at home), Bill Clinton turned his attention increasingly to the making of peace in the world. Early in his administration, his principal challenges came in the Balkans, where the dissolution of Yugoslavia rekindled centuries-old ethnic hatred. The Serbs, led by strongman Slobodan Milosevic, went to war against their Croatian and Bosnian neighbors, producing fatalities in the hundreds of thousands. Rape, murder, and other atrocities became so commonplace that the United States finally felt compelled to intervene. Specifically, U.S.-led NATO air strikes targeted Serbian forces in Bosnia, and their success compelled Milosevic to attend peace talks convened at a Dayton, Ohio, air force base in November 1995.

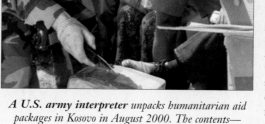

A U.S. army interpreter unpacks humanitarian aid packages in Kosovo in August 2000. The contents— including clothing, school supplies, and toys—were donated by families in the United States.

The peace plan that emerged in Dayton required President Clinton to approve the inclusion of twenty thousand U.S. troops in a UN peacekeeping force. Fortunately for the president, the Dayton accords produced peaceful, free elections in Bosnia in September 1996—although Milosevic continued to make trouble elsewhere in the Balkans. Frustrated in Bosnia, the Serbs next sought to "purify" Kosovo, a southern Serbian province that Milosevic's minions began to "cleanse" of its mostly Albanian population. Again, the United States and its NATO allies intervened with air raids in early 1999, compelling Milosevic to withdraw. This time, however, Milosevic's government fell as well, and he was ultimately extradited to the International Criminal Tribunal in The Hague for prosecution as a war criminal.

Perhaps because of eventual U.S. success in the Balkans and elsewhere, Clinton felt confident enough during his second term to become deeply involved in two of the most intractable conflicts of the late twentieth century: the dispute between Catholics and Protestants in Northern Ireland and the fighting between Israelis and Palestinians in the Middle East.

With regard to Northern Ireland, the U.S. president (with the indispensable aid of former senator George Mitchell) spent several years painstakingly putting together the so-called Good Friday Agreement, signed in April 1998. He concluded these negotiations personally with a round of telephone calls, during which he employed some judicious White House arm-twisting. In the Middle East, however, Clinton's efforts fell short. As he entered office, Israeli prime minister Yitzhak Rabin and Palestinian leader Yasir Arafat signed the September 1993 Oslo "land for peace" accords, which established a Palestinian "authority" in the Israeli-occupied West Bank and Gaza Strip as a prelude to Palestinian statehood. Thereafter, Clinton attempted to keep the Oslo process on track as the two sides negotiated the numerous details intentionally left unaddressed by that agreement, such as the future status of Jerusalem. The president's efforts peaked in July 2000, during the final months of his administration, when the president led an extraordinary marathon negotiating session at Camp David. Unfortunately, Arafat and Israeli prime minister Ehud Barak could not reach a final agreement—and afterward, the situation in the Middle East deteriorated badly.

stopgap spending bills, Gingrich forced a confrontation with the president that resulted in a partial government shutdown in mid-November. Federal offices were closed around the country, and eight hundred thousand workers were sent home. The shutdown ended six days later, apparently with a Gingrich victory, when Clinton agreed to accept the Speaker's goal of balancing the budget within seven years, and Congress appropriated the necessary temporary spending.

However, when Congress and the president couldn't agree on how to reach the new goal, the government shut down again in mid-December. This time, the closure lasted three weeks, during which time it became clear that Gingrich had substantially miscalculated. Frustrated voters who had once applauded Gingrich's efforts to dismantle the federal government now praised Clinton's courage in protecting programs such as Medicare from a reckless congressional majority. Nevertheless, Republicans kept control of both houses throughout the remainder of the Clinton presidency, even voting to impeach the president in December 1998 for perjuring himself to conceal an embarrassing sexual relationship with a White House intern, but the momentum generated by Gingrich's 1994 "revolution" vanished. Of course, President Clinton lost influence as well.

Although the numerous shameful revelations that had led to his impeachment proved insufficient to warrant his removal from office (the Senate voted to acquit him on both counts in February 1999), they were sufficient to rob him of most of his moral authority to lead. As a result, much of his second term was wasted, at least from a domestic point of view.

Meanwhile, the stock market soared. On the day that Bill Clinton took office, the Dow Jones Industrial Average closed at 3241.95. On December 5, 1996—the day that Federal Reserve chairman Alan Greenspan suggested in a widely quoted speech that the financial markets were suffering from "irrational exuberance"— the Dow closed at 6437.10. On January 14, 2000, as the campaign to replace the retiring Clinton got under way, the Dow peaked at 11722.98, or more than triple its January 1993 level and nearly double the level at which Greenspan had first expressed his concern. The market took some hits after the disputed 2000 election—which the Supreme Court decided in favor of Texas governor (and presidential son) George W. Bush by ruling, 5–4, to discontinue recounts in Florida. Nevertheless, the Dow would have opened at 9605.51 on the morning of September 11, 2001, had American Airlines Flight 11 not crashed into the ninetieth floor of the North Tower at 8:48 A.M. Eastern Standard Time, closing the New York Stock Exchange, the American Stock Exchange, and the Nasdaq.

Alan Greenspan in March 1998. He was first appointed chairman of the Federal Reserve by President Reagan in August 1987, then reappointed by Bush in 1992 and by Clinton in 1996 and again in 2000.

FOR THE NEXT FIFTEEN MINUTES, it was possible to believe that some dreadful accident had occurred; then, at 9:03 A.M., a second hijacked airplane, United Airlines Flight 175 (also out of Boston and bound for Los Angeles) crashed into the South Tower near its eightieth floor. Within moments of each plane's impact, the thousands of pounds of jet fuel in its nearly full tanks caused the upper

The September 11 attacks weren't the first time al-Qaeda had struck at the United States. It had exploded car bombs outside U.S. embassies in Africa in August 1998 and used a speedboat to blast a hole in the USS Cole *in October 2000.*

floors of each tower to explode in flames. Unable to descend, all the people who had been working above the point of impact in each building died. Furthermore, the heat of the flames gradually weakened each building's superstructure until it buckled, causing the floors above the fire to drop down onto those below. Not designed to withstand such force, the lower floors collapsed, and the building pancaked.

It took mere seconds for the South Tower to collapse at 9:59 A.M., and at 10:28, the North Tower followed, killing hundreds more people. Meanwhile, another group of hijackers turned around American Airlines Flight 77, which had taken off from Washington's Dulles Airport earlier that morning, and crashed the plane into the Pentagon at 9:37 A.M. Only aboard a fourth jet, United Airlines Flight 93 out of Newark, were the passengers able to frustrate the hijackers' aim. Having learned

of the World Trade Center and Pentagon attacks from cell phone conversations with family members, and realizing that their own chances for survival were low, a group of passengers apparently rushed the cockpit and forced the plane down. The Boeing 757 crashed at 10 A.M. in rural Somerset County, Pennsylvania, southeast of Pittsburgh, killing everyone aboard but no one on the ground.

Government agencies in both New York City and Washington responded by evacuating most major public buildings. In New York City, the Port Authority of New York and New Jersey ordered all of its bridges and tunnels closed; meanwhile, at 9:40 A.M., the Federal Aviation Administration shut down the nation's entire air traffic system, closing every U.S. airport and restricting American airspace— the first time it had ever taken such an extreme action. The president— in Florida at the time, making a routine public appearance—was hurried onto Air Force One and flown to Barksdale Air Force Base in Louisiana, then to Offutt Air Force Base in Nebraska. It would be nearly 7 P.M. before he returned to the White House. Ninety minutes later, he addressed the nation on television. "These attacks shattered steel," he said, "but they cannot dent the steel of American resolve."

While Bush was still in the air, New York City mayor Rudolph W. Giuliani held a press conference around 3 P.M. Answering a question about how many people had died, he said that the number of fatalities wasn't yet known, but that it would certainly be "more than any of us can bear." Where the Twin Towers had once stood, jutting up into the sky, there were now only enormous piles of rubble, with thousands of bodies of workers, firefighters, police, and other rescue personnel buried underneath. The first official estimates suggested that perhaps six thousand people had died as a result of the September 11 attacks. However, as Pentagon and World Trade Center workers found their way home (a difficult task in New York City given the bridge closures and mass-transit shutdowns) and duplicate names were removed from the lists of the missing, that number fell by half. It was still more than anyone could bear.

Al-Qaeda

BY LATE IN THE DAY on September 11, it had become clear from calls made by passengers and crew members aboard the doomed flights that the hijackers had been young Islamic men. Further investigation revealed that there had been nineteen hijackers in all, fifteen of them Saudis, and that the terrorists who had flown the planes into the buildings had received the bulk of their training at American flight schools. The money they used to pay for their tuition and other expenses was eventually traced to Saudi exile Osama bin Laden's al-Qaeda terrorist network. Presumably, the group's leadership targeted the World Trade Center and the Pentagon because those structures represented American financial and military might, respectively.

Hardly had Americans begun to respond to the airplane hijackings when they were subjected to another, possibly related, terrorist assault. This time, the weapons used were ordinary first-class envelopes, containing deadly anthrax spores along with letters threatening further attacks. (Although the texts of these letters made use of militant Islamic rhetoric, a non-Muslim may well have been responsible for them.) The anthrax-loaded missives were sent to media figures in New York City and Florida, as well as to top Washington political leaders. Before the damage was contained several weeks later, a number of postal workers and others who had come into contact with the weaponized spores had died; meanwhile, hundreds of thousands of other Americans had rushed to receive antibiotic treatments to counter possible exposure. Congressional office buildings and mail-sorting facilities were closed pending decontamination, and the integrity of the entire U.S. postal system was at issue for a time.

Although George W. Bush had spent the first eight months of his presidency pursuing a unilateral approach to foreign policy—disengaging from the December 1997 Kyoto global warming accord and preparing to abrogate the 1972 Anti-Ballistic Missile Treaty with Russia so that he could move ahead with his revised version of Reagan's Strategic Defense Initiative—he reacted to the September 11 attacks much as his father had responded to the Iraqi invasion of Kuwait. The events of the day gave the suddenly popular Bush his presidential mission. Rather than acting precipitously, he spent nearly two months gathering intelligence, formulating policy, and building an international coalition to support his new "war on terrorism." As expected, that war's first major battles came in Afghanistan, where the fanatically Islamic Taliban government had been sheltering Bin Laden and his terrorist training camps for years.

"You could hear the building cracking. It sounded like when you have a bunch of spaghetti, and you break it in half to boil it."

—

Bob Shelton, an architect whose office was on the fifty-sixth floor of the South Tower

In October 2001, with crucial support from neighboring Pakistan, the United States and its allies began military operations against the Taliban and al-Qaeda. Rather quickly, the Taliban were driven from power, and the larger al-Qaeda bases were overrun—yet most key personnel escaped, including Bin Laden and Taliban chief Mullah Omar. So did enough Taliban and al-Qaeda rank-and-file to pose an ongoing threat to U.S. troops and other international peacekeepers working in Afghanistan. The situation in that unruly country remains (as this book goes to press) far from stable. Meanwhile, the threat from al-Qaeda persists elsewhere. Although the anxiety produced by the September 11 attacks has slowly subsided within the United States, President Bush and other government officials have consistently warned Americans that future attacks must be anticipated—and that some of these will likely succeed.

"IN THE SPASMS OF A FEW HOURS," *Time* essayist Lance Morrow has written, the United States "became a changed country. It turned the corner, at last, out of the 1990s. The menu of American priorities was rearranged." Yet much more has endured. The United States remains throughout the world economically dominant, politically stable, militarily unchallenged, technologically innovative, and culturally pervasive. These are realities with which any foe (and we ourselves) must contend.

Yet the September 11 attacks do seem to have added a new, unexpected dimension to American (and global) life. As nineteenth-century French anarchist Pierre-Joseph Proudhon once remarked, "The fecundity of the unexpected far exceeds the prudence of statesmen." Certainly, the country has entered a new and probably lengthy period of heightened security and greater national vigilance— which will, in turn, pose threats to civil liberties, as wartime situations always do. Of course, we cannot predict a future devoid of deep anguish and tragedy, whether due to fresh terrorist onslaughts or to our own inadequacies. "History," Arthur M. Schlesinger Jr. has written, "is not a redeemer promising to solve all problems in time." Today, Americans have entered a new testing time, one that bears close resemblance to other crucial moments in our past. How we confront these tests in the years ahead remains to be seen and will determine whether the present generation of leaders and citizens can rise to the current challenge with courage and effectiveness.

Unlike most other people, Americans have traditionally welcomed the unexpected. "America was discovered accidentally," historian Samuel Eliot Morison reminds us, "by a great seaman who was looking for something else; when discovered, it was not wanted; and most of the exploration for the next fifty years was done in the hope of getting through or around it. America was named after a man who discovered no part of the New World. History is like that, very chancy."

* * *

AT RIGHT: *On March 11, 2002, two powerful beams of light rose skyward from a point just north of where the Twin Towers had stood. The Tribute in Light shone each night for the next month from dusk until 11 P.M.*

ABOUT THE CONTRIBUTORS

JAMES AXTELL is William R. Kenan Jr. Professor of Humanities at the College of William and Mary. He is the author of eleven books in ethnohistory and the history of education. His most recent publications are *The Pleasures of Academe: A Celebration and Defense of Higher Education* (1998) and *Natives and Newcomers: The Cultural Origins of North America* (2001). He is at work on a history of twentieth-century Princeton University, which he did not attend.

IRA BERLIN is Distinguished University Professor at the University of Maryland. He is the author of *Many Thousands Gone: The First Two Centuries of Slavery in North America* (1998) and is the coeditor of *Remembering Slavery: African Americans Talk about Their Personal Experiences of Slavery and Freedom* (1998). He is a member of the Council of the National Endowment for the Humanities and president of the Organization of American Historians.

MICHAEL BARONE is a senior writer for *U.S. News and World Report*, having formerly been a member of the *Washington Post*'s editorial-page staff. He is also the principal coauthor of *The Almanac of American Politics* (published biannually) and the author of *Our Country: The Shaping of America From Roosevelt to Reagan* (1990) and *The New Americans: How the Melting Pot Can Work Again* (2001).

ANN BRAUDE is director of the Women's Studies in Religion program at Harvard Divinity School. Her book *Radical Spirits: Spiritualism and Women's Rights in Nineteenth-Century America* (1989) explores the overlap between the early women's rights movement and spiritualism. She is also coeditor of *Root of Bitterness: Documents of the Social History of American Women* (1996).

CATHERINE CLINTON is the author of *The Plantation Mistress* (1982); *Tara Revisited* (1995); and, most recently, *Fanny Kemble's Civil Wars* (2000). She is currently at work on a biography of Harriet Tubman, scheduled to be published in 2004.

ROBERT DALLEK is currently Professor of History at Boston University, having taught for thirty years at UCLA. In 1994–1995, he was Visiting Harmsworth Professor of American History at Oxford. An elected fellow of the American Academy of Arts and Sciences, Dallek is the author of numerous books on American diplomatic and presidential history, including a two-volume life of Lyndon B. Johnson.

JOHN W. DOWER is Elting E. Morison Professor of History at the Massachusetts Institute of Technology. His numerous books include *Empire and Aftermath: Yoshida Shigeru and the Japanese Experience, 1878–1954* (1979); *War Without Mercy: Race and Power in the Pacific War* (1986), which won the National Book Critics Circle Award for Nonfiction; and *Embracing Defeat: Japan in the Wake of World War II* (1999), which won the Pulitzer Prize for General Nonfiction, the National Book Award in Nonfiction, and the Bancroft Prize.

JOSEPH J. ELLIS is the author of six books on American history, including *American Sphinx: The Character of Thomas Jefferson* (1997), which won a National Book Award, and *Founding Brothers: The Revolutionary Generation* (2000), which won the Pulitzer Prize for History.

ERIC FONER is DeWitt Clinton Professor of History at Columbia University. He is the author of numerous works, including *Reconstruction: America's Unfinished Revolution, 1863–1877* (1988), which won the Parkman and Bancroft Prizes.

He is also a past president of the American Historical Association.

THOMAS FLEMING writes both history and historical novels. His most recent work of history is *The New Dealers' War: FDR and the War Within World War II* (2001). His recent novel *When This Cruel War Is Over* (2001) deals with a little-known plot to revolutionize the Midwest during the last summer of the Civil War.

JOAN HEDRICK is Charles A. Dana Professor of History at Trinity College. She is the author of *Harriet Beecher Stowe: A Life* (1994), which won the Pulitzer Prize for Biography, and *Solitary Comrade: Jack London and His Work* (1982).

DANIEL J. KEVLES, a professor of history at Yale University, has written widely on the history of science and its relationship to society. His books include *In the Name of Eugenics: Genetics and the Uses of Human Heredity* (1985); *The Physicists: The History of a Scientific Community in Modern America* (1995); and, most recently, *The Baltimore Case: A Trial of Politics, Science, and Character* (1998). He is a coauthor of *Inventing America* (2002), a history of the United States that integrates science and technology into the narrative of American development.

ALICE KESSLER-HARRIS is R. Gordon Hoxie Professor of History at Columbia University. Her books include *Women Have Always Worked: A Historical Overview* (1981); *Out to Work: A History of Wage-Earning Women in the United States* (1982); *A Woman's Wage: Historical Meanings and Social Consequence* (1990); and *In Pursuit of Equity:*

Women, Men, and the Quest for Economic Citizenship in Twentieth-Century America (2001), which won the Bancroft Prize.

WILLIAM E. LEUCHTENBURG is William Rand Kenan Jr. Professor Emeritus of History at the University of North Carolina at Chapel Hill. His many books include the prize-winning *Franklin D. Roosevelt and the New Deal, 1932–1940* (1963) and *In the Shadow of FDR: From Harry Truman to Bill Clinton* (1993). He has been elected president of the American Historical Association, the Organization of American Historians, and the Society of American Historians.

DAVID LEVERING LEWIS is Martin Luther King Jr. University Professor at Rutgers. Among his publications are *King: A Biography* (1978); *When Harlem Was in Vogue* (1981); *The Race to Fashoda: European Colonialism and African Resistance in the Scramble for Africa* (1987); and the two-volume biography of W. E. B. Du Bois awarded the Pulitzer Prizes for Biography in 1994 and 2001.

JACK N. RAKOVE is Coe Professor of History and American Studies and Professor of Political Science at Stanford University, where he has taught since 1980. He is the author, among other books, of *The Beginnings of National Politics: An Interpretive History of the Continental Congress* (1979) and *Original Meanings: Politics and Ideas in the Making of the Constitution* (1996), which won the Pulitzer Prize for History.

RICHARD REEVES, the author of *President Kennedy: Profile of Power* (1993) and *President Nixon: Alone in the White House* (2001),

writes a syndicated newspaper column and teaches at the Annenberg School for Communications at the University of Southern California.

GEOFFREY C. WARD, the former editor of *American Heritage*, is the author of a dozen books, including *Jazz: A History of America's Music* (2000) and *A First-Class Temperament: The Emergence of Franklin Roosevelt* (1989), which won the Parkman Prize. He also writes historical documentaries for public television.

ELLIOTT WEST is Distinguished Professor of History at the University of Arkansas. The most recent of his five books, *The Contested Plains: Indians, Goldseekers, and the Rush to Colorado* (1998), received the Parkman Prize. He is currently writing a book on the 1876 Sioux and 1877 Nez Perce Wars.

*   *   *

INDEX

PHOTO CREDITS

All the images in *The Story of America* are from the collections of the Library of Congress, the National Archives, or Agincourt Press, with the exception of those reprinted with the permission of the following:

Corbis: 16 (top), 18, 27, 73, 412 (top), 413, 463, 464, 468, 477, 500, 503, 509, 541, 563, 566, 568, 569, 571, 581, 595, 596, 606–607, 609, 613, 614, 615, 626, 635, 637, 639 (top), 642, 644, 645, 646, 648, 650 (top), 651, 652, 654 (top), 655, 656, 660, 661, 663

Seaver Center for Western History Research, Los Angeles County Museum of Natural History: 29

Ashmolean Museum, Oxford: 39 (bottom)

Folger Shakespeare Library: 41 (top), 42

Association for the Preservation of Virginia Antiquities: 41 (bottom), 44 (bottom), 46 (top)

Architect of the Capitol Collection: 44 (top), 313

Enoch Pratt Free Library: 45

Library of Virginia: 49, 198–199 (bottom), 200 (bottom)

North Wind Picture Archives: 50–51

Friends Historical Library, Swarthmore College: 57 (both), 216 (bottom)

Pilgrim Hall Museum, Plymouth, Massachusetts: 61 (both)

Smithsonian Institution, NNC, Douglas Mudd: 64, 140 (bottom), 184 (top), 288 (top), 381, 386 (bottom)

Commonwealth of Massachusetts, Archives Division: 67

Clements Library, University of Michigan: 78 (bottom)

Massachusetts Historical Society: 80 (bottom)

Boston Public Library: 87 (bottom)

Pennsylvania Capitol Preservation Committee: 97 (top)

U.S. Senate Collection: 108, 112 (bottom), 239 (top), 244 (top), 420

Independence Hall National Historic Park: 122 (bottom)

Albany Institute of History and Art: 123

Missouri Historical Society, St. Louis: 128, 144 (top), 145, 478

Academy of Natural Sciences of Philadelphia: 136 (top left, top right)

Beinecke Rare Book and Manuscript Library, Yale University: 136 (bottom), 147 (top)

Ernst Mayer Library of the Museum of Comparative Zoology, Harvard University: 138

Virginia Military Institute: 141 (top), 289 (bottom)

Buffalo Bill Historical Center, Cody, Wyoming: 142–143

Smithsonian Institution, National Museum of American History: 147 (bottom)

The Hermitage, Home of President Andrew Jackson, Nashville, Tennessee: 162 (bottom), 187

American Antiquarian Society: 176

University of North Carolina Library at Chapel Hill: 191

North Carolina Division of Archives and History: 201

Waterloo Library and Historical Society: 208 (top)

Swarthmore College Peace Collection: 211 (top)

Oberlin College Archives, Oberlin, Ohio: 213 (bottom), 220 (bottom), 254 (top)

Church of Jesus Christ of Latter-day Saints Historical Archives: 214 (bottom)

First Church of Christ, Scientist, Mary Baker Eddy Library for the Betterment of Humanity, Inc.: 217

Oneida Community Mansion House, Oneida, New York: 218 (top left, top right)

Center for American History, University of Texas at Austin: 232 (top)

Franklin Delano Roosevelt Library: 236 (bottom), 484, 490, 494, 497 (top), 527, 530

Society of California Pioneers: 236–237

John F. Kennedy Library: 241 (bottom), 560 (bottom)

Kansas State Historical Society: 253 (right), 254 (bottom), 265 (top), 268 (bottom)

Abraham Lincoln Library and Museum, Lincoln Memorial University, Harrogate, Tennessee: 281 (top)

Alabama Department of Archives and History, Montgomery, Alabama: 294 (top)

Little Bighorn Battlefield National Monument: 333 (top), 334 (top), 339 (top)

University of Wisconsin–Madison Archives: 339 (bottom)

Nebraska State Historical Society: 342–343, 377 (bottom), 392, 395

Eugene V. Debs Foundation: 352 (both), 369, 546 (top)

George Meany Memorial Archives: 370 (bottom)

UNITE Archives, Kheel Center, Cornell University, Ithaca, New York: 435, 436 (top), 445 (both), 446 (bottom), 448, 449 (both)

Minnesota Historical Society: 457 (both), 458 (top), 475, 616, 617

Denver Public Library: 480

Martin Luther King Jr. Memorial Library, District of Columbia Public Libraries: 513 (top), 544, 554, 564, 565, 567, 570, 575, 587, 594, 602, 618, 620, 621, 627, 628 (top), 629, 632 (top), 633, 647

Defense Visual Information Center: 653, 662

Tilman Rietzle: 654 (bottom)

David Plakke: 658, 664, 667